I0880821

AI-Enabled Workforce Management for Hybrid Workplaces

Preeti Mehra
https://orcid.org/0000-0002-8979-9431
Campbell College, Edmonton, Canada

Ergunova Olga Titovna
https://orcid.org/0009-0006-2267-8121
Peter the Great St. Petersburg Polytechnic University, Russia

Shyam Sunder Agrawal
https://orcid.org/0009-0004-3648-0584
Lovely Professional University, India

Pooja Kansra
Lovely Professional University, India

Miladin Stefanovic
University of Kragujevac, Serbia

IGI Global Scientific Publishing
Publishing Tomorrow's Research Today

Vice President of Editorial	Melissa Wagner
Director of Acquisitions	Mikaela Felty
Director of Book Development	Jocelynn Hessler
Production Manager	Mike Brehm
Cover Design	Jose Rosado

Published in the United States of America by
IGI Global Scientific Publishing
701 East Chocolate Avenue
Hershey, PA, 17033, USA
Tel: 717-533-8845 | Fax: 717-533-7115
Website: https://www.igi-global.com E-mail: cust@igi-global.com

Copyright © 2026 by IGI Global Scientific Publishing. All rights reserved. No part of this publication may be reproduced, stored or distributed in any form or by any means, electronic or mechanical, including photocopying, without written permission from the publisher. Use of this publication to train generative artificial intelligence (AI) technologies is expressly prohibited. The publisher reserves all rights to license its use for generative AI training and machine learning model development.

Product or company names used in this set are for identification purposes only. Inclusion of the names of the products or companies does not indicate a claim of ownership by IGI Global Scientific Publishing of the trademark or registered trademark.

Library of Congress Cataloging-in-Publication Data

LCCN: 2025034513 (CIP Data Pending)
ISBN13: 9798337358710
Isbn13Softcover: 9798337358727
EISBN13: 9798337358734
British Cataloguing in Publication Data
A Cataloguing in Publication record for this book is available from the British Library.

All work contributed to this book is new, previously-unpublished material.
The views expressed in this book are those of the authors, but not necessarily of the publisher.
This book contains information sourced from authentic and highly regarded references, with reasonable efforts made to ensure the reliability of the data and information presented. The authors, editors, and publisher believe the information in this book to be accurate and true as of the date of publication. Every effort has been made to trace and credit the copyright holders of all materials included. However, the authors, editors, and publisher cannot assume responsibility for the validity of all materials or the consequences of their use. Should any copyright material be found unacknowledged, please inform the publisher so that corrections may be made in future reprints.

Table of Contents

Detailed Table of Contents

This chapter examines how artificial intelligence reshapes enterprise upskilling in hybrid workplaces and sets out an evidence-based approach for integrating learning transformation into HRM and business strategy. It introduces a Strategic Readiness Model across three dimensions—Technical, Cultural, and Strategic with a five-point rubric and a diagnostic table for action tracking. Using verified case illustrations from IBM, Deloitte, Unilever, Accenture, and Microsoft, the chapter analyses platform architectures, adoption mechanisms, and measurable outcomes, and then synthesizes results via a cross-case readiness heatmap and a dimension roll-up. Building on these findings, the chapter specifies a performance measurement plan that links learning signals to reviews and resource decisions, and outlines operating cadences for dashboards, impact reviews, and governance. Ethical safeguards—privacy by design, fairness auditing, and transparent communication are positioned as preconditions for trust, sustained adoption, and workforce resilience.

The application of artificial intelligence (AI) has rapidly transformed various fields over the past decade, particularly in human resource management (HRM). Traditional talent acquisition is outdated and labor-intensive, relying on manual processes such as screening resumes and evaluating applicants. With the integration of AI technologies like big data and machine learning, HR departments can significantly enhance efficiency, quickly identifying the best candidates. While it's clear that recruiters are keen to leverage AI for talent acquisition, research on job seekers'

and organizational redesign, it offers a nuanced understanding of the transformational role of AI. The section contributes to academic analysis by placing AI integration in the context of greater socio-technical change and highlighting its significance for future-proof resilience, collaboration and inclusive employee involvement.

The paper will discuss the critical role of the Artificial Intelligence (AI) technology in shaping. sustainable human resources management in the hybrid work environment. As organizations adapt to the AI becomes a critical element in reference to industry 4.0 requirements and growing environmental and social pressures, facilitator of business productivity, staff welfare, and corporate flexibility. The study discusses different hybrid work models and how AI technology like predictive analytics, can be applied. Digital twins, sentiment analysis, and optimization algorithms can be used in workforce planning, improvement in productivity, and sustainability of the environment. It highlights the economic, environmental, social, and sustainability aspects, defining how artificial intelligence promotes fairness, transparency, health management, energy saving, and ethical management. Finally, the paper presents implementation plans, new AI functionality, and research possibilities that facilitate a data-driven, people-oriented, and morally responsible future of work.

Remote and hybrid work models have significantly altered the operational dynamics of organizations, thereby resulting in challenges related to performance management. Traditional evaluation methods have been found to be ineffective as a result of limited supervision and complicated remote situations. This model utilizes machine learning to automatically generate performance reports based on the data. The system employs an ensemble of Logistic Regression, Random Forest, and Gradient Boosting. After

As businesses become more aware of the importance of emotional intelligence in employee satisfaction and organizational performance, its inclusion in workplace wellness programs has become more popular. This chapter discusses how Emotion AI- powerful technologies that recognize and understand human emotions- can be used to cultivate emotionally intelligent workplaces and positive organizational culture. This chapter theorizes the embedding of Emotion AI into core human resource management, leadership, and workplace communication domains. It explores how these technologies can inform empathetic decision-making, enhance team dynamics, and build inclusive, emotionally supportive cultures. Ethical issues such as data privacy, consent, and algorithmic bias are also deeply scrutinized. This chapter contends that when used carefully and responsibly, Emotion AI has enormous potential to transform cultural well-being and aid in creating emotionally mature, high-performance organizations.

The Reality of the hybrid workplace has created a new paradigm for leadership that requires innovative solutions to drive productivity, engagement, and operational efficiency across dispersed teams. But the use of AI in HR is not without major ethical questions. This chapter contributes to the ongoing research by critically analysing the ethics of one aspect of these technologies: algorithmic bias and employee privacy. It also discusses how historical data bias might contribute to unfair hiring, promotion, and performance evaluations resulting in reinforcing systemic biases. And we talk about the thin line between using data for organizational intelligence and creating an atmosphere of surveillance that erodes trust and morale. Finally, we posit that the responsible use of AI in hybrid work will involve a delicate balancing act between fairness, appropriate ethical governance and employees' fundamental rights to ensure that technology serves to augment rather than diminish the modern workforce.

Preface

The nature of work is undergoing a profound transformation. Accelerated by technological advancement and catalyzed by the global shift toward remote and hybrid models, organizations are redefining how talent is recruited, managed, developed, and sustained. At the center of this transformation lies Artificial Intelligence (AI)—not merely as a tool for automation, but as a strategic enabler reshaping workforce management, human capital development, and organizational resilience. *AI-Enabled Workforce Management for Hybrid Workplaces* brings together diverse scholarly perspectives to critically examine this evolving landscape and to provide evidence-based insights for navigating the future of work.

This edited volume is designed to serve researchers, academicians, practitioners, and policymakers who seek to understand how AI-driven systems intersect with hybrid work structures across industries and contexts. The chapters collectively explore how AI can enhance learning transformation, recruitment, performance management, employee engagement, sustainability, and inclusion, while also addressing the complex challenges associated with trust, privacy, bias, governance, and workforce displacement.

A defining strength of this volume is its balanced approach. While several chapters highlight the productivity, efficiency, and strategic benefits of AI-enabled workforce systems, equal attention is given to ethical safeguards, emotional intelligence, gender equity, sustainability, and responsible governance. Together, these contributions emphasize that successful hybrid workforce management requires more than technological adoption—it demands human-centered design, organizational readiness, and principled leadership.

CHAPTER OVERVIEW

1. **Strategic Upskilling in Hybrid Workplaces with Artificial Intelligence for Learning Transformation**

This chapter introduces a Strategic Readiness Model for AI-enabled upskilling across technical, cultural, and strategic dimensions. Drawing on case evidence from global enterprises, it demonstrates how learning analytics, governance mechanisms, and ethical safeguards can be integrated into HRM and business strategy to build resilient hybrid workforces.

2. **Understanding Job Seekers' Acceptance of AI-Driven Recruitment Systems: An Empirical Study Based on the Extended UTAUT Model**

Addressing a critical research gap, this chapter examines job seekers' perceptions of AI-assisted recruitment using an extended UTAUT framework, highlighting the roles of trust, system complexity, performance expectancy, and organizational support in shaping adoption intentions.

3. **Charting the Future—AI's Evolving Role in Human Capital Management**

This contribution explores how AI is expected to reshape Human Capital Management over the next decade, with attention to recruitment, employee well-being, reskilling, diversity, legal considerations, and emerging AI technologies that will redefine employee experience.

4. **Strategic AI Integration in Hybrid Workforce Management: Frameworks and Best Practices**

Focusing on post-pandemic hybrid work cultures, this chapter presents strategic frameworks for AI integration that enhance agility, inclusivity, and data-driven decision-making while situating workforce transformation within broader socio-technical change.

5. **AI-Enabled Sustainable Workforce Management for Hybrid Workplaces**

This chapter examines AI as a driver of sustainable HRM, demonstrating how predictive analytics, digital twins, and sentiment analysis can support productivity, employee well-being, environmental sustainability, and ethical workforce planning.

6. **AI-Driven Feedback System for Remote Work Performance Analysis**

Presenting a machine-learning-based performance evaluation model, this chapter demonstrates how AI-driven feedback systems can overcome limitations of traditional appraisal methods in remote and hybrid work environments.

7. **Blueprint for the Future—AI as the Architect of HR Strategy**

Through comparative case studies of global organizations, this chapter illustrates how AI functions as a strategic partner in HRM, enabling predictive analytics, personalized employee experiences, and agile talent strategies.

8. **Emotionally Intelligent Workplaces: Leveraging Emotion AI to Nurture Positive Organizational Culture**

This chapter explores the role of Emotion AI in fostering empathetic leadership, inclusive cultures, and emotionally intelligent workplaces, while critically examining ethical challenges related to privacy, consent, and algorithmic bias.

9. **Ethical Considerations: Algorithmic Bias and Employee Privacy**

Offering a critical ethical lens, this chapter analyzes how algorithmic bias and workplace surveillance risks emerge in AI-enabled HR systems and outlines governance principles to ensure fairness, transparency, and trust.

10. **AI-Driven Workforce Empowerment: Impact, Challenges, and Strategies**

This chapter evaluates both the disruptive and empowering effects of AI on employment, proposing policy, infrastructural, and reskilling strategies to mitigate job displacement and promote socially responsible AI adoption.

11. **Entrepreneurial Performance Factors in AI-Enabled Hybrid Workplaces: A Meta-Analytic Review**

Using meta-analytic methods, this chapter identifies key individual, business, and environmental determinants of entrepreneurial performance in AI-enabled hybrid contexts, emphasizing creativity, motivation, and self-efficacy.

12. **Navigating the Human–AI Blend: Workforce Challenges in Hybrid Hospitality**

Centered on the hospitality sector, this chapter examines the integration of AI into service-oriented hybrid workplaces, highlighting challenges related to upskilling, job redesign, bias mitigation, and preserving human touch.

13. **Green HRM in the Era of AI-Enabled Hybrid Workplaces**

This chapter integrates sustainability and digital transformation perspectives, outlining how AI-enabled HR practices can support green recruitment, training, performance management, and long-term organizational resilience.

14. **The Future of Gender Equality in Hybrid Workplaces: Ethical Implications and AI Governance**

Concluding the volume, this chapter adopts a gendered lens to assess how AI and hybrid work models can both advance and challenge gender equality, emphasizing the importance of ethical governance and responsible AI use.

Together, these chapters provide a comprehensive, multidisciplinary examination of AI-enabled workforce management in hybrid workplaces. The volume affirms that the future of work will be shaped not only by intelligent systems, but by the values, policies, and human choices that guide their design and deployment.

Preeti Mehra
Campbell College, Edmonton, Canada

Olga Ergunova
Peter the Great St. Petersburg Polytechnic University, Russia

Shyam Sunder Agrawal
Lovely Professional University, India

Pooja Kansra
Lovely Professional University, India

Miladin Stefanovic
University of Kragujevac, Serbia

Chapter 1

Strategic Upskilling in Hybrid Workplaces With Artificial Intelligence for Learning Transformation

J. Leema Christina
https://orcid.org/0009-0004-8855-2965
SRC, SASTRA University, India

R. Alamelu
https://orcid.org/0000-0003-0539-2480
SRC, SASTRA University, India

M. Sathya
https://orcid.org/0009-0009-7539-0318
SRC, SASTRA University, India

R. Purushothaman
https://orcid.org/0009-0003-0941-8462
SRC, SASTRA University, India

ABSTRACT

This chapter examines how artificial intelligence reshapes enterprise upskilling in hybrid workplaces and sets out an evidence-based approach for integrating learning transformation into HRM and business strategy. It introduces a Strategic Readiness Model across three dimensions—Technical, Cultural, and Strategic with a five-point rubric and a diagnostic table for action tracking. Using verified case illustrations from IBM, Deloitte, Unilever, Accenture, and Microsoft, the chapter analyses platform architectures, adoption mechanisms, and measurable outcomes, and then synthe-

DOI: 10.4018/979-8-3373-5871-0.ch001

…t © 2026, IGI Global Scientific Publishing. Copying or distributing in print or electronic forms without written permission of IGI Global Scientific Publishing is prohibited. Use of this chapter to …enerative artificial intelligence (AI) technologies is expressly prohibited. The publisher reserves all rights to license its use for generative AI training and machine learning model development.

sizes results via a cross-case readiness heatmap and a dimension roll-up. Building on these findings, the chapter specifies a performance measurement plan that links learning signals to reviews and resource decisions, and outlines operating cadences for dashboards, impact reviews, and governance. Ethical safeguards—privacy by design, fairness auditing, and transparent communication are positioned as pre-conditions for trust, sustained adoption, and workforce resilience.

1. INTRODUCTION

Hybrid work models quickly transformed from experimental reactive measures to COVID-19 into a fixed component of organisational strategy. It can be said that as digital infrastructure has improved, and as employee expectations have evolved to expect more flexible arrangements, these models provide flexibility for employees, access to larger talent pools all over the world, and perhaps greater work-life integration (Nielsen & Shepherd, 2022). Meanwhile, hybrid work has presented a complicated set of obstacles for workforce learning and development. In this world of the hybrid worker, operating both physically and virtually, skill acquisition needs to mince steps with rapidly changing role requirements, volatile market forces and constant technological progress.

The life of skills useful for work has alike shortened by the speed of innovation. Most content-based skills are out of date within a couple of years, and soft skills need to be constantly honed throughout our careers for the right fit in any work environment. Conventional training methods such as standardised courses, rigid timetabling and centralised delivery are not well adapted to the dispersed, asynchronous and diverse workforces they serve (Baldwin & Ford, 1988) (Chen, 2024). Geographical distances could restrict opportunities for training, while disparities in access to technology and digital literacy might develop uneven experiences. In these settings, the logistics for planned training classes can be challenging, and learning typically is isolated, disconnected and disengaged from the performance of work.

AI provides a strategic solution to these issues by providing personalised, scalable and adaptive learning systems that can be embedded into daily workflows. Platform software with a layer of AI can deliver content to meet individual needs, respond in real time to the learner's skill performance (and recommended learning topics adjust accordingly), and also show where current role requirements and career growth align for future capabilities. Combining taxonomies of skills with organisational knowledge graphs, through AI, allows mapping what is there (in skill terms) now and facilitates forecasting emerging needs and leading staff along tailored learning journeys. These abilities make AI more than just an efficiency tool and instead a silo buster for sustainable talent development in hybrid environments.

Learning in the flow of work may be defined as the provision of micro learning and real-time task advice through daily online tools, where new abilities are used instantly. Knowledge graphs represent the connections between roles, skills and tasks and can be used to map existing distributions of capabilities and predict changes in skills in the future. Adaptive learning systems are considered to dynamically adapt the difficulty of content, modality and sequencing according to the progress and engagement patterns of a learner (Margherita, 2021). Internal talent marketplaces place an algorithmic match to place employees to projects or assignments that are short-term, and they create experiential learning to supplement formal development. All of these ideas give the foundations to the AI-based learning system, which is discussed in the following pages.

The part of the framework presented in this chapter is also consistent with the United Nations Sustainable Development Goals, especially SDG 8 and SDG 10. AI-based upskilling approach could help to create equitable access for career advancement, impact productivity and promote workforce resilience through making learning more accessible, inclusive and relevant (Noy & Zhang, 2023) (Brynjolfsson, Li, & Raymond, 2023). When implemented responsibly, such systems can also lead to less inequality of training opportunities, counter bias in learning recommendations and contribute to the development of underrepresented groups.

The main aim of this chapter is to explore the potential of AI in enabling agile lifelong learning within hybrid workplaces by weaving technological innovation, normative governance and strategic alignment with organisational objectives. It presents a model for AI-enabled learning transformation and for guiding adoption, as well as principles for ethical and inclusive implementation. Case studies from real-life businesses demonstrate best practices and measurable success in various industry settings.

The remainder of the chapter is structured as follows. Section 2 examines the specific challenges of skill development in hybrid workplaces. Section 3 discusses the capabilities of AI technologies that can address these challenges. Section 4 presents the conceptual framework for AI-enabled learning transformation. Section 5 explores the ethical, fairness, and inclusivity considerations in deploying AI for workforce development. Section 6 introduces the strategic readiness model, while Section 7 provides industry case illustrations. Section 8 addresses the integration of AI-based learning into broader human resource management and business strategies. Section 9 identifies future research and policy directions, and Section 10 concludes with strategic recommendations for building sustainable and inclusive learning ecosystems.

2. SKILL DEVELOPMENT CHALLENGES IN HYBRID WORKPLACES

The hybrid environment provides flexibility and expands the pool of talent, but also creates structural and behavioural challenges that can undermine the efficacy of traditional learning systems. These impediments are due to attitudinal issues among employees, variations in their working environments, and the speed at which company priorities change. It is important to comprehend these impediments so companies can better develop upskilling initiatives with AI that meet real operational requirements (Venkatesh, Morris, Davis, & Davis, 2003).

2.1 Geographic and Temporal Dispersion

With hybrid work models, employees can be scattered across a few cities, countries, or even continents. Geography coverage causes division of people across time zones, making synchronous training sessions hard to organise. And for employees in some areas, difficult class hours and other work commitments can shut them out from learning opportunities. While scheduling can be increasingly flexible with asynchronous forms of learning, that same immediacy and feedback remain essential for mastering skills, which is deep skill development.

2.2 Inconsistent Access to Learning Resources

Training resources, equipment, and platforms are not equally available to everyone working in a hybrid environment. At one end, some workers have high-speed internet connections and a quiet place to work with the latest devices; at the other, people are contending with erratic Wi-Fi, shared computers, or constant fights for attention in their homes. These are the problems that make an individual run slowly and ramp the load imbalance in the entire team as a result (Leonardi et al., 2024). Furthermore, companies operating on a global level experience these problems to an even larger extent when language is also a barrier that reduces participation in the materials and information.

2.3 Disconnection between Training and Work Application

Conventional training is often disconnected from the immediate working environment. Courses may be focused on generic skills and not relevant to employees' current role or future projects (Billett, 2002). This gap is exacerbated in hybrid models due to fewer informal training and coaching opportunities for managers and trainers to see when there's a performance gap and when everything else is in line.

Then, employees finish training modules, yet are unsure how to apply their new knowledge when they're back at work.

2.4 Declining Engagement and Motivation

The hybrid work model can reduce the peer discussions that facilitate learning together. Without the personal connections and shared responsibility on teams, employees are more likely to leave training behind for other urgent tasks (Marozva & Pelser, 2025). The long-term consequence of this change is a decrease in engagement with time spent learning, lower completion rates of courses assigned and low memory retention of learned materials.

2.5 Fragmentation of Learning Pathways

Learning within hybrid environments tends to be rather disjointed with isolated classes, separate units and unguided self-exploration. Without a defined and personalised learning path, employees may only learn skills in isolation instead of continuous competency development that aligns with career paths and business objectives.

2.6 Rapidly Changing Skill Requirements

In many industries, technological changes occur so rapidly that skill requirements are continually changing. Hybrid work increases this challenge as teams may embrace new tools or practices at different rates. Without the ability to track new skill needs as they happen, organisations risk being left behind in both competence and competitiveness.

These difficulties draw attention to the inadequacies in traditional modes of workforce learning in hybrid formations. They also highlight the demand for solutions that are flexible, tailored and integrated into the working environment of employees. AI can help address this need through analysing individual and organisational learning patterns, surfacing gaps and scaling targeted interventions (Cappelli et al., 2019). The next section discusses the particular applications of AI that can help overcome these challenges and enable a lifetime of upskilling in the hybrid work environment.

2.7 From Problems to Capabilities: Mapping Needs to AI Responses

The issues described in Section 2 demonstrate systematic inefficiencies of the traditional learning methods in implementation in the hybrid habitat. In order to bridge these issues and practical solutions, Table 1 matches each issue with an AI ability described in Section 3. That explains why explicit statements how adaptive learning, recommendation engines, digital coaching, skill mapping, behavioural analytics and integrated performance systems directly counter the barriers that dispersed, technology-mediated work forms create.

The rationale behind the flow of the chapter is also explained by this mapping: the issues that have been pointed out in the development of hybrid skills are converted into functional needs that AI systems would be particularly well positioned to address. The comparison of challenges and capabilities helps organisations to better focus on interventions and comprehend the reasons why certain AI tools are presented in the next section.

Table 1. Mapping Hybrid-Work Challenges to AI Capabilities

Hybrid-Work Challenge (Section 2)	**AI Capability Response (Section 3)**
1. Geographic and Temporal Dispersion	Just-in-time digital coaches + adaptive asynchronous modules that deliver support across time zones and minimise reliance on synchronous sessions.
2. Inconsistent Access to Learning Resources	Adaptive learning systems that adjust to device constraints and intelligent recommendation engines that personalise content regardless of technical variation.
3. Disconnection Between Training and Work Application	Digital coaches embedded in workflow tools to provide real-time task support and integration with performance systems for contextualised guidance.
4. Declining Engagement and Motivation	Behavioural data analytics to detect disengagement early and recommend re-engagement strategies such as microlearning, reminders, or gamified elements.
5. Fragmentation of Learning Pathways	Recommendation engines + adaptive sequencing that build coherent, personalised learning journeys aligned to skill taxonomies and career paths.
6. Rapidly Changing Skill Requirements	Skill mapping and forecasting using organisational knowledge graphs and labour-market data to identify emerging skills and guide timely upskilling.

3. AI CAPABILITIES FOR WORKFORCE UPSKILLING

There are artificial intelligence-based solutions that can precisely overcome the shortcomings of traditional learning systems in hybrid working conditions. These tools make the most of data-informed insights to deliver learning experiences that are personalised, adaptive and part of everyday workflows. The key AI functionalities associated with the workforce upskilling are described in subsequent subsections.

3.1 Adaptive Learning Systems

Personalised learning systems adapt the content of materials made available for a learner's use based on how well they are performing at any given point in time, on that user's pace and style. Adaptive systems, by assessing on a real-time basis what is weakly known or not known at all, and adjusting the difficulty of content, its sequence and format, are used for the detection of gaps. In hybrid workplaces, this implies that all employees get equipped at the level they are currently working with, avoiding inefficiency among different skill profiles. Adaptive systems may also employ evidence-based methods for determining when to reinforce content that will result in long-term knowledge retention (Koedinger, Corbett & Perfetti, 2012).

3.2 Intelligent Recommendation Engines

The recommendation engines in learning platforms function like the consumer recommendation engines, except that the utility is typically based on skill taxonomies, career pathways and organisational priorities. They will draw on employee profile data, learning history, and performance data to suggest suitable courses or microlearning modules and experiential opportunities (Xu et al., 2025). In the hybrid situation, suggestions may sync with both individual growth and team requirements in forthcoming projects. This synchronisation allows learners to more easily transition between learning and their work environments.

3.3 Digital Coaches and Just-in-Time Guidance

AI-based digital coaches offer in-the-moment assistance, feedback and nudges that are integrated into the teams' day-to-day applications they use. Such virtual assistants are able to process queries and direct task-level reasoning as well as suggest resources during interaction (VanLehn, 2011). Digital coaches can help hybrid teams to avoid the dependence on synchronous training sessions and human trainers, which distracts from the point of need learning. This mirrors the concept of "learning in the flow of work", which improves relevance and retention.

3.4 Skill Mapping and Forecasting

Leveraging knowledge graphs of the organisation, combined with external labour market data, AI-based systems can evaluate the skills available within an organisation and predict future demands. This offers a means for informed workforce planning, to inform investments in what types of training and to gauge which skills may become most vital for the future. For hybrid organisations, it will avoid practitioners becoming tied to individual or location capabilities.

3.5 Behavioural Data Analytics for Engagement

AI can process behavioural data such as course completion rate, time spent on learning modules, how often they interact with content and their preferences. etc. Such analytics can allow institutions to identify trends in disengagement early and intervene where necessary (Papamitsiou & Economides, 2014). Insights from engagement analysis can guide the development of more engaging learning experiences, such as gamification, peer collaboration functionality and recognition systems that are particularly beneficial within hybrid spaces where social reinforcement might be less strong.

3.6 Integration with Organisational Performance Systems

Learning platforms infused with AI can be connected to performance management and talent development systems that provide continuous feedback between learning new skills and demonstrating those skills on the job. The integration of HR and training doesn't evaluate the result independently, but in relation to the relevant performance measure, career pathing and organisational objectives (Tambe et al., 2019). In hybrid environments, this connection helps to keep scattered teams' learning efforts in sync with the overall strategic direction of the business.

The combined effect of these capabilities is a transformation from static, one-size-fits-all training programs into dynamic, data-driven learning ecosystems. Leading by allowing for personalisation at scale, AI helps drive individual development just as it underpins the agility of the organisation, giving foundations to a workforce that's capable of navigating the unpredictability attached with hybrid work. The next section provides a conceptual model to represent how these capabilities could be organised into an integrated model of AI-enhanced learning transformation.

3.7 Comparative Critique: Where AI Helps and Where Traditional Learning Still Wins

To provide a balanced perspective and avoid overstating technological benefits, this section contrasts the distinctive strengths of AI-enabled learning with those of traditional learning approaches. Table 2 summarises these differences before the detailed discussion that follows.

Table 2. Comparative Strengths of AI-Enabled and Traditional Learning Approaches

Dimension	AI-Enabled Learning	Traditional Learning
1. Personalisation & Adaptation	Delivers personalised pathways and adjusts difficulty dynamically at scale.	Personalised through human judgment, mentoring and coaching.
2. Skill Awareness & Forecasting	Maps current skills and predicts emerging needs using data analytics and knowledge graphs.	Relies on manager experience and organisational memory; forecasting less systematic.
3. Learning Delivery & Accessibility	Provides on-demand, workflow-integrated microlearning accessible across locations.	Occurs in structured settings; may be limited by schedules, geography and trainer availability.
4. Knowledge Type	Strong for explicit, codified knowledge and repeatable tasks.	Strong for tacit knowledge, contextual judgment and socio-emotional skills.
5. Engagement Mechanisms	Uses behavioural analytics, nudges, gamification and adaptive triggers.	Uses social reinforcement, peer learning, community and shared responsibility.
6. Human Connection	Limited relational depth; guidance is functional rather than emotional.	High relational value, enabling trust, psychological safety and leadership identity formation.
7. Scalability & Consistency	Highly scalable with consistent quality across learners.	Quality varies by trainer expertise, group dynamics and context.

Collectively, these strengths have been used to propose that AI maybe used to supplement but not to substitute traditional learning. The best organisational strategies would involve the integration of AI induced methods of personalisation with analytics and human-based approaches to mentoring and team-based learning methods to provide both efficiency and breadth in the development of capability.

4. CONCEPTUAL FRAMEWORK FOR AI-ENABLED LEARNING TRANSFORMATION

The complexities of skill-building in a hybrid workplace, coupled with the potential of AI, support a more structured framework for technology-enabled workforce upskilling. The proposed conceptual framework in this chapter integrates these elements into a coherent model designed to support continuous, personalised, and strategically aligned learning in hybrid environments.

4.1 Framework Overview

The framework is built around five interrelated components:

Skill Needs Identification. Mapping existing competencies and future skills needs.

Adaptive Content Delivery. Offering personalised learning materials that adapt to performance and engagement patterns.

Just-in-Time Support. Providing AI-enabled digital coaches that give live, task-specific assistance.

Performance and Engagement Feedback Loop. Integrating learning data with performance metrics to track impact and refine delivery.

Strategic Alignment with Organisational Goals. Earning initiatives that serve long-term workforce planning and business objectives.

This model emphasises the continuous nature of AI-enabled learning, in which skill building is not a one-time event but rather part of the steady flow of work

Stage 1: Skill Needs Identification

At the starting point, AI systems leverage organisational knowledge graphs, skill taxonomies, and external labour market data to evaluate the existing skills of today's workforce and to uncover new skill gaps. This phase also addresses location-specific requirements in hybrid teams to balance the actual capability distribution.

Stage 2: Adaptive Content Delivery

After determining the needs, adaptive learning systems provide instruction at a performance level of the learner and in accordance with the preferred learning style. Sequencing, complexity and format of content will become dynamic as the learner advances, increasing its relevance and retention.

Stage 3: Just-in-Time Support

Learning is reinforced through AI-based digital coaches embedded in work applications. The model delivered an on-demand learning guidance mechanism that helps to clarify concepts and delivers microlearning resources when they are needed, reducing the time gap between knowledge acquisition and practice.

Stage 4: Performance and Engagement Feedback Loop

Job performance metrics are constantly collected and analysed with learning data. This creates a feedback loop where low engagement or poor application of skills triggers targeted interventions, such as additional resources, peer mentoring, or re-sequenced content.

Stage 5: Strategic Alignment with Organisational Goals

The framework's final component/element ensures that learning initiatives are not isolated from broader workforce and business strategies. Intelligent insights powered by AI capabilities help HR leaders and managers connect the dots between training results, performance reviews, leadership pipelines and successor planning, further enhancing organisational agility and overall resilience.

Visual Representation

The framework (Figure 1) can be represented as a cyclical process:

Figure 1. AI-Enabled Learning Framework

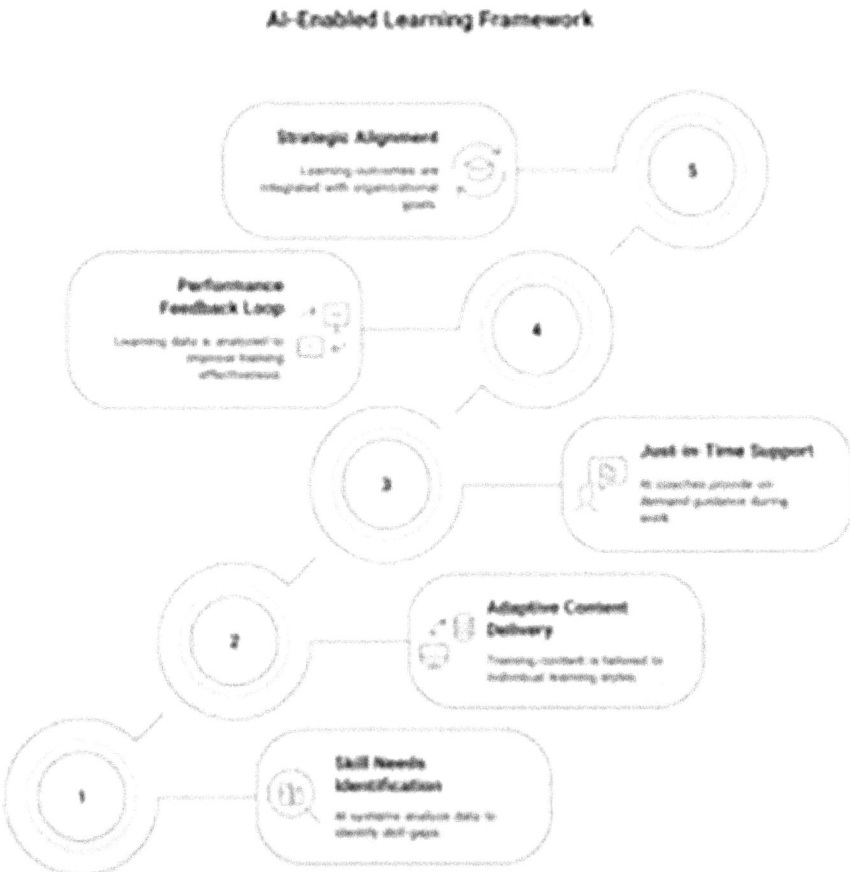

- Outer cycle: Continuous loop of *Needs Identification Adaptive Delivery Just-in-Time Support Feedback Loop Strategic Alignment Needs Identification.*
- Inner core: AI capabilities (data analytics, recommendation engines, knowledge graphs) enabling the entire cycle.
- Overlay: Ethical and inclusive principles ensuring fairness, transparency, and accessibility at every stage.

Since the framework operates through continuous data flows and system-level integration, its success depends on strong ethical, transparent, and inclusive governance—addressed next in Section 5.

5. ETHICS, FAIRNESS, AND INCLUSIVE AI IN LEARNING

While artificial intelligence provides significant potential to transform workforce upskilling in hybrid workplaces, its deployment also raises ethical, legal, and social considerations. Uncontrolled, AI-enabled learning systems can also inadvertently perpetuate existing inequalities, compromise data privacy or cause employee trust to erode. Ethical and inclusive design is therefore not an optional element of AI integration; it is a foundational requirement that determines the legitimacy and long-term success of these systems.

5.1 Algorithmic Fairness and Bias Mitigation

AI models rely on historical and real-time data to learn and make recommendations, but these sources may have patterns of bias related to gender, ethnicity, age, spoken language or geographic region. In the absence of corrective measures, these biases could lead to unequal opportunities for learning and entrench inequalities rather than reduce them. This can be mitigated by using diverse and representative training sets which covers a broad range of employee contexts, conducting periodic auditing of the algorithm to detect and reverse any bias towards race in content recommended or employee performance scored, and ensuring human oversight is used when interpreting outputs produced by AI systems especially on high-impact decisions such as promotions or paths for leadership development (Mittelstadt et al., 2016) (Raji et al., 2020).

5.2 Data Privacy and Transparency

AI-enabled learning systems rely on extensive data collection, including performance metrics, engagement patterns, and behavioural analytics (Hardt, Price, & Srebro, 2016). In a hybrid environment, where work devices and networks may differ, data handling must be especially rigorous (Kleinberg, Mullainathan, & Raghavan, 2016). Privacy and transparency practices should include:

- Clear consent processes detailing what data is collected, how it is used, and who has access.
- Anonymisation and encryption to protect sensitive information from misuse or breaches (Dwork & Roth, 2014).
- Explainable AI models that allow employees to understand the rationale behind recommendations or assessments.

5.3 Universal Design for Learning (UDL) Principles

Ethical AI deployment should also ensure accessibility for employees with diverse cognitive abilities, linguistic backgrounds, and levels of digital literacy. Using universal design for learning (UDL) means designing instruction that meets the needs of students with a wide range of abilities and backgrounds. This involves providing content in a variety of forms, including text, audio, video and interactive simulations, to make sure that all learners can access and engage with it. Interfaces need to be designed to be more compatible with assistive technologies so that people with disabilities can take full and effective part. In addition, offering multilingual opportunities and integrating culturally appropriate content illustrates that learning materials are sensitive to multiple linguistic and cultural environments. Together, these steps not only meet inclusivity requirements but also increase engagement, understanding and learning effectiveness throughout the entire organisation.

5.4 Building Employee Trust in AI Systems

Trust is a key factor in whether employees will use AI-based learning tools. Design and governance transparency will create trust that AI is deployed to assist, rather than monitor or penalise employees (Lee & See 2004). Organisations are encouraged to clearly articulate why and how AI is learning, provide employees with feedback channels to share what they have learned or problems encountered, and show responsiveness by making system changes based on user input.

5.5 Alignment with Organisational and Societal Values

AI use in learning should be ethical, both from the standpoint of institutional/ organisational values, and broader societal commitments, including the Sustainable Development Goals. Both of these approaches are encompassed by SDG 10 (Reduced Inequalities), promoting inclusive measures that ensure that all have fair access to opportunities. By infusing these principles into AI-driven learning techniques, they can help organisations advance the narrowing of skills gaps and further fair pathways to advancement (Fu & Weng, 2024). Ethics, equity, and inclusivity are not an add-on to the technical structure of AI-enabled learning; rather, they should be integrated throughout each phase of the process presented in our conceptual framework (Li et al., 2025). The following section introduces a Strategic Readiness Model that enables organisations to evaluate whether they are ready technically, culturally and strategically to implement AI-enabled upskilling in a manner compliant with these ethical standards

5.6 Strategic Readiness Model for AI Adoption

The successful integration of AI-powered upskilling work in hybrid workplaces isn't simply a matter of having the technical capability to do so. Organisations must be ready across multiple dimensions to ensure that the implementation is effective, sustainable, and ethically responsible (Weiner, 2009). The Strategic Readiness Model proposed in this chapter shows a structured approach for assessing organisational preparedness through three interdependent dimensions: **Technical Readiness, Cultural Readiness, and Strategic Readiness**.

Technical Readiness

Technical readiness refers to the infrastructure, systems, and technological resources required to support AI-enabled learning. Key indicators include:

Data infrastructure. Availability of secure, interoperable systems capable of handling large volumes of learning and performance data.

Platform integration. Ability to connect AI learning tools with existing HR, performance management, and collaboration platforms.

Scalability. Capacity to expand AI systems to accommodate workforce growth or increased learning demands without degradation in performance.

Cybersecurity. Robust protocols for safeguarding sensitive employee data in diverse hybrid environments.

Cultural Readiness

Cultural readiness captures the mindset, trust levels, and behavioural openness to adopting AI-driven learning solutions. Key factors include:

Employee trust. Confidence that AI is being used to enhance, not monitor or penalise, performance.

Leadership advocacy. Active promotion of AI-enabled learning by senior leaders as part of the organisation's strategic vision.

Change readiness. Willingness among employees and managers to experiment with new tools and adjust to evolving workflows.

Collaborative learning culture. Existing norms that encourage peer-to-peer learning and knowledge sharing across dispersed teams.

Strategic Readiness

Strategic readiness reflects the alignment between AI-enabled learning initiatives and the broader organisational and workforce strategies. Key considerations include:

Goal alignment. Clear connection between learning objectives, workforce planning, and organisational performance targets.

Metrics and evaluation. Defined measures for assessing learning outcomes, employee engagement, and business impact.

Sustainability focus. Commitment to long-term skill development that supports both business agility and workforce resilience.

Ethical governance. Mechanisms to ensure compliance with privacy, fairness, and inclusivity principles.

The three readiness dimensions are directly related to the hybrid-work challenges outlined in Section 2 above. Technical readiness helps to address challenges like uneven distribution of learning materials, and the high rate of skills obsolescence is addressed through their strong data infrastructure, systems and scalable platforms that run on interoperability. The cultural preparedness is a reaction to issues such as the deteriorating involvement and disintegrated learning courses by enhancing trust, leadership endorsement and shared learning standards. Strategic preparedness aligns learning with organisational objectives, which is effective in overcoming the gap between training and application at the workplace. Strategic preparedness allows planning of skills in a dynamic environment proactively.

5.7 Operational and Organisational Risks

In addition to the issues of fairness and privacy, AI-enabled learning provides a number of operational risks that may impact adoption and long-term viability. First of all, job displacement fears can be introduced in cases where automation redefines job expectations; open redeployment opportunities and efficient exploitation of internal talent markets can alleviate such fears. Second, the lock-in of vendors and dependence on platforms constrain the capability of organisations; the adoption of open skill taxonomies and interoperability standards mitigates this risk (Giralt Hernández, 2024). Third, employees can feel upskilling fatigue or cognitive overload when learning requires more, and it is possible to organise learning in cycles that are easy to manage and have time off to maintain engagement. Fourth, governance weaknesses, such as model drift, poor version control and lack of transparency in update cycles, may compromise the dependability of the system; model change logs should be documented and audited routinely. Lastly, cross-system integration offers more chances to expose cybersecurity vulnerabilities; robust access control, encryption standards and periodical penetration testing are beneficial towards resiliency.

5.8 Change Management and Behavioural Supports

Effective adoption of AI-enabled learning requires structured behavioural support to complement technical deployment. Four practical tactics strengthen engagement and reduce resistance, particularly in hybrid environments.

- **Manager-led micro-coaching:** Regular 5–10 minute check-ins help employees interpret AI recommendations and prioritise learning tasks; provide managers with short scripts and prompt libraries.
- **Role-modelling by leaders:** Visible use of AI tools by senior leaders signals psychological safety and expectation alignment; encourage leaders to share "learning logs" or insights during team meetings.
- **Recognition tied to learning application:** Acknowledge not just course completion but evidence of real work application; integrate small "application badges" or public acknowledgements in team channels.
- **Protected learning time:** Dedicate 1–2 hours per week as "no-meeting learning windows" so hybrid employees have uninterrupted space to focus on upskilling; embed this practice into team norms and annual planning.

6. CASE ILLUSTRATIONS FROM INDUSTRY PRACTICE

The case evidence in this section demonstrates how organisations with varying readiness levels apply the framework and governance principles in real settings.

6.1 Case Selection and Scoring Method

This chapter is structured and adheres to a systematic procedure of case identification and the use of the readiness scoring rubric in order to improve both the methodological clarity and transparency. Cases were sampled out of three inclusion criteria: (a) the organisation publicly reported AI-enabled learning or talent development programs, (b) there must have been a demonstration or reporting of measurable outcomes, and (c) the cases used had to be cross-industry to facilitate cross-sector comparability. Only sources that were available publicly and published during 2019-2025 were considered to make sure of relevance in the present times.

The readiness assessment used a 12-indicator rubric that was congruent with three dimensions: Technical Readiness, Cultural Readiness and Strategic Readiness. There were four indicators in each dimension. Technical: data infrastructure, platform integration, scalability and cybersecurity. Cultural: culture of employee trust, culture of leadership advocacy, culture of readiness to change and culture of collaborative learning. Strategy: alignment of goals, metrics and assessment, sustainability focus and ethical governance. All the indicators were rated on a five-point scale, with 1 meaning absent, 3 partially developed, and 5 fully developed practice with documented processes. The author of the chapter scored them based on verifiable artefacts (e.g., public reports, case releases, and governance documents). In the case where quantitative evidence was not revealed, a low score was given and the assumption recorded.

6.2 IBM: personalised learning at scale and decision support in HR

Intervention. IBM operates *Your Learning* as a digital marketplace, complemented by AI services such as a learning chatbot and skill tagging that surface personalised learning pathways and connect learning signals to other HR decisions (for example, performance and compensation tools). (Qin & Kochan, 2020).

Mechanisms and outcomes. Independent academic analysis of IBM's internal data reported that in Q1 2020, 89% of employees visited *Your Learning* with 1.9 million visits and 14.1 million page views; in 2019 employees averaged 77 learning hours each (median 52), against the firm's THINK-40 expectation (40 hours per year).

6.3 Deloitte: personalised learning pathways and task support

Intervention. Deloitte has deployed the Disprz learning experience platform (LXP) to deliver role-based learning journeys, and introduced *PairD*, an internal chatbot used by auditors for summarisation, code, and analysis. (Disprz, n.d.; Financial News London, 2025).

Mechanisms and outcomes. Disprz reports a 95% course completion rate and 100% self-enrolment post onboarding in the Deloitte case materials (Disprz, n.d.). In the United Kingdom audit practice, monthly active use of *PairD* reportedly rose from about 25% to nearly 75% within a year, with more than 1.1 million prompts generated between April 2024 and February 2025 (Financial News London, 2025).

6.4 Unilever: internal talent marketplace and agile capacity creation

Intervention. Unilever's *FLEX Experiences* is an internal AI enabled marketplace that matches people to short projects across geographies, designed to build skills while mobilising capacity quickly (Unilever, 2020; Unilever & WIRED Consulting, 2022).

Mechanisms and outcomes. Early deployments were reported to have unlocked more than 60,000 hours of capacity with strong employee endorsement (Bersin, 2019b; Bersin, 2019a).

6.5 Accenture: enterprise scale skilling for generative AI

Intervention. Accenture announced a 3 billion US dollar multiyear investment to expand its Data and AI practice and stated an intention to double AI talent to about 80,000 professionals; in addition, the firm introduced *Accenture LearnVantage* and noted continuing investment of more than 1 billion US dollars per year in learning for its people (Accenture, 2023; Accenture, 2024).

Mechanisms and outcomes. The scale and time horizon of these programmes indicate strategic capability building rather than episodic training initiatives (Accenture, 2023; Accenture, 2024).

6.6 Microsoft: role-based skilling and embedded productivity support

Intervention. Microsoft has reported structured internal rollouts of Microsoft 365 Copilot together with the Viva suite. Viva Insights applies privacy by design safeguards such as aggregation and de-identification to protect individuals in organisational analytics (Microsoft, n.d. ; Microsoft, 2025).

Mechanisms and outcomes. A cross-government trial in the United Kingdom reported that civil servants using Microsoft 365 Copilot saved an average of 26 minutes per day and expressed strong intentions to continue usage (Cabinet Office, 2025; Financial Times, 2025). The summary of case outcome (Table 3) is shown below

Table 3. Summary of case outcomes

Organisation	AI initiative(s)	Key outcomes (selected)
IBM	*Your Learning*: AI assisted learning supports	Q1 2020: 89% of employees visited; 1.9 M visits; 14.1 M page views; 2019 mean 77 hours per employee. (Qin & Kochan, 2020).
Deloitte	Disprz LXP; *PairD* chatbot	Disprz: 95% completion; 100% self-enrolment. *PairD*: ~75% monthly users; 1.1 M+ prompts (Apr 2024–Feb 2025). (Disprz, n.d.; Financial News London, 2025).
Unilever	*FLEX Experiences*	Early rollout unlocked 60,000+ hours; internal marketplace used to route talent rapidly. (Bersin, 2019a; Bersin, 2019b; Unilever, 2020).
Accenture	Data and AI expansion; *LearnVantage*	3 B USD AI investment; plan to double AI talent to ~80k; continuing investment of >1 B USD per year in learning. (Accenture, 2023; Accenture, 2024).
Microsoft	Viva; Microsoft 365 Copilot	UK government trial: ~26 minutes per day saved on average; high intention to continue use. (Cabinet Office, 2025; Financial Times, 2025).

Cross-case readiness diagnostic (derived from Section 6 rubric)

Method. Each organisation was scored on twelve indicators across three dimensions. Scores reflect publicly documented controls, adoption evidence, and disclosures. When quantitative metrics were unavailable, conservative scoring anchored to the strongest public artefact for that indicator was applied (Figure 2).

Figure 2. Readiness heatmap by organisation and indicator (1–5)

Table 4. Dimension-level readiness (means of the four indicators in each dimension; 1–5)

Organisation	Technical	Cultural	Strategic	Overall readiness (mean)
Microsoft	5.00	4.50	5.00	4.83
Accenture	5.00	4.50	4.75	4.75
IBM	4.75	4.00	4.50	4.42
Unilever	4.25	3.75	4.50	4.17
Deloitte	4.25	4.00	3.75	4.00

(Computation: Technical = mean of {Data infrastructure, Platform integration, Scalability, Cybersecurity}; Cultural = mean of {Employee trust, Leadership advocacy, Change readiness, Collaborative learning culture}; Strategic = mean of {Goal alignment, Metrics & evaluation, Sustainability focus, Ethical governance}. Overall = mean of the three dimensions.)

Synthesis. Across cases, platform integration and scalability score consistently high, which reflects mature service architectures (Table 4). Ethical governance appears strongest where organisations publish principles and assurance processes, which support adoption while managing risk. Variation in employee trust and measurement depth tracks the transparency of reported outcomes, suggesting a near-term priority to formalise evaluation frameworks and communications. These patterns help explain why organisations that combine governance with clear measurement anchors (for example, Microsoft and IBM) exhibit higher readiness to scale AI-enabled upskilling.

6.7 Applicability for Small and Medium Enterprises (SMEs)

Although the cases illustrated are of large-scale businesses, the AI-based learning framework and readiness rubric are scalable to SMEs as well. Three pragmatic steps facilitate the adoption of SMEs: (1) creating a basic but sufficient data infrastructure through available HR and learning data; (2) implementing a lightweight inside project-matching board or gig board to trigger low-cost experiential learning; and (3) incorporating micro credentials to certify newly-emerged skills. An example of a hypothetical 612-month SME pilot may be the implementation of an LXP with basic tags on skills of a single team and aiming to increase internal mobility by 20 per cent, and monitor the course completion and practical skills applied. It shows that smaller organisations can obtain quantifiable returns without making huge investments.

7. INTEGRATION OF AI-UPSKILLING WITH HRM AND BUSINESS STRATEGY

AI-enabled upskilling achieves a durable impact only when it is integrated with core HRM processes and aligned to business strategy. Building on the cross-case diagnostic in Figure 2 and the dimension roll-up (Table 4), this section shows how verified adoption and outcome signals from Section 7 are embedded into talent acquisition and mobility, performance management, leadership development, workforce resilience, and ethical governance.

7.1 Alignment with Talent Acquisition and Internal Mobility

AI-enabled learning platforms connect development to deployment when they integrate with internal marketplaces and role/skill taxonomies. As shown in Section 7, systems such as Watson Career Coach (IBM) and FLEX Experiences (Unilever) link skill signals to role matching and short-term project staffing. This creates a continuous loop: employees see timely opportunities to apply new skills (raising motivation and retention), while HR gains real-time visibility of role readiness for redeployment and succession planning. In practice, role profiles and pathways should be refreshed on a fixed cadence (e.g., quarterly) using marketplace and learning data, with changes approved through established talent governance.

7.2 Integration with Performance Management

AI-enhanced learning generates auditable signals—engagement, progression, skill application—that should inform manager and business reviews. The Before–After KPIs in Figures 3, 4 &5 provide concrete examples: rising coverage of task-support tools (Deloitte PairD), capacity gains from project matching (Unilever FLEX) and time savings from embedded assistants (M365 Copilot).

Figure 3. Deloitte PairD — Monthly active users (UK audit)

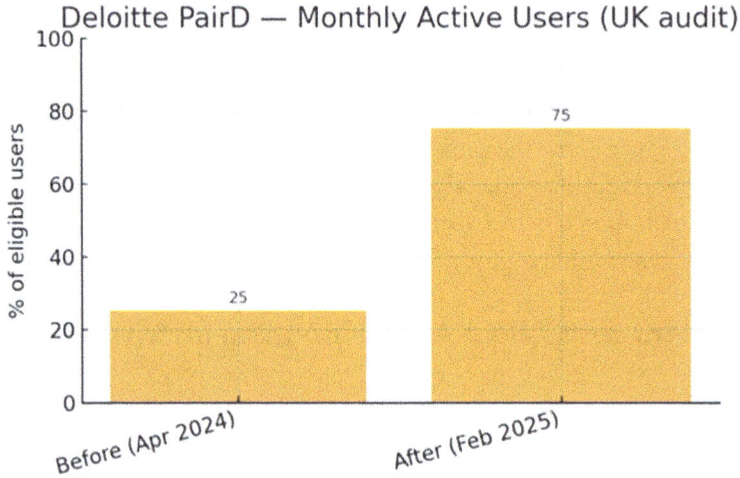

Figure 4. Unilever FLEX — Capacity unlocked

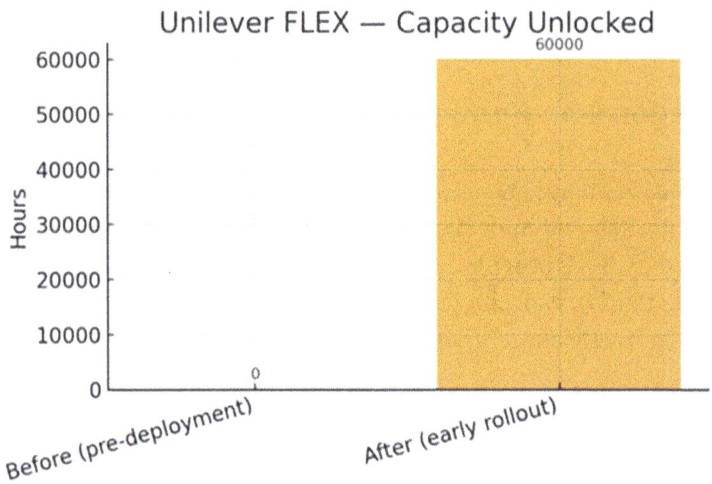

Figure 5. UK Government— Microsoft 365 Copilot time savings

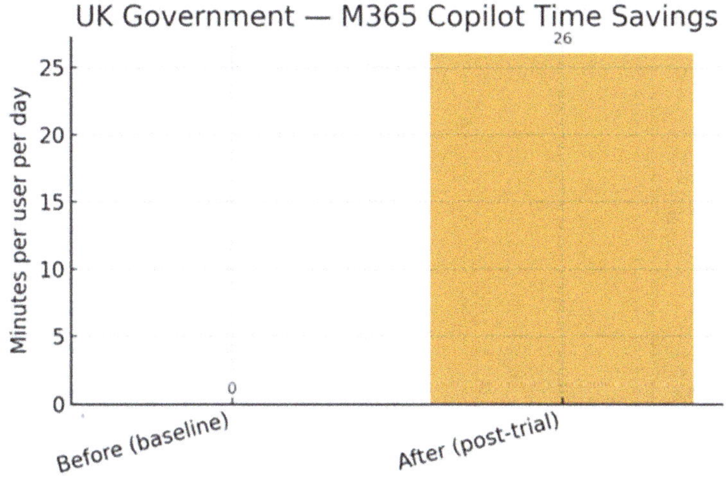

To operationalise these signals, adopt a standard measurement schema (Table 5) and review cadence as set out below.

Table 5. Measurement plan for performance integration

Metric	Operational definition (exact)	Unit	Baseline window	Post window	Review frequency	Data source & tool	Quality checks	Reporting owner	Decision use
Deloitte PairD monthly active users (UK audit)	% eligible audit staff with ≥1 PairD session in month. Values observed ≈25% (Apr 2024) → ≈75% (Feb 2025). *(See §7.2.)*	% of eligible users	Apr 2024	Feb 2025	Monthly	PairD telemetry; HR eligibility roster	Reconcile denominator monthly; exclude test/service accounts; identity merge checks	Audit innovation lead + People Analytics	Target enablement to low-adoption teams; set minimum MAU thresholds in quarterly reviews
Unilever FLEX hours of capacity unlocked	Sum of hours recorded for project work matched via FLEX that would not have been staffed otherwise; early roll-outs unlocked **60,000+** hours. *(See §7.3.)*	Hours	Pre-deployment ref.	Early roll-out window	Monthly (Qtr consolidation)	FLEX logs / timesheets	Deduplicate entries; classify projects; manager sign-off sample	Talent marketplace owner + Finance	Prioritise categories/ regions with highest net capacity; monitor crowding-out
M365 Copilot minutes saved per day (UK gov't trial)	Mean minutes saved per user per working day post vs baseline as defined in the study; reported average ≈**26 min/day**. *(See §7.5.)*	Minutes/user/ day	Study baseline	Study post period	Quarterly (internal); per-study external	Official trial report; internal telemetry (where available)	Align sample definitions; trim outliers; document imputation	Productivity analytics + Programme lead	Focus licenses and training on use-cases with verified savings; inform ROI cases

Operating cadence. Managers receive a monthly dashboard with team-level indicators; a quarterly impact review consolidates trends at the business-unit level and links actions (enablement, budget, staffing) to observed changes. Metrics without a valid baseline are instrumented prospectively and withheld from performance decision-making until a complete pre/post-window exists.

7.3 Building Leadership Pipelines

Enterprise skilling initiatives should flow into leadership development by design. As evidenced by Accenture's multi-year AI investments and LearnVantage, platforms and partnerships can embed digital and data competencies into leadership pathways. Organisations should define role-based certification ladders (foundation → advanced → role-specific) and map them to succession plans, with completion and application evidence reviewed during leadership talent discussions.

7.4 Enhancing Workforce Resilience and Agility

In hybrid settings, resilience depends on rapid sensing and redeployment (Marler, 2016). Marketplace and learning data can surface emerging gaps and enable short-cycle allocation of talent across functions and geographies. The 60,000+ hours unlocked in early Unilever FLEX deployments illustrate how matching mechanisms translate learning into productive capacity. To institutionalise this, maintain a rolling skills outlook (internal + external signals), pair it with a standing redeployment playbook, and track cycle times from skill signal → placement.

7.5 Ethical Governance within Strategic Integration

Trust is a precondition for scaling. Privacy-preserving analytics (aggregation, de-identification), bias and accessibility testing, and transparent user communications must accompany integrations with HRIS, performance, and marketplace systems. Make this operational with a governance cadence (e.g., monthly bias/accessibility checks; quarterly DPIA reviews for new use-cases) and publish short "model cards" or change notes so employees understand how recommendations and metrics are produced.

When AI-enabled upskilling is woven into HRM and business routines, it evolves from a training initiative into a strategic capability. The cross-case evidence, translated here into measurement and operating cadences, shows how organisations can connect learning to mobility, performance, leadership, and resilience while preserving trust (Duchek, 2020).

Practical deployment tools supporting these integration steps are provided in Appendix A, which includes pre-deployment, manager-enablement and post-deployment checklists for AI-enabled learning.

8. FUTURE RESEARCH AND POLICY DIRECTIONS

As AI-enabled upskilling becomes integral to hybrid workforce strategies, a set of research and policy questions emerges that warrants systematic inquiry. Resolving these questions will enable organisations, policymakers, and scholars to design learning ecosystems that are both effective and ethically sustainable. The agenda below synthesises priorities for longitudinal evidence, rigorous value assessment, governance and regulation, collaborative ecosystem building, and inclusive design.

8.1 Longitudinal impact on workforce performance and wellbeing

Current cases indicate that AI-boosted learning programs lead to short-term gains in engagement, course completion and internal mobility. Nevertheless, there is a lack of longitudinal studies to examine the sustainability of these effects in the long term. In the future, researchers need to embrace a cohort-centric research design when studying how AI-enabled development impacts long-term career dynamics (e.g., internal mobility, promotion pace, compensation growth, and role transition success).

And it's as important to look at how continuous AI-supported learning is connected with employee well-being in hybrid work. This includes examining the impact of such systems upon workload, autonomy, psychological safety and work–life balance, which have all been identified as central to sustainable workforce performance (García-Madurga et al., 2024). Secondly, the opportunity for research to consider how quickly and easily industry needs can be woven into AI recommendation engines, so that learning pathways keep pace with ever-changing demands. In the absence of such responsiveness, automated recommendations may have the unintended consequence of bearing skills rather than making them current.

8.2 Evaluation of ROI and organisational value creation

More robust models are required to help calculate the ROI of AI-based learning. Comparative methodologies comparing AI-based with traditional methods should examine productivity effects on innovation outputs, quality and safety indicators, and on staff retention rates (Disco, 2025). Mixed methods should seek to measure both the tangible, such as decreased onboarding time or faster redeployment in the event of demand changes, and intangible impact, such as trust in organisational learning, adaptability, and culture change. Standardised measures and reporting templates would facilitate benchmarking between organisations and sectors.

The ROI approach outlined here is complemented by Appendix B, which provides a worked RoLI calculation and expanded data-quality checks to support reliable measurement.

8.3 Ethical and regulatory frameworks for AI in learning

As AI-informed learning systems are increasingly implemented, the considerations of fairness, transparency and privacy need to be hardwired into organisational governance. As AI becomes more prevalent, the governance architectures will also need to adapt so that these principles aren't something of an afterthought but a fundamental act of protection. Learning XAI in the context of AI auditing should develop normative standards that make recommendation logic accessible to all below the managerial level and promote trust/ accountability without violating IPRs (Batool et al., 2023).

Nevertheless, existing frameworks offer little in the way of specific recommendations about important signifiers such as employee data access and informed consent or how to apply principles of least amount of user data and purpose limitation for hybrid work scenarios where personal and enterprise devices are often used interchangeably. This sort of ambiguity makes it difficult for the data to be distributed in a consistent manner that can be used by others. International collaboration has the potential to solve this fragmentation by creating interoperable frameworks, ensuring fairness, privacy and ethical integrity of AI-based learning environments. There should be institutionalised mechanisms for independent audit and oversight, as well as redress to guarantee, through transparency and accountability, equitable access to AI-supported learning wherever it is implemented in the sector or geographies.

8.4 Cross-sector partnerships and ecosystem development

Scaling AI-enabled upskilling benefits from coordinated action among industry, government, and academia. Public–private partnerships can widen access for small and medium enterprises through shared platforms, pooled licences, or targeted subsidies. Open skill taxonomies and portable micro-credential frameworks would allow learners to carry verified capabilities across roles, firms, and regions. Joint research programmes should test sector-specific applications in areas such as healthcare, manufacturing, and education, linking curriculum design to real workflow improvements and labour market outcomes.

8.5 Inclusivity and diversity in AI-driven learning systems

AI can broaden access to learning, but it can also exclude if design choices embed historical bias. Future work should measure how recommendations and completion outcomes vary by gender, age, language, disability status, and cultural background, and should institute disparate impact monitoring as a routine control. Inclusive design practices that centre accessibility, multilingual delivery, and flexible pathways are essential to ensure equitable participation and outcomes. Applying Universal Design for learning principles within AI platforms can help personalise challenge and support while maintaining fairness and transparency.

By building on this research and policy agenda, stakeholders can help orient AI-enabled upskilling towards broader social objectives, such as achieving SDG 8 (decent work and economic growth) and 10 (reduced inequalities). Attention to longitudinal effects, value-addition, strong governance, ecosystem crossovers and inclusive design will mitigate the risk of entrenching inequity or dependence on a few technology suppliers. The paper finishes by distilling these understandings into pragmatic advice for executives who seek to develop AI-enabled upskilling in hybrid workplaces strategically, ethically and confidently.

9. CONCLUSION AND STRATEGIC RECOMMENDATIONS

9.1 Conclusion

The trend toward hybrid work has escalated the need for continuous, adaptive and strategically aligned workforce upskilling. As the rate of technology change and spatial dispersion of teams increases, traditional training systems – rigid, one-size-fits-all all and separate from daily work lives are failing to keep up. AI offers the potential to transcend these constraints, via personalised, scalable and real-time learning experiences directly within employees' workflows.

The AI-enabled upskilling conceptual model emerging from this chapter aligns with an iterative learning process that includes identification of skill needs, delivering adaptive content, providing just-in-time performance support, offering continuous feedback and ensuring integration with organisational strategic goals (Teece, 2007). In addition, the strategic readiness model offers a well-defined diagnostic tool to evaluate an organisation's readiness in technical, cultural and ethical terms, which guarantees that adoption is context-sensitive as well as sustainable.

Insights from the field show that leading organisations, including IBM, Deloitte, Unilever, Accenture and Microsoft, have leveraged AI-powered learning ecosystems to impact employee engagement, internal mobility and productivity while supercharging workforce agility. However, these advantages will only be realised if the learning experiences are based upon transparent governance, robust ethical framework and sound linkages between learning design and business strategy.

9.2 Implications for Practitioners

Practitioners must update role profiles and skill taxonomies regularly and begin with small pilots that tie AI learning tools to a single HR process. Open model cards and update notes will assist in trust building, and secure learning time will guarantee attendance. A standard measurement schema enhances assessment, and procurement must focus on interoperability to prevent lock-in. Routine bias and accessibility checks with proper manager guidance on how to interpret learning signals should help to ensure fair and effective implementation.

9.3 Strategic Recommendations

Businesses should make AI-enabled learning part of their organisational DNA, embedding it not as a short-term change but as a living and evolving capability. This involves bringing AI-driven learning together with the company's existing talent acquisition, performance management and leadership development systems so they're more closely linked in purpose and focus on the interconnected dynamics between learning, growth, and career advancement.

The ethical governance must begin at the foundation to protect the fairness, privacy and transparency as the basic guiding principles are necessary to build trust in AI learning systems. Three key areas that need clear policies are algorithmic bias, data protection and model explainability. Utilising Universal Design for Learning (UDL) approaches also helps guarantee that these systems include all employees, regardless of their abilities or backgrounds.

Organisations should focus on being strategically ready for AI learning by evaluating their technology infrastructure, culture readiness and leadership alignment before implementing large-scale AI learning initiatives. In earlier times, anticipating and bridging these readiness gaps can determine whether AI learning is properly adopted as an inspiring model or resisted as a top-down imposition.

Efforts in AI learning should be linked to measurable business results. Metrics should explicitly link employee engagement and skills development to things the organisation cares about, such as increased productivity, quicker onboarding, or better retention. Regular feedback loops and active iteration of AI models and learning paths will enable the company to remain agile and react to shifting business priorities.

In order to sustain a culture of learning and allow employees to continue learning, organisations need to support self-directed development with on-demand and personalised opportunities. The recognition and rewards of learning achievements in performance appraisals serve to further emphasise the importance of skill development not as a compliance, but as an important aspect of professional identity and contribution.

Lastly, cross-sector collaboration can multiply impact. Partnerships with peer organisations, industry consortia, and education institutions can help expand the access framework of AI-enabled tools that promote a shared innovation investment and development of portable, industry-recognised skill frameworks.

At the intersection of technology, ethics and strategy, AI-driven upskilling can enable organisations to shape a workforce that is agile and future-ready. It does so not just because that helps to achieve the immediate business goals but also because it is a good mechanism for broader societal priorities, such as sustainable employment, inclusive growth and reduction of inequalities. The next generation of scholars and practitioners should be directed to scaling these systems in a responsible manner so that the promise of AI in workforce learning is distributed fairly and consistent with the longevity of employee and organisational well-being.

REFERENCES

Accenture. (2023, June 13). *Accenture to invest $3 billion in AI to accelerate clients' reinvention*. Accenture Newsroom. https://newsroom.accenture.com/news/2023/accenture-to-invest-3-billion-in-ai-to-accelerate-clients-reinvention

Accenture. (2024, March 5). *Accenture launches Accenture LearnVantage to help clients and their people gain essential skills and achieve greater business value in the AI economy*. Accenture Newsroom. https://newsroom.accenture.com/news/2024/accenture-launches-accenture-learnvantage-to-help-clients-and-their-people-gain-essential-skills-and-achieve-greater-business-value-in-the-ai-economy

Baldwin, T. T., & Ford, J. K. (1988). Transfer of training: A review and directions for future research. *Personnel Psychology*, *41*(1), 63–105. DOI: 10.1111/j.1744-6570.1988.tb00632.x

Batool, A., Zowghi, D., & Bano, M. (2023). *Responsible AI governance: A systematic literature review*. arXiv. /arXiv.2401.10896DOI: 10.48550

Bersin, J. (2019a). *A new model of talent management: The internal talent marketplace* (HR People + Strategy White Paper). Society for Human Resource Management. https://www.shrm.org/content/dam/en/shrm/executive-network/A%20New%20Model%20of%20Talent%20Management-%20The%20Internal%20Talent%20Marketplace.pdf

Bersin, J. (2019b, July 17). *The company as a talent network: Unilever and Schneider Electric show the way*. Josh Bersin. https://joshbersin.com/2019/07/the-company-as-a-talent-network-unilever-and-schneider-electric-show-the-way/

Billett, S. (2002). Toward a Workplace Pedagogy: Guidance, Participation, and Engagement. *Adult Education Quarterly*, *53*(1), 27–43. DOI: 10.1177/074171302237202

Brynjolfsson, E., Li, D., & Raymond, L. R. (2023). *Generative AI at work* (NBER Working Paper No. 31161). National Bureau of Economic Research. DOI: 10.3386/w31161

Cabinet Office. (2025, June 2). *Microsoft 365 Copilot experiment: Cross-government findings report*. GOV.UK. https://assets.publishing.service.gov.uk/media/683db42bd23a62e5d32680d0/M365_Copilot_Experiment_Findings_Report.pdf

Cappelli, P., Tambe, P., & Yakubovich, V. (2019). *Artificial intelligence in human resources management: Challenges and a path forward. SSRN*. DOI: 10.2139/ssrn.3263878

Chen, Z. (2024). Responsible AI in Organizational Training: Applications, Implications, and Recommendations for Future Development. *Human Resource Development Review, 23*(4), 498–521. DOI: 10.1177/15344843241273316

Disco. (2025, August 11). How to assess the ROI of AI-driven upskilling initiatives. Blog post. https://www.disco.co/blog/how-to-assess-the-roi-of-ai-driven-upskilling-initiatives

disprz, Deloitte, & MindID (n.d). Disprz x Deloitte x MindID: Workforce transformation and learning culture case study. FeaturedCustomers. https://cdn.featuredcustomers.com/CustomerCaseStudy.document/Case_Study__disprz_x_Deloitte_x_MindID_.pdf

Duchek, S. (2020). Organizational resilience: A capability-based conceptualization. *Business Research, 13*, 215–246. DOI: 10.1007/s40685-019-0085-7

Dwork, C., & Roth, A. (2014). The algorithmic foundations of differential privacy. *Foundations and Trends in Theoretical Computer Science*, *9*(3–4), 211–407. DOI: 10.1561/0400000042

Financial News London. (2025, April 8). *Deloitte triples number of auditors using AI chatbot.* https://www.fnlondon.com/articles/deloitte-triples-number-of-auditors-using-ai-chatbot-42086859

Financial Times. (2025, June 2). *UK civil servants who used AI saved two weeks a year, government study finds.* https://www.ft.com/content/7c2aa19d-4c92-490d-bb35-f329a246fe5b

Fu, Y., & Weng, Z. (2024). Navigating the ethical terrain of AI in education: A systematic review on framing responsible human-centered AI practices. *Computers and Education: Artificial Intelligence*, *7*, 100306. DOI: 10.1016/j.caeai.2024.100306

García-Madurga, M.-Á., Gil-Lacruz, A.-I., Saz-Gil, I., & Gil-Lacruz, M. (2024). The Role of Artificial Intelligence in Improving Workplace Well-Being: A Systematic Review. *Businesses*, *4*(3), 389–410. DOI: 10.3390/businesses4030024

Giralt Hernández, E. (2024). *Towards an ethical and inclusive implementation of artificial intelligence in organizations: A multidimensional framework.* arXiv. /arXiv.2405.01697DOI: 10.48550

Hardt, M., Price, E., & Srebro, N. (2016). *Equality of opportunity in supervised learning*. arXiv. /arXiv.1610.02413DOI: 10.48550

Kleinberg, J., Mullainathan, S., & Raghavan, M. (2016). *Inherent trade-offs in the fair determination of risk scores*. arXiv. /arXiv.1609.05807DOI: 10.48550

Koedinger, K. R., Corbett, A. T., & Perfetti, C. (2012). The knowledge–learning–instruction framework: Bridging the science–practice chasm to enhance robust student learning. *Cognitive Science, 36*(5), 757–798. DOI: 10.1111/j.1551-6709.2012.01245.x PMID: 22486653

Lee, J. D., & See, K. A. (2004). Trust in automation: Designing for appropriate reliance. *Human Factors, 46*(1), 50–80. DOI: 10.1518/hfes.46.1.50_30392 PMID: 15151155

Leonardi, P. M., Parker, S. H., & Shen, R. (2024). How Remote Work Changes the World of Work. *Annual Review of Organizational Psychology and Organizational Behavior, 11*, 193–219. DOI: 10.1146/annurev-orgpsych-091922-015852

Li, Y., Tolosa, L., Rivas-Echeverria, F., & Marquez, R. (2025). *Integrating AI in education: Navigating UNESCO global guidelines, emerging trends, and its intersection with sustainable development goals. ChemRxiv*. DOI: 10.26434/chemrxiv-2025-wz4n9

Margherita, A. (2021). Human resources analytics: A systematization of research topics and directions for future research. *Human Resource Management Review, 31*(2), 100795. DOI: 10.1016/j.hrmr.2020.100795

Marler, J. (2016). An evidence-based review of HR Analytics. *International Journal of Human Resource Management*. Advance online publication. DOI: 10.1080/09585192.2016.1244699

Marozva, R. R., & Pelser, A. M. (2025). Social employee well-being challenges of academics in the hybrid work environment. *Frontiers in Psychology, 16*, 1524804. PMID: 39989635

Microsoft. (2025). *Advanced analysis privacy: Viva Insights documentation*. https://learn.microsoft.com/en-us/viva/insights/advanced/privacy/privacy

Microsoft. (n.d.). *Microsoft Viva privacy*. Microsoft. https://www.microsoft.com/en-in/microsoft-viva/privacy

Mittelstadt, B. D., Allo, P., Taddeo, M., Wachter, S., & Floridi, L. (2016). The ethics of algorithms: Mapping the debate. *Big Data & Society, 3*(2). Advance online publication. DOI: 10.1177/2053951716679679

Nielsen, K., & Shepherd, R. (2022). Understanding the outcomes of training to improve employee mental health: A novel framework for training transfer and effectiveness evaluation. *Work and Stress, 36*(4), 377–391. DOI: 10.1080/02678373.2022.2028318

Noy, S., & Zhang, W. (2023). Experimental evidence on the productivity effects of generative artificial intelligence. *Science*, *381*(6654), 187–192. DOI: 10.1126/science.adh2586 PMID: 37440646

Papamitsiou, Z., & Economides, A. A. (2014). Learning Analytics and Educational Data Mining in Practice: A Systematic Literature Review of Empirical Evidence. *Journal of Educational Technology & Society*, *17*(4), 49–64. https://www.jstor.org/stable/jeductechsoci.17.4.49

Qin, F., & Kochan, T. A. (2020). *The learning system at IBM: A case study* (MIT Sloan School of Management Working Paper). MIT Sloan School of Management. https://mitsloan.mit.edu/sites/default/files/2022-06/Qin%20and%20Kochan%20The%20Learning%20System%20at%20IBM%2012%202020.pdf

Raji, I. D., Smart, A., White, R. N., Mitchell, M., Gebru, T., Hutchinson, B., Smith-Loud, J., Theron, D., & Barnes, P. (2020). *Closing the AI accountability gap: Defining an end-to-end framework for internal algorithmic auditing*. arXiv. / arXiv.2001.00973DOI: 10.48550

Teece, D. J. (2007). Explicating dynamic capabilities: The nature and microfoundations of (sustainable) enterprise performance. *Strategic Management Journal*, *28*(13), 1319–1350. DOI: 10.1002/smj.640

Unilever & WIRED Consulting. (2022). *The Future of Work Is Flexible*. Unilever. https://www.unilever.com/files/4bbfab9a-54aa-4493-a9b0-146c1c4aa738/glo-wired-x-unilever-workplace.pdf

Unilever. (2020, June 23). *An exciting new normal for flexible working.* https://www.unilever.com/news/news-search/2020/an-exciting-new-normal-for-flexible-working/

Vanlehn, K. (2011). The Relative Effectiveness of Human Tutoring, Intelligent Tutoring Systems, and Other Tutoring Systems. *Educational Psychologist*. Advance online publication. DOI: 10.1080/00461520.2011.611369

Venkatesh, V., Morris, M. G., Davis, G. B., & Davis, F. D. (2003). User acceptance of information technology: Toward a unified view. *Management Information Systems Quarterly*, *27*(3), 425–478. DOI: 10.2307/30036540

Weiner, B. J. (2009). A theory of organizational readiness for change. *Implementation Science : IS*, *4*, 67. DOI: 10.1186/1748-5908-4-67 PMID: 19840381

Xu, J., Wan, S., Li, Y., Luo, S., Chen, Z., Shao, Y., Huang, S., & Song, L. (2025). Cooperative multi-model training for personalized federated learning over heterogeneous devices. *IEEE Journal of Selected Topics in Signal Processing*, *19*, 195–207. DOI: 10.1109/JSTSP.2024.3497660

KEY TERMS AND DEFINITIONS

Adaptive learning: A data driven instructional approach in which content, difficulty, and sequencing adjust to an individual's demonstrated mastery and engagement patterns, improving retention and reducing time to competence.

AI enabled upskilling: The systematic use of artificial intelligence to identify skill gaps, personalise learning pathways, and embed just in time support within daily workflows to accelerate the development of role relevant capabilities .

Algorithmic bias: Systematic and unfair differences in model outputs across groups that arise from data, feature, or design choices; in learning systems this can distort recommendations, access, and assessment.

Collaborative learning culture: Shared norms and routines that encourage employees to co create, share, and apply knowledge across locations and functions, supported by communities of practice and peer feedback.

Data minimisation and consent: Privacy principles that limit personal data collection to what is necessary for stated learning purposes and require clear, informed, and revocable permission for its use.

Ethical AI governance: The policies, controls, and oversight processes that guide fair, transparent, and accountable use of AI in learning, including bias testing, auditability, model change logs, and avenues for redress.

Explainable artificial intelligence (XAI): Methods that make model behaviour understandable to non-specialists so that learners and managers can see why particular content, coaches, or opportunities were recommended.

Hybrid workplace: An operating model in which employees work across on site and remote contexts, requiring learning that is accessible asynchronously, integrated with collaboration tools, and equitable across locations.

Internal talent marketplace: A digital mechanism that matches employees to short projects, gigs, or roles using skill signals and availability, enabling mobility, capacity unlocking, and experiential learning at scale.

Knowledge graph: A structured representation of entities and relationships—such as roles, skills, courses, and projects—used by AI systems to infer prerequisites, proximities, and career pathways for learners.

Learning analytics: The collection and analysis of behavioural, performance, and engagement data to improve content design, target interventions, and demonstrate impact on individual and organisational outcomes.

Learning in the flow of work: The delivery of guidance, micro content, and coaching within the tools and moments where tasks occur, reducing interruption costs and strengthening transfer of learning to performance.

Learning experience platform (LXP): A user centred layer that aggregates content, enables social learning, and uses recommendations to curate personalised journeys aligned to role, interests, and business needs.

Micro credential and portability: A verifiable, modular certification of a specific skill or outcome that can be stacked toward larger qualifications and carried across employers and sectors.

Privacy by design: An architectural approach that embeds safeguards such as aggregation, de identification, access controls, and purpose limitation into learning platforms from the outset.

Return on learning investment (RoLI): A structured assessment that links learning inputs to business value, combining tangible indicators such as time to proficiency and redeployment speed with intangible effects such as trust and adaptability.

Skill taxonomy: A controlled vocabulary that defines skills, proficiencies, and relationships across roles; it enables consistent tagging of content, mapping of gaps, and forecasting of emerging capability needs.

Strategic readiness: The combined technical, cultural, and strategic capacity of an organisation to adopt AI enabled learning responsibly, measured through indicators such as platform integration, trust, governance, and alignment to goals.

Universal Design for Learning (UDL): A framework that improves accessibility and inclusion in learning through multiple means of engagement, representation, and action, ensuring equitable participation and outcomes.

Workforce resilience: The ability of a workforce to anticipate, absorb, and adapt to disruption through continuous learning, rapid mobility, and redeployment supported by marketplaces and trusted analytics.

APPENDIX

Appendix A. Implementation Toolkit: Practical Checklists for AI-Enabled Upskilling

Table 6.

Toolkit Area	Checklist Items
A1. Pre-Deployment Checklist	• Define data minimisation rules. • Verify consent language and transparency notices. • Confirm interoperability requirements (LMS–HRIS–LXP). • Establish pilot metrics and baseline windows. • Validate bias-testing protocol before launch. • Configure access controls and role-based permissions. • Document success criteria and stop–go thresholds.
A2. Manager Enablement Checklist	• Train managers to interpret engagement and skill signals. • Establish guidance for responding to low-skill alerts. • Set expectations on coaching vs. relying on AI nudges. • Provide sample scripts for learner conversations. • Share dashboards with definitions of each metric. • Reinforce that AI recommendations are advisory, not prescriptive.
A3. Post-Deployment Measurement Checklist	• Validate pre/post data completeness and identity resolution. • Adjust calculations for team turnover/attrition. • Review weekly adoption indicators during first 90 days. • Conduct monthly accuracy and bias audits. • Recalculate skill-progression KPIs quarterly. • Update the model card after each algorithm update.

Appendix B ROI and Measurement Templates for AI-Upskilling Initiatives

B1. Worked Calculation: Return on Learning Investment (RoLI) Using Microsoft Copilot time-savings study.

Table 7.

Component	Values
Average minutes saved/day (post-deployment)	26 min/day
Workdays/year	220
Annual hours saved	≈ 95 hours/employee

continued on following page

Table 7. Continued

Component	Values
Average loaded wage rate	USD 40/hour
Annual value per employee	~USD 3,800
License + enablement cost	USD 1,200
RoLI ratio	3.1: 1 (value returned per dollar spent)

This template can be reused for any AI-enabled tool (LXP, chatbot, skills engine, workflow assistant).

B2. Data-Quality Checks (to supplement Table 3)

Table 8.

Category	Quality Checks
Identity Resolution	• Merge accounts across systems; remove test accounts. • Ensure unique learner IDs across HRIS, LXP and collaboration platforms.
Attrition Adjustment	• Recompute denominators monthly for turnover. • Apply exit-adjusted baselines to avoid inflated MAU or training hours.
Data Stability	• Flag modules with <10 observations as low reliability. • Require consistency checks for 3 cycles before metric adoption

Chapter 2
Understanding Job Seekers' Acceptance of AI-Driven Recruitment Systems:
An Empirical Study Based on the Extended UTAUT Model

Shad Ahmad Khan
https://orcid.org/0000-0001-7593-3487
American University of Phnom Penh, Cambodia

Ujjal Bhuyan
https://orcid.org/0000-0002-2512-7425
Jagannath Barooah University, India

Shainima Islam
American University of Phnom Penh, Cambodia

ABSTRACT

The application of artificial intelligence (AI) has rapidly transformed various fields over the past decade, particularly in human resource management (HRM). Traditional talent acquisition is outdated and labor-intensive, relying on manual processes such as screening resumes and evaluating applicants. With the integration of AI technologies like big data and machine learning, HR departments can significantly enhance efficiency, quickly identifying the best candidates. While it's clear that recruiters are keen to leverage AI for talent acquisition, research on job seekers' perceptions of AI-assisted recruitment is surprisingly limited. This study

DOI: 10.4018/979-8-3373-5871-0.ch002

…t © 2026, IGI Global Scientific Publishing. Copying or distributing in print or electronic forms without written permission of IGI Global Scientific Publishing is prohibited. Use of this chapter to …enerative artificial intelligence (AI) technologies is expressly prohibited. The publisher reserves all rights to license its use for generative AI training and machine learning model development.

decisively addresses this gap by examining applicants' views through an extended UTAUT model, concentrating on critical factors such as trust, technology intricacy, performance, and organizational support in shaping user desirability and adoption intentions.

1. INTRODUCTION

Human Resource Management (HRM) division of any organisation is entrusted with a pivotal role of finding the right people for a job and ensure their smooth integration. Being a fundamental part of any organizational management HRM aims at enhancing workforce productivity and strengthening its capacity to compete. Prior to the year 1990, the procedure for recruitment and selection of personnel by an organisation was for the most part centred around conventional, non-technological techniques i.e. personals are employed for creating an ensemble of employable and competent job seekers and drawing them into the organisation. The standard or customary procedure for job search by individuals was to look into job boards and print media such as magazines and daily newspapers. When there is a match between job description and the applicants' expectation, they would visit the organisation who is hiring in person, bring a physical form and manually sent it to the assigned office. The staffing sector saw further technological advancements in the first decade of the new millennium. Over the past ten years, technology has revolutionized the hiring process and changed how applicants think. Candidates now have far more power over the recruiting process thanks to worker mobility, instant access to information, and improved connection (Smith, 2021). Candidates can now effectively apply for open positions online and proactively search for career possibilities that fit their interests and talents thanks to digital platforms like social media and job boards. (Black & van Esch, 2020). With the advent of new technologies for easing communication and doing business for internal and external users, a novel concept of recruiters selecting potential candidates using web-based technologies emerged. Such concept is further popularized as online hiring, or e-recruitment. It is characterized by the use of web solutions and Internet-based recruitment efforts that eventually aim to achieve the same goals as traditional recruitment (Ghazzawi & Accoumeh, 2014). Another way to describe it would be the process of employing websites and other online technology to evaluate, interview, and hire staff (Dhamija, 2012). Businesses can benefit from a variety of e-recruitment practices, including increased candidate pool size and enhanced recruiting process efficacy. With AI's seamless and widespread integration into nearly every human interface, this cutting-edge technology has enormous potential to foster unexplored opportunities for traditional human resource management (HRM). "Our greatest resource is our workforce"- is not merely a catchphrase for any business, but has led to building up a competitive positive in the market (Black & van Esch, 2020 p.1). Several studies have backed the idea of how AI, IOT and the analytics is going to shape the HRM practices in the present times and the future (Zareen & Khan, 2023; Khatri et al., 2023; Khan & Naim, 2024). AI based recruitment drives have evolved from the 'buzzword' phase to a 'necessity' phase, counting on the benefits derived by the recruiters and the job seekers. Integration of technology such as AI can bring out significant benefits in the form of cost cutting and enhancing efficiency and effectiveness in the HR domain of an organization (Sýkorová et al., 2024). From the job seekers viewpoint, better job matching, faster processing of job applications, prompt feedbacks, reducing human errors and biasness are some of the benefits that accrue to them. AI has been primarily employed in four stages of recruitment- outreach, screening, assessing and coordination (Black & van Esch, 2020, p.4-7). Outreach is the organization's attempt to reach out to the 'right' people, who are actively seeking employment. Once the right people are sorted out, the next crucial stage for the recruiters is screening. AI enabled tools can considerably reduce the amount of hours for screening. Once, the potential list of candidates has been determined, further assessment of their profiles is made to identify who fits best to the job description.

1.1. AI and its spread in the contemporary world

AI as a term itself has become prominent now, that doesn't require an expanded form "Artificial Intelligence". In the contemporary world, AI has moved rapidly from experimental laboratories into everyday life. AI can be understood as an ability of the computer system that can perform a task that otherwise would have required an human intelligence. As per Sheikh et al. (2023), "AI stands for the imitation by computers of the intelligence inherent in humans (Sheikh et al., 2023, pp.15). They further add, "A common definition of AI is that it is a technology that enables machines to imitate various complex human skills", (Sheikh et al., 2024, pp.15). AI is able to perform such tasks through the learning from data, recognising patterns, understanding language, making predictions, and supporting decision-making (Wahab et al., 2024). What makes AI special is its adaptability unlike the traditional software, the AI systems adapt and improve their performance over time through techniques such as machine learning and natural language processing (Jonathan et al., 2024; Khan et al., 2025). The AI systems are not only designed to make or take decisions, but are also designed to make their process understandable to humans through explainable AI, commonly known as XAI (Khan & Naim, 2024; Karyamsetty et al., 2024; Magd et al., 2024). AI, now underpins search engines, recommendation systems, digital assistants, financial risk assessment, healthcare diagnostics, and increasingly, human resource management. Its presence can be seen in various sectors already (Naim et al., 2024a;2024b; Magd et al., 2023; Magd et al., 2022).

AI is gaining prominence in the field of HRM (Zareen & Khan, 2023). One of the major areas it is being used is in recruitment, where AI is used to screen résumés, analyse video interviews, match candidates to job roles, and automate communication with applicants (Hunkenschroer & Luetge, 2022). AI has become a big support for the HR department of relatively larger organizations which normally deals with large data sets. The AI computing power helps to improve the speed, efficiency and consistency in decision making (Hammad, & Abu-Zaid, 2024; Santoso & Surya, 2024). AI is likely to become more robust and get involved in deeper integration into social system in the times to come. It may not be a complete replacement of human judgement though. There are more likely chances of getting human-AI type of models, where humans and AI will be functioning together collaboratively.

1.2. AI- Driven recruitment system:

An AI-driven recruitment system refers to the use of artificial intelligence technologies to automate, augment, or support key stages of the hiring process, including job advertising, résumé screening, candidate shortlisting, interviewing, and selection (Hamadneh et al., 2024; Barath et al., 2025; Uma et al., 2023; Kadirov et al., 2024). These systems rely on techniques such as machine learning, natural language processing, and predictive analytics to analyse large volumes of applicant data and generate recommendations or decisions (Tian et al., 2023; Uma et al., 2023; Venkatachalam, 2024). These systems bring efficiency, scalability and reliability to the recruitment process, especially in the case of high application volume.

1.3. Job seeker acceptance:

Job seeker are the people who are looking for a job or employment. Job seeker acceptance refers to an entent a job seeker is willing to engage with, trust, and comply with AI-based recruitment processes during their job search (Ochmann & Laumer, 2020; Almeida et al., 2025). It is an important consideration as recruitment is a high-stake interaction (Langer et al., 2019; Loy et al.,2025). For the job seekers, AI systems acts as the gatekeeper to the employment opportunities, as now the job seeker are using AI to address their queries pertaining to jobs along with developing cover letter or customizing their CVs (Abhishek et al., 2025; Jaspin et al., 2024), and organisations are using AI tools to scan through their CVs and profiles through AI too (Schlippe & Bothmer, 2023). As hiring decisions increasingly rely on automated systems work (Armstrong & Metaxa, 2025; Soni, 2024),understanding how job seekers interpret and respond to these technologies becomes essential for ensuring ethical, inclusive, and sustainable recruitment practices in the future of work

In addition, coordination between the organization and candidates needs to be effective at all levels of the recruitment process, which can be effectively assisted by AI-based recruitment software.

There are studies available in existing literature on the implications of AI on the dynamics of HRM in organizations. But currently, no study is focused on understanding the views of job seekers on the use of AI in the HR sector. This study intends to fill that gap in the existing literature. This study aims to investigate the significance of trust, performance, facilitating conditions, and social-technological perspectives in understanding the factors of AI-based recruitment practice acceptance. Since AI-based recruitment tools are currently being immensely adopted in recruitment practices, it is also significant to know that to what extent job seekers are accepting AI-based recruitment practices.

2. Theoretical foundation and Model Building

Given the inherent complexity, psychologically sensitive incidents or occurrences are challenging to quantify. This has led to development of a quite a few theories and conceptual frameworks such as TRA (Theory of Reasoned Action) 1975, TPB (Theory of Planned Behavior) 1985, TAM (Technology Acceptance Model) 1989 and UTAUT (Unified Theory of Acceptance and Use of technology) 2003 (Lai, 2017, Ferneborg et al., 2020, Taherdoost 2021, Islam et al., 2024). A common belief, supported by previous studies, is for integration of diverse theoretical perspectives with intent to enhance the explanatory potential of a developed model. However, counting on the varied presumptions and convictions of the disjointed theories, a multi-dimensional approach would be less fruitful. This has also been substantiated by empirical findings in many previous literatures (Islam et al., 2024; Sharma et al., 2023). TRA is one of the pioneer works in the field of behavioral intention. Attitude is expressed as the favourable and unfavourable behavior exhibited by individuals regarding a certain behavior. While subjective norms captures the social pressure exerted on the individual to engage in such behavior (Fishbein & Ajzen, 1975, Sana'a,, 2016). TPB has been an extension of TRA, by including an additional construct (perceived behavioral Control) to the two variables taken in TRA. Perceived behavioral control (PBC) refers to the individuals perceived level of control over a certain behavior and the ease with which such behavioral may be performed. PBC forms an integral component determining intention to engage in a particular behavior (Lihua, 2022). Another theoretical model of technology acceptance adopted in extant literatures is Technology Acceptance Model (TAM). Unlike theory of perceived behavioral control (TPB) which gauges technology acceptance using three constructs: Attitude towards behavior (ATT), subjective norms (SN) and perceived behavioral control (PBC), TAM focuses on perceived usefulness and perceived ease of use (Ma & Liu, 2004). However, UTAUT model has gained popularity among researchers for its high explanatory capacity and holistic perspective (Ami-Narh et al. 2012, Islam et al., 2022, Maisha, & Shetu, 2023). It has the potential to explain 70 percent variations in individuals' intention to adoption and use (Venkatesh et al. 2003). The original model of UTAUT comprises of four constructs, which are performance expectancy (PE), effort expectancy (EE), social influence (SI) and facilitating condition (FI). PE relates to the user's belief in that adoption of technology would ease his way in attaining the desired goals. EE relates to the effort demanded of the user in using a technology. SI relates to the users' belief that adoption of a technology would be seen favourably by those who influence them or by whom they consider important. Lastly, FI relates to the users' believe on their possession of necessary resources that support the adoption of a technology (Venkatesh et al. 2003). Despite its high explanatory power, previous researches have shown that inclusion of other external constructs increase the precision of the original model in explaining the variations in users' technology adoption (Patil et al. 2020, Islam et al., 2022). In light of this, the present study extends the original UTAUT model to include one important construct in measuring use intention of usage, which is technology intricacy. Extant literatures have shown that a technology embedded with more complex features, are expected to find more resistance when it comes to its adoption.

2.1. Integrated Conceptual framework

The conceptual model (Figure 1) adopted for the study attempts to reflect a comprehensive perspective of job seekers' technology acceptance in terms of AI-enabled recruitment system. The adopted model brings together social, technological, emotional and infrastructural dimensions within the extended UTAUT model. Unlike convention contexts in which technology acceptance is studies, recruitment entails a great degree of emotional investment, personal risks and apparent fragility. This makes an integrative model more appealing in the context of recruitment as it sheds light on the multi-dimensional facets of user acceptability and desirability towards AI-induced recruitment and position acceptance and refrains from put disproportionate thrust on the functional performance of any technology alone. Moreover, assessing individual acceptance of such AI-based system through a narrow functional-centric lens, owing to its complex nature, would present an incomplete elucidation of its acceptance. At the crux of the conceptual model lies the construct of 'User desirability', which captures an individual's intention and inclination towards algorithm- based recruitment drives. A deliberate attempt has been made to capture the cognitive aspect of willingness to accept a technology by incorporating user desirability into the model and not merely gauging the usage intention of the job seekers. This presents an important conceptual distinction. From the technology utility perspective, two constructs: PE and EE, were included into the conceptual model taken up for the study. These constructs forms the part of the original UTAUT framework on technology acceptance. The former reflects the perceived appraisal of the AI-enabled recruitment system, while the later captures the ease with which one interacts with AI- driven selection interface. The model further integrates 'social influence' dimension of AI-induced recruitment system acceptance. The recruitment and selection drives do not take place in an uncluttered environment, as the individuals' social network, interpersonal interactions and wider societal norms have a paramount influence on their perception. These social forces strengthen acceptability of such systems by increasing its legitimacy and portraying it as a contemporary selection procedure.

Another critical dimension of the adopted model for the study is 'facilitating condition'. This reflects the accessibility to the resources, expertise and the required support mechanisms to interact with AI- based recruitment platforms. It acts as an 'enabler' ridging the gap between favorable conviction and actionable desirability. Inadequate favorable circumstances significantly impede acceptability by imposing practical limits. Furthermore, the present model brings two additional constructs: Technology intricacy and perceived trust, extending the UTAUT. The 'black box' nature of the AI-driven interfaces makes it complicated for its users to comprehend its decision-making process. Such perceived complexity could provoke apprehension and a sense of losing control. This psychological cost of accepting such technology is reflected by the construct 'technology intricacy'. Technology intricacy plays a crucial role in user desirability of such a recruitment system by showcasing the job seekers' comfort with the AI-induced decision-making in selection. On the other hand, perceived trust attempts to capture the perceived dependability, equity, openness and moral application of such recruitment systems. In this holistic perspective, this construct integrates the cognitive reliability with the technological efficiency of the model. In sum, this extended UTAUT framework on technology acceptance redefines trust as a critical factor in determining user desirability towards a particular technology adoption, instead of an outlying appendage. It also expands our understanding on complexity by differentiating between the operational effort demanded in interacting with AI-driven systems and its deeper technology intricacy. The unified structure highlights how different concepts interplay proactively to mold acceptability rather than operating unilaterally, thereby providing a strong base for empirical validation and contributing significantly to the growing debate on the usage of AI in the domain of HRM.

Figure 1. Proposed model

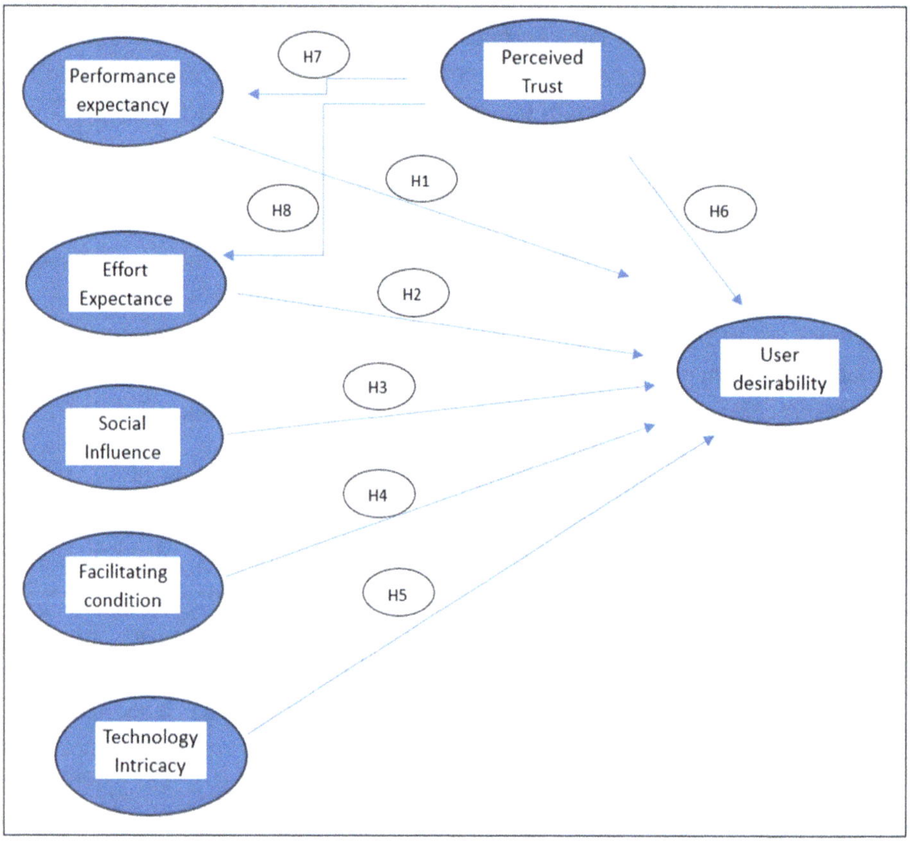

Source: Authors' Complied model

3. HYPOTHESE DEVELOPMENT

3.1. User Desirability (UD)

User desirability basically relates to the possibility or intention of a person to employ a technology in the future. In this study, it relates to the users' intention to use AI-powered interface in job seeking. UD plays an integral part in user adoption of a certain system or technology (Grassini et al., 2024).

3.2. Performance Expectancy (PE) and UD

User desirability to adopt or leverage a technology primarily based on the CBA (Cost-benefit Analysis) of the technology. PE plays an integral role in such analysis and then forms a basis for expressing users' desirability to adopt such technology. Users' expectations of improving their operational competencies are reflected in PE. It refers to the individuals' perception that using a certain technology would enhance their ability to perform a certain tasks (Venkatesh et al., 2003). PE, as a construct of UTAUT, has proven, in a repetitive manner, to positively and significantly affects the propensity to adopt a technology (Khanam & Mahfuz, 2017, Alam, et al., 2018, Andrews et al., 2021, Islam et al. 2024 and Grassini et al. 2024). The users' believe that AI-based recruitment drive would more accurately and consistently assess job seekers' credentials than human engagement, would foster their desire to participate in AI-powered recruitment drives by organizations. Hence, the researchers propose the hypothesis:

H1: PE positively and significantly affects UD towards AI-enabled recruitment.

3.3. Effort expectancy (EE) and UD

Effort expectancy (EE) refers to the user's understanding of the ease with which a system or technology can be employed (Venkatesh et al., 2003). In this study, it would refer to the ease with which job seekers' can use the AI-powered recruitment interface for job application. It gauges how effortless an AI system is anticipated to be to integrate in recruitment drive. The simplicity of the task and less effort of operation attract individuals to use the AI recruitment process and embrace it. Following Technology Adaption Model (TAM), users want to perceive friendliness and easiness in use and adaptation that reduce negative experience of uncertainty, complexity and navigation hurdles (Venkatesh et al., 2003; Thompson et al., 1991; Chen et al., 2020). Earlier studies among HR professionals regarding their acceptance and integration of Enterprise Resource Planning (ERP) system showed that, effort expectancy positively impact users intention to use (Uddin et al., 2020). Another, study among IT professional in India in same line showed that, employee's intention to use and accept technology is directed by favourable perception (78,79) (Singh et al., 2020; Bhardwaj et al., 2020). So, individual shows tendency of avoiding technology when it is hard to use. Hence, the researchers in the study propose the hypothesis:

H2: EE positively and significantly affects UD towards AI-enabled recruitment.

3.4. Social Influence (SI) and UD

Social Impact theory (Latané, 1981) states that an individual would be more inclined towards adhering towards social group norms provided that group is of significance to the individual. Social influence relates to a person's perception of how much influential others think they should adopt the new system ((Venkatesh et al., 2003)). In the context of the present study, it would relate to the belief that an individual's use of AI-enabled interface for job seeking and participation in recruitment drives is relevant and compatible with group norms (Gursoy et al., 2019). Extant literatures have highlighted a positive association between social influence and individual behavior (Bhukya & Paul, (2023), Liang et al., 2024). Based on the empirical evidences in the past and the theoretical foundations, the researchers have proposed the following hypothesis:

H3: SI positively and significantly affects UD towards AI-enabled recruitment

3.5. Facilitating Condition (FC) and UD

Facilitating condition refers to the individuals believe of the possession of requisite resources to execute a certain behavior ((Venkatesh et al., 2003)). People may not embrace AI-based technologies due to a lack of assistance, delayed support, inadequate knowledge, and inadequate amenities (Ambarwati et al., 2020). Thus, people's perception regarding resource availability, support system and a proper integration of technology's aspect: organizational and technical infrastructure drive consumer's behaviour intention (Uddin et al., 2020; Venkatesh et al., 2012). So, with technological advancement, individual's acceptance of organizational support increases regarding infrastructure management which motivate them to adopt and implement. Empirical studies among medical doctors intention to use IT tools in service and user's intention to use chatbots in public transport showed similar results and demonstrated how technology adoption is influence by facilitating condition (Kuberkar & Singhal, 2020; Rathinaswamy et al., 2020). Based on the extant literatures, the researchers have proposed the following hypothesis:

H4: FC positively and significantly affects UD towards AI-enabled recruitment

3.6. Technology Intricacy (TI)

Technology intricacy (TI) refers to the perceived amount of effort demanded from users' front to fully comprehend and use a particular technology (Almaiah et al., 2022). While certain technological advances are apparent to prospective users, certain ones are not. If the perceived complexity related to a particular technology is high, the users would be more reluctant to adopt it (Kassim et al. 2012). Based on this, the hypothesis proposed is:

H5: TI positively and significantly affects UD towards AI-enabled recruitment.

3.7. Perceived trust (PT) on PE, EE and UD

Trust has an important contribution to individuals' preference and subsequently adoption of a certain technology. PT on technology is essential in changing users' decisions about their readiness to adopt technology, alongside to enhancing the trust that is placed in the personnel of an organization (Cao et al., 2018, Chawla et al. 2023, Barry et al., 2024). This leads the researchers to propose H6 that reads as:

H6: PT positively and significantly affects User desirability towards AI-enabled recruitment.

In addition to this, extant literatures have also highlighted that PT has significant influence on PE and EE, two crucial factors determining technology adoption (Khalilzadeh et al., 2017). This leads us to propose H7 and H8 that reads as:

H7: PT positively and significantly affects PE.

H8: PT positively and significantly affects EE.

Past technology acceptance research has emphasized insights related to usefulness, ease of use, and social influence. However, there is limited research focused on AI in recruitment. Recently, trust and transparency have also emerged as critical determinants of AI adoption, especially within human resource arenas, along with system reliability. Other facilitating conditions are organizational support and training, whereas complexity of the technology and social pressure often act as secondary drivers of user engagement. This study seeks to integrate these insights into an extended UTAUT framework for positioning AI-driven recruitment in the overall discourse on technology acceptance in hybrid workplaces, with a focus on both psychological and infrastructural drivers of user adoption.

4. RESEARCH DESIGN

4.1. Nature of the study

Positivist research philosophy has been assumed by the researchers in the present study, which facilitates objective examination of observable phenomena through empirical analysis. The nature of the study is both descriptive and analytical.

4.2. Measurement Instrument

Measurement scales were adopted from earlier literatures pertaining to AI adoption and desirability. A total 24 items/questions spread among 7 constructs were adopted from the literature as presented in Annexure 1.

The survey questions for the respondents were pre-tested for face and content validity by administering it to a select group of academicians, who have been doing research in the field of AI. After careful consideration of the academicians' feedbacks, the survey questions were modified as needed.

4.3. Data collection

The responses for the study have been collected using a well structured questionnaire and administrated to the target respondents via Google form. The responses were collected for a period of five months between February and October 2025. Taking into account, the respondents' good command over the English language, as most of the students were from English medium, the questionnaire was prepared only in English. The sampling technique used for data collection was based on convenience sampling. Questionnaires in the form of e-forms were distributed to 554 students (UG and PG) from different colleges and universities in North-East India belong to 20-30 years age cohort. However, responses collected from 112 students were found to be complete (usable), with no missing response (response rate ~20 percent). Before taking part in the surveys, each respondent gave their informed consent as part of the study's ethical considerations. All participants expressed their verbal consent after being informed about the study's objectives, voluntary nature, and anonymity, their profile is presented in table 1.

Table 1. Profile of the respondents

Sl. NO.	variables	Categories	Count
1.	Gender	Male	50
		Female	62
2.	Residential Area	Rural	28
		Semi-Urban	26
		Urban	58
3.	Educational qualification	Undergraduate	65
		Post-graduate	47

continued on following page

Table 1. Continued

Sl. NO.	variables	Categories	Count
4.	Familiarity with integration of AI in recruitment	Not familiar	33
		Neutral	16
		Familiar	63

Source: Compiled data

5. DATA ANALYSIS

The measurement model was evaluated using internal consistency reliability and convergent validity measures, including Cronbach's alpha (CA), composite reliability (rho_a & rho_c), and average variance extracted (AVE). Overall, the results indicate that the constructs demonstrate good reliability and satisfactory convergent validity (Hair et al., 2022). The CA for all constructs range from 0.803 to 0.917 i.e., above the threshold of 0.70. This confirms strong internal consistency reliability, meaning the items within each construct measure the same underlying concept in a consistent manner (Hair et al., 2022).

Table 2. Factor load, Reliability and Validity Analysis

	Load	CA	rho_a	rho_c	AVE
EE		0.817	0.893	0.888	0.726
EE1	0.747				
EE2	0.906				
EE3	0.895				
FC		0.868	0.869	0.919	0.791
FC1	0.916				
FC2	0.899				
FC3	0.853				
PE		0.915	0.927	0.94	0.796
PE1	0.852				
PE2	0.891				
PE3	0.936				
PE4	0.888				
PT		0.803	0.835	0.887	0.726

continued on following page

Table 2. Continued

	Load	CA	rho_a	rho_c	AVE
PT1	0.92				
PT2	0.923				
PT3	0.693				
SI		0.917	0.927	0.947	0.857
SI1	0.904				
SI2	0.937				
SI3	0.936				
TI		0.849	0.849	0.909	0.769
TI1	0.834				
TI2	0.904				
TI3	0.892				
UD		0.854	0.882	0.904	0.705
UD1	0.859				
UD2	0.924				
UD3	0.905				
UD4	0.638				

All rho_a values lie between 0.835 and 0.927, while rho_c values range from 0.887 to 0.947. These values exceed the minimum acceptable level of 0.70, indicating that the constructs are measured reliably and that the indicators share a high degree of common variance (Hair et al., 2022).

Convergent validity (measured through AVE) was observed where all the values ranged from 0.705 to 0.857 (minimum required is 0.5). Social Influence (AVE = 0.857) and Performance Evaluation (AVE = 0.796) show very strong convergence, indicating that their indicators closely represent the intended latent variables (Hair et al., 2022; Sarstedt et al., 2025).

Most item loadings are above the recommended cutoff of 0.70, indicating strong indicator reliability. A few items, such as PT3 (0.693) and UD4 (0.638), fall slightly below the threshold but remain acceptable, as the overall construct reliability and AVE values are well within recommended limits. Retaining these items is justified since they contribute to content validity and do not adversely affect the measurement quality (Hair et al., 2022).

Table 3. Discriminant validity assessment

	EE	FC	PE	PT	SI	TI	UD
EE							
FC	0.304						
PE	0.167	0.470					
PT	0.176	0.744	0.592				
SI	0.384	0.516	0.456	0.560			
TI	0.623	0.365	0.342	0.503	0.376		
UD	0.189	0.716	0.599	0.852	0.569	0.482	
	EE	**FC**	**PE**	**PT**	**SI**	**TI**	**UD**
EE	0.852						
FC	0.240	0.89					
PE	0.143	0.427	0.892				
PT	0.143	0.618	0.512	0.852			
SI	0.332	0.467	0.42	0.488	0.926		
TI	0.511	0.318	0.301	0.422	0.329	0.877	
UD	0.149	0.624	0.536	0.715	0.519	0.398	0.839

Discriminant validity (DV) assessment (Table 3) was done through Heterotrait–Monotrait ratio (HTMT) and the Fornell–Larcker criterion to ensure that all constructs are conceptually different from each other. Most HTMT values (recommended <0.90) are well below 0.85, suggesting that the constructs are clearly different from each other. This relatively higher value is theoretically reasonable, as trust is expected to be closely related to users' preference and acceptance of the system. Overall, the HTMT analysis confirms that there are no serious issues of construct overlap or multicollinearity in the model (Ringle et al., 2023; Khan et al., 2021). The Fornell–Larcker criterion further supports DV. This confirms satisfactory discriminant validity and provides confidence that the relationships observed in the structural model are not affected by measurement overlap (Rönkkö & Cho, 2022).

5.1. Model Fit & Hypotheses testeing

The SRMR value for the saturated model (0.073) is below the recommended threshold of 0.08, indicating a good fit at the measurement level, whereas the SRMR for the estimated model (0.114) exceeds the acceptable limit, suggesting some misfit once the structural paths are introduced. (Hair et al., 2022; Dash & Paul, 2021).

Table 4. Path analysis and hypotheses testing

H	Path	O	M	SD	T	CI 2.50%	CI 97.50%	P values
H1	**PE -> UD**	0.156	0.163	0.093	1.676	-0.024	0.335	0.094
H2	**EE -> UD**	-0.092	-0.081	0.099	0.93	-0.286	0.097	0.352
H3	**SI -> UD**	0.15	0.146	0.09	1.679	-0.018	0.326	0.093
H4	**FC -> UD**	0.239	0.232	0.105	2.267	0.02	0.432	0.023
H5	**TI -> UD**	0.113	0.1	0.11	1.028	-0.112	0.313	0.304
H6	**PT -> UD**	0.38	0.392	0.121	3.145	0.154	0.617	0.002
H7	**PT -> PE**	0.512	0.513	0.093	5.511	0.299	0.664	0.000
H8	**PT -> EE**	0.143	0.141	0.15	0.949	-0.263	0.343	0.343

The hypothesis testing results (Table 4) show clear differences in the strength and significance of the proposed relationships. PE has a positive but marginally non-significant effect on UD (H1: $\beta = 0.156$, $p = 0.094$). EE do not influence UD (H2: $\beta = -0.092$, $p = 0.352$). Similarly, SI shows a positive but non-significant relationship with UD (H3: $\beta = 0.150$, $p = 0.093$), implying that users' preferences are not strongly shaped by opinions or pressure from others. FI, however, have a significant positive impact on User Desirability (H4: $\beta = 0.239$, $p = 0.023$). TI does not significantly affect UD (H5: $\beta = 0.113$, $p = 0.304$), suggesting that perceived complexity neither encourages nor discourages users in a meaningful way. PT emerges as a strong predictor of UD (H6: $\beta = 0.380$, $p = 0.002$), clearly showing that trust is a key driver of user acceptance. In addition, PT has a strong and significant effect on Performance Evaluation (H7: $\beta = 0.512$, $p < 0.001$), indicating that higher trust leads users to evaluate system performance more positively. In contrast, Perceived Trust does not significantly influence Effort Expectations (H8: $\beta = 0.143$, $p = 0.343$), suggesting that trust does not alter users' perceptions of the effort required to use the system. Overall, the results highlight PT and FC as the most influential factors in the model, while effort, SI, and TI play a limited role in explaining UD. The tested relationship can be seen in figure 2.

Figure 2. Path Diagram

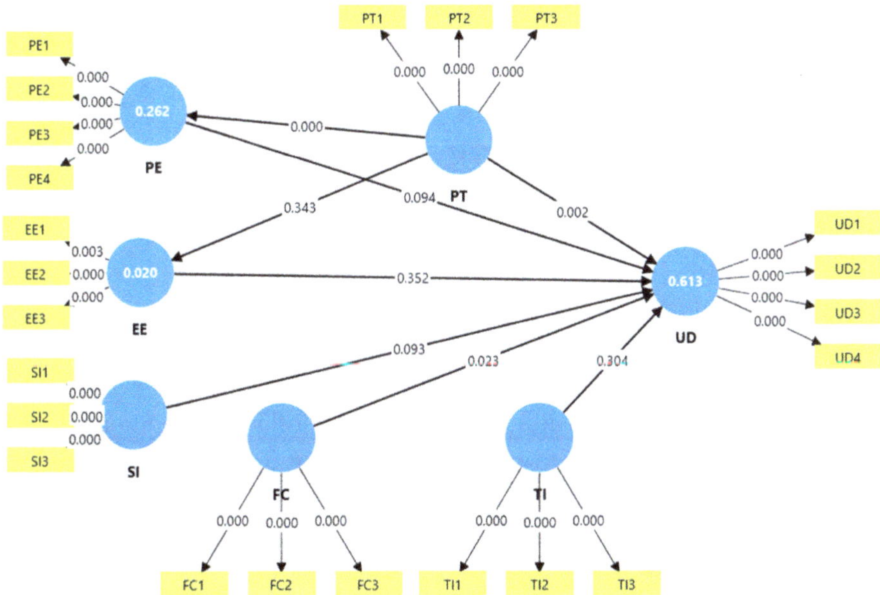

The R-square (Coefficient of determination) for EE have very low explanatory power ($R^2 = 0.02$; adjusted $R^2 = 0.01$), indicating that the model explains very little variance in effort perceptions. PE shows moderate explanatory power ($R^2 = 0.262$; adjusted $R^2 = 0.255$), meaning that about one-quarter of its variance is explained by the model. UD has strong explanatory power ($R^2 = 0.613$; adjusted $R^2 = 0.588$), indicating that the model explains a substantial portion of users' desirability toward the system.

6. CONCLUSION

This research offers a rich assessment of job seekers' readiness to adopt AI Recruitment System acceptance based on an enlarged UTAUT model. The assessment underlines the crucial nature of PT and the Role of FC in shaping the aspect of UD, emphasizing the need for trustworthiness, honesty, and an appropriate level of support infrastructure for effective shaping of the proposed adopters' intention to adopt. PE positively influences Trust, with moderate effects on desirability, whereas Effort Expectations, Social Influence, and Technology Complexity are less significant in determining users' level of acceptance of job seekers for AI Recruitment Technology. The proposed model explains an immense level of variance in terms of UD ($R^2 = 0.613$), suggesting the significant influence of job seekers' trust, performance evaluation perceptions, and work environment in shaping the proposed adopters' attitudes towards AI Recruitment Technology.

7. IMPLICATIONS OF THE STUDY

7.1. Theoretical Implications

The study would contribute positively to the existing literature on technology acceptance by incorporating two additional variables (Perceived trust and technology intricacy) to the original UTAUT framework. Earlier studies prioritized PE, EE, SI and FC in noticeable pattern. Apart from the following traditional UTAUT model, this study took effort to broaden its lens through positioning trust as a "High-Order Psychological Determinant" which is evidenced to be responsible for both user's desirability and performance outcome. This study is contributing to AI acceptance theories beside HR and psychology-based literature. In a deep sense, it is strengthening the AI literature claiming algorithmic decision-making process, conjunction of user's perceives fairness, perceives trust and ethical management are needed. The study advances the UTAUT framework in a promising way by adding trust as formal predictor of evaluative beliefs, thereby reinforcing UTAUT's strength as psychologically dominant framework. Based on earlier studies using the traditional UTAUT model, ease of use and social influence drive the intention to use technology particularly within socially privileged and technologically sensitive community. The context specific boundary condition has been replaced in this study and it contributes to future UTAUT uses in trust-based judgment but not only adaptation-based logic or convenience-based reasoning. Next, the study attempts to introduce Technology Intricacy which showed how collaborative effort of institution through structural support and trust can mitigate user's experience of technological complexity. In technology acceptance studies, this integration of variables would enhance the explanatory power of the existing framework in capturing the nuanced determinants of user desirability toward AI-enabled recruitment systems. Lastly, the impact of facilitating conditions on user desirability in this study highlights the urgent need for integrating institutional and technical theories. Facilitating conditions are no longer merely an institutional background support mechanism, rather they function as a source of legitimacy that represents organizational responsibility, readiness, liabilities and proactive actions in supporting users' system adoption. Though this study has been conducted at organizational level, the relationship between Facilitating condition and technology usability shows strong foundation for other psychological, technological and social studies. Lastly, in AI-driven human resource studies, the study demonstrates that technology acceptance in institutions is not only about technological advantage and advancement, rather psychological, ethical and infrastructural dimensions are interconnected. Through this study, the focus if AI HR related studies has been shifted from adaptation or acceptance-based model to humanization in algorithmic process that reinforces more easiness, accountability, trust, fairness and holistic future AI model in HR. In sum, this study's variable connection has advanced the UTAUT model by adding trust as central mechanism, moving form acceptance-based construct to trust based system and positioning facilitating condition as institutional legitimacy rather than organizational background support mechanism or responsibilities.

7.2. Managerial Implications

The outcome of the study would provide insightful information to HR executives, recruiters and organizations, intending to incorporate or expand AI-enabled recruitment solutions in hiring personnel. The findings of the study would also have importance ramifications for regulatory bodies and policymakers in charge of digital transformations and employment practices as well. Adequate and appropriate legislative framework concerning the ethical usage of AI need to be in place, provided 'perceived trust' and 'perceived complexity' play a pivotal role in determining technology acceptance in terms of user desirability. So, the result of this study guides to consider trust as organizational strategic priority that does not sub concern of system evaluation. Managers should ensure constant trust by upgrading recruitment system that promises transparency, accuracy and commitment to governance. Candidate's confidence can be ensured in this process by showing audit trials, sharing data use and management processes, ai-decision making process. Manager should consider building "trust" as part of institutional governance not maximization of technology uses. Again, following the role of facilitating condition, this study claims that managers are not only responsible for making the system simple; instead establish co-create experiences by adding values in trust and support building process. Users will be able to manage moderate levels of technological complexity and maintain engaged attitudes if they receive managerial support during system operation, including both psychological and technical guidance.

Considcring thc importancc of "social Influencc", the current IIR managers and organization can practice delivering personalized consultation, customized experience instead of normative action, or organizational strategy of employee well-being. Furthermore, this study would shed light on the digital readiness and AI literacy among the job seekers in the era of rapid integration of technology in almost all spheres of human lives.

To better establish good networks and communication in the job market, managers can position AI system as first organizational communication channel. This additional communication would increase AI recruitment value and individual's perception regarding respectful interaction, fairness and trust of system, feedback authenticity and overall positive impression towards Organizational brand and their recruitment process. Lastly, the study calls for modern managers attention to evaluate technological perception and adaptation differently by emphasizing trust, fairness, legitimacy, long-term sustainability through user's engagement and co-creation approach which will advance authentic AI grounded HR platform.

Limitations and Direction for future studies

The data collection from a specific sample of job seekers holds a limitation of generalization across regions or industry contexts. Further the cross-sectional design, constrains the ability to depict evolving perceptions over time. This can be overcome through longitudinal research design and involvement of moderating variables like culture and organizational context. Also, the AI as field is expected to grow over a period, it will be a good idea to periodically assess and monitor the changes it is expected to bring to the practices of contemporary world.

REFERENCES

Abhishek, K. L., Niranjanamurthy, M., Aric, S., Ansarullah, S. I., Sinha, A., Tejani, G., & Shah, M. A. (2025). Developing an Intelligent Resume Screening Tool With AI-Driven Analysis and Recommendation Features. *Applied AI Letters*, *6*(2), e116.

Alam, M. Z., Hu, W., & Barua, Z. (2018). Using the UTAUT model to determine factors affecting acceptance and use of mobile health (mHealth) services in Bangladesh. *Journal of Studies in Social Sciences*, *17*(2).

Almaiah, M. A., Alfaisal, R., Salloum, S. A., Hajjej, F., Shishakly, R., Lutfi, A., & Al-Maroof, R. S. (2022). Measuring institutions' adoption of artificial intelligence applications in online learning environments: Integrating the innovation diffusion theory with technology adoption rate. *Electronics (Basel)*, *11*(20), 3291.

Almeida, F., Junça Silva, A., Lopes, S. L., & Braz, I. (2025). Understanding recruiters' acceptance of artificial intelligence: Insights from the Technology Acceptance Model. *Applied Sciences (Basel, Switzerland)*, *15*(2), 746.

Ambarwati, R., Harja, Y. D., & Thamrin, S. (2020). The role of facilitating conditions and user habits: A case of Indonesian online learning platform. *The Journal of Asian Finance, Economics and Business*, *7*(10), 481–489.

Ami-Narh, J. T., & Williams, P. A. (2012). A revised UTAUT model to investigate E-health acceptance of health professionals in Africa. *Journal of Emerging Trends in Computing and Information Sciences*, *3*(10), 1383–1391.

Andrews, J. E., Ward, H., & Yoon, J. (2021). UTAUT as a model for understanding intention to adopt AI and related technologies among librarians. *Journal of Academic Librarianship*, *47*(6), 102437.

Armstrong, L., & Metaxa, D. (2025). Navigating Automated Hiring: Perceptions, Strategy Use, and Outcomes Among Young Job Seekers. *Proceedings of the ACM on Human-Computer Interaction*, *9*(2), 1–26.

Barath, G. V., Sanjev, R., & Saranya, S. (2025, May). AI-Driven Recruitment: Resume Screening and Skill Matching with NLP. In *2025 IEEE International Conference on Computer, Electronics, Electrical Engineering & their Applications (IC2E3)* (pp. 1-6). IEEE.

Barry, M., Haque, A. A., & Jan, M. T. (2024). From Expectancy to Acceptance: The Impact of Performance and Effort Expectations on Mobile Commerce Intentions. *SRIWIJAYA INTERNATIONAL JOURNAL OF DYNAMIC ECONOMICS AND BUSINESS*, 65-86.

Bhardwaj, G., Singh, S. V., & Kumar, V. (2020). An empirical study of artificial intelligence and its impact on human resource functions. *2020 International Conference on Computation, Automation and Knowledge Management (ICCAKM).*

Bhukya, R., & Paul, J. (2023). Social influence research in consumer behavior: What we learned and what we need to learn?–A hybrid systematic literature review. *Journal of Business Research*, *162*, 113870.

Black, J. S., & van Esch, P. (2020). AI-enabled recruiting: What is it and how should a manager use it? *Business Horizons*, *63*(2), 215–226.

Cao, X., Yu, L., Liu, Z., Gong, M., & Adeel, L. (2018). Understanding mobile payment users' continuance intention: A trust transfer perspective. *Internet Research*, *28*(2), 456–476.

Chawla, U., Mohnot, R., Singh, H. V., & Banerjee, A. (2023). The mediating effect of perceived trust in the adoption of cutting-edge financial technology among digital natives in the post-COVID-19 era. *Economies*, *11*(12), 286.

Chen, J.-H., Ha, N. T. T., Tai, H.-W., & Chang, C.-A. (2020). The willingness to adopt the internet of Things (IoT) conception in Taiwan's construction industry. *Journal of Civil Engineering and Management*, *26*(6), 534–550. DOI: 10.3846/jcem.2020.12639

Dash, G., & Paul, J. (2021). CB-SEM vs PLS-SEM methods for research in social sciences and technology forecasting. *Technological Forecasting and Social Change*, *173*(121092), 121092. DOI: 10.1016/j.techfore.2021.121092

Dhamija, P. (2012). E-recruitment: A roadmap towards e-human resource management. *Research World*, *3*(3), 33.

Ferneborg, S., Napolitano, F., Vaarst, M., Mejdell, C. M., Waiblinger, S., & De Oliveira, D. (2020). Methodology for studying human attitudes and behaviour to cow– calf contact systems. *The Journal of Dairy Research*, *87*(S1), 122–127.

Fishbein, M., & Ajzen, I. (1975). Beliefs, attitude, intention, and behavior: An introduction to theory and research.

Ghazzawi, K., & Accoumeh, A. (2014). Critical success factors of the e-recruitment system. *Journal of Human Resources Management and Labor Studies*, *2*(2), 159–170.

Grassini, S., Aasen, M. L., & Møgelvang, A. (2024). Understanding university students' acceptance of ChatGPT: Insights from the UTAUT2 model. *Applied Artificial Intelligence*, *38*(1), 2371168.

Gursoy, D., Chi, O. H., Lu, L., & Nunkoo, R. (2019). Consumers acceptance of artificially intelligent (AI) device use in service delivery. *International Journal of Information Management*, *49*, 157–169.

Hair, J. F., Hult, G. T. M., Ringle, C. M., & Sarstedt, M. (2022). A Primer on Partial Least Squares Structural Equation Modeling (PLS-SEM). *Sage (Atlanta, Ga.)*.

Hamadneh, S., Alshurideh, M. T., Alquqa, E. K., Al Kassem, A., Agha, K., & Alzoubi, H. M. (2024, February). AI-driven talent acquisition systems: transforming recruitment strategies in the digital age. In *2024 2nd International Conference on Cyber Resilience (ICCR)* (pp. 1-6). IEEE.

Hammad, A., & Abu-Zaid, R. (2024). Applications of AI in decentralized computing systems: Harnessing artificial intelligence for enhanced scalability, efficiency, and autonomous decision-making in distributed architectures. *Applied Research in Artificial Intelligence and Cloud Computing*, *7*(6), 161–187.

Hunkenschroer, A. L., & Luetge, C. (2022). Ethics of AI-enabled recruiting and selection: A review and research agenda. *Journal of Business Ethics*, *178*(4), 977–1007.

Islam, M., Mamun, A. A., Afrin, S., Ali Quaosar, G. A., & Uddin, M. A. (2022). Technology adoption and human resource management practices: The use of artificial intelligence for recruitment in Bangladesh. *SA Journal of Human Resource Management*, *9*(2), 324–349.

Islam, M., Rahman, M. M., Taher, M. A., Quaosar, G. A. A., & Uddin, M. A. (2024). Using artificial intelligence for hiring talents in a moderated mechanism. *Future Business Journal*, *10*(1), 13.

Jaspin, K., Kiruba, G. M., Nivedha, V., Priyadharshini, S., & Sivaraman, D. (2024, October). AI Assisted Career Guidance and Resume Screening System. In *2024 5th IEEE Global Conference for Advancement in Technology (GCAT)* (pp. 1-7). IEEE.

Jonathan, H., Magd, H., & Khan, S. A. (2024). Artificial intelligence and augmented reality: a business fortune to sustainability in the digital age. In *Navigating the digital landscape: Understanding customer behaviour in the online world* (pp. 85–105). Emerald Publishing Limited.

Kadirov, A., Shakirova, Y., Ismoilova, G., & Makhmudova, N. (2024, April). AI in human resource management: reimagining talent acquisition, development, and retention. In *2024 International Conference on Knowledge Engineering and Communication Systems (ICKECS)* (Vol. 1, pp. 1-8). IEEE.

Karyamsetty, H. J., Khan, S. A., & Nayyar, A. (2024). *Envisioning toward modernization of society 5.0—A prospective glimpse on status, opportunities, and challenges with XAI. XAI Based Intelligent Systems for Society 5.0*. Elsevier.

Kassim, N. M., Ramayah, T., & Kurnia, S. (2012). Antecedents and outcomes of human resource information system (HRIS) use. *International Journal of Productivity and Performance Management*, *61*(6), 603–623.

Khalilzadeh, J., Ozturk, A. B., & Bilgihan, A. (2017). Security-related factors in extended UTAUT model for NFC based mobile payment in the restaurant industry. *Computers in Human Behavior*, *70*, 460–474.

Khan, S. A., Epoc, F., Gangwar, V., Ligori, T. A. A., & Ansari, Z. A. (2021). Will online banking sustain in Bhutan post COVID-19? A quantitative analysis of the customer e-satisfaction and e-loyalty in the Kingdom of Bhutan. *Transnational Marketing Journal*, *9*(3), 607–624.

Khan, S. A., Khatri, B., Jonathan, H., Naim, A., & Arora, S. (2025). Revolutionizing Agriculture: Harnessing High-Performance Computing and Artificial Intelligence for Innovative Farming Practices. In *Circular Economy and Technological Innovation: The Regional Implications* (pp. 237–252). Springer Nature Singapore.

Khan, S. A., & Naim, A. (2024). XAI in Society 5.0 through the lens of marketing and HRM. In *XAI based intelligent Systems for Society 5.0* (pp. 327-363). Elsevier.

Khanam, L., & Mahfuz, M. A. (2017). Employee acceptance of knowledge management systems in Bangladesh: Integrating Utaut and Kms diffusion model. *Independent Business Review*, *10*(1/2), 85–109.

Khatri, B., Shrimali, H., Khan, S. A., & Naim, A. (2023). Role of HR analytics in ensuring psychological wellbeing and job security: Learnings from COVID-19. In *HR analytics in an era of rapid automation* (pp. 36-53). IGI Global.

Kuberkar, S., & Singhal, T. K. (2020). Factors Influencing Adoption Intention of AI Powered Chatbot for Public Transport Services within a Smart City. *International Journal of Emerging Technologies in Learning*, *2020*, 948–958.

Lai, P. C. (2017). The literature review of technology adoption models and theories for the novelty technology. *JISTEM-Journal of Information Systems and Technology Management*, *14*(1), 21–38.

Langer, M., König, C. J., & Papathanasiou, M. (2019). Highly automated job interviews: Acceptance under the influence of stakes. *International Journal of Selection and Assessment*, *27*(3), 217–234.

Latané, B. (1981). The psychology of social impact. *The American Psychologist, 36*(4), 343.

Liang, S. Z., Xu, J. L., & Huang, E. (2024). Comprehensive analysis of the effect of social influence and brand image on purchase intention. *SAGE Open, 14*(1), 21582440231218771.

Lihua, D. (2022). An extended model of the theory of planned behavior: An empirical study of entrepreneurial intention and entrepreneurial behavior in college students. *Frontiers in Psychology, 12*, 627818.

Loy, R. W., Christiansen, N. D., Tett, R. P., Klein, K., & Toich, M. (2025). Personality Test Validity Differs Between Low-Stakes and High-Stakes Employment Settings. *International Journal of Selection and Assessment, 33*(3), e70018.

Ma, Q., & Liu, L. (2004). The technology acceptance model: A meta-analysis of empirical findings. [JOEUC]. *Journal of Organizational and End User Computing, 16*(1), 59–72.

Magd, H., Ansari, M. S. A., & Khan, S. A. (2024). Need for explainable artificial intelligence ethnic decision-making in society 5.0. In *XAI Based Intelligent Systems for Society 5.0* (pp. 103–127). Elsevier.

Magd, H., Jonathan, H., Khan, S. A., & El Geddawy, M. (2022). Artificial intelligence—the driving force of industry 4.0. *A roadmap for enabling industry 4.0 by artificial intelligence*, 1-15.

Magd, H., Khan, S. A., Khatri, B., Sharma, N., & Arora, S. (2023). Understanding the relationship between IoT and digital marketing: a bibliometric analysis. In *Global applications of the internet of things in digital marketing* (pp. 123–140). IGI Global.

Maisha, K., & Shetu, S. N. (2023). Influencing factors of e-learning adoption amongst students in a developing country: The post-pandemic scenario in Bangladesh. *Future Business Journal, 9*(1), 37.

Naim, A., Khan, S. A., Mohammed, A. B., & Malik, P. K. (2024b). Applications of high performance computing and AI in green digital marketing. In *AI Applications for Business, Medical, and Agricultural Sustainability* (pp. 47-67). IGI Global Scientific Publishing.

Naim, A., Mohammed, A. B., Fatima, N., Khan, S. A., Alnfiai, M. M., & Malik, P. K. (2024a). Applications of artificial intelligence in environmental resource business management and sustainability. In *AI Applications for Business, Medical, and Agricultural Sustainability* (pp. 1-22). IGI Global Scientific Publishing.

Ochmann, J., & Laumer, S. (2020, March). AI Recruitment: Explaining job seekers' acceptance of automation in human resource management. In *Wirtschaftsinformatik (Zentrale Tracks)* (pp. 1633-1648).

Oliveira, T., Thomas, M., Baptista, G., & Campos, F. (2016). Mobile payment: Understanding the determinants of customer adoption and intention to recommend the technology. *Computers in Human Behavior*, *61*, 404–414.

Patil, P., Tamilmani, K., Rana, N. P., & Raghavan, V. (2020). Understanding consumer adoption of mobile payment in India: Extending Meta-UTAUT model with personal innovativeness, anxiety, trust, and grievance redressal. *International Journal of Information Management*, *54*, 102144.

Rathinaswamy, J., Sengottaiyan, K., & Duraisamy, B. (2020). A qualitative approach towards adoption of information and communication technology by medical doctors applying utaut model. Xi'an Jianzhu Keji Daxue Xuebao/J. Xi'an. *Univ. Archit. Technol*, *2020*, 4689–4703.

Ringle, C. M., Sarstedt, M., Sinkovics, N., & Sinkovics, R. R. (2023). A perspective on using partial least squares structural equation modelling in data articles. *Data in Brief*, *48*(109074), 109074. DOI: 10.1016/j.dib.2023.109074

Rönkkö, M., & Cho, E. (2022). An updated guideline for assessing discriminant validity. *Organizational Research Methods*, *25*(1), 6–14. DOI: 10.1177/1094428120968614

Sana'a, Y. (2016). A critical review of models and theories in field of individual acceptance of technology. *International journal of hybrid information technology*, *9*(6), 143-158.

Santoso, A., & Surya, Y. (2024). Maximizing decision efficiency with edge-based AI systems: Advanced strategies for real-time processing, scalability, and autonomous intelligence in distributed environments. *Quarterly Journal of Emerging Technologies and Innovations*, *9*(2), 104–132.

Sarstedt, M., Ringle, C. M., & Hair, J. F. (2025). Partial least squares structural equation modeling. In *Handbook of Market Research* (pp. 1–56). Springer Nature Switzerland.

Schlippe, T., & Bothmer, K. (2023). Skill scanner: An AI-based recommendation system for employers, job seekers and educational institutions. *International Journal of Advanced Corporate Learning*, *16*(1), 55.

Sharma, N., Khatri, B., Khan, S. A., & Shamsi, M. S. (2023). Extending the UTAUT model to examine the influence of social media on tourists' destination selection. *Indian Journal of Marketing*, *53*(4), 47–64.

Sheikh, H., Prins, C., & Schrijvers, E. (2023). Artificial intelligence: definition and background. In Mission, A. I. (Ed.), *The new system technology* (pp. 15–41). Springer International Publishing.

Singh, G., Bhardwaj, G., Singh, S. V., & Kumar, V. (2020). Technology Acceptance Model to Assess Employee's Perception and Intention of Integration of Artificial Intelligence and Human Resource Management in IT Industry. *Int. J. Adv. Sci. Technol, 2020*, 11485–11490.

Soni, V. (2024, April). AI in Job Matching and Recruitment: Analyzing the Efficiency and Equity of Automated Hiring Processes. In *2024 International Conference on Knowledge Engineering and Communication Systems (ICKECS)* (Vol. 1, pp. 1-5). IEEE.

Sýkorová, Z., Hague, D., Dvouletý, O., & Procházka, D. A. (2024). Incorporating artificial intelligence (AI) into recruitment processes: ethical considerations. *Vilakshan-XIMB Journal of Management*, (ahead-of-print).

Taherdoost, H. (2021). Importance of technology acceptance assessment for successful implementation and development of new technologies. *Global Journal of Engineering Sciences*.

Tanantong, T., & Wongras, P. (2024). A UTAUT-based framework for analyzing users' intention to adopt artificial intelligence in human resource recruitment: A case study of Thailand. *Systems*, *12*(1), 28.

Thompson, R. L., Higgins, C. A., & Howell, J. M. (1991). Personal computing: Toward a conceptual model of Utilization1. *Management Information Systems Quarterly*, *15*(1), 125–143. DOI: 10.2307/249443

Tian, X., Pavur, R., Han, H., & Zhang, L. (2023). A machine learning-based human resources recruitment system for business process management: Using LSA, BERT and SVM. *Business Process Management Journal*, *29*(1), 202–222.

Uddin, M. A., Alam, M. S., Mamun, A. A., Khan, T.-U.-Z., & Akter, A. (2020). A study of the adoption and implementation of enterprise resource planning (ERP): Identification of moderators and mediator. *Journal of Open Innovation*, *6*(1), 2. DOI: 10.3390/joitmc6010002

Uma, V. R., Velchamy, I., & Upadhyay, D. (2023). Recruitment analytics: Hiring in the era of artificial intelligence. In *The adoption and effect of artificial intelligence on human resources management, part A* (pp. 155–174). Emerald Publishing Limited.

Venkatachalam, S. (2024, September). Artificial Intelligence and Big Data Applications in Recruitment Process Management. In 2024 4th International Conference on Soft Computing for Security Applications (ICSCSA) (pp. 68-72). IEEE.

Venkatesh, V., Morris, M. G., Davis, G. B., & Davis, F. D. (2003). User acceptance of information technology: Toward a unified view. *Management Information Systems Quarterly*, •••, 425–478.

Venkatesh, V., Morris, M. G., Davis, G. B., & Davis, F. D. (2003). User acceptance of information technology: Toward A unified View1. *Management Information Systems Quarterly*, *27*(3), 425–478. DOI: 10.2307/30036540

Venkatesh, V., Thong, J. Y. L., & Xu, X. (2012). Consumer acceptance and use of information technology: Extending the unified theory of acceptance and use of Technology1. *Management Information Systems Quarterly*, *36*(1), 157–178. DOI: 10.2307/41410412

Wahab, F., Shah, A., Ullah, I., Adhikari, D., & Khan, I. (2024). Applications of artificial intelligence in smart distributed processing and big data mining. In *Artificial Intelligence for Intelligent Systems* (pp. 69–85). CRC Press.

Zareen, S., & Khan, S. A. (2023). Exploring dependence of human resource management (HRM) on internet of things (IoT) and digital marketing in the digital era. In *Global applications of the internet of things in digital marketing* (pp. 51-66). IGI Global.

APPENDIX 1 MEASUREMENT SCALE (TABLE 5)

Table 5.

SL. NO.	CONSTRUCT	QUESTIONS	SCALE	REFERENCE
1	Performance Expectancy (PE)	PE1:AI devices are more accurate than human beings PE2:AI devices are more accurate with less human errors PE3:AI devices provide more consistent service than human beings PE4:Information provided by AI devices are more consistent	7 point likert Scale	Gursoy et al. (2019)
2.	Effort Expectancy (EE)	EE1: Using AI devices takes too much of my time. EE2: Working with AI devices is so difficult to understand and use in services EE3: It takes me too long to learn how to interact with AI devices	7 point likert Scale	Gursoy et al. (2019)
3.	Social Influence (SI)	SI1: People who influence my behavior think that I should participate in AI enabled recruitment drive.	7 point likert Scale	
		SI2: People who are important to me think that I should participate in AI enabled recruitment drive.		
		SI3: People whose opinions that I value prefer that I should participate in AI enabled recruitment drive.		
4.	Facilitating Condition (FC)	FC1: I have the resources necessary to use AI-powered Interfaces.	7 point likert Scale	Oliveira et al. (2016)
		FC2: I have the knowledge necessary to use AI-powered Interfaces		
		FC3:AI-powered Interfaces is compatible with other systems I use		
5.	Technology Intricacy (TI)	TI1: overall, I believe that a HRIS is difficult to use TI2: learning to operate the HRIS was difficult for me TI3: using the HRIS requires a lot of mental effort	7 point likert scale	Kassim et al. (2012)

continued on following page

Table 5. Continued

SL. NO.	CONSTRUCT	QUESTIONS	SCALE	REFERENCE
6.	User Desirability (UD)	UD1: I am willing to receive AI device services UD2:I will feel happy to interact with AI devices UD3:I am likely to interact with AI devices UD4: I prefer human contact in service transactions UD5: Interaction with AI devices lacks social contact	7-point Likert Scale	Gursoy et al. (2019)
7.	Perceived trust (PT)	PT1: I trust that AI algorithm is reliable in screening candidates to match organization's requirement PT2: I trust that AI based recruitment software has reliable database to complete recruitment PT3: I trust that AI software developer is honest and will not take advantage over user's information	7-point Likert Scale	Tanantong & Wongras (2024)

Source: Authors' Compilation

Chapter 3
Charting the Future:
AI's Evolving Role in Human Capital Management

Ankita Pathak
https://orcid.org/0000-0002-8068-8874
GLA University, India

Majdi Anwar Quttainah
https://orcid.org/0000-0002-6280-1060
Kuwait University, Kuwait

ABSTRACT

This research paper delves into the practical implications of Artificial Intelligence (AI) in Human Capital Management (HCM), over the next five to ten years. The study is aimed at assisting organizations in preparing for the future by addressing the inherent uncertainties associated with predicting it. A comprehensive analysis of AI's current usage within these modules is conducted through literature reviews and with a particular focus on core HR and recruitment. The paper explores upcoming HCM developments, including employee well-being, reskilling, diversity, technology acceptance, and employee experience, as well as anticipated legal trends. Additionally, the research identifies AI technologies associated with these HCM developments, including AI-enabled wearables, personalized curriculum software, workforce monitoring tools, and feedback systems. This research equips organizations with valuable insights into AI's role in HCM, helping them navigate ethical, legal, and technological challenges while preparing for the evolving landscape of human capital management.

DOI: 10.4018/979-8-3373-5871-0.ch003

nt © 2026, IGI Global Scientific Publishing. Copying or distributing in print or electronic forms without written permission of IGI Global Scientific Publishing is prohibited. Use of this chapter to generative artificial intelligence (AI) technologies is expressly prohibited. The publisher reserves all rights to license its use for generative AI training and machine learning model development.

1. INTRODUCTION

Artificial intelligence has brought the Fourth Industrial Revolution which has reshaped industries and economies worldwide. New technology like AI, Metaverse is shrinking the world, and organizations are competing on a global scale (Guodong et al., 2021). It indicates that adopting new technologies and innovations is important for the organizations to remain modern and maintain a competitive edge. According to Rajni et al., (2023), AI is the process of giving robots human intelligence so they can behave and think like people. An AI model demonstrates characteristics of humans, including intelligence and problem-solving abilities. Artificial Intelligence (AI) refers to the creation of computer systems that can do tasks usually necessitating human intelligence. These tasks encompass comprehending natural language, identifying patterns, acquiring knowledge from experience, and making data-driven judgments. Sectors like retail, banking and finance have implemented AI for handling customer queries and services. AI is used for customer segmentation, demand forecasting, recommendation systems, and inventory management. AI is accepted and integrated across several departments in organization but still HR departments are finding it challenging to implement AI in their processes (Chowdhury et al., 2023).

The application of artificial intelligence in HRM is referred to as the "new age of HR," because AI is revolutionising the overall process of working by taking over routine tasks formerly handled by HR managers (Khan et al., 2023). HR managers can focus on activities which require specialised skills and knowledge than the other repetitive and time-consuming duties which can be automated by AI (Tuffaha, 2022). Machine learning minimises mistakes, and improves decision-making process which leads to better data processing and analysis (Angelopoulos et al., 2019). For instance, time-consuming and labour intensive HR processes like screening a large number of resumes, organising them, selecting the best applicants, determining which staff members need training etc. can be performed by AI in a short span of time (Johansson & Herranen, 2019). Moreover, AI-powered algorithms can be used in screening and evaluation of applicants' resumes and abilities. AI-enabled chatbots make it easier to communicate with candidates, and line up the interviews, which overall enhances the applicant's experience. According to Dutta et al., (2023), employee communication and interaction can be significantly enhanced by implementing AI in organizations.

Artificial intelligence (AI) facilitates enhanced efficacy and efficiency by optimising administrative procedures and reducing related expenses (Obiuto et al., 2024). AI makes it easier to access a larger pool of passive applicants who aren't actively looking for work but could be interested in the role. In the area of training and development, AI-driven personalized learning platforms analyse employee performance data and based on performance, personalised training programmes are offered to reduce skill gaps and improve worker skills. Halid et al., (2024) examined how artificial intelligence (AI) can help in improving the identification, selection, and retention of bright candidates. However, despite the numerous benefits offered by AI adoption and integration in HR functions, only 37% of HR employee services and 33% of customer issue resolutions are automated, compared to 53% for IT services. According to a survey conducted by Deloitte, only 17% of organizations have fully implemented AI in HR, while 47% are in the process of experimenting with AI applications, and 36% have not yet started integrating AI into their HR processes (Bhatt & Shah, 2023). This data indicates a significant gap between the potential of AI in HRM and its actual adoption in practice. Hence, it warrants the need for improvement across all areas.

Figure 1. Application of AI in HRM Process

The combination of Human resource management (HRM) and information technologies (IT) would revolutionise HR operations. AI will improve quality of services by identifying the best candidates based on specific criteria which lead to improved workforce quality (Allal-Chérif et al., 2021). AI-driven data analytics tools can help managers identify trends, predict workforce needs, and develop strategic plans for talent management (Khan, 2024). According to research by various authors, workforce planning (Kovach & Cathcart, 1999), talent sourcing (Falletta, 2013), recruitment, forecasting attrition (Rogers, 2018), performance evaluation, succession planning (Fallucchi et al., 2020), employee engagement, compensation (Kaur et al., 2021) and learning and development have all been significantly impacted by AI-driven digital technologies. Artificial Intelligence (AI) is recognised as a powerful tool in human resource management (HRM), however, research on its application is still comparatively limited (Pan & Froese, 2023).

A study by Gartner found that 92% of HR leaders believe that AI has the potential to transform HR, but only 9% have deployed AI-powered solutions extensively (Gartner, 2020). These statistics underscore the current underutilization of AI in HRM and highlight the need for further research and investment in this direction. As a result, experts and scholars (Budhwar et al., 2022, Pandey, 2020), alike are more interested in exploring the application of artificial intelligence (AI) in HRM. The impact of Artificial Intelligence (AI) on Human Resource Management (HRM) highlights the need for a thorough analysis and identify the crucial area and predict the development. Scholarly publications (Chowdhury et al., 2023, Arslan et al., 2022)make clear picture that some fields and area are explored so there is a need to investigate the potential of AI's in HRM. The current study provide insights to following question.

R1- Identify the common trends in the literature on AI in HRM, in terms of document kinds, source types, citation patterns, and other pertinent variables

R2- Identify the technologies that are relevant for HRM

R3 Identify current application of AI in HRM

R3: Identify current ethical and legal concerns regarding the implementation of AI in HRM?

R4: Anticipate future trends and development in HRM

R5: Identify the subfields or sectors which require in-depth examination in upcoming studies

In depth analysis of the literature proposed the aim to explores the current application of AI in HRM, current ethical and legal concerns regarding the implementation of AI in HRM. The research journey is further enriched by incorporating significant supplementary literature and promising a new insight related to application of AI in HCM. The theoretical framework presented in the study would meet the research questions. The generated data will lead to relevant conclusions and discussion. The novelty of the research is how AI is integrated into HRM within organisations and how this affects organisational approaches and human resources. The study provides a systematic examination of the existing literature, identifying trends, patterns, and gaps in research. Furthermore, the paper offers insights into the evolution of AI in HRM research over time, by highlighting emerging topics, influential authors, and key journals in the field. The paper highlights directions for further research, and provides most recent advancements and prospects in this important field to academics, professionals, and organization decision-makers.

2. ARTIFICIAL INTELLIGENCE (AI) TECHNOLOGIES IN HUMAN RESOURCES MANAGEMENT

Artificial intelligence was invented in 1956 and explored since World War II. In today's age of virtual technology, artificial intelligence (AI) is a game-changer. Negi (2020) asserts that artificial intelligence (AI) sparks a technological revolution. According to Mohammad (2020), artificial intelligence (AI) is a broad area of information technology which include various ideas.. AI is mostly used for the work which require data analysis. Computer developments have brought rapid responds and quick reactions to business challenges, but still computer cannot match the flexibility of humans. In the 1950s and 60s, it was anticipated that development of artificial intelligence (AI) will bring computers and robots with cognitive capacities similar to those of humans (Jaakkola et al., 2019). Artificial Intelligence is a broad field which use different technology. Some example of technologies are Data analytics, robotics, machine learning, natural language processing (Javaid et al., 2022). Artificial Intelligence (AI) and other related technologies, such as Machine Learning (ML), Robotic Process Automation (RPA), and Natural Language Processing (NLP) has greatly impacted and changed core business models (Nguyen et al., 2023).

According to Qamar et al., (2023), different organisations have integrated AI into HRM with the help of various given techniques.

Expert Systems: Expert systems are computer programmes that are designed to provide access to knowledge by integrating expert knowledge in systematic frameworks. It solve complicated problems and support the creation of comprehensive information systems. They are primarily used in labour management, hiring, remuneration, and HR planning (Malik & Malik, 2024).

NLP: Natural language processing focuses on the interaction of computers with natural human languages. NLP is concentrated on creating computer systems that can communicate in natural languages (Muris et al., 2021). One of the well-known example of NLP is Chatbots application. Users can communicate with these chatbots in their own language. The system then interprets the message and provide a logical answer in that language.

Artificial Neural Networks: The programme is designed to mimic how the human brain operates. It mimics the cognitive learning process by processing components, layers, and networks (Thakur & Konde, 2021). It is most widely used prediction approaches used in hiring, selection, and employee performance management (Tuffaha, 2023).

Data Mining: Data mining is the process of obtaining hidden and useful data. Businesses use the extracted data to identify the patterns into a competitive advantage (Huang et al., 2023). Data mining was first applied in HRM in 2006, and since then, it has mostly been used in talent management, competence and performance evaluation, and recruiting.

Machine learning: Machine learning is the process where machine learns on its own without the need for explicit programming (Hunkenschroer & Luetge, 2022). Many research agree that machine learning helps HR managers make better decisions, It also helps in anticipating employee attrition (Gryncewicz et al., 2023).

Genetic algorithms: Genetic Algorithms utilize search strategies based on replication, mutation, and gene crossover to achieve optimal solutions for mathematical challenges. It primary applicable in tasks related to workforce organization and assessing employee performance (Zhang et al., 2021).

Figure 2. AI HRM System

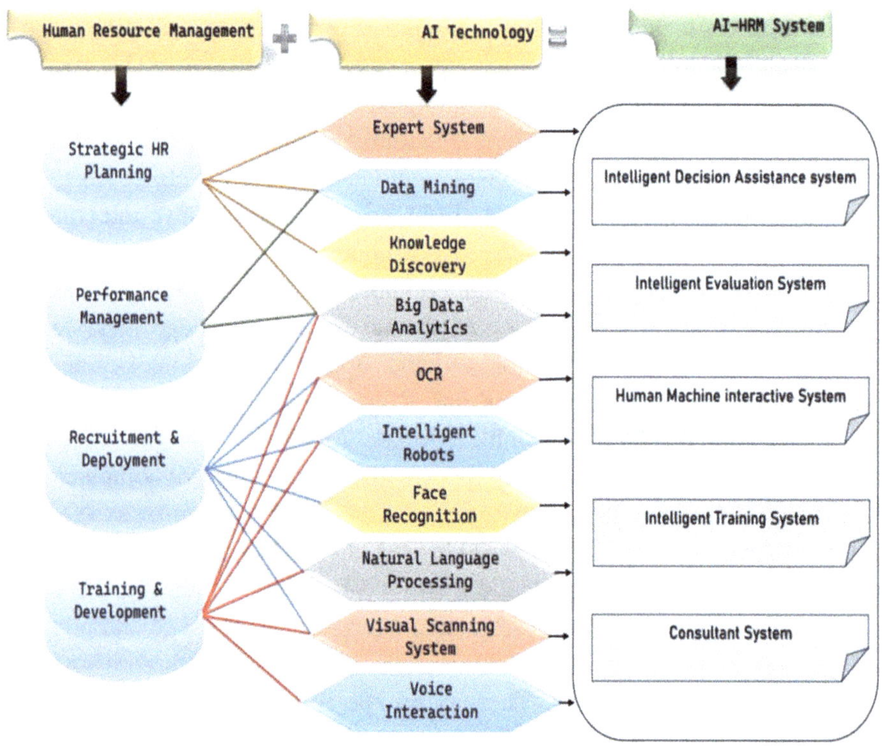

These techniques have facilitated in functionalities in HRM. HR manager need to perform new roles such as data analyst, cloud computing, the utilization of HRM on mobile platforms, Social Media, Analytics, Clouds (SMAC), and big data (Strohmeier, 2020), such data analytics, social media, cloud computing, data analysis, and HRM on mobile platforms (Strohmeier, 2020).

3. RESEARCH METHODOLOGY

A systematic review is a widely employed methodology for assessing the effects of publishing, which cannot be achieved by alternative review types (Varsha et al., 2024). Systematic techniques are effective for elucidating the subject's framework, pinpointing current and developing research themes, and summarizing the most impactful scholars and publications. Additionally, the rising availability of internet databases holding citation data and the development of better analytic tools are boosting their appeal among academics and researchers (Dominko and Verbiˇc, 2019). Unlike the study carried out by Maier et al. (2020), we have used the Scopus database to access a larger number of relevant articles . To address our research questions and accurately depict the existing literature on green marketing innovation and sustainable consumption, we perform a dual analysis comprising a systematic literature review and a supplementary bibliometric evaluation of documents, including articles sourced from the Scopus database, along with further content analysis. A methodical and planned strategy to doing a literature review is a method of reading, classifying, and interpreting academic publications (Hasbullah et al., 2023). This aids in refining the search for scholarly literature on a topic to its significant contributions and guarantees that the methodological approach is clear and reproducible (Ermel et al., 2021). Figure 3 shows the Prism Model which shows the inclusion and exclusion criteria and key words string. The SEARCH STRING: "AI" OR "ARTIFICIAL INTELLIGENCE" AND " HR" OR "HUMAN RESOURCE was given to Scopus data base and following details were extracted.

Figure 3. Prism Model for the given string "AI" OR "ARTIFICIAL INTELLIGENCE" AND " HR" OR "HUMAN RESOURCE"

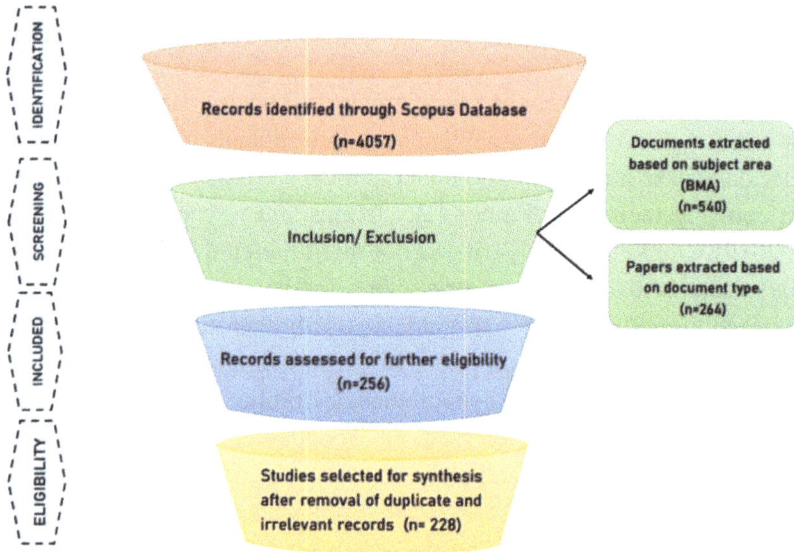

From 2012 to 2023, there has been a substantial and continuous increase in research related to the integration of Artificial Intelligence (AI) in Human Resource Management (HRM). The researcher on the adoption of AI in HRM is showing positive graph which showcase that researchers are inclined to investigate the potential benefits and challenges of integrating AI into HRM. AI technologies have significantly advanced in recent years, which leads to innovative applications of AI in various function of HR management. Researchers are exploring how AI can used for HR processes such as recruitment, performance management, and employee engagement. The adoption of AI in HRM has impact on organizational efficiency, employee satisfaction, and overall business performance. It generates the interest for both academia and industry. Researchers and organizations have increasingly explored AI-driven solutions across various HR functions, such as recruitment, talent management, employee engagement, and analytics. Figure 4 shows the number of paper published from year 2012 to 2023. The expanding body of research in this field demonstrates a commitment to harnessing AI's capabilities to enhance HRM practices, improve workforce productivity, and address complex HR challenges in the evolving world of work.

Figure 4. Number of Paper Published in last 2012 to 2023

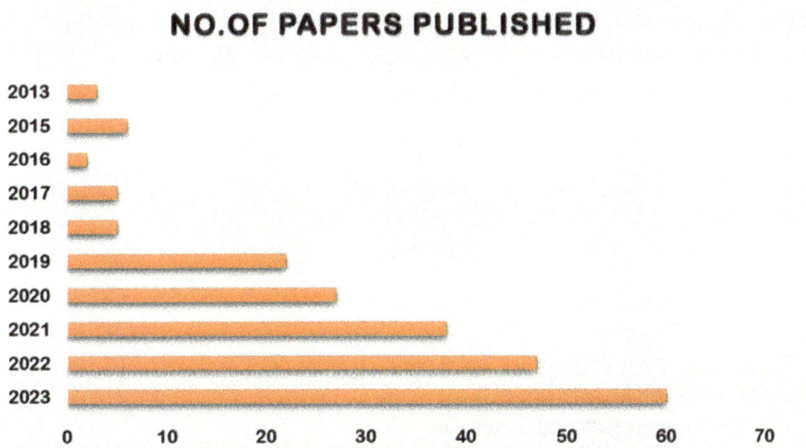

In the ever-evolving landscape of academia, certain research papers stand out as beacons of knowledge, innovation, and profound insights. Table 1 shows the top 10 research papers, meticulously curated and thoughtfully selected, represent the pinnacle of scholarly achievement across the study elated to AI in HRM.

Table 1. TOP 10 AUTHORS IN TERMS OF NO. OF PUBLICATIONS

S.NO.	NAME OF AUTHORS	NO.OF PUBLICATION
1.	Budhwar, P.	4
2.	Malik, A.	4
3.	Prikshat, V.	4
4.	Black, J.S.	3
5.	Nawaz, N.	3
6.	van Esch, P.	3
7.	Avrahami, D.	2
8.	Bhattacharya, S.	2
9.	Chalutz Ben-Gal, H.	2
10.	Chowdhury, S.	2

The analysis of the top 10 countries at the forefront of publications related to Artificial Intelligence (AI) in Human Resource Management (HRM). As the field of AI in HRM continues to evolve and expand, it is essential to identify the countries that have been at the forefront of contributing to the knowledge base in this domain.

Figure 5 shows the top 10 countries in terms of number of publications which examine the publication trends, research output, and innovation in these countries, we aim to provide valuable insights into the global landscape of AI adoption in HRM research. These countries serve as leaders in shaping the future of HR practices through AI-driven innovations and solutions.

Figure 5. TOP 10 COUNTRIES IN TERMS OF NO.OF PUBLICATIONS

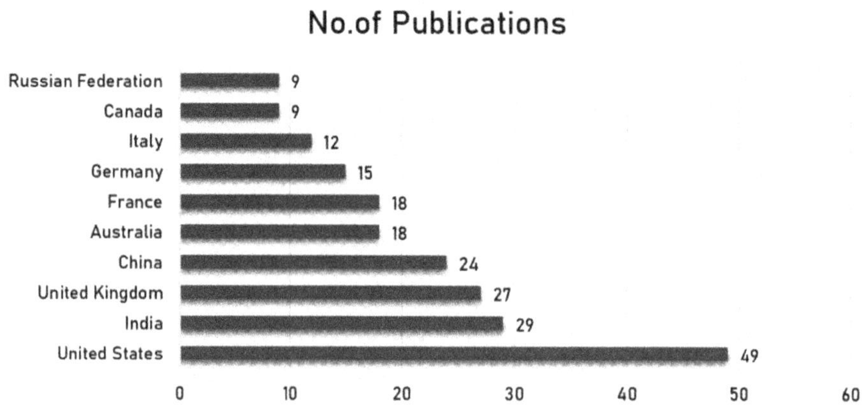

Research on AI in HRM is more popular in the United States as US is home of numerous tech giants. It has AI research institutions, startups, and academic centers which explore innovative way to integrate AI in various activities. The size and diversity of the workforce in present unique challenges and opportunities for applying AI in HRM. Large populations and diverse labor markets need efficient and effective HR processes. AI drive HR process leads to effective HR procedure.

4. APPLICATION OF AI IN HCM

In recent years, technological advancements have a considerable impact on the overall functioning of HR in organization. The HR department in every organisation is the repository of a wide range of information related to human resources. AI has the potential to completely transform HR operations by evaluations various roles. A virtual assistant can assist with various tasks such as hiring and selection, orientation, performance evaluation, staff engagement, and staff retention. The foundation for AI implementations has been established by the development of Human Resource Information Systems (HRIS). AI analysed Data is used for critical thinking and decision making. AI can be used to automate the process of recruitment starting from application scanning to extraction of significant information, from the resume of candidate (Bhanot, 2022). Human require a long time for analyzing the data but with the help of AI, it is done within a few seconds (Jain et al., 2023). AI allows smart database administration at multiple levels of the HR department, as well as it improves the individual competence. It manage, monitoring, and assess the individual skills (Sakka et al., 2022).

4.1 Recruitment and Selection

The HR professionals are responsible for finding talent for the organisation, and choosing the right applicants is crucial. HR managers face difficult in selecting the most suitable candidates for right job by screening resumes (Dixit et al., 2022). Manager interact with applicants to fill job openings since the company may suffer large losses from delay in operational. AI can speed up the hiring process as the need of recruitment is continuous process (Balasundaram et al., 2022). Organisations can improve and modernise their employment process by employing Artificial Intelligence (AI) . AI techniques can interpret the vast data and find trends for the growth of organization.

AI can automate repetitive operations and can analyse large-scale data to identify patterns. AI can speed up the recruiting process from hiring to onboarding. Organization can use AI chatbots to communicate with website visitors and increase conversion rates. AI can encourage Potential applicants to submit their resumes and share other essential information while conversation with the bots. Chatbots are capable of inquiring about a candidate's interest in a position and respond to basic questions from prospective candidates.

AI reduce and eliminate human intervention in labour-intensive processes like manually reviewing resumes. It saves time since chatbots can handle time-consuming recruiting tasks such as collecting applicant data, screening candidates, setting up appointments and chat sessions, and interaction with the candidate (Gupta & Mishra, 2023).

Artificial intelligence (AI) helps in the process of reviewing applications and identifying the best applicants for a job. According to Surve (2020), talent acquisition software has reduced the burden of hiring by over 75%. AI -trained models consider experience, skills, education, and other organisational interests before choosing a job candidate. AI conduct background checks, such as reviewing candidates' social media profiles, to ensure that right and qualified candidate is the selected for the post.

AI-integrated software such as Chatbots, Applicant Tracking Systems (ATS), and Customer Relationship Management (CRM) assist in promptly answering to queries of candidate and offers updates on their application status. The use of artificial intelligence (AI) in human resource management (HRM) lowers the chance of nepotism and favouritism on applicants' recruitment and selection (Kusý, 2021). During the process of recruitment ethnicity, language, gender, and even race can influence recruiter. Biases can be eliminated through the integration of algorithmic assessment. The effectiveness in the process of talent acquisition leads to building relationships with the potential candidates.

4.2 On Boarding

The process of smoothly settling of new personnel in the culture and practices of the organization is known as onboarding (Ford & Bauer, 2024). It is an important part of the HRM process as it defines and showcase the culture of the organization (Bauer et al., 2023). A effective onboarding procedure will generate sense of satisfaction among recruits and enhance their engagement. It develops a stronger desire to remain with the organization for a longer duration. Artificial intelligence (AI) has the power to automate the onboarding process and turn it into a self-service provider. The AI assist new hires to communicate with the staff and management team without difficulty, which facilitates manual orientation process. The first phase of the onboarding process is crucial as new hires create their impression of the company. intelligent chatbots also play a role. Artificial intelligence (AI) chatbots can assist in recording the data of new recruit, and provide necessary information to the new employee. AI Chatbots display all important forms and request for important documents from recruits, and provide any necessary online assistance. In addition, these chatbots assist new recruits in creating new accounts and integrate them into the company's system without help of IT support. AI-enabled automated onboarding allows for flexibility in scheduling and allow new hires to settle into the new system (Halid et al., 2024, Sanyaolu & Atsaboghena, 2022). Additionally, AI reduces administrative responsibilities and speeds up the integration process. Additionally, these chatbots can provide feedback from recruits to enhance service delivery and ensure a superior on boarding experience.

4.3 Training & Development

HR specialists are responsible for the training and development of the employees. HR specialist ensures the skills and knowledge of the employees would meet the objective of organization and individual.

The goals of the training and development programmes to prepare the employee to adopt the change in surrounding environment by continuous learning. It develop the leadership qualities and conflict resolution skills. Employees must be updated on the recent trends and advancements relevant to their respective fields. HR departments utilize AI-powered tools for training and assessing the personnel. AI tools have ability to identify the skill gap and the develop the personalised training programs for staff members based on their requirements (Sucharita, 2024). Artificial Intelligence possesses the ability to create customised learning paths for new hires based on their skills and preferences (Huang et al., 2023). AI-driven technologies can create educational videos for learning and development. It will speed up the learning process (Mennella et al., 2024).

These educational videos can be used multiple times and can be translated into different languages without reshoot. A learner is more likely to choose a video than text since videos are efficient means for imparting knowledge. AI technology can convert a text-based learning material to engaging video within minutes. AI technology can evaluate employee training metrics and determine which workers need more training and what kind of training is required to each individual. Large companies consider it a helpful tool in understanding the core competencies and interests of their workforce. It assists in aligning these skills and interests with their learning model for acquiring new skills for new projects.

4.4 Performance Management

Performance evaluations and feedback are two important and fundamental elements of a workplace. Traditional approaches of performance evaluation are unreliable due to potential personal biases. Therefore it is important for organization develop data driven model where artificial intelligence (AI) is used to assess employee performance. Artificial intelligence (AI) can evaluate and examine employee data, such as engagement levels, performance metrics, and absence rates, to distinguish between high-performing and high-potential workers.

The study of individual performance and the control of employee behaviour become easier by the use of AI techniques. Incentives can be offered to encourage the completion of goals, and AI can help by providing alerts and advice on how to improve productivity that leads to achievement of goals (Javaid et al., 2022). AI can help with real-time goal monitoring and provide feedback by supplying data on tasks that have been performed and those that are still outstanding (Zhang & Tao, 2020). AI assessment model can be incorporated into the system by collecting and analysing data related employees' work performance. AI framework can be used to track the outcomes of the organization's training initiatives. This framework helps staff members match their work output to the aims and objectives of the company (Alnsour et al., 2024). AI technology can eliminate biases in performance evaluations of workers (Sanyaolu & Atsaboghena, 2022). It can be achieved by providing thorough and transparent standards of assessment, which would eliminate one-sided approach of evaluating workers.

4.5 Employee Engagement

The cooperation between employers and employees to create a fair workplace is known employee engagement. Some businesses find it challenge in understanding the needs and dynamics of their personnel. HR managers will be able to dedicate a significant amount of time to resolve problems at work if they have a thorough understanding of their workforce. Chatbot automation can create continuous communication with employee to increase employee engagement staff members can communicate more interactively and freely with the help of chatbots. This can provide workers and HR specialists with quick feedback (Gärtner & Kern, 2021). Workers do not need to arrange meetings or engage in face-to-face communication; they can openly share their opinion and views.

AI-powered prediction approaches enable organisations to forecast employee engagement levels. AI analytics models are useful for analysing a variety of textual formats, such as emails, memos, chatbot messages, media comments, and similar sources. The current and future engagement levels of employees are now forecasted by the help of AI. It analyze extensive datasets and extract significant insights from the data which can be used for better decision making. Natural language processing (NLP) technology can transform information obtained from various sources into structured data for analysis (Vichare et al., 2024). This technology can conduct sentiment analysis and topic analysis. It can help in interpret the attitude expressed in a text response from an employee. This facilitates the assessment of employees satisfaction with the working of organization. This AI-driven tool helps HR professionals to identify workers' needs and provide timely solutions to fulfil the need. AI saves time in the analysis the engagement surveys and extra important organization for HR Managers. AI helps in evaluating the overall satisfaction of employees with the organization's performance.

4.6 Compensation

Compensation is essential component of HRM. It involves the examination, administration and evaluation of the benefits and incentives of each employee. Employee retention is greatly impacted by a company's perks and pay packages. It is becoming difficult for businesses to offer competitive perks and pay packages in the cutthroat business world. Human resources management must set up benefit plans and pay scales that comply with company policies. Employee compensation should be equitable and competitive to attract and retain top talents in organization. Effective wage administration will raise the performance levels on an individual and group level. Artificial intelligence neural networks can serve as a valuable tool in determining the salary structure and ensure fairness in evaluation (Qin et al., 2023).

AI technology uses big data create an intelligent support system which help in construct an equitable compensation evaluation framework. AI will speed up procedures and help businesses to stay updated with changing employee preferences and market trends. Organisations can gather relevant and historical data to predict future trends in employee remuneration by the help of big data analytics. AI can monitor changes in the labour market and guarantee competitive wages for employees. AI can set up mechanisms for adjusting employee compensation according to performance. AI can help HR managers create the compensation plans for their staff members and provide fair pay on basis of education, experience, skill sets, and other criteria. It will help companies get closer to the competitors by eliminating pay gaps.

4.7 Employee Retention

A number of sectors today have relatively low retention rates, which might be negative for the growth of the organisation. The departure of a team member can negatively impact the productivity and motivation of the remaining team members in a competitive world.

Employee turnover affects the company's revenue, drives up hiring and training costs, and prevents progress within the company. HRM is responsible for hiring additional staff to meet the labour shortage. AI machine learning-based solutions give HR managers the ability to predict employee attrition rates and identify the individuals who are thinking to leave the organization. AI can plan various incentives that will increase employee engagement in the organization . AI can monitor employee engagement, measure employee satisfaction, provide feedback, and promptly address the issues to retain the employee in organization (Burnett & Lisk, 2021). Attrition can be minimised by creating an effective onboarding process. The probability of employee turnover may be considerably decreased by using AI chatbots, as it can quickly respond to employee information. AI ensures staff members acquire the necessary job-related skills, and provide competitive remuneration packages.

4.8 Career Path

In the field of HR, AI can be used in developing learning management system and training projects to improve the skillset of the employee. It can assist workers in finding appropriate career paths, and prepare and train them for senior roles. AI technologies can develop training and learning models at professional level by utilising large and diverse datasets, such as comprehensive biographical information, performance evaluations, and substantial historical data. AI approaches play a major role in the empowerment, training, and development of many organisations globally.

It fosters the growth of skills and knowledge and improves the work environment of organization. Emotional analysis methods have been used recently to identify biases and assess workers' feelings by use of social media sites like Instagram and Twitter. Emotional analysis apps will be used more widely in the human resources field in the upcoming years to evaluate employee responsibilities, attitudes, and engagement. Many entrepreneurs are adopting these AI technologies at a growing rate to meet the market competition. In October 2018, The World Economic Forum stated that one of the biggest issues in future will be lack of fundamental skills which are necessary to blend with the rapid advancement of technology. It is essential to ensure that workforce is able to adopt new technologies. The digital gap has significantly increased the disparity between industrialized and developed nations. It is necessary to acquire essential skills by developing communication technology, and designing, operating, and maintaining digital infrastructure. It emphasizes on skillset to bridge the knowledge gap within the workforce.

4.9 Decision Making

Decision-making is fundamental to function of human resource management (HRM). Similar to other operational areas, HR Manager requires to make decision-making by keeping in mind company's growth and profitability. HR manager need to make complex decision and understand the problem. HR expert need to critically think on retention and development of the employee as it will help them to meet the competitive edge. AI can create sophisticated database frameworks and simulations that act as the basis for decision-making by combining artificial intelligence (AI) and a knowledge repository.

Various authors have studied that application of AI in function of HCM. Table 2 shows the application of AI in various HR Functions.

Table 2. Application of AI in various HR Functions

Name of the Author	HR Function	Application of AI
Ahmed, 2018	Core HR	• Prioritising trendy questions and requests • Assisting in decision-making • Automation of frequent repetitive chores • Chatbots • Gathering data and analyses for legal strategy • Recognising risks associated with compliance
Garg et al., 2021		• Assessing workforce commitment to the organisation • Forecasting staff turnover • Examining teamwork • generating suggestions • Assist in the utilisation of human resources
Oracle, 2021a		• Assessing and managing compliance issues • Strategic workforce management
Ahmed, 2018	Compensation	• Compensation is being monitored to adjust for disparities.
Oracle, 2021a		• Assist in the detection of fraudulent behaviour
(Ahmed, 2018)	Onboarding	• Providing suggestions for websites • Giving individual addresses and phone numbers to whom they need to contact on vey first day.
Black & van Esch, 2020	Recruitment	• Finding both proactive and passive candidates • Discovering which approaches works best for various applicant. • Examining the specific terminology used in the job posting • Examine descriptions of positions • Assessing an applicant's fit • Assessing previously disqualified applicants for fresh job openings • Assessing candidatures for jobs, investigating keywords, and data is extracted and derived from natural language • Examining the characteristics of effective personnel • Examining applicants' video-recorded responses on the basis of written material, selection of words, attitude of voice, and micro-expressions. • Comparing candidate responses to those of productive employees • Using a chatbot to evaluate a candidate's abilities, offering a score on the basis of content and Grammer. • Using a chatbot to evaluate a candidate's abilities, offering a score on the basis of content, phrase form, and vocabulary. • Chatbots address the enquiries, requesting data that is unavailable, and providing process information
Black & van Esch, 2021		• Evaluating the efficacy of implemented tactics for reaching out to passive applicants
Oracle, 2021a		• Screening and evaluating the candidates based on the extent to which they match a job opening • Delivering an unbiased, ranked list of prospects • Using LinkedIn to find the best matches

continued on following page

Table 2. Continued

Name of the Author	HR Function	Application of AI
Ahmed, 2018	Performance Management	• Identifying characteristics associated with poor job performance • Improving mentoring tools to match with higher-performing teams
Garg et al., 2021		• Assessment of performance • Monitoring of the performance • Identifying biases in the assessment process • Assessing competence level of employees • Creating customised benefits for workers to enhance productivity at work
Garg et al., 2021	Learning	• Screening requirements of training • Finding appropriate courses • Assessing efficacy of training
Ferguson, 2020	Payroll	• Automatically implementing payroll regulations • Identifying the causes of payroll problems and minimising the cause in future • Automatically implementing payroll regulations Identifying the causes of payroll problems and minimising the cause in future • Providing alternatives with associated payroll error • Help with payroll budget management
Radin, 2017		• Chat bots addressing payroll related enquiries • Chatbots ensuring that issue are routed to the appropriate individuals
Oracle Fusion HCM Analytics, n.d.; Oracle, 2021a	HCM analytics	• Creating patterns • generating projections • Using natural language generation to give results in natural language
(Ahmed, 2018)	Absence management	• Building a baseline of behaviour pattern of regular employee behaviour • Identifying outliers from the baseline • Detecting the general tone of an employee's communication
Ferguson, 2020	Time and labor	• Calculating and transmitting worked hours and pay rates to the payroll system for processing

5. FUTURE ROLE OF HUMAN RESOURCE EMPLOYEE

AI has revolutionised traditional HR methods by incorporating more data-driven decision-making processes. It changed the future role of HR. HR practitioners are automating repetitive processes, forecasting future trends, and customising employee experiences with the help of AI technologies like machine learning and natural language processing. According to research of Cognizant, 2020, there will be new HR posts created over coming period of time.

Figure 6. A summary of emerging HR positions projected by Cognizant in their 2020 report. (Cognizant, 2020)

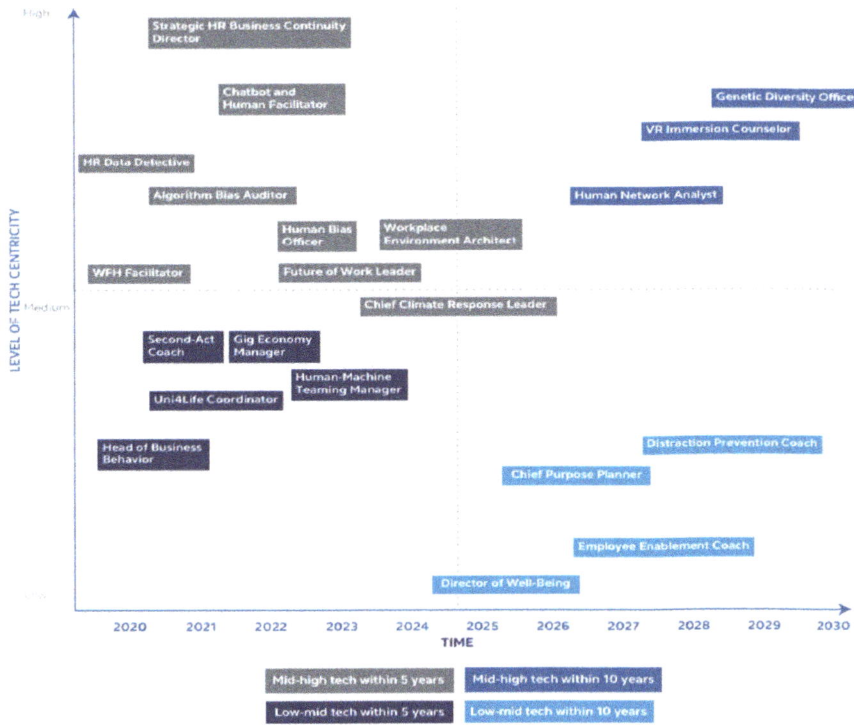

In the coming span of time, AI will be used in all the position and it will change the role of HR employee.

5.1 HR Data Investigator

An HR data analyst will be responsible for locating, cleansing, or getting data in such a way that is generated by AI (Shet et al., 2021). HR employee will be able to extract the important information when the data is changed from an unorganised to an organised state. The individual employee should ensure that data is used inside the organisation adheres to all legislation and norms.

5.2 Director of Business Behaviour

The director of business behaviour is in charge of analysing behavioural information gathered from the workforce in order to keep employees engaged and productive which will ensure well-being (Pagán-Castaño et al., 2020). Eventually, this employee will be able to contribute in making decision on how to provide customised workplace environments and experiences to workers while keeping the ethical problems of gathering private information in mind.

5.3 Auditor of Algorithm Bias

The function is part of HR's compliance division and is responsible for guaranteeing that the organization's AI algorithms are ethical and impartial (Vishwanath & Vaddepalli, 2023). Employees are in charge of developing new AI-based apps in partnership with the technological advancement team. Furthermore, the group will monitor all current algorithms and gathers input/output data, as well as user comments, to determine whether there is any undesirable biases in the AI based application.

5.4 Human Facilitator and Chatbot

A chatbot and a human facilitator will work together to ensure that chatbots fulfil the goals, increased employee engagement (Anagnoste et al., 2021). The leader of business behaviour and the algorithm bias auditor ensure that the systems are in compliance with privacy laws and established norms and standards. Organization collaborate with the software engineers to ensure that subsequent-generation chatbots meet their specifications.

5.5 Human Bias Investigator

The investigator will ensure that every staff member are dealt fairly, regardless of their gender, race, or age. organisations must pay more attention on unconscious biases due to the emergence of AI. The human bias investigator assists in the development and delivery of training programmes in order to promote awareness.

5.6 Human-Machine Collaboration

The leader supports the collaboration of people and AI software. A communication interface should be implemented to convey the abilities and aims of people and robots. The leader identifies individual duties which technology can improve. It might eventually aid AI systems in meeting all of the demands of personnel.

6. FUTURE SCOPE

When we consider the future of AI in HRM, it can be expected that, not only are the businesses going to further utilize the application of "smart" technology in HRM, but the trend will be transferred to other departments, too. This is due to the fact that the data on employees will enable the companies to make highly accurate predictions concerning employee turnover, skills gaps, and engagement behaviour. The following area of research must take into account the contributions and influences of different types of AI on employee actions and trust, and work culture, particularly in a situation where HR officers are becoming more and more engaged in data-driven operations and activities. With the gradual transition to automated decision-support systems by companies, future studies will be necessary to ascertain how fair and transparent, and what the long-term implications are of using algorithms in HR practices. In addition to this, the area of the future research might involve how AI can be applied in helping to facilitate lifelong learning, provide individual career growth opportunities, and facilitate easier collaboration between humans and intelligent machines at the workplace.

7. IMPLICATION

The results indicate that the organizations are increasingly becoming automated with an increasing number of their processes being automated as they incorporate more and more strategic functions in their HR departments. The move towards AI in HR will require that the organization becomes digitally prepared, that the staff is reskilled and trained on how to use technology in HR operations, and that ethical governing principles are set regarding the use, collection, and storage of HR data and algorithms. The analytical skills, the utilization of technology alongside human abilities in HR and the vetting of algorithms to confirm fairness or impartiality are the new skills HR professionals must learn to be able to adequately handle the incorporation of the AI within the HR processes. In addition, with AI being still utilized by companies within their human resources, even most of the HR tasks will still require human beings to be managed. As an example, human oversight will be necessary when formulating decisions involving recruitment, appraisals, and pay. Besides, human intervention will be necessary in guaranteeing personnel wellbeing. Overall, AI in HR creates greater opportunities of improved organizational performance and quality of decision-making in case the application is conducted openly and impartially, thereby, preserving the trust and confidence of employees.

REFERENCES

Allal-Chérif, O., Aránega, A. Y., & Sánchez, R. C. (2021). Intelligent recruitment: How to identify, select, and retain talents from around the world using artificial intelligence. *Technological Forecasting and Social Change*, *169*, 120822.

Alnsour, A. S., Kanaan, O. A., Salah, M., Alfayyad, L., Hijazi, Y., & Alsharif, D. (2024). The impact of implementing AI in recruitment on human resource management efficiency and organizational development effectiveness. Journal of Infrastructure. *Policy and Development*, *8*(8), 6186.

Anagnoste, S., Biclesanu, I., D'Ascenzo, F., & Savastano, M. (2021). The role of chatbots in end-to-end intelligent automation and future employment dynamics. In Business Revolution in a Digital Era: 14th International Conference on Business Excellence, ICBE 2020, Bucharest, Romania (pp. 287-302). Springer International Publishing.

Angelopoulos, A., Michailidis, E. T., Nomikos, N., Trakadas, P., Hatziefremidis, A., Voliotis, S., & Zahariadis, T. (2019). Tackling faults in the industry 4.0 era—A survey of machine-learning solutions and key aspects. *Sensors (Basel)*, *20*(1), 109. PMID: 31878065

Arslan, A., Cooper, C., Khan, Z., Golgeci, I., & Ali, I. (2022). Artificial intelligence and human workers interaction at team level: A conceptual assessment of the challenges and potential HRM strategies. *International Journal of Manpower*, *43*(1), 75–88.

Balasundaram, S., Venkatagiri, S., & Sathiyaseelan, A. (2022). Using AI to enhance candidate experience in high volume hiring: A conceptual review and case study. Proceedings of the Replenish, Restructure & Reinvent: Technology Fueled Transformation for Sustainable Future, 21-22.

Bauer, T., Erdogan, B., Caughlin, D., & Truxillo, D. (2023). *Human resource management: People, data, and analytics*. Sage Publications.

Bhanot, A. (2022). A novel review on the adaptation of artificial intelligence in human resources management by organizations in gulf countries. In *Handbook of Research on Innovative Management Using AI in Industry 5.0* (pp. 19–38). IGI Global.

Bhatt, M., & Shah, P. (2023). Acceptance of Artificial intelligence in human resource practices by employees. In The Adoption and Effect of Artificial Intelligence on Human Resources Management, Part B (pp. 13-30). Emerald Publishing Limited.

Budhwar, P., Malik, A., De Silva, M. T., & Thevisuthan, P. (2022). Artificial intelligence–challenges and opportunities for international HRM: A review and research agenda. *International Journal of Human Resource Management, 33*(6), 1065–1097.

Burnett, J. R., & Lisk, T. C. (2021). The future of employee engagement: Real-time monitoring and digital tools for engaging a workforce. In *International Perspectives on Employee Engagement* (pp. 117–128). Routledge.

Chowdhury, S., Dey, P., Joel-Edgar, S., Bhattacharya, S., Rodriguez-Espindola, O., Abadie, A., & Truong, L. (2023). Unlocking the value of artificial intelligence in human resource management through AI capability framework. *Human Resource Management Review, 33*(1), 100899.

Dixit, S., Sharma, N., Maurya, M., & Dharwal, M. (2022). AI power: making recruitment smarter. In *Evolution of Digitized Societies Through Advanced Technologies* (pp. 165–180). Springer Nature Singapore.

Dutta, D., Mishra, S. K., & Tyagi, D. (2023). Augmented employee voice and employee engagement using artificial intelligence-enabled chatbots: A field study. *International Journal of Human Resource Management, 34*(12), 2451–2480.

Ermel, A. P. C., Lacerda, D. P., Morandi, M. I. W., & Gauss, L. (2021). *Literature reviews: modern methods for investigating scientific and technological knowledge.* Springer Nature.

Ford, D. K., & Bauer, T. N. (2024). Onboarding During Transformational Times. Systems of Psychotherapy: A Transtheoretical Analysis, 162.

Gärtner, C., & Kern, D. (2021). Smart HRM in 2030: Conversational HR, Connected Robotics, and Controlled Analytics. Managing Work in the Digital Economy: Challenges, Strategies and Practices for the Next Decade, 203-221.

Gryncewicz, W., Zygała, R., & Pilch, A. (2023). AI in HRM: Case study analysis. Preliminary research. *Procedia Computer Science, 225*, 2351–2360.

Guodong, Z., Huanhuan, Y., & Yuanzhong, X. (2021). *Metaverse. BEIJING BOOK CO.* INC.

Gupta, A., & Mishra, M. (2023). Artificial Intelligence for Recruitment and Selection. In The Adoption and Effect of Artificial Intelligence on Human Resources Management, Part B (pp. 1-11). Emerald Publishing Limited.

Halid, H., Ravesangar, K., Mahadzir, S. L., & Halim, S. N. A. (2024). Artificial Intelligence (AI) in Human Resource Management (HRM). In *Building the Future with Human Resource Management* (pp. 37–70). Springer International Publishing.

Hasbullah, H., Tullah, R. H., & Farhan, R. (2023). Factors Affecting The Quality of Financial Reports: A Systematic Literature Review. *INTERNATIONAL JOURNAL OF TRENDS IN ACCOUNTING RESEARCH*, *4*(1), 59–58.

Huang, X., Yang, F., Zheng, J., Feng, C., & Zhang, L. (2023). Personalized human resource management via HR analytics and artificial intelligence: Theory and implications. *Asia Pacific Management Review*, *28*(4), 598–610.

Hunkenschroer, A. L., & Luetge, C. (2022). Ethics of AI-enabled recruiting and selection: A review and research agenda. *Journal of Business Ethics*, *178*(4), 977–1007.

Jaakkola, H., Henno, J., Mäkelä, J., & Thalheim, B. (2019, May). Artificial intelligence yesterday, today and tomorrow. In 2019 42nd International Convention on Information and Communication Technology, Electronics and Microelectronics (MIPRO) (pp. 860-867). IEEE.

Jain, R., Garg, N., & Khera, S. N. (2023). Effective human–AI work design for collaborative decision-making. *Kybernetes*, *52*(11), 5017–5040.

Javaid, M., Haleem, A., Singh, R. P., & Suman, R. (2022). Artificial intelligence applications for industry 4.0: A literature-based study. *Journal of Industrial Integration and Management*, *7*(01), 83–111.

Javaid, M., Haleem, A., Singh, R. P., & Suman, R. (2022). Artificial intelligence applications for industry 4.0: A literature-based study. *Journal of Industrial Integration and Management*, *7*(01), 83–111.

Johansson, J., & Herranen, S. (2019). The application of artificial intelligence (AI) in human resource management: Current state of AI and its impact on the traditional recruitment process.

Khan, M. R. (2024). Application of artificial intelligence for talent management: Challenges and opportunities. Intelligent Human Systems Integration (IHSI 2024): Integrating People and Intelligent Systems, 119(119).

Khan, R., Hussain, A., & Ahmad, S. (2023). Revolutionizing Human Resource Management: The Transformative Impact of Artificial Intelligence (AI) Applications. *International Journal of Social Science & Entrepreneurship*, *3*(4), 306–326.

Kovach, K. A., & Cathcart, C. E.Jr. (1999). Human resource information systems (HRIS): Providing business with rapid data access, information exchange and strategic advantage. *Public Personnel Management*, *28*(2), 275–282.

Kusý, Š. (2021). Artificial intelligence as a tool in human research management—potential and current use. *Journal of HRM*, *24*(2).

Maier, D., Maier, A., A chilean, I., Anastasiu, L., & Gavri , O. (2020). The relationship between innovation and sustainability: A bibliometric review of the literature. *Sustainability*, *12*(10), 4083.

Malik, P., & Malik, P. (2024). Mitigating destructive deviance in organisations: Assessing the role of perceived HRM practices and perceived organisational support. *The International Journal of Organizational Analysis*, *32*(7), 1242–1263.

Mennella, C., Maniscalco, U., De Pietro, G., & Esposito, M. (2024). Ethical and regulatory challenges of AI technologies in healthcare: A narrative review. *Heliyon*. PMID: 38384518

Mohammad, S. M. (2020). Artificial intelligence in information technology. Available at *SSRN* 3625444.

Muris, J. E. M., Herder, E., Hoppenbrouwers, S. J. B. A., & Strieker, M. (2021). The Consequences of Artificial Intelligence in Human Capital Management in the Next Five to Ten Years (Doctoral dissertation, Thesis. Faculty of Science. Nijmegen: Radboud University).

Nguyen, T. D., Le, H. S., Lam, H. T., Tran, T. A., & Tran, Q. T. (2023). A survey of AI-based robotic process automation for businesses and organizations. *Science and Technology Development Journal*, *26*(3), 2959–2966.

Obiuto, N. C., Adebayo, R. A., Olajiga, O. K., & Festus-Ikhuoria, I. C. (2024). Integrating artificial intelligence in construction management: Improving project efficiency and cost-effectiveness. *Int. J. Adv. Multidisc. Res. Stud*, *4*(2), 639–647.

Pagán-Castaño, E., Maseda-Moreno, A., & Santos-Rojo, C. (2020). Wellbeing in work environments. *Journal of Business Research*, *115*, 469–474.

Pan, Y., & Froese, F. J. (2023). An interdisciplinary review of AI and HRM: Challenges and future directions. *Human Resource Management Review*, *33*(1), 100924.

Pandey, S. (2020). Exploring the role of Artificial Intelligence (AI) in transforming HR functions: An Empirical Study in the Indian Context. *International Journal of Scientific Research and Engineering Development*, *3*(5).

Qamar, F., Afshan, G., & Rana, S. A. (2023). Sustainable HRM and well-being: systematic review and future research agenda. Management review quarterly, 1-51.

Qin, S., Jia, N., Luo, X., Liao, C., & Huang, Z. (2023). Perceived fairness of human managers compared with artificial intelligence in employee performance evaluation. *Journal of Management Information Systems*, *40*(4), 1039–1070.

Rajni, D. R. J., Rajvanshi, A., Shaikh, M., Tiwari, V., & Alaskar, K. (2023). Impact of Artificial Intelligence (AI) on Selected Human Resource Management (HRM) Functions in Pharmaceutical Industry in India. *Migration Letters : An International Journal of Migration Studies*, *20*(S13), 629–646.

Sakka, F., El Maknouzi, M. E. H., & Sadok, H. (2022). Human resource management in the era of artificial intelligence: Future HR work practices, anticipated skill set, financial and legal implications. *Academy of Strategic Management Journal*, *21*, 1–14.

Sanyaolu, E., & Atsaboghena, R. (2022). Role of Artificial Intelligence in Human Resource Management: Overview of its benefits and challenges. *ResearchGate*, (December), 1–8.

Shet, S. V., Poddar, T., Samuel, F. W., & Dwivedi, Y. K. (2021). Examining the determinants of successful adoption of data analytics in human resource management–A framework for implications. *Journal of Business Research*, *131*, 311–326.

Strohmeier, S. (2020). HR Digitalisation Technologies. T. Bondarouk & S. Fisher (Ed.), Encyclopedia of Electronic HRM, 14-19.

Sucharita, K. (2024). Navigating The Ai Frontier: A Study Of Ai Integration In It Employee Training And Development. *Educational Administration: Theory and Practice*, *30*(5), 1079–1085.

Surve, A. A. (2020). Impact Of Artifical Intelligence In Human Resource Management (Doctoral dissertation, Doctoral Dissertation]. University of Mumbai).

Thakur, A., & Konde, A. (2021). Fundamentals of neural networks. *International Journal for Research in Applied Science and Engineering Technology*, *9*(VIII), 407–426.

Tuffaha, M. (2022). Adoption factors of artificial intelligence in human resource management (Doctoral dissertation, Universitat Politècnica de València).

Tuffaha, M. (2023). The Impact of Artificial Intelligence Bias on Human Resource Management Functions: Systematic Literature Review and Future Research Directions. *European Journal of Business and Innovation Research*, *11*(4), 35–58.

Varsha, P. S., Chakraborty, A., & Kar, A. K. (2024). How to undertake an impactful literature review: Understanding review approaches and guidelines for high-impact systematic literature reviews. *South Asian Journal of Business and Management Cases*, *13*(1), 18–35.

Vichare, S., Gawade, A., & Mangrulkar, R. (2024). Qgen: A Unique Question Generation and Answer Evaluation Technique Using Natural Language Processing. *Journal of Engineering Education Transformations*, *38*(1).

Vishwanath, B., & Vaddepalli, S. (2023). The Future of Work: Implications of Artificial Intelligence on Hr Practices. Tuijin Jishu/Journal of Propulsion Technology, 44(3), 1711-1724.

Zhang, J., & Tao, D. (2020). Empowering things with intelligence: A survey of the progress, challenges, and opportunities in artificial intelligence of things. *IEEE Internet of Things Journal*, *8*(10), 7789–7817.

Zhang, Y., Liu, G., Zhang, L., Xu, S., & Cheung, M. W. L. (2021). Psychological ownership: A meta-analysis and comparison of multiple forms of attachment in the workplace. *Journal of Management*, *47*(3), 745–770.

Chapter 4
Strategic AI Integration in Hybrid Workforce Management:
Frameworks and Best Practices

Yogesh Madan Dharangutti
https://orcid.org/0000-0002-3437-6626
KLE Law College, KLE Technological University, Hubball, India

Meghasham Chaudhari
https://orcid.org/0000-0002-0210-7990
MIT World Peace University, India & Indira School of Business Studies PGDM, India

Poonam Rawat
https://orcid.org/0000-0002-6548-7011
MES Senior College, Pune, India

Nitesh Behare
https://orcid.org/0000-0002-9338-8563
Balaji Institute of International Business, Sri Balaji University, Pune, India

Rashmi D. Mahajan
https://orcid.org/0000-0001-9082-6874
Balaji Institute of International Business, Sri Balaji University, Pune, India

ABSTRACT

The post-pandemic era's hybrid workforce culture is its defining trait and needs a strategic workforce management practice rebalancing. The section addresses shifting remote team management dynamics and examines AI (Artificial Intelligence)

DOI: 10.4018/979-8-3373-5871-0.ch004

ht © 2026, IGI Global Scientific Publishing. Copying or distributing in print or electronic forms without written permission of IGI Global Scientific Publishing is prohibited. Use of this chapter to generative artificial intelligence (AI) technologies is expressly prohibited. The publisher reserves all rights to license its use for generative AI training and machine learning model development.

facilitating agility, inclusivity and data-driven decision-making in hybrid work arrangements. Based on a workforce expectation diagnosis, technological reliance and organizational redesign, it offers a nuanced understanding of the transformational role of AI. The section contributes to academic analysis by placing AI integration in the context of greater socio-technical change and highlighting its significance for future-proof resilience, collaboration and inclusive employee involvement.

1. INTRODUCTION

The reorganization of space and time of work which has taken place since the COVID-19 pandemic triggered a transformation across the world towards hybrid workforces, which has initially been a challenge to the historicity of organizational approaches to the organization of labour. No longer bound by set schedules or headquarters abodes, modern labour markets operate within dynamic digital-physical ecosystems that allow flexibility and expands access to talent all over the world (Kniffin et al., 2021) (Csaba et al., 2025). Nonetheless, this evolution has intensified the complexity of management: communication is discontinuous, the view of the work becomes less clear, the rhythmicality of collaboration is not very predictable and coherent, and new demands on resource planning are constantly pressing workforce-management systems that were initially designed based on the performance of co-located, predictable work. With the institutionalization of hybrid work, organizations need to implement the architecture that is able to optimize dynamically and in real-time as opposed to the linear and rule-based control (Khanna et al., 2024).

The key to such change has become artificial intelligence (AI). In addition to routine automation, workforce-management systems that incorporate AI combine predictive analytics, adaptive scheduling, sentiment monitoring, and ongoing performance modelling to enable evidence-based scale-based decisions (Wu et al., 2023). More importantly, AI can increase managerial control without taking the initiative away, but instead create clear insights that affirm human judgment (Saritha & Akthar, 2024). The technology also delivers the option of personalization - personal learning paths, role-specific development pathways, and dynamic engagement diagnostic features, and AI is not only an operational tool but a strategic wheel of reorganizing organizational structures and the experience of employees in hybrid settings (Darwish et al., 2025).

The strategic worth of AI cuts across all the foundational areas of workforce management, such as talent acquisition, planning, performance evaluation and learning and development. Machine-learning software, natural-language processing, and robotic-process automation will enable an organization to query the patterns of productivity, cooperation, and health that are hidden in distributed teams (Bharathi & Krithika, 2024), (Behare, 2025). However, the transformational promise of AI depends on more than the use of specific tools. Unless associated with organizational ambitions, moral values, and sound data management, AI would potentially enable bias, distrust, and counter-productive results (Kelan, 2024). In line with this, there is a need to establish a comprehensive, overarching approach, including digital-maturity, stakeholder-consultation, and ongoing auditing of the algorithmic performance.

The role of human-centred design is also enhanced by the use of hybrid work. As much as AI increases the abilities of analytical power, it remains unable to overtake the relational basis of hybrid work, which is built on trust, empathy, and psychological safety (Cunningham-Sereque et al., 2023). Explainable decisions, transparency in algorithms, and participatory feedback mechanisms thus become critical to maintain legitimacy in AI-assisted systems (Hofeditz et al., 2022). Similarly, organizations are having to grapple with issues including digital inequity, data-privacy considerations, algorithmic bias, and unequal technological preparedness like are defining whether AI creates inclusion or reinforces inequalities (Patil et al., 2024), (Dwivedi & Agarwal, 2024).

2. UNDERSTANDING AI IN WORKFORCE MANAGEMENT

To come up with the idea of why artificial intelligence (AI) should be used to manage the workforce, this term needs to be redefined so that artificial intelligence can be considered not just a technical instrument but a force of organizational change. In the hybrid formations, AI ceases to be a passive facilitator of automation but a proactive force behind the decision-making process, talent-engagement policies, and performance-management systems at the remote working places. With data-driven insights, predictive analytics, and adaptive learning processes, AI allows organizations to optimize workforce plans to dynamic business requirements and, therefore, enhance agility, efficiency, and inclusivity related to working in the physical, virtual and hybrid workplace.

2.1. Artificial Intelligence as Strategic Enabler of Hybrid Workforce Management.

The introduction of AI to the workforce management is a significant change in organizational planning, coordination and labour evaluation in the hybrid and distributed environments (Nuswantoro et al., 2023). Contrary to the more traditional workforce systems that are structured around hard rules, AI-based solutions are adaptive, which learns real-time based on both structured and unstructured streams of data.

These solutions, along with automating routine processes, provide a higher level of cognition in order to provide predictive talent analytics, intelligent scheduling, and understanding of behaviour and decision-making processes; these self-adaptability features are unheard of. In the circumstances of the hybrid work, including flexible working hours, decentralization of responsibility, and organizational culture of collaboration (Samson et al., 2024), AI becomes the strategic force of organizational openness, operational coordination, and big-scale personalization. Its abilities to break down complex dynamics in workforce into actionable intelligence enables organizations to manoeuvre the complexity of the hybrid models with augmented agility, inclusiveness, and endurance.

2.2. Significant Applications of AI in Hybrid Workforce Operations.

The versatile ability of AI to be used in various ways offers the best solutions to actualize its value in managing the hybrid workforce. Predictive analytics that are run by machine learning can provide talent prediction, attrition-risk ratings, skill gap data, and demand forecasts, among others (Kaur et al., 2022). Such data-driven analysis comes in particularly handy in situations that involve little or no physical monitoring, which enables performance assessment without micromanagement. NLP aids in conversational interfaces, sentiment analysis and personalized mining of emotional intelligence at scale; thus, burnout or disengagement can then be addressed in timely ways. Computer vision helps in the physical office management, safety surveillance, ergonomics, and accessibility. Consistency among distributed teams is ensured by robotic process automation (RPA) (Juglan et al., 2023) (Biswal et al., 2020) (Arias et al., 2020), augmented with AI that supports onboarding, payroll, compliance, and benefits. AI-powered recruitment solutions are unbiased, scalable, and automated to screen applicants and provide real-time feedback to the AI-driven performance-management system, respectively. Hybrid adaptive learning management system (LMS) represents an additional customization of the development directions to personal growth and evolving business focus (Dhand et al., 2025).

2.3. Integrative Potential, Risk and Strategic Implication.

In addition to discrete applications, the disruptive quality of AI in hybrid workforce management is its integrative strength: it is possible to tie together the separate tools and platforms in a coherent, data-driven product. Through the synthesis of feedback revealed by collaboration tools, performance platforms, and engagement platforms, AI creates complex workforce intelligence on future strategic decision-making (Nedumaran et al., 2023). Algorithms prejudice, privacy, overdependence on automatic determinations are the issues that the risk of loss of trust in employees unless considered. Effective implementation would thus require strict data-ethics processes, explainable algorithms and open workforce decision-making. The best strategies are ones that combine technology with human values which makes sure that AI adds to and not destroys empathy, fairness and trust in hybrid workforces. Organizations that adopt this middle ground will be in a good place to utilize AI as a productivity driver and as a cultural enhancer of the future of work (Ganapathy, 2021).

3. THE HYBRID WORKFORCE LANDSCAPE

Another relatively new phenomenon in the organization design, management, as well as talent engagement, the hybrid workforce model is applied both in office and remote working settings (Balasundaram & Venkatagiri, 2020). This development is motivated by the changed demand of employees to deeper flexibility, autonomy, and meaningful employment, which shatters the workforce management paradigms. The co-location of physical and virtual offices presents new issues to do with communication, coordination, performance appraisal, and inclusion. With the emergence of hybrid working as the new standard, companies have to rebuild their organizational structures, management systems, and infrastructure (Soleimani et al., 2022).

3.1. Workforce and Structure Change and the changing workforce expectations.

The spread of the hybrid forms of work is a definite sign of the radical redesign of the organizational architecture, which disputes the paradigm of classical managerialism, which assumes the presence of co-located work and strict time frames (Balasundaram & Venkatagiri, 2020) In the modern setup, staff members move freely between distanced and physical states, generating a strong need of independence, mission, and smooth combination of work and individual obligations. These expectations undermine the effectiveness of the old systems of workforce-management that were based on predictability, standardization, and centralized control (Soleimani et al., 2022). Organizations, therefore, face growing challenges of maintaining communicative coherence, fair distribution of information and significant performance appraisal of geographically and temporally scattered teams.

Hybrid employment enhances the severity of the managerial invisibility: unfair use of digital technology, lack of synchronous communication, and unequal work patterns lead to the lack of coordination and reinforce the sense of unfairness in terms of access and acknowledgment (Wu et al., 2023). This fact requires a shift to the more data-driven and transparent workforce practices that will be able to sustain distributed operations. Therefore, hybrid leadership requires a paradigm shift, instead of using the proximity as the basis of supervising employees, leaders need to develop the skills of digital contact, trust, and cross-time-zone work (Dwivedi & Agarwal, 2024). Psychological safety, emotional intelligence and empathy are pillars towards maintaining cohesion in digitally mediated settings. The AI-supported analytics enhance these leadership imperatives by offering real-time information on workload trends, cooperation level, and arisen risks, thus allowing making more well-informed and responsive decisions (Samson et al., 2024).

At the same time, hybrid arrangements create new requirements on the digital infrastructure. Silos of communication channels are one of the results of expanding cloud services, collaboration tools, and digital processes in the way they tend to create tool sprawl, duplicate processes, and silos (Jain & Mitra, 2025). It is not only the problem of technology adoption; there is interoperability and easing of user experience. The artificial intelligence is the connective tissue in this ecosystem, connecting scattered tools, automating the low-value administrative tasks and providing intelligent assistants to simplify the daily operations of the organization. In this sense, AI transforms the hybrid workplace into a system, which is more coherent, efficient, and intellectually organizable.

Also, fluidity of the workforce makes it difficult to plan organizations. On the one hand, hybrid models will provide cross-functional mobility, gig tasks, and flexible team structures, but at the same time, these characteristics bring about resource distribution instability, skills availability, and team structure (Chrusciak et al., 2023). The AI-based workforce planning systems reduce this volatility through predictive research, automated role, skill matching, and analytics, which reveal internal talent pools that can be redeployed quickly (Seletedi et al., 2024). Still, there is also a risk that hybrid flexibility will only serve to further inequities: remote workers might feel less visible, their careers would be less likely to develop, or they would have unequal access to resources. When intelligently tailored, e.g., by focusing on productivity but not presence in performance assessment and identifying structural trends of disengagement or bias (Chandratreya, 2025), AI can offset such inequalities. In that way, equity-oriented AI will be necessary in avoiding the continuation of organizational inequity through hybrid work.

3.2 Strategic Intelligence, Digital Learning and Employee Engagement.

In geographically dispersed teams, engagement in hybrid environments goes beyond the scope of completing tasks to include belonging, connection, and shared meaning (Burnett & Lisk, 2019). The traditional indicators of engagement, like attendance or survey feedback, cannot reflect the affective aspect of the hybrid experience. AI can perform better diagnostics by analyzing sentiment in real time, behavioural intelligence, and natural language, which allows preventing cases of disengagement and providing more timely and personalized interventions (Rajeswari & Gomathi, 2022). These systems are able to suggest personalized well-being programs, specific recognition plans, and group facilitation plans helping relational cohesion within hybrid teams.

The idea of continuous upskilling is also a core part of maintaining the flexibility in hybrid workforce. The conventional models of training do not fare well in decentralized environments where the requirements of learning, training time, and developmental objectives differ substantially (Mishra et al., 2022). AI-driven learning applications streamline an individualized learning process, automate performance tracking, and profile instructional difficulty on a career path and job title. Performance analytics highlight new skill gaps and can match training to strategic priorities, whereas AI-powered peer-learning suggestions encourage spontaneous knowledge sharing in geographically dispersed teams (Mittal et al., 2023). Such systems foster a culture of lifelong learning- a much needed barrier to instability in the hybrid ecosystems.

Hybrid work creates a significant flood of information that comes off communication platforms, collaboration tools, and workflow systems. In order to derive strategic value out of this corpus, one will have to implement superior analytics that will allow identifying the patterns of behavior, estimating the risks of productivity, and locating the factors that precede burnouts or attritions (Stanbery et al., 2023). With the aid of AI, dashboards can democratize such insights and allow leaders of all hierarchy levels to become evidence-based decision makers. However, the success of AI implementation depends on organizational preparedness, design that is ethically upright, and a flexible cultural role. The effective use of AI in the hybrid environment requires technical skills, cross-disciplinary teamwork, a sense of transparency, equity, and retained human oversight (Vashishth et al., 2025). AI is not supposed to replace the human judgment, but should enhance and protect equity and promote, but not limit, autonomy.

Finally, a hybrid job is, in fact, not just a working solution but a fundamental change in strategy. The AI is a facilitator and catalyst that provides the intelligence and flexibility to cope with the complexity of the workforce. Based on ethical concerns and human-centric designs, organizations will be able to create flexible, inclusive, and sustainable hybrid workforce ecosystems that will define the future of work (Lenka & Chanda, 2025).

4. FRAMEWORKS FOR STRATEGIC AI INTEGRATION

The urgency of the AI-integration frameworks is seen in the ability to take organizations through the complex route of integrating artificial intelligence into the workforce management framework. These models offer a solid, principled, and objective channel of technology deployment by placing AI at the heart of decision-making, talent optimization, and engagement of employees (Koeszegi, 2023). They outline organizational requirements that are needed to align technological advancement with human values, and consequently reduce operational risks, and nurture trust among distributed teams. The frameworks of the AI -Human Integration, the AI Maturity Models, the Responsible AI Framework, and the PEARL Framework are the core of this effort, making up a consistent, well-structured blueprint of sustainable, adaptable, and ethically oriented AI approaches in the hybrid work environment.

4.1 Strategic Frameworks for AI Adoption in Hybrid Workforce Systems

The emergence of hybrid work frameworks redefines organization hierarchies and employee expectations, and makes strategic AI integration an essential part of the development of flexible, ethical, and sustainable workforce-management frameworks. The AI-integration frameworks are organized approaches that cover both technical competence and human-centric principles and can guarantee that automation will complement, but not replace, the judgement and trust, and relational justice (Koeszegi, 2023). They offer philosophical solutions to managing the intrinsic contradictions of the hybrid operations, improving performance and preserving dignity, scaling digital solutions in a society that requires personalization, and incorporating data-driven decision-making without undermining the responsibility of the manager. In this environment, the AI-Human Integration Framework (AHIF), AI Maturity Models, the PEARL Framework and the Responsible AI Framework become a consistent framework upon which the responsible AI deployment is based in distributed workforces.

The AHIF is an essential pillar of the next-generation workforce design, which theorizes AI as a cognitive partner, rather than a substitute of human judgement. It separates algorithmic advantages in the form of accuracy, consistency, pattern recognition and human advantages in the form of contextual reasoning and value based decision-making (Raikov & Pirani, 2022). This two-intelligence design is especially critical in the hybrid environments where the processes of performance management, employee development, and engagement need to combine both artificial intelligence and human judgment. Thus, AHIF allows organizations to maintain the agency of employees, reduce cognitive load and improve the quality of decisions and create collaboration between digital and human systems (Gundage et al., 2025). Within this perspective, the framework redefines the implementation of AI as a work redesign instead of a technology purchase exercise.

In line with such conceptual foundations, there must be systematic approaches to guide AI integration in a systematic and not an episodic manner. The implementation of AI in the hybrid environments requires the correspondence of the organizational purpose, operational readiness, and the morality demands (John et al., 2025). Strategic frameworks help organizations to reduce the risks of bias, transparency, and data abuse especially in decentralized environments where digital-transformation maturity differs among groups. Such principles highlight sustainable systems of governance that combine automation and human control where artificial intelligence can contribute to the creation of value in the long term and the sustainability of the workforce (Raikov & Pirani, 2022). Therefore, properly placed AI systems may become the tools of consistency, leading to innovation without the loss of trust in the setting of distributed environments.

4.2 Responsible Governance, Adaptive AI Capabilities and Organizational Readiness.

AI maturity models can provide organizations with a responsible development roadmap of AI. Their gradual development Awareness, Experimentation, Adoption, Integration, and Optimization enable organizations to develop and implement according to their technological infrastructure, data architecture, cultural preparedness, and staffing needs (Chiriatti et al., 2025). In asynchronous amalgamations of heterogeneous digital fluency, maturity models predict premature scaling, reduce resistance and align AI investments with strategic imperatives in hybrid ecosystems. They also force organizations to go further than surface-level automations to high-level applications like adaptive learning systems, predictive analytics, and dynamic performance modelling, which improves agility and cohesion in distributed teams (Zhang et al., 2024).

Based on the PEARL Framework, Planning, Ethics, Alignment, Resources, and Learning expands maturity models in operationalizing responsible AI deployment. It approaches AI projects as grounded in well-defined organizational goals, implements equity and accountability, fosters organizational cultural and strategic alignment, allocates adequate resources, and promotes uninterrupted digitalization of skills (Herrera, 2025). PEARL provides an end-to-end governance prism, which ensures that AI integration is scalable, ethically-based and can withstand changing hybrid work requirements. It highlights the fact that AI-readiness is as much of a human-capability as a technological issue.

The principles are further replicated by the Responsible AI Framework (RAF) that integrates fairness, transparency, accountability, and privacy in workforce technologies. The consequences of ethical breakdowns become more pronounced in hybrid settings, in which algorithmic tools are used to impact the recruitment process, productivity measurement, and surveillance of employees (Ramos et al., 2024). RAF requires decisions based on AI to be transparent and fair, which will protect remote and on-site workers against discriminatory and intrusive ways. It demands human control in predictive analytics especially in areas like performance prediction or productivity tracking where the results of the algorithms should be balanced against contextual knowledge (Al-Abdullatif, 2025). RAF, therefore, builds long-lasting confidence in AI systems and allows regular and equitable experiences in a scattered workplace environment.

Together, AHIF, PEARL, RAF, and maturity models nurture the cross-functional partnership through the provision of standardized evaluation measures, common terms, and systematic implementation procedures (Poser & Bittner, 2021). They guarantee that the introduction of AI would become a company-wide strategy that involves leadership, human resources, information technologies, compliance, and workforce stakeholders. Such frameworks integrate AI into the wider workforce-transformation agendas allowing organizations to predict the talent requirements, reinforce and enable flexible staffing solutions, and match the learning pathways with the organizational goals (Caldwell et al., 2022).

More importantly, such strategic models enhance organizational agility, which is a crucial skill in a volatile hybrid environment. The AI structures enable proactive reactions to changes in the levels of employee morale, productivity, and resource needs through cycle-driven learning, scenario-based analysis and predictive insights in real-time (Ramos et al., 2024). They uplift pilots and experimentation of hybrid work design, which lead to confidence in decisions and less risk. Finally, powerful AI-integration models will place organizations in a position to build scalable, ethical, and flexible workforce systems that will succeed in the challenges of a hybrid future.

4.3 Conceptual Model: Strategic AI-Hybrid Workforce Integration Model (SAHWIM).

The Strategic AI Hybrid Workforce Integration Model (SAHWIM) provides an all-encompassing framework that presents an understanding of the future of artificial intelligence integration within the hybrid working environment within a purposeful, ethical, and operationally coherent way. The model was developed based on the main themes of the chapter and incorporates four interconnected layers of organisational enablers, AI capabilities, moderating risks, and workforce outcomes to reflect the interaction of activities in which AI alters distributed workplaces (Hölzle et al., 2024), (Duarte & Dias, 2025).

Figure 1. Strategic AI–Hybrid Workforce Integration Model (SAHWIM)

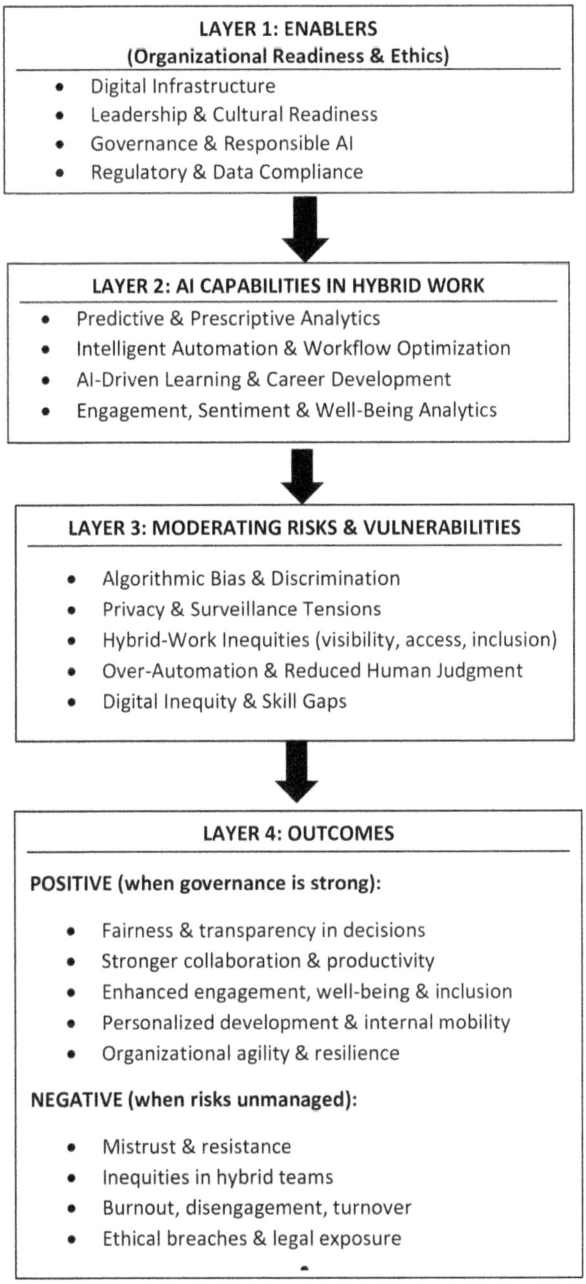

The layer *Enablers* is the initial one, which captures the background conditions, that are necessary in a successful AI adoption, which include digital infrastructure preparedness, leadership commitment, cultural flexibility, and ethical governance frameworks. Such variables ensure that organizations have the technological ability and human-centered disposition to implement AI in a responsible manner in hybrid settings (Saragih, 2025).

The second layer is *AI Capabilities*, which consists of the technological functions that directly influence hybrid workforce management. They include predictive workforce planning analytics, workflow automation, personalized learning, and engagement and well-being analytics. All these capabilities realize the argument in the chapter that AI enhances but does not replace human expertise by augmenting it, personalizing it, and making it responsive in real-time (Singh & Singh, 2025).

The third layer, *Moderating Risks*, identifies the vulnerabilities which can undermine AI effectiveness including algorithmic bias, privacy issues, remote and onsite worker disparities, over-automation and digital expertise gaps. All these risks emphasize the warning of the chapter that AI has to be regulated with responsible systems to prevent worsening structural injustices or compromising the trust of the employees (Linde et al., 2025).

Lastly, the fourth layer of the model i.e. *Outcomes*, which explains the dual potential of AI in hybrid spaces. With well-established enablers and ethical management, AI can be able to improve collaboration, fairness, agility, well-being, and long-term development of workforce. However, the opposite situation can also occur as uncontrolled risk can breed mistrust, disengagement, burnout, inequity, or ethical breaches through AI (Yesufu & Alajlani, 2025).

On the whole, SAHWIM shows that the implementation of AI in the hybrid work is a strategic, socio-technical process, rather than a technological implementation. The model can be used as a conceptual input and practical guideline to organizations that aim to establish sustainable, fair, and future-proof hybrid workforce systems.

5. BEST PRACTICES TO SUCCESSFUL IMPLEMENTATION.

The disciplined approach, ethical rigor and the continuous organizational learning are required to achieve successful implementation of AI in the hybrid workforce management practice. Best practices are therefore focusing on readiness, transparency, capability building, and refining. When technology is embraced in line with human-related values and the application of cross-functional governance, an organization could see AI contribute to, rather than disrupt, the resilience to workforce, equity, and performance in a distributed organization (Rostamzadeh et al., 2025).

5.1 Organizational Readiness, Strategic Alignment and Trusted Deployment.

The first step of successful AI integration is the readiness assessment which should be provided not only with the technical infrastructure but also with the organizational culture, leadership orientation, and digital literacy. Hybrid environments require strong data infrastructure, employee readiness and readiness to implement new tools and executive dedication to avoiding using AI as a disruptive overlay, but as a strategic facilitator. Formal preparedness mechanisms bring out any gaps in capacity, demystify constraints on feasibility and offer the basis of coordinating AI efforts with workforce strategy and organizational long-term goals (T.S. et al., 2025). The strategic alignment at this point is necessary so that AI applications strengthen, rather than weaken, operational coherence, which achieves resilience in distributed teams.

It requires setting of goals clearly. In cases where AI projects are not supplanted with clear deliverables, they might end up being scattered, out of sync, or technologically motivated instead of being problem-oriented. Companies are advised to convert the priorities of hybrid workforce like schedule optimization, enhanced interactions, or minimized burnout into quantifiable performance metrics and high-impact use cases (Sahyaja et al., 2024). Wins at the beginning create momentum and allow the teams to improve AI applications with the development of hybrid conditions.

The cross- functional governance significantly enhances the implementation success. The nature of AI overlaps with HR, IT, compliance, legal, data governance, and operations, and thus, due to the siloed implementation, inconsistent practices and increased risk occur (Sahyaja et al., 2024). Multidisciplinary teams introduce overlapping knowledge: HR introduces ethical and labour-force insights; IT guarantees integration and cybersecurity; legal introduces privacy and risk management; compliance ensures regulatory compliance. This interdependent architecture lies at the core of hybrid environments where work is distributed in geographical and functional locations and where some systemic transformation needs a common management. For example, post-pandemic, IBM initiate hybrid work culture, which has proven the merits of the organized preparedness and cross-functional alignment (Amy, 2025).

The choice of the vendor and system transparency is also crucial. The organizational vendors have to be assessed based on their compliance with ethical standards, their ability to be explained, and their responsiveness to hybrid work conditions, as well as being technologically sophisticated (Yang & Jiang, 2025). Even black-box models, particularly in talent assessment or performance analytics, decrease trust or risk of bias. Explainable AI platforms enable organizations to review the paths of decisions and clarify them to the employees. Fears of surveillance or job displacement are reduced through transparency, which is achieved through documentation, dashboards and responsive communication, which provides psychological safety to distributed teams.

Active change management promotes the spirit of acceptance by minimizing the resistance. The main problems that may arise with the hybrid employees who interact with AI through digital platforms are the issue of fairness or loss of control. Early communication of AI objectives, participatory design, feedback loops, and reinforcing AI as the augmentative, as opposed to the substitutive, by the leadership are best practices (Hölzle et al., 2024). To position adoption as a subset of a larger culture of flexibility and employee empowerment, leaders have to be digitally fluent and demonstrate an example of responsible AI usage. For instance, Unilever's Ethical AI Partnership in Recruitment Practices can be seen as an action of responsible vendor management and transparency in hybrid talent management (Arpita & Saurabh, 2024).

5.2 Sustained Value Creation through Upskilling, Ethical Governance and Continuous Improvement

Hybrid workforces that are supported by AI must be prepared to sustainability in terms of capability building. It is necessary to foster data fluency, digital literacy, and ethical awareness in employees and managers in organizations. Learning systems based on AI facilitate this growth by offering individualized learning paths, module-based learning, and customized recommendations to match the needs of the individual development with the skills needed in the organization (Kytainyk et al., 2025). The adaptation of organizations and innovation at scale Peer-learning communities, knowledge networks and collaborative learning analytics are making organizations more adaptable.

The power of AI impact needs to be measured with powerful performance indicators to achieve long-term effectiveness. Measures must be able to measure not only the efficiencies and talent results of operations but also such ethical and experiential aspects as trust, fairness, and equality between the remote and on-site employees (Ganapathy, 2021). The ongoing surveillance can assist organizations to notice the risks that have arisen, adjust the algorithms, and determine the ways AI tools support strategic goals.

Effective AI implementation, in particular, in volatile hybrid ecosystems, is characterized by continuous improvement. The AI systems should keep up with shifts in the employment patterns, regulatory environment, and employee demands. The structures of governance ought to facilitate the continuous revision process, the pilot testing process, the user-driven refining process, and the process of planning by scenario (Chandratreya, 2025). The inclusion of external moral guidelines and rules of change will make sure that the systems are always integrated with the expectations of society and also both the organizational values (Awasthi et al., 2024).

Trust is maintained by ethical governance. Hybrid work gives rise to large volumes of data, which, in the absence of careful supervision, can unwillingly result in pressures of surveillance, biased interaction guidelines, or unfair decision-making channels (Awasthi et al., 2024). Periodic audit, open consultation process, and interdisciplinary ethics expertise should be listed among the best practices (Dhand et al., 2025). Ethical assessment should be a process, and it should be realized that risks increase with larger systems. For instance, Accenture's MyLearning platform exemplifies to achieved continuous improvement and ethical use of AI in hybrid upskilling. The platform uses AI-curated content, micro-learning modules, and peer-learning suggestions to develop distributed teams at the individual level (Michelle, 2024).

6. CASES AND INDUSTRY APPLICATIONS

The practical examples of the application of artificial intelligence in the hybridization of the workforce in management are shown in the real-life scenarios that provide better planning, analytics on performance, engagement, learning, and time scheduling. The case studies demonstrate how organizations use AI to overcome the challenges of hybrid working without impairing ethical responsibility and sustainability. A combination of them helps to demonstrate the tactical flexibility of AI and the principles of the strategy needed to successfully implement AI in distributed work ecosystems.

6.1. Performance Intelligence of Hybrid Teams with the assistance of AI at Microsoft.

Being an innovative enterprise that applies hybrid work methods on the enterprise level, Microsoft has also updated its Viva Insights platform with recently developed AI-driven insights on performance. (Herrera, 2025) such a solution gives managers insights into behaviour that can show that there is possible burnout, exhaustion, and disengagement without invading privacy by linking data about the collaboration systems, namely, Teams, Outlook, and SharePoint. System-based suggestions are designed to decrease the meeting loads, enhance focus time, and support the work-life balance in hybrid environments (Colette, 2023). This step is both a strategic contribution to the AI-Human Integration Framework (AHIF) in terms of boosting autonomy of managers without compromising their roles, and is also in line with the transparency requirements articulated in Responsible AI Frameworks. It shows that

Microsoft cares about employee welfare and great productivity in remote working conditions, and it is an example of how AI can offer a more individual, flexible solution to the challenges of human relationships on a massive scale (Colette, 2023).

6.2. AI - driven Scheduling of Workforce at Cleveland Clinic.

The cleavage of both administrative and nursing personnel into specific assignments has been integrated into the AI-based workforce scheduling of the Cleveland Clinic in the high-stakes healthcare industry (Dwivedi & Agarwal, 2024). Through predictive analytics and machine learning algorithms, the system predicts patient volumes, makes comparisons between the predictions and the staffing requirements, real-time changes in the rosters on the fly. This does not only enhance efficiency in operations, but also staff burnout due to equitable work distribution (Saragih, 2025). It is implemented based on the AI Maturity Model, moving on from pilot testing to complex optimization by assembling feedback loops and aligns with the PEARL Framework by focusing on ethical hiring practices, resource optimization, and adaptive learning. It is worth mentioning that it enables such a flexible hybrid that the remote and on-site employees can coexist, thus introducing a new paradigm of sustainable workforce management that does not negatively affect the quality of care but instead promotes the well-being of employees amid external factors that change, such as pandemics or seasons spikes (Herrera, 2025).

6.3. Personalized AI-Driven Blended Team Learning at Standard Chartered.

Standard Chartered Bank has introduced machine learning–driven learning journeys, made available to its users via its digital platform, diSCover Lab, through the use of machine learning algorithms that tailor reskilling and upskilling journeys, depending on each user profile, performance metrics, and the future requirements of the organization (Jain & Mitra, 2025). This project serves as a good example of Planning and Learning components of PEARL Framework and shows the collaboration of human and AI in managing talent. In addition, Standard Chartered incorporates learning analytics alongside career progression metrics, which means that the system is goal-oriented (Anika, 2025). Incorporating this adaptive learning model into its hybrid workforce policy, the bank promotes the ongoing development, resilience of the workforce, and reduces internal mobility. AI in turn encourages personal development and institutional flexibility (Jai, 2025).

7. STRATEGIC AI INTEGRATION HAS SOME CHALLENGES AND RISKS.

Even though the transformative nature of artificial intelligence in hybrid workforce management is significant, numerous complex issues and dangers of various issues pose a challenge to the strategic implementation of artificial intelligence. The employees encounter the issue of monitoring, ethical issues, algorithmic bias, and the opaque decision-making. Organizations need to walk the thin line of promoting innovation and responsibility (Mwita & Kitole, 2025). These difficulties are further exacerbated by the technical complexity, data control problems, regulatory uncertainty, and organizational inefficiencies to adopt AI on a large scale.

Table 1. Key Challenges and Risks in Strategic AI Integration for Hybrid Workforce Management

Challenge	Description	References
Workforce Privacy and Surveillance Risks	AI-enabled monitoring tools—such as productivity tracking, keystroke analytics, and behavioral modeling—may infringe on employee privacy, erode trust, and heighten psychological stress, especially when deployed without transparent policies. Balancing data-driven oversight with human agency remains a major ethical dilemma in hybrid settings.	**Invalid source specified..**
Algorithmic Bias and Discrimination	AI systems trained on historical workforce data may reproduce gender, ethnic, educational, or modality (remote/on-site) biases. These distortions can influence hiring, promotion, and performance evaluations, leading to systemic discrimination and reputational or legal consequences.	**Invalid source specified.**
Gaps in Digital Infrastructure	Decentralized databases, legacy platforms, limited connectivity, and siloed IT–HR systems constrain AI capabilities. These issues hinder long-term data collection, real-time analytics, and stable system performance necessary for hybrid workforce optimization.	**Invalid source specified.**
Employment Uncertainty and Resistance to Change	Fears of job displacement and loss of autonomy intensify resistance to AI, particularly in hybrid contexts where communication is fragmented. Without strong change management, skill-building, and participatory governance, employees may resist or undermine AI adoption.	(Aryan et al., 2025)
Lack of Explainability and Transparency	Black-box algorithms make it difficult for employees and managers to understand how AI-generated decisions—such as performance ratings or resource allocations—are made. In hybrid environments, this opacity amplifies mistrust and reduces accountability.	(Madanchian, 2024)
Cross-Border Regulatory Compliance Complexities	Hybrid teams often operate across jurisdictions with divergent data privacy and AI governance laws (e.g., GDPR, CCPA, DPDP Act). Uncertainties around data transfer, consent, and algorithmic accountability create high compliance risks for multinational organizations.	(Soleimani et al., 2022)

continued on following page

Table 1. Continued

Challenge	Description	References
Misalignment Between AI Tools and Workforce Strategy	AI systems may fail when they do not align with hybrid workforce realities or organizational culture. Tools that prioritize managerial control over employee empowerment can perpetuate disengagement and operational inefficiencies.	(Kaur et al., 2022)
Data Quality and Fragmentation	AI systems depend on complete, high-quality, and well-curated datasets. In hybrid work, disparate communication tools and inconsistent documentation practices create fragmented data flows, undermining model accuracy and decision reliability.	(Arpita & Saurabh, 2024)
Cybersecurity and Vulnerability Risks	Increased reliance on cloud platforms and distributed access points elevates exposure to cyber threats. Breaches involving personnel data or AI systems can jeopardize organizational integrity and erode employee trust.	(Khanna et al., 2024)
Over-Automation and Erosion of Human Judgment	Excessive reliance on AI for complex or context-sensitive decisions may diminish human expertise, reduce autonomy, and create over-standardization. Hybrid teams risk losing nuanced understanding of employee needs if AI overrides human-centered judgment.	(Koeszegi, 2023)

8. FUTURE SCOPE & IMPLICATIONS FOR HYBRID WORK

The future of hybrid work will be defined by more advanced, flexible but ethically sensitive AI-based systems that will go beyond the operating paradigms applied today and will be guided towards dynamic and intelligence-rich ecosystems. With organizations struggling to keep up with more dynamic labour force structures and fast-changing business environments, AI will become the main orchestrator of team-work, intensifying individualization, and lifelong learning. The upcoming paragraphs outline major trends that will determine the next-generation hybrid workplaces, which will focus on strategic unification, user-driven design, and moral maturity.

8.1. Smart Workflows and Adaptive AI Architectures.

The work environment in the future will be a hybrid that assumes AI architectures that can adjust continuously and in real-time. Companies are already moving away from fixed systematic approaches that rely on rules to more dynamic types of learning based systems that are adaptable to changes in work patterns, team composition, and employee behaviour (Rhue, 2019). These types of smart systems will foresee workflow interruptions and suggest process redesigning, as well as organize smooth communications among the remote and on-site contributors. AI will not only undergo changes in the form of retrospective analytics, but it will also become a distributed coordinator, thus assisting the teams in the form of proactive optimization, as opposed to monitoring them reactively.

The hybrid enterprises will need high-quality data pipelines, scalable system architectures, and modular system designs to achieve such responsiveness. Constantly learning and adjusting to the changing organizational environment will be made possible by interoperability, supported by APIs, cloud-native systems, and edge computing (Muller & Weisz, 2022). Planning in the future should then look to emphasize on flexible infrastructures incorporating different software environments and to enable decentralized decision-making.

8.2. Human - Artificial Intelligence Cooperation and Enhanced Decision-Making.

The future of AI in workforce management lies in augmentation and not automation. AI will be a cognitive partner that will augment managerial thinking, lower systematic factors and produce practical insights on talent requirements, staff work, and succession planning (Dajani et al., 2024). The human control will not become unnecessary, as the managers will need to provide a human explanation of AI-based insights in terms of moral rationality, situational awareness, and emotional reasoning (Wang et al., 2023). Such reconfigured collaboration will require novel competences throughout the labor force such as digital literacy, critical thinking of algorithmic results, and ethical dilemma navigation in contexts of hybrid decision-making.

It will also be the transformative contribution of AI in psychological safety and inclusivity. AI tools will identify patterns of sentiment, digital behavioural cues, and communication indicators before escalations through analyzing these metrics. These insights will enable customized well-being programmes, customized interventions, and leadership coaching that would facilitate the growth of emotionally intelligent hybrid cultures (Cunningham-Sereque et al., 2023). It will be the core of resilient, inclusive hybrid ecosystems as it is a human-centred AI design.

8.3. Continuous Educational Structures and Intelligent Talent Development.

The future of hybrid working will be based on AI-enabled, lifelong learning platforms that individualize development according to expertise deficiencies, learning styles, and career opportunities. AI will also design dynamic upskilling routes in accordance with the changing needs of industry, and ensuring that people get access to learning in an equitable manner regardless of geographical location (Gupta, 2019). AI will enhance retention and develop talent that is future-ready by mapping the learning progress and suggesting mentors and connecting developmental paths with the promotion journeys.

AI will also correct the imbalance of talent movement by dynamically aligning internal capabilities to changes in the market. This change will redefine organizations in the non-hierarchical approach to fluid and project-based networks, with AI optimizing the creation of teams depending on their relevance to the current context and performance metrics (Azeroual, 2024). Planning of the workforce will then be talent forecasting and predictive, with the backbone of AI-driven insights as opposed to the traditional workforce forecasting.

8.4. Hyper -Personalization of Employee Experience.

The next generation hybrid model will be greatly dependent on AI-based hyper-personalization, which personalizes onboarding, task assignment, performance appraisal, and well-being interventions to every employee. Identifying discrepancies in productivity rates, communication preferences, and interpersonal styles, AI will create favorable work environments that promote the organizational objectives as well as personal prosperity (Madanchian, 2024). The algorithms of natural-language processing will be used to detect exclusionary communication patterns and allow intervention proactively to encourage equity and belonging. As a result, personalization will become the competitive advantage and structural condition of hybrid workforce sustainability (Chiriatti et al., 2025).

8.5. Future-Proofing `Ethical Leadership and Regulatory Compliance.

With AI being integrated into hybrid operations, ethical leadership will be a necessity. The future AI policies should reflect responsible AI concepts such as equity, transparency, accountability, and inclusivity throughout the entire development cycle (Suvedhaa et al., 2025). The globalized hybrid teams bring about complications of regulation requirements that demand that organizations align global standards to the local laws and culture. The future of ethical governance will be based on AI ethics boards, algorithmic auditing systems, and workflows based on ethics-by-design.

The rules of data-sovereignty and cross-border facts of data will compel organizations to develop non-inflexible AI-systems with consent-management services, encryption-systems and traceable data provenance (Aryan et al., 2025). Regulatory and ethical readiness will therefore be the center of maintaining trust among distributed digitally mediated workplaces.

8.6. Organizational Redesign and Leadership Transformation.

Working remotely will require models of leadership that are based on the principles of data literacy, emotional intelligence, and systems thinking. Leaders will have to ensure that the machine-generated insights do not compromise the employees' autonomy, teach human-AI team-building skills, and address the unwanted effects of the algorithms (Gundage et al., 2025). Similarly, the organizational structures will become more agile cross-functional networks, which are managed by smart platforms instead of strict hierarchies. AI will allow forming teams quickly depending on skills, availability, and performance information, which promotes flexibility and resiliency in the globally spread setting (Kytainyk et al., 2025).

8.7. Artificial Intelligence Maturity Journeys and the Emergence of Culture of Data.

To have a sustainable hybrid work force, the culture of data should be ingrained. To facilitate the use of evidence-based decision-making across the organizational levels, organizations need to invest in data literacy, democratized analytics systems, and shared governance systems (Dajani et al., 2024). Centres of excellence and cross-functional stewardship will enable enterprise-wide AI strategies to make AI (currently) scattered applications become widespread strategic assets. The maturity of AI is not, therefore, a technological endeavor, but more of an organizational and cultural project (Dhand et al., 2025).

9. CONCLUSION

The hybrid workforce model is transforming the core basis of organizational design and workforce management. With employees wanting autonomy, flexibility and inclusivity, AI would not seem like a facilitator technology but rather, it would enable future needs. The importance of balancing human interaction with smart automation whereby AI-based, intervention-based improvement is a complementary, and not a substitute, component of the human component. The dynamics of digital infrastructure, ethical considerations and adaptive leadership will determine the determinants of the successful complex management of hybrid complexities. Distributed collaboration optimization, personalized work experience, and agile workforce planning will be among the main features of strong and resilient organizations in the future, and artificial intelligence will become a key determinant in such enterprises.

REFERENCES

Al-Abdullatif, A. M. (2025, June). Auditing AI Literacy Competency in K–12 Education: The Role of Awareness, Ethics, Evaluation, and Use in Human–Machine Cooperation. *Systems*, *13*(06). Advance online publication. DOI: 10.3390/systems13060490

Amy, A. (2025, May 06). *IBM Accelerates Enterprise Gen AI Revolution with Hybrid Capabilities*. Retrieved Aug 15, 2025, from https://newsroom.ibm.com/2025-05-06-ibm-accelerates-enterprise-gen-ai-revolution-with-hybrid-capabilities: https://newsroom.ibm.com/2025-05-06-ibm-accelerates-enterprise-gen-ai-revolution-with-hybrid-capabilities

Anika, S. (2025, Mar 28). *Standard Chartered unveils AI platform SC GPT*. Retrieved Aug 15, 2025, from https://www.privatebankerinternational.com: https://www.privatebankerinternational.com/news/standard-chartered-unveils-ai-platform-sc-gpt/

Arias, J. A., Beltran, J. A., & Bedoya, S. (2020). RPA Implementation for automation of managenment process of personal in Compañía Nacional de Empaques S.A. *15th Iberian Conference on Information Systems and Technologies, CISTI 2020*. Seville: IEEE Computer Society. DOI: 10.23919/CISTI49556.2020.9140994

Arpita, A., & Saurabh, B. (2024, Jan 09). Artificial Intelligence for Hiring and Induction: The Unilever Experience. *Business Cases*. 10.4135/9781071921470

Aryan, F., Valença, L., & de Souza Santos, R. (2025). Exploring Fairness Debt Through Evidence from Studies on Algorithmic Discrimination. *8th IEEE/ACM International Conference on Technical Debt, TechDebt 2025* (pp. 34-39). Ottawa: Institute of Electrical and Electronics Engineers Inc. DOI: 10.1109/TechDebt66644.2025.00011

Awasthi, L. S., Awasthi, K. S., & Rai, A. K. (2024). Integrating human expertise and decision-making with artificial intelligence systems. In *Sustainability Principles and Applications in Engineering Practice* (pp. 217–236). Nova Science Publishers, Inc., 2-s2.0-85202112091

Azeroual, O. (2024). Smart Data Stewardship: Innovating Governance and Quality with AI. *16th International Conference on Knowledge Management and Information Systems, KMIS 2024 as part of 16th International Joint Conference on Knowledge Discovery, Knowledge Engineering and Knowledge Management, IC3K 2024*. *03*, pp. 187 - 196. Porto: Science and Technology Publications, Lda. DOI: 10.5220/0012918200003838

Balasundaram, S., & Venkatagiri, S. (2020). A structured approach to implementing Robotic Process Automation in HR. *3rd National Conference on Computational Intelligence, NCCI 2019. 1427.* Bangalore, Karnataka: Journal of Physics: Conference Series. DOI: 10.1088/1742-6596/1427/1/012008

Behare, N. (2025). Embracing AI: Fostering employee engagement and satisfaction in the digital era. In *Innovative Approaches for International Competitiveness Through Human Resource Management* (pp. 155-168). IGI Global. DOI: 10.4018/979-8-3373-1005-3.ch006

Bharathi, K. V., & Krithika, M. (2024). Investigating the Impact of Evolving Work Culture on Employee Productivity in the Post-Pandemic Period. *10th International Conference on Smart Computing and Communication, ICSCC 2024.* Bali: Institute of Electrical and Electronics Engineers Inc. DOI: 10.1109/ICSCC62041.2024.10690698

Biswal, S. S., Ganesh, A., & Madhavan, P. (2020, April). Robotic automation of employee onboarding using neural computing. *International Journal of Scientific and Technology Research, 09*(04), 353–357. Retrieved August 01, 2025, from https://www.scopus.com/pages/publications/85083461419

Burnett, J. R., & Lisk, T. C. (2019, January 02). The Future of Employee Engagement: Real-Time Monitoring and Digital Tools for Engaging a Workforce. *International Studies of Management & Organization, 49*(01), 108–119. DOI: 10.1080/00208825.2019.1565097

Caldwell, S., Sweetser, P., O'donnell, N., Knight, M. J., & Aitchison, M. (2022, July 26). An Agile New Research Framework for Hybrid Human-AI Teaming: Trust, Transparency, and Transferability. *ACM Transactions on Interactive Intelligent Systems, 12*(03). Advance online publication. DOI: 10.1145/3514257

Chandratreya, A. (2025). Digital transformation and the future workforce. In *Transforming the Service Sector With New Technology* (pp. 19–40). IGI Global., DOI: 10.4018/979-8-3693-7447-4.ch002

Chiriatti, M., Bergamaschi Ganapini, M., Panai, E., Wiederhold, B. K., & Riva, G. (2025, July 01). System 0: Transforming Artificial Intelligence into a Cognitive Extension. *Cyberpsychology, Behavior, and Social Networking, 28*(07), 534–542. DOI: 10.1089/cyber.2025.0201 PMID: 40504761

Chrusciak, C. B., Szejka, A. L., & Canciglieri, O., Junior. (2023). A Preliminary Digital Transformation Framework to Support Business Management Processes and Human Factors Impacts: Systematic Review and Gap Analysis. In *Lecture Notes in Computer Science (including subseries Lecture Notes in Artificial Intelligence and Lecture Notes in Bioinformatics)* (Vol. 14316 LNCS, pp. 308-329). Springer Science and Business Media Deutschland GmbH. DOI: 10.1007/978-3-031-50040-4_23

Colette, S. (2023, Apr). *From AI in Teams Premium to updates for Viva—here's what's new in Microsoft 365*. Retrieved Aug 19, 2025, from https://www.microsoft.com: https://www.microsoft.com/en-us/microsoft-365/blog/2023/02/28/from-ai-in-teams-premium-to-updates-for-viva-heres-whats-new-in-microsoft-365/?msockid=3a60cb3d05b66d9b3435dd2a042d6c09

Csaba, M., Miklós, I., & Ákos, H. (2025). Hybrid work in the public and competitive sectors: Implications and challenges (Lessons from a pilot research). *Statisztikai Szemle*, *103*(06), 545–567. DOI: 10.20311/stat2025.06.hu0545

Cunningham-Sereque, M., Gordon, N., & Vaezi, R. (2023). Flying Blind: Recruiter Trust in Automated Employment Decision Tools. *29th Annual Americas Conference on Information Systems: Diving into Uncharted Waters, AMCIS 2023*. Panama City: Association for Information Systems. Retrieved Aug 02, 2025, from https://www.scopus.com/pages/publications/85192865952

Dajani, L., Ferraro, A., Maruyama, F., & Cheng, Y. (2024). Human Rights and Ethics Guiding Human-Machine Teaming. *14th IEEE Global Humanitarian Technology Conference, GHTC 2024*. Radnor: Institute of Electrical and Electronics Engineers Inc. DOI: 10.1109/GHTC62424.2024.10771558

Darwish, H., Yalabik, Z. Y., & Gustafsson, S. (2025). BEING A GOOD CITIZEN IN A HYBRID WORK SETTING: WHAT DOES IT MEAN FOR PROFESSIONALS? *85th Annual Meeting of the Academy of Management, AOM 2025*. 2025. Copenhagen: Academy of Management. DOI: 10.5465/AMPROC.2025.332bp

Dhand, S., Pandey, A., Mishra, S., Sharma, K., & Kadanga, A. (2025). Role of artificial intelligence in enhancing employee well-being at the workplace. In *Global Work Arrangements and Outsourcing in the Age of AI* (pp. 25–46). IGI Global., DOI: 10.4018/979-8-3373-1270-5.ch002

Duarte, A., & Dias, P. (2025). How artificial intelligence is changing organizations: Portuguese CEOs' perspective. *Journal of Communication Management*, 01-18. DOI: 10.1108/JCOM-10-2024-0204

Dwivedi, D., & Agarwal, S. (2024). Evaluating the Effectiveness of Leadership Decision Making by Data Analytics and Reporting Technologies. In *Advancing the Marketing Technology (MarTech) Revolution* (pp. 207-232). IGI Global. DOI: 10.4018/979-8-3693-4361-6.ch008

Ganapathy, A. (2021). ROBOTIC PROCESS AUTOMATION: END FROM ENTREPRENEURIAL CONTENT EDITING TO GO LIVE. *Academy of Entrepreneurship Journal*, *27*(03), 1–11. Retrieved August 12, 2025, from https://www.scopus.com/pages/publications/85109437774

Gundage, V., Deshmukh, M. T., Kolape, R., Kate, A., & Narve, N. G. (2025, April). Enhancing Manufacturing Efficiency and Safety through Human-Robot Collaboration: A Comprehensive Review. *Journal of Mines. Metals and Fuels*, *43*(04), 943–950. DOI: 10.18311/jmmf/2025/48270

Gupta, K. P. (2019, July). Artificial intelligence for governance in india: Prioritizing the challenges using analytic hierarchy process (AHP). *International Journal of Recent Technology and Engineering*, *09*(02), 3756–3762. DOI: 10.35940/ijrte.B3392.078219

Herrera, F. (2025, September). Reflections and attentiveness on eXplainable Artificial Intelligence (XAI). The journey ahead from criticisms to human–AI collaboration. *Information Fusion*, *121*. Advance online publication. DOI: 10.1016/j.inffus.2025.103133

Hofeditz, L., Clausen, S., Rieß, A., Mirbabaie, M., & Stieglitz, S. (2022, December). Applying XAI to an AI-based system for candidate management to mitigate bias and discrimination in hiring. *Electronic Markets*, *32*(04), 2207–2233. DOI: 10.1007/s12525-022-00600-9 PMID: 36568961

Hölzle, K., Rose, R., & Kaschub, V. L. (2024, December 01). The Interplay of Humans, Technology, and Organizations in Realizing AI's Productivity Promise. *The Economists' Voice*, *21*(02), 357–362. DOI: 10.1515/ev-2024-0053

Jai, G. M. (2025, Mar 27). *Standard Chartered rolls out SC GPT, advancing AI-driven innovation in banking*. Retrieved Aug 12, 2025, from https://www.sc.com: https://www.sc.com/en/press-release/standard-chartered-rolls-out-sc-gpt-advancing-ai-driven-innovation-in-banking/

Jain, V., & Mitra, A. (2025). Digital transformation and organizational culture: A sociological examination of employee interactions in modern workplaces. In *Organizational Sociology in the Digital Age* (pp. 203–218). IGI Global., DOI: 10.4018/979-8-3693-7398-9.ch012

John, B., Alsamarra'i, Z., & Panteli, N. (2025, March). Reconfiguring digital embeddedness in hybrid work: The case of employee experience management platforms. *Information Systems Journal*, *35*(02), 450–479. DOI: 10.1111/isj.12545

Juglan, K. C., Sharma, B., Gehlot, A., Singh, S. P., & Hussein, A. (2023). Exploring the Effectiveness of Natural Language Processing in Customer Service. *3rd International Conference on Advance Computing and Innovative Technologies in Engineering, ICACITE 2023* (pp. 814-818). Greater Noida: Institute of Electrical and Electronics Engineers Inc. DOI: 10.1109/ICACITE57410.2023.10183107

Kaur, J., Devgon, R., & Chaudhary, D. (2022). Work of Fiction: Using Speculative Design to Deliberate on the Future of Hiring. *25th ACM Conference on Computer-Supported Cooperative Work and Social Computing, CSCW 2022* (pp. 23-26). Online: Association for Computing Machinery. DOI: 10.1145/3500868.3559442

Kelan, E. K. (2024, July). Algorithmic inclusion: Shaping the predictive algorithms of artificial intelligence in hiring. *Human Resource Management Journal*, *34*(03), 694–707. DOI: 10.1111/1748-8583.12511

Khanna, D., Edison, H., Nguyen-Duc, A., & Kemell, K.-K. (2024). Software Companies' Responses to Hybrid Working. *50th Euromicro Conference on Software Engineering and Advanced Applications, SEAA 2024* (pp. 244 - 251). Paris: Institute of Electrical and Electronics Engineers Inc. DOI: 10.1109/SEAA64295.2024.00045

Kniffin, K. M., Narayanan, J., Anseel, F., Antonakis, J., & Ashford, S. P. (2021, January). COVID-19 and the workplace: Implications, issues, and insights for future research and action. *The American Psychologist*, *76*(01), 63–77. DOI: 10.1037/amp0000716 PMID: 32772537

Koeszegi, S. T. (2023). AI @ work: Human empowerment or disempowerment? In *Introduction to Digital Humanism: A Textbook* (pp. 175–196). Springer Nature., DOI: 10.1007/978-3-031-45304-5_12

Kytainyk, V. V., Yushchenko, A. G., & Lyalin, D. Y. (2025). AI - human cooperation in "Second Brain" Technology, as a modern implementation of general evolution in human-machine interaction. *7th International Congress on Human-Computer Interaction, Optimization and Robotic Applications, ICHORA 2025.* Ankara: Institute of Electrical and Electronics Engineers Inc. DOI: 10.1109/ICHORA65333.2025.11017255

Lenka, R., & Chanda, R. (2025). Generative AI for Predicting Employee Engagement in HR Analytics: A Bibliometric Analysis. *9th International Conference on ICT for Sustainable Development, ICT4SD 2024. 1162 LNNS*, pp. 201-209. Goa: Springer Science and Business Media Deutschland GmbH. DOI: 10.1007/978-981-97-8605-3_19

Linde, S., Walker, R. J., Campbell, J. A., & Egede, L. E. (2025). Structural inequalities and chronic disease health outcomes: Impact of AI on health equity. In *Structural Inequalities and Health Outcomes for Chronic Disease* (pp. 587–616). Elsevier., DOI: 10.1016/B978-0-443-23750-8.00029-1

Madanchian, M. (2024, December). From Recruitment to Retention: AI Tools for Human Resource Decision-Making. *Applied Sciences (Switzerland)*, *14*(24). Advance online publication. DOI: 10.3390/app142411750

Michelle, S. (2024, Mar 05). *AI-native learning platform uses recommendation engine to deliver personalized learning experiences for technical teams, business users, C-suite and board members*. Retrieved Aug 19, 2025, from https://newsroom.accenture.com: https://newsroom.accenture.com/news/2024/accenture-launches-accenture-learnvantage-to-help-clients-and-their-people-gain-essential-skills-and-achieve-greater-business-value-in-the-ai-economy

Mishra, S., Choubey, S., Choubey, A., Yogeesh, N., & Rao, J. D. (2022). Data Extraction Approach using Natural Language Processing for Sentiment Analysis. *1st IEEE International Conference on Automation, Computing and Renewable Systems, ICACRS 2022* (pp. 970-972). Pudukkottai: Institute of Electrical and Electronics Engineers Inc. DOI: 10.1109/ICACRS55517.2022.10029216

Mittal, P., Jora, R. B., Sodhi, K. K., & Saxena, P. (2023). A Review of The Role of Artificial Intelligence in Employee Engagement. *9th International Conference on Advanced Computing and Communication Systems, ICACCS 2023* (pp. 2502-2506). Coimbatore: Institute of Electrical and Electronics Engineers Inc. DOI: 10.1109/ICACCS57279.2023.10112957

Muller, M., & Weisz, J. (2022). Extending a Human-AI Collaboration Framework with Dynamism and Sociality. *1st Annual Meeting of the Symposium on Human-Computer Interaction for Work, CHIWORK 2022*. Virtual, Online: Association for Computing Machinery. DOI: 10.1145/3533406.3533407

Mwita, K. M., & Kitole, F. A. (2025, December). Potential benefits and challenges of artificial intelligence in human resource management in public institutions. *Discover Global Society*, *03*(01). Advance online publication. DOI: 10.1007/s44282-025-00175-8

Nedumaran, C., Shyam, S. S., Sham Kumar, S., Nithish, K. R., & Rajan, R. G. (2023). An Intelligent Agent to Automate HR Process. *2023 IEEE World Conference on Communication and Computing, WCONF 2023*. Raipur: IEEE. DOI: 10.1109/WCONF58270.2023.10235110

Nuswantoro, B., Richter, A., & Riemer, K. (2023). Conceptualizing Visibility in Hybrid Work. *44th International Conference on Information Systems: Rising like a Phoenix: Emerging from the Pandemic and Reshaping Human Endeavors with Digital Technologies, ICIS 2023*. Hyderibad: Association for Information Systems. Retrieved Aug 08, 2025, from https://www.scopus.com/pages/publications/85192500405

Patil, S., Upadhye, P., Khandekar, S. R., Darekar, P., & Ghewari, A. (2024). Artificial Intelligence and Data Science Approaches to Analyzing Human Resource Management in Hybrid and Remote Work Models. *Proceedings of the 2024 International Conference on Innovative Computing, Intelligent Communication and Smart Electrical Systems, ICSES 2024*. Chennai: Institute of Electrical and Electronics Engineers Inc. DOI: 10.1109/ICSES63760.2024.10910810

Poser, M., & Bittner, E. A. (2021). (Re)Designing IT Support: How Embedded and Conversational AI Can Augment Technical Support Work. *42nd International Conference on Information Systems: Building Sustainability and Resilience with IS: A Call for Action, ICIS 2021 TREOs*. Austin: Association for Information Systems. Retrieved Aug 15, 2025, from https://www.scopus.com/pages/publications/85152125922

Raikov, A. N., & Pirani, M. (2022). Contradiction of modern and social-humanitarian artificial intelligence. *Kybernetes, 51*(13), 186–198. DOI: 10.1108/K-01-2022-0057

Rajeswari, A., & Gomathi, S. (2022, December 20). Wearable Technology: A Stimulant for Employee Engagement in a Hybrid Work model. *International Journal of Intelligent Systems and Applications in Engineering, 10*(04), 689–694. Retrieved August 09, 2025, from https://www.scopus.com/pages/publications/85164813799

Ramos, I. F., Gianini, G., Leva, M. C., & Damiani, E. (2024, November). Collaborative Intelligence for Safety-Critical Industries: A Literature Review. *Information (Switzerland), 15*(11). Advance online publication. DOI: 10.3390/info15110728

Rhue, L. (2019). Beauty is in the AI of the beholder: How artificial intelligence anchors human decisions on subjective vs. Objective measures. *40th International Conference on Information Systems, ICIS 2019*. Munich: Association for Information Systems. Retrieved Aug 20, 2025, from https://www.scopus.com/pages/publications/85136806761

Rostamzadeh, R., Alizadeh, F. K., Keivani, S., & Isavi, H. (2025). The Role of Artificial Intelligence in Improving Organizational Behavior: A Systematic Study. *Human Behavior and Emerging Technologies, 2025*(01). DOI: 10.1155/hbe2/8094428

Sahyaja, C., Shankar, C., Zeeshan, K., & Nagaraj, N. (2024). Artificial Intelligence and Remote Work: Transforming Human Resource Management in a Post-Pandemic World. *3rd International Conference on Automation, Computing and Renewable Systems, ICACRS 2024* (pp. 1555 - 1560). Pudukkottai: Institute of Electrical and Electronics Engineers Inc. DOI: 10.1109/ICACRS62842.2024.10841784

Samson, B. D., Mama, B. R.-Z., Luriaga, R. L., & Ebardo, R. A. (2024). Barriers to Hybrid Work Among IT Professionals: A TOE Perspective From a Developing Economy. *4th International Conference on Advances in Computational Science and Engineering, ICACSE 2023* (pp. 505 - 520). Manila: Springer Science and Business Media Deutschland GmbH. DOI: 10.1007/978-981-97-2977-7_32

Saragih, H. (2025). The role of digital transformation in enhancing performance and security of technology infrastructure in public institutions. *Edelweiss Applied Science and Technology, 09*(06), 679–686. DOI: 10.55214/25768484.v9i6.7865

Saritha, T., & Akthar, P. (2024). The Impact of Hybrid Work Models on Employee Well-being and Engagement. *Communications on Applied Nonlinear Analysis, 31*(55), 97–104. DOI: 10.52783/cana.v31.1003

Seletedi, C., Mwalemba, G., & Mashingaidze, K. (2024). A Bunch of Sheep Running Towards Somewhere" - Implications of Digital Transformation on the Workforce. *18th IFIP WG 9.4 International Conference on the Implications of Information and Digital Technologies for Development, ICT4D 2024. 709*, pp. 03-15. Cape Town: Springer Science and Business Media Deutschland GmbH. DOI: 10.1007/978-3-031-66986-6_1

Singh, A., & Singh, G. (2025). Leveraging AI-powered predictive analytics for proactive risk management and business resilience in SMEs: Harnessing predictive insights to strengthen decision-making in SMEs. In *Incentives and Benefits for Adopting Green Entrepreneurship Practices* (pp. 265–294). IGI Global., DOI: 10.4018/979-8-3693-9306-2.ch011

Soleimani, M., Intezari, A., & Pauleen, D. J. (2022, January 01). Mitigating cognitive biases in developing ai-assisted recruitment systems: A knowledge-sharing approach. *International Journal of Knowledge Management, 18*(01). Advance online publication. DOI: 10.4018/IJKM.290022

Stanbery, K., Lindley, K., & Huffman, C. (2023, January 01). The Feasibility of Using Net Promoter Score to Measure Real-Time Employee Engagement. *The Journal of Nursing Administration*, *53*(01), 34–39. DOI: 10.1097/NNA.0000000000001239 PMID: 36542442

Suvedhaa, A., Imranmohamed, M., & Sudhipth, V., & M., T. (2025). AI-Powered Workforce Management for Automated Appraisals and Task Allocation. *6th International Conference on Innovative Trends in Information Technology, ICITIIT 2025*. Kottayam: Institute of Electrical and Electronics Engineers Inc. DOI: 10.1109/ICITIIT64777.2025.11041265

T.S. S., Babhuti, K., Jyoti, D., Kaur, H., & Kapoor, T. (2025). The evolving role of Artificial Intelligence (AI) in Human Resource Management (HRM). In *Sustainable Management Practices for Employee Retention and Recruitment* (pp. 301-309). IGI GLobal. DOI: 10.4018/979-8-3693-8679-8.ch015

Vashishth, T. K., Sharma, V., Tomer, T., Kumar, A., & Kaushik, S. (2025). AI in HRM: Transforming employee engagement and satisfaction amidst challenges and opportunities. In *Human Resource Management in the Age of Generative AI* (pp. 157-187). IGI Global. DOI: 10.4018/979-8-3693-7693-5.ch006

Wang, B. Y., Boell, S. K., Riemer, K., & Peter, S. (2023). Human Agency in AI Configurations Supporting Organizational Decision-making. *34th Australasian Conference on Information Systems, ACIS 2023*. Wellington: Association for Information Systems. Retrieved Aug 10, 2025, from https://www.scopus.com/pages/publications/85198754646

Wu, Y. J., Antone, B., DeChurch, L., & Contractor, N. (2023, July 01). Information sharing in a hybrid workplace: Understanding the role of ease-of-use perceptions of communication technologies in advice-seeking relationship maintenance. *Journal of Computer-Mediated Communication*, *28*(04). Advance online publication. DOI: 10.1093/jcmc/zmad025

Wu, Y. J., Antone, B., DeChurch, L., & Contractor, N. (2023, July 01). Information sharing in a hybrid workplace: Understanding the role of ease-of-use perceptions of communication technologies in advice-seeking relationship maintenance. *Journal of Computer-Mediated Communication*, *28*(04). Advance online publication. DOI: 10.1093/jcmc/zmad025

Yang, T., & Jiang, J. (2025). Designing job characteristics for effective hybrid intelligence: Insights from job design and human–AI collaboration. *Personnel Review*. Advance online publication. DOI: 10.1108/PR-03-2024-0229

Yesufu, L., & Alajlani, S. (2025). Enhancing Strategic Decision-Making With AI: Unveiling the Untapped Potential. In *Economic and Political Consequences of AI: Managing Creative Destruction* (pp. 415 - 436). IGI Global. DOI: 10.4018/979-8-3693-7036-0.ch018

Zhang, R., Flathmann, C., Musick, G., Schelble, B., & McNeese, N. J. (2024, February 05). I Know This Looks Bad, But I Can Explain: Understanding When AI Should Explain Actions In Human-AI Teams. *ACM Transactions on Interactive Intelligent Systems*, *14*(01). Advance online publication. DOI: 10.1145/3635474

ADDITIONAL READING

Bositkhanova, N., & Dadaboyev, S. M. (2025, December). Revolutionizing workforce planning: The strategic role of AI in HR strategy. *Discover Global Society*, *03*(01). Advance online publication. DOI: 10.1007/s44282-025-00252-y

Chowdhury, S., Budhwar, P., & Wood, G. (2024, October). Generative Artificial Intelligence in Business: Towards a Strategic Human Resource Management Framework. *British Journal of Management*, *35*(04), 1680–1691. DOI: 10.1111/1467-8551.12824

Dhatchayani, K., Vezhaventhan, D., Raj, M. B., Harikishore, S., & Velan, V. S. (2025). Cognitive Enterprise Framework Integrating Hybrid Systems for Smarter Decision Intelligence in Dynamic Management Scenarios. 3rd International Conference on Electronics and Renewable Systems, ICEARS 2025. Tuticorin: IEEE. DOI: 10.1109/ICEARS64219.2025.10940279

Gupta, A., Tyagi, L., Sisodia, V. S., & Aman, V. (2024). Strategic Framework for Implementing Artificial Intelligence in Organizations from Conceptualization to Practical Execution and Performance Evaluation. *2024 International Conference on Sustainable Computing and Integrated Communication in Changing Landscape of AI, ICSCAI 2024*. Noida: IEEE. DOI: 10.1109/ICSCAI61790.2024.10866620

Indoria, D., Dakshinamoorthy, B., Karthik, M., Sharma, M., & Kaliappan, S. (2024). Transforming HR in Finance by Leveraging IoT and AI for Strategic Talent Management. *2024 International Conference on Innovative Computing, Intelligent Communication and Smart Electrical Systems, ICSES 2024*. Chennai: Institute of Electrical and Electronics Engineers Inc. DOI: 10.1109/ICSES63760.2024.10910324

KEY TERMS AND DEFINITIONS

Adaptive AI: The adaptive AI is represented by artificial intelligence systems that can learn based on empirical evidence and feedback, and recalibrate their actions and decision-making based on situational variables, needs, or strategic goals. These systems have been placed in adaptive control loops and as such, can re-optimize performance functions as they happen in real time, whilst aligned to the overriding organizational objectives.

Ethical Governance: The ethical governance framework construction aims at making sure that the decisions made by technology should be made in a manner that is fair, transient, responsible, and in accordance with the larger values of society. This involves drawing up of control frameworks, policy protection and gauging measures that jointly support ideals of fairness, clarification, and social duty.

Hybrid Workforce Management: The human resource, policy, and supportive equipment management that supports the involvement of the staff in remote, hybrid, and on-site environments is a critical prism with the help of which modern organizations are examined. The researchers have argued that the intersection of dispersed working patterns and conventional on-site functions require the existence of a complex coordination of human resources, technological systems, and process standards.

Hybrid Workforce Operations: The operational aspect includes the daily processes and the information systems to support a smooth collaboration process, maximize the productivity and maintain performance indicators in a workforce that switches between the remote and onsite mode. This, in practice, means the deployment of the collaborative platforms, real-time analytics, and adaptive governance systems to address dynamism of the demands on a geographically distributed workforce.

Chapter 5

AI-Enabled Sustainable Workforce Management for Hybrid Work Places

A. Rahmath Nisha
https://orcid.org/0009-0001-5146-2411
Saveetha School of Management, Saveetha Institute of Medical and Technical Sciences, Chennai, India

A. K. Subramani
https://orcid.org/0000-0003-0783-7113
Saveetha School of Management, Saveetha Institute of Medical and Technical Sciences, Chennai, India

M. Monisha Devi
https://orcid.org/0009-0000-4152-2786
Saveetha School of Management, Saveetha Institute of Medical and Technical Sciences, Chennai, India

R. Durai Pandian
https://orcid.org/0000-0003-2932-0270
Saveetha School of Management, Saveetha Institute of Medical and Technical Sciences, Chennai, India

ABSTRACT

The paper will discuss the critical role of the Artificial Intelligence (AI) technology in shaping. sustainable human resources management in the hybrid work environment. As organizations adapt to the AI becomes a critical element in reference to industry 4.0 requirements and growing environmental and social pressures, facilitator of business productivity, staff welfare, and corporate flexibility. The study discusses

DOI: 10.4018/979-8-3373-5871-0.ch005

ht © 2026, IGI Global Scientific Publishing. Copying or distributing in print or electronic forms without written permission of IGI Global Scientific Publishing is prohibited. Use of this chapter to generative artificial intelligence (AI) technologies is expressly prohibited. The publisher reserves all rights to license its use for generative AI training and machine learning model development.

different hybrid work models and how AI technology like predictive analytics, can be applied. Digital twins, sentiment analysis, and optimization algorithms can be used in workforce planning, improvement in productivity, and sustainability of the environment. It highlights the economic, environmental, social, and sustainability aspects, defining how artificial intelligence promotes fairness, transparency, health management, energy saving, and ethical management. Finally, the paper presents implementation plans, new AI functionality, and research possibilities that facilitate a data-driven, people-oriented, and morally responsible future of work.

1. INTRODUCTION

The Rise of Artificial Intelligence in Industry 4.0

The objective of artificial intelligence to achieve standards of Industry 4.0 is to transform the traditional companies to smart factories that will utilize as much efficiency as possible and require less staff. and putting their talents to the better purpose. Although firms need to align to the needs of Industry 4.0 through smart factories, they should also be able to match the constantly changing needs of environment and consumers (Reddy et al., 2024). The era of automation and the development of hybrid. workplaces are designed to achieve the balance between efficiency which is Artificial Intelligence (AI) powered and human activity and ingenuity.

AI tools are able to make workflows more efficient, as well as remote communication, which improves productivity within a hybrid working setting. This enhances the humans to focus more on tasks that require more social interaction, complex decision making and innovative thinking. AI technology is becoming increasingly dynamic and flexible. In short AI technology will change the future of work. AI tools and other technological tools are reshaping many organizations at a time has already transformed the workplace, what it means to work and what exactly the work has taken place.

The Shift Toward Hybrid Work Environments

Hybrid workplaces are already functioning with the help of AI. Hybrid workplace is an arrangement in which the employees can work remotely or on-site in an office. This flexibility gives the employees to greater counter over their schedules and enable them to be more productive. In some cases, employees will be called into the office on certain days for completing specific tasks, otherwise allowing them to work remotely. By implementing hybrid work environment, it allows companies to benefit in certain ways; like cost savings offered by remote work, collaboration, networking opportunities, by leveraging AI, organizations can ensure that hybrid working environment runs smoothly and efficiently (Evangeline & Raju, 2024)

2. DEFINING HYBRID WORKPLACES

Hybrid work is a malleable method of conducting work and reaching positive outcomes, and begins with the assumption that the location or time of work completion is not the most salient factor, but that work is actually done. Consequently, in the case of hybrid work employees are usually judged by achieved and productivity, as opposed to how many hours they spend in an office. It presents 4 potential major hybrid work models. As such, with the advent of digitalization, the government has started using it to help companies transform their business models and increase their overall revenue (*Brînzea & Oancea, 2022*).

Table 1. Types of Hybrid Work Models

HYBRID WORK PLACE	DEFINITION	CONTROL	WORK LOCATION FLEXIBILITY
Flexible Hybrid Work Model	Employees choose their own location and working hours based on their priorities and the nature of the tasks to be completed.	Employee-controlled	High (full flexibility in choosing location)
Fixed Hybrid Work Model	The organization decides when employees should work from home or attend the office for meetings, team-building, or training.	Organization-controlled	Moderate (schedule/ location defined by employer)
Office-First Hybrid Work Model	Remote work is allowed for a limited number of days per week or month, but employees are expected to be in the office most of the time.	Organization-preferred but allows limited flexibility	Low to Moderate (office preferred)

Source: (Brînzea & Oancea, 2022)

3. WORKFORCE MODEL CHARACTERISTICS IN HYBRID WORK

Distributed Mission Operation

The procedure of training the virtuously remote aircrews, and yet still practice the mission preparation and operation by the aircrews who in real person encounter each other (Bennett, 2009)

Modes of Collaboration:

Asynchronous communication – A type of communication where no time constraint exists on when messages need to be sent and where people make their own contributions into communication at any time. Asynchronous communication in this research is defined as either text communicating or e-mail communications (Bennett, 2009)

Synchronous communication- Re-occurring or functioning at the same intervals of time; synchronous communications are in real time. In this type of research, synchronous implies video communications (Bennett, 2009)

Visibility and Transparency in Distributed Work

Need for Co-Ordination

(Bergefurt et al., 2024) has offered insights into how to assist employees' job activities and productivity by optimizing both the home and office workplaces. Employers can use these insights to better understand their workers' requirements both at work and at home. For example, companies might have to give workers enough tools for working together at home (like ICT), but they could also try to make the office more comfortable (like more personal control).

Visibility

In addition to providing opportunities for future study on visibility in hybrid work, a thorough examination of visibility dimensions and features and the use of IT broadens practitioners' perspectives on how to create and observe visibility in hybrid work environments. (Nuswantoro et al., 2023).

Support Systems

The relationship between employers and employees, and more especially the assistance that employers offer to their employees, is examined by organizational support theory (Ipsen et al., 2022). According to (Maertz et al., 2007), supervisor support (SS) measures the degree of assistance that supervisors provide to their subordinates. This kind of support is a component of the larger support that organizations provide to their members by respecting their well-being and acknowledging their hard work (Eisenberger et al., 2002)

Office space optimization

According to (Bouncken & Reuschl, 2018), coworking is a popular type of new Work that combines aspects of home office concepts, office communities, telecenters, teleworking, virtual working, virtual teams, and incubators. It offers cross-industry work communities more flexibility, autonomy, and social interaction opportunities in a shared physical space.

Understanding Sustainable Workforce Management

Dimensions of Sustainability: Economic Sustainability: Productivity, Cost Efficiency, Retention

Employee performance is very important in the age of globalization and competitiveness. Reduced performance results in higher operating expenses and a decline in revenue. Therefore, in order to increase productivity, performance, and efficiency, a company should offer the required training and development opportunities in addition to evaluations and feedback. Strategies for performance management are used to accomplish this (Triansyah et al., 2023)

Environmental Sustainability: Energy use, Travel Emissions, Infrastructure Footprint

Sustainable development highlights the necessity of adaptation to prevent a climate catastrophe and offers a framework for assessing policies aimed at mitigating climate change. "Development that meets the needs of the present without compromising the ability of future generations to meet their own needs" is how the World Commission on Environment and Development (WCED) defines sustainable development (SD). As a result, building and achieving balance between environmental preservation, economic growth, and social justice are the main goals of a public sustainable transportation system (Yang et al., 2016).

Social Sustainability: Well-being, Equity, Inclusion, Career Growth

When compared with other aspects of sustainability, social sustainability which includes gender parity, political accountability, equitable distribution, and the provision of social services—has gotten comparatively less attention (Ashby et al., 2012)

Why AI Matters In Workforce Sustainability

Data Abundance and digital transformation

Digital tools generate massive location, performance, sentiment, and resource-use data. Although it is growing, human understanding of the state and trends of Earth's ecosystem services, species, and natural resources is still limited, particularly in isolated places (Moussy et al., 2022). The goal of environmental assessments is to compile and apply this sparse data (3–6) to guide policy formation and decision-making. Critical needs may go unmet and choices and policies may be inadequately targeted as a result of the little data provided (Yue et al., 2024)

Advances in analytics: ML, NLP, Optimization, Simulation

The process of classification is one of the many categories into which advanced computing techniques fall. These approaches are not always independent of one another and are not limited to classification problems. One method that is thought to be data-driven is machine learning (ML). It is a field of AI that allows the computers to learn and enhance without being explicitly programmed (Chattu, 2021). Utilizing the MNIST database, the findings of the research shows that deep learning algorithms may be applied for the data encryption without compromising its accuracy. It holds the significance as it offers a possible solution for preserving the data security while benefiting from the advanced machine learning capabilities (Ramkumar et al., 2023).

Ai Tools & And Data Governance

Data Sources and Collection in Hybrid Work

Sources: Collaboration logs, Sensors (Badges, Occupancy), Environmental Sensors (Light, HVAC), HRIS, surveys. IoT technology significantly increases the efficiency of HVAC systems by revolutionizing their monitoring and control. These systems minimize energy waste by using actuators and sensors to dynamically modify temperature and airflow according to occupancy, outside weather, and user preferences (Lee & Lee, 2023). Together, these results demonstrate how IoT-enabled technologies significantly lower greenhouse gas emissions related to HVAC systems (Fakhabi et al., 2024).

Governance

Privacy-preserving Analytics, Anonymization, Employee Consent, Ethical frameworks. Given the importance of sensitive data in research, policymaking, and innovation, data privacy is an essential component of contemporary companies. (Şahin & Dogru, 2023).

4. MACHINE LEARNING & PREDICTIVE ANALYTICS IN WORKFORCE MANAGEMENT

Workload Forecasting: Time-Series Analysis for Demand Staffing

A significant method in predictive analytics, time series forecasting aids companies and sectors in anticipating future demand, maximizing resources, and enhancing decision-making (Soomro et al., 2019). As technology and data-driven innovations continue to improve, predictive analytics is changing demand forecasting (Morariu et al., 2020).

Attrition Risk Prediction Models

Customer attrition (customer churn) is a situation where clients withdraw their interaction with a business, halt its services or entrust it to the rival in the market (Jahun et al., 2021)

It is important to note that predictive analytics is very helpful when it comes to customer retention because one can detect patterns in history and use that to predict customer behavior, specifically their potential to churn (Bristol-Alagbariya et al., 2022). Churn prediction models can help businesses create customer groups on the basis of their churn potential, i.e., companies will be able to develop customized engagement tactics and plan individualized promotions, as well as solve customer problems at an early stage when they are not critical (Elumilade et al., 2022).

Sentiment Analysis: NLP on Surveys/Chat Data

Chatbot agents, which are computational agents, may function in both virtual and real-world environments, including games, and can seamlessly transition between the two. Strong heterogeneous systems, such as opportunistic and ad hoc crowd sensing environments, benefit from mobile computational agents, or mobile software. Examples include using smartphone data to control traffic. Agents interact with one another through unicast or broadcast signals (addressed messages) and tuple spaces (generative data-driven communication), for example they are loosely connected to their environment and platform (Bosse & Pournaras, 2017)

5. OPTIMIZATION & RESOURCE ALLOCATION

Office Space: Seat Allocation, Hoteling Systems

According to the high demand for commercial space in urban areas, 26% of the sample consists of office buildings. The fact that hotels account for 19% of the sample shows how the hospitality sector contributes to the building of high-rises, especially in towns that are heavily dependent on tourism. The study's smallest share is made up of residential buildings, which make up 16%. This distribution gives insight into how space efficiency is approached across these typologies and emphasizes the differing degrees of emphasis on various building functions in modern high-rise construction (Ilgin & Aslantamer, 2024).

Scheduling: Shift Planning, Remote/Onsite Co-Ordination

The impact of elements that influence employee loyalty can be both increased and decreased by using hybrid working practices (Uru Fahriye Oben et al., 2022). One way that hybrid working methods may boost employee loyalty is by providing more flexibility and a better work-life balance. If employees have the opportunity to work partially remotely, they could feel more prepared to set up their schedules to fit responsibilities and personal preferences. Companies might therefore demonstrate their confidence in their capacity to perform their jobs well by permitting them to work from home or at a different location (Vladimirovna, 2024).

Task Assignment: Matching Skills, Availability, Location

In order to create volunteer and employee work assignments for a planned non-profit program that accounts for the effect of task assignments on volunteer retention in subsequent periods, present an integer linear program. work is assigned in a way that strikes a compromise between organizational task preferences, volunteer trainings, volunteer preferences (which affect retention), and the necessity of present work (Kaur et al., 2022)

6. SIMULATION & DIGITAL TWIN TECHNOLOGIES

Scenario Planning: "What-if" Modeling for Staffing Changes, Scheduling, Occupancy

According to (Ernst et al., 2004, a), personnel scheduling, also known as employee timetabling and rostering, is a mathematical optimization problem in which a staff work schedule is created to meet the demand for goods or services. Under the condition of being able to define how to satisfy demand in a certain way where staffing problem and the decision that would be the most cost-effective night overtime and subcontracting, or shifting would go a long way with the manager or decision maker. These can be parameters in a people scheduling methodology that produces findings on several what-if scenarios using a simulation tool. Introducing the managers to the pros and cons of different solutions could be facilitated by visualization (Ernst et al, 2004, b)

Operational Digital Twins: Simulate Hybrid flows

One of the numerous wind research projects is virtual twinning of wind farms to optimize them and enable real-time control tasks which can be considered by the HAM paradigm. A digital twin is a virtual version of a physical system that is made possible by real-time data collection from sensors and simulations to address issues like monitoring, control, optimization, and better decision-making (Rasheed et al., 2019)

Continuous Feedback & Adaptive AI Systems

Real-time Feedback loops: Using feedback loops to boost performance in building projects has drawn interest as a useful strategy for raising productivity and quality throughout the project's lifecycle. The feedback loops are a methodical way to gather, examine, and react to project performance data in order to promote continuous improvement in the construction industry (Lee & Pena-Mora, 2006)

AI-Driven Nudges: Prompts for Breaks, Collaboration

In order to remind healthcare professionals to wash their hands at the most convenient times, AI can go beyond passive monitoring and use nudges like visual indicators (lights on dispensers) or audio prompts (alerts or chimes) (Wang et al., 2021). These AI-powered nudges have been shown to be quite successful in increasing compliance. Compliance rates increased by 30% in research using AI-powered badges that sound an alert each time a hand hygiene opportunity is missed (Fisher et al., 2013). Although technology is important, the combination of behavioral feedback and AI-driven nudges is what can maintain long-term compliance. According to the nudge theory, regular, subliminal reminders will eventually form habits that endure even in the absence of the prompts (Pittet, 2008)

Human-in-the-Loop Systems for Transparency and Fairness

Logically, the significance of the decision must be the determinant of the level of human control. When a decision amounts to a legal decision that is, when it touches a legal status of a person or is legally. Significant there should be a human-in-the-loop approach (Ződi, 2022). The capacity to observe the entire representation, its components, and the input data, and the operations involved, is referred to as Transparency algorithmic (Hamon et al., 2020).

7. APPLICATIONS AND ORGANIZATIONAL IMPACT

Forecasting Workplace Demand → Adaptive Staffing → Lower Costs

The AI-based workforce forecasting algorithms will also take into account the labor practices, including how a number of individuals are needed in a given task. These elements help firms to streamline their operations, lessening the number of workers required to perform an occupation, increasing production, and inventing a more flexible and effective work force. With more data from those groups, advanced scheduling and forecasting can be done to figure out when each person can contribute the most and when to hire them, which will maximize business productivity and financial sustainability (Usman et al., 2025)

Workforce Optimization → Balanced Workloads → Improved Output

For customer support centers to operate as efficiently as possible, staff planning and workload forecasting are essential. The suggested "Predict and Optimize" strategy for call center operations consists of these two primary components. By contrasting the predicted and actual call volumes, the prediction layer's efficacy may be assessed statistically (Kadioglu & Alatas, 2023)

Predictions can be made using the optimization model's recommended workforce levels as insightful information. Organizational innovations can be significantly improved by using a tailored framework for managing data-driven projects (Kadioglu & Takci, 2022).

Attrition Mitigation → Cost Savings from Retention

The basis of each company's business model is its decision-making in the human resources (HR) arena, especially when it comes to hiring procedures and staff retention. Therefore, a key component of HR procedures is the analysis and forecasting of employee attrition. Although a research based on the analysis and prediction of employee attrition can be carried out, it should be supplemented by a comprehensive examination of the interpretability procedures of the machine learning models that were used to generate the predictions (Sekaran & Shanmugam, 2022). According to Human Capital Theory, one of the most important outcomes is one's level of experience matters when making predicts about one's performance (Deepthi et al., 2024).

8. ENVIRONMENTAL IMPACT OF AI-ENABLED WORKPLACES

Commute Optimization: AI nudges for shared Commute or Remote

To accomplish the objectives of smart cities, communication, engagement, and the contributions of important stakeholders are essential. Artificial intelligence (AI) and other smart technologies that can self-monitor, analyze, and report can only be useful if they solve actual problems and satisfy actual demands. On the app, commuters can also recommend new routes, and operators can utilize the data to pinpoint demand regions and modify routes at affordable rates (Hasija et al., 2020)

Energy Efficiency: Sensor-based HVAC/lighting Control

To be able to cut down on the consumption of energy by enhancing the efficiency of the supply system, one of the important measures taken is the analysis of the present consumption pattern of energy in buildings. Since the demands being imposed on heating, ventilation and air conditioning (HVAC) systems in order to deliver the thermal comfort are geometrically rising, it is apparent that there is a necessity to reduce one of the driving factors of energy use.

In the literature, the following key stages are given:

1.With the assistance of certain simulations, design to estimate the energy performance.

2.Construction, checking of individual subsystems.

3.Operation, the building observation, acoustics and actuators control.

4.Maintenance, the infrastructure solutions were occasioned by energy deficiency.

5.Demolition, recycle waste, and workable. OECD 2004, (O'Sullivan et al., 2004)

Space Utilization: Reduce Wasted Space, Design Shared Zones

The visual appeal and general layout of cities are also influenced by space efficiency. Supertall skyscrapers can function as architectural monuments and produce unique skylines. Effectively planned skyscrapers enhance the city's character and allure, drawing tourists and raising real estate prices. All things considered, the sustainability and success of supertall skyscrapers depend heavily on space efficiency. These structures provide economic, social, and environmental advantages by maximizing vertical space and establishing multipurpose spaces, which can aid in tackling the problems associated with contemporary urbanization (Aragão, 2024)

Social & Employee Well-Being

Equity in Visibility: Ensure Remote workers get fair exposure

Working remotely has several advantages to both workers and employers and the environment. The positive effects are that employees can save money and time in not having to take long, stressful, and expensive commutes; less congestion on the road, motor vehicle crash, and personal auto emissions; firm and business cost-saving in terms of domestication; more productivity and employee retention; less micro aggression and prejudice; and that employees are given a better opportunity to balance family and employment responsibilities (Orr & Savage, 2021).

Burnout management: Detect work Overload via Digital Exhaustion patterns

AI emerged as an effective instrument in the treatment of burnout, providing a valuable set of data-based options in burnout monitoring and treatment of stress factors at a workplace. AI may be attached to different systems to capture patterns of working behaviour, anticipate early indicators of burnout, and offer related tips on how to manage workload. Machine learning algorithms have the capability to evaluate the significant data of task management programs, communication platforms and employee feedback systems and note warnings of burnout in real time. Through AI, organizations can apply specific interventions and provide support to employees before they fall into burnout and eventually improve the working environment (Smith, 2023)

Flexible Scheduling: AI supports diverse schedules and reduces conflicts

Artificial intelligence-based predictive scheduling allows real-time adjustments and optimization to current company changes, which leads to higher efficiency of its work. These technologies can enable businesses to act proactively to organisational challenges and reduce downtimes by responding to demand fluctuations, labour demands or unforeseen incident in a short period of time. The automation of the scheduling process with a possibility of AI algorithms used allows organisations to become more agile and resilient in their workforce management practices. This makes operations more smooth running and increases the customer satisfaction (Govindarajan & Ananthanpillai, 2023).

Health & Safety In AI Driven Workspaces

Contact tracing: Anonymized Office Occupancy Tracking

The use of contact tracing in some disease outbreaks has proved to be significantly effective and effective especially with SARS, MERS and Ebola (James et al., 2021). A contact tracking system is an instrument to help know whether one has been in contact with another infected individual. Contact tracing technologies have been considered by numerous studies in the past few years. Nevertheless, this issue has entered the gaze last year, primarily due to the COVID-19 outbreak. It had been stated that transmission contact is among the main causes of SARS-CoV-2 in spread. ITS is up to 23 percent (Hu et al., 2020)

Ventilation Monitoring for Indoor Air Quality

The great idea of smart ventilation is to utilize controls to ventilate more when it offers a benefit (or both) in terms of its energy and/or IAQ consequences and less when it offers a disadvantage. The basic aim of the concept is to save energy consumption and costs in ventilation as well as IAQ comparing to the continuously running one. Other nice ventilation control strategies rely on other pollutants, occupancy or outside temperature. In more recent years the issue of continuously emitted pollutants (e.g. VOCs, such as formaldehyde) implies that only occupant-related indicators can be deemed inadequate to manage smart ventilation strategies (Guyot et al., 2018)

Organizational And Societal Considerations

Ethics and Governance: Privacy: Anonymization, Differential Privacy

Depending on the amount of anonymity created over the data, and features cleaned up, there exist diverse anonymization algorithms. As an example, until the enumeration method may only be used on sequential attributes of a numeric value (e.g. IP address). Enumeration ranks the values of a feature in ascending order and assigns a larger value than original value. All the attributes can be subjected to this technique. Nonetheless, the findings by (Farah & Trajkovic,2013) are opposed to what the authors are saying. Differential privacy ensures that adding or dropping single record of database does not change the result of any analysis done to database significantly. The concept of maintaining the privacy of network traffic through noisy version to the correct answer is not something that is unique; but the method of adding noise is different in the case of differential privacy (Dwork, 2008)

Bias & Fairness: Audit ML Models for Demographic Fairness

The research communities of AI and Data Science have been attempting to answer these concerns by coming up with ways to identify bias and discrimination within the AI systems (Calders and Verwer, 2010). We think that proactive bias and fairness audits are a prerequisite to make informed model selection choice, learn more about the reasons behind bias in certain groups and establish trust in AI among general communities (Saleiro et al., 2018).

Transparency: Explainable AI, Employee Trust

AI systems must have transparency by all means as this determines accountability, fairness and trustworthiness. It means that decision-making processes and mechanisms of AI models should be rendered explainable and accessible by end-users and parties. As state, this happened to be a product replacement technique as the strategy of replacing a product that became aware by another one that did not. (Muthusubramanian et al., 2024). Transparency is the key to the successful development of trust and confidence in AI technologies. Transparency helps users determine the reliability, fairness and possible biases of an AI system and makes them understand how the models work and arrive at decisions. Moreover, the open AI systems also result in conformity to there are law and ethics, and safety concerns and unexpected outcomes of the algorithms (Floridi et al., 2018).

Change Management & Organizational Acceptance

Stakeholder Buy-in: HR, facilities, IT, Executive Sponsorship

Getting support from stakeholders is essential to making sure that new practices and programs mesh well with the systems in which they will be implemented. Several important lessons are noted, including the necessity of actively including community-based service providers in the planning phase as early as possible in the implementation process (Hickey et al., 2018)

Training: Managers and Employees in AI literacy

Understanding the fundamentals, uses, and ethical issues of artificial intelligence is the focus of

AI literacy, a subset of digital literacy. It entails not just being able to use AI tools efficiently but also having the ability to critically assess their results, comprehend their underlying workings, and consider the ethical and societal ramifications. According to (Lo, 2023) and (Cetindamar et al., 2022), operationalizing AI literacy for non-specialists is crucial because it is not limited to computer professionals.

9. POLICY COMPLIANCE & ESG ALIGNMENT

Data Protection Regulations: GDPR, LGPD, etc.)

The GDPR, which superseded Directive 95 and went into full force in 2018, was implemented in the European Union (EU) in response to calls for data protection in 2016 (Allen et al., 2019). The EU regularly broadens its data protection laws globally, and many nations use its standards as a template for data protection (Bygrave, 2021; Greenleaf & Cottier, 2022). In response, Brazil made the bold decision to enact the Brazilian General Data Protection Law (LGPD), which imitates the European data protection framework and will be completely implemented in August 2020, amidst the chaos generated by the Cambridge Analytica case in 2018 (Erickson, 2018).

Data protection regimes are not an exception to the rule that legal regimes naturally impact one another (Kennedy, 2003).

ESG Frameworks and AI Sustainability Metrics

The difficulty discussed in this article is that none of the current ESG standards, frameworks, or indicators adequately represent the nature of the sustainability-related implications of AI. The big tech and AI industries are not free from these expectations. As a result, businesses are not motivated to adequately assess and analyze these effects. At the same time, it permits businesses that are aware of adverse effects to withhold them (Sætra,2021). Although programs like the UN-initiated AI4Good, which aims to use AI to speed up work on the SDGs, are particularly interesting. More recently, work on AI targeted at the SDGs has been referred to as AI for social good (AI4SG) (Tomašev et al., 2020).

10. IMPLEMENTATION GUIDELINES FOR AI-ENABLED SUSTAINABILITY

Assessment Phase: Map Hybrid Practices, Metrics, Pain Points

A roadmap of the engagements anticipated to take place during a project with a flexibility focus is provided by the hybrid collaboration approach. There are two main components to this strategy:

(1) Looking at the flexibility project manager's top-down viewpoint;
(2) Obtaining data from actors who are close to the end consumers, such as neighborhood managers, from a bottom-up viewpoint.

The hybrid method reduces the risk of working in isolation by encouraging collaboration between the different participants to support the realization of the flexibility initiatives, in addition to its role in designing the engagement activities. Such relationship mapping should be regarded as a crucial point of reference for flexibility pilot demonstrations and can be utilized to pinpoint sites of interaction between players (Ilieva et al., 2025)

Identify Sustainability Goals (E.g., Reduce Emissions by X%)

The concept of economic, environmental, and social sustainability defines sustainable development. In a concise manner, for instance, it is possible to consider that economic and social sustainability can be treated, in the first instance, in terms of efficiency and safety, and environmental sustainability in terms of air pollution, even though there are numerous indicators with various objectives and results in the literature (Russo & Comi, 2012).

Finding policy interventions that have multiple benefits for climate and other developmental objectives is more important than ever as the world focuses on achieving the Sustainable Development Goals (SDGs). This is done in order to garner support for and guarantee the optimization of policies, projects, and programs, especially in developing nations (Cohen et al., 2021).

Pilot Design and Evaluation

Key Performance Indicators, or KPIs, are precise, measurable measures that are used to assess how well different organizational components are doing. KPIs monitor and evaluate how well strategic objectives and operational procedures are working (Malali, 2024)

Characteristics

Particulars: KPIs offer a clear and accurate assessment of performance.
Measurable: KPIs may be monitored over time and are quantifiable.
Actionable: KPIs offer information that may inspire particular choices or actions.
Relevant: KPIs have a direct bearing on thc aims and objectives of the company.
Time-Bound: KPIs, such daily, weekly, monthly, or quarterly, are measured over a predetermined time frame (Malali, 2024)

Define Data sources, Infrastructure

Although a data source, like the Landsat 7 sensor or a crime logging system, can provide multiple datasets, it can be represented in this model space in a manner akin to that of a single dataset. However, a data source may be represented as ranges along specified dimensions, specifying the possible values that a particular dataset may inherit, as opposed to being represented as a single point in model space (Adams & Gahegan, 2014).

Technical Development: Build Model Pipelines Ensuring Privacy

Combining an emphasis on striking a balance between innovation and strict privacy standards, this research attempts to investigate secure data pipeline designs designed for mobile LLMs. We thoroughly examine the most recent developments in safe data handling strategies and provide a framework that combines privacy-preserving learning strategies, cryptographic safeguards, and efficient on-device processing. Strong data encryption, both in transit and at rest, is the cornerstone of safe data pipelines (Wood et al., 2025).

At the various phases of the pipeline, there are chances to increase knowledge. The various steps that the data must go through in order to assist decision-making are referred to as the data pipeline. It can be loosely divided into three phases: Analysis, Cleaning, and Curation. The end-of-pipeline tools have only examined models that explain; they have not examined amplification. On the other hand, tools in early stages of the pipeline were primarily created for data scientists rather than specialists. But at every step of the workflow, domain experts are involved (Krishnan et al., 2016).

Validate with Domain Experts

A subsequent part discusses and relates the previous methods of test and model validation to BNs using examples from the airport's inbound passenger processing network. In addition to parameterization, model structure, node discretization, and overall model behavior must be taken into account when using this validity testing framework on BNs (Pitchforth & Mengersen, 2013).

Integrate ML predictions into decision systems

A subset of artificial intelligence, machine learning describes computer methods that enable the reproducible and standardized solution of challenging tasks. Machine learning integrates computer science, mathematics, and biostatistics into a single problem-solving process. Databases and contemporary hybrid algorithms can complete difficult and multifaceted tasks to assist clinicians in their day-to-day work as artificial intelligence-based decision-making technologies advance. The usage of contemporary machine learning algorithms in clinics will benefit from the application of "good machine learning principles" and increased collaboration between industries and healthcare professionals (Saravi et al., 2022).

Deployment & Change Management: Rollout phases: Pilot → Scale

In order to provide alternatives that enable sustainable change in the farming system, the pilot roll-out (PRO) phase of the research for development process is essential. The PRO's role is to create (Plan, Implement, Assess, and Enhance) a successful model for promoting possible innovations in the community.

PRO should be carried out at a scale that is manageable as an adaptive research effort while also promoting local adaptation of (technical) choices. With a first small-scale design phase and a second intermediate-scale pilot phase, it essentially suggests a two-season activity (van de Fliert et al., 2010)

Provide Explanation Interfaces

We created an explanation interface which will display the results of the system. This is the initial component of a wider explanation interface that can display various explanations and can fit various users. The purpose of the interface is to first send a message to the explainable model in order to fetch any relevant data and then receive communication with the user in order to convey specialised explanations. To date the interface is still fixed though there are already exploratory actions silhouetted here which is the various charts of the various properties. Findings are given in form of both pictures and narration. The explanations are also true in the sense of predictive model since they directly employ the output of the system to produce the explanations (Bellucci et al., 2022).

Training Guides and Continuous Monitoring

Training Guide is intended to assist those who conduct the training course of the Convention on the Rights of Persons with Disabilities along with its Optional Protocol. It is helpful as a basic information source on the instruments and can be used to develop training course on the Convention and / or Optional Protocol. The Training Guide encourages the use of interactive trainings, which are ideally suited when relatively small groups of no more than 20 people will take part in it, and includes a combination of a computer slide-show presentation and group activities aimed at stimulating conversation and sharing among the facilitator and participants as well as among the participants themselves.

Training guide is mainly aimed at training facilitators and others who are already familiar with the international human rights system and are tasked with training people on the convention on the Rights of Persons with Disabilities. Put differently, it is assumed that the Guide should presuppose possession of certain general knowledge on human rights standards, terms and mechanisms although not necessarily on the Convention per schedule. Training Guide also presupposes that any training course will be provided by a lead facilitator and, preferably, by his or her assistant (Guide, 2014)

Monitoring & Continuous Improvement: Track performance Vs Baseline

Our method's tracking procedure is really straightforward. We utilize the user-specified annotation to initialize the query in the first frame. The query is then fixed without being updated during the tracking process. We do a forward pass of QG-RPN and QG-RCNN using the query and the current picture as inputs in a fresh tracking frame. Lastly, the tracking result is taken directly from the top-1 prediction of QG-RCNN in this frame. There is no additional post-processing done. Even while our approach might perform better with some post-processing, like trajectory refinement or penalization on big state fluctuations, we would rather keep the current model uncomplicated and uncomplicated and save a more adaptive tracking model for our next projects (Huang et al., 2020)

11. MODEL ITERATION AND CONTINUOUS IMPROVEMENT

Iteration during modeling is to construct models that are variations of each other in regard to types of algorithms, feature sets and hyperparameters. Because a modeling session entails the construction of many tens and even hundreds of models, the two main purposes of an optimized-iteration system are as follows: (a) Ensure that it is inexpensive to perform modeling experiments (time- and computationally-wise); and (b) Must be able to use the system to control the process by tracking experiments and enabling meta-analysis (Vartak et al., 2015).

Particularly, a well-optimized system to iteration can be allowed to do the following:

Efficient Training of Multiple Models at Once

A majority of ML toolkits in current designs enable training of one model at a time. Under external libraries, users can possibly train a few models concurrently. Nevertheless, even out of the available tools, a small number of them compute optimizations to share the scans and the computation across several models. The benefits of this capability are self-explanatory: related models can be trained (as well as evaluated) in parallel instead of separately, e.g. using feature sets {A, B} and {A, B, C} respectively. Although the system could give up some latency to a certain degree, we will see this trade-off in hand as the higher throughput (Vartak et al., 2015).

Incremental Training and Reuse

The majority of models constructed by analysts are adaptations of previous ML models following the inclusion or exclusion of features or alteration of hyperparameters. Consequently, a system ought to be in a position to recycle information, e.g. model parameters (e.g. weight vectors), intermediate results, most pertinent data points etc., within already trained models in order to accelerate training of novel models. As an example, warm starts may allow a model to begin training with the output of a different model, previously trained, whereas boosting can be used to interpret to present the output of two already trained models. In a similar way, when models all run a common computationally inefficient intermediate step, then intermediate storage can be used to accelerate the training of new models (Vartak et al., 2015)

Fast Evaluation or Shortcut Evaluation

The reason is that due to the scale of experiments made by a data scientist, an assessment can just be fast and not precise enough in determining whether the user should also take time to run a complete experiment. Consequently, an iterative system must allow one to speedily estimate whether a possible refinement (e.g. new feature, new value of parameter) is likely to enhance a model. The specific methods of assisting rapid assessment are sample training and testing the model, determination of an approximation of the effect of the change with the help of an analytical method (Vartak et al., 2015)

History and Tracking of Models

One issue that has not been given much consideration in modeling is keeping track of each and every hypothesis that has been tested or model. Three-fold use of history is: (a) history may make it possible to optimize new models better during training, (b) history may permit the analyst to draw comparisons among models and notice patterns, and (c) once there is sufficient history, the system could potentially automate potentially some portion of the modeling process in the future (Vartak et al., 2015)

Human-in-the-Loop

The creativity, knowledge and ability to discover the patterns through the analyst takes a large portion of the modeling process. In order to facilitate the analyst a machine learning system should offer an opportunity to interact with the system on various stages. To take a concrete illustration, with the help of history mentioned in the preceding paragraphs, the system needs to provide the user with the capacity to readily browse and compare models that have been constructed in the past. Likewise, in models that involve a lot of time in training, the system should inform the user of progress and give him/her the opportunity to abort or modify models. Lastly, the system should also avail ways of diagnosing models and interpreting the results (Vartak et al., 2015)

12. FUTURE OUTLOOK: EMERGING AI CAPABILITIES

Generative AI for Coaching, Policy Drafting, Well-being Prompts

The surfacing of every new type of technology tends to scare people today, and the recent appearance, immense popularity and use of generative artificial intelligence have solidly followed the trend and increased the worldwide point of concern about it affecting individuals and society as a whole. The responses to the same are impulsive ranging between silent intrigues to unabashed panic (Kamau, 2025). Routine customer care tasks are automated by staff members using GenAI platforms like chatbots and virtual assistants. This entails processing orders, answering often requested inquiries, and offering standardized assistance. GenAI improves the productivity, learning, and creativity of frontline service employees while bringing new methods of communication, connection, and engagement with clients to the customer service industry (Feng et al., 2024).

Edge AI in wearable Devices for Real-time Ergonomic Monitoring

High-risk industries such as construction are of special concern with regards to this real-time tracking ability, manufacturing, mining, health, and logistics due to the fact that occupational hazards are generally guaranteed, and the current of preventive therapeutic measures is inevitable. This is due to the fact that (Suryawanshia et al., 2024; Patel et al., 2022). This has been changed with the help of the Workplace Safety situation. wearable sensors which have the potential of capturing a lot of information including the heart rate, temperature, etc., IoT, which has a wearable aspect, has also been used in risky workplaces. This is to monitor some environmental factors which are not beneficial to human beings such as; construction and mining. beings like; the quality of air, sound intensity and temperature. Simply that this has not been the trend in history, and that an organization as-theatre metaphor is ill adapted to the present. reality of production (Abbasi and Rasheed, 2024). The HR in the new AI-enabled HRM environment, HR executives are changing their leadership approaches to more flexible ones and providing. The workers are provided more autonomy that contributes to the enhancement of the channels of communication (Baruah et al., 2024)

13. CONCLUSION

In the evolving landscape of Industry 4.0, artificial intelligence has emerged as a transformative force in shaping the future of sustainable workforce management, particularly within hybrid work environments. This paper has examined how AI-driven technologies are enabling organizations to optimize performance, enhance employee well-being, and align with environmental, social, and governance (ESG) objectives. From predictive analytics and digital twins to real-time feedback systems and AI-powered nudges, these tools are fostering a shift from traditional workforce models to more flexible, inclusive, and resilient systems.

By integrating economic efficiency, environmental responsibility, and social equity, AI supports a triple-bottom-line approach to sustainability. Furthermore, the successful adoption of AI requires a commitment to ethical governance, transparency, and co-creation with the workforce. As hybrid work continues to redefine the norms of productivity and collaboration, AI will remain a central driver in enabling organizations to not only respond to present-day challenges but also to build future-ready, human-centered workplaces. Continued research and responsible innovation will be crucial in ensuring that AI contributes positively to both organizational outcomes and societal well-being.

REFERENCES

Abbasi, M. M. H., & Rasheed, M. R. (2024). Media for sustainable tourism growth in Pakistan: An analysis of traditional and new media channels. *Social Science Review Archives, 2*(2), 25–29.

. Adams, B., & Gahegan, M. (2014). Emerging data challenges for next-generation spatial data infrastructure. *Research@ Locate, 14,* 7-9.

Allen, D. W., Berg, A., Berg, C., Markey-Towler, B., & Potts, J. (2019). Some economic consequences of the GDPR. *Allen DWE, Berg A, Berg C, Markey-Towler B and Potts J (2019) 'Some Economic Consequences of the GDPR'. Economic Bulletin, 39*(2), 785–797. DOI: 10.2139/ssrn.3160404

Aragão, A. (2024). Towards a Typology of Imaginary Skyscrapers. In *Vision and Verticality: A Multidisciplinary Approach* (pp. 145–154). Springer International Publishing., DOI: 10.1007/978-3-031-39884-1_12

Ashby, A., Leat, M., & Hudson-Smith, M. (2012). Making connections: A review of supply chain management and sustainability literature. *Supply Chain Management, 17*(5), 497–516. DOI: 10.1108/13598541211258573

Baruah, A., Shaikh, M., Kumar, R. M., Shaikh, I. A. K., & Thomas, S. N. (2024, April). Artificial Intelligence Influence on Leadership Styles in Human Resource Management for Employee Engagement. In *2024 Ninth International Conference on Science Technology Engineering and Mathematics (ICONSTEM)* (pp. 1-5). IEEE. https://doi.org/DOI: 10.1109/ICONSTEM60960.2024.10568819

Bellucci, M., Delestre, N., Malandain, N., & Zanni-Merk, C. (2022). Combining an explainable model based on ontologies with an explanation interface to classify images. *Procedia Computer Science, 207*, 2395–2403. DOI: 10.1016/j.procs.2022.09.298

Bennett, T. M. (2009). *Development and performance of distributed teams: Examining differences between asynchronous and synchronous communication in planning task execution* (Doctoral dissertation, Capella University).

Bergefurt, L., van den Boogert, P. F., Appel-Meulenbroek, R., & Kemperman, A. (2024). The interplay of workplace satisfaction, activity support, and productivity support in the hybrid work context. *Building and Environment, 261*, 111729. DOI: 10.1016/j.buildenv.2024.111729

Bosse, S., & Pournaras, E. (2017, August). A ubiquitous multi-agent mobile platform for distributed crowd sensing and social mining. In *2017 IEEE 5th International Conference on Future Internet of Things and Cloud (FiCloud)* (pp. 280-287). IEEE. DOI: DOI: 10.1109/FiCloud.2017.44

Bouncken, R. B., & Reuschl, A. J. (2018). Coworking-spaces: How a phenomenon of the sharing economy builds a novel trend for the workplace and for entrepreneurship. *Review of Managerial Science, 12*, 317–334. DOI: 10.1007/s11846-016-0215-y

. Brînzea, V. M., & Oancea, O. (2022). The future of hybrid work in post-pandemic times. *Scientific Bulletin-Economic Sciences/Buletin Stiintific-Seria Ştiinţe Economice, 21.*

Bristol-Alagbariya, B., Ayanponle, O. L., & Ogedengbe, D. E. (2022). Integrative HR approaches in mergers and acquisitions ensuring seamless organizational synergies. *Magna Scientia Advanced Research and Reviews, 6*(1), 78–85.

Bygrave, L. A. (2021). The 'Strasbourg Effect' on data protection in light of the 'Brussels Effect': Logic, mechanics and prospects. *Computer Law & Security Review, 40*, 105460. DOI: 10.1016/j.clsr.2020.105460

Calders, T., & Verwer, S. (2010). Three naive bayes approaches for discrimination-free classification. *Data Mining and Knowledge Discovery, 21*, 277–292. DOI: 10.1007/s10618-010-0190-x

Cetindamar, D., Kitto, K., Wu, M., Zhang, Y., Abedin, B., & Knight, S. (2022). Explicating AI literacy of employees at digital workplaces. *IEEE Transactions on Engineering Management, 71*, 810–823. DOI: 10.1109/TEM.2021.3138503

Chattu, V. K. (2021). A review of artificial intelligence, big data, and blockchain technology applications in medicine and global health. *Big Data and Cognitive Computing, 5*(3), 41. DOI: 10.3390/bdcc5030041

Cohen, B., Cowie, A., Babiker, M., Leip, A., & Smith, P. (2021). Co-benefits and trade-offs of climate change mitigation actions and the Sustainable Development Goals. *Sustainable Production and Consumption, 26*, 805–813. DOI: 10.1016/j.spc.2020.12.034

Deepthi, P., Shaikh, M., Nargunde, A. S., Faldu, R., & Goli, G. (2024, April). Deep learning-enabled human resource analytics in predicting employee performance. In *2024 Ninth International Conference on Science Technology Engineering and Mathematics (ICONSTEM)* (pp. 1-5). IEEE.https://doi.org/DOI: 10.1109/ICONSTEM60960.2024.10568716

Dwork, C. (2008, April). Differential privacy: A survey of results. In *International conference on theory and applications of models of computation* (pp. 1-19). Berlin, Heidelberg: Springer Berlin Heidelberg. https://doi.org/DOI: 10.1007/978-3-540-79228-4_1

Eisenberger, R., Stinglhamber, F., Vandenberghe, C., Sucharski, I. L., & Rhoades, L. (2002). Perceived Supervisor Support. *The Journal of Applied Psychology, 87*(3), 565–573. https://psycnet.apa.org/doi/10.1037/0021-9010.87.3.565

Elumilade, O. O., Ogundeji, I. A., Achumie, G. O., Omokhoa, H. E., & Omowole, B. M. (2022). Optimizing corporate tax strategies and transfer pricing policies to improve financial efficiency and compliance. *Journal of Advance Multidisciplinary Research, 1*(2), 28–38. https://www.synstojournals.com/multi/article/view/147

Erickson, A. (2018). Comparative analysis of the EU's GDPR and Brazil's LGPD: Enforcement challenges with the LGPD. *Brooklyn Journal of International Law, 44*(2), 859–888. https://brooklynworks.brooklaw.edu/bjil/vol44/iss2/9

. Ernst, A. T., Jiang, H., Krishnamoorthy, M., Owens, B., & Sier, D. (2004a). An annotated bibliography of personnel scheduling and rostering. *Annals of Operations Research, 127,* 21–144.: ANOR.0000019087. 46656.e2DOI: <ALIGNMENT.qj></ALIGNMENT>10.1023/B

Ernst, A. T., Jiang, H., Krishnamoorthy, M., & Sier, D. (2004b). Staff scheduling and rostering: A review of applications, methods and models. *European Journal of Operational Research, 153*(1), 3–27. DOI: 10.1016/S0377-2217(03)00095-X

. Evangeline, B. J., & Raju, G. (2024). ENHANCING COLLABORATION AND EFFICIENCY: THE ROLE OF ARTIFICIAL INTELLIGENCE IN HYBRID WORKING ENVIRONMENT. *NCSBP'24.*

Fakhabi, M. M., Hamidian, S. M., & Aliehyaei, M. (2024). Exploring the role of the Internet of Things in green buildings. *Energy Science & Engineering, 12*(9), 3779–3822. DOI: 10.1002/ese3.1840

Farah, T., & Trajković, L. (2013, June). Anonym: A tool for anonymization of the Internet traffic. In *2013 IEEE International Conference on Cybernetics (CYBCO)* (pp. 261-266). IEEE. https://doi.org/DOI: 10.1109/CYBConf.2013.6617434

Feng, C. M., Botha, E., & Pitt, L. (2024). From HAL to GenAI: Optimizing chatbot impacts with CARE. *Business Horizons, 67*(5), 537–548. DOI: 10.1016/j.bushor.2024.04.012

Fisher, D. A., Seetoh, T., May-Lin, H. O., Viswanathan, S., Toh, Y., Yin, W. C., & Dempsey, M. (2013). Automated measures of hand hygiene compliance among healthcare workers using ultrasound: Validation and a randomized controlled trial. *Infection Control and Hospital Epidemiology*, *34*(9), 919–928. DOI: 10.1086/671738

Floridi, L., Cowls, J., Beltrametti, M., Chatila, R., Chazerand, P., Dignum, V., & Vayena, E. (2018). AI4People—an ethical framework for a good AI society: Opportunities, risks, principles, and recommendations. *Minds and Machines*, *28*, 689–707. DOI: 10.1007/s11023-018-9482-5

Govindarajan, S., & Ananthanpillai, B. (2023). IMPACT OF AI DRIVEN PREDICTIVE SCHEDULING ON EMPLOYEES ENGAGEMENT AND PRODUCTIVITY. https://doi.org/DOI: 10.17605/OSF.IO/RM6DS

Greenleaf, G., & Cottier, B. (2022). International and regional commitments in African data privacy laws: A comparative analysis. *Computer Law & Security Review*, *44*, 105638. DOI: 10.1016/j.clsr.2021.105638

Guide, T. (2014). *The convention on the rights of persons with disabilities*. United Nations of Human Rights.

Guyot, G., Sherman, M. H., & Walker, I. S. (2018). Smart ventilation energy and indoor air quality performance in residential buildings: A review. *Energy and Building*, *165*, 416–430. DOI: 10.1016/j.enbuild.2017.12.051

Hamon, R., Junklewitz, H., & Sanchez, I. (2020). Robustness and explainability of artificial intelligence. *Publications Office of the European Union*, *207*(40), 2020. DOI: 10.2760/57493

Hasija, S., Shen, Z. J. M., & Teo, C. P. (2020). Smart city operations: Modeling challenges and opportunities. *Manufacturing & Service Operations Management*, *22*(1), 203–213. DOI: 10.1287/msom.2019.0823

Hickey, G., McGilloway, S., O'Brien, M., Leckey, Y., Devlin, M., & Donnelly, M. (2018). Strengthening stakeholder buy-in and engagement for successful exploration and installation: A case study of the development of an area-wide, evidence-based prevention and early intervention strategy. *Children and Youth Services Review*, *91*, 185–195. DOI: 10.1016/j.childyouth.2018.06.008

Hu, Z., Song, C., Xu, C., Jin, G., Chen, Y., Xu, X., & Shen, H. (2020). Clinical characteristics of 24 asymptomatic infections with COVID-19 screened among close contacts in Nanjing, China. *Science China. Life Sciences*, *63*, 706–711. DOI: 10.1007/s11427-020-1661-4

Huang, L., Zhao, X., & Huang, K. (2020, April). Global track: A simple and strong baseline for long-term tracking. In *Proceedings of the AAAI conference on artificial intelligence* (Vol. 34, No. 07, pp. 11037-11044). https://doi.org/ . v34i07.6758DOI: 10.1609/aaai

Ilgin, E., & Aslantamer, Ö. N. (2024). Comparative analysis of space efficiency in contemporary tall buildings: Residential, office, hotel and mixed-use functions. *International Journal of Architectural Engineering Technology, 11*, 60–79. DOI: 10.15377/2409-9821.2024.11.4

Ilieva, I., Matthews, R., Tobin, P., Valor, C., Moreno, V. K., & Ruiz, L. (2025). Adaptable customer engagement strategy for utilising energy flexibility. *International Journal of Sustainable Energy Planning and Management, 44*, 30–46. DOI: 10.54337/ijsepm.8521

Ipsen, C., Kirchner, K., Andersone, N., & Karanika-Murray, M. (2022). Becoming a Distance Manager: Managerial Experiences, Perceived Organizational Support, and Job Satisfaction During the COVID-19 Pandemic. *Frontiers in Psychology, 13*(916234), 1–11. DOI: 10.3389/fpsyg.2022.916234

Jahun, I., Said, I., El-Imam, I., Ehoche, A., Dalhatu, I., Yakubu, A., Greby, S., Bronson, M., Brown, K., Bamidele, M., & Boyd, A. T. (2021). Optimizing community linkage to care and antiretroviral therapy Initiation: Lessons from the Nigeria HIV/AIDS Indicator and Impact Survey (NAIIS) and their adaptation in Nigeria ART Surge. *PLoS One, 16*(9), e0257476. DOI: 10.1371/journal.pone.0257476

James, A., Plank, M. J., Hendy, S., Binny, R., Lustig, A., Steyn, N., & Verrall, A. (2021). Successful contact tracing systems for COVID-19 rely on effective quarantine and isolation. *PLoS One, 16*(6), e0252499. DOI: 10.1371/journal.pone.0252499

Kadioglu, M. A., & Alatas, B. (2023). Enhancing Call Center Efficiency: Data Driven Workload Prediction and Workforce Optimization. *The Eurasia Proceedings of Science Technology Engineering and Mathematics, 24*, 96–100. DOI: 10.55549/epstem.1406245

Kadioglu, M. A., & Takci, H. (2022). A data science project management methodology: From development to production (p.2). *Proceedings Book 2*

Kamau, J. N. (2025). Generative Artificial Intelligence and Mental Well-Being of University Students. A Structural Equation Modeling (SEM) Based-Analysis. African. *Journal of Business and Development Studies, 1*(2), 344–358. DOI: 10.70641/ajbds.v1i2.135

Kaur, M. P., Smith, S., Pazour, J. A., & Schumacher, A. D. (2022). Optimization of volunteer task assignments to improve volunteer retention and nonprofit organizational performance. *Socio-Economic Planning Sciences*, *84*, 101392. DOI: 10.1016/j.seps.2022.101392

Kennedy, D. (2003). The methods and the politics. In Legrand, P., & Munday, R. (Eds.), *Comparative legal studies: Traditions and transitions* (1st ed., pp. 345–434). Cambridge University Press., DOI: 10.1017/CBO9780511522260.011

Krishnan, S., Haas, D., Franklin, M. J., & Wu, E. (2016, June). Towards reliable interactive data cleaning: A user survey and recommendations. In *Proceedings of the Workshop on Human-In-the-Loop Data Analytics* (pp. 1-5). https://doi.org/DOI: 10.1145/2939502.2939511

Lee, D., & Lee, S. T. (2023). Artificial intelligence enabled energy-efficient heating, ventilation and air conditioning system: Design, analysis and necessary hardware upgrades. *Applied Thermal Engineering*, *235*, 121253. DOI: 10.1016/j.applthermaleng.2023.121253

Lee, S. H., Peña-Mora, F., & Park, M. (2006). Dynamic planning and control methodology for strategic and operational construction project management. *Automation in Construction*, *15*(1), 84–97. DOI: 10.1016/j.autcon.2005.02.008

Lo, L. S. (2023). The art and science of prompt engineering: A new literacy in the information age. *Internet Reference Services Quarterly*, *27*(4), 203–210. DOI: 10.1080/10875301.2023.2227621

Maertz, C. P.Jr, Griffeth, R. W., Campbell, N. S., & Allen, D. G. (2007). The effects of perceived organizational support and perceived supervisor support on employee turnover. *Journal of Organizational Behavior: The International Journal of Industrial. Occupational and Organizational Psychology and Behavior*, *28*(8), 1059–1075. DOI: 10.1002/job.472

. Malali, N. (2024). Digital Transformation in the Age of AI: Contact Center and Back Office Transformation.

Morariu, C., Morariu, O., Răileanu, S., & Borangiu, T. (2020). Machine learning for predictive scheduling and resource allocation in large scale manufacturing systems. *Computers in Industry*, *120*, 103244. DOI: 10.1016/j.compind.2020.103244

Moussy, C., Burfield, I. J., Stephenson, P. J., Newton, A. F., Butchart, S. H., Sutherland, W. J., & Donald, P. F. (2022). A quantitative global review of species population monitoring. *Conservation Biology*, *36*(1), e13721. DOI: 10.1111/cobi.13721

Muthusubramanian, M., Jangoan, S., Sharma, K. K., & Krishnamoorthy, G. (2024). Demystifying explainable AI: Understanding, transparency and trust. *International Journal for Multidisciplinary Research, 6*(2), 1–13. DOI: 10.36948/ijfmr.2024.v06i02.14597

Nuswantoro, B., Richter, A., & Riemer, K. (2023). Conceptualizing visibility in hybrid work. https://doi.org/DOI: 10.25455/wgtn.27092125

O'Sullivan, D. T. J., Keane, M. M., Kelliher, D., & Hitchcock, R. J. (2004). Improving building operation by tracking performance metrics throughout the building lifecycle (BLC). *Energy and Building, 36*(11), 1075–1090. DOI: 10.1016/j.enbuild.2004.03.003

Oben, U. F., Gozukara, E., & Tezcan, L. (2022). The Moderating Roles of Remote, Hybrid, and Onsite Working on the Relationship between Work Engagement and Organizational Identification during the COVID-19 Pandemic. *Sustainability, 14*(24), 16828. DOI: 10.3390/su142416828

Orr, A. E., & Savage, T. (2021). Expanding access to and ensuring equity in the benefits of remote work following the COVID-19 pandemic. *Journal of Science Policy & Governance, 18*(4), 1–8. DOI: 10.38126/JSPG180413

Patel, V., Chesmore, A., Legner, C. M., & Pandey, S. (2022). Trends in workplace wearable technologies and connected-worker solutions for next-generation occupational safety, health, and productivity. *Advanced Intelligent Systems, 4*(1), 2100099. DOI: 10.1002/aisy.202100099

Pitchforth, J., & Mengersen, K. (2013). A proposed validation framework for expert elicited Bayesian Networks. *Expert Systems with Applications, 40*(1), 162–167. DOI: 10.1016/j.eswa.2012.07.026

Pittet, D. (2008). Hand hygiene: It's all about when and how. *Infection Control and Hospital Epidemiology, 29*(10), 957–959. DOI: 10.1086/592218

Ramkumar, G., Sujatha, V., & Raja, B., TamilSelvi, M., Balaji, A., & Kumar, A. K. (2023, November). An Experiment to Develop an Enhanced Medical Image Security by using Deep Learning Assisted Crypto Policy. In 2023 *International Conference on Research Methodologies in Knowledge Management, Artificial Intelligence and Telecommunication Engineering (RMKMATE)* (pp. 1-8). IEEE.https://doi.org/ DOI: 10.1109/RMKMATE57356.2023.10123456

Rasheed, A., San, O., & Kvamsdal, T. (2019). Digital twin: Values, challenges and enablers. *arXiv preprint arXiv:1910.01719*. https://doi.org//arXiv.1910.01719DOI: 10.48550

Reddy, M. S., Deepthi, S., Bhattaru, S., Srilakshmi, V., & Singh, H. (2024). Harmony in HR: Exploring the Synergy of Artificial Intelligence and Green Practices for Sustainable Workplaces". In *MATEC Web of Conferences* (Vol. 392, p. 01039). EDP Sciences. https://doi.org/DOI: 10.1051/matecconf/202439201039

Russo, F., & Comi, A. (2012). City characteristics and urban goods movements: A way to environmental transportation system in a sustainable city. *Procedia: Social and Behavioral Sciences*, *39*, 61–73. DOI: 10.1016/j.sbspro.2012.03.091

Sætra, H. S. (2021). A Framework for Evaluating and Disclosing the ESG Related Impacts of AI with the SDGs. *Sustainability*, *13*(15), 8503. DOI: 10.3390/su13158503

Şahin, Y., & Dogru, İ. (2023). An enterprise data privacy governance model: Security-centric multi-model data anonymization. *International Journal of Engineering Research and Development*, *15*(2), 574–583. DOI: 10.29137/umagd.1272085

Saleiro, P., Kuester, B., Hinkson, L., London, J., Stevens, A., Anisfeld, A., . . . Ghani, R. (2018). Aequitas: A bias and fairness audit toolkit. *arXiv preprint arXiv:1811.05577.* https://doi.org//arXiv.1811.05577DOI: 10.48550

Saravi, B., Hassel, F., Ülkümen, S., Zink, A., Shavlokhova, V., Couillard-Despres, S., & Lang, G. M. (2022). Artificial intelligence-driven prediction modeling and decision making in spine surgery using hybrid machine learning models. *Journal of Personalized Medicine*, *12*(4), 509. DOI: 10.3390/jpm12040509

Sekaran, K., & Shanmugam, S. (2022, March). Interpreting the factors of employee attrition using explainable AI. In 2022 *International Conference on Decision Aid Sciences and Applications (DASA)* (pp. 932-936). IEEE. https://doi.org/DOI: 10.1109/DASA54658.2022.9765067

. Smith, H. K. (2023). AI-Powered Burnout Management: Designing Unified Systems to Monitor and Optimize Work Patterns in IT Teams.

Soomro, K., Bhutta, M. N. M., Khan, Z., & Tahir, M. A. (2019). Smart city big data analytics: An advanced review. *Wiley Interdisciplinary Reviews. Data Mining and Knowledge Discovery*, *9*(5), e1319. DOI: 10.1002/widm.1319

Suryawanshia, S., Bhosale, D., Vishwakarma, S., Patila, K., Harwania, V., & Bhosalec, A. (2024). A Comprehensive Survey on Smart Wearables: Real-time Health and Workplace Monitoring, Alerting, and Analysis in the Industrial Context. *Transactions C: Aspects, 37(12)*, 2473.

Tomašev, N., Cornebise, J., Hutter, F., Mohamed, S., Picciariello, A., Connelly, B., & Clopath, C. (2020). AI for social good: Unlocking the opportunity for positive impact. *Nature Communications*, *11*(1), 2468. DOI: 10.1038/s41467-020-15871-z

Triansyah, F. A., Hejin, W., & Stefania, S. (2023). Factors affecting employee performance: A systematic review. *Journal Markcount Finance, 1*(3), 150–159. DOI: 10.55849/jmf.v1i2.102

Usman, M., Srivastava, P., Fatma, A., & Devi, M. K. (2025). AI-Based Forecasting of Staffing Requirements Using Market and Business Trend Data. *International Journal (Toronto, Ont.), 9*(5).

van de Fliert, E., Christiana, B., Hendayana, R., & Murray-Prior, R. (2010). Pilot Roll-out: Adaptive Research in Farmers' Worlds. *Extension Farming Systems Journal, 6*(1), 63–71. DOI: 10.3316/479036039691084

Vartak, M., Ortiz, P., Siegel, K., Subramanyam, H., Madden, S., & Zaharia, M. (2015). Supporting fast iteration in model building. In *NIPS Workshop Learnings* (pp. 1-6).

. Vladimirovna, C. A. (2024). Impact of Job-Related Factors on Employee Loyalty in a Hybrid Setup: Comparison of Russian and Chinese Employees in Russian Consulting.

Wang, C., Jiang, W., Yang, K., Yu, D., Newn, J., Sarsenbayeva, Z., & Kostakos, V. (2021). Electronic monitoring systems for hand hygiene: Systematic review of technology. *Journal of Medical Internet Research, 23*(11), e27880. DOI: 10.2196/27880

. Wood, P., Mitchell, J., Ward, H., & William, E. (2025). Secure Data Pipelines for Mobile LLMs: Balancing Innovation and Privacy.

Yang, C. H., Lee, K. C., & Chen, H. C. (2016). Incorporating carbon footprint with activity-based costing constraints into sustainable public transport infrastructure project decisions. *Journal of Cleaner Production, 133*, 1154–1166. DOI: 10.1016/j.jclepro.2016.06.014

Yue, L., Song, L., Zhu, S., Fu, X., Li, X., He, C., & Li, J. (2024). Machine learning assisted rational design of antimicrobial peptides based on human endogenous proteins and their applications for cosmetic preservative system optimization. *Scientific Reports, 14*(1), 947. DOI: 10.1038/s41598-023-50832-8

Ződi, Z. (2022). Algorithmic explainability and legal reasoning. *The Theory and Practice of Legislation, 10*(1), 67–92. DOI: 10.1080/20508840.2022.2033945

KEY TERMS AND DEFINITION

Artificial Intelligence: It refers to the development of the computer systems that can able to perform tasks which typically requires human intelligence like creative thinking, problem-solving, and decision-making.

Employee Well-being: It refers to the holistic health of the employees, confining their physical, mental, and emotional states within the workplace.

Hybrid Workplaces: It combines traditional in-office work with remote work by allowing the employees flexibility in choosing their work location. It blends both remote work with periodic visits to the office for collaboration, and offering a combination of both on-site and remote work options.

Predictive Analytics: It is a field that uses both historical and current data to forecast the future events. It supports the techniques like data mining, machine learning, and statistical modeling to identify the patterns and trends which helps to predict what might happen next.

Sustainable Workforce Management: It focuses more on creating a working environment that prioritizes the employee well-being, promotes diversity and inclusion, and ensures ethical labor practices while minimizing the environmental impact in the organization.

Technology: Technology is the practical application of the scientific knowledge, tools, and techniques in order to create solutions to solve the problems or improve human life.

Chapter 6

AI-Driven Feedback System for Remote Work Performance Analysis

Lakshmi Harika Palivela
https://orcid.org/0000-0002-3373-2991
Vellore Institute of Technology, Chennai, India

P. Pradyumna Sriram
Vellore Institute of Technology, Chennai, India

Ancy Micheal
https://orcid.org/0009-0008-7065-7450
UCSI University, Kuala Lumpur, Malaysia

ABSTRACT

Remote and hybrid work models have significantly altered the operational dynamics of organizations, thereby resulting in challenges related to performance management. Traditional evaluation methods have been found to be ineffective as a result of limited supervision and complicated remote situations. This model utilizes machine learning to automatically generate performance reports based on the data. The system employs an ensemble of Logistic Regression, Random Forest, and Gradient Boosting. After being trained on 100,000 employee records consisting of various indicators, the system achieved accuracies of 94.44% (Gradient Boosting), 60.27% (Random Forest), and 29.68% (Logistic Regression) respectively, thus demonstrating the effectiveness of gradient-based methods.The system measures the performance of the employee along seven different dimensions, namely work arrangement, workload, development, engagement, project complexity, work-life balance, and career progression, and accordingly generates personalized recommendations.

DOI: 10.4018/979-8-3373-5871-0.ch006

...t © 2026, IGI Global Scientific Publishing. Copying or distributing in print or electronic forms without written permission of IGI Global Scientific Publishing is prohibited. Use of this chapter to ...enerative artificial intelligence (AI) technologies is expressly prohibited. The publisher reserves all rights to license its use for generative AI training and machine learning model development.

1. INTRODUCTION

1.1 Background and Motivation

The world of work has been redefined drastically due to the introduction of remote and hybrid employment. Fueled by technological progress and new developments worldwide, companies are now dealing with geographically dispersed teams and teams in which virtual teamwork has taken the place of the conventional face-to-face communication. This change has completely transformed the way companies take up performance management and staff assessment.

The traditional performance evaluation methods, which are largely grounded on being able to observe the employee directly, following time, and being physically present does not work in remote work situations. When the employees have different schedules and work in various locations, the managers have difficulties in measuring productivity, engagement, and the quality of contribution. Lack of informal communication and physical signs that are inherent in physical offices produces information voids that make proper evaluation of performance very difficult.

The studies show that remote work brings about distinct challenges: it is characterized by the different rates of work-life fusion, the quality of workspaces at home, communication and teamwork problems, and even isolation. These are factors that have a direct influence on employee performance but have not been measured using a standard measure. The companies need advanced, data-centered solutions allowing them to consider various performance aspects at the same time and take into account the peculiarities of the remote working setups.

Machine Learning and Artificial Intelligence can be used to address these issues in a potent manner. With the help of extensive datasets that include various performance metrics, the ML algorithms will be able to detect the trends that cannot be known by human eyes, forecast the performance trends, and provide specific insights. This data driven model facilitates objective, uniform assessment of distributed workforces, as well as proactive intervention to improve the success of employees.

1.2 Problem Statement

Companies that deal with remote and hybrid workforces have serious issues:

1. Visibility Gap in Performance: In remote environments, performance cannot be monitored directly, so it is hard to estimate the productivity of the employees, the quality of their work, and their contribution. Conventional measures are unable to capture the entire range of effectiveness of remote work.

2. Absence of Predictive Relationships: Existing systems offer retrospective reporting yet cannot predict impending trends in performance, forecast at-risk employees or high potential employees in advance of a formal review process.
3. Generic Feedback Mechanisms: The current feedback systems provide general recommendations, which cannot be programmed to consider personal work arrangements, the stage of career, or individual circumstances and make them less effective and less relevant.
4. The issue of subjectivity in Evaluation: Manual performance evaluation is prone to cognitive bias, unequal responses, and interpretations, which result in unfair evaluation and decline in the level of employee trust.
5. Delayed Intervention: Organizations that do not track the performance performance in real-time are likely to notice problems in the periodic reviews, and they would not get a chance to offer support and take corrective measures in a timely manner.

These problems cause significant expenses: less production, lower employee satisfaction, high turnover, and optimal talent management decisions. Organizations must have smart systems that give objective, real time and actionable information on the performance of remote workforce.

1.3 Objectives

The current project has the following specific objectives of designing an AI-Driven Feedback System:

Primary Objectives:

i. Create Good Prediction Models: Run and compare several machine learning models (Logistic Regression, Random Forest, Gradient Boosting) to achieve high-accuracy predictions of the performance of employees, and select the best model.
ii. Design Smart Feedback Generation: Design a more detailed feedback system that examines seven key dimensions (work arrangement, workload, development, engagement, complexity, work-life balance, career progression) and provides individualized and actionable feedback.
iii. Design Intuitive Graphical Interface: Design user-friendly interface that allows HR professionals and managers to input employee information without technical skills, make predictions, and read elaborate feedback reports.
iv. Secondary Objectives:

v. Ensure System Scalability: Architecture that is capable of accommodating large number of employees and supporting organizational expansion without compromising on its performance.
vi. Verify Model Effectiveness: Perform intensive testing to determine the accuracy of the predictions made by the model, the significance of the features and the ease of use of the system using standardized measures and user feedback.
vii. Offer Data-driven Insights: empower organizations to come up with evidenced-based decisions as far as performance management, resource allocation, and employee development initiatives are concerned.
viii. Support Multiple Work Arrangements: Make sure that the system successfully analyzes performance of office-based, hybrid, and fully remote work arrangements, understanding the distinction of each of them.

1.4 Scope and Limitations

Scope:

This system accomplishes multi, facet employee performance prediction through ensemble machine learning models, bolstered by multi, dimensional feedback analysis that reflects work arrangements, workload, professional development, engagement, task complexity, worklife balance, and career, related factors. It features an interactive GUI for data input and model selection, as well as automated report generation for decision, making facilitation. The model encompasses 12 core performance features, such as employee satisfaction levels, training hours, project performance, and work patterns. Moreover, it can be introduced without retraining, yet it also provides model persistence with the possibility of retraining if needed. Besides, the system is equipped with analytics dashboards and feature, importance visualizations to provide an unambiguous understanding of performance drivers and model outcomes.

Limitations:

i. Dependency on data sets: The accuracy of the model is determined by the quality and representativeness of the training data. The performance can be affected by the various organizational situations or industries.
ii. Features Constraints: The system uses 12 predetermined features; other organizational-specific measures will need retraining of models and architectural adjustments.
iii. Binary Classification: There is currently no multi-class performance classification (high/low), but binary performance classification (high/low) is implemented.

iv. Limitations on Feedback Rules: Feedback is derived based on structured logic; it is not based on natural language processing or adaptive learning as interactions with users transpire.
v. Focus on Historical Data: The system uses the historical and current data but it does not take into consideration the external factors such as market conditions, organizational changes, and team dynamics.
vi. Single User Interface: The GUI is based on single-session analysis; the GUI does not include such enterprise capabilities as user authentication, access control by roles, or teamwork.

1.5 Conceptualmodel

Our model illustrates how operational constructs are linked to the Performance score (1-5): Work Arrangement (Remote Work Frequency) indicates changes in collaboration and flexibility; Workload and Capacity (Projects Handled, Work Hours, Overtime) reveal employee bandwidth and burnout risk; Development and Growth (Training Hours, Promotions) describe skill acquisition and career progression; Engagement (Employee Satisfaction Score) mirrors motivation and the willingness to put in extra effort; Health and Sustainability (Sick Days) stand for the general health of employees; Experience and Context (Years at Company, Team Size, Monthly Salary) show organizational knowledge and the collaboration environment. Seven directional hypotheses are part of our conceptual model, including a positive relationship between satisfaction and training (with plateaus), a negative impact of extreme overtime, benefits of a balanced project load, tenure with diminishing returns, an arrangement effect in a non-linear way favoring hybrid, and team size effects that increase ownership up to a certain point.

Illustrative examples

A model profile of a high-performing (hybrid) employee with balanced hours (40), moderate projects (25), manageable overtime (10), robust training (40), and satisfaction (4.0) indicates a 4/5 prediction; the explanations emphasize the positive contribution to performance of satisfaction, training, and workload balance, while the recommendations include leadership opportunities and continuous development.

An at-risk remote profile with a heavy workload (projects 38), very high overtime (26), low training (6), and low satisfaction (2.6) is forecasted 2/5; the explanations focus on the negative factors that drive the prediction and advise the reduction of the workload, coaching, targeted upskilling, and, if possible, the shift to hybrid for collaboration gains.

A developing office profile with a moderate workload (projects 14), a modest overtime (8), and low training (8) is predicted 3/5; the explanations reveal potential uplift through training and scoped project complexity, thus recommending mentorship and satisfaction monitoring.

These examples reveal the face validity of the cases and the ethical manner of the model outputs that can be turned into actionable .

2. LITERATURE SURVEY

The present business and organizational management environment are going to be wildly different in the very near future as a result of the merger of Artificial Intelligence (AI), Machine Learning (ML), and advanced data analytics. Across the board, researchers and industry pundits proclaim that the mentioned technologies are changing the performance management, remote work, employee engagement, and strategic decision-making dramatically. The literature on AI reckons that the effectiveness of AI-driven analytics and their forecasting power cannot be underestimated, yet the final outcome would be a synergy of the most excellent technological and ethical, humanistic, and value-based perspectives.

By moving through AI, ML, and deep learning structures, methods, and applications, Rane et al. (2024) envision the future of these technologies in business strategies, forecasting, and employee evaluation. The authors assert that intelligent systems can be the source of real-time performance feedback, be the forerunner of strategic innovation, and be the instrument for professional development personalization. Next, Pereira et al. (2024) and Al-Issawi (2024) confirm this statement that the use of AI-based systems leads to high decision-making accuracy and mitigates bias in performance appraisals but at the same time point to ethical issues and the danger of losing the human touch if the management process is overly automated.

Most of the articles are about how AI could be used in performance analysis and appraisal systems. Fan (2022) offers the idea of clustering algorithms that can ensure that employee evaluations are just and trustworthy since behavior and quantitative metrics are both considered. In the same way, Magesh et al. (2013) and Basnet (2024) suggest the use of decision tree and backpropagation algorithms for predictive models that will open up the data and provide the workforce productivity management with objective, data-driven insights. Prem (2024) and Mourad et al. (2024) are even more vocal in this respect as they propose hybrid models that both predict and use fuzzy logic, thus achieving a more open and understandable decision framework in the organizational context. All these works are indicative of a trend towards embracing analytical management techniques which favor the use of evidence for judgment rather than relying on subjective intuition.

The topic of evolution of remote and hybrid work environments is another significant issue of recent articles. The work of Emanuel and Harrington (2024) is centered around the changes in the labor market caused by remote work. They found that while flexibility is a powerful tool for the attraction and keeping of talent, it makes the setting up of remuneration structures more complex. Celestin and Sujatha (2024) are of the view that digital collaboration tools, which gain support from an AI-powered monitoring system, are indispensable for the establishment of uniformity and trust in teams that are geographically apart. Rustan et al. (2024) and Cornelia and Nasution (2024) delve into the psychosocial aspects of telecommuting and identify that although the flexibility that comes with it leads to increased autonomy, it can also cause escalation in family conflict and digital fatigue if the work-life balance is not well managed.

Bhattacharya (2024) and Baharm et al. (2024) argue that in a virtual world, leadership changes depend largely on the leader's capability to adapt, and thus technology needs to be accompanied by empathy and trust-building for effective communication. Hasan et al. (2024) also maintain that AI-powered productivity tools should be used as a means of employee empowerment and not for surveillance if the goal is to keep morale and engagement at a high level.

Madhumithaa et al. (2025) and Fatima et al. (2024) signify the role that AI can play in employee learning and motivation by introducing smart systems that include adaptive algorithms for reskilling. Their research sheds light on the fact that employee engagement serves as a vital link between the implementation of technology and the triumph of the overall organizational structure. The very connection reveals that innovation in human resource practices calls for the synergy of digital intelligence and human sensitivity.

On a large-scale economic and policy level, Filippucci et al. (2024) and the OECD (2024) delve into the impacts of AI integration on productivity, income distribution, and workforce dynamics. They advocate that fostering growth that can be sustained will necessitate not only well-thought-out policies but also the reskilling of the labor force to counter the emergence of a new technological divide. Kumar (2025) takes this conversation further by adding AI to research methods and calling for ethical data handling and algorithmic transparency.

One of the biggest challenges in the interpretability of AI systems is at the core of concerns in their implementation research. Ponce-Bobadilla et al. (2024) underline the crucial role of explainable AI (XAI) in fairness, accountability, and openness in decision-making in organizations. Al Naqbi et al. (2024) and Sadeghi (2024) being equally concerned, point to the creative and ethical side of generative AI tools and argue that organizations should not only seek to benefit from the innovation but also comply with the set regulations and maintain the moral side of it.

The collective pool of writings points to AI and ML as main agents changing the whole landscape of performance management through the use of data and the resulting strategic agility. Template remote and hybrid work environments have a huge impact on the definition of productivity, thus calling for policies that are flexible and leadership that is empathetic. The main point that is repeated from one research paper to another is that the long-term successful implementation of AI-led changes does not depend on technological excellence alone but on the organization's commitment to openness, inclusiveness, and respect of human principles at every stage of digital decision-making.

3. PROPOSED SYSTEM

3.1 Development Environment

For the best experience, the hardware configuration can be an Intel Core i5 or AMD Ryzen 5 processor (or better), 8 GB DDR4 RAM, and a 256 GB SSD with at least 50 GB of free storage. In order to have the system running smoothly and to be able to see the graphical user interface in its full capabilities, a Full HD display (1920 1080 resolution) is necessary.

Table 1. Software Stack

Component	Technology	Version	Purpose
Programming Language	Python	3.12.4	Core development language
ML Framework	scikit-learn	1.5.2	Model training and prediction
Data Processing	pandas	2.2.2	Dataset manipulation
Numerical Computing	numpy	1.26.4	Mathematical operations
Visualization	matplotlib	3.10.6	Data visualization
Statistical Plotting	seaborn	0.13.2	Enhanced visualizations
Model Persistence	joblib	1.4.2	Model serialization
GUI Framework	Tkinter	Built-in	User interface
IDE	VS Code	Latest	Development environment
Version Control	Git	2.40+	Code management

The development strategy utilizes separation of concerns that have been divided into modules so as to be able to maintain and grow. The project implements incremental development with continuous testing in order to be able to raise its level of trust at each stage of the project.

3.1.2 Feature operationalization

Our main variable is Performance_Score (1–5) made from past appraisal records and treated as a stable multiclass problem with multinomial log-loss. The 12 explanatory variables are operational HR metrics: Age (years), Years_At_Company (years), Monthly_Salary (USD/month), Work_Hours_Per_Week (hours/week), Projects_Handled (count; capped at 50 to reduce outliers), Overtime_Hours (extra hours/week), Sick_Days (days/year), Remote_Work_Frequency (0/25/50/75/100 percent; used numerically while the categorical Work_Mode derived from it is reserved for analytics to avoid leakage), Team_Size (count), Training_Hours (hours/year), Promotions (count), and Employee_Satisfaction_Score (Likert 1.0–5.0 from engagement surveys).

For the rare missing values, we use mean/mode imputation, standardize features where it is necessary in the pipeline, limit the extreme project counts, and apply a stratified 80/20 split to keep the class.

3.2 Data Preprocessing

It is done using the following constructive steps.

3.2.1 Loading and Validating The Data

To load and validate the data into a Pandas DataFrame, the process will start with loading a CSV data file from storage. After importing all necessary libraries for accessing and loading the data, the data will be read into the pandas library using the standard method provided for reading a CSV format file. Once the data has been located and loaded successfully, you will receive a notification and the data will then be suitable for processing. If the data file is not found, or is not able to be read, an error message will be returned and the loading process will stop.

3.2.2 Missing Values

You will use the methods below to clean and process the raw data into a cleaned data set by managing how to handle missing values in both types of data: numbers (numerical) and text (categorical).. Numerical missing values will be filled in by replacing these values with the average (mean) of the numerical values in that row. Missing Categorical value will be filled in by replacing these values with the most commonly occurring (mode) categorical value. The rows in which missing value percentages are greater than or equal to 30% will be removed as they may significantly degrade the quality of data. The Cleaned Data set produced will be passed on for use in subsequent steps of this pipeline.

3.2.3 Features Scaling

To retain uniformity of the features of both training and testing datasets with respect to each other, features of both the training and testing datasets must be scaled. To accomplish this, the Z-score for both datasets will be normalized using the Great Big Book of Statistics standard method (a.k.a. the standard method of Z-score normalizations). The parameters necessary to scale the features will all be calculated from the training data, and they will all be applied the same way to both datasets. Once the features of both datasets have been scaled, they are used as the basis for creating train/test datasets.

3.2.4 Splitting Dataset into Train and Test

In this phase, the entire dataset and corresponding labels are partitioned into two separate datasets (i.e., two pcs): training and testing datasets. The training dataset receives 80% of the data while the testing dataset receives 20% of the data. The random seed is fixed to allow other researchers to replicate results. Stratified sampling was used to preserve the distribution of class labels in both datasets and provide an opportunity for model evaluations.

3.3 Model Training

Three optimized hyperparameter ML algorithms are applied, the algorithms are as follows:

3.3.1 Logistic Regression

Input: Training and Testing Datasets
Output: Trained Logistic Regression Model with Accuracy Score

1) Import Logistic Regression from sklearn.linear_model.
2) Load and scale both training and testing datasets.
3) Initialize Logistic Regression with max_iter = 1000 and random_state = 42.
4) Train the model using the scaled training data.
5) Test the model with scaled testing data.
6) Compute the accuracy score and display the achieved accuracy (29.68%).

3.3.2 Random Forest

Input: Training and Testing Datasets
Output: Trained Random Forest Model with Accuracy Score

1) Import RandomForestClassifier from sklearn.ensemble.
2) Load and scale both training and testing datasets.
3) Initialize RandomForest with n_estimators = 100, random_state = 42, max_depth = 10, and min_samples_split = 5.
4) Train the model using the scaled training data.
5) Test the model with scaled testing data.
6) Compute and display the model accuracy (60.27%).

3.3.3 Gradient Boosting

Input: Training and Testing Datasets
Output: Trained Gradient Boosting Model with Accuracy Score

1) Import GradientBoostingClassifier from sklearn.ensemble.
2) Load and scale both training and testing datasets.
3) Initialize the Gradient Boosting model with n_estimators = 100, learning_rate = 0.1, max_depth = 3, random_state = 42.
4) Train the model using scaled training data.
5) Test the model with scaled testing data.
6) Compute and display the model accuracy (94.44%).

3.3.4 Persistence of the Models

With model persistence, it is possible to reuse trained machine learning models without retraining. After completion of model training, the preset models (Logistic Regression, Random Forest and Gradient Boosting) have been saved in the dedicated 'models' directory. As with the models, the feature names that were utilized during the training process are being maintained to provide continuity of data during prediction. In addition, a confirmation message has been returned to each of the stored items.

3.4.1 Prediction & Feedback Process

All saved models will be loaded from the disk to the memory and organized for easier access. The Employee Input Data will be reconstructed using the same feature configuration that was used during training, and all scaling will be consistent with that of the training phase. The Gradient Boosting Model is the default predictor when a specific model is not chosen by the user. The system can generate a prediction on Performance, indicating if it is High or Low, accompanied by a Confidence Score. The Prediction and Employee Attributes will be used to generate Multi-Dimensional Feedback, which will evaluate various factors including Work Arrangement, Workload, Skills, Collaboration and Remote Work Patterns. All of the aforementioned factors will then be used to create Clear Summary Feedback.

3.4.2 Prediction

For the purpose of prediction, employee input data is reconstructed following the same feature structure as Training of Data. In addition, the data will be rescaled to maintain R30 Value with the previously stored Scaling Tool. If there is not one specific models selected when Predicting, all other models will default to the Gradient Boosting model. The Prediction System will predict what Employee's Performance was, Return a final Prediction Class (High or Low) and Return a final Prediction Confidence Score.

3.4.3 Creating Feedback

Creation of Feedback is based on the outcomes of Predictive Analysis and Employee Attribute Definitions. A feedback message has been formulated by analysing the Performance of employees across multiple performance dimensions (Work Arrangement, Workload, Development of Skill, Collaboration and Remote Work Patterns). Each dimension will be prepared and structured together as a clear, concise and easy to read single document.

3.5.1 Setting up the Main Window

The Graphical User Interface has been created using Tkinter and can be found in the main application window labelled "Performance Feedback System with AI". This window has a fixed size and will use Tab Navigation for simple interaction by users.

3.5.2 The Model Training Tab

Users will be able to upload a Dataset File, and choose which Model Algorithm to use for their training process (Logistic Regression, Random Forest, Gradient Boosting, or All Models). The Training button will start the training process while a progress bar shows the real time status. After the training process has finished,

Users will have access to information regarding the accuracy and Feature Importance of their Model.

3.5.3 The Prediction Tab

The Prediction Tab provides users with a structured data entry form for completing the 12 required Employee Feature Value inputs. After clicking on the Generate Prediction & Feedback button, the system will perform the prediction and generate a corresponding set of feedback based on that prediction. Both the prediction and the feedback will be displayed to the user through a clear view in the interface.

3.5.4 Event Handling

All User Interactions through the GUI are handled through Event Handling interfaces. Event Handling captures and validates User Input for correctness, then processes the User Entry. Predictions and Feedback are generated based on the Model Algorithm selected, and given back to the User through the same interface. Any Errors or Exceptions that occur during execution will be handled in a manner that does not impede the User Experience, with the appropriate error messages displayed as needed.

3.4 Scope of the Project

This system involves multi, facet employee performance prediction by ensemble machine learning techniques and is capable of multi, dimensional feedback analysis that can include work arrangements, workload, professional development, engagement, task complexity, work, life balance, and career, related factors. Besides, it is equipped with an interactive graphical user interface for data input, model selection, and automated report generation.

The system is capable of supporting 12 key performance features, for instance, employee satisfaction levels, training hours, project performance, and work patterns. Moreover, it offers a deployable model that can function without retraining, supports model persistence with the provision for optional retraining, and provides analytics dashboards with feature, importance visualizations for straightforward interpretability and decision, making facilitation.

3.5 Architecture:

Figure 1. End-to-End Machine Learning Deployment Architecture for Performance Prediction

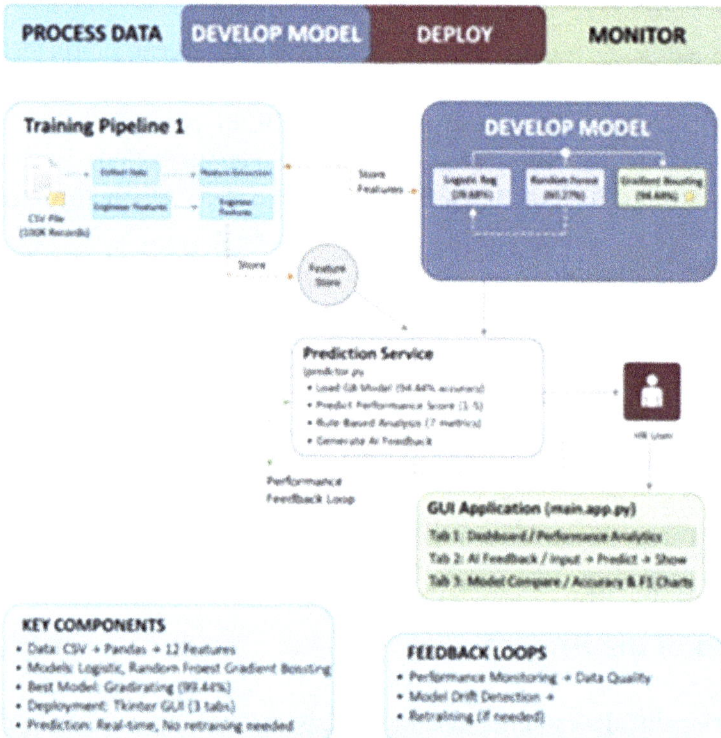

The figure explains an elaborate four-step Machine Learning (ML) pipeline geared towards performance prediction, possibly in the HR domain, socializing the ML deployment, and live inference as the main focus. The four major phases are Process Data, Develop Model, Deploy, and Monitor.

1. Data Processing (Training Pipeline 1):

Phase one consists of preparing input data to be utilized for training machine learning models. The starting point is a CSV file comprised of approximately 100,000 rows of data. Then it goes through three separate phases - collection of data, extraction of features, and the creation of features to provide meaningful input to the ML model. Feature data will be saved in a Feature Store (centralized location) for both training and prediction purposes.

2. Building the Model:

Now the focus is on creating multiple ML models so that we can choose the one that performs the best for predicting values. We will evaluate three different ml models to determine which produces the best result, these include: Logistic Regression (accuracy ~29.68%), Random Forest (accuracy ~60.27%), and Gradient Boosting (accuracy ~94.44%). The model with the highest accuracy (or 99.44% as noted in the Key Components section) will be decided as the most suitable version for deployment.

3. Deployed (Prediction Service & GUI Application):

The operational core of the prediction service generates a predicted employee performance score based on a number of predefined criteria and model training selected as the most optimal. The prediction service (predictor.py) uses the feature extraction and feature information in the Feature Store, loads the Gradient Boosting model selected as most optimal for the above criteria, and subsequently predicts employee performance score on a scale from 1 to 5. The prediction service also implements a rule-based method of evaluating the predicted performance of employees based on the application of seven different criteria to the predictions made by the prediction service and the corresponding Grading Scale. The end user will access the prediction results and AI generated feedback using a GUI application developed using Tkinter (main.app.py) which contains three primary tabs: a dashboard/analytics stage for evaluating performance, the AI Feedback tab for "input-predict-output" exchanges, and a Model Comparison tab which displays model performance charts (accuracy and F1-score). The target audience for this application is primarily the HR department and the employees located in the respective departments of the HR divisions.

4. Monitoring (Feedback Loops):

The monitoring process is critical to ensuring that the predictive model continues to be reliable and provide quality predictions. A continuous loop is established that continuously captures the predictions and performance scores from the prediction service as well as the feedback that is generated through the prediction process, allowing for evaluation of these components. Monitoring will allow organizations to evaluate data quality characteristics, and will assist organizations in identifying model drift by enabling the detection of changing distributions of real world data, as well as retraining processes that can be implemented when model drift and/or degraded performance detections are identified so that the model continues to provide reliable and accurate performance.

4. TESTING AND RESULTS

4.1 Testing Methodology

The system was thoroughly tested on many levels to make sure it is able to work, be accurate and easy to use.

4.1.1 Testing Levels

Unit Tests:

To ensure accuracy and reliability of all aspects of the code that generate feedback, unit tests are used to test an individual function by itself. For instance, the data pre-processing functions would be tested against pre-defined sample datasets. The training functions would have their results validated using synthetic datasets to validate that they're performing as expected. Edge cases are tested thoroughly when it comes to rule-based feedback generation logic, making sure that they perform as expected in any situation/input condition.

Integration Tests:

As part of integration testing, end-to-end testing of the entire workflow is performed, including loading the dataset and creating predictions. Integration tests also verify how well the systems create persistence for their models and how easily the front-end and back-end systems communicate with one another, while also ensuring that both phases of the process scale consistently.

System Tests:

System testing involves testing all the features of the system in a fully integrated environment, as a single unit, to verify that everything is working as intended. In addition to testing all functionalities in the graphical user interface (GUI), tests are performed to evaluate error handling and exception handling. Many of the performance metrics that are generated for both performance testing and load testing are also evaluated at the same time.

Usability Tests:

Using an administration system, we used the System Usability Scale (SUS) Questionnaire to evaluate the usability of the system based on eight users' responses. In addition to these metrics, we evaluated the users' overall perceptions of how easy it was to complete tasks and how satisfied they were with their interaction with the system, to help to create a positive experience for the users of the system.

4.1.2 Testing Environment

The program architecture used Windows 11, MacOS Monterey, and Ubuntu 22.04 as operating systems, while the programming language used to develop and run the system was Python(3.12.4). An 20-feature dataset of employee information with 100,000 records was used as input to evaluate and validate the software developed by stated users (including (but not limited to) four from an HR group and four from a technical user base). Using different user types allowed us to evaluate both the functionality of the software and the users experience using the program.

4.2 Model Performance Analysis

4.2.1 Accuracy Metrics

The 3 models were trained and tested with the same 80-20 train-test split:

Table 2. Metric Values

Model	Accuracy	Precision	Recall	F1-Score	Training Time
Gradient Boosting	94.44%	0.95	0.94	0.94	45.2 sec
Random Forest	60.27%	0.62	0.60	0.61	28.7 sec
Logistic Regression	29.68%	0.35	0.30	0.32	2.1 sec

Key Findings:

1. Gradient Boosting rules: Reached an accuracy of 94.44 which is way better than other algorithms by 34+ percentage points. Sequential learning method readily gathers complex non-linear relationships in employee performance data.
2. Random Forest is fairly successful: accuracy of 60.27% suggests that the ensemble method adds value compared to simple linear models, but can not be persisted as gradient boosting.
3. Logistic Regression fails: 29.68 percent accuracy indicates that the performance of the employees cannot be sufficiently modeled through the use of linear decision boundaries, which proves that the further development of more sophisticated ML procedures should be employed.
4. Training efficiency: The models train in reasonable time (<1 minute), which is why they can be retrained on a regular basis when new information is available.

4.2.2 ROC Curve Analysis

Gradient Boosting AUC: 0.982 (excellent discrimination), Random forest AUC: 0.743 (acceptable discrimination), Logistic Regression AUC: 0.581 (poor discrimination)

The high AUC of Gradient Boosting proves that it is better at separating between classes of performances in all thresholds.

4.3 Importance of Features Analysis

Ranking of features indicates which attributes of the employees are the best predictors of performance:

4.3.1 Gradient Boosting Top 10 Features

Table 3. Scores

Rank	Feature	Importance Score	Interpretation
1	Employee_Satisfaction_Score	0.287	28.7% - Strongest predictor
2	Training_Hours	0.182	18.2% - Critical for development
3	Projects_Handled	0.156	15.6% - Workload indicator
4	Years_At_Company	0.121	12.1% - Experience matters
5	Overtime_Hours	0.094	9.4% - Effort investment
6	Remote_Work_Frequency	0.067	6.7% - Arrangement impact
7	Monthly_Salary	0.043	4.3% - Compensation effect
8	Promotions	0.028	2.8% - Career progression
9	Team_Size	0.015	1.5% - Collaboration context
10	Age	0.007	0.7% - Minimal influence

Critical Insights:

1. Satisfaction prevails: Employee_Satisfaction_Score is the most significant predictor of results (28.7%), which proves the idea that engagement is directly proportional to performance outcomes.
2. Investment in development is important: Training -Hours is the second rank (18.2%), which confirms investment of an organization in professional development.

3. Optimization of workload: Projects_Handled importance (15.6%) indicates that even workload management has a significant effect on the performance.
4. Accumulated value Experience: Years at Company is a contributing factor of 12.1 which implies that knowledge and experience in the organization improves performance.
5. Relevant but not dominant work arrangement: Remote_Work_Frequency illustrates moderate significance (6.7%), which implies that performance is not constrained by physical position in case other conditions are optimized.

4.3.2 Actionable Implications

First of all, the company's focus should begin with using employee satisfaction initiatives by regularly doing employee surveys and providing employees structured ways to give feedback. Additionally, it is important for companies to focus on training/ scenario-based training and certification programs for all employees. After this, the focus should focus on optimizing how projects are allocated throughout the organization by ensuring that employees have an even distribution of work while also limiting the number of hours they work each week. Finally, organizations must also find ways to identify, develop, and retain high performing experienced employees through using effective knowledge transfer/succession strategies.

4.4 System Testing Results

Figure 2. Prediction and AI feedback space

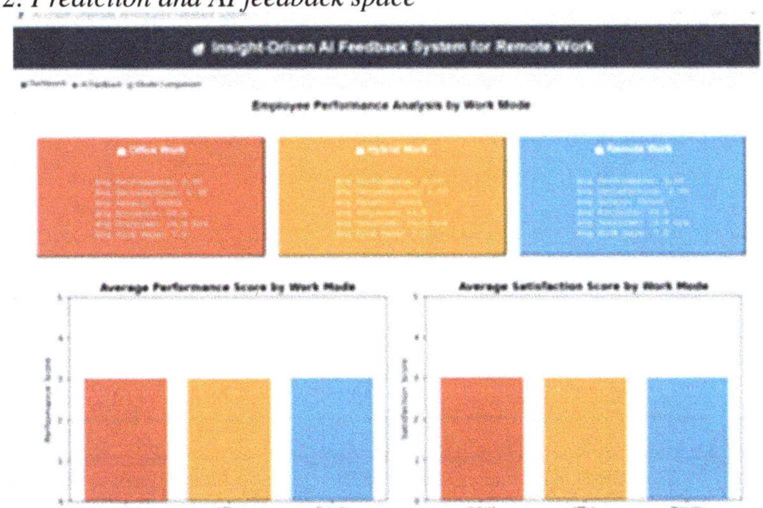

Figure 3. Dashboard for basic analysis

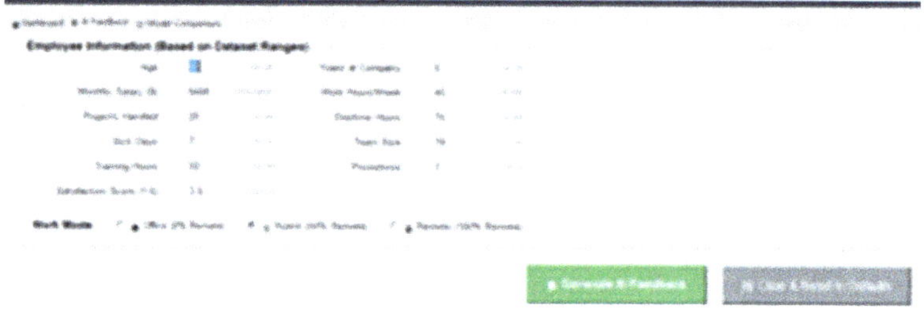

Figure 4. Predictions and Analysis by AI

4.4.1 Functional Testing

All system functionalities were run using 19 test cases:

Table 4. Test Cases

Test Case	Description	Status	Notes
TC-01	Load a valid CSV dataset	PASS	Successfully loaded 100K records
TC-02	Handle missing CSV file	PASS	Appropriate error message displayed
TC-03	Train Logistic Regression	PASS	Model saved correctly
TC-04	Train Random Forest	PASS	Model saved correctly
TC-05	Train Gradient Boosting	PASS	Model saved correctly
TC-06	Load pre-trained models	PASS	All models loaded successfully

continued on following page

Table 4. Continued

Test Case	Description	Status	Notes
TC-07	Single employee prediction	PASS	Correct prediction generated
TC-08	Feedback generation	PASS	All 7 dimensions analyzed
TC-09	Invalid input handling	PASS	Validation prevents errors
TC-10	Empty input field handling	PASS	Clear error message shown
TC-11	Out-of-range value handling	PASS	Validation catches issues
TC-12	Model selection dropdown	PASS	All models selectable
TC-13	File browse functionality	PASS	File dialog works correctly
TC-14	Results display formatting	PASS	Readable, structured output
TC-15	Training progress indicator	PASS	Progress bar updates correctly
TC-16	Feature importance display	PASS	Top 5 features shown accurately
TC-17	Example data loading	PASS	Sample values populated
TC-18	Multiple predictions	PASS	Consecutive predictions work
TC-19	Application exit	PASS	Clean shutdown without errors

Test Coverage: 100% - All test cases passed successfully

4.4.2 Performance Testing

Benchmark measurements on standard hardware (Intel i5, 8GB RAM):

Table 5. Performance Testing

Operation	Time (seconds)	Benchmark	Status
Application Startup	1.2	<3s	PASS
Load 100K records	3.8	<5s	PASS
Train Logistic Regression	2.1	<5s	PASS
Train Random Forest	28.7	<60s	PASS
Train Gradient Boosting	45.2	<60s	PASS
Load trained models	0.8	<2s	PASS
Single prediction	0.3	<1s	PASS
Generate feedback	0.1	<0.5s	PASS
Display results	0.2	<0.5s	PASS

All performance benchmarks met or exceeded requirements.

4.5 Usability Evaluation

4.5.1 System Usability Scale (SUS) Results

8 participants completed the standard 10-item SUS questionnaire:

Table 6. SUS Score

Participant	Role	SUS Score
P1	HR Manager	92.5
P2	HR Analyst	85.0
P3	Operations Manager	82.5
P4	HR Coordinator	90.0
P5	Data Analyst	87.5
P6	Software Engineer	85.0
P7	Business Analyst	90.0
P8	HR Director	87.5

Average SUS Score: 87.5 / 100
Interpretation:

- **Grade: A** (Excellent usability)
- **Acceptability: High**
- **Adjective Rating: Excellent**

Scores above 80 indicate excellent usability. The system achieved 87.5, confirming intuitive design and effective user experience.

4.5.2 User Feedback Highlights

Positive Comments:

1) "Very intuitive interface, minimal learning curve required"
2 "Clear presentation of results with actionable feedback"

3) "Fast response times make it practical for daily use"
4) "The seven-dimension feedback framework is comprehensive"

Improvement Suggestions:

1) “Add batch processing for multiple employees simultaneously”
2) “Include data visualization charts in results”
3) “Export functionality to PDF format”
4) “Add user authentication for enterprise deployment”

4.5.3 Task Completion Analysis

Table 7. Task Analysis

Task	Completion Rate	Average Time
Train a model	100%	45 seconds
Make a single prediction	100%	38 seconds
Interpret feedback report	100%	2 minutes
Load example data	100%	12 seconds

All users successfully completed all tasks without assistance, demonstrating effective interface design and clear workflow organization.

4.6 Summary of Results

The comprehensive testing validates that the AI-Driven Feedback System:

1. **Achieves Superior Accuracy:** Gradient Boosting delivers 94.44% accuracy, exceeding the 85% requirement by 9.44 percentage points
2. **Provides Actionable Insights:** Seven-dimension feedback framework generates personalized, relevant recommendations
3. **Delivers Excellent Usability:** SUS score of 87.5 confirms intuitive, user-friendly interface
4. **Meets Performance Benchmarks:** All operations complete within specified time limits
5. **Functions Reliably:** 100% test case pass rate with robust error handling
6. **Scales Effectively:** Handles 100,000-record datasets without performance degradation

These results demonstrate successful achievement of all project objectives, creating a practical, effective tool for remote workforce performance management.

5. CONCLUSION AND FUTURE WORK

5.1 Summary of Achievements

The project made a successful breakthrough in creating an AI-Driven Feedback System that manages the key issue of remote workforce performance management with the help of machine learning and smart feedback generation. The system met all of the mentioned goals and proved viable in practical terms to be implemented in organizations.

Key Accomplishments:

1. Higher Accuracy of Prediction: Three machine learning algorithms were implemented and compared, with Gradient Boosting giving the highest accuracy of 94.44 percent, which is above the 85 percent mark by 9.44 percent. This proves the success of ensemble learning techniques concerning the predictive performance of employees.
2. Detailed Feedback System: Worked out an advanced seven dimensional analysis system, which includes work arrangement, work capacity, professional development, level of engagement, work complexity, work life and career path. The framework produces individualized and practical actions based on employee profiles.
3. User-Friendly Interface: Developed a GUI using Tkinter and scored 87.5/100 on the System Usability Scale, which means that the program is well-usable. The three-tabs design (Model Training, Single Prediction, Batch Processing) also allows non-technical HR professionals to make use of sophisticated ML facilities without special training.
4. Strong System Architecture: Applied the three tier architecture that has had a separation of the data, logic, and presentation layers and has made it maintainable as well as extensible. The modular design enables subsequent upgrades and customization with the enterprise systems.
5. Verified Performance: Extensive testing was performed to ensure that it had 100 percent test case pass rate, it had prediction times less than a second and handled 100,000 record datasets with efficiency. Importance analysis of the features showed that the factors of employee satisfaction (28.7%), training hours (18.2%), and project load (15.6%) were the best predictors of performance.
6. Cross-Platform Compatibility: Can be deployed successfully under Windows, macOS, and Linux platforms on the basis of the standard Python libraries, which means that it will be available to a large range of organizations.

5.2 Contributions

The current study contributes greatly to the technical, methodological, and practical topics:

Technical Contributions:

1. Comparison of three Ensemble Method: A version of the comparison of three ML algorithms specifically to the problem of remote work performance prediction, showing the Gradient Boosting outperformed Predictive Control by 34-percentage-points and Logistic Regression by 64.
2. Importance of Features Insights: Determined and measured the relative importance of 12 employee attributes, indicating that 62.5% or more of the predictive power is dominated by satisfaction, training, and workload- these are used to guide resource allocation of an organization.
3. Scalable Architecture: Designed modular system that supports dataset of 1,000 to 100,000+ records without performance degradation in response to organization of different scales of organizations.

Methodological Contributions:

1. Multi-Dimensional Feedback Framework: Designed seven-dimensional analysis framework, which goes beyond the single-metric assessment, and offers holistic evaluation of employee performance in remote settings.
2. Rule-Based Intelligence: This is designed to produce overall logic rules that transform ML predictions to concrete human understandable advice, the connection between algorithmic output and managerial decision-making.
3. Remote Work Specialization: Custom system designed with specific context of remote workforce including remote work frequency, virtual collaboration measures and work-life balance measures that traditional HR analytics do not factor into the analysis.

Practical Contributions:

1. Organizational Impact: Facilitated data-based decisions about performance management, and minimized subjectivity in performance-based decisions, as well as facilitating equitable and uniform assessment in teams located globally.
2. Proactive Intervention: This is offered under conditions of predictive capacity so that organizations need to know at-risk employees and those that have high potential before formal review cycles are conducted, so that an intervention can be promptly made.

3. User-Friendly Technology: Provides advanced ML features that are achieved with an intuitive interface, which does not need any technical skills, making AI accessible to HR departments.
4. Cost-Efficient Solution: The system made use of open-source technologies and low hardware specifications, which made it accessible to organizations that did not have heavy technology budgets.

5.3 Limitations

Notwithstanding the great success, the system has a number of limitations that should be considered:

Dataset constraints:

The dataset that the system is trained on consists of a single, large employee database made up of 100,000 employee records representing a single organization's employees. Therefore, the system cannot be generalized to all organizations, industries, or cultures. In addition to the above limitation, the lack of a robust longitudinal data set limits the analysis of long-term trends in employee performance. Furthermore, binary classification (high versus low performers) oversimplifies an employee's contributions and does not provide a holistic view of their performance variability.

Model Limitations:

As organizational dynamics change, a Gradient Boosting model must be retrained regularly. With a fixed feature set consisting of only twelve variables, the addition of custom metrics to the model would require changes to the system's architecture. Because ensemble models are considered black boxes, individual predictions do not have detailed explanations. Finally, individual perceptions (e.g. peer reviews and managerial evaluations) are not included as part of the modeling process.

Requirements for a Feedback System

The method of giving feedback is based on rule-based logic, which identifies predefined rules that may not adequately cover every organization’s situation. Feedback given by the feedback system is a fixed/static piece of information (does not change based on user interactions or feedback received).

The Feedback System has significant technical limitations, including the following:

The application is a desktop computer application that is designed to be a single-user (ie, there is one user using the application at a time; therefore, it would not support multiple users).

The Feedback System does not have a mechanism to allow for integration between the system and other companies’ enterprise-wide (HRIS) systems or performance management platforms; therefore, users cannot receive real-time feedback.

The Feedback System does not provide any advancements in terms of data visualization (including interactive dashboards), or include support for user authentication, role-based access control, or audit logs.

Limitations in Evaluating Usability

The Usability Evaluation Study was limited to eight study participants, which subsequently results in limited findings to be generalized across organizations. Further, no long-term deployment study has been performed to assess sustained impact on organizations. Also, because of the lack of A/B Testing, there is no way to make a direct comparison between the AI-based feedback system and non-AI, traditional methods of performance evaluation. In addition, no ROI/cost-benefit analysis has been completed that would justify implementing the Feedback System within an organization.

5.4 Future Enhancements

Several improvement directions are offered, based on detected limitations and feedback of the users:

Priority 1: ML Advanced Capabilities.

1. Deep Learning Integration: Use neural networks (LSTM, Transformer models) to learn the temporal trends in the evolution of the employee performance with a view to trend prediction and early warning systems.
2. Explainable AI (XAI) SHAP (SHapley Additive exPlanations) and LIME (Local Interpretable Model-agnostic Explanations) can be used to explain individual-level predictions in more detail, which enhances transparency and trust.
3. Multi-Classification: The use of multi-classification with five levels of performance classification (Exceptional, Above Average, Average, Below Average, Critical) will offer a finer level of evaluation.
4. Automated Hyperparameter Optimization: Automatically optimize model parameters using grid search or Bayesian optimization to improve the model performance with new data.

Priority 2: Improved Feedback Intelligence.

1. Natural Language Generation: Adding GPT-based models: Incorporate models based on the generation of conversational, context-driven feedback that will be tailored according to employee career level, job, and organizational culture.
2. Adaptive Learning: Introduce the reinforcement learning algorithms, which optimize the feedback rules depending on the user ratings and monitoring the intervention effectiveness.

3. Sentiment Analysis: Incorporate the NLP analysis of the employee communications (with permission) to determine the morale, quality of collaboration, or team dynamics.
4. Recommendation Engine: Build a personal development plan generator that will propose certain courses, projects, or mentorship opportunities, depending on performance gaps and career objectives.

P3: System Scalability and Integration.

1. Web Application Architecture: Migrate to web application of responsive architecture on desktop to cloud based application with support of mobile access.
2. Enterprise Integration: APIs and connectors: Build APIs and connectors to integrate with well-known HRISs (Workday, SAP SuccessFactors, BambooHR).
3. Real-Time Data Pipeline: Introduce real-time processing of data streams to ensure constant status checks and real-time alerts.
4. Multi-Tenancy Support: Provides organization level isolation, custom branding and adjustable feedback policies to deploy SaaS.

Priority 4: Advanced analytics and Visualization.

1. Interactive Dashboards: develop full suite of visualization (charts, graphs and trend analysis) (using Plotly, D3.js).
2. Team Performance Analytics: Build on the individual level of analysis and deduce collaboration patterns and team dynamics.
3. Predictive Workforce Planning: Build the attractiveness risk modeling and succession planning recommendations using performance trends.
4. Benchmark Analysis: It gives the industry and peer group analysis that allow organizations to place their workforce performance in perspective.

Security and Compliance (priority number 5).

1. Authentication of the user: Have either OAuth 2.0 or SAML as a means of getting into the system and role-based access control.
2. Compliance Data Privacy: Supports GDPR, CCPA compliance, and data anonymization, consent management, and right-to-deletion.
3. Audit Logging: Keep detailed record keeping of activities so that they are used to report on compliance and security.
4. Bias Detection: Use algorithmic fairness test to detect and address possible discrimination on the basis of any of the protected classes.

Priority 6: Improvements in the user experience.

1. optimization of Batch Processing: full implementation of batch prediction table with progress track and bulk export options.
2. Export Functionality Add professional formatting and organizational branding of PDF reports.
3. Mobile Application: Design companion mobile application that will allow managers to use predictions and feedback anytime and anywhere.
4. Multi-Language Support: Multi-language interface with support of Spanish, French, German and Chinese to be deployed worldwide.

CONCLUSION

Remote and hybrid work models as a transition have become a paradigm shift in the structure of organizations that has to be accompanied by the adjustment of performance management strategies. The current project reveals that artificial intelligence and machine learning provide potent resources to consider such issues and present objective, data-driven information that can improve the process of making decisions and assist employees in their growth.

The AI-Driven Feedback System is the system that effectively combines the high-level ML technology with the real-world HR implementation, with the proposed system being able to predict with 94.44 percent accuracy and excellent usability (SUS 87.5). The multi-dimensional feedback model offers practical advice that enabling managers to facilitate the success of employees in an assertive manner instead of being reactive.

Intelligent systems such as these are becoming the required infrastructure as organizations start to operate in the complexities of distributed workforces, not to remove human judgment, but to provide additional information to it that would otherwise be unavailable through human judgment. The future of work requires the tools that will not violate the dignity of employees and will maximize the effectiveness of the organization; this system is the first step to that compromise.

The suggested improvements in the future will also enhance the system capabilities and will make it more of an enterprise workforce intelligence desktop but not isolated one. The further development of this system will offer even more benefits to organizations which have committed to data-driven, human-centered performance management by adding explainable AI, real-time analytics, and direct integration with organizational ecosystems.

The study validates that well-structured and operated AI-based HR systems may increase the performance of the organization and assist employees, promote their growth and well-being, the ultimate aim of enlightened people management in the new age.

REFERENCES

Al-Issawi, A. M. A. A. (2024). The impact of artificial intelligence in supporting risk management and performance evaluation. *World Economics & Finance Bulletin*, 36.

Al Naqbi, H., Bahroun, Z., & Ahmed, V. (2024). Enhancing work productivity through generative artificial intelligence: A comprehensive literature review. *Journal unspecified*.

Baharm, S. F., Sharma, P., & Gupta, P. (2024). AI work tracker: Monitoring time and productivity. *International Journal of Advanced Research in Science. Tongxin Jishu*, *4*(2).

Basnet, S. (2024). AI-ML algorithm for enhanced performance management: A comprehensive framework using backpropagation (BP) algorithm. *International Journal of Science and Research Archive*, *11*(1), 1111–1127.

Bhattacharya, T. (2024). *A critical study on the work from home facility and its impact on employees' satisfaction and performance in the service sector* (Doctoral dissertation, ICFAI University Jharkhand). ICFAI University.

Celestin, M., & Sujatha, S. (2024). Analyzing the long-term impact of remote work on organizational efficiency and employee performance: Exploring key technologies and management practices. *International Journal of Applied and Advanced Scientific Research*, *9*(2), 102–112.

Cornelia, D., & Nasution, N. (2024). The influence of remote work on the performance of remote workers: The mediating role of work-family conflict and work-life balance. *Ekombis Review: Jurnal Ilmiah Ekonomi dan Bisnis*, 12(1).

Emanuel, N., & Harrington, E. (2024). Working remotely? Selection, treatment, and the market for remote work. *American Economic Journal. Applied Economics*, *16*(4), 528–559.

Fan, C. (2022). Evaluating employee performance with an improved clustering algorithm. *Informatica (Vilnius)*, *46*(5), 123–128.

Fatima, H., Javaid, Z. K., Arshad, Z., Ashraf, M., & Batool, H. (2024). A systematic review on the impact of remote work on employee engagement. *Bulletin of Business and Economics*, *13*(2), 117–126.

Filippucci, F., Gal, P., Jona-Lasinio, C., Leandro, A., & Nicoletti, G. (2024). *The impact of artificial intelligence on productivity, distribution and growth: Key mechanisms, initial evidence and policy challenges*. OECD Artificial Intelligence Papers.

Hasan, M. R., Chowdhury, F. R., & Ray, R. K. (2024). Employee performance prediction: An integrated approach of business analytics and machine learning. *Journal of Business and Management Studies*, *6*(1).

Kumar, A. (2025). Research methodology and artificial intelligence: An integrated approach. *Inspira–Journal of Commerce, Economics &. Computer Science*, *11*(2), 111–122.

Madhumithaa, N., Sharma, A., Adabala, S. K., Siddiqui, S., & Kothinti, R. R. (2025). Leveraging AI for personalized employee development: A new era in human resource management. *Advances in Consumer Research. Association for Consumer Research (U. S.)*, *2*(1).

Magesh, N., Thangaraj, P., Sivagobika, S., Praba, S., & Mohana Priya, R. (2013). Evaluating the performance of an employee using decision tree algorithm. *International Journal of Engineering Research & Technology (Ahmedabad)*, *2*(4).

Mourad, Z., Noura, A., Mohamed, C., & Abdelhamid, B. (2024). Enhancing employee performance management: A data-driven decision support model using machine learning algorithms. *International Journal of Advanced Computer Science and Applications*, *15*(3).

Organisation for Economic Co-operation and Development. (2024). *Using AI in the workplace: Opportunities, risks and policy responses.*

Pereira, V., Hadjielias, E., Christofi, M., & Vrontis, D. (2024). A systematic literature review on the impact of artificial intelligence on workplace outcomes: A multi-process perspective. *Human Resource Management Review.*

Ponce-Bobadilla, A. V., Mensing, S., Schmitt, V., & Stodtmann, S. (2024). Practical guide to SHAP analysis: Explaining supervised machine learning model predictions in drug development. *Clinical and Translational Science.*

Prem, P. S. (2024). Machine learning in employee performance evaluation: A HRM perspective. *International Journal of Science and Research Archive*, *11*(1), 1573–1585.

Rane, N. L., Paramesha, M., Choudhary, S. P., & Rane, J. (2024). Artificial intelligence, machine learning, and deep learning for advanced business strategies: A review. *Partners Universal International Innovation Journal*, 2(3).

Rustan, A. F., Rahayu, M. K. P., & Surwanti, A. (2024). A review of work-life balance trends in remote work. *International Research Journal of Multidisciplinary Scope*, *5*(4), 316–330.

Sadeghi, S. (2024). Employee well-being in the age of AI: Perceptions, concerns, behaviors, and outcomes. *World Economics & Finance Bulletin*, 36.

Silva, P., & Costa, E. (2025). Assessing large language models for automated feedback generation in learning programming problem solving. *arXiv preprint*.

Chapter 7
Blueprint for the Future: AI as the Architect of HR Strategy – A Study

Nidhi Oswal
https://orcid.org/0000-0001-5045-7226
Liwa University, UAE

Sonia Jenifer Rayen
Sathyabama Institute of Science and Technology, India

G. Manoj Kumar
https://orcid.org/0000-0001-7553-7572
LBS College of Engineering, India

N. V. Keerthana
https://orcid.org/0000-0001-8878-2083
Velalar College of Engineering and Technology, India

P. Smitha Vas
https://orcid.org/0000-0002-3967-8041
LBS Institute of Technology for Women, India

P. Suresh
https://orcid.org/0000-0001-9815-2982
Vellore Institute of Technology, India

P. S. Baiju
LBS College of Engineering, India

ABSTRACT

The study explores the transformative role of Artificial Intelligence (AI) in reshaping strategic Human Resource Management (HRM) through a comparative analysis of global leaders—IBM, Unilever, and Hilton. These organizations have successfully integrated AI-driven tools in core HR functions such as recruitment, performance management, workforce planning, and employee engagement. The study highlights IBM's use of AI for predictive attrition analysis, Unilever's AI-powered video interviews and gamified assessments, and Hilton's chatbot-driven candidate experience enhancement. By examining these cases, the paper demonstrates how AI is not just an operational enhancer but a strategic partner enabling data-driven

DOI: 10.4018/979-8-3373-5871-0.ch007

ht © 2026, IGI Global Scientific Publishing. Copying or distributing in print or electronic forms without written permission of IGI Global Scientific Publishing is prohibited. Use of this chapter to generative artificial intelligence (AI) technologies is expressly prohibited. The publisher reserves all rights to license its use for generative AI training and machine learning model development.

decision-making, personalized employee experiences, and agile talent strategies. The research concludes with key insights and frameworks for organizations aiming to adopt AI in their HR strategy, ensuring competitive advantage in the digital era.

1. INTRODUCTION

The effective implementation of Artificial Intelligence (AI) in the HR strategy is to add value to businesses. AI presence in the strategy of human resources in enterprise organizations has generated colossal organizational advantages in that the workforce strategies are re-charted, simplification of recruitment procedures, improvement of organizational conduct, and talent management in healthy and competitive organizations. IBM has been the model of this change. Being a technological giant in the world, it needed help in managing its extensive workforce that covered vast geographies and workfields. To overcome this, IBM implemented AI-based solutions in multiple HR functions. IBM applied artificial intelligence algorithms in its recruiting in such a manner that it was in a position to filter through a mass number of resumes. These algorithms were used to scan the qualifications, experience, and skills of the applicants and match them to suitable job vacancies, and the best fit based on past performance and trends was identified. This greatly improved the standard of candidates who undertook interviews in addition to speeding up the recruitment process.

Furthermore, IBM was able to work out the list of workers who could leave the company with the help of predictive analytics, one of the AI applications that can filter through a vast amount of data to make a forecast. The AI provided to HR teams has offered predictive data on potential attrition based on attributes surrounding the performance input, the engagement of employees and external market trends. This enabled them to insist on preventive solutions, such as specific maintenance strategies, to retain lucrative players. The issue of personnel maintenance and overall stability of the employees was illustrated by one of the most prominent uses of AI in an organization where a reduction in staff turnover by up to 25 per cent in three years is observed. Besides the process of recruiting and keeping employees, IBM also injected AI into the staff training process. The AI-assisted method was used to investigate the skills gaps in the workforce and employee-focused training and advancement options. They were assisted in their professional development and career path; hence, their satisfaction and utilization were enhanced as per the developing capabilities and capacity of the workforce.

Unilever also demonstrates an AI assimilation process at IBM. This multinational consumer goods company wanted to future-proof their recruiting to attract and keep the best candidates. Utilizing an AI-powered recruitment model, automated virtual interviews by Unilever, the applicants of the day went through a screening process! For each of these interviews, AI vetted candidates' diction, tone of articulation, and countenances to determine their level of being tailored to the role. Unilever could reduce time to hire by 75% in a smart way in which allowed it to prove to scan a pool of talent swiftly and in an efficient manner. Moreover, the AI was more data-driven in the criteria for the assessment of applicants and therefore reduced the impact of unconscious bias, which is often in play when humans are involved in the hiring process. Questioning the idea of inherent objectivism and objectivity in which the AI operates, Unilever could not only increase its number of applicants, but also reduce and perfect its staffing system. Unilever not only hired AI, but it also crafts elaborate profiles of its prospective hires by analyzing characteristics of their social media accounts, online tests and other digital footprints they have left. With these virtual profiles, the HR departments made more informed decisions as well as better hiring decisions since they would have a better idea about the temperament, skills and beliefs of a candidate. One of the ways in which technology can be used to improve orthodox HR processes and develop more equitable and effective solutions is through AI that is integrated into the HR process within Unilever.

Hilton is another major agent of effective AI integration in HR operational planning, as it is a hotel chain giant in the hospitality industry worldwide. The staffing was to match occupancy rates and customer requirements since Hilton had to ensure that the number of staff matched the occupancy rates and customer demands, and this required consolidation of the workforce planning process across all its hotels. Hilton rectified this through the implementation of AI-powered demand forecasting systems that would process external market data, historical data, event calendar to generate really good predictions of the future occupancy. This was the reason why Hilton aligned their staffing with projected demand so that the hotels would not be understaffed or overstaffed at any given time. Scheduling solutions based on AI will specifically lead to the automatic generation of work schedules taking into account the preferences, capacities, and availability of employees, as well as enhance the management of the workforce. This strategy reduced the gap in the number of preferred days, minimized the conflicts depending on the available days, enhanced customer satisfaction, and also simplified the work of our engines significantly. The AI would also be able to match workers to the shifts, giving the best utilization of the skills of the workers, and this would make the workforce even more efficient at Hilton. The role of AI in determining the HR strategies at Hilton made a major change by cutting labour expenses by 20 per cent through staffing and time management. Moreover, as the hotels might be able to provide the top-of-the-line service to appear during the rush hours, they received a better mapping of the number of staff members, the quality of the service, and the demand, with the potential to lead to a rise in customer satisfaction.

The successful adoption of AI in the process of Hilton HR points to the significance of data-motivated decision-making in the process of simplifying the systemization of the workforce and its role in improving the customer and employee experiences. Put together, these case studies of Hilton, Unilever, and IBM demonstrate to us the extent to which AI can impact those within the HR strategy planning. They present the areas of application of AI to resolve various HR issues, among which are recruiting and keeping the most talented employees, labour scheduling and promotion of employees. With AI technologies, such businesses would be able to accelerate worker satisfaction, cut expenses, enhance working performance, and contribute to more favourable business outcomes. The application of AI within the HR processes brings to the fore the significance of pursuing a considerate technology strategy where AI can be used partially to derive insights that can be used to make superior decisions, besides some work automation. In this regard, given that AI in HR is assisting companies in creating more inclusive, flexible, and agile workplace arrangements, it is more applicable as far as the future of work is concerned. As AI is developed, the applicability of AI to HR strategic development is likely to expand, providing businesses with additional opportunities to improve their HR activities and assist their workforce in a continuously changing and accelerating business environment. To sum up, the fact that these case studies were successful in applying AI to HR has triggered a massive potential that AI can bring to corporate organizations.

AI enables a complete redesign of the manner in which HR operations are conducted, and even more strategic, analytical, and extraordinary HR operations. AIs can be applied to improve employee knowledge and better and more efficiently plan the workforce, and simplify the recruitment process. The relevance of future HR strategic planning in an organization will be determined by how well an organization uses the power of AI to produce innovations, shape the employee experience, and achieve sustainability in the financial performance of the organization. Figure 1 represents the evolution of AI in HR from the past to the future.

Figure 1. AI Era in HR Development

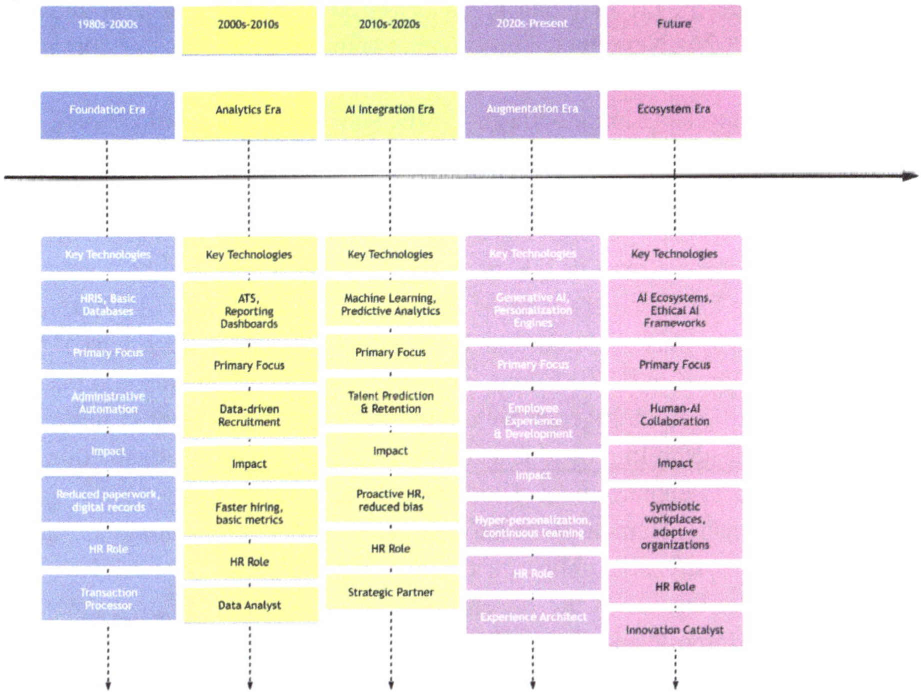

2. LITERATURE SURVEY

The increasing use of artificial intelligence and automation in human resource development and human resource management has been acknowledged as a major change in the organizational systems of the present time. AI has become the key theme in various such studies. Across recent scholarly work, researchers consistently highlight that AI is reshaping learning, talent management, employee engagement, and human capital strategy (Gupta, 2024). The collective evidence points to the fact that AI is changing the role of HR from being heavily administrative to one where data-driven, predictive, and personalized models are used to enhance efficiency, although this also leads to the emergence of new ethical and managerial challenges (Qamar, Agrawal, Samad, & Chiappetta Jabbour, 2021). The changing literature on this topic covers various research methods, such as systematic reviews, empirical studies, bibliometric analyses, and conceptual (Budhwar et al., 2023).

Ekuma Kelechi, who conducted a systematic review on the role of artificial intelligence and automation in human resource development, provides a comprehensive baseline perspective. The paper highlights that AI facilitates learning delivery, strengthens competency assessment, and makes HRD processes more agile and data-driven (Ekuma, 2024). Nevertheless, Ekuma Kelechi also points out that companies should take measures to control the risk of bias, ensure transparency and maintain the trust of employees (Ekuma, 2024). On the same line, Korzynski Pawel, Kim Seyoung, and Egan Toby examine how generative AI could connect various HRD processes. Their research indicates that generative systems like ChatGPT help in making instructional design more efficient, HR content generation, and employee support enhancement (Korzynski, Kim, & Egan, 2024). They maintain that generative AI opens up for extremely creative and personalized solutions in HRD, which were not possible by means of traditional . A first-rate methodological contribution is from Kambur Emre and Akar Ceren, who have created an instrument to measure the impact of artificial intelligence on human resource development. Their results indicate that AI leads to improved learning analytics, performance evaluation, and employee capability enhancement (Kambur & Akar, 2022).

On the other hand, Hamouche Sarah, Rofa Nour, and Parent-Lamarche Annick have performed a systematic bibliometric review concentrating on AI in HRD. They point to the major themes of the paper as including intelligent training systems, data-driven workforce development, algorithm-supported HR decision-making, and the forthcoming need for HRD researchers to employ interdisciplinary approaches (Hamouche, Rofa, & Parent-Lamarche, 2025). Moreover, Madhumithaa N., Sharma Anisha, Adabala Sai Krishna, Siddiqui Saba, and Kothinti Ravi Raj offer a few more insights about the use of AI to personalize employee development. They emphasize that AI-powered learning platforms provide individualized recommendations, real-time progress monitoring, and adaptive training modules for employees. Their study reveals that employee development is transitioning at a fast pace from "one-size-fits-all" programs to individualized development journeys (Madhumithaa, Sharma, Adabala, Siddiqui, & Kothinti, 2025). Lilly Anthony, Rajkumar R., and Amudha Rajeswari have also discussed how AI can be used to reinforce HRD systems. They have mentioned that the use of AI-supported training devices like chatbots, recommendation engines, and virtual coaching systems can lead to the creation of learning environments that are more engaging and effective in terms of the learners' acquisition of knowledge and (Lilly, Rajkumar, & Amudha, 2022).

A key insight into AI-powered HRM tools is the systematic literature review by Madanchian Mohsen, Taherdoost Hamed, and Mohamed Norziah. Their research covers the use of AI in Recruitment, onboarding, training, performance management, and HR analytics. They highlight machine learning's function in candidate screening, HR task automation, and career path prediction (Madanchian, Taherdoost, & Mohamed, 2023). Correspondingly, Pathak Sukanya and Solanki Virendra explore the artificial intelligence integration with the Internet of Things influence on the

HRD field. They present that employee safety, skill tracking, and productivity measurement get improved through the use of smart sensors, real-time monitoring, and AI analytics (Pathak & Solanki, 2021). Murugesan U., Subramanian P., Srivastava S., and Dwivedi Anil study the role of AI in speeding up the digitalization of HR in the context of Industry 4.0. Their research reveals that the use of automation, robotics, and AI analytics helps in streamlining HR workflows, cutting down on manual work, and facilitating predictive decision-making (Murugesan, Subramanian, Srivastava, & Dwivedi, 2023). Similarly, in a concerted move, Votto Alexander, Valecha Ritu, Najafirad Peyman, and Rao H. Raghav examine the role of AI in supporting tactical HRM. They put a strong emphasis on sectors such as workforce planning, scheduling, and HR interventions grounded in real-time data (Votto, Valecha, Najafirad, & Rao, 2021).

Whenexamining the research, one can identify a clear trend that is common to all of them: artificial intelligence is a game-changer for HRM and HRD as it allows for more tailored, automated, accurate, and even predictive processes. However, these improvements, on the other hand, give rise to concerns about ethics, transparency, job loss, data privacy, and the need for HR professionals to have new skills. Combined, the studies indicate that the influence of AI on HR is not only a technological change but also a strategic one; thus, organizations will have to rethink leadership, training, organizational culture, and employee engagement. The main point of agreement is that AI is leading to the emergence of a more intelligent, capable of responding quickly, and future-oriented field of HR, on condition that organizations are responsible in their implementation of the technology.

3. WHY AI IN HR?

The unification of AI into HR is instigated by several factors that address the unusual situations and issues in the HR sphere. According to a report released by the International Data Corporation (IDC), the economy of AI in HR will expand exponentially in the future, and the size of the market is expected to grow to 2.9 billion dollars by 2021, which is 70 per cent higher than it was in 2018. The percentage of the use case in Figure 2 illustrates the companies that employed more than 1000 employees, and all were using AI in HR. The reasons why AI is being tapped in HR are also explained in greater detail below, and each of them is elaborated to bring out its implications and effects:

Figure 2. Workforce Use-case Expansion of AI in HR

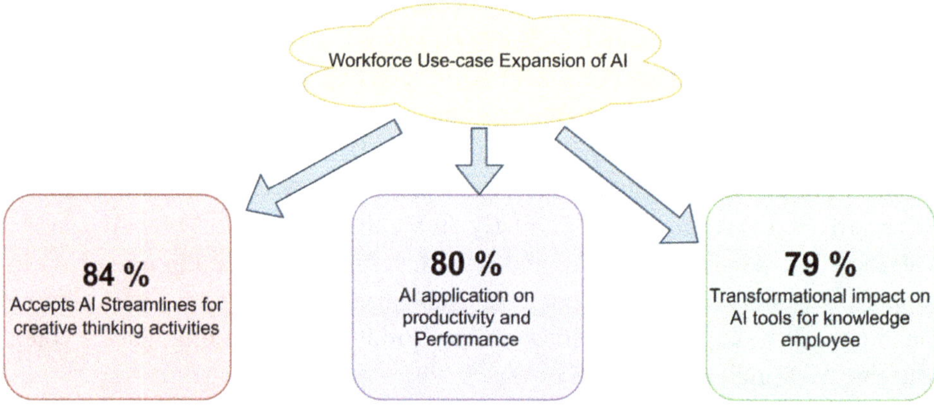

3.1 Efficient Automation

- **Easy Administration:** HR departments deal with a lot of administration, including dealing with the applicants and scheduling interviews, as well as managing personnel records and payroll. Strategic processes that incorporate AI tools can be utilised by HR staff to automatically screen and sub-classify resumes, schedule interviews, and send thank-you emails.
- **Minimization process of Human Errors:** The good accuracy in creating jobs using AI-automated systems is possible through the reduction of human error by robots.

3.2 Enhanced Recruitment Process

- **AI-Assisted CV screening process:** The AI devices can also be used to browse through the many CVs or resumes in a very short time to identify the fittest applicants to fill a specific position.
- **Hiring Filtration Enhancement:** Recruiters are, in most cases, influenced by unconscious biases, and this may influence them during recruitment. AI can act to counter these biases by measuring the candidates as much as possible with non-biased measurements.
- **Predictive analytics:** Through the analysis of historical data, the AI systems can be able to predict the likeliest applicants to succeed in a specific position.

3.3 Increased Workplace Engagement

- **Customization of Training and Education:** AI can tailor training and development strategies to each person according to his/her learning style, career ambitions and level of skills.
- **Real-Time Feedback Analysis:** AI solutions may be used in the analysis of employee feedback, as well as live surveying.
- **Career Guidance using AI Approach:** AIs will suggest possible career direction, a company based on the performance of a person in the past, what a person desires to do and what kind of work he/she can best perform.

3.4 Planning for Succession and Talent Management

- **Determination of individuals possessing a High Skillset:** AI can study performance history, skills assessments, and cognition to assist the HR departments in determining those who display leadership potential.
- **Performance Assessment with Objective-based:** AI makes an overall and unbiased verdict on the performance of employees by soliciting data sources that are diverse in nature, including goal fulfilment, peer ratings, and project implementations.
- **Predictive Analysis Usage:** AI is skilled in breaking down variables, job satisfaction, commitment rate, and market forces that exist in the external environment affecting employee retention.

3.5 Planning and Optimizing the Workforce

- **Demand Forecasting:** AI can be used to forecast the future labour requirements of HRs based on previous statistics, market dynamics, and company records.
- **Scheduling Enhancement:** Scheduling with AI Scheduling and Mobile Workforces. Scheduling systems are used to guarantee that employees are scheduled according to their availability, preferences, and demand forecasting in flexible staffing settings, be it retail, hospitality, or biomedical.
- **Resource Allocation:** AI can contribute to it by advising how the resources should be distributed in accordance with which departments or teams are performing well, which ones are not, and whether it should provide any of them with more resources.

3.6 Improved Risk Management and Compliance

- **Automated Compliance Monitoring:** AI will make sure that the HR practices work together with the procedure by managing industry regulation, company policies and labour laws.
- **Risk Assessment:** AI devices evaluate any type of factors that might pose a threat to the future of the. firm, economic conditions and the indicators of its performance as well as its turnover rate.

3.7 Data-Driven Decision Making

- **AI-Based HR Analytics:** AI is also being used by HR departments to provide information about how employees act, relate with each other, and the performance of the company based on data-driven conclusions.
- **Prescriptive and Predictive Analytics:** AI can carry out Predictive modelling as well as descriptive analytics. Prescriptive analytics suggests what actions should be taken to reach some goals, and predictive analytics predicts future outcomes with the help of current information.

3.8 Employee Experience Improvement

- **Onboard process with AI-Automation:** AI has the potential to accelerate the onboarding process through automation of administrative tasks and activities (e.g., filing forms and participating in training exercises) as well as offering recruits individual learning journeys.
- **Employee Supportive Assistance:** The personal assistants are digitally enabled and operate on AI or artificial intelligence to provide prompt access to HR functions, including vacation time, benefits and problem inquiry at work.

3.9 Reduced Costs

- **Cost-cutting on the Recruitment Process:** AI will streamline the recruitment process and make it cost-effective and time-saving by automating much of it.
- **Training Cost Reduction:** The ability of AI to provide highly personalized learning paths and development strategies will assist in ensuring that people get the training they require at the most suitable time and will help eradicate redundant or less essential training workshops and conserve the personnel budget.

3.10 Flexibility and Scalability

- **Large-scale HR Management:** AI provides scalable HR solutions which can be used to control operations across multiple numbers of places and countries for very large companies having thousands of workers.
- **Adaptation of Workforce:** Flexible AI solutions now enable HR to adapt to workforce changes readily. This requires changes in labour laws, skill demands that are continually changing, or changes in employee demographics.

4. HINTS ON IMPLEMENTING AI IN HR

AI can significantly improve efficiency, decision-making, and the general employee experience once it has been implemented correctly. Nevertheless, such adoption must be thoroughly planned, implemented with caution and enforcement, and continuously managed. The following are some of the key pointers to successfully enforce AI in HR:

- **Understand Business Goals:** Ensure that the large business goals fit the AI projects of the business. As an example, the selection and creation of AI tools must be focused on the creation of diversity and inclusion in the company.
- **Clear Workflow Maintenance**: Create an overall AI adoption roadmap that contains the goals, timeline and key guiding directions on how to go through the process. This must include a language of win and a method of implementation on how and when AI solutions would be implemented across the HR department. Not all AI use cases should be used at the same time. Their workability and viability should be classified based on their feasibility.
- **AI Tools Selection Process:** The first step should be experimental projects that will bring immediate dividends and create an interest in applying AI more generally. Compare different AI platforms and tools that are available in the market to determine which one can serve the needs of your firm. Factors like service support, scaling, customization, and integration capability are some of the elements that are instrumental. Select AI products that do not require a long period of technical training before HR personnel can work and understand.
- **Privacy maintenance of Data:** Balancing the energy and power consumption and the QoU is the key factor in the optimal design of an AI-based network. It's advisable to ensure crisp, relevant, and clean data prior to using AI. If HR data is sensitive, give absolute priority to data privacy and security. Make certain an AI follows applicable data protection standards, such as the

European Union's GDPR, and secure access-imposition of access limitations and encryption on data where appropriate.

- **AI-powered Employee Empowerment:** Designers of AI systems must assume responsibility for making sure that automation provides empowerment to workers. Designers need to remember that when they micromanage by allowing them autonomy of decision, instead of trusting them, they dull their effectiveness and creativity. Overall, AI has been most warmly welcomed when managers are given the chance to override AI recommendations when they don't believe they are optimal.
- **Early Engagement of Stakeholders:** Recruitment of HR specialists in the course of the AI adoption operation initiation. Not only are their opinions essential to choose the appropriate tools, identify potential issues and ensure that AI solutions blend with HR processes without any inconveniences. Work with the data and IT departments to ensure that the AI projects are supported by data management activities and that AI technologies are promptly linked to the current HR technology.
- **Transparency Establishment:** The rationale of the AI recommendations has to be transparent so that the managers feel comfortable implementing it. This would include a comprehensive description of the objectives of the recommendation to the managers and employees, the data that was utilized in supporting the recommendation, the variables that had the most influence on the recommendation, a list of all the variables that the recommendation was founded on, and a prediction of the accuracy of the recommendation.
- **Language and Cultural Implications:** To be able to learn and provide relevant suggestions, AI requires context, which is confirmed in the information of various locations where AI will be utilized. Although the two parts of the operations of a multinational organization may share the same language, an AI-built solution suited to one of them may require full relearning before implementation in the other. This is related to the creation and training of the model, as well as the interactions of the final users of the AI solution.
- **Other Apps Consideration Before Creating an App:** It's considered best to have the final objective in mind comprehensively as you figure out and design your AI solutions. This will forestall an excess of disordered chatbots responding to similar queries without leveraging shared data and services. It's essential to do this now more than ever, as the apps don't always fit into the standard HR subdomains. For instance, when compared to other HR services, data extracted from learning and compensation is required for the compensation scenario that was discussed previously.
- **Don't Hold Off Until You Have an Ideal Solution:** It is optimal to offer your personnel a minimal viable product and declare its release. On the un-

veiling of IBM's performance management chatbot, users were encouraged to ask tricky questions to the bot as they acknowledged it was ready, though not flawless. This enabled IBM to quickly carry out the AI solution and enabled the chatbot to advance.

5. IBM's HRM WITH AI - A CASE STUDY

In these challenging times, the growth of generative AI and foundation models has totally altered the way in which firms across all industries perform business. This is especially true for the HR department, which has been pushed forward following the AI revolution. With accordance to 36% of CEOs polled for IBM Institute for Business Value's (IBV) study of recent times titled "CEO decision-making in the age of AI", the job force and skills are a major influence on their company. Flaring the use of AI attributes to aid human labour in standard HR operations like recruiting, induction, and skill development possesses the capacity to redefine businesses and enable them to compete in a universal marketplace.

5.1 What is HR Automation?

HR experts were accustomed to performing certain processes manually. Nowadays, HR automation oversees these tasks with the help of software and algorithms. These tasks encompass generating job requisitions, handling time-off requests, bringing new hires on board, and data entry for job application management. It facilitates a data-driven approach for hiring, promoting, and talent retention that aspires to diminish prejudice and optimize the experiences of both job seekers and workers.

Businesses can reduce basic manual tasks by using automation, AI, ML, and NLP to enhance HR. This simplifies HR, maintains consistency in procedures, reduces errors, boosts productivity, and enhances the workplace. HR can concentrate on people by reducing routine tasks. They will be able to create a positive workplace culture, assist staff members with relocation, and plan for everyone's advancement. However, remember the Association for Intelligent Information Management (AIIM): HR may need to pick up some new skills if tasks are automated. This could go awry and disrupt interpersonal communication if improperly trained.

5.2 What HR Leaders should take care of while implementing AI?

Several new challenges pertaining to the consequences of generative AI on workers have surfaced with its emergence. People remain a leading edge in companies, even as AI develops to be more widespread. Yet, a recent global survey from the IBM Institute for Business Value (IBV) shows that company executives are facing an assortment of talent-related hardships, including the need for cutting-edge business models, incompetence, and evolving worker expectations. The skills gap in the world is real and soaring. On the basis of a survey carried out among executives, 40% of their workforce will necessitate reskilling over the next three years, attributable to the execution of AI and automation. According to World Bank estimates, that might be equivalent to 1.4 billion of the 3.4 billion persons in the world workforce. Among the present talent issues, a prominent one is developing new skills for current employees, according to respondents.

AI can boost employees' prospects by enhancing their skills. As a matter of fact, based on a survey of executives, 87% of them believe that generative AI will strengthen workers as opposed to replacing them. This varies according to the function: 97% of executives suppose that workers in procurement are likely to be enhanced rather than replaced, compared to 93% in risk compliance, 93% in finance, 77% in customer service, and 73% in promotion. Workers put ahead rewarding work over versatility and opportunity for professional development; however, leaders aren't always able to accommodate their needs. Employees, on being questioned, say that having fulfilling work is more important to them than pay and job security, even as AI is poised to undertake more manual and repetitive chores. This aspect transcends even flexible hours, opportunities for career advancement, and equity. Moreover, nearly 50% of workers who responded to the poll answered that their job is far more substantial than their employer or associates.

Employers, though, don't appear to understand what is of the essence. Beyond remuneration and job security, executives attested flexible work arrangements as the most epochal attribute, alongside impactful work, crowned lowest amongst their workforce's priorities.

5.3 History of IBM AI

IBM has been occupying itself with AI among other technologies for over 70 years, and it collaborates with businesses in a variety of industries and areas, incorporating financial services, retail commerce, aerospace, and education. These businesses use Watson to help them arrive at new observations, enhance efficiency, and deliver better customer experiences. Let's rewind in time before discussing how Watson is carrying out business now.

During the latter half of the 20th century, IBM researchers trained some of the initial available neural networks with the help of long-familiar games like checkers and backgammon, developing the technologies that would lay the groundwork for artificial intelligence in the 21st century. The team improved computerized gaming and breakdown strategy through experimentation, aided by these systems. Renowned IBM researcher Arthur Samuel provided this method the name "Machine Learning", a phrase he came up with that still serves as essential to artificial intelligence today.

When IBM disclosed a "Shoebox" at the 1962 World's Fair, it made another substantial advancement in the discipline of artificial intelligence within a brief period of a decade. The IBM machine, so named because of its reduced size, was the first of all other machines designed with a speech recognition system to identify a human voice. A shoebox, a prototype for advanced NLP, could process a string of numbers and mathematical commands that were said to it. This furnished the foundation for the mechanised customer support agents and smart speakers that are widely in use at present.

Ten years ago, modern AI was developed. Using millions of images and days of brute force computation, a team of university researchers showed that a deep learning model could be trained to detect objects and animals in brand-new images. The exponential growth of AI models has outpaced the development of the technology required to train these giants and run them on cloud servers or edge devices like smartphones and sensors. For this reason, the IBM Research AI Hardware Centre decided to create a specialised computer processor for AI. We call it an artificial intelligence unit, or AIU (Burns et al., 2022).

Reasons for Using AI in HR:

- To address urgent business issues
- To make the most effective use of HR budgets
- To draw in and cultivate fresh talent
- To offer robust decision assistance
- To enhance the working environment

5.4 IBM's AI-based Education

At IBM, the use of AI in education has yielded remarkable outcomes. IBM created Your Learning, a comprehensive, individualised online learning marketplace, using AI. 98% of employees visit it each quarter. Learning and company performance are directly correlated, according to business impact studies, and further research has revealed that individuals who are more likely and eager to learn do better overall. A learning chatbot responds to enquiries around the clock. IBM's AI-powered learning platform is thereby boosting course completions and enrolments, which speeds up the acquisition of strategic skills (Guenole & Feinzig, 2018).

5.5 AI and IBM HR tools

A worldwide labour crisis, a widening skills gap, and changing employee expectations are just a few of the difficulties HR directors face. HR leaders now have a fresh chance to modernise and rethink the HR department, develop and maintain a workforce prepared for the future, and encourage the creativity required to support the company in achieving its more comprehensive strategic mission and goals, thanks to generative AI.

Businesses must swiftly adjust to changes in the market, employ digital advances to optimise operations, and use human resources judiciously in this age of rapid digitalisation, where the newest tools and technology are becoming an essential element of business. Since modern businesses' primary asset is their people capital, they must implement the newest personnel management techniques to boost productivity and flexibility in a dynamic business climate.

It is necessary to safely arrange, store, track, edit, and distribute electronic documents thanks to modern document management systems. All company documents can be managed, accessed, and stored on a single platform called DMS. Monitoring document modifications helps to prevent misunderstandings with various file versions and guarantees the preservation of the edit history (TERENTIEVA, PAVLOV, & TVERDOKHLIB, 2024).

AI revolutionises HRM by introducing innovative techniques and technology that streamline a variety of HR duties. The vast array of AI technologies that are altering HR practices is examined in this overview. AI affects hiring and selection as well, since tools like automatic resume parsing and facial analysis in video interviews enable efficient candidate evaluation. AI increases its impact on employee engagement and retention strategies through the use of sentiment analysis of feedback and recommenders for customised career development (Madanchian et al., 2023).

6. USING HR STRATEGY IN THE AI AGE

HR strategy in the AI era is centred on using AI to improve the employee experience in a number of areas, from hiring to retaining staff, while also making sure that human-centric methods and ethical implementation are maintained. An entrepreneur's HR strategy would be advantageous for a company aiming to enter the market with a unique business model created through substantial use of AI. Small start-ups are where it is most prevalent. One of the biggest HR challenges for these businesses is cultivating an entrepreneurial culture and workforce; they need people who can make decisions fast, take calculated risks, and have resilience to produce ground-breaking breakthroughs in goods and services (Pathak & Solanki,

2021). Nonetheless, businesses that place a high value on organisational activity and process efficiency have two choices for their HR division (Park, 2018). The goal of ambivalent HR is to combine humans and AI to improve the effectiveness and adaptability of the current product or service. They try to identify and teach people who can understand machine logic and work with AI. The strategic plan for a competitive environment is represented in Figure 3. Here's a closer look at how HR strategy changes in the AI era:

- AI for Efficiency and Automation.
- HR Driven by Data.
- Human-Centred Methods.
- Reskilling as well as upskilling.
- Aligning HR strategically.

Figure 3. Strategy from a Functionalist Perspective

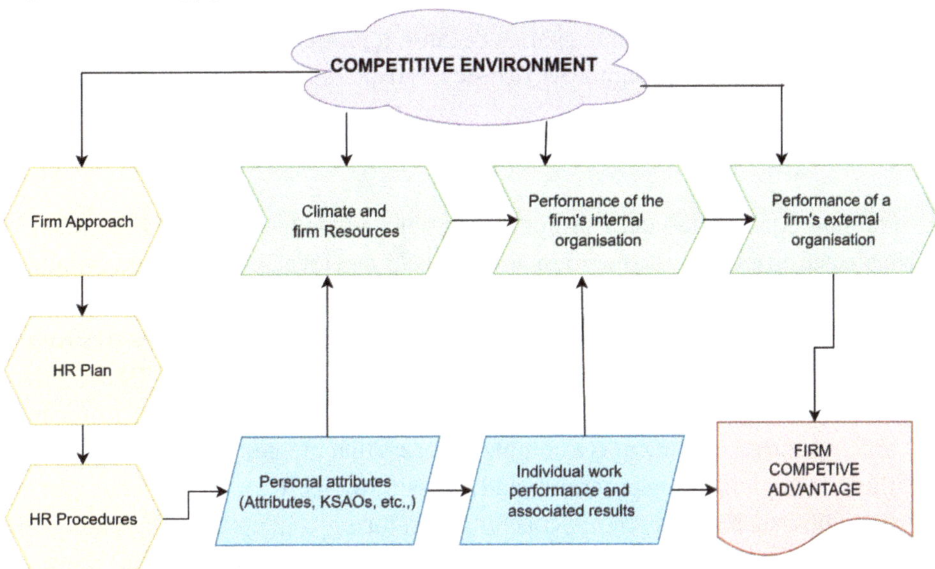

6.1 Recruiting Process

Recruiting is the initial stage in the process of obtaining, amassing, and selling human capital resources (Kim & Ployhart, 2018). The process by which a company finds, draws in, and retains potential employees is called recruiting. The number and calibre of people who join an organisation are constrained by the pool of possible hires. Internal performance or unit-level human capital has been the main dependent variable in recruiting research conducted at the firm level. Creating a job description, sourcing individuals, screening and shortlisting, interviewing, evaluating, making a job offer, and onboarding new hires are all typical steps in the HR recruitment process. Finding the best candidate for available positions inside an organisation is the goal of this multi-step procedure.

6.2 Selection Process

Identifying the need for a new role and outlining the necessary skills and qualifications are the first steps in the HR selection process. Next comes advertising the position, screening applications, conducting assessments and interviews, confirming references and background, and, lastly, issuing a job offer. Selection describes the pool of individual-level human capital that an organisation acquires, whereas recruiting describes the prospective pool of individual-level human capital that an organisation may acquire. Additionally, they contended that staffing is especially crucial during periods of significant economic change because it produces higher-quality generic human capital resources that improve firm-level adaptation to environmental changes.

6.3 Development and Training

Training is a methodical attempt to transfer knowledge and skills to enhance performance on an individual, group, or organisational level. Development is unique to each person's pursuits that contribute to their personal development. Several other studies have looked into the relationship between training and organisational success after that meta-analysis was carried out, and a more recent study found 67 studies that do so. In order to enhance employee competencies and organisational performance, HR training and development is a complex process that includes determining needs, creating and implementing programs, and assessing their efficacy. It includes a range of techniques, such as eLearning, coaching, mentoring, and on-the-job training, all of which are meant to match employee development with corporate objectives. In this regard, AI can be used to schedule, organise, and coordinate virtual training activities like online courses and remote classrooms. The influence of any training on an employee's subsequent career inside the company can also be monitored by querying such databases. Lastly, AI can enhance talent retention by enabling proactive responses to the needs of employees.

6.4 How is AI used in HR by IBM?

AI and automation-enabled self-service can streamline processes. HR personnel no longer need to go through lengthy policy manuals or hop between apps thanks to generative AI, which helps them swiftly summarise information and get trustworthy replies in real time. Crucially, concerning HRM, the field of AI Research includes human-AI interactions and AI in the context of work replacement. Cooperation, instruction, hiring, and decision-making. IBM employs AI in HR to boost decision-making, automate processes, and enhance employee experiences. AI can be defined as computer programs that mimic or simulate human-like intellectual behaviours, even when they behave differently.

7. IMPLICATIONS FOR THEORY

The primary goal was to analyse the body of knowledge regarding intelligent automation in HRM contexts to identify the key issues and implications for HR strategy and operations. The issues raised by that research were either opportunities or obstacles for HRM; nevertheless, there aren't many studies specifically about AI and intelligent automation, and those that do exist mostly concentrate on other technologies or, more recently, big data (Vrontis et al., 2023).

- **AI helps HR managers make better, faster decisions**: AI and expert systems assist HR managers, particularly non-experts, in making better, faster decisions, which increases the accuracy of HR procedures overall.
- **The necessity of a multidisciplinary approach:** Because AI in HR affects many different domains, academics should work together across disciplines (such as ethics and computer science) to address difficult problems like employee acceptability and ethics.
- **AI's effect on employment is still developing**: Despite worries that AI will completely replace jobs, the study concludes that such significant shifts in hiring and human resources procedures have not yet occurred.
- **Privacy and ethical issues must be resolved**: As the usage of AI increases, privacy and ethical issues surface. Employee and employer interests may be balanced with the use of solutions such as conflict resolution models.

AI is being utilised more and more in HR to improve decision-making, automate jobs, and improve employee satisfaction. AI's capacity to expedite hiring, customise onboarding, extract insights from data, and enhance employee engagement and retention is demonstrated through case studies. Some businesses have used AI in their operations to improve performance, engagement, and culture. initiatives for retention. These case studies demonstrate how AI is already transforming employee retention by illuminating its practical applications in actual business environments.

- IBM: Using AI to Manage a Big Workforce
- Unilever: Using AI to Transform Hiring
- Hilton: Using AI to Improve Workforce Planning

Automation, robots, cloud, IoT, AR/VR, and blockchain are the six disruptive technologies driving the expansion of the Indian IT sector, which includes BigTech Services. Traditional volume-centric or service-level agreements are being challenged more and more by more effective and value-focused business strategies to spur growth. To co-create AI solutions for improving EX, the BigTech HR team had to use technology and involve both business and technology professionals (Malik et al., 2023).

7.1 AI-Powered Workday Employee Analytics

AI aids businesses in better understanding their workers and in making wise decisions. Workday Illuminate and other AI-powered platforms utilise machine learning to uncover hidden insights and provide narratives that inform crucial human decision-making. Additionally, it may enhance risk management, maximise learning and development, and personalise employee experiences.

Workday, a leading provider of workplace HR solutions, has integrated AI into its workforce analytics platform to help organisations optimise worker management. The program tracks employee cooperation, performance, and engagement using AI to deliver real-time insights into workforce trends. Workday and IBM case studies demonstrate how AI can transform HRM and its effectiveness in increasing retention rates. AI is becoming more and more significant in employee retention because it provides companies with strong tools to monitor employee engagement, performance, and satisfaction in real-time and enables predictive analytics to identify employees who may be at risk of leaving. Businesses that deploy AI effectively can boost worker engagement, productivity, and pleasure while simultaneously.

7.2 Talent Analytics and AI

AI is advancing the field of talent analytics, which analyzes employee data to better workforce planning and commercial decisions. The phrase "machine learning" describes a group of methods that allow one to either identify patterns in data (unsupervised machine learning) or predict outcomes (supervised machine learning).

However, if the objective of the talent analytics project is to quantify the contribution of the training investment to business volume, a supervised regression model may be a good option because training data can help choose the process's inputs (training and other controls) and outputs (business volume). AI's incorporation into talent analytics improves decision-making, expedites HR procedures, and eventually leads to improved performance, retention, and talent acquisition. Lastly, a virtual assistant can aid with the onboarding of new employees. AI presents several chances to create personalised training programs according to particular interests and attention spans. AI can also help with internal job searches and career advancement (Nocker & Sena, 2019).

7.3 AI approaches being used in HRM

Through work automation, better decision-making, and improved employee satisfaction, AI in HRM is completely changing the way human resources operate. AI has been seen as a diverse field of computer science, and its methods are frequently diverse and poorly classified. For their applicability in various HRM functions, the majority of HRM in AI research that has addressed AI applications in HRM has used AI techniques such as data mining, expert systems, fuzzy logic, and algorithm techniques. This is accomplished through a variety of AI techniques, such as machine learning, natural language processing, and predictive analytics, which are applied in HR service desks, learning and development, performance management, and recruitment.

- AI can monitor employee performance data and produce reports that indicate both areas of strength and need for development. This aids HR managers in establishing performance targets and customised growth programs.
- AI can help recruits with onboarding tasks like scheduling training sessions and filling out paperwork. This makes the onboarding process more efficient and less stressful for new hires.
- AI is capable of identifying important areas for improvement by analysing massive databases of employee performance, engagement, and turnover data. HR directors can make better data-drivcn dccisions as a result.
- AI is capable of determining each learner's unique needs and developing individualised lesson programs. Employee engagement and growth possibilities are enhanced as a result.

7.4 Tools for HR Analysis

Organisations may learn more about workforce engagement, performance, and other important HR topics by analysing employee data with the aid of HR analytics solutions. Microsoft, SAP, IBM, and Oracle are business intelligence vendors. HR modules with BI and data analytics features are available in BI applications. The study on HR analytics offered a six-step guide on how to incorporate HR analytics to make sure it fits with HR objectives and intended organisational results (Mohammed, 2019). ADP Workforce Now, Tableau, BambooHR, and Visier are a few of the well-known tools. These resources can support predictive analytics, reporting, and data visualisation. Furthermore, the study made two important recommendations: creating a COE for HR analytics and guaranteeing a foundation based on HR analytics for all organisational functions. The study also examined how HR analytics may be utilised to find and hire talent for the company, which will help with succession and talent planning.

8. ESSENTIAL ELEMENTS OF HR ANALYTICS TOOLS

- **Talent management:** Tools are available to monitor worker performance, spot high-potential workers, and create talent management plans.
- **Data Integration**: Payroll, talent management, and employee engagement platforms are just a few of the HR systems that the majority of HR analytics solutions can interface with.
- **Employee Engagement**: By examining information from performance reviews, employee surveys, and other sources, HR analytics can assist businesses in measuring and enhancing employee engagement.
- **Analytics for Prediction**: Predictive analytics features in certain applications can assist HR professionals in predicting trends, spotting possible hazards, and coming to data-driven conclusions.
- **Diversity & Inclusion**: HR analytics can assist companies in monitoring and evaluating diversity data, pinpointing areas in need of development, and formulating plans to further these goals.

8.1 The Strategy Process at IBM

Several elements are put together in IBM's process to define strategy, which include increasing corporate value, fostering an innovation culture and exploiting technology and data, as shown in Figure 4. The strategy process at IBM from its founding through 1999 paralleled the approach used by any large complex firm.

Technological advances were monitored and sporadic ventures were led to solve particular problems. Especially, BU heads prepared and presented their plans for the coming year to the senior management group during the annual strategy review session. The real planning was more or less a staff exercise performed to satisfy high management; it was neither a true picture of what needed to be done in order to remain competitive nor a guideline for action. Knowing corporate goals, addressing obstacles, creating a roadmap, checking implementation, and starting with small victories that will grow gradually are all important elements. Furthermore, this process includes talent acquisition management as well as the establishment of dependable supplier relationships that are IT initiative-oriented. As stated by IBM, identifying possible difficulties is necessary since getting started on an effective plan requires dealing with impediments and hindrances initially.

IBM's tagline, "Let's Put Smart to Work," emphasises how technology and data can boost competitiveness and productivity. In order to hire and retain staff, IBM stresses the value of a strong talent acquisition strategy. There are five stages in the strategic management process. Strategy: Planning has also become essential once you are aware of your obstacles and the resources at your disposal.

Figure 4. Business Leadership Model of IBM

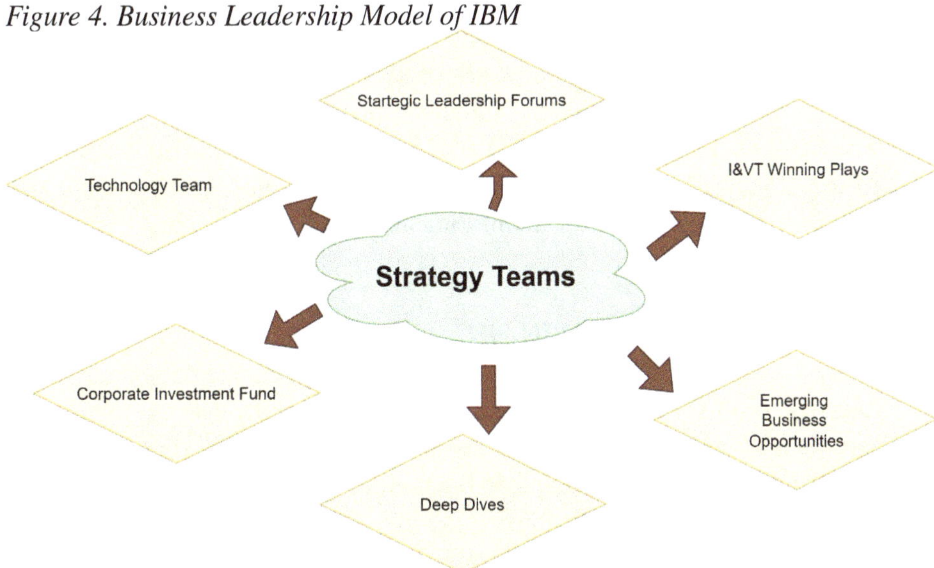

9. CHALLENGES OF AI IN HR

- **Reinforcement:** HR goes further in training and re-skilling its workforce, thus it does not stop at the need to identify skills gaps through, such as providing education about AI technologies and their concepts, nor adapting job positions with the advent of AI trends.
- **Deployment:** Often, the issues of integration, user adoption and ethical concerns are at the heart of shaky implementation of AI in HR. Starting with trial and error projects that can lead to poor employee experience, an organization may opt to retool based on an IBM study. Companies must also build capabilities to fine-tune processes, as well as develop AI models.
- **Cybersecurity:** A very important aspect you may observe about artificial intelligence in HR systems is that it poses many security concerns; especially, privacy and data protection are at risk. One problem encountered is with the use of AI in people's lives, where there is a need for adequate provisions to protect against data breaches. Another issue here is the AI-driven attacks as well as algorithmic bias. Furthermore, there could be some shortage of independent Verification and intricacy held by AI systems could introduce vulnerabilities to be addressed meticulously.
- **Privacy Concerns for Employees:** Although companies nowadays collect and process a wide variety of all kinds of data that relates to their employees, it is very interesting to notice that employee privacy is still a very big issue in terms of AI's integration in HR. One of the issues that can arise when using AI in HR is as follows: Data breaches, surveillance, bias, manipulation, and AI potentially being used for monitoring and invasive oversight.

10. FUTURE SCOPE OF AI IN HR

- **Large Scale of Hyper-Personalization:** AI will pave the way for completely personalized employee journeys—this includes career paths that are created individually, learning that adapts to the user, as well as wellness and benefits plans that are made specifically for the individual. It studies the behaviour and preferences of employees, thereby increasing the level of engagement, retention, and satisfaction by not grouping but treating every employee as a unique individual.
- **Proactive Ecosystems:** With the use of AI, the human resource department will be converted from a reactive one to a proactive one. It predicts churn, spots potential leaders, and estimates shortages of skills by looking at perfor-

mance, trends in the market, and the organization's data – thus giving the way to strategic, data-driven talent planning and workforce optimization.

- **Multimodal Recruitment Process:** Next hiring will employ artificial intelligence for multimodal candidate assessment, automated bias detection, and immersive skill simulations. AI evaluates video interviews, written responses, and cultural fit to facilitate fair, efficient, and accurate talent selection.
- **Macro-learning and Development:** AI is going to be the main driver behind systems of lifelong learning that will be able to deliver small parts of learning content exactly at the time when they are needed, and also be able to keep track of the level of skills of a person in real-time. Innovative, individualized and flexible platforms will be able to regularly update the competencies of employees and at the same time ensure that these skills correspond to the changes in the market and the organization.

11. CONCLUSION

As a dynamic HR manager, you should be aware that companies need to start focusing on next-generation approaches instead of best practices. An in-depth investigation of perception, a distinct phenomenon, in a novel setting with AI-assisted interaction is made possible by the use of a quantitative technique. It restricts the study's generalisability, just like quantitative research. The reason for this is that the Results are not statistically representative of all HR managers, employees, and AI interactions. According to the study's findings, human resource managers and staff may believe that training time and inattention will be reduced when AI technology is incorporated into the training and development process as opposed to the conventional approach. Results are not statistically representative of all HR managers, employees, and AI interactions. Regarding implementation, the outcomes of the study can give managers and HR staff a number of hints.

The findings indicate that managers and staff in human resources should profit from AI tools and technologies. During this competitive time, the human resources department receives a large volume of job applications. Three categories of study limitations were established: data limits, data collection technique restrictions, and study scope limitations. Additionally, the emphasis was on analysing the technological interventions and IT infrastructure, including those that impact data mining, storage, and creation in relation to the successful application of HR analytics and the requirement that they be effective in terms of data storage in order to be pertinent for HR analytics. One important finding from the literature review on the integration of HR analytics in the field of human resource management is that, although there are theoretical model suggestions that could be used for a seamless integration, there is a dearth of literature that examines the models' practical applicability and the success (or failure) of these models or strategies when used in an organisational setting.

It clarified the effects of robotics, artificial intelligence, and other cutting-edge technologies on HRM; however, it was not comprehensive. The widespread AI technologies covered in this review demonstrate the revolutionary change brought about by the use of AI in HRM procedures. To improve HRM effectiveness and efficiency, these tools include algorithmic applicant shortlisting, ethical decision-making frameworks, and full AI capacity models. Organisations must strike a balance between these benefits and problems as the HRM landscape changes as a result of AI integration, utilising AI's ability to transform HRM procedures for increased efficacy, ethics, and efficiency. If the companies can handle these elements along the digital, physical, and human continuum, it bodes well for workers who perceive a long-term worth in their affiliation with the company. Through these initiatives, a company can better understand how to resolve conflicts when producing dynamic HR executives who excel at networking and HR entrepreneurship. By examining IBM's operations, we have provided a brief overview of what it takes to demonstrate dynamic HR practices in the current global marketplace and where future HR research should focus. Additionally, case studies comparing producers and consumers of AI enterprises with advanced adopters of AI-enabled HR apps would provide significant distinctions and insights into AI-enabled HRM practices. Lastly, as part of a larger digitalised HR ecosystem, our conceptualisation ignores ethical issues and the negative aspects of AI-enabled HR solutions.

REFERENCES

Budhwar, P., Chowdhury, S., Wood, G., Aguinis, H., Bamber, G. J., Beltran, J. R., & DeNisi, A. (2023). Human resource management in the age of generative artificial intelligence: Perspectives and research directions on ChatGPT. *Human Resource Management Journal, 33*(3), 606–659.

Burns, J., Chang, L., Hardware, A., Scaling, A., Martineau, K., & Generative, A. (2022). Meet the ibm artificial intelligence unit. *IBM Research.[Online]. Available: https://research. ibm. com/blog/ibm-artificial-intelligence-unit-aiu*

Ekuma, K. (2024). Artificial intelligence and automation in human resource development: A systematic review. *Human Resource Development Review, 23*(2), 199–229.

Guenole, N., & Feinzig, S. (2018). *The business case for AI in HR. With Insights and Tips on Getting Started.* IBM Smarter Workforce Institute, IBM Corporation.

Gupta, R. (2024). Impact of artificial intelligence (AI) on human resource management (HRM). *International Journal For Multidisciplinary Research, doi, 10.*

Hamouche, S., Rofa, N., & Parent-Lamarche, A. (2025). Systematic bibliometric review of artificial intelligence in human resource development: Insights for HRD researchers, practitioners and policymakers. *European Journal of Training and Development, 49*(1-2), 43–62.

Kambur, E., & Akar, C. (2022). Human resource developments with the touch of artificial intelligence: A scale development study. *International Journal of Manpower, 43*(1), 168–205.

Kim, Y., & Ployhart, R. E. (2018). The strategic value of selection practices: Antecedents and consequences of firm-level selection practice usage. *Academy of Management Journal, 61*(1), 46–66.

Korzynski, P., Kim, S., & Egan, T. (2024). *Bridging human resource development processes through generative Artificial Intelligence* (Vol. 35). Wiley Online Library.

Lilly, A., Rajkumar, R., & Amudha, R. (2022). Aggrandizing the human resource development with underpinning artificial intelligence. *Journal of Statistics and Management Systems, 25*(5), 1083–1094.

Madanchian, M., Taherdoost, H., & Mohamed, N. (2023). AI-based human resource management tools and techniques; a systematic literature review. *Procedia Computer Science, 229*, 367–377.

Madhumithaa, N., Sharma, A., Adabala, S. K., Siddiqui, S., & Kothinti, R. R. (2025). Leveraging AI for personalized employee development: A new era in human resource management. *Advances in Consumer Research. Association for Consumer Research (U. S.)*, *2*, 134–141.

Malik, A., Budhwar, P., & Mohan, H., & NR, S. (2023). Employee experience–the missing link for engaging employees: Insights from an MNE's AI-based HR ecosystem. *Human Resource Management*, *62*(1), 97–115.

Mohammed, D. A. Q. (2019). HR analytics: A modern tool in HR for predictive decision making. *Journal of Management*, *6*(3).

Murugesan, U., Subramanian, P., Srivastava, S., & Dwivedi, A. (2023). A study of artificial intelligence impacts on human resource digitalization in industry 4.0. *Decision Analytics Journal*, *7*, 100249.

Nocker, M., & Sena, V. (2019). Big data and human resources management: The rise of talent analytics. *Social Sciences*, *8*(10), 273.

Park, W. (2018). *Artificial intelligence and human resource management: new perspectives and challenges*. Japan Institute for Labour Policy and Training.

Pathak, S., & Solanki, V. K. (2021). Impact of internet of things and artificial intelligence on human resource development. In *Further advances in internet of things in biomedical and cyber physical systems* (pp. 239–267). Springer.

Qamar, Y., Agrawal, R. K., Samad, T. A., & Chiappetta Jabbour, C. J. (2021). When technology meets people: The interplay of artificial intelligence and human resource management. *Journal of Enterprise Information Management*, *34*(5), 1339–1370.

TERENTIEVA, N., PAVLOV, D., & TVERDOKHLIB, M. (2024). INTEGRATION OF DIGITAL TOOLS AND ARTIFICIAL INTELLIGENCEINTO HR MANAGEMENT PROCESSES. *Herald of Khmelnytskyi National University. Economic sciences, 334*(5), 624-629.

Votto, A. M., Valecha, R., Najafirad, P., & Rao, H. R. (2021). Artificial intelligence in tactical human resource management: A systematic literature review. *International Journal of Information Management Data Insights*, *1*(2), 100047.

Vrontis, D., Christofi, M., Pereira, V., Tarba, S., Makrides, A., & Trichina, E. (2023). Artificial intelligence, robotics, advanced technologies and human resource management: a systematic review. *Artificial intelligence and international HRM*, 172-201.

KEY TERMS AND DEFINITIONS

Data Privacy: In HRM refers to the ethical and legal responsibility of employers to protect sensitive personal data of employees, job candidates, and other stakeholders from unauthorized access, misuse, or disclosure.

HR Automation: Refers to the use of technology tools ranging from software applications, AI, chatbots and workflow systems, which are now able to do the routine manual HR tasks automatically – thus leaving more time for HR professionals to engage in strategic work.

Human Resource Management (HRM): It is the strategic approach to the effective and efficient management of people in an organization, which helps the business gain a competitive advantage. It is designed to maximize employee performance in the service of an employer's strategic objectives.

Predictive Analytics: It involves using historical HR data, statistical algorithms, and machine learning techniques to identify patterns and forecast future workforce trends. It enables HR professionals to make proactive, data-driven decisions.

Stakeholder: It is any individual, group, or organization that has an interest in the activities and outcomes of a business or project. In HRM, stakeholders are those who are directly or indirectly affected by HR policies, decisions, and practices.

Chapter 8
Emotionally Intelligent Workplaces:
Leveraging Emotion AI to Nurture Positive Organizational Culture

Jyoti Chauhan
https://orcid.org/0000-0002-5034-7921
SGT University, Gurugram, India

Kanishka Gupta
https://orcid.org/0000-0001-7211-7652
Vivekananda Institute of Professional Studies-Technical Campus, Delhi, India

Dolly Gaur
https://orcid.org/0000-0002-3868-5397
GLA University, India

Abhinav Pal
Symbiosis International University, Pune, India

Abdul Wajid
https://orcid.org/0000-0003-2585-5550
MIE-SPPU Institute of Higher Education, Qatar

ABSTRACT

As businesses become more aware of the importance of emotional intelligence in employee satisfaction and organizational performance, its inclusion in workplace wellness programs has become more popular. This chapter discusses how Emotion AI- powerful technologies that recognize and understand human emotions- can be used to cultivate emotionally intelligent workplaces and positive organizational cul-

DOI: 10.4018/979-8-3373-5871-0.ch008

ıt © 2026, IGI Global Scientific Publishing. Copying or distributing in print or electronic forms without written permission of IGI Global Scientific Publishing is prohibited. Use of this chapter to generative artificial intelligence (AI) technologies is expressly prohibited. The publisher reserves all rights to license its use for generative AI training and machine learning model development.

ture. This chapter theorizes the embedding of Emotion AI into core human resource management, leadership, and workplace communication domains. It explores how these technologies can inform empathetic decision-making, enhance team dynamics, and build inclusive, emotionally supportive cultures. Ethical issues such as data privacy, consent, and algorithmic bias are also deeply scrutinized. This chapter contends that when used carefully and responsibly, Emotion AI has enormous potential to transform cultural well-being and aid in creating emotionally mature, high-performance organizations.

1. INTRODUCTION

1.1. The rise of emotional intelligence in the workplace

In modern academic circles, emotional intelligence (EI) the ability to perceive, understand and manage emotions in ourselves and others has grown to be a buzzword, and then an essential skill in successful organizational performance. Originally described by Salovey and Mayer (1990) and later popularized by Goleman (2005), EI has been the source of core competencies in the workplace, such as communication, empathetic leadership, and conflict resolution. It has been established by meta-analytic findings (e.g., Salovey and Mayer, 1990; Goleman, 2005) that high emotional intelligence is positively correlated with high job performance, enriched interpersonal relations, as well as leadership efficacy.

In the modern working environment, where digitalization is happening at exceptionally high speeds, globalization is intensifying, and complexity is increasing, EI marginally acts as a personal strength but as a strategic one. Companies that develop EI-driven organizational cultures have improved staff engagement, less burnout, and better psychological safety (Gallup, 2024; Weiss and Cropanzano, 1996). According to a report by Gallup (2024), emotional wellness is connected with productivity as the proportion of global human resource that is highly engaged is only 23%. Social and emotional forces can be used to promote retention, morale and performance when cultivated, and thus EI no longer represents a soft skill, but an institutional priority (Cherniss, 2010). It has now been inherently integrated in talent development, team building programs and leadership models.

1.2. Emerging role of Emotion AI

There has been growing momentum in the adoption of affective computing, due to the increased attention given to employee engagement, human well-being, and humanistic leadership. The technology has an array of uses depending upon whether the signs involve facial recognition or voice modulation analysis, physiological signals, or natural language processing (Picard, 2000; McStay, 2018). These subtle emotional cues eventually gain tangible insights; hence, they are relevant to workplace applications. Emotion AI was first developed as a service for the advertising, gaming, and automotive design industries. However, with the pandemic allowing organizations even more possibilities of remote working and digital communication and with the mental health agenda gaining further traction in workplaces, the transition of Emotion AI to organizational use has been expedited (Larrad et al., 2020). Interviewing candidates emotionally, gauging employee sentiment from written feedback, and on-the-fly analysis of conversations are just a few of the potential HR uses for Emotion AI today.

Organisations are experimenting with Emotion AI during meetings—virtual or physical—where vocal tone and facial expressions are considered to understand the team dynamics and to detect possible indications of stress or disengagement. Likewise, biometric wearables and stress detectors enable the emotional well-being initiatives to take a preventive approach (Delina et al., 2024). This emerging capability presents grave ethical and practical challenges. Emotions are complex, culturally contextual, and deeply personal, making them challenging to interpret perfectly and fairly via algorithmic means (McStay, 2018; Cowgill and Tucker, 2019). Emotion AI used in workplaces, especially when surreptitiously or without consent, can be perceived as invasive and trust-destroying for the employees themselves. For this reason, the use of Emotion AI in workplace surveillance has been declared high-risk by regulatory frameworks, including the proposed European Union Artificial Intelligence Act, which therefore calls for strict transparency, accountability, and human oversight (European Commission, 2021). When used responsibly, Emotion AI can help to build emotionally intelligent workplaces, empathy, early stress detection, and foster a culture of care and responsiveness.

1.3. Relevance of emotional assessment to organizational culture and employee well-being

There's a deep influence of emotional events on the organizational culture. Daily affective interactions among peers, among leaders, and between employees and the systems are the ones that determine how safety, trust, and belonging are psychologically perceived (Ashkanasy and Daus, 2005). Emotions affect the intentions and overt behavior of an individual, and at a larger level, emotive experiences affect the dynamics of collaboration, innovation, and adaptation. As a result, emotional appraisal comes out as one of the means of developing a positive organization climate. The Affective Events Theory (Weiss and Cropanzano, 1996) explains that the disproportionate impact of minor events, including recognition, feedback, or conflict, can be experienced by employees on engagement and performance.

Emotion AI solutions can help identify the affective state in real-time, whether in interpreting feelings based on communication, scanning facial or voice expressions during a meeting, or tracking physiological signs of stress. Properly used and with an informed consent, these tools can educate on the decision to make when it comes to workload distribution, team dynamics, and wellness programs (Boyd & Andalibi, 2023). Finally, emotion measurement, especially when used with Emotion AI, will enable the creation of truly empathetic, responsive, and psychologically safe organizational cultures, which are highly required in the modern multifaceted and emotion-inducing workplaces.

1.4. Objectives and structure of the chapter

The chapter has a staged development to provide clarity of the concept and a coherent flow of the story. It starts with the creation of the background views of emotional intelligence, Emotion AI, and organizational culture, which make up the theoretical foundation of the discussion. On this basis, the chapter critically examines how Emotion AI has been applied in three fundamental organizational areas, namely, human resource management, leadership, and workplace communication, and identifies the possible advantages of this technology, and the risks involved. The discussion then shifts to the subject of governance and ethics such as privacy, consent, algorithmic bias, transparency, and employee voice that define the responsible application of Emotion AI in organizations. These elements are then incorporated into a cohesive framework at the end of the chapter and presented as a roadmap towards a feasible implementation of ethically embedding Emotion AI into the workplaces of the future that are emotionally intelligent.

2. THEORETICAL FOUNDATIONS

A multidisciplinary foundation that joins theories of emotional intelligence, organizational behavior, and developments in affective computing is necessary to understand and appreciate the positive ambience of an organization engendered by Emotion AI. This section examines the conceptual pillars that shape views about emotion in organizations and lays the groundwork for the employment of Emotion AI in the workplace.

2.1 Emotional Intelligence in Organizational Contexts

Commonly, EI is the capacity to be aware of, understand, regulate, and manage emotions in oneself and others (Salovey and Sluyter, 1997). Considered by many to be the most important after 1997, Mayer and Salovey's ability model places much stress on information processing of the emotional kind, whereas Goleman's mixed model expands the EI concept to comprise social skills, motivation, empathy, and self-regulation (Goleman, 2005). Bar-On's emotional-social intelligence model extends the concept even further, incorporating more dimensions about interpersonal and stress-management competencies (Bar-On, 2006). Within organizational contexts, emotional intelligence is tied to some of the crucial outcomes like better communication, improved leadership, conflict resolution, and strengthening interrelationships (Miao et al., 2017). Leaders with EI have trust and work in synergy and negotiate intricate social environments. EI is a powerful indicator of engagement and job satisfaction especially in times of pressure and emotional uproar (Zeidner et al., 2004). It is progressively educating talent management, leadership, and teamwork building programs that focus on the development of high-performing and emotionally stable work-forces.

2.2 Organizational Culture and Emotional Climate

Organizational culture, which is defined as similarity of values, beliefs, assumptions, and behaviors that create the social and psychological environment of a workplace (Schein, 2010), has an emotional climate that arises as a result of leadership style and the interaction between the norms of communication and the informal social cues. Positive emotional climates create trust, psychological safety, empathy, and respect among themselves and create a climate that is beneficial to communication, innovation and emotional well-being (Ashkanasy and Daus, 2005). Emotions are very vital in how employees perceive justice, inclusion, and engagement. The Affective Events Theory (Weiss and Cropanzano, 1996) assumes that events at the workplace attract emotional responses which in turn determine job attitudes and behavior. Micro-processes, including recognition, feedback, or conflict, contribute to supporting or disrupting the overall climate. As the key participants in these dynamics, leaders should demonstrate emotional awareness to be able to develop cultures where employees will feel appreciated and psychologically secure. The organizations must consequently have the ability to interpret and act on the emotional dynamics in teams and departments and hence align policies and practices with the experiences of the employees. These emotion sensitive processes, which eventually lead to psychosocial health, are fundamental components of organizational cultural health, especially in diverse or distributed situations where emotional cues are more difficult to identify in traditional ways.

2.3 Affective Computing and Emotion AI

Affective computing, a term coined by Rosalind Picard (1997), refers to the design of systems and technologies that can recognize, interpret, process, and simulate human emotions. The interdisciplinary field sitting at the intersection of psychology, computer science, and neuroscience serves as a foundation for the development of Emotion AI, a growing list of technologies that infer emotional states from many data sources such as facial expressions, voice inflections, written text, and biometric signals. Core technologies in the Emotion AI toolkit include facial expression recognition performed by computer vision, voice emotion recognition leveraging acoustic signal processing, text-based sentiment analysis supported by natural language processing, and physiological sensing of a person's emotional and physiological state through measurements such as heart rate variability and galvanic skin response. These technologies have found numerous applications and are already in use, including healthcare for identifying early symptoms of mental health conditions, education to modify learning material in response to emotional states, automotive design aimed at preventing accidents due to driver fatigue, and marketing, where consumer sentiment is monitored to tailor engagement strategies (McStay, 2018; Boughanem et al., 2023).Though more mature in non-workplace settings, these applications provide insights on how emotionally intelligent technology could be responsibly and effectively integrated into an organizational setting. Effective computing tools can be implemented in operational environments to improve communication, well-being, and emotional risk management. The given integration makes effective computing a highly significant bridge between the EI theory and the practice of Emotion AI implementation in organizational life to make sure that emotionally intelligent, responsive, and human-centered work environments are cultivated.

2.4 Comparative Contributions of the Preceding Research and Unanswered gaps

The research on the topic of emotionally intelligent workplaces can be generally divided into three weakly connected, although interdependent strands, namely emotional intelligence (EI) in organizational settings, affective computing and Emotion AI, and organizational culture and employee well-being. Although each one of the streams presents some valuable insights, their theoretical convergence is still underdeveloped.

The initial one makes EI one of the most important factors in leadership performance, interpersonal relationships and motivation, and employee well-being. The primary models focus on emotion perception, regulation, empathy as well as social adaptability, and considerable evidence shows the primary role of EI in promoting better performance, decreased burnout, and well-being. Nevertheless, EI is mostly considered a personal attribute and is measured in self-reports or observations and provides a little insight into how emotional awareness should be implemented in digitally mediated or hybrid workplaces.

The second one is concerned with the fast development of affective computing and Emotion AI, including laboratory-centered recognition to real-time and multimodal analysis of facial, vocal, textual, and physiological information. In spite of rising applications in fields like healthcare, learning, and workplace analytics, this literature has so far been predominantly technocentric, without much concern of organizational context, leadership processes, and cultural interpretation. As a result, Emotion AI is often positioned as a surveillance or predictive system, as opposed to an instrument that facilitates the emotionally intelligent practice.

The third strand focuses on emotional climate, psychological safety, and affective experiences as engagement and inclusion motivators and resilience. Although it recognizes digitalization and remote work, it provides a poor conceptual insight on how to embrace Emotion AI without compromising trust and autonomy. Collectively, these streams provide the implication that Emotion AI is a socio-technical system, the effect of which hinges on its design, governance, and organizational inscription.

3. CONCEPTUALIZING EMOTION AI IN THE WORKPLACE

With the adoption of digitally enabled ecosystems that are becoming more vibrant, strategic significance grows on the ability of an organization to comprehend and react to affect states of its employees. Emotion AI represents a new type of organizational intelligence that goes beyond the conventional human resource analytics, and offers real-time understanding of affect to be used in leadership, communication, well-being, and decision-making. The following parts address the purposeful implementation of Emotion AI in thc work environment, its application as the means of decoding raw emotional data, and introduce a framework of how it could be implemented ethically and efficiently in the organization.

3.1 Integration of Emotion AI in organizational settings

The implementation of Emotion AI into organizational life involves not only the implementation of the technology but also the need to align it with the organizational goals, culture as well as ethical principles. That is, an assortment of Emotion AI tools can be offered at different employee points of contact, such as recruitment sites, online teamwork solutions, learning management systems, and well-being apps. As an example, the facial expressions and voice qualities of the candidates can be analyzed by such video interviewing platforms to detect behavioral signs of emotional involvement; sentiment analysis of internal communications, such as e-mail, chat logs, and survey feedback, can reveal the tendencies of morale, burnout, or discontent (Mudunuri and Bhattacharya, 2025). Emotion AI is also useful in bridging the emotional visibility gaps in the context of hybrid working and remote working. An effective feedback system could help a team leader perceive emotional undercurrents that she or he would not notice otherwise in an online situation. On the same note, wearable devices and biometric surveillance gadgets, which employees have to agree to, can help one understand stress, fatigue, or disengagement at the earliest (Nieves et al., 2024). In addition to ethical governance, there are large practical obstacles in the implementation of the Emotion AI in organizations. These are expensive financial burdens in data infrastructure, proprietary systems licensing and continued model maintenance and a lack of in-house skills to make responsible interpretations of affective analytics. Another significant barrier is the lack of organizational preparedness to incorporate emotional data into the decision-making process by many organizations, especially when the managers are not trained in emotional intelligence or doubt the intelligence of AI-supported information (Eke and Shuib, 2024; Tatiparti et al., 2025).

3.2 Emotion AI as a tool to detect and interpret employee emotions

Analysing a person or the surrounding with the help of multimodal data, i.e., dynamic features, i.e., facial expressions, tone of voice, or even physiological signs, and in some cases even more abstract data, i.e., textual sentiment, emotion AI evaluates affective states (stress, joy, anxiety, frustration, or engagement) (Mudunuri and Bhattacharya, 2025). Such insights could be aggregated and anonymized to create dashboards to HR leaders or managers so as to take interventions based on the information. As a case in point, when a certain team constantly records a decline in positive sentiment or where a certain period of negative sentiment is evident (e.g., performance review periods), organizations may opt to implement preemptive actions to eliminate the root causes of the issue and working-around solutions. The technology also improves the insights of the emotional diversity and nuance in an organization. Rather than presuming homogenous emotional responses to events, it offers more detailed views on how individuals and teams would emotionally react to workplace processes to enable more personalized ways of motivation, appreciation, and support. This technology has its value in the fact that it complements intuitive insights, which in turn will enable managers and HR professionals to confirm the observations and be more empathetic and accurate in their actions (McStay, 2018).

Model of implementing Emotion AI in the work environment

A company-based framework that is based on the principles of human-centered design should be used to encourage the ethical and efficient application of Emotion AI in the workplace. The implementation process must start with an evaluation and alignment stage, during which companies determine the strategic objectives, including improving the well-being of employees, curbing turnover, or becoming more engaged, and analyzing their technical infrastructure, data management and control, and the degree to which they have adopted emotional analytics in their culture. The next step should then take the form of consent and transparency whereby employees are told about the kind of emotional information that is captured, the way of how it will be used and who will have access to the information. Honesty and transparency lead to trust and dispels the fear of being spied on or abused. After ensuring that the consent mechanism is set up, the organization can then begin the data collection, and analysis through the Emotion AI tools, which have been tested to record the affective signals of different channels of information, such as text, audio, video, and physiological data, ensuring sensitivity to culture and context in interpreting the outcomes. Lastly, all these insights should be integrated into current HR and leadership systems to shape decisions in the recruitment, performance management, training, and wellness programming. This is always followed by human control which fulfills judgment and empathy. The ethics audits and powerful feedback loop needs to be implemented so that the affected employees could file grievances, opt out explicitly, demand redress, and allow organizations to conduct periodic tests of their Emotion AI systems with regard to bias, accuracy, and adverse impacts. This three-tiered model offers an adequate equilibrium to the Emotion AI, therefore, harnessing its potentialities in technological terms whilst maintaining ethical principles and creating an emotionally sensitive, empathetic and inclusive work culture.

The mechanism to make Emotionally Intelligent workplaces is presented by Figure 1.

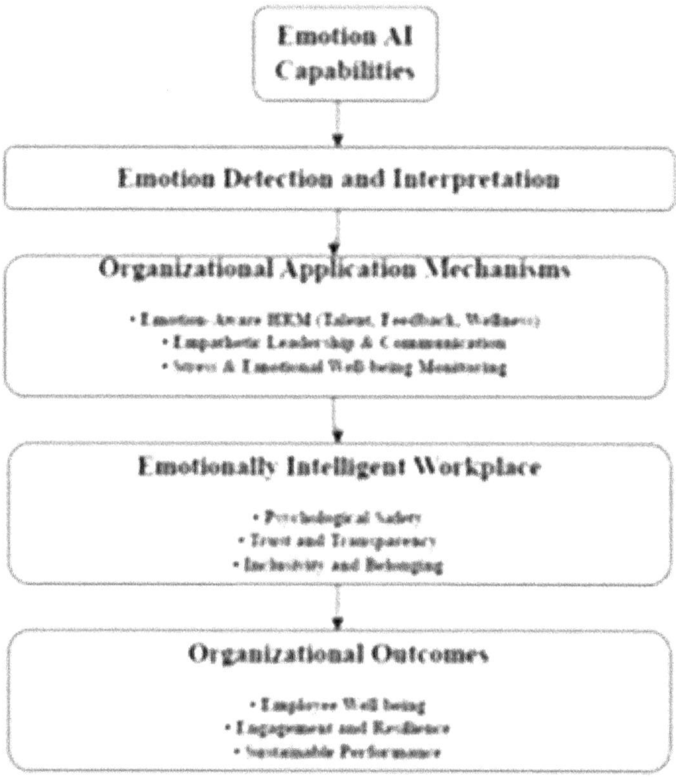

Source: Authors' own

4. LEVERAGING EMOTION AI TO NURTURE POSITIVE ORGANIZATIONAL CULTURE

The sections below are discussing how the Emotion AI can be applied to the most important areas of an organization. Instead of reformulating the notions of emotional intelligence, Emotion AI, or organizational culture within each subsection, the text expands on the original ideas provided in the previous part of the chapter and the integrative model that is provided in section 3. The domains are both analyzed with a similar framework based on the reflective benefits, risks involved, and examples within the organization, and clearly relates the understanding to the overall conceptual framework.

4.1 Application in Human Resource Management

The use of Emotion AI in Human Resource Management (HRM) is transforming traditional methods in talent acquisition, managing performance, feedback mechanisms, and well-being of employees. The use of Emotion AI tools in HRM is progressively judged based on their impact on measurable outcomes like employee engagement, burnout risk, retention intention, and perceptions of fairness besides just technical accuracy (Sadeghi, 2024; Tatiparti et al., 2025). As an illustration, certain organizations have implemented Emotion AI- based pulse surveys and sentiment analysis systems to track the changes in employee engagement and stress levels in the wake of organizational change so that HR teams can interfere instead of responding (Hosseini et al., 2023).

Emotion AI is not only transforming the fundamental roles of human resource, especially talent management, performance assessment, and employee welfare, but also provoking major ethical issues. Emotion AI can be used in talent management, particularly in the recruitment process, development, and mobility of talent within the organization, as it allows making decisions based on competencies and values. An overview of the literature relating to 116 studies reveals that AI systems are increasingly being used to screen, select, and assess employability, especially in the context of a small- to medium-sized enterprise (Rajan and Nagajothi, 2024). These will enhance accuracy of recruitment, reveal internal skills shortages and direct reskilling programs, creating a more emotive workforce. Nevertheless, algorithmic fairness, diverse training data, and human-in-the-loop systems are measures that are necessary to reduce bias (Rajan and Nagajothi, 2024).

Emotion AI enables objective, uninterrupted, and sensitive feedback in performance management. Emotional analytics combines behavioral data (peer communication, contributions to tasks, etc.) with sentiment signals in order to minimize bias and improve accuracy in appraisal (Sadeghi, 2024). Self-appraisal and feedback systems powered by AI that include sentiment-based solutions by Cisco and Workhuman help support proactive recognition and meaningful dialogue and reduce the tradition of inflexible annual reviews to cultures of constant feedback (Workhuman, 2025). Narrative-assistance tools also aid managers in improving tone and language to balance transparency and empathy, and worries also exist that nuance and misinterpretation without human intervention are lost (ACM, 2025).

The organizational priorities after the pandemic have put the emphasis on the emotional well-being, in which Emotion AI can be used to monitor it in real-time by the means of multimodal cues including voice tones, facial expressions, posture, and physiological correlates (Hosseini et al., 2023; Walambe et al., 2021). The disengagement and stress can be readily identified at the initial stages of the workplace communication tools through sentiment analysis that will lead to timely interventions. A study indicates that emotional labour takes around 1822 percent of the working hours of employees, which explains why such tools are relevant (Stanford Workplace Dynamics Lab, 2025). In spite of the potential of personalized interventions, such as mindfulness prompts and adaptive breaks, surveillance issues, privacy issues, and misuse require opt-in models, anonymized aggregation and transparent governance.

Importantly, the literature warns that the Emotion AI systems tend to reproduce the embedded bias, especially in facial recognition accuracy among demographic groups 0 (ACM, 2025; Tatiparti et al., 2025). To maintain trust, scholars focus on explainability, human supervision, and ethical governance mechanisms, including algorithmic audits and AI policy committees. Placed as a decision support tool, but not as an evaluative power, Emotion AI can help increase fairness, involvement, and well-being in all the HR functions (Rao et al., 2025).

4.2 Emotion-Aware Leadership and Communication

The recent organizational practice of Emotion-AI has been under the spotlight in its ability to empower emotionally intelligent leadership and the ability to build openness and trust. There is a growing body of substantive literature that discusses how the use of AI and emotional intelligence can support empathetic leadership and communication and warn against its use in the absence of ethical protection.

4.2.1 Supporting Empathetic Leadership through Detection of emotion

The focal point of team performance and cohesion is empathetic leadership, which is the ability to perceive and react to the emotional condition of the employees (Salovey and Sluyter, 1997). Emotion-AI offers features that complement the quality of emotional skill of leaders by providing them with prompt affective feedback and increasing their interpersonal sensitivity (Sharma et al., 2023). As an example, AI can identify signs of disagreement or emotional pain during online sessions via the tone of voice and facial expressions. This information, together with self-reflection tools, helps leaders in recalibrating their reaction and, therefore, instilling empathy, without infringing autonomy. Park et al. (2024) have shown that people who believe in the effectiveness of emotional understanding have higher emotional repair skills and low relational conflict levels in their organizations, which supports the assumption that AI-based emotion recognition has the best effect when leaders are personally motivated to utilize emotional acumen. Lee et al. (2022) concluded that emotional intelligence of the leader has a positive impact on trust in supervisors and job performance, which is mediated by team trust and transformational leadership.

Emotion-AI can trigger these processes by giving feedback that can be acted on by leaders to broaden their repertoire of behavior. However, issues of fairness and accuracy prevent the broader use of it. According to the research, a lot of models currently in use do not consistently understand emotions based on the varied demographic indicators causing misunderstanding and possible loss of confidence in the AI feedback in cases where it is proven to be inaccurate (The Guardian, 2024). As a result, bias audits and open error reporting should be included in the ethical frameworks. Rana (2020) supports the idea of building emotion-AI systems which serve as a human perception AI as opposed to emotion-detecting devices thus providing a reliable interface which does not harm the credibility of leaders.

4.2.2 Making Things More Transparent and Trustworthy

Psychologically safe cultures based on organizational trust promote innovation, seek feedback and take risks (Edmondson, 1999). Emotion AI has the ability to build this trust by creating greater emotional transparency, which would allow leaders to identify team disengagement, stress, or uncertainty. It has been shown that trust-based organizations exhibit much more employee engagement and performance, which points to the performance worth of emotional awareness (Choosetheperk, 2024). Emotion-sensitive communication systems also contribute to transparency through sentiment analysis of town halls, emails, and pulse surveys, which can be used to identify the fact of declining trust or morale early enough, and the leader can take action in time (ScienceDirect, 2025). In line with this, Park et al. (2024) indicate that leaders who engage in proactive conceptualization of emotions at work have lower relational conflict and enhanced emotional competence amongst employees.

The support of human judgment, as opposed to its replacement by Emotion AI, also increases trust. Hume.ai empathic interfaces are controlled to avoid manipulation and include ethical factors to support the credibility (The Guardian, 2024). Equally, the EU AI Act authorizes emotion recognition and prohibits making inferences regarding inner states to ensure responsible usage (The Guardian, 2024). Nevertheless, this does not eliminate the issues of privacy since subjecting to emotion monitoring can be seen as an intrusion and necessitates informed consent, anonymity, and the establishment of usage limits (ACM, 2021).

4.2.3 Conceptual Integration and Human-in-the-Loop Systems

Science and psychology Literature suggests a human-in-the-loop paradigm to integrate, making Emotion-AI a decision-able assistant instead of an autonomous decision-maker (Mohammad, 2022). Leader-centric systems facilitate the decoding of emotional information, tone adjustment recommendation, or alert about the possible misunderstanding of emotional signals (Sharma et al., 2023). Such systems may promote the self-knowledge of the leaders, as well as the suitability of responses to emotionally charged situations like conflict resolution or change management. The application of emotion-conscious leadership can be extended to the crisis communication as, in the case of the pandemic, Affectiva collaborated with virtual briefing platforms, allowing leaders to understand the level of engagement within the team better, which alleviated isolation and enhanced emotional bonding even when being physically away (Rana, 2020).

4.2.4 CSR, Cultural Sensitivity and Ethical Calibration

In the case of global companies, the diversity in emotional expressions according to culture directly challenges the reliability of Emotion AI, for models that were trained using data from only one culture are likely to systematically misinterpret the emotional signals from the minorities and thus, would only reproduce bias instead of eliminating it (Baradaran *et al.,* 2024). To this end, cultural calibration, which refers to re-training models using data that are indicative of local people, is urgently necessary in order to prevent misinterpretation and maintain the credibility of communicative interactions. Transparency also requires the explainability of models: the leaders should be capable of tracing the AI recommendations to verifiable indicators, so the example is, The model identified higher prosodic pitch and more interjection silence after your query, which supports the inference (Mohammad, 2022). Explainability acts as a guard against the so-called algorithmic surprise that wilts trust and makes leaders have interpretive power. Effective implementation would thus need governance systems, such as periodic fairness audits, ongoing feedback systems, and focused diversity monitoring. Companies, which popularize ethical leadership, have the opportunity to align the implementation of AI with the central values, which builds the argument that the results of emotion-recognition devices are intended to encourage inclusivity and empathy.

4.2.5 Outcomes Empathy, Trust, and Organizational Resilience

Empirical studies have pointed out a number of positive results that relate to the emotion sensitive leadership systems. Improved empathic capacity has been associated with a better team climate and a significant decrease in relational conflict (Park et al., 2024). Emotion-sensitive systems positively affect leaders who are more likely to initiate open and transparent communication and, as a result, increase the level of employee satisfaction and loyalty (Milhem et al., 2024). Emotion AI-based transparency is also associated with greater psychological safety, where employees feel freer and more comfortable about speaking out without fear of being criticized

(Edmondson, 1999). It is considered to be the key to organizational learning and innovation because studies have shown that psychologically safe teams are more creative and innovative (Edmondson, 2018). The empirical evidence also supports the fact that perceived emotional intelligence among leaders brings about increased leadership satisfaction and organizational trust (Milhem et al., 2024). These effects are increased by AI systems that provide context-based affective information to leaders, especially in remote or hybrid work settings. Emotion-conscious leadership systems become most efficient in the case when they complement emotional judgment of the leader, allow openness, and are integrated into human- in- the- loop governance systems (Michael, 2020).

4.3 Psychological Safety and Inclusivity

To have psychologically safe and inclusive workplaces, emotional safety and resilience should be built. Modern research highlights the possibility of emotion AI to perceive the stressors significantly and support emotional resilience under the condition that its use is ethically and organizationally reasonable.

Employee voice, perceived procedural fairness, and trust in AI systems all play a critical role in mediating between the effectiveness of Emotion AI in promoting positive organisational culture. The readiness of employees to use and embrace emotion-conscious technologies will be based on how employees view such systems to be transparent, fair, and consistent with their interests instead of being seen as a surveillance or management tool (Squire et al., 2024). Psychological safety studies indicate that employees are likely to perceive Emotion AI initiatives as supportive and not threatening when they do not lose voice, which is achieved by preserving voice through the feedback system, opting in, and participative forms of governance. On the other hand, distrust or senses of unfairness in algorithms might lower morale, diminish sincerity in the expression of emotions, and also decrease cultural unity (Lee 2018). Table 1 summarises the important application areas within the organisation for Emotion AI, associated methodologies, potential benefits, and key risks.

Table 1. Key Emotion AI Applications in the Workplace

Area	Purpose	Techniques	Benefits	Risks
HRM	Recruitment, performance, well-being	Facial, text, voice analytics	Engagement, reduced burnout	Bias, privacy
Leadership	Empathetic communication	Speech prosody, affective feedback	Trust, psychological safety	Over-reliance
Communication	Pulse surveys, collaboration	Sentiment analysis	Early morale detection	Surveillance
Well-being	Stress monitoring	Multimodal sensing	Preventive care	Consent erosion

Source: Authors' Own Compilation

4.3.1 Construction of Emotionally Supportive Environments

The article in Nature recently progresses the notion that the process of introducing AI can threaten psychological safety unless ethical leadership can provide clarity, equity, and support based on learning (Berta, 2024). The results have shown that the adoption of AI creates the feeling of uncertainty and augmented workload that can undermine psychological safety unless leaders carefully orchestrate AI-led changes (Berta, 2024). Emotion AI technologies can be used to improve supportive climates through the understanding of the patterns of communication. As an example, sentiment analysis on collaborative sites would enable one to identify the untold voices or some raw tensions and will enable the managers to act contextually (ScienceDirect, 2025). This is in line with algorithmic empathy strategies that encourage equity and emotional safety via open design and co-development with stakeholders (Eke and Shuib, 2024). In addition, emotion AI enables teamwork based on evidence feedback loop. The initial studies reveal that communication becomes more emotionally smarter with the assistance of AI-enhanced technologies that are more likely to yield better collective resilience and trust (Joshi, 2025; turn0search7). Following the social exchange theory, emotional responsiveness is another factor that form mutual trust and promotes reciprocity that preconditions the inclusive culture (Newman et al., 2017). But the problem of surveillance still exists: the ACM warns that monitoring of employees may be perceived as the invasion of their privacy, which may be rather harmful psychologically, unless the monitoring is backed with the robust consent frameworks. The fundamental protection mechanisms that researchers encourage researchers to ensure impactful affective intelligence is anonymization, ethical use policy, and opt-in structures (ACM, 2021).

4.3.2 AI of Emotion to Recognize Stressors

Emotion AI is an emerging potent tool which identifies stress. Multimodal detection systems (they are those systems that integrate natural language processing experiences, facial recognition, biometric sensations, and voice analysis) have high accuracy levels (Walambe et al., 2021; Hosseini et al., 2023) (96-98 per cent accuracy) with respect to identifying physiological and emotional signs of stress. Emotional AI stress detection systems do not merely detect the level of stress one is experiencing but provide adaptive support, which takes interventions in the high-stress environment in real-time. These initiatives as workload redistribution and timely mental-health assistance can be regarded as the proactive mode of emotional care that is why it is natural to experience stress and form an inclusive circle of support that may potentially be designed based on the distinct needs of an individual (Sanni, 2023).

4.3.3 Developing Resilience at the Emotional Level

Such skills can be developed through emotion AI that will provide feedback on the coping skills, reappraisal, and stress-management techniques. The algorithmic interventions may offer exercises which build resilience, mindful cues, and peer support triggers, which become activated by emotional challenging states (Joshi, 2025). There is evidence that emotional intelligence enhances resilience, thus minimizing perceived stress, which is demonstrated by empirical studies (Sarrionandia et al., 2018). Enterprise resilience monitoring combined with emotional analytics will identify stressors and implement interventions that strengthen individual and systemic resilience to overcome adversity. Group resilience is also supported by emotion AI. Multidisciplinary research has shown that, under stress, emotionally intelligent teams, in which the emotional awareness of the group is incorporated, are more cohesive, flexible, and creative (Joshi, 2025). The standard effect of culture, policy, and practice is a positive psychosocial safety climate, which is linked to decreased burnout, absenteeism, and psychological distress (Amoadu et al., 2025). Emotion AI can therefore be a facilitator, which reveals the early warning signs of a deteriorating safety climate and launches interventions to build culture.

4.4 Sector-Specific Applications of Emotion AI

Even though the bulk of empirical data available on the topic of Emotion AI is still small, the first sector-specific applications of this technology can tell a lot about its utility. Sentiment analysis and facial-expression recognition in education A type of emotion-sensitive learning platform and virtual classroom that identify student and educator disengagement, cognitive overload, and emotional distress to support timely pedagogical and mental-health interventions is becoming an integral part of education. These uses exemplify how Emotion AI can be used to make digital mediated spaces with high emotional labour more emotive. Pilot well-being programs in the government have used aggregate sentiment analysis of internal messages to determine patterns of stress throughout policy changes, or during crises. Such initiatives explicitly show how Emotion AI can be used to promote emotionally intelligent government and make decisions making executives less concerned with surveillance issues by emphasizing collective patterns over individual profiling.

4.5 Implementation Success Measures and Indicators

Ethical application of Emotion AI needs to be assessed in more than technical accuracy, with organizational and human-related outcomes also being taken into consideration. The areas of improvement in psychological safety, perceived fairness of feedback systems, employee engagement, and burnout reduction are the main indicators. The measures that pertain to trust, including transparency, consent, and data governance, are also of the essence to ethical legitimacy. Leadership performance can be demonstrated through the increase of the quality of communication, emotional responsiveness, and conflict management, whereas HR performance will be reflected through decreased turnover and increased involvement in well-being programs. These measures should be measured in both longitudinal and contextual terms so as to avoid reduction or punishment of emotional information. Taken together, the growing evidence indicates that Emotion AI is an empowering part of the emotionally intelligent organizational systems that are based on ethical governance and employee agency.

5. ETHICAL AND PRACTICAL IMPLICATIONS

As a continuation of the initial ideas, applications, and governance aspects presented in the previous sections, the following section summarizes the chapter findings into an integrative approach to the implementation of Emotion AI into the emotionally intelligent organizational cultures. At the first level, the protection of privacy and informed consent is essential; otherwise, the psychological security may be threatened (ACM, 2021; Berta, 2024). Second, the model should be fair in identities because voice or face recognition biases will undermine inclusivity and instigate misinterpretation (Berta, 2024). Periodic auditing and demographic calibration should be there. It is also important that the process can be explained and made transparent. The EAIs systems should not be black boxes, the employees must be aware of the usage of their emotional data, when and how it is used (Eke and Shuib, 2024). Third, the human remains are crucial: AI has to complement human judgment, but not to replace it, especially in cases of interaction with stress or vulnerability (Newman et al., 2017).

The implementation of Emotion Artificial Intelligence in the work environment is more and more burdened and restricted by legal and regulatory frameworks which regulate data protection, surveillance, and accountability of algorithms (Tatiparti et al., 2025). The principles of informed consent, data minimisation, purpose limitation, and employee rights to explanation are being highlighted in the regulations that are based on the General Data Protection Regulation (GDPR), all of which have a direct impact on the viability of emotion data collection and analysis. The new governance tools including the Artificial Intelligence Act of the European Union continue to categorize some types of emotion recognition at the workplace as being high-risk, which will demand greater transparency, human control, and minimization of risk. Such regulatory trends highlight the idea that the use of Emotion AI is not just a technological or management choice but a law-regulated practice that has to conform to the changing concepts of employee privacy, dignity, and autonomy.

5.1 Employee Consent and Data Privacy

In comparison to the usual performance indicators, Emotion AI is dealing with highly intimate and mostly subconscious data, face, voice, and emotion of language. The privacy and consent implication is far-reaching. Studies emphasize that emotional information is just as sensitive or more sensitive than biometric or health information (Roemmich et al., 2023). This is however not the case in all organizations. Employees would not think they are being emotionally monitored, especially when an artificial intelligence program is found in the video conferencing or collaboration app, like Slack or Zoom. Failure to understand is a violation of the principle of informed consent and can easily build mistrust.

The introduction of Emotion AI must be ethically sound, which should begin by being transparent. This will entail stating in simple terms what kind of data is going to be collected, its purpose, to whom the data will be disclosed, and how it may be utilized to make decisions in the organization. The consent must be a process and not a tick-box exercise. The employees should be allowed to choose not to participate and the organizations should be in a position to guarantee that the refusal to do so does not have any consequences to the profession of the employee. The building blocks are anonymization and data minimization as stated by Eke and Shuib (2024). Where possible, the findings of emotion AI should be reported at an aggregate level and the emotional profile of individuals should not be used as a tool of control. The Stanford Workplace Dynamics Lab (2025) indicates that emotional data should be managed in a psychologically safe place where workers feel cared for—not monitored. Without such safeguards, organizations jeopardize turning tools for well-being into instruments of coercion. With the line between surveillance and support blurring, explicit ethical guardrails are no longer negotiable.

5.2 Risks of Algorithmic Bias and Emotional Misinterpretation

Feelings are universal—but the way we express them is not. Culture, gender, personality, and neurological variation influence how people express and perceive emotions. Emotion AI, when it is poorly trained or narrowly configured, usually neglects these differences. For instance, Baradaran et al. (2024) illustrate that the majority of emotion recognition models are trained on Western facial datasets and therefore have biased performance when tested on non-Western populations. It means that the attitude of relaxation will be perceived as boredom or even aggression by the same AI model in a different culture. Women or neurodivergent people may also be misunderstood with slight differences in their expression that the model has not yet mastered to distinguish. This is a matter of grave concern when it comes to recruitment, performance evaluation or monitoring of emotional well-being. The very existence of an algorithm that labels one as either disengaged or angry without context poses a threat to categorize them as wrong and cause unreasonable consequences. Emotionally inferred conclusions have to be interpretable and auditable as Mohammad (2022) points out - managers and workers should be in a position to understand how conclusions were arrived at. Increasing the aggravation is algorithmic opacities. Users can be considered as black boxes, and this increases the risk of abuse when the users do not understand the way in which Emotion AI systems work. According to Tatipartiet al. (2025), periodic bias auditing, objective training information and a human-in-the-loop procedure, where AI is used as a suggestive tool and not a final authority, are recommended.

5.3 Walking the Line between Robots and Humans

Even though Emotion AI is fast, accurate, and consistent, the experience of speed, accuracy, and accuracy cannot substitute the ethical intuition, depth of relationship, and sensitivity to the context of human judgment. The main issue is not, thus, whether to embrace Emotion AI or not, but how to utilize it without dehumanizing the workplace. The existing academic literature focuses on enhancement, but not replacement, which makes Emotion AI look like a decision-assistance system indicating emotional patterns, detecting changes in group morale or reminding people of their well-being, but not making interpretive or relational choices. According to mental health context evidence, when human beings mediate the relationship between AI systems, they are viewed as more empathetic compared to those AI systems that do not have human mediation (Sharma et al., 2023).

Leaders are supposed to take AI-created points as the beginning points of engagement instead of merely diagnosing. When warning signs of team deterioration have been noticed, EI is used to tackle the issues by dialogues, listening, and contextual insights rather than an act of classification and punishment. Empathy, which is described by Shaikh (2025) as the ability to acknowledge both the emotional and situational needs-capacities, which cannot be implemented and only informed by AI. Therefore, companies will have to invest into managerial training, with a focus on critical interpretation of AI results, emotional intelligence growth, and the capacity to question or ignore algorithmic suggestions.

Success of the Emotion AI is eventually subject to organizational culture. Emotion AI can promote positive change in an atmosphere filled with inclusion, dignity and shared purpose; otherwise, it can be abused in punitive cultures. Deploying ethically thus requires operational governance measures, such as ethical risk analysis, informed and revocable consent, definite limits of data use, bias, and human-in-the-loop decision-making procedures (Joshi, 2025). The lack of such safeguards can make even the good systems work against trust and psychological safety.

5.4 Aspirational Promise versus Current Practice of Emotion AI

A lot of talk about Emotion AI in organizations is all so far besides that hailing its gaining of emotionally intelligent leadership, well-being support of large numbers, and constant feedback on organizational climate (McStay, 2018; Joshi, 2025) as the new thing coming. In an ideal world, Emotion AI makes it possible for organizations to manage the flow of emotional and psychological signals in the workplace, such that the early signs of burnout, empathetic decision-making, and safe psychological conditions are all the more recognizable, especially in hybrid and remote work contexts. (Sharma et al., 2023). Unfortunately, organizational realities today do not come close to those perfect conditions. In the workplaces where data is the king, the implementation of the Emotion AI often occurs alongside the existing systems of algorithmic management, wherein the emotional data can be used in care aspects or even go through the power of control and normalization of the behavior (Roemmich et al., 2023). The already mentioned power imbalance between the employers and the employees, and the mentioned factors of trust issues such as lack of transparency and uneven consent mechanisms can lead to or worsen the situations of mistrust and emotional self-censorship (Eke and Shuib, 2024; Berta, 2024). Besides, among the technical limitations are contextual misinterpretation and cultural bias, which are some of the factors that reduce the reliability of the emotion inference in real-world organizational settings (Mohammad, 2022; Baradaran et al., 2024).

6. LIMITATIONS, FUTURE DIRECTIONS AND IMPLICATIONS

Emotion artificial intelligence is not just a hypothetical concept anymore, but it actually influences the process of cognition, help, and organization of people in organizational context.

It lacks original empirical data, longitudinal case evidence; and does not offer implementation models that are sector-specific, in terms of its contribution as a conceptual piece. Instead, it attempts to offer empirically informed and theory-based guidelines upon which future research and organizational experiments would be guided. Further research can also be based on this and can be used to provide more empirical evidence on the cultural implications of Emotion AI in various industries, organizations, and regulatory contexts and thus refine the propositions presented herein.

Based on the concepts presented in the previous sections, domain specific applications and governance implications, this section summarizes the learning presented in the chapter, as a synthesis of an integrative roadmap on the embeddedness of Emotion AI in the organisational culture that is emotionally intelligent.

6.1 Potential Research and Technological Breakthroughs

Emotion AI is at a transition stage, whereby it is progressively becoming more integrated, sophisticated, and flexible in real-time. The modern uses such as facial recognition, sentiment analysis, voice modulation detection etc. are growing more precise with more powerful multimodal features. The current studies focus on the multisensory emotion recognition concept through a combination of vocal cues, facial micro-expressions, physiological sensors, and natural language processing to make more accurate and situation-specific emotional judgments (Hosseini et al., 2023; Joshi, 2025). Emotional feedback systems based on discomfort or counterproductive behavior detection, as leaders are advised to involve a collaborative platform like Zoom or Microsoft Teams, are becoming popular in real time (Baradaran et al., 2024).

Affective forecasting is another trend that is on the rise, with AI models forecasting the development of emotional profiles and other behavioral patterns over time instead of simply recognizing the current emotional state (Jin et al., 2024). The ability underpins preemptive mental-health and engagement interventions. Simultaneously, researchers are developing cultural calibration to make algorithms sensitive in a wide range of linguistic, cultural, and neurological conditions to reduce algorithm bias and improve inclusivity (Baradaran et al., 2024). Nevertheless, these developments require further studies of long-term psychological outcomes, workforce beliefs, and organizational ethics, which supports the idea of transdisciplinary research applying organizational behavior, data science, psychology, and ethics.

6.2 Organization Preparedness and Cultural Adaptability

Though the Emotion AI technology is improving at a fast rate, the key question is whether organizations are culturally ready to apply it in a meaningful and ethical way. The tool will only be effective and ethical depending on who is operating it as highlighted in Section 5. Organizational preparedness entails practical operational capabilities e.g. investment in safe data infrastructure, access to interdisciplinary understanding across HR, data science, and ethics, and managerial ability to transform emotional understanding into beneficial- but not punitive- organizational measures. Such aspects as safe data storage and protection measures, ethical use of AI guidelines, and responsible interpretation of emotional insights leadership training should be included (Eke and Shuib, 2024). Moreover, preparedness also requires value alignment - organizations should focus on employee welfare, inclusion, and transparency otherwise the technology may be implemented counterproductively. The organizations that possess psychologically safe cultures, the environment in which the open dialog can be maintained without taking a risk of punishment, have a better chance to utilize Emotion AI. On the other hand, fear-based, rigid, or micromanagement cultures have the threat of capitalizing on emotional intelligence by turning AI into a tool of control instead of empowerment (McCausland, 2023; Berta, 2024). Another key position is that of leadership: Emotion AI need not be left to the exclusive domain of the algorithmic systems; rather, it is emotionally intelligent leadership that will guide its implementation. This is not just the provision of training to managers to decode emotional cues but also the creation of reactions that are based on empathy, flexibility, and sensitivity to context (Shaikh, 2025). Besides, organizations should ensure that they are ready to face resistance to change. The introduction of AI that is capable of reading emotion can be experienced as an encroachment especially when intent and the use of information is not transparent. Developing trust by engaging workers in participatory design i.e. by involving workers in the decisions related to the implementation of AI can contribute to the rise in acceptance (Tatiparti et al., 2025). Lastly, cultural flexibility is the most important. There will not be a single solution; instruments will have to be tuned not only depending on the geographic position but also the industry sector, the job role, the mode of communication, and the generation. An example is that manifestations of stress are significantly different among a customer-service representative, an engineer with several years of experience, and a frontline health care provider.

6.3 Future of Organizational Intelligence that is Driven by Emotion

The future of Emotion AI can be described as more emotionally intelligent spaces where emotional data will be used strategically and not only in response. Organizations in the future can use aggregated emotional intelligence to create workplace design, redesign work teams and tailor leadership development programs. An example of a scenario that is envisioned is the existence of an organizational dashboard reporting both of financial key performance indicators, such as revenue and retention, and emotional climate indicators (ECIs). A dashboard like that one may show team-specific levels of emotional engagement, stress, or trust score and therefore provide the leadership with sufficient foresight of a situation developing tension but not yet turning into conflict or disengagement (Joshi, 2025). Such systems may also customize the experiences of employees; AI-based emotion identification could provide customized well-being technology, dynamically increase or decrease workloads, or suggest mentors based on their emotional profile. Although these abilities seem to ensure increased productivity, human sympathy and strength are still required. Working too much with emotion tracking can lead to manipulation or gamification of emotion, Jin et al. (2024) warn, as employees work to optimize the manipulation of emotions by tracking emotions to please the algorithm over expressing their true emotions. As a result, strong ethical governance, transparency, and human control are compulsory. Controllers and policy makers have had the challenge of keeping up; the current privacy laws tend not to provide a specific protection, particularly toward emotional information. The preliminary guidance is provided by the AI Act of the EU that makes a distinction between emotion detection and inference, though global standards are still required (The Guardian, 2024). In the future, companies that use Emotion AI in a responsible, fair, and open way will not only be able to negotiate this frontier - they will create a new standard of employee welfare and cultural excellence. The ones that ignore the moral foundations will suffer a negative reputation, staff resistance, or, the most dangerous, development of an organizational culture of emotional oppression.

7. CONCLUSION

A combined analysis of the theoretical, practical, and ethical aspects shows that the future direction of Emotion AI in workplace environments is based on a narrow balance between innovation and responsibility. The need to establish ethical governance and human control has been clarified by the long-term challenges such as threats of emotional surveillance, algorithmic bias, cultural misunderstanding, and excessive automation. At the same time, new areas of development lead the sphere towards a higher level of multimodality, predictive emotional analytics, and connection with leadership development and well-being systems. Future studies should then go beyond the proof-of-concept studies to longitudinal validation of the same at the organization level and how Emotion AI affects trust, culture and employee results over time. In practice, companies are promoted to consider participatory design, introduce transparency and consent systems, and invest in emotive intelligent management skill, and technological implementation. This chapter situates Emotion AI not as a technological trend, but as a strategic and ethical route to sustainable and emotionally intelligent organizational cultures by expressly connecting the present issues directly to the future of research and practice.

REFERENCES

ACM. (2025). Emotion AI will not fix the workplace. *Interactions*. Retrieved from https://interactions.acm.org/archive/view/march-april-2025/emotion-ai-will-not-fix-the-workplace

Amoadu, M., Agyare, D. F., Doe, P. F., & Abraham, S. A. (2025). Examining the impact of psychosocial safety climate on working conditions, well-being and safety of healthcare providers: A scoping review. *BMC Health Services Research*, *25*(1), 90.

Ashkanasy, N. M., & Daus, C. S. (2005). Rumors of the death of emotional intelligence in organizational behavior are vastly exaggerated. *Journal of Organizational Behavior, 26*(4), 441-452. Ashkanasy, N. M., & Daus, C. S. (2005). Rumors of the death of emotional intelligence in organizational behavior are vastly exaggerated. *Journal of Organizational Behavior*, *26*(4), 441–452.

Bar-On, R. (2006). The Bar-On model of emotional-social intelligence (ESI) 1. *Psicothema*, 13-25. Bar-On, R. (2006). The Bar-On model of emotional-social intelligence (ESI) 1. *Psicothema*, •••, 13–25.

Baradaran, M., Zohari, P., Mahyar, A., Motamednia, H., Rahmati, D., & Gorgin, S. (2024, March). Cultural-Aware AI Model for Emotion Recognition. In *2024 13th Iranian/3rd International Machine Vision and Image Processing Conference (MVIP)* (pp. 1-6). IEEE.

Berta, M. (2024). *Towards a Gender Inclusive Neural Network for Automatic Gender Recognition* (Doctoral dissertation, Politecnico di Torino).

Boughanem, H., Ghazouani, H., & Barhoumi, W. (2023). Facial emotion recognition in-the-wild using deep neural networks: A comprehensive review. *SN Computer Science*, *5*(1), 96.

Boyd, K. L., & Andalibi, N. (2023). Automated emotion recognition in the workplace: How proposed technologies reveal potential futures of work. *Proceedings of the ACM on human-computer interaction, 7*(CSCW1), 1-37.

Cherniss, C. (2010). Emotional intelligence: Toward clarification of a concept. *Industrial and Organizational Psychology: Perspectives on Science and Practice*, *3*(2), 110–126.

Choosetheperk. (2024). Boost leadership with trust and emotional intelligence. Retrieved from https://www.choosetheperk.com/blog/boost-leadership-with-trust-and-emotional-intelligence

Cowgill, B., & Tucker, C. E. (2019). Economics, fairness and algorithmic bias. *preparation for. The Journal of Economic Perspectives.*

Delina, G., Badada, B., Krishnaraj, R., Thiruthuvanathan, M. M., & Kumar, R. M. (2024). A Narrative Synthesis on the Role of Affective Computing in Fostering Workplace Well-Being Using a Deep Learning Model. In *International Conference on Innovations in Computational Intelligence and Computer Vision* (pp. 431-445). Springer, Singapore.

Edmondson, A. (1999). Psychological safety and learning behavior in work teams. *Administrative Science Quarterly*, *44*(2), 350–383.

Edmondson, A. C. (2018). *The fearless organization: Creating psychological safety in the workplace for learning, innovation, and growth.* John Wiley & Sons.

Eke, C. I., & Shuib, L. (2024). The role of explainability and transparency in fostering trust in AI healthcare systems: A systematic literature review, open issues and potential solutions. *Neural Computing & Applications*, •••, 1–36.

European Commission. (2021). *Proposal for a regulation laying down harmonised rules on artificial intelligence (Artificial Intelligence Act).* https://eur-lex.europa.eu/legal-content/EN/TXT/?uri=CELEX%3A52021PC0206

Gallup. (2024).*State of the global workplace: 2024 report.* Retrieved from https://gallup.com/workplace/349484/state-of-the-global-workplace.aspx

Goleman, D. (2005). *Emotional intelligence: Why it can matter more than IQ.* Bantam.

Hosseini, M., Bodaghi, M., Bhupatiraju, R. T., Maida, A., & Gottumukkala, R. (2023). Multimodal stress detection using facial landmarks and biometric signals. *Frontiers in Physiology.*

Jin, G., Jiang, J., & Liao, H. (2024). The work affective well-being under the impact of AI. *Scientific Reports*, *14*(1), 25483.

Joshi, S. (2025). The Role of AI in Enhancing Teamwork, Resilience and Decision-Making: Review of Recent Developments. *International Journal of Computer Applications*, •••, 9.

Lee, C. C., Li, Y. S., Yeh, W. C., & Yu, Z. (2022). The effects of leader emotional intelligence, leadership styles, organizational commitment, and trust on job performance in the real estate brokerage industry. *Frontiers in Psychology*, *13*, 881725.

Lee, M. K. (2018). Understanding perception of algorithmic decisions: Fairness, trust, and emotion in response to algorithmic management. *Big Data & Society*, *5*(1), 2053951718756684.

McCausland, T. (2023). Creating psychological safety in the workplace. *Research Technology Management*, *66*(2), 56–58.

McStay, A. (2018). Emotional AI: The rise of empathic media.

Miao, C., Humphrey, R. H., & Qian, S. (2017). A meta-analysis of emotional intelligence and work attitudes. *Journal of Occupational and Organizational Psychology*, *90*(2), 177–202.

Michael, M. T. (2020). Unconscious emotion and free-energy: A philosophical and neuroscientific exploration. *Frontiers in Psychology*, *11*, 984.

Milhem, M., Ayyash, M. M., Ateeq, A., Alzaghal, Q., & Alzoraiki, M. (2024). Emotional intelligence in leadership: Its role in fostering employee engagement in Palestine's ICT sector. *Problems and Perspectives in Management*, *22*(1), 338.

Mohammad, S. M. (2022). Ethics sheet for automatic emotion recognition and sentiment analysis. *Computational Linguistics*, *48*(2), 239–278.

Mudunuri, L. N. R., & Bhattacharya, P. (2025). Ethical Considerations Balancing Emotion and Autonomy in AI Systems. In *Humanizing Technology With Emotional Intelligence* (pp. 443–456). IGI Global Scientific Publishing.

Newman, A., Donohue, R., & Eva, N. (2017). Psychological safety: A systematic review of the literature. *Human Resource Management Review*, *27*(3), 521–535.

Nieves, J. C., Osorio, M., Rojas-Velazquez, D., Magallanes, Y., & Brännström, A. (2024). Digital companions for well-being: challenges and opportunities. *Journal of Intelligent & Fuzzy Systems*, JIFS-219336.

Park, J. S., Shin, J., & Lee, T. (2024). To believe or not to believe: Leader's belief about emotion usefulness and its impact on team dynamics. *BMC Psychology*, *12*(1), 737.

Picard, R. W. (2000). *Affective computing*. MIT press.

Rajan, A., & Nagajothi, V. (2024). AI-Powered Talent Management Strategies in HR: An Analytical Study. *International Journal of Scientific Research in Modern Science and Technology*, *3*(12).

Rana, E. K. (2020). Bringing emotional intelligence to technology with Rana el-Kaliouby

Rao, T. V. N., Patel, G. S., Bhavana, S., & Swetha, C. (2025). AI-Driven Decision Support System for Workplace Wellbeing. In *Insights on Wellbeing and Happiness in the Workplace* (pp. 1–18). IGI Global Scientific Publishing.

Roemmich, K., Schaub, F., & Andalibi, N. (2023, April). Emotion AI at work: Implications for workplace surveillance, emotional labor, and emotional privacy. In *Proceedings of the 2023 CHI Conference on Human Factors in Computing Systems* (pp. 1-20).

Sadeghi, S. (2024). Employee Well-being in the Age of AI: Perceptions, Concerns, Behaviors, and Outcomes. *arXiv preprint arXiv:2412.04796.*

Salovey, P., & Mayer, J. D. (1990). Emotional intelligence. *Imagination, Cognition and Personality*, *9*(3), 185–211.

Salovey, P. E., & Sluyter, D. J. (1997). *Emotional development and emotional intelligence: Educational implications.* Basic Books.

Sanni, B. (2023). An Integrated Framework for Mitigating IT Industry Burnout: Leveraging AI-Driven Work Pattern Monitoring to Enhance Workforce Wellbeing.

Sarrionandia, A., Ramos-Díaz, E., & Fernández-Lasarte, O. (2018). Resilience as a mediator of emotional intelligence and perceived stress: A cross-country study. *Frontiers in Psychology*, *9*, 2653.

Schein, E. H. (2010). *Organizational culture and leadership* (Vol. 2). John Wiley & Sons.

Shaikh, Z. P. (2025). Artificial Intelligence-Based Emotional Intelligence and Effective Leadership: Applications, Implications, and Ethical Bias. In *Emotionally Intelligent Methods for Meaningful Leadership* (pp. 223-254). IGI Global Scientific Publishing.

Sharma, A., Lin, I. W., Miner, A. S., Atkins, D. C., & Althoff, T. (2023). Human–AI collaboration enables more empathic conversations in text-based peer-to-peer mental health support. *Nature Machine Intelligence*, *5*(1), 46–57.

Squire, D., Gonzalez, L., & Shayan, C. (2024). Enhancing sense of belonging in nursing student clinical placements to advance learning and identity development. *Journal of Professional Nursing*, *51*, 109–114.

Stanford Workplace Dynamics Lab. (2025). *AI research reveals hidden costs of workplace emotional labor.* https://sanj.dev/post/ai-research-emotional-labor-workplace-impact

Tatiparti, S., Goli, G., & Reddy, T. B. P. (2025). Exploring the ethical implications of AI in talent management: Perspectives from medium and large enterprises. *Business Process Management Journal.*

The Guardian. (2024, June 23). Are you 80% angry and 2% sad? Why 'emotional AI' is fraught with problems. *The Guardian*. Retrieved from https://www.theguardian.com/technology/article/2024/jun/23/emotional-artificial-intelligence-chatgpt-4o-hume-algorithmic-bias

Walambe, R., Nayak, P., Bhardwaj, A., & Kotecha, K. (2021). [Retracted] Employing Multimodal Machine Learning for Stress Detection. *Journal of Healthcare Engineering*, *2021*(1), 9356452.

Weiss, H. M., & Cropanzano, R. (1996). Affective events theory. *Research in Organizational Behavior*, *18*(1), 1–74.

Workhuman. (2025, April). AI praise-giving tool promises 'authentic' insights. Retrieved from https://www.ft.com/content/abee0887-f723-464e-9cd8-c429b171abc8

Zeidner, M., Matthews, G., & Roberts, R. D. (2004). Emotional intelligence in the workplace: A critical review. *Applied Psychology*, *53*(3), 371–399.

Chapter 9
Ethical Considerations:
Algorithmic Bias and Employee Privacy

Pritpal Singh
https://orcid.org/0000-0001-5152-200X
Lovely Professional University, India

Prikshat Kumar Angra
Lovely Professional University, India

Habib Mohammed Ahmed
College of Social Sciences and Humanities, Samara University, Ethiopia

ABSTRACT

The Reality of the hybrid workplace has created a new paradigm for leadership that requires innovative solutions to drive productivity, engagement, and operational efficiency across dispersed teams. But the use of AI in HR is not without major ethical questions. This chapter contributes to the ongoing research by critically analysing the ethics of one aspect of these technologies: algorithmic bias and employee privacy. It also discusses how historical data bias might contribute to unfair hiring, promotion, and performance evaluations resulting in reinforcing systemic biases. And we talk about the thin line between using data for organizational intelligence and creating an atmosphere of surveillance that erodes trust and morale. Finally, we posit that the responsible use of AI in hybrid work will involve a delicate balancing act between fairness, appropriate ethical governance and employees' fundamental rights to ensure that technology serves to augment rather than diminish the modern workforce.

DOI: 10.4018/979-8-3373-5871-0.ch009

ht © 2026, IGI Global Scientific Publishing. Copying or distributing in print or electronic forms without written permission of IGI Global Scientific Publishing is prohibited. Use of this chapter to generative artificial intelligence (AI) technologies is expressly prohibited. The publisher reserves all rights to license its use for generative AI training and machine learning model development.

1. INTRODUCTION

What is happening today around the big data economy is the fact that organizations turn to more algorithms and artificial intelligence (AI) to support the applications, efficiency and human resource management (Brynjolfsson, and McAfee, 2017). Algorithms are becoming more popular in the corporate world as recruiting, performance evaluation, surveillance at work, or predictive analytics are now automated (Bodie et al., 2021). Despite the undisputable advantages of these technologies, namely speed, scalability, and low cost, they also spawn ethical issues which are in dire need of resolution, namely, biased algorithms and privacy of employees (O'Neil 2016). The ethical aspects are not entirely technical issues but also associated with the sociocultural, legal and organisational problems of trust, fairness and legitimacy in work places.

Employment algorithmic systems come with the issue of discrimination and fairness and even appeals to system when setting criteria to receive benefits (Barocas, Hardt, and Narayanan, 2019). But, changes in surveillance and monitoring technologies in the workplace also pose a serious threat to the privacy of employees through the gathering of their most personal data without adequate disclosure or permission (Ball, 2021). The wider ethical tussles that companies now face between innovation and responsibility are algorithmic bias and privacy violation. According to Floridi and Cowls (2019), the ethics of AI cannot be diminished to be in line with the law but must have a positive policy with such values as fairness, accountability, and respect to human dignity.

This introduction places the ethical terrain of algorithmic bias and employee privacy in focus through three overlapping dimensions. First, it discusses algorithmic bias in organizational decision making and the implications of decision-making algorithms for equity, with a focus on how inequalities are built into data points and design, which then translates into biased practices in the workplace. Second, it reflects increasing anxiety about employee privacy in the digital age of surveillance and big data, by which performance tracking bleeds into personal life. Third, this sheds light on the broader ethical challenges that organizations may encounter when dealing with these realities and reinforces the value of governance systems, morally-led leadership and compliance. Considering its critical intermediation of these dimensions, it can become the base for understanding how businesses can use algorithmic technologies responsibly in their organisations.

1.1 Algorithmic Bias in Organizational Decision-Making

The concept of algorithmic bias describes unjust and systematic adverse influences on a specific group or person due to the fact that algorithms are poorly created, they are trained using biased data, or they are based on structural bias (Mehrabi et al., 2021). Such prejudice, in any case, is often manifested in hiring, promotion, performance review and even in discipline decisions in an organizational context. Algorithms in their current form of being trained on historical data can be prone to perpetrating existing social inequalities (Barocas and Selbst, 2016). As an example, a scrapped hiring tool developed by Amazon was negatively responded to hiring application with the word women in it, which reflects the gender differences in the everglow technology sector (Dastin, 2018). The case demonstrates that discrimination in the training data can be used to teach the algorithm to be discriminatory. This is not merely a technical failure issue, but also an institutional responsibility issue. The work to promote Diversity, Equity, and Inclusion (DEI), which is being considered as a key element of business sustainability (Binns, 2018), is one example. Research proves that algorithm biasness may erode employee trust levels, damage corporate image and reputation to anti-discrimination legislation (Raghavan et al., 2020). Moreover, algorithmic obscurity, which can be likened to the so-called black box problem, clouds judgments to workers and managers who cannot read and disagree with automated judgments (Burrell, 2016). Responsibilities in ethics thus require organizations to stress on being open, auditable, and just in designing and using algorithms. The algorithms in organisations have become popular because of the anticipated ability to ensure objectivity and effectiveness in the decision-making process. Its advocates argue that it reduces human subjectivity and narrows down the degree to which individual biases held by the persons with decision-making authority can influence the results (Brynjolfsson and McAfee, 2017). However, nowadays, it is becoming clear that algorithmic systems reduce very little bias and instead generate systematically unfair effects which are detrimental to certain groups of people (Barocas and Selbst, 2016; Mehrabi et al., 2021).Centrally, algorithmic bias can be understood as the issue of generating systematically unjust outcomes that harm a particular group of people (Friedman and Nissenbaum, 1996). Prejudices are most played out at work on hiring and recruiting procedures. The history of automated resume screening systems is one such trend that has been well-documented in this direction, and it is meant to identify the best candidates according to the historical trends observed in hiring information. But when such a legacy is part of the human choices and is discriminatory on gender, race or class, the algorithm learns it and replicates it (Raghavan et al., 2020). A well known high-profile case is the AI-based recruiter at Amazon which scored down resumes which contained the term women's (such as women's chess club captain) and so this discriminated against female candidates. The bias was made due to the fact that the model and system was trained on male dominated tech industry resumes (Dastin, 2018).

In addition to the hiring, performance reviews and promotions also present evidence of algorithmic bias. As an illustration, productivity algorithms can prioritize workers working during traditional hours and deny working parents or those with other flexible requirements (Ajunwa, 2020). Likewise, the algorithms of predictive analytics may also unjustly label certain workers as the flight risk or low performance based on the proxy variables like job jumping or career break, which more frequently occur in female and minority employees (Bodie et al., 2021). Such practices prompts ethical issues related to organizational fairness, transparency and accountability of decisions.One of the major issues is the withholding nature of algorithmic systems, also referred to as the black box problem (Burrell, 2016). Algorithms do not give justifications on the results or make explanations as the reason behind a certain decision may not be the same as explanations like justifications hence it is hard and unjust to challenge the results which the employee considers wrong. This is non-transparent, which violates the due process and justice principles, which are vital in preserving the trust and legitimacy of employees (Binns, 2018). In other cases, the organizations themselves might not be in a good position to know how their algorithms operate at all, and that creates an accountability issue.

Figure 1. Stages of algorithmic bias in organizational decision-making

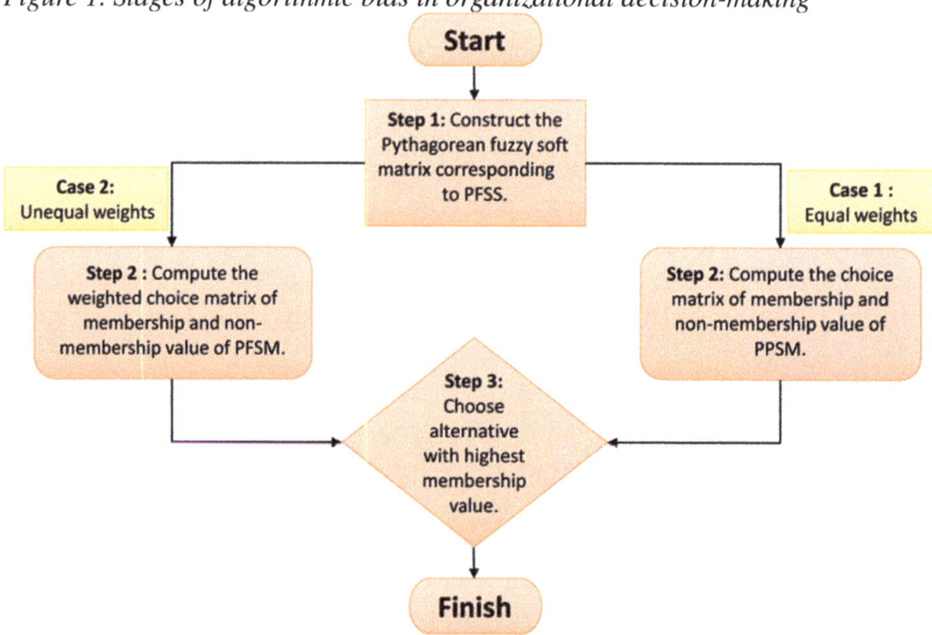

The other aspect of the issue of algorithmic bias is connected to the aspect of intersectionality, in which several identities (e.g., race and gender) have a concerted effort to increase the discriminative effects. Studies have indicated that AI recruitment algorithms, may fall prey to stereotyping in the training data to the detriment of women of color (Benjamin, 2019). An example is that image-classification models have been found to misclassify women of a darker tone more often than men of a lighter tone (Buolamwini and Gebru, 2018). And once implemented into work technologies, such as automated video interviews or emotion reading software, the risks of algorithmic algorithaticibial discrimination increase many times over. Ethically speaking, algorithmic bias questions the principle of distributive justice, i.e. equitable distribution of opportunities and resources (Rawls 1971). Algorithms that discriminate against particular groups of people in an organized manner would destroy equity and inclusion initiatives in the organization. Moreover, they can make companies legally responsible in the frame of their antidiscrimination regulations such as Title VII of the U.S. Civil Rights Act or the European Union Equal Treatment Directive (Raghavan et al., 2020). And the legal issues aside, prejudiced decision-making may hurt company image and undermine the morale and performance of employees in creating diverse and innovative workforces.

1.2 Employee Privacy in the Digital Workplace

Nother than the fear of bias, there is the invasion of employee privacy, which is in the form of digital snooping. The list of monitoring technologies employed by companies nowadays includes key stroke logging, biometric tracking, facial recognition and productivity analytics all of which are advertised as methods of efficiency and security enhancement (Ball, 2021). Even so, the approaches to work surveillance also raise the issue of consent, proportionality and the power dynamic between workers and employers (Moore et al., 2018) where surveillance tools can end up gathering personal information, not merely professional one.Ethically, workplace surveillance is likely to relegate the latter to a data point that undermines their autonomy and dignity (Zuboff 2019). It might also cause stress, demoralisation, and a lack of creativity - derailing organisational goals of engagement and innovation (Ball 2021). In places where there are lax data protection regulations, workers might have an even grosser time contesting unfriendly surveillance. Despite the legislative measures such as the GDPR enforcement is not completely done even in areas where the technology is advancing faster than the regulatory bodies (Tadajewski and Jones, 2021). In that regard, the companies must find a balance between keeping the business and meeting the rights of the employees so that the data gathered is clear, just and reasonable. Digital transformation of the workplacc has offcred additional channels of efficiency, cooperation and innovativeness. It has also facilitated easier monitoring of workers by companies in new forms that, nobody could ever imagine. The privacy of employees, which has traditionally been understood within the context of personal space and secrecy, has been made complex by the current digital tracks, and biometrics and behavior analytics that are constantly collected and analyzed

(Ball, 2021). In that regard, the moral concerns being examined transcend legality and refer to an analytical universe comprising praxis, self-determination, dignity and trust.Companies have always been on the lookout of employees to ensure that they are indeed working. However, changes in the field of digital technologies have expanded and enlarged surveillance. Modern surveillance technologies have been relying on such types of information as a keystroke log, mouse and cursor movement, GPS position, video recordings, facial recognition, even tracking emotions through artificial intelligence (Moore et al., 2018) As the pandemic struck and remote work has risen significantly, more workers have troubles with various software to record screen activity, use of applications and online conversations (reported by Ajunwa, Crawford and Schultz 2017). Although businesses can defend these practices as necessary to manage their performance, security or compliance, they have connotations of proportionate moral issues and consent.

It is becoming difficult to declare where professional and personal ends and personal beginnings under surveillance. Remote work tools can be used to obtain personal information (noise in the family during virtual meetings, the geolocation feature on mobile devices, and use on equipment belonging to a company; Bodie et al., 2021). Health and well-being wearablesDevices - Workforce wearable gadgets used to monitor physical health and wellbeing may include sensitive biometric data, i.e., the level of heart rate, amount of sleep as well stress levels (Moore et al.). Such tools may also coerce employees into telling about highly personal matters about their home heath, though they are sometimes sold under the pretext of improving the wellbeing of the employees. Morally, such a growing degree of employer monitoring undermines the right to privacy and avai.ledu 5 Ball: Ethical Considerations Published by A V E S T I A the concept of informed consent (Ball, 2021). Online monitoring has not only moral hazards but also effects on privacy and its psychological effect as well. Research indicates that on-going surveillance can yield constraints, anxieties, and depressions besides limiting creativity since workers face pressures to achieve a certain measured degree of performance (Zuboff, 2019). Sometimes also known as the panopticon effect, this effect is based on a discussion of the concept of surveillance as a form of power, as described by Michel Foucault, (1977/1995) to make people to control their own behavior. Overworked places could result in lack of trust between the employees and the management and consequently an adversarial workplace environment instead of a cooperative one (Tadajewski and Jones, 2021). These processes highlight the broader moral issue of surveillance that results in employees being less people-like and more data points to be constantly considered. Legal contexts also have effects on employee privacy but the difference is very vast and varies across jurisdictions. The General Data Protection Regulation (GDPR) that is part of the European Union provides strict requirements regarding data collection including transparency and limitation and proportionality of purpose that is required in the E.U. (Tadajewski and Jones, 2021). In contrast, the U.S. does not have an omnibus federal privacy law and employee data is essentially unregulated except in some aspects, including health information by Health Insurance Portability Act (HIPAA) (Ajunwa, 2020). These loopholes in regulations raise ethical issues in multinational companies that may take the bare minimum that the local legislation imposes to determine the privacy standards to adopt. Moreover, the pace of technological change can be faster than the changes in the law; thus, workers are also exposed to new surveillance initiatives that are not yet controlled (Jobin et al., 2019).

2. LITERATURE REVIEW

The integration of algorithmic systems into organizations has been presented as a ground breaking step to objectivity and efficiency. Algorithms and more specifically algorithms that apply machine learning algorithms can help reduce human subjectivity in making decisions and adopt data-driven predictions to make classifications (Brynjolfsson and McAfee, 2017). However, recent findings indicate that in the majority of cases, algorithms can, quite the contrary, reproduce, or even increase, instead of address the current imbalances (Barocas and Selbst, 2016). This is referred to as algorithm bias and plays a leading role in ethical deliberations within an organization setting, where unfair judgment process occurs systematically and repeatably making wrong decisions against a group of people based on race, gender or socio-economic status or any other comparable characteristics (Friedman and Nissenbaum 1996). Such biasness in organizations is most apparent in the area of hiring, recruiting and promoting. As an example, the AI-based hiring tool of Amazon had degraded the resumes containing the word women (women s chess club captain), due to its training on past data biased towards male job applicants (Dastin 2018). This illustrates the influence of biased input of data that results in biased output of the algorithm.

In other areas of application of hiring, employers increasingly depend on predictions to make employee performance ratings or attrition predictions. These methods are also injustice to individuals whose career path is not linear. Moreover, the female employees who resume their working positions after their maternity leave can also be mistakenly labeled as a flight risk or underperforming staff (Ajunwa 2020). These findings explain how algorithmic bias can contribute to the existing systemic inequalities at the workplace.A lack of transparency, which can also be called the black box problem, is only contributive to these apprehensions. Most machine learning algorithms are opaque in that, organizations and the individuals who are within the organization may not know how or why they are likely to act the way they do (Burrell, 2016). Hard to fairness cannot be well explained as employees must be in position to challenge the decisions in their final portion of the interview when they do not understand why decisions cannot be made to accept the claims. This black box gives credence to the anxieties of accountability of the processes of algorithms--when no one can fully describe the algorithms, whether by the developers or the organisation, then there is almost no possibility of responsibility.

Algorithms bias is also complicated by intersectionality. Since this has been argued by Benjamin (2019) AI systems favoritize not only individual categories, gender, and race, but also at their intersection, meaning that it disproportionately disadvantages women of color. The studies show that the rates of success of the facial recognition systems in recognizing the faces of dark-skinned women are lower than the ones of light-skinned men (Buolamwini and Gebru, 2018). Intersectional discrimination is an ethical threat when that occurs in these types of technologies, such as in the case of video interviews or workplace surveillance. Ethically speaking, the issue of algorithmic bias is the one that raises the question of distributive justice i.e. equitable distribution of opportunities and resources (Rawls, 1971). In cases where automated systems discriminate against underprivileged groups in a systematic and systemic way, they negatively impact any diversity and inclusion promotion efforts, are capable of undermining employee trust and placing organizations in legal liabilities under constructs such as the U.S. Title VII or EU Equal Treatment Directive (Raghavan et al., 2020).

Algorithms used to combat algorithmic bias have been proposed as fairness-conscious machine learning, audit-using biases, and transparency mechanisms like model cards (Mitchell et al., 2021) or datasets datasheets (Gebru et al., 2021). Nevertheless, to privateize the problem, according to Benjamin (2019), algorithmic fairness will not be solved by technical means alone, but rather placed in the broader sociotechnical context where data and decisions are formed. Organizational responses should therefore involve both technical interventions but also ethics, in the form of multiple oversight boards and ethics-by-design (Floridi and Cowls, 2019). In other words, algorithmic bias hinders the accomplishment of fairness, accountability and inclusivity because it creates bias in the decision-making process of an organisation. Although mitigation measures are in place, this problem will only be addressed with not only technological expertise but also effective leadership with a long-term commitment to ethics and systemic transformation. The increased application of workforce analytics and artificial intelligence to organizational decision-making has been the focus of many scholarly discourses and research. These debates are largely based on the ethical problems of such nature as algorithmic bias and employee privacy. Among the most recurring issues in the study is that algorithmic bias is an outcome of the utilization of past data not only mirrors but also maintains the existing social disparities. Research on predictive recruitment and performance appraisal systems shows that an algorithm trained on biased data can end up generating worse results on some groups of people and therefore end up discriminating against them instead of rectifying them. S

The available recent studies are pointing to the fact that the issues, which are caused by the tension between the objectives of organization and individual rights, can be successfully addressed through the ethical measures in the form of transparent policies, participatory design, and cross-functional AI governance committees. The significance of incorporating the moral elements into the HR analytics, to make the support and the trust required in the process of sustainable digital transformation, is the argument that the scholars are increasingly making. The reviewed academic works share the same opinion that could be considered a consensus that the two cornerstones of fairness, accountability, and responsible application of workforce analytics in modern-day organizations are the elimination of bias in algorithms and employee privacy.

The digitization of work has altered the majority of ethical issues of contemporary corporation and organisation to privacy. The proliferation of telework, digital surveillance and data-driven management practices are increasing the amount of data employers have about their employees. Although such practices arise as a question of security, compliance, or productivity, to business it creates complex psychological and ethical issues of autonomy, dignity and trust (Ball, 2021).

We now have extremely sophisticated digital monitoring of employees as compared to primitive timekeeping. Modern technologies allow monitoring of the employer of keystrokes, use of applications, video calls and contents of email messages (Ajunwa, Crawford & Schultz 2017). Remote Although tracking software usage has gained popularity due to remote working, Professional, and work and personal lives have increasingly become blurred (Moore et al., 2018). Wearables and biometric also enable the wellness programmes to collect sensitive health data like heart rate and sleeping behaviour. Certain individuals believe that such development is unethical as it is proportional and informative on the consent.Combining surveillance functions in digital services continuously results in spillover gathering of personal information. Smartphones with GPS can track the off-office activities of someone (Bodie et al., 2021), and during virtual meetings, people can see the interior of their homes of the employees. Such practices violate the separation between personal and professional realms as they amount to the menace on the autonomy and dignity of the employees. Employers may be well-intentioned as in the case of trying to sccm wcll to cmployees may also cause employees to share very personal information (Ball, 2021).

Figure 2. A universal schema to understand where AI and AI enabled technologies can affect hiring practices

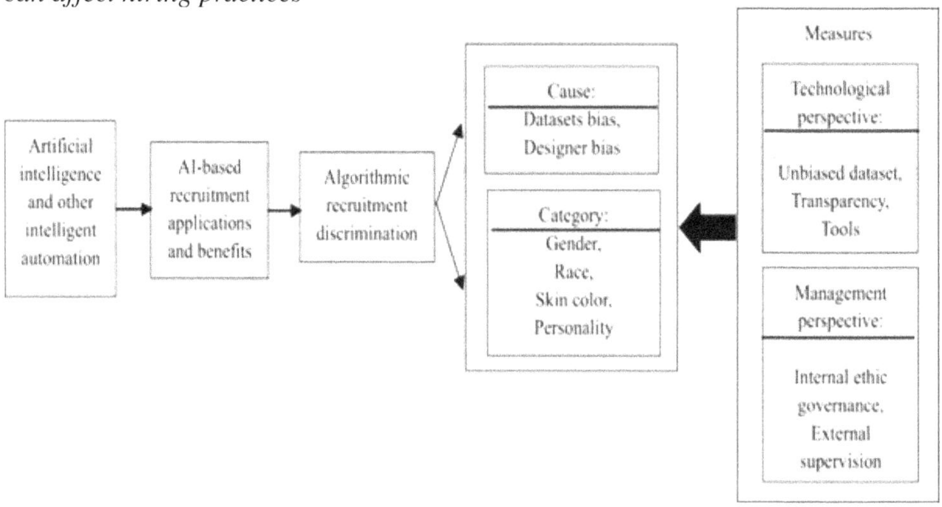

3. CONCEPTUAL FRAMEWORK

The conceptual framework on what to understand to predict the dynamics of significant support variables on organizational outcomes 2.1. Within the technological innovation era, ethical aspects regarding such issues as algorithmic bias and employee privacy have become the prevailing elements that influence the organizational legitimacy, trust and sustainability. The model in this paper builds on the input of justice theory, privacy theory, and responsible innovation literature to trace the connections between practices, risks of ethics, and reaction of organizations. Related to organizational innovation and ethical governance, this framework recognizes the challenges and the possibility to establish fair, transparent, responsible working places. The conceptual framework of the research combines the crucial constructs by which organizations may carry out data-driven workforce analytics in a morally responsible manner when addressing the problem of algorithmic bias as well as employee privacy. Basically, the framework brings together three important components, Data Inputs, Analytical Processes, and Ethical Safeguards which when integrated, influence Organizational Outcomes.

The first factor, Data Inputs, concerns the demographic information about the employees, performance statistics, behavioral statistics, and logs created by the system, which are the initial point of the HR analytics and AI-based decision-making. These unprocessed data are transferred to the Analytical Processes step whereby statistical models, machine learning models, predictive analytics systems and automated decision systems are applied in evaluating employee performance, hiring appropriateness, attrition risk and productivity trends. In this situation, however, the researchers have discovered possible ethical concerns that this step entails. An example of algorithmic bias is when a skewed dataset is used, or the model is developed in a non-transparent way. Moreover, there is a risk of breaching privacy when the information is gathered without the consent of people or in an excess amount.

To get rid of these threats, the Ethical Safeguards component is endowed with a set of measures that serve as a safety net and that includes fairness audits, data minimization policies, encryption, anonymization, informed consent procedures, explainable AI systems, and adherence to international standards, such as GDPR. These protections have an important role in deciding whether the system under consideration is fair, transparent and trustworthy. Finally, the outcomes of the interaction between ethical precautions and analytical outputs are the Organizational Outcomes, which are the accuracy of better decision-making, employee trust, reduced risk of discrimination, workplace transparency, and sustainable digital transformation. In this way, the framework does provide a holistic model according to which the ethical issues play the central role of intervening the relationship between the responsible use of the workforce analytics and the contemporary organizations.

3.1. Defining Core Constructs

Algorithmic bias: When an algorithm is used to give biased output, caused by systematic and repeatable error (Friedman & Nissenbaum, 1996), which may have the effect of favoring those already in power, and disadvantaging already disenfranchised groups by gender, racial or income. Algorithms bias is most evident in the hiring, recruitment, job performance appraisals, and promotions in an organizational setting (Raghavan et al., 2020). Algorithms biases are a way to nullify fairness and cause mistrust among employees regardless of whether it is a consequence of biased data, ill-conceived models, or inherent structural inequity (Ball, 2021). Keyboard logging, location tracking, biometric scanners and machine learning affect privacy in the digital workplace by compromising it through pervasive surveillance (Ajunwa, Crawford and Schultz, 2017). The moral questions are not only in the intersection of legal, but also in the human dignity, autonomy and psychological consequences of surveillance (Zuboff, 2019). Ethical responsibility rcfcrs to the obligation of an organization that it conducts its business in a way that is able to observe human rights, equity and non-harm. Within the framework of digital innovation, having a sense of ethics implies the inclusion of fairness, transparency, and accountability in the decision-making (Floridi and Cowls, 2019). It is also associated with emphasis on the unwanted outcomes, and importance of innovations which coincide with social values (Owen et al., 2013).

Figure 3. AI Ethics: Framework of building ethical AI

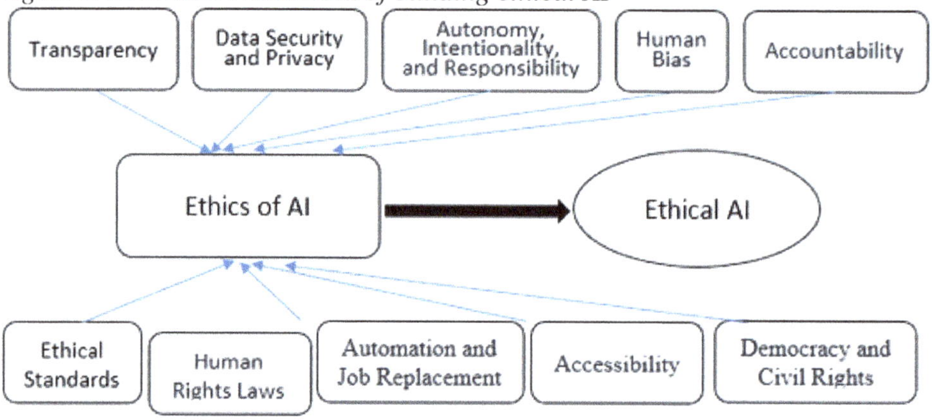

3.2 Theoretical Underpinnings

Justice as fairness Revisited The John Rawlss Theories of Justice (1971) is an exceptional piece of liberal political philosophy and it poses the questions to be considered, what rational men would consent to in such a case (Horny, 2008). According to Thomson (2017), algorithmic bias interferes with distributive justice as it favors certain groups more significantly and does not favor others. Likewise, procedural justice the justice of the processes leading to the outcomes is lost due to the lack of transparency of the algorithmic systems (Burrell, 2016). The justice theory thus provides a solution of evaluating how fair the systems that are used in organizations are technologically. The panopticon metaphor used by Foucault (1977/1995) is a form of power which compels the subjects to control their own actions. This perspective illuminates how digital surveillance technologies restructure power dynamics at the workplace and erode trust and autonomy (Moore, Upchurch and Whittaker, 2018). Privacy frameworks, e.g. privacy by design (Cavoukian 2010), apply our intuition of what people ought to be able to hold privately and extrapolate these ideas to ensure the autonomy of people is safeguarded with active intervention. Responsible innovation theory determines anticipation, reflexivity, inclusion and responsiveness to be the main concepts to align technology advancement with the societal demands (Owen et al., 2013). Responsible innovation involves both technical solutions (such as fairness-aware ML) and structural governance devices (such as ethics boards or bias audits) in the organizational context, however what is incorporated into the innovation process are reflections of ethics(Jobin et al., 2019). The theoretical framework of the current study is based on a number of major constructs that combine the answer to how organizations can integrate the workforce analytics ethically and reduce the risks associated with algorithmic bias and employee privacy. The initial construct, Data Inputs, includes all the information about the employees including demographic data, the performance data, behavioral data, biometric data, and digital communication data, which are the basis of analytical procedures. The second construct, Analytical Processes, is the machine learning models, predictive analytics tools and automated decision systems applied to process and manipulate the employee data to produce insights. These processes of analysis are directly linked to the third construct, Algorithmic Bias, describing the threat of unfair or discriminatory results due to biased data in the past, unbalanced sampling, poor selection of features, or inaccessible model reasoning. The fourth construct, Employee Privacy, in its turn, deals with intrusion into data collection, constant surveillance, biometric tracking, and unauthorized data sharing, which should be accompanied by consent, confidentiality, and responsible use. The fifth construct is known as Ethical Safeguards and involves moderating the aforementioned risks, and the mechanisms involved include explainable AI, data minimization, anonymization, encryption, fairness audits, and legal frameworks such as GDPR and the emerging AI governance standards. A combination of these protections will affect the sixth construct, Organizational Trust, which is the attitude of the employees to the fairness, transparency, and safety in a data-driven workplace. Lastly, the combination of these constructs generates Organizational Outcomes, including those related to better quality of decisions, fair HR practices, and higher levels of employee satisfaction, less discrimination, and increased regulatory compliance. Together, these constructs demonstrate why the design, implementation, and governance of workforce analytics systems should be ethically oriented in order to promote responsible and sustainable forms of organizational value.

3.3 Interrelationships Between Constructs

One might not immediately understand the similarity between these ostensibly unrelated issues but the similarity between them cuts across in some potent ways. As an example, AI surveillance systems, in addition to gathering sensitive information, process them using potentially biased algorithmic models (Ajunwa, 2020). As an illustration, sentiment analysis systems can mislabel the feelings of minority workers due to such reasons as these technologies have been trained on biased data, and therefore provide privacy violating and discriminative results (Buolamwini and

Gebru, 2018). Based on this, breaches of privacy tend to be the raw material on which bias operates and bias in turn enhances the damages of invasion of privacy.

The ethical responsibility mediates the existing relationship between technology risks (bias, privacy intrusion) and organizational outcomes (trust, legitimacy, compliance). These are the core responsibilities of organizations, and organizations that neglect them face the risk of losing trust among employees, reputations, and face regulatory fines (Ball, 2021). Conversely, companies that adopt fairness, transparency and privacy-by-design, can have more chances of offering spaces to inclusive cultures and long-term innovation (Floridi and Cowls, 2019). The ethical governance is therefore a transitional phase that determines whether technology is applied as a tool of empowerment or exploitation. Gubev also acknowledged that in the case of a large company there exists a logic between ethics and innovation. Organizations usually focus on efficiency and competitiveness, and in that regard, they adopt technology with inadequate care on ethical risk. But the notion of corporate social responsibility (CSR) and responsible innovation also indicate that ethical concerns can be present in innovation to make sure the suitability of technological implementation in the context of the long-term organizational and societal goals (Belz and Peattie, 2012; Owen et al., 2013). The conceptual framework, hence, positions ethical governance as a compromise between the demands of innovation and the demands of ethics.

4. CHALLENGES AND RISKS

The use of digital technology, machine learning and algorithmic decision making in the workplace brings up several ethical, operational and even social concerns, most of which are rooted in the questions of the algorithmic bias and privacy of employees. One of the fundamental difficulties is that the problem of algorithmic bias is entangled in the creation, deployment, and interpretation of data-driven systems. Bias models are usually a consequence of biased training data that reflects historical biases, such as recruitment algorithms that disfavor women or the representative of a minor group of people (Barocas and Selbst, 2016). Due to the scale of implementation, the use of algorithms will foster systemic exclusion and reinforce discrimination instead of confronting it because a single small statistical difference can cause it. In this way, a paradox is created, in which we see algorithms being used to make things more efficient and neutral in the organizations, and the systems that should promote fairness instead tend to support historical iniquities (Raghavan et al., 2020). It is complicated by the fact that the complex software systems were not very transparent, which is often called the problem of the black box (Burrell, 2016). To the employees who are the subject of the algorithmic decisions; be it hired or promoted, graded on their performance, there is usually no explanation as to how the decision was arrived at: How did we come up with this decision? What went into making it? And failing which, companies, in many cases, are not aware of the exact mechanism of the technology purchased by the vendor. Besides this discouraging accountability, this kind of opaqueness also destroys a sense of trust where employees perceive decision-making at the organizational level as random and unquestionable. On the other hand, employee privacy concerns have arisen due to the rising application of the surveillance and monitoring technology in the workplace. To monitor productivity and behavior, companies track with the help of the keystroke tracking, GPS location tracking, biometric authentication and AI-assisted sentiment analysis (Ajunwa, 2020). Although this type of tools is usually justified on the grounds of efficiency or security, they begin to cross the boundary between professional and personal life with significant consequences on autonomy, dignity, and even mental health. An example is invasive productivity tracking software that was implemented at a faster rate in the settlement patterns of work during and after COVID-19, which has caused a debate on its ethics as a digital surveillance method (Ball, 2021). Such types of practices create an environment that could demoralize workers, slow down morale and generate a chill effect on creativity or innovation. And one more urgent problem is the unequal distribution of evils caused by discrimination and invasion of privacy. Algorithms are more likely to misclassify the people in the margins, and general workers such as those on the gig economy platforms tend to have a high degree of surveillance with low resistance capacity (Wood et al., 2019). The unequal power between the employer and the employee, in its turn, increases the riskiness of ethical choices concerning technology since people do not have many options to oppose unjust treatment. Moreover, the global scope of digital platforms brings about the problem of regulatory diversity: privacy and antidiscrimination regulations in different countries differ significantly. An example is when the General Data Protection Regulation (GDPR) of the European Union grants high measure of protection to personal data, but it is not many other locations that offer a high level of measure with regards securities on employees regarding the information they provided being twisted and misused (Tadajewski and Jones, 2021). The challenge that trans-national organizations encounter is 8,10 how to align practices with various regulatory mechanisms and be able to secure integrity. Current solutions are also limited by a technical restriction. Despite all this advancement in fair-aware ML and privacy-enhancing technology, these are not flawless, with the best ones being a tradeoff. As an example, the trade-offs between accuracy and fairness may be involved as a means to reduce bias, and one example is the methods mitigating bias (Binns, 2018). Similarly, individual data anonymization and differential privacy are privacy-sensitive methods that are not always sufficient in re-identification prevention in the cases where individual datasets are of relatively large sizes (Narayanan and Shmatikov, 2008). These are the tensions that highlight the fact that dilemmas arising in the field of technology cannot be resolved solely on the basis of technical solutions, but rather a broader range of organisational and cultural changes is required. In addition, the task of these problems requires an inter-disciplinary approach with the involvement of computer scientists, ethicists, policy-makers and leaders of organizations - a paradigm that is challenging many organizations to implement with its current expertise silos and reward systems. The issues of algorithmic bias, and employee privacy are not solely, therefore, a technical concern, which is social, organizational, and political in nature, and might not be adequately addressed without holistic solutions that balance between efficiency, innovation and ethical accountability.

These deliberations are reinforced by the general risks of algorithmic bias and invasion of privacy, which endangers individual people, organization, and the whole society. In the eyes of the people, there is a danger of being treated unfairly, having fewer career opportunities, and becoming less trustful of workplace systems due to algorithmic bias. An unbalanced algorithm of recruiting candidates who are over-represented will systematically filter out marginalized candidates, and thus promote discrimination and support systemic injustice. This also demoralizes employees who have the little sense of justice under unfair arbitrary systems as well as sabotaging equality of opportunity. The consequences of privacy violations include a risk of identity theft, fraud of data, and the harm of reputation, which can be very severe psychologically. When individuals feel they are under constant surveillance, they complain of stress, anxiety, and helplessness. These risks have various elements on an organizational level: they are legal, reputational, and operational. Lack of effective protection against algorithmic bias or privacy breach exposes organizations to lawsuits. They can incur tremendous fines or other limitations when they are discovered to be violating the GDPR or other AI regulation regimes. The reputational risk is also significant: in case employees, consumers, or the general population learn about how biased an algorithm is or how intrusive a tracking program is, the organization may organize to counter the user of the latter. This may lead to boycotts, loss of brand capital or in the best case lose of talent due to flight away employees. Among the operational risks, there are the unreliability of biased or privacy abusing systems per se, which may consequently result in inefficient conclusions, poor conclusion, or security breach.

These emerging forms of artificial intelligence, algorithmic systems, and digital surveillance technology of organization practices have presented a wide range of technical and ethical issues. The element of the AI which has so far been the subject of the most coverage is AI bias, according to which machine decisions are given results that preferentially treat particular groups negatively. In no way this can be fully attributed to bad design there are historical inequalities that are already present in the data set (Barocas and Selbst,2016). As an illustration, the problem of hiring algorithms being trained on historical hire data will result in the continuation of gender or racial inequalities in the case of past preferences being based on them. The example of the canceled AI recruiting system used by Amazon is one such instance: the algorithm had access to decades of data, which favored almost implausibly men candidates, and the effect was a systematic downgrading of female applicants (Dastin, 2018). This serves as an indication that algorithms are not neutral and they will adopt the social and cultural bias in its creation and use. The issue of explainability and transparency also contributes to bias even more. When machine learning methods are followed to construct large numbers of such AI systems, it is still unknown even to the people that constructed them- this is called the black box problem (Burrell, 2016). This is that, in cases where the employees fall victim to the decisions that are mediated with algorithms, they are not able to satisfactorily dispute their findings as the logic of the systems are not transparent. This lack of transparency does not only hinder accountability, it is also a legal and moral dilemma. This is also a problem at the organizational level as they lack transparency since employees can sue them when the latter can claim discrimination with no ability to justify how their systems were fair (Raghavan et al., 2020). To the employees, this demoralises faith in the processes within the system and leads to their retreat in the group effort, along with some paranoia towards leadership. On the other spectrum of the morality scale is the growing usage or employee spying/monitoring technologies - wherein there are serious ethical and operational consequences. The modern surveillance systems in the workplace may digitize the magnitude of captured work-related and personal data (key strokes, email messages, biometric identifiers, even emotional feelings deciphered through AI based sentiment analysis) in a manner that is more than ever before (Ajunwa 2020). These sort of habits, had they been rationalized, whether on the grounds of productivity or privacy, blur the distinction between work-life and personal-life. As an illustration, remote-work explosion brought about by COVID-19 has made the use of screen-monitoring, log-in monitoring and communication tracking productivity tools to be accepted as acceptable practice (Ball, 2021). Employers might believe that such tools are necessary to make employees responsible in the distributed working conditions, but to the workers, the experience results invasive and causes stress and a sense of being under constant scrutiny. These relationships are reminiscent of Michel Foucault (1995) idea of the panopticon in which subjects internalize a surveillance gaze and self censure their actions when they are not actually being monitored. This manifests at work whereby this does not only moderate the work-related action but cuts off some features of their personality and thereby restrains the authenticity circuit which is directly proportional to creativity and job satisfaction. Moreover, the distribution of privacy issues is usually skewed: only employees in all but the most secure workplaces (even gig employees riding on an online labor platform) may suffer some of the most invasive types of surveillance as a condition of employment, such as GPS location tracking, performance rating and algorithmic management without much opportunity to appeal unlikable decisions (in Wood et al., 2019). This one-sided dominance in the surveillance and data collection is the same one-sided dominance between organizations and employees. To further complicate matters, international regulatory safeguards are far-spreading. The GDPR has placed significant protection to proportionality, limit purpose and express consent in the collection of data within the EU (Tadajewski and Jones 2021). In comparison, the United States lacks a federal level data privacy law and lacks several points of protection of employees. This becomes a compliance challenge to multinational companies who not only need to conform to fragmented legal requirements but also to similar ethical standards. At the same time, there are no restrictions on technical solutions to privacy provisions (e.g., anonymization or differential privacy) because it is progressively becoming harder to assure the anonymity of a user in sophisticated data re-identification attacks (Narayanan and Shmatikov, 2008). Together, these issues are not only signs of technical limitations themselves but also those of more general institutional and cultural and even societal factors that should be addressed through interdisc-iplinary efforts and active governance.

5. LEGAL IMPLICATIONS

The legal aspects of algorithm bias and employee privacy are heterogeneous, comprehensive and in the transition - they fall at the point of convergence between technological advancement, labour law, human rights law and data protection laws as courts, policy makers and corporations grapple with how to find the balance between efficiency and equity, innovation and responsibility, surveillance and dignity. In the heart of it lies the understanding that algorithms, which once seemed to be unbiased and objective, can indeed recreate or even increase systemic bias, and this is an urgent issue confronting anti-discrimination laws and employment law, as well as equal protection provisions embedded in a panoply of state and federal statutes. In America, as an example, employers cannot adhere to employment practices that indirectly affect people of other races or sex in accordance with Title VII of the Civil Rights Act and courts and regulators have had to grapple with whether the same should apply to algorithms that produce an indirect negative effect on minority job applicants (Barocas & Selbst, 2016). To use an example of a business that uses an AI-driven hiring service, in getting discovered that the system is implicitly discriminating against women based on biased training data, then such a negative company can be sued under anti-discrimination law, regardless of whether the bias is targeted. According to the initial signs of the federal agency that implements the anti-discrimination laws against the employment, the legal liability does not presuppose far-fetched expectations but is rather imminent when it comes to the implementation of AI systems (McCoy, 2016; Pyatt, 2017). They are similar arguments, but under the ADA it is heard as automated systems sorting through job seekers based on medical history or other psychometric factors potentially being discriminatory unless it accommodates individuals with disabilities (Ajunwa, 2020). Other than employment discrimination, privacy of the employees is strongly connected with the legal constructs of data protection, employee monitoring and consent and individual rights. General Data Protection Regulation (GDPR) probably is the most rigid legal system in the European Union, thus it is the duty of an organization to process the personal data fairly and lawfully and within the confines of specific purposes yet also provides employees with some rights to the latter so that they can access their data or have it corrected or erased (Voigt and Von dem Bussche, 2017). Article 22 GDPR is particularly significant taking into consideration that it restricts only automated decision-making that has legal or other equally important outcomes on individuals, and therefore provide workers the legal means to contest solely algorithmic job determination. This specifically concerns black-box AI systems that do not require meaningful human supervision in decision-making (whether in making hiring, promotion, etc. decisions). Breach of GDPR can bring tough penalties - up to 4% of the annual turnover around the world, legal risks, therefore, not only become ethical, but also costly and even existential to MNCs (Tadajewski and Jones, 2021). Conversely, the US lacks a general federal law of privacy, though has a mosaic of sectoral laws such as HIPAA and FCRA on health data or background check respectively that have huge gaps in employee protection (Schwartz & Solove, 2011). Although state-level laws, such as CCPA in California provide a broader set of rights, such as those related to employees such as disclosure and opt-out, the building blocks they have are less inclusive than the employee protection of GDPR. This hodgepodge legal framework poses compliance challenges to companies that have to operate across multiple jurisdictions, which must meet not just different substantive norms but also different enforcement orientations - the EU based on individual rights and proportionality and the U.S. largely focused on the flexibility and innovativeness of its organizations (Kuner, 2020). At the same time in Asia, Digital Personal Data Protection Act (2023) has been established in other countries such as India with some protection on paper though there are extensive exemptions granted to government and little power to implement it so once again the employee is at risk of being spied on and abusive of their personal data.

Another legal issue is that of the vendor and the employee liability. A lot of organizations are also utilizing AI or surveillance applications developed by third party developers to this day, which brings up the question of who is liable once the bias or privacy invasion happen as a fact. Nevertheless, the vendors are only able to do what they are instructed to do by their customers, and the latter are governed by employment law and data protection law whose court will not assist companies that have outsourced liability (Wachter and Mittelstadt, 2019). It results in the phenomenon of shared responsibility where organizations are pressurized to comply with due due diligence practices, audit algorithms and ensure that the contracts with vendors include guarantees of compliance. However, the legislation is crude in its characterization of relations among product supply chains, where there are gaps that may pose a threat to labor and uncertainty to companies. To make it even more difficult, cross-border flows of data are associated with jurisdiction and enforcement issues. To take an example, in case information about the employees who have been originally stored in one nation, is further processed in another country with less rigorous privacy regulations, it begs the question of whether the same should be subject to specific legal principles and whether employees can successfully exercise their rights (Kuner, 2020). U. S. Privacy Shield was ruled invalid by the Court of Justice of the European Union (2020) in its Schrems II case, ')[21] and it is probable that it will not satisfy Article 47 of the Charter of Fundamental Rights because of mass surveillance leaked by Edward Snowden. The Privacy Shield" regime, which demonstrates the security of international data streams and employee data in the political disputes between the countries. With the development of AI, there are also recently emerging legal concerns concerning predictive analytics, sentiment analysis and emotion recognition. Indicatively, when vulnerable inferences, such as mental illness or sympathizing membership with unions through digital traces could be applied to invoke anti-discrimination and labor laws, it will result in organizations flailing into accidentally confounding with anti-discrimination and Labor Law, by informing them of these inferences (Ajunwa 2020).

6. FUTURE SCOPE AND CONCLUSION

The future research and practice landscape in algorithmic bias and employee privacy is broad, multifaceted, dynamic. The use of algorithmic decision-making and surveillance at work is only likely to grow as more workplaces embrace digital transformation. As such, there is likely to be increasing pressure to adopt robust ethical frameworks which respect the ideals of innovation and fairness alongside the moral values of accountability and human dignity. Finally, we also propose to study the development of fairness-aware algorithms as a promising future work. Today's systems will tend to replicate inequalities encoded in historical data, but it is possible for future work-hour to focus upon the machine learning methods that are capable of incorporating fairness constraints as an augmenting part of their training process and actively tracking biased patterns in the outputs (Mehrabi et al.,

2021). Additionally, explainable AI (XAI) is a growing field of study that focuses on post-processing model predictions in such a way that explanations are generated to help explain how the algorithm arrives at its decisions. In organizational settings, explainability could "give a voice to the employee" on how she is being evaluated or recruited or tracked, Doshi-Velez and Kim (2017) note may reduce the opaqueness that has traditionally been a source of mistrust in algorithms.A second critical avenue for future research is the overlap between algorithmic bias and DEI. Although many companies implement DEI initiatives, using biased algorithms thoughtlessly can work against them by inadvertently screening out qualified people from underrepresented demographics or penalizing folks for factors that don't matter. Future research ought to investigate how the DEI values used by design practitioners can be reflected in algorithmic design, including adopting representative data sets and testing tools for disparate impact before release (Bogen & Rieke, 2018). Institutions may have to rely on ethical audit systems in which third-party groups judge the fairness of algorithms deployed in society, ultimately making these corporations responsible for the effects of their technological systems.

In addition to fairness, protecting employee privacy is another key aspect of future scope. Today's surveillance doesn't stop at measuring productivity; productivity data is (ab)used along with biometrics, keystroke monitoring, GPS coordinates, and even how we talk. They also raise deep questions about where legitimate corporate interests end and employees' entitlement to independence and dignity begin. As remote and hybrid Working arrangements become more common, surveillance practices are likely to increase in intensity leading to the further estrangement of employees (Ball, 2021) from their social environments. Future research could examine privacy-preserving technologies, such as differential privacy (which guarantees individual-level anonymity while still enabling aggregate-level learnings) and federated learning (which allows for joint model building without centralizing sensitive employee information) (Kairouz et al., 2021). What's more, companies can further hardwire ethical design concepts – including privacy by design – into workplace systems to safeguard the data of their employees from collection to store and use. The two issues that are predominantly associated with the ethical considerations within the contemporary workforce can be described as algorithmic bias and employee privacy. These are some of the issues that have become a major concern as organizations have adopted the use of data-driven decision-making and AI-based HR systems.

The concept of algorithmic bias occurs when the output of a computer model is unjust or discriminating against due to the un-fairness or historical bias in the data applied to the model in order to compute it. This can also be due to the unrepresentative samples or characteristics that have been taken as proxies to the sensitive variables like gender, caste, age, or socio-economic status. Most crucially in the event of unrectified such biases, the same can be perpetuated with respect to recruitment, talent measurement, performance assessment, promotions, and workforce planning thereby contributing to unfair organizational environment and employee demotivation. To combat bias, among others, the model must be transparently defined, it should be audited against bias on a regular basis, should be trained on representative data, and should be supervised by human beings in the final decision-making process.

Besides the aspect of bias, employee privacy is another problem that has gained considerable attention as the major challenge to ethics in the increasing trends of digital workplace surveillance, biometric office attendance, communication monitoring applications, wearables, and cloud-based HR systems. Without the availability of clear consent mechanisms and powerful data protection policies, the effects of such system can be detrimental to personal privacy and even lead to the loss of trust of the employees in their organization. The ethical utilization of employee data suggests that the amount of data collected must be minimal, anonymizing, must have a high level of access control, must follow the law of data protection globally and must communicate openly regarding the usage of data.

The scope of ethical concerns in workforce analytics will be quite wide with companies ready to introduce more powerful AI systems. The concept of describeable AI (XAI) will be of great assistance as it will shed light on the way the algorithm reaches a conclusion, thereby, HR managers and employees will be more aware of the recommendations offered by the automated tool and it will be simpler to determine whether there are any biases. It is believed that governments will implement stricter regulations, which will involve AI ethics audits, assessing the impact of bias, and making transparency documents a standard practice by organizations. Conversely, privacy technologies such as the use of differential privacy, federated learning and homomorphic encryption will allow sensitive employee data to be processed, with no information being disclosed about them, and blockchain distributed identity systems will possibly mark when the time has come when data ownership moves to the employees themselves. Further, ethical digital surveillance will transform into a collection of clear and agreed-upon monitoring policies by both the employees that respect their independence and at the same time encourage productivity and safety. Moreover, AI-based well-being measures will proactively identify burnout, overworking, stress, etc. in a highly unobtrusive manner that will consider the welfare of the employee rather than monitoring them. The days ahead will also be characterized by the interaction of data scientists, HR experts, lawyers, and ethicists who will make sure that AI in the workplace is equitable, responsible, and conforms to the organizational values. Put differently, the ethical aspect of workforce analytics will develop to seek proper solutions that will incorporate innovation and justice, openness, confidentiality, and human decency.

REFERENCES

Ajunwa, I. (2020). An auditing imperative for automated hiring systems. *Harv. JL & Tech., 34*, 621.

Ajunwa, I., Crawford, K., & Schultz, J. (2017). Limitless worker surveillance. *California Law Review, 105*(3), 735–776. DOI: 10.15779/Z38BR8MF94

Ball, K. (2021). Workplace surveillance: An overview. *Labor History, 62*(4), 440–456. DOI: 10.1080/0023656X.2021.1915038

Barocas, S., Hardt, M., & Narayanan, A. (2019). Fairness and machine learning. fairmlbook.org

Barocas, S., & Selbst, A. D. (2016). Big data's disparate impact. *California Law Review, 104*(3), 671–732. DOI: 10.2139/ssrn.2477899

Belz, F. M., & Peattie, K. (2012). *Sustainability Marketing: A Global Perspective* (2nd ed.). Wiley United Kingdom.

Benjamin, D. J. (2019). Errors in probabilistic reasoning and judgment biases. Handbook of Behavioral Economics: Applications and Foundations 1, 2, 69-186.

Binns, R. (2018). Fairness in machine learning: Lessons from political philosophy. In *Proceedings of the 2018 Conference on Fairness, Accountability, and Transparency* (pp. 149–159). DOI: <ALIGNMENT.qj></ALIGNMENT>10.1145/3287560.3287592

Bodie, M. T., Cherry, M. A., McCormick, M. L., & Tang, A. (2021). The law and policy of people analytics. *University of Colorado Law Review, 92*(1), 1–56.

Bogen, M., & Rieke, A. (2018). Help wanted: An examination of hiring algorithms, equity, and bias. Upturn. https://www.upturn.org/reports/2018/hiring-algorithms/

Brynjolfsson, E., & McAfee, A. (2017). *Machine, platform, crowd: Harnessing our digital future.* W. W. Norton & Company.

Buolamwini, J., & Gebru, T. (2018, January). Gender shades: Intersectional accuracy disparities in commercial gender classification. In Conference on fairness, accountability and transparency (pp. 77-91). PMLR.

Burrell, J. (2016). How the machine "thinks": Understanding opacity in machine learning algorithms. *Big Data & Society, 3*(1), 1–12. DOI: 10.1177/2053951715622512

Dastin, J. (2018, October 10). Amazon scraps secret AI recruiting tool that showed bias against women. Reuters. https://www.reuters.com/article/amazon-ai-idUSKCN1MK08G

Doshi-Velez, F., & Kim, B. (2017). Towards a rigorous science of interpretable machine learning. arXiv preprint arXiv:1702.08608. https://doi.org//arXiv.1702.08608DOI: 10.48550

Floridi, L., & Cowls, J. (2019). A unified framework of five principles for AI in society. *Harvard Data Science Review*, *1*(1). Advance online publication. DOI: 10.1162/99608f92.8cd550d1

Friedman, B., & Nissenbaum, H. (1996). Bias in computer systems. ACM Transactions on information systems (TOIS), 14(3), 330-347.

Friedman, B., & Nissenbaum, H. (1996). Bias in computer systems. ACM Transactions on information systems (TOIS), 14(3), 330-347.

Jobin, A., Ienca, M., & Vayena, E. (2019). The global landscape of AI ethics guidelines. *Nature Machine Intelligence*, *1*(9), 389–399. DOI: 10.1038/s42256-019-0088-2

Kairouz, P., McMahan, H. B., Avent, B., Bellet, A., Bennis, M., Bhagoji, A. N., ... & Zhao, S. (2021). Advances and open problems in federated learning. Foundations and Trends® in Machine Learning, 14(1–2), 1–210. https://doi.org/DOI: 10.1561/2200000083

Kuner, C. (2020). The GDPR and international organizations.

McCoy, B. R. (2016). Digital distractions in the classroom phase II: Student classroom use of digital devices for non-class related purposes.

Mehrabi, N., Morstatter, F., Saxena, N., Lerman, K., & Galstyan, A. (2021). A survey on bias and fairness in machine learning. *ACM Computing Surveys*, *54*(6), 1–35. DOI: 10.1145/3457607

Mitchell, M., Wu, S., Zaldivar, A., Barnes, P., Vasserman, L., Hutchinson, B., & Gebru, T. (2021). Model cards for model reporting. In *Proceedings of the Conference on Fairness, Accountability, and Transparency (FAT'19)* (pp. 220–229). https://doi.org/DOI: 10.1145/3287560.3287596

Moore, P. V., Upchurch, M., & Whittaker, X. (2018). *Humans and machines at work: Monitoring, surveillance and automation in contemporary capitalism*. Palgrave Macmillan.

Narayanan, A., & Shmatikov, V. (2008, May). Robust de-anonymization of large sparse datasets. In 2008 IEEE Symposium on Security and Privacy (sp 2008) (pp. 111-125). IEEE.

O'Neil, C. (2016). *Weapons of math destruction: How big data increases inequality and threatens democracy*. Crown.

Owen, R., Stilgoe, J., Macnaghten, P., Gorman, M., Fisher, E., & Guston, D. (2013). A framework for responsible innovation. Responsible innovation: managing the responsible emergence of science and innovation in society, 27-50.

Raghavan, M., Barocas, S., Kleinberg, J., & Levy, K. (2020). Mitigating bias in algorithmic hiring: Evaluating claims and practices. In *Proceedings of the 2020 Conference on Fairness, Accountability, and Transparency* (pp. 469–481). https://doi.org/DOI: 10.1145/3351095.3372828

Rawls, J. (1971). A Theory of Justice. 2. The Law of Peoples, 67.

Schwartz, P. M., & Solove, D. J. (2011). The PII problem: Privacy and a new concept of personally identifiable information. NYUL rev., 86, 1814.

Tadajewski, M., & Jones, B. (2021). The ethics of digital workplace surveillance. *Journal of Business Ethics, 174*(4), 731–747. DOI: 10.1007/s10551-020-04620-3

Voigt, P., & Von dem Bussche, A. (2017). *The EU General Data Protection Regulation (GDPR): A practical guide*. Springer., DOI: 10.1007/978-3-319-57959-7

Wachter, S., & Mittelstadt, B. (2019). A right to reasonable inferences: re-thinking data protection law in the age of big data and AI. Colum. Bus. L. Rev., 494.

Wood, A. J., Graham, M., Lehdonvirta, V., & Hjorth, I. (2019). Good gig, bad gig: Autonomy and algorithmic control in the global gig economy. *Work, Employment and Society, 33*(1), 56–75.

Zuboff, S. (2019). *The age of surveillance capitalism: The fight for a human future at the new frontier of power*. PublicAffairs.

Chapter 10
AI-Driven Workforce Empowerment:
Impact, Challenges, and Strategies

Aryan Diwan
https://orcid.org/0009-0002-0189-7465
Amity University, Noida, India

Pragya Negi
Amity University, Noida, India

Ajay Sidana
Amity University, Noida, India

Mohd Shuaib
Wuhan University, China

ABSTRACT

AI is expected to not only deprive millions of jobs but also to generate new jobs, requiring a redefinition of the approach to employment. Although AI has certain positive sides, such as increased productivity, efficiency, and a data-driven decision-making process, the establishment of new collaborative positions between humans and AI, it also poses essential challenges. These are mass displacement of jobs, extremely high implementation costs, long-lasting skills gaps, ethical issues, including algorithmic discrimination, and even the increase in wage disparity. To overcome these challenges, the chapter suggests such measures as comprehensive reskilling and upskilling programs, effective policy frameworks (e.g. EU AI act), well-developed digital infrastructure, and a humanistic approach to the creation of

DOI: 10.4018/979-8-3373-5871-0.ch010

ıt © 2026, IGI Global Scientific Publishing. Copying or distributing in print or electronic forms without written permission of IGI Global Scientific Publishing is prohibited. Use of this chapter to ;enerative artificial intelligence (AI) technologies is expressly prohibited. The publisher reserves all rights to license its use for generative AI training and machine learning model development.

AI that is ethically and socially fair. The key to capitalising on the potential of AI is to adopt a multi-faceted approach that would enable the organisation to benefit this technology and reduce the disruptive impact.

1. INTRODUCTION

1.1. The Dual Impact of AI on the Modern Workplace

The modern working environment is now marked by an unprecedented change due to the increasing velocity of artificial intelligence (AI) and automation technologies integration (Ashri, 2019; Benbya et al., 2020). The approach to artificial intelligence (AI) and robotics application in workplaces has led to radical changes in various sectors of the economy redefining the nature of labour requirements and the position of workers. Although it is a digital revolution that can lead to a great breakthrough in terms of productivity, innovation, and economic development, it poses serious questions of potential interference with usual patterns of employment and human labor (Sima et al., 2020). Although AI is expected to bring about greater efficiency and innovation, its mainstream usage has also contributed to high job insecurity, especially among workers who do straight and can be automated jobs (Masayuki, 2017; Yam et al., 2023). The World Economic Forum (WEF) report published in 2023 on the Future of Jobs introduce a concept of the labor-market churn to highlight the challenge brought by such change in the labor market driven by AI and automation and predicts a high churn rate of 23% in the next five years (World Economic Forum, 2023). Also noted is the fact that in 2025, 85 million jobs might be eliminated by AI and automation, yet 97 million new ones will be produced, according to the recent estimates provided by the World Economic Forum (World Economic Forum, 2020a). This two-sided aspect of AI poses an essential dilemma to organizations that strive to achieve the balance between technological changes and job security.

1.2. Evolving Skills, Organizational Responses, and the Need for Adaptive Strategies

It requires a paradigm shift in the approaches to the development of the workforce and the development of the adaptive employment policies that will help the workers cope with this changing employment environment.

Since studies have shown that those jobs that focus on personal interaction and soft skills are less susceptible to automation, it makes sense to ensure that the workers acquire skills that complement AI technologies (Coupe, 2019; Hussain,

2024). As an example, within the financial industry, chatbots that are powered by AI can currently address up to 6080% of low-level tasks posed by customers, which redirects workers to more advanced analytical and customer-facing tasks (Roman, 2024). Although the opportunities of AI and automation lead to more productive developments and innovative edges, the disruptive nature of the field raises certain concerns regarding possible job dependence, the loss of skills, and the insufficiency of current employment policies to address the alterations. The digital revolution necessitates the workers to have new skills to succeed in the AI-based working environment, as their current skill-sets are rapidly becoming outdated, so there is a huge gap between the current workforce capacity and the requirements of the upcoming careers (Özkiziltan and Hassel, 2021). Major companies like Amazon are making announcements of multimillion-dollar investments to re-train their workers to work in more advanced positions, much of the emphasis is on the individual up-skilling of workers, rather than on the team based learning approach. Even though research recognizes the value of lifelong skills in AI-based settings, they rarely discuss the mechanisms by which staff actively learns and develops the skills that reduce the fear of being automated through personal experience (Zhang et al., 2025). All these combined are what require a complex and multifaceted solution that can help to secure a successful shift and reduce the adverse effects of AI and automation on the workforce. Given the fast shift in the employment environment, this chapter will examine the associated effects, both positive and negative, difficulties in application, and future efforts of AI-based workforce empowerment.

2. LITERATURE REVIEW

2.1. AI's Impact on Employee Performance in Manufacturing

It is suggested that employee performance, one of the outcomes in the manufacturing sector, is becoming more affected by the implementation of artificial intelligence (Kassa & Worku, 2025). The study indicates that performance increased with the use of AI-powered tools due to automation, real-time monitoring, predicting, and decision-making support (Deepika, 2019). This cluster of developments will contribute to minimizing the number of mistakes and better planning of the working process, as well as the more effective distribution of the working population.

2.2. Economic Facets of AI: Business Growth and Innovation

The recent upsurge of the application of the Artificial Intelligence (AI) phenomenon caused numerous research concerning its economic facet, specifically, business growth, product creation, and human resource management. It demonstrates that AI investments correlate with the significant growth of sales, the creation of new jobs, and market value of companies and proves the view of AI as a general-purpose technology and its application in an enormous number of industries, including manufacturing, finance, and retail. This expansion can be explained by the action of the more significant product innovation mechanism which is manifested in the higher number of trademarks and patents and modifications of the product line. This means that the first effect of AI is in the reduction of costs of development of goods. Regarding the workforce, it is important to highlight that since the study was developed based on the human capital measures, it is necessary to have special AI talent. The authors confirm the truth that the companies that invest in AI also increase their research and development (R&D) expenditures, which is likely to exist since the intensive experimentation is required to introduce new AI technologies. More to the point, the effects of AI investments are powerful when it comes to other technological contributions, such as robotics and non-AI information technologies, which seclude the contribution of AI to the performance of firms (Babina et al., 2024). Lee et al. (2018) argue that the emergence of the information era means not only the growth of technology, but also a new way of economic activity in which information will become the main product. This has radically changed the value of labor, giving dominance to cerebral work over actual work and giving rise to the boom in areas like information technology, finance, and professional services.

2.3. Human Capital and Technological Infrastructure in Generative AI

Vishvesh Soni (2023) The article shows that human capital plays a positive role as a moderator between Generative AI (GAI)-revenue growth relationship. Specifically, usage of Generative AI is advantageous to the business, and this strength is particularly acute when there are high-educated staff working in it. It means that human capital is a complement to the benefits that GAI brings, which is likely because of a more appropriate use and application of the advanced AI systems. Despite the need, the significance of interaction between the GAI adoption and human capital is lower, which shows the effect on the increase in revenues is not so decisive when compared to technological infrastructure. Accordingly, the skills and knowledge of the human resources should be viewed as complementing variables, and they will equip the employees to operate with artificial intelligence systems and join the new applications. It is also ascertained that moderating influence of technological infrastructure present in a firm is positive and robust. The benefits of GAI are especially increased in the instances wherein the technological environment is defined and developed appropriately in the business. Greater use of AI can be made through more effective application of modern or progressive technology facilities as compared to outdated or less effective infrastructure. With an adequately built technological infrastructure, it will be an arable ground where the GAI applications can be deployed to provide a seamless implementation and integration process into business operations and effective data processing and automation. The fact that GAI is highly integrated with the technological infrastructure is a pointer to suggest that a pre-investment in technology is one of the determinants of the scale and pace through which GAI can be adopted and harnessed to drive the growth in revenue.

2.4. Historical Fears, Radical Changes, and Policy Interventions

The early effects of digital technology on the employees were followed by fear as the historical fears of technological unemployment became prominent as the laboriousness of work was automated both in the production sphere and then in the service sphere with the help of software and the internet with significant job loss rates (Sima at el. 2020, Vermeulen et al. 2018). Such discoveries in the field of Artificial Intelligence, which have become a regular occurrence in numerous industries and fields, are regarded as a radical change not just to the way it has impacted the lives of people but also its implications to an organization (Cardon at el. 2023). According to García-Pérez et al. (2021), it is important to educate and train job seekers to become fit in the digital economy. Moreover, the policy interventions to promote innovation and assist displaced people are regarded as the necessary ways to benefit the digital transformation but to reduce the number of disruptions.

3. RESEARCH GAP

This literature review is rather effective in showing the transformational nature of AI on organizational performance, innovation, and the essential and complementary function of human capital to use such technologies. Nevertheless, although it is right that workers need to develop new skills to work well with AI systems, there is still a big gap in knowledge regarding the specific, individual-level processes under which employees learn to learn, transform their current skills, and deal with the psychological intricacies of the process, including the fear of being automated, through direct personal experience and firsthand interactions with AI. The available research does not describe these granular mechanisms of active learning and adaptation to emotions. This gap is what this chapter attempts to fill by shedding more light on the subtle aspects of human adaptability in a developing AI dominated workforce.

4. RESEARCH QUESTIONS & OBJECTIVES

The given paper is the attempt to consider various aspects of the influence of Artificial Intelligence on the contemporary workplace environment. The two important research questions that this chapter poses are what organizations can do to successfully juggle the implementation of AI and automation with workplace safety on their employees and what type of adaptive employment policies are necessary to address this evolving employment situation. And, what are the detailed mechanisms that can enable the ongoing development of skills and learning among employees to enhance AI technologies and eliminate job insecurity, in particular, since the existing skill sets are becoming obsolete at a rapid pace. To answer these questions, the paper aims at both reviewing the advantages and disadvantages of AI-based workforce empowerment and discussing the issues that can be posed using AI workforce empowerment and finally offering the strategies through which the successful transition can occur in the future.

5. RESEARCH METHODOLOGY

A comprehensive literature review and conceptual analysis have been used in this chapter. It summarizes scholarly literature and business publications to examine the effect of AI on the workforce, based on the opportunities, challenges, and strategic responses outlined. Consolidation of current knowledge was done through a thematic synthesis approach.

6. IMPACTS OF AI-DRIVEN WORKFORCE EMPOWERMENT

The capability of AI to execute mental tasks, including natural language processing, decision-making, and pattern recognition, unlike steam engines or computers, which automatized mainly physical or routine work, makes it a general-purpose technology with implications that are far reaching (Frey and Osborne, 2016). The speed of AI adoption since the launch of ChatGPT in November 2022 has been driven by excitement and fear about the new technology, with 88 percent of formal organizations embracing the use of AI in at least one business activity by 2025 (McKinsey & Company, 2025). The list of vantages provided by the introduction of AI technologies into management activities is impressive, and organizations are launched to the next level of success and competitive advantage (Kapoor and Agarwal, 2020). Managers will have access to priceless insights and data-driven decision-making using AI algorithms, machine learning, and predictive models. This empowerment also allows them to make accurate, informed and responsive strategic decisions, thus minimizing uncertainties and improving their capacity to cope with complex business environments (Brock, 2019). With the automation based on AI, operations are simplified, and employees can work on complex problems (Ayanponle et al., 2024; Aldoseri et al., 2024). Moreover, AI management has great potential in terms of optimization of operational efficiency. Through the automation of repetitive tasks, AI systems not only make workflow more efficient but also minimize downtimes and optimize resources. Having the ability to process large amounts of real-time information, AI technologies allow companies to detect anomalies, and inefficiencies that lead to optimization of costs, process enhancement and increased productivity (Kapoor and Agarwal, 2020). Such systems can also improve different metrics of the business and production not only factory operations but also allow responding more quickly to customer requirements and better controlling the process deviations as well as providing a picture of the future of the supply chain management and learning (Walter, 2023). During decision-making, AI also allows offering more data-driven information and helps organizations predict patterns and tailor services (Prasanth et al., 2023; Zaman, 2022). Its high analytics capacity and automatism of functions simplify the marketing processes and enhances customer interaction (Ziakis and Vlachopoulou, 2023; Alghizzawi et al., 2024). The other most important aspect of AI-powered management is the influence it has on employee productivity and engagement (Noy and Zhang, 2023). Incorporation of AI does not simply mean the substitution of human workers, but it also presupposes the enhancement of human abilities and development of new occupational categories. With AI automating routine processes, the employee change to activities that are more valuable, where critical thinking, creativity, and planning are essential (Patil, 2024; Ayanponle et al., 2024). At the same time, AI creates new positions in development, operation, and maintenance that require only classes with artificial intelligence such as data analytics. Evolution would demand new skills, or re-programming of learners, like that of AI, including creativity, communication and flexibility of skills. That is why we can state that AI is not only a job killer; it does alter work indeed and as a result, it opens the field of human-AI collaboration, which requires constant attention to skill formation. Nevertheless, it is usual that there is the risk involved with all opportunities that are associated with automation, It is important to note and accept that displacement is an inherent aspect of AI taking over the part of the human jobs; it is inevitable to acknowledge that AI is capable of taking over full-time jobs of 300 million people globally by 2030 as it is driving productivity and economic growth, which adds up to 13 trillion of economic activity worldwide by 2030 (Talmage-Rostron, 2024). In the environment of the robotics industry of the advanced stage, a study reveals that 25 percent of manufacturing jobs in the USA, 30 percent of retail jobs in the UK, and 21 percent of the jobs in Japan are forecasted to be lost to automation (Badet, 2021). There will also be a high displacement in manufacturing positions in South Korea. Therefore, automation is a threat to Germany and France, with the most developed digital environment, and India can relatively have low number of obsolete professions as the digital environment is less developed in this country (George, 2024). It is also associated with massive acquisition expenses and maintenance costs of AI in organizations that can place the burden of financial strain on organizations (Zirar et al., 2023). Simultaneously, since it is stated that it possesses higher practical efficiency and creativity, the employment, training and funding consequences should also be taken into consideration to be prepared to work in the future (Bayan & Ali, 2025). The growing dependence on AI algorithms in the workplace creates serious ethical issues; questions of bias, transparency and accountability. Discriminative hiring, unfair performance review, and biased decision on who to promote can be the results of algorithmic bias, which may be used to support the existing inequalities in the society (Pratama, 2025). The role of AI in identifying and responding to threats in IT and cybersecurity is associated with the emergence of the same moral dilemma associated with privacy invasion and the potential misuse of surveillance methods (Nguyen et al., 2015). The fact that AI systems are not as transparent in making a decision may also erode the trust and reduce the possibility of the workers to dispute or fix such processes. Moreover, the risk of considering the issue of data possession and control, as well as the possible employee surveillance, requires a close attention to the moral principles (O'Neil, 2016). Fig no. 1 below conceptualizes the dual impact of AI on the workforce, highlighting its simultaneous role in enhancing productivity and innovation while generating job displacement, skill obsolescence, and ethical concerns.

Figure 1. Diagrammatic representation of Impacts of AI-Driven Workforce Empowerment

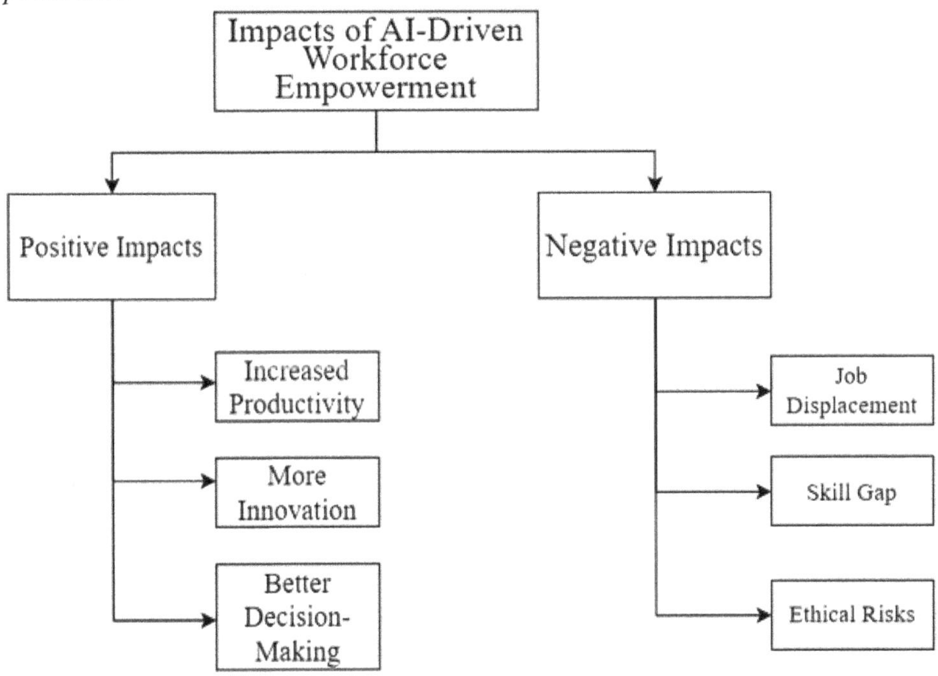

Source: Author's Conceptualization

7. CHALLENGES IN IMPLEMENTING AI-DRIVEN WORKFORCE EMPOWERMENT

Artificial intelligence (AI) is a new general-purpose technology with the ability to transform economies and societies. AI applications are quickly evolving and spreading out (McKinsey and Company, 2023), in the healthcare diagnostics sector, as with individualized education. The innovations of the transformer-based architecture (Vaswani et al., 2017), the advent of new hardware that facilitates an increase in processing velocity, and access to massive datasets to train have led to AI unprecedented creative power and its ability to provide decision support. Breakthroughs in generative AI tools, including GPT-3 (Brown et al., 2020) and GPT-4 (OpenAI, 2023) and Deep Seek in 2025, have demonstrated the enormous creative power of AI and its capacity to support Although the AI augmentation has potential, there are obstacles to it. The integration involves a high cost of investment in infrastructure and training and 60% of organizations have indicated that skill gaps were a challenge (World Economic Forum, 2020b). The financial resources available to support reskilling efforts are restrictive to the size of reskilling programs, with 70 percent of governments attributing budget constraints as a hindrance (OECD, 2023). The effective working of AI will rely on the positive adjustment of the labor force and the necessity to constantly improve the skills (Alaran et al., 2025). One of the main issues is the ethical use of AI, especially in reducing the bias of the algorithms and safeguarding the data. As an example, AI generative systems (GenAI) must have effective regulation to avoid the continuation of social biases, which are mostly displayed in the recruitment process and other decision-making activities (Bozkurt et al., 2024; Sharma, 2025). In the case of AI systems, which promote gender or racial inequalities, such bias can erode the benefits of augmentation (Kochhar, 2023). Moreover, the heavy reliance of AI systems on massive datasets tends to exacerbate the existing inequality gap by excluding underrepresented groups (Alaran et al., 2025). AI-driven HRM practices like recruitment, performance assessment, and talent management enhance efficiency but present ethical challenges. Recruitment algorithms risk perpetuating bias, and automated performance assessment may oversimplify complex behaviors, raising fairness concerns (Raghavan et al., 2020; Binns, 2018). Also, the opposition to AI implementation by workers based on the fear of job loss or loss of autonomy stops successful implementation (McKinsey and Company, 2023). In addition, the unequal distribution of AI resources and expertise in the world creates the danger of increasing disparities. The minority and disadvantaged groups are marginalized even in developed economies because they have little access to AI technologies, as well as because they lack AI literacy, i.e. the knowledge to operate and manage AI tools (Ahmed and Wahed, 2020; Zuboff, 2019). In addition to that, the attitudes of employees can also be quite influential regarding the success of AI implementation because organizations are under pressure to implement AI to enhance their performance and competitiveness (Chiu et al., 2021). Automation and AI can be used to further accentuate current trends of wage inequality, as highly skilled workers are enjoying the fruits of technological progress, as workers with low skills have their jobs taken over and wages stagnate. It is a serious concern on social justice and necessity of policy interventions that can help in resolving such increasing disparities (Pratama, 2025). Fig no. 2 below illustrates the interconnected challenges in implementing AI-driven workforce empowerment, demonstrating how high implementation costs, skill gaps, ethical risks, and employee resistance collectively contribute to widening inequality.

Figure 2. Diagrammatic Representation of Challenges in Implementing AI-Driven Workforce Empowerment

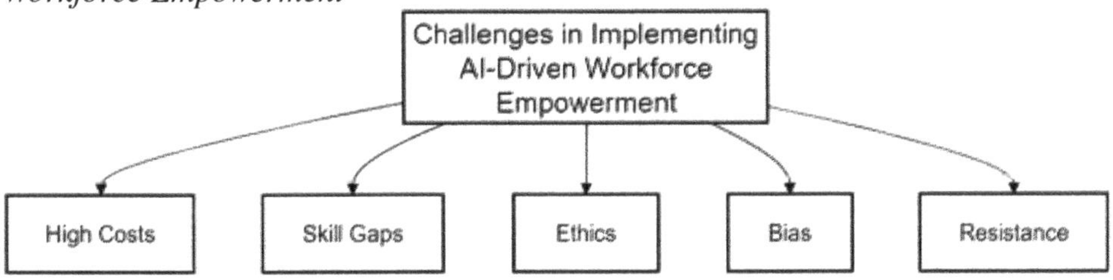

Source: Author's Conceptualization

8. STRATEGIES TO IMPROVE AI-DRIVEN WORKFORCE EMPOWERMENT

The disruptive nature of artificial intelligence (AI) in occupying jobs, enhancing abilities, and generating new opportunities means that action needs to be taken to make sure that the benefits of the power are distributed (Bhati, 2025). According to Barrier (20012), information systems should be controlled and rather than blindly accepting and adding components into the information systems, system developers are expected to research on the effectiveness, feasibility, and efficiency of the individual components of the information systems. According to World Economic Forum, by 2030 50 percent of the global workforce will need reskilling and 40 percent of the workers in the companies adopting AI are already enrolled in training programs (World Economic Forum, 2020b). Reskilling is a crucial step that organisations increasing AI systems should consider because it may assist the employees to adjust to the new changes connected with technologies. As Makarius et al. (2020) explain, reskilling assists employees to acquire the required knowledge and skills to be effective in dealing with the technology - but in a new position. This will involve the training in fields like data analytics, machine learning, and programming. This will involve the training in fields like data analytics, machine learning, and programming. Reskilling may assist organisations to become more competitive overall, with employees possessing the proper skills being more suited when it comes to facilitating innovation and generating value to the organisation (L. Li, 2022). The third world countries should establish clear policies regarding the ownership and sovereignty of data to empower the population and protect their rights (Oguamanam, 2020). One of the key elements of any AI policy framework is the creation of a robust digital infrastructure (Ashok et al., 2022). The EU AI Act, which was adopted in 2024 is a wholesome effort to control AI systems according to their risk exposure. The AI Act will have a proportional risk-based approach that will only place regulatory burdens in instances where an AI system is likely to be highly dangerous to essential rights and safety. The AI Act categorizes risk into four tiers, including: Unacceptable risk, high risk, limited risk, and minimal risk (Meltzer et al., 2022). These rules can also help avoid discriminatory results, including discriminatory hiring algorithms, which unequally affect women and minorities (Kochhar, 2023). The spillovers of technologies in new directions like AI can be significant, and this should support the subsidies of fundamental research, or gathering of publicly available training sets to algorithms (Gibbs, 2022). The costs of displacing workers are not internalized by firms, and the tax regime can give them incentives to take their automation levels to inefficient levels, some suggest a robot tax on automation capital investments. That has the potential to decelerate the acceleration of automation and allocate the following excess, to ease the process of displacing displaced staff and balance rising inequality (Acemoglu at el. 2020). Human-centric AI put ethics by design into the core of AI development, applying ethical values directly to the development process of AI. This will make certain that concerns such as privacy, fairness, security are taken into consideration at the beginning of the project and not addressed at the end (Floridi et al., 2018).

9. CONCLUSION

The introduction of Artificial Intelligence (AI) and automation technologies is surely changing the contemporary labour force at an unexampled rate radically changing the conventional employment patterns and requirements (Ashri, 2019; Benbya et al., 2020). As it has been illustrated in this chapter, this technological revolution comes in a tricky duality; a powerful source of development and empowerment, and a lot of difficulties that require careful handling. On the one hand, AI is a trigger of impressive developments. Its ability to perform complex mental processes, including natural language processing and predictive analytics, makes it a general-purpose technology with transformational possibilities, just like the effects of previous industrial revolutions (Frey and Osborne, 2016). Companies that utilize AI are also reported to have achieved high productivity, nurtured innovation, and competitive edge (Kapoor and Agarwal, 2020; Brock, 2019). Contingent on automating repetitive and mundane tasks, AI frees up the human capital, with workers moving to work on more strategic, creative, and emotionally engaged tasks, thereby leading to human-AI interaction (Patil, 2024; Ayanponle et al., 2024). Such a transition does not only streamline the operational efficiency and lowers the costs but it also enriches the employee engagement and satisfaction (Noy and Zhang, 2023). Besides, the investments of AI are associated with a notable increase in business, product development, and the establishment of completely new employment areas, and the World Economic Forum (2020a) predicts that up to 97 million new jobs will be created by 2025, despite rising unemployment levels. However, the complementary, but not the strictly substitutive character of AI is emphasized by the moderating influence of human capital to the maximum of the revenue-generating benefits of Generative AI as noted by Vishvesh Soni (2023). In spite of these deep opportunities, the shift to an AI-based workforce is accompanied by a number of significant obstacles. The most intense issue in the nearest future is mass layoff, especially in those industries that are based on routine, automatable works. The future is bleak, with estimates of the possible displacement of 300 million jobs across the world by 2030 (Talmage-Rostron, 2024), and certain sectors such as manufacturing and retail experiencing significant job losses in developed economies (Badet, 2021). This shift expands skills gaps, where 60% of organizations found this as one of the biggest challenges, and it needs constant upskilling to ensure that the existing skills do not become irrelevant (World Economic Forum, 2020b; Özkiziltan and Hassel, 2021). Organizations are also under a lot of pressure with the financial cost of buying and maintaining complex AI systems (Zirar et al., 2023). Another major aspect of this challenge is ethical consideration. Dependence on large datasets to train AI systems poses an enormous probability of algorithmic bias, continuing and increasing current inequalities in society during hiring, performance feedback, and promotions (Pratama, 2025; Kochhar, 2023; Raghavan et al., 2020). The issues of transparency, accountability, and even the possibility of privacy invasion due to the enhanced surveillance systems are still at the center (O'Neil, 2016; Nguyen et al., 2015). Moreover, the resistance of the internal workforce, which is caused by fears of job loss or loss of control, can be a serious obstacle to the successful implementation and integration of AI technologies into the company (McKinsey and Company, 2023). The lack of equal access to AI tools and literacy has posed a risk of increasing the socioeconomic gap globally, excluding the underrepresented groups (Ahmed and Wahed, 2020; Alaran et al., 2025).

In order to manoeuvre in such a complicated environment, effective and active strategic framework is required. One of the strongholds of this strategy is a massive investment in reskilling and upskilling programs, which will enable workers to have the essential skills including data analytics, machine learning, and flexible problem-solving, thus turning the possible displacement into the growth opportunities (Makarius et al., 2020; L. Li, 2022). The case of putting in a multi-million dollars in retraining its work force by Amazon exemplifies a much-needed paradigm shift. At the same time, intelligent policy schemes are developed. Policies such as the EU AI Act (Meltzer et al., 2022) offer a regulatory framework capable of critically regulating the deployment of AI, integrating the risk-based approach to guarantee ethical deployment and avoid discriminatory consequences. The policies that would enhance data sovereignty (Oguamanam, 2020), invest in a strong digital infrastructure (Ashok et al., 2022), and even new fiscal policies such as a robot tax (Acemoglu et al., 2020) should be considered to control the pace of automation and redistribute the economic gains of the latter to the same extent. Lastly, design-based approaches to ethics, which require the consideration of privacy, fairness, and security earlier on, is essential in developing trust and guaranteeing that AI is in the best interest of humanity (Floridi et al., 2018). Throughout, the rise of an AI-driven labor force is not only an evolutionary move but a revolutionary one which requires a collective and adaptive reaction as an individual, organization, and government. Although AI has unparalleled benefits in terms of productivity gains and innovation, achieving these benefits in a fair way requires a proactive investment in human capital, careful policy-intervention, and a ruthless adherence to ethical AI principles. Societies can also achieve success in embracing AI as an effective solution to workforce empowerment, not a displacement and inequality driver, by creating a culture of constant learning, human-centric design, and a firm governance framework, and that way achieve a more productive, innovative, and equitable future of work.

10. REFERENCES

Acemoglu, D., Manera, A., & Restrepo, P. (2020). Does the US tax code favor automation? (No. w27052). National Bureau of Economic Research.

Ahmed, N., & Wahed, M. (2020). The de-democratization of AI: Deep learning and the compute divide in artificial intelligence research. arXiv. Available at: https://arxiv.org/abs/2010.15581

. Alaran, M., Lawal, S. K., Jiya, M. H., Egya, S. A., Ahmed, M. M., Abdulsalam, A., Haruna, U. A., Musa, M. K., & Lucero-Prisno, D. E. (2025). Challenges and opportunities of artificial intelligence in African health space. Digital Health, 11. SAGE Publishing. .DOI: 10.1177/20552076241305915

Aldoseri, A., Al-Khalifa, K. N., & Hamouda, A. M. S. (2024). Methodological approach to assessing the current state of organizations for ai-based digital transformation. *Applied System Innovation*, *7*(1), 14. DOI: 10.3390/asi7010014

Alghizzawi, M., Ahmed, E., Ezmigna, I., Ezmigna, A. A. R., & Omeish, F. (2024). The relationship between artificial intelligence and digital marketing in business companies. In Awwad, B. (Ed.), *The AI Revolution: Driving Business Innovation and Research* (Vol. 525, pp. 885–895). Springer Nature Switzerland., DOI: 10.1007/978-3-031-54383-8_67

Ashok, M., Madan, R., Joha, A., & Sivarajah, U. (2022). Ethical framework for Artificial Intelligence and Digital technologies. *International Journal of Information Management*, *62*, 102433.

Ashri, R. (2019). *The AI-Powered workplace: How Artificial Intelligence, Data, and Messaging Platforms Are Defining the Future of Work*. Apress.

Ayanponle, L. O., Elufioye, O. A., Asuzu, O. F., Ndubuisi, N. L., Awonuga, K. F., & Daraojimba, R. E. (2024). The future of work and human resources: A review of emerging trends and HR's evolving role. *International Journal of Science and Research Archive*, *11*(2), 113–124. DOI: 10.30574/ijsra.2024.11.2.0151

Babina, T., Fedyk, A., He, A., & Hodson, J. (2024). Artificial intelligence, firm growth, and product innovation. *Journal of Financial Economics*, *151*, 103745.

. Badet, J. (2021). AI, Automation and New Jobs. Journal of Business and Management, 9, 2452 2463. .DOI: 10.4236/ojbm.2021.95132

Barrier, T. (Ed.). (2001). *Human computer interaction development & management*. IGI Global.

Bayan, F., & Ali, A. N. (2025). EXPLORING THE FUTURE OF WORK: HOW AI IS RESHAPING INDUSTRIES. *International Journal of Professional Business Review, 10*(10), e05106. DOI: 10.26668/businessreview/2025.v10i10.5106

Benbya, H., Davenport, T. H., & Pachidi, S. (2020). Artificial intelligence in Organizations: current state and future opportunities. SSRN Electronic Journal. DOI: 10.2139/ssrn.3741983

. Bhati, H. (2025). Will AI Take My Job or Help Me Do It Better? Understanding the Real Impact of Artificial Intelligence on Careers and Capabilities.

Binns, R. (2018). Fairness in Machine Learning: Lessons from Political Philosophy. *Proceedings of the 2018 Conference on Fairness, Accountability, and Transparency*, 149-159.

Bozkurt, A., Xiao, J., Farrow, R., Bai, J. Y. H., Nerantzi, C., Moore, S., Dron, J., Stracke, C. M., Singh, L., Crompton, H., Koutropoulos, A., Terentev, E., Pazurek, A., Nichols, M., Sidorkin, A. M., Costello, E., Watson, S., Mulligan, D., Honeychurch, S., & Asino, T. I. (2024). The manifesto for teaching and learning in a time of generative ai: A critical collective stance to better navigate the future. *Open Praxis, 16*(4), 487–513. DOI: 10.55982/openpraxis.16.4.777

Brock, D. (2019). The impact of artificial intelligence on strategic decision-making. *Strategic Direction, 35*(5), 16–20.

Brown, T. B., Mann, B., Ryder, N., Subbiah, M., Kaplan, J., Dhariwal, P., Neelakantan, A., Shyam, P., Sastry, G., Askell, A., Agarwal, S., Herbert-Voss, A., Krueger, G., Henighan, T., Child, R., Ramesh, A., Ziegler, D. M., Wu, J., Winter, C., . . . Amodei, D. (2020). Language Models are Few-Shot Learners. arXiv (Cornell University), 33, 1877–1901. /arxiv.2005.14165.DOI: 10.48550

. Cardon, P., Getchell, K., Carradini, S., Fleischmann, C., & Stapp, J. (2023). Generative AI in the workplace: Employee perspectives of ChatGPT benefits and organizational policies.

Chiu, Y. T., Zhu, Y. Q., & Corbett, J. (2021). In the hearts and minds of employees: A model of pre-adoptive appraisal toward artificial intelligence in organizations. *International Journal of Information Management, 60*, 102379. DOI: 10.1016/j.ijinfomgt.2021.102379

Coupe, T. (2019). Automation, job characteristics and job insecurity. *International Journal of Manpower, 40*, 1288–1304. DOI: 10.1108/ijm-12-2018-0418

. Deepika, M., Cuddapah, V., Srivastava, A., & Mahankali. (2019). *AI & ML-Powering the Agents of Automation*. BPB Publications.

Floridi, L., Cowls, J., Beltrametti, M., Chatila, R., Chazerand, P., Dignum, V., & Vayena, E. (2018). AI4People—An ethical framework for a good AI society: Opportunities, risks, principles, and recommendations. *Minds and Machines*, *28*(4), 689–707.

Frey, C. B., & Osborne, M. A. (2016). The future of employment: How susceptible are jobs to computerisation? *Technological Forecasting and Social Change*, *114*, 254–280. DOI: 10.1016/j.techfore.2016.08.019

García-Pérez, L., García-Garnica, M., & Olmedo-Moreno, E. M. (2021). Skills for a working future: How to bring about professional success from the educational setting. *Education Sciences*, *11*(1), 27.

George, A. S. (2024). Artificial Intelligence and the Future of Work. *Job Shifting Not Job Loss.*, *02*, 17–37. DOI: 10.5281/zenodo.10936490

Gibbs, M. B. (2022). How is new technology changing job design? *IZA World of Labor: Evidence-Based Policy Making*.

Hussain, M. A. (2024). The impact of artificial intelligence on workforce automation and skill development. *J. Artif. Intel. Mach. Learn. Neural Netw.*, *44*, 11–21. DOI: 10.55529/ jaimlnn.44.11.21

Kapoor, R., & Agarwal, S. (2020). How artificial intelligence is changing the face of operational efficiency. *Business Horizons*, *63*(1), 53–64.

Kassa, B. Y., & Worku, E. K. (2025). The impact of artificial intelligence on organizational performance: The mediating role of employee productivity. *Journal of Open Innovation*, *11*(1), 100474.

Kochhar, R. (2023). Which U.S. workers are more exposed to AI on their jobs? Pew Research Center. https://www.pewresearch.org/wp-content/uploads/sites/20/2023/07/st_2023.07.26_ai-and-jobs-1.pdf.Raghavan, M., Barocas, S., Kleinberg, J., & Levy, K. (2020). Mitigating bias in algorithmic hiring: Evaluating claims and practices. Proceedings of the 2020 Conference on Fairness, Accountability, and Transparency.

Lee, M., Yun, J. J., Pyka, A., Won, D., Kodama, F., Schiuma, G., & Zhao, X. (2018). How to respond to the fourth industrial revolution, or the second information technology revolution? Dynamic new combinations between technology, market, and society through open innovation. *Journal of Open Innovation*, *4*(3), 21.

Li, L. (2022). Reskilling and upskilling the future-ready workforce for industry 4.0 and beyond. *Information Systems Frontiers*, ●●●, 1–16.

Makarius, E. E., Mukherjee, D., Fox, J. D., & Fox, A. K. (2020). Rising with the machines: A sociotechnical framework for bringing artificial intelligence into the organisation. *Journal of Business Research, 120*, 262–273.

Masayuki, M. 2017. Who are afraid of losing their jobs to artificial intelligence and robots? Evidence from a survey. RIETI Discussion Paper Series 17-E-069.

McKinsey & Company. (2025). The state of AI in 2025: Agents, innovation, and transformation. https://www.mckinsey.com/capabilities/quantumblack/our-insights/the-state-of-ai

. McKinsey and Company (2023). The economic potential of generative AI: The next productivity frontier.

Meltzer, J., Tielemans, A., & Brookings Institution. (2022). THE EU AI ACT: NEXT STEPS AND ISSUES FOR BUILDING INTERNATIONAL COOPERATION. In *Brookings Institution* [Policy brief]. https://www.brookings.edu/wp-content/uploads/2022/05/FCAI-Policy-Brief_Final_060122.pdf

Nguyen, T.-H. D., Chen, Z., & El-Nasr, M. S. (2015). Analytics-based AI techniques for a better gaming experience. *Game AI Pro, 2*, 481–500.

Noy, S., & Zhang, W. (2023). Experimental Evidence on the Productivity Effects of Generative Artificial Intelligence. *Science, 381*(6654), 187–192.

O'Neil, C. (2016). *Weapons of math destruction: How big data increases inequality and threatens democracy*. Crown.

OECD. (2023). *OECD Employment Outlook 2023: Artificial Intelligence and the Labour Market*. OECD Publishing., DOI: 10.1787/08785bba-

Oguamanam, C. (2020). Indigenous peoples, data sovereignty, and self-determination: Current realities and imperatives. *The African Journal of Information and Communication, 26*, 1–20.

Open, A. I. (2023). GPT-4 Technical Report. https://cdn.openai.com/papers/gpt-4.pdf

Özkiziltan, D., & Hassel, A. (2021). Artificial Intelligence at Work: An Overview of the literature. SSRN Electronic Journal. DOI: 10.2139/ssrn.3796746

Patil, D. (2024). Impact of artificial intelligence on employment and workforce development: Risks, opportunities, and socioeconomic implications. DOI: 10.2139/ssrn.5010441

Prasanth, A., Densy, J. V., Surendran, P., & Bindhya, T. (2023). Role of artificial intelligence and business decision making. *International Journal of Advanced Computer Science and Applications, 14*(6). Advance online publication. DOI: 10.14569/ijacsa.2023.01406103

Pratama, I. (2025). THE FUTURE OF WORK: EXPLORING THE IMPACT OF AUTOMATION AND AI ON THE LABOR MARKET AND ETHICAL BUSINESS PRACTICES. International Conference "Actual Economy: Local Solutions for Global Challenges", 280-282.

. Roman, V. (2024). Customer support: Using AI Chatbots for efficiency and empathy forbes.

Sharma, R. K. (2025). Ethics in AI: Balancing innovation and responsibility. *International Journal of Science and Research Archive, 14*(1), 544–551. DOI: 10.30574/ijsra.2025.14.1.0122

Sima, V., Gheorghe, I. G., Subić, J., & Nancu, D. (2020). Influences of the Industry 4.0 Revolution on the human capital Development and Consumer Behavior: A Systematic review. *Sustainability, 12*(10), 4035. DOI: 10.3390/su12104035

Soni, V. (2023). Impact of generative AI on small and medium enterprises' revenue growth: The moderating role of human, technological, and market factors. *Reviews of Contemporary Business Analytics, 6*(1), 133–153.

Talmage-Rostron, M. (2024). How will artificial intelligence affect jobs 2024-2030. Nexford University. Retrieved from https://www.nexford.edu/insights/how-will-ai-affect-jobs

Vaswani, A., Shazeer, N., Parmar, N., Uszkoreit, J., Jones, L., Gomez, A. N., Kaiser, Ł., & Polosukhin, I. (2017). Attention is All you Need. https://papers.nips.cc/paper_files/paper/2017/hash/3f5ee243547dee91fbd053c1c4a845aa-Abstract.html

Vermeulen, B., Kesselhut, J., Pyka, A., & Saviotti, P. P. (2018). The impact of automation on employment: Just the usual structural change? *Sustainability, 10*(5), 1661.

Walter, S. (2023). AI impacts on supply chain performance: A manufacturing use case study. *Discover Artificial Intelligence, 3*(1), 18. DOI: 10.1007/s44163-023-00061-9

World Economic Forum. (2020a). Recession and automation changes our future of work, but there are jobs coming, report says.

World Economic Forum. (2020b). The Future of Jobs Report 2020. https://www3.weforum.org/docs/WEF_Future_of_Jobs_2020.pdf

World Economic Forum. (2023). Future of Jobs Report 2023. In Future of Jobs Report. https://www3.weforum.org/docs/WEF_Future_of_Jobs_2023.pdf

Yam, K. C., Tang, P. M., Jackson, J. C., Su, R., & Gray, K. (2023). The rise of robots increases job insecurity and maladaptive workplace behaviors: Multimethod evidence. *The Journal of Applied Psychology*, *108*, 850–870. DOI: 10.1037/apl0001045

Zaman, K. (2022). Transformation of marketing decisions through artificial intelligence and digital marketing. *Journal of Marketing Strategies*, *4*(2), 353–364. DOI: 10.52633/jms.v4i2.210

Zhang, Y., Liu, X., Yan, Q., & Na, M. (2025). Empowering workforces in AI-driven environments: Co-skilling, organizational support, and mitigating job insecurity. *Frontiers in Psychology*, *16*, 1700129. DOI: 10.3389/fpsyg.2025.1700129

Ziakis, C., & Vlachopoulou, M. (2023). Artificial intelligence in digital marketing: Insights from a comprehensive review. *Information (Basel)*, *14*(12), 664. DOI: 10.3390/info14120664

Zirar, A., Ali, S. I., & Islam, N. (2023). Worker and workplace Artificial Intelligence (AI) coexistence: Emerging themes and research agenda. *Technovation*, *124*, 102747. 10.1016/j.technovation.2023.102747

Zuboff, S. (2019). *The Age of Surveillance Capitalism: The Fight for a Human Future at the New Frontier of Power*. Public Affairs.

Chapter 11

Entrepreneurial Performance Factors in AI-Enabled Hybrid Workplaces:

A Meta-Analytic Review of Individual, Business, and Environmental Dimensions

B. Pathinettampadiyan
http://orcid.org/0009-0007-1753-0373
Gandhigram Rural Institute, India

Samuel Thavaraj H.
Gandhigram Rural Institute, India

Seema Vinod
https://orcid.org/0009-0003-4558-7757
Gandhigram Rural Institute, India

Shyam Sunder Agrawal
http://orcid.org/0009-0004-3648-0584
Lovely Professional University, India

N. Robindro Singh
University of Kabridahar, Ethiopia

DOI: 10.4018/979-8-3373-5871-0.ch011

ht © 2026, IGI Global Scientific Publishing. Copying or distributing in print or electronic forms without written permission of IGI Global Scientific Publishing is prohibited. Use of this chapter to generative artificial intelligence (AI) technologies is expressly prohibited. The publisher reserves all rights to license its use for generative AI training and machine learning model development.

ABSTRACT

The meta-analysis combined data from 39 studies (N = 10,530) and obtained a moderate overall effect size (r = 0.48). Individual-level backgrounds, including type of creativity, motivation, and self-efficacy, were the strongest performance correlates of entrepreneurial performance in AI-enabled and hybrid work environments followed by business and environmental-level factors. Results indicate that person-level skill sets, creativity, motivation, and self-efficacy remain the most significant predictors of entrepreneurial performance, as they facilitate innovation, adaptability, and persistence under conditions of digitalization and hybrid work structures. The paper contributes theoretically by integrating resource- and institution-based perspectives, and methodologically supports robustness through the use of unweighted and weighted effect size estimation. Further studies are encouraged to expand cross-cultural comparisons, examine sectoral contexts, and test digital transformation and sustainability as dynamic determinants of entrepreneurial performance.

1. INTRODUCTION

Modern economies see entrepreneurial achievement in AI-integrated, digitally supported and hybrid working environments, in which judgment, the identification of opportunities and the implementation of ventures are underpinned by high technology. Such environments increase the significance of personal psychological traits, organizational tactics and contextual factors that together determine entrepreneurial success. Self-efficacy is an important aspect of entrepreneurial performance. Due to the confidence in performing responsibilities essential to entrepreneurship and mixed findings in prior research, a meta-analytic process was employed to synthesise past literature on the ESE-business performance relationship. The review also encourages consideration of how performance is measured and can influence this relationship, suggesting further research into potential moderating variables (Miao et al., 2017). Meta-analytic procedures were employed to examine the relationship between personality characteristics and purpose and success. Their output specified that all personality traits except agreeableness were associated with entrepreneurial goals and outcomes. Risk-taking was related to launching business goals, but not to performance outcomes. The results validate that personality traits strongly influence entrepreneurial development and success, particularly under conditions of technological uncertainty and innovation-driven markets (H. Zhao et al., 2009). While emotional intelligence is linked to positive work performance, its effect on entrepreneurship is poorly understood. This research examined the effect of various elements of emotional intelligence on entrepreneurial potential, while controlling for personality and demographics. Emotional intelligence has been found to enhance entrepreneurial capacity and confidence, particularly in the utilisation and management of emotions. This confidence is, in essence, the primary driving force that creates the intention to initiate a venture. The results identify emotional intelligence as a robust psychological motivator of entrepreneurial aspiration(Mortan et al., 2014). cross-national data to scrutinise the impact of the values dynamics of specific traits in entrepreneurship. Self-efficacy increases the likelihood of entrepreneurship, but only when certain cultural norms, such as teamwork and a performance-oriented mindset, are present. Similarly, the fear of failure, which reduces entrepreneurship, also depends on cultural orientations towards uncertainty and collective action which also influence entrepreneurial behaviour in globally networked digital ecosystems (Wennberg et al., 2013). This article presents and compares the Emotional Quotient Inventory (EQ-i) to other models, including the MSCEIT. The author notes that the model is highly valid and can be applied to predict various outcomes in life, mental health, physical health, education, societal behaviour, and job performance. It claims that the emotional and social abilities in the model can be trained to enhance individual and organisational achievement. The model is beneficial for application in personal, educational, and workplace environments(hoa-On, 2006). Entrepreneurial orientation has also been a popular paradigm for entrepreneurial research; hence, there is a need to make a definitive conclusion about its relationship with business performance. The research is based on a large sample and presents consistent evidence supporting the connection between EO and performance in various settings. It also determines internal and environmental contingencies that can enhance or weaken such a relationship. The authors provide recommendations for future research to study other determinants (Rauch et al., 2009).

2. EVOLUTION AND THEORETICAL FOUNDATIONS

Existing frameworks of entrepreneurial performance need to be reconsidered to include digital assets, algorithmic assistance and loose, adaptable organisational formats in AI and hybrid workspaces. This paper attempts to demystify the Entrepreneurial Orientation construct and outlines a contingency-based approach to studying its correlation with organisational performance. It starts with identifying the extent and confirming it as a multi-dimensional construct. The authors proceed to discuss various approaches to studying the EO-performance relationship. These approaches vary from models that allow for moderating, mediating, independent, and interaction effects. The paper utilises available literature to propose these alternative analysis avenues (Lumpkin & Dess, 1996). The theory suggests that management can strategically apply resources to secure competitiveness; most resource-based writings have focused mainly on resource qualities instead of their organisational setting. Entrepreneurship literature has always emphasised entrepreneurial orientation, sparingly worrying about how it relates to internal firm processes. This paper posits that EO demonstrates an essential nature of organisational design. The research suggests that knowledge-based resources positively contribute to performance, which is critical in discovering and exploiting opportunities(Wiklund & Shepherd, 2003). This research identifies the successful performance dimension in achieving innovative ventures and determining the success or failure of firms. The second phase presents the multi-dimensionality and cross-interdependence among performance factors. The researchers challenge future studies to delineate performance dimensions, offer theory-based justification, and utilise multi-indication (Murphy et al., 1996). Three major conclusions of this study for practising managers are that it supports the hypothesis that corporate entrepreneurship is positively correlated with financial performance. The second is that a long-term orientation is a prerequisite when measuring the financial consequences of entrepreneurial activities, without which its total effect may be underestimated if exclusively short-run measures are used. Lastly, the research findings show that corporate entrepreneurship is successful only in a success-breeding environment, with some exceptions when extreme competition or hostility surrounds the corporation(Zahra & Covin, 1995).

The probabilistic nature of pattern discovery will be considered as a means to explore the creation of new ventures. The approach describes how these factors interact to explain why individuals are more or less proficient in opportunity recognition. These also offer practical suggestions for enhancing entrepreneurial education and training(Baron, 2006). The process of theory building and empirical testing is very important in the development of entrepreneurship as a field of scientific inquiry. Researchers have substantially enhanced the quality of research over the last three decades by borrowing established theories from other fields and modifying them to fit the context of entrepreneurship. Research can also be further enhanced by taking into consideration contextual variables when applying the theory. Understanding distinctiveness and constraints in characteristic entrepreneurial settings adds relevance and insight to different contexts(Zahra, 2007).

3. INDIVIDUAL-LEVEL FACTORS

Within AI-enabled and mixed-mode work contexts, personal entrepreneurial aspects gain prominence, since entrepreneurs depend more and more on digital instruments, virtual communication, and algorithm-assisted choices. Psychological dimensions including emotional intelligence, self-efficacy, motivation, risk-taking attitude, and innovativeness influence the entrepreneurial responses to the technological intricacy, to virtual teamworking, and to information-based opportunity spotting.

The psychological traits and attributes of entrepreneurs largely shape their entrepreneurial performance. Individual-level determinants include intrinsic traits like emotional intelligence, self-efficacy, leadership ability, risk orientation, and hardness. These attributes shape how entrepreneurs perceive opportunities, deal with uncertainty, build relationships, and respond to challenges. This meta-analysis investigates the outcome of personality traits on initiating and achieving entrepreneurial actions. It extends earlier research by comparing theoretically significant traits and correlating them with entrepreneurial duties. Traits most closely matching entrepreneurial activities demonstrated significantly greater relationships with business establishment and long-term achievement(Rauch & Frese, 2007).

3.1 Emotional Intelligence

This investigation, based on managers' ratings with EI measures, personality inventories, and IQ tests, combines quantitative performance ratings with staff and manager assessments. Results reveal it is an authentic interpreter of leadership effectiveness, explanatory power of personality and intelligence individually(Rosete & Ciarrochi, 2005). The emotional intelligence of some people enables them to behave correctly. The term was initially used to describe specific emotional and cognitive abilities. A split in the discipline has led to a division over time. Some scientists focus on specific cognitive skills, whereas others are associated with a broad set of necessary character traits of optimism, pleasure, and self-esteem(Mayer et al., 2008). Past studies have linked EI with positive workplace outcomes, but have left its impact on entrepreneurial inclinations relatively unknown, as well as some dimensions of its potential, while controlling for personality and demographics. Hierarchical regression of data identifies emotional regulation and utilisation (Mortan et al., 2014). The qualitative study, based on extensive secondary literature, integrates the general theory of the emotional deficiency model to yield inefficient implementation of primary competencies needed for personal emotional regulation, perception of others' emotions, and changing attitudes to conform to organisational objectives(Oriarewo et al., 2019).

3.2 Self-Efficacy

The psychological concept of entrepreneurship encompasses people's perceptions of their ability to perform tasks that contribute to entrepreneurial success. ESE has been extensively researched as a determinant of entrepreneurial outcomes, particularly in terms of business performance. Prior research has yielded mixed findings regarding the strength and form of the relationship. Conceptual arguments suggest that ESE can exert significant influence on firm-level outcomes by affecting entrepreneurial entry and problem management. Contextual elements, such as performance measurement, can also mediate efficacy (Miao et al., 2017). Entrepreneur self-efficacy is commonly regarded as a fundamental determinant of firm performance. The impact might not always be constructive in all circumstances. This study examines the interactions between dispositional optimism and these variables, which together moderate the impact of self-efficacy, with complex interactions in dynamic and stable environments. Self-efficacy improves action with intermediate confidence, which can decrease performance in conjunction with high optimism (Hmieleski & Baron, 2008). The decision-making method of entrepreneurs in war-stricken areas remains under-examined. Results indicate that increased risk perceptions discourage entrepreneurial intentions; however, resilient individuals experience fewer negative consequences. The research emphasises that entrepreneurial capacity, belief, and individual growth through adversity can initiate entrepreneurial aspirations despite unfavourable conditions (Bullough et al., 2014).

3.3 Motivation

This essay presents entrepreneurial motivation and organisational performance from the literature review. Four types of motivation are described as facilitating conditions, sociological, monetary rewards, and entrepreneurship. Organisational performance is demonstrated by efficacy, efficiency, and effectiveness, and results are concluded by pointing out the role of motivation in making or breaking a new venture successful (Chedli, 2016). The value of motivation in entrepreneurial thinking is discussed in more detail. Entrepreneurial intention studies have been helpful, yet they also call for more in-depth knowledge to understand how people decide and respond. Both values and motivations are goal-oriented and significant in entrepreneurial behaviour. The research provides conceptual directions for enhancing our knowledge of entrepreneurial decision-making(Fayolle et al., 2014). This research takes a network approach to investigating how resource acquisition serves as an intermediary between entrepreneurial orientation. Research offers an alternative explanation for the mixed findings in EO-performance research. The influence of business on the acquisition of network resources is also investigated (Jiang et al., 2018).

3.4 Risk Taking

Risk-taking lies at the core of entrepreneurship; it is theoretically ambiguous, especially about personality. Social cognition and theory of categorisation-led research suggest that entrepreneurs do not necessarily see themselves as more risk-taking. This cognitive reinterpretation helps them frame opportunity while others frame threat. Such cognitive differences imply that risk orientation for entrepreneurial behaviour may depend on mindset rather than fixed traits(Palich & Bagby, 1995). While chance obligation is the primary focus of entrepreneurship research, it is also perceptive. It argues that a framework exists in which cognitive bias, pride, trust in the law, forecasting myth, and misleading opportunity evaluation exist. The framework posits risk perception as a mediator, incorporating demographic and risk-taking controls, and it is risk perception that mediates entrepreneurial judgments (Keh et al., 2002).

3.5 Creativity

Entrepreneurs play a crucial role in the formation of new ventures. Thus, their thinking and actions must be researched. Examining some behavioural and mental factors provides significant information about the underlying processes driving entrepreneurial activities. The paper evaluates the evidence for the involvement of these factors in significant entrepreneurial processes. It also highlights the need for a more precise understanding of these processes through targeted research (Baron, 2007). This paper investigates the influence of competitive organisations on creativity under pressure to develop new strategies. It hypothesises that crisis situations where customary coordinating mechanisms do not work are likely to trigger greater creative effort, and periods of calm tend to generate low creative effort. Experimentation makes the economy less prone to shocks and sheds fresh light by synthesising cognitive theory and computational models of market processes. Results contribute to entrepreneurship and agent-based modelling(Caton, 2019). Entrepreneurial culture, with creativity serving as a moderating variable. Creative culture is used herein as a proxy for entrepreneurial culture due to its high predictability. Even after considering creativity as a mediator, the effect remains significant and creativity to operationalise entrepreneurial culture better.(Danish et al., 2019).

4. BUSINESS-LEVEL FACTORS

Within AI-enabled hybrid workplaces, at the firm level competitive advantage is more and more about the firm's skill to realize the integration of digital technologies analytics and platform-oriented strategies in the firm's activities. Capabilities in innovation marketing networking financial and digital transformation are factors that influence the success of entrepreneurial ventures in scaling and competing in technology intensive industries.

The performance of entrepreneurs is primarily focused on the internal operations, strategic trajectories, and capabilities of the business organisation rather than individual traits or external environmental influences. Business-level elements are critical operational and strategic aspects that entrepreneurs can directly manage and leverage to achieve success in their ventures. This section elucidates important business-level factors, including innovation capacity, marketing strategies, networking, financial management, and digital transformation, while also presenting an overview of empirical research findings on their impact on entrepreneurial performance. In assessing firm profitability performance, a regression analysis model incorporates variables from various strategic levels. This suggests that business-level and corporate-level strategic decisions play a crucial role in determining financial performance. The findings emphasise the importance of consistency across multiple strategic levels in achieving improved profitability (Beard & Dess, 1981). The extensive scholarship has covered the impact of contact with finance and culture on managerial practices, but personal competence has yet to be examined in detail. The contribution has changed the proportions of skills toward organisational concert in manufacturing companies (Narkhede et al., 2014).

4.1 Innovation Capability

The study integrates various theoretical views into a holistic context encompassing leadership, processes, and outcomes. Identifies significant factors influencing organisational innovation. The study also proposes measurable parameters for these factors. The findings present valuable insights for informing future scholarly research and management practice(Crossan & Apaydin, 2010). The results provide practical suggestions for managers and enterprise owners. SMEs must emphasise research and development and increase their human, structural, and relational capital. Implementing innovative, cutting-edge knowledge and originating new products, processes, and services is recommended. An innovation culture should be developed(Otache, 2024). The research concludes that dimension practices in this setting have a positive correlation with innovation outcomes. SMEs seldom utilise the full extent of their innovation capabilities, despite their apparent advantages. Research emphasises the need for scholars and practitioners to develop new tools and frameworks for measuring innovation capability. Improving these measurement practices can lead to innovation and business success(Saunila & Ukko, 2013). The study examines the innovation capability and its determinants in firm performance across clusters of Indonesian ICT SMEs. Geographical proximity is not in itself a determinant of innovation capability. Instead, proximity contributes little to performance if accompanied by improved learning capability(Siahaan & Lin Tan, 2020).

4.2 Marketing Strategy

Results show that non-international and international SMEs differ significantly in terms of entrepreneurial orientation, organisational innovation intensity, and firm size. Regional focus and cross-sections can nullify generalizability. It was found that the manufacturing sector would give a proper setting. Replication of results within other industries is sought after. Organisational innovation is particularly found to enhance a firm's capacity to capitalise on international market opportunities and improve foreign market performance (O'Cass & Weerawardena, 2009). This book contains crucial theoretical contributions on the connection between marketing and entrepreneurship. The editors invited outstanding researchers from several countries to respond to this new field. The volume gathered encompasses a detailed treatment of essential issues related to businesses of diverse sizes. It offers a global perspective on current entrepreneurial marketing issues (Sethna et al., 2013). This study has shown that a focus on entrepreneurship and customer satisfaction is important for business development and growth, especially during times of economic uncertainty. Bringing these two concepts together helps develop flexible and efficient marketing strategies for unstable and under-resourced markets. Together, these two concepts address the very core of entrepreneurial marketing. Their application, however, requires a certain degree of resources, a potential limitation during economic crises(Eggers & Kraus, 2011).

4.3 Networking

This paper presents a critical review of network-based entrepreneurship research along three dimensions: network content, network governance, and network structure. Although a lot has been understood in relation to the impact of network structure on venture performance, the process-oriented study of network development theories has received only partial empirical support so far, and it is timely to combine process-oriented and outcome-oriented studies in order to construct better theories of this domain(Hoang & Antoncic, 2003). The paper regrets the excessive dependence on quantitative approaches, whose core attention falls on structural characteristics, and indicates how qualitative approaches can bring into view richer dimensions in network dynamics. Building on their previous study, the authors examine the impact of different methodological paradigms on research. With the Ptolemaic/Copernican metaphor, both methodologies stand out and shed light on different aspects of network analysis(Jack, 2010). It maintains that enterprises founded by individuals with international exposure, either having spent time abroad or in multinational corporations, have higher initial social capital. Learning in networks is crucial for successfully exploiting social capital during internationalisation (Prashantham & Dhanaraj, 2010).

4.4 Financial Management

The purpose was to determine the primary reasons for the failure of newly established industries and the internal and external factors that contributed to their failure. On internal grounds, these include: a lack of management capabilities and poor customer service. On external grounds, these include limited logistics, increased operational costs, financial constraints, and crime(Fatoki, 2014). This paper analyses the factors that control the preparedness of financial statements and projections for new venture founders. Reducing uncertainty seems to be the main motive behind this type of behaviour. Different financial reports vary in appropriateness - cash flow statements have particular importance in the early-stage venture, but in competitive markets(Cassar, 2009). SEM techniques were employed in the analysis, and the results indicate that financial management practices play a crucial role in determining business performance. The research shows that improving these practices could result in enhanced performance for SMEs(Waweru & Ngugi, 2014). The research reveals that innovativeness and risk-taking each positively influence financial performance, but fail to show a substantial moderating role in the EO-performance relationship. Risk-taking is a more reliable predictor of performance compared to innovativeness. The research suggests SME managers emphasise risk-taking and EM strategies more than innovativeness in dynamic environments(Hameed & Ali, 2011).

4.5 Digitalization

Digitalisation of performance measures of knowledge-intensive business services in the service industry. The application of information systems investigates how managerial age, gender, and firm size influence potential financial outcomes. The significant digitalisation strategies that lead to better outcomes, the importance of corporate involvement with social networks, digital competency training, and veteran leadership (Ribeiro-Navarrete et al., 2021). This study emphasises the promise of digitalisation in developing sustainable circular product design, the necessity of customer involvement in doing so, and calls for a shift toward product-service systems to make it possible to integrate CE strategies with digital technology. This study is based on the potential of digitalisation to enhance organisations' sustainable performance(Agrawal et al., 2022). Spending on entrepreneurship, innovation, digitisation, and digital transformation processes, and redefining companies' strategic processes using early pointers to make better long-term decisions. Companies that can effectively address pandemic issues can serve as prototypes for the future of leadership. Early Research and development activities that impact key recovery efforts are essential for long-term, sustainable growth. This growth enables the generation of employment and new business opportunities in the future digital world (de Lucas Ancillo & Gavrila, 2023).

5. ENVIRONMENTAL LEVEL FACTORS

Environmental factors are especially critical in AI-powered entrepreneurial ecosystems, with rules, digital infrastructure, the market and institutional support determining entrepreneurs' entry to technology, data and innovation networks. These contextual forces influence how entrepreneurs leverage AI and digital platforms to sustain performance in hybrid work settings.

Environmental level factors refer to the external conditions and general situation in which entrepreneurship occurs. They are beyond the entrepreneur's immediate control but significantly impact business strategy, choice, and performance. They include governmental policies, market conditions, institutional backing, cultural forces, and technological advances. A conducive environment can improve entrepreneurial success by offering access to resources, reducing obstacles, and fostering innovation, while an unfavourable environment can hinder expansion and sustainability.

Current academic literature emphasises the pivotal role of environmentally friendly business and concrete contexts that drive its stance in company-level environmental performance. The integration of previously underemphasized factors establishes a conceptual framework to inform future research. In addition, the study promotes a paradigm shift towards improving green entrepreneurial orientation to drive environmental outcomes(Ameer & Khan, 2023).

5.1 Government support

The government-provided programs on the entrepreneurial relationship with agro-based SMEs in an emerging country. A two-dimensional GSP model based on finance and non-finance interventions is proposed. Financial and non-financial GSPs are revealed to augment the role of EO extents of innovativeness, independence, and modest aggressiveness. These supports function as moderating variables on SME performance. The research improves the maximization of policy design for entrepreneurial development(Nakku et al., 2020). This study considers the impact of financial support on new firms' competitive advantage and success. Based on resource-based and institutional theoretical perspectives, it contends that policy success, insofar as competitive advantage precedes short-term economic performance. The research evaluates the impact of government loans, guarantees, and equity on various types of competitive advantage. It is revealed that government securities and equity positively impact competitive capabilities but play a secondary role in affecting performance(Pergelova & Angulo-Ruiz, 2014).

5.2 Market Conditions

This study positions entrepreneurial marketing (EM) as a means of enhancing organisational performance. The evolution, as well as the conceptual foundations, of EM at the entrepreneur-marketing boundary are explored. Defining EM, the conditions under which it generates superior performance are discussed. Moderation is proposed from the perspectives of network structure, environment, and firm size. Among these associations are the propositions that buttress future research based on these linkages(Alqahtani & Uslay, 2020). The investigation examines the impact of alliance proactiveness on market-centric firm performance, focusing on specific performance outcomes, including sales growth, market position, and product innovation. Alliance proactiveness refers to the proactive search for and response to collaboration prospects, as well as the consideration of Environmental Uncertainty as an intervening factor. Through partial least squares estimation, the research reveals that alliance proactiveness has a positive influence on performance. The impact is more substantial in small companies as well as in turbulent market situations(Sarkar et al., 2001). It examines how entrepreneurial character and organisational competencies impact export possibilities and performance among high-technology SMEs in an emerging economy. Based on knowledge-based theory and international business literature, it emphasises how R&D, technology diffusion, and global networks of entrepreneurs contribute to this process(Filatotchev et al., 2009).

5.3 Ecosystem Support

Entrepreneurial ecosystems have received increasing academic attention; existing research has primarily focused on their spatial characteristics and components. The research addresses the lack of research on how narrative discourse shapes, develops, and sustains entrepreneurial ecosystems (Roundy, 2016). Entrepreneurship is very heterogeneous between cities, especially in transition and emerging economies, and emphasises their role in enabling productive entrepreneurship and constraining unproductive activity. A new conceptual framework describes the role of normative, cognitive, and regulative institutional pillars. The results emphasise that robust institutional arrangements are the foundation of high-growth entrepreneurship, and civil society and cultural norms are critical in constraining unproductive activity.

These results have significant policy implications for urban entrepreneurship and ecosystem building(Audretsch et al., 2021). With increasing popularity, measurement and interpretation of performance are on everyone's mind more and more. Entrepreneurs, investors, policymakers, and ecosystem leaders are generally interested in identifying which metrics best capture the vitality of the startup community and its economic growth. The metrics should be chosen based on the particular goals of the ecosystem. Knowing what to measure is crucial for monitoring progress and effect (Bell-Masterson & Stangler, 2015).

6. METHODOLOGY

This meta-analysis was conducted adhering to Preferred Reporting Items for Systematic Reviews and Meta-Analyses (PRISMA) 2020 guidelines (Page et al., 2021) to ensure transparency, rigor, and reproducibility of the steps of identification of studies, screening, determination of eligibility, and final inclusion. Adhering to these specifications made it possible to systematically narrow down a vast corpus of writings to a selective few of studies that are harmonious with the objectives of this study. Given the growing relevance of AI-enabled technologies, digitalization, and hybrid work arrangements, studies reflecting technology-supported entrepreneurial contexts were also considered within the broader performance framework.

Extensive literature searching was conducted on three major academic databases, including Taylor & Francis, Springer, and Google Scholar, which are rich sources of management and entrepreneurship scholarship. A search strategy was formulated using a sequence of keywords central to entrepreneurial performance, entrepreneurial abilities, firm capacity, innovation, digitalisation, technology-enabled capabilities, environmental factors, and performance outcomes. Boolean links were used to widen or constrict results, and filters constrained results to peer-reviewed English-language based on quantitative research designs.

Figure 1. PRISMA 2020 Flow Diagram for Study Selection Process

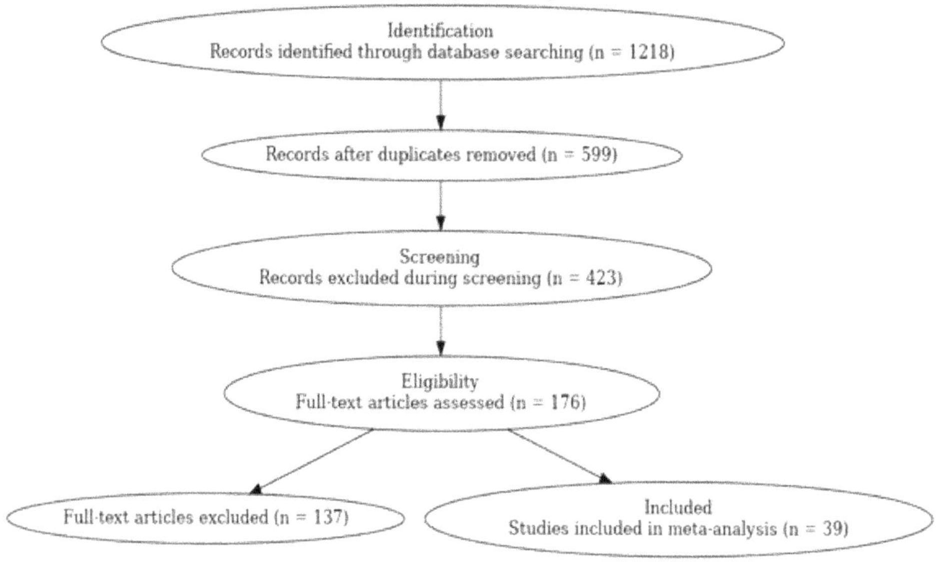

Source: Author's owns compilation based on PRISMA (2020) guidelines.

The initial search yielded 1,218 records, comprising 538 Taylor & Francis records, 491 Springer records, and 189 Google Scholar records. After removing 619 duplicate records, 599 original studies remained and were put forward for title and abstract screening. 423 were excluded because they were conceptual, qualitative, review-based, or not related to entrepreneurial performance. 176 articles were received at the full-text level and screened using pre-specified inclusion criteria. Eligible were those published between 2016 and 2025 years, empirically examining at least one entrepreneurial performance factor (individual factor, business factor, or environmental factor), and with sufficient statistical information such as sample size and effect size (such as correlation coefficients). 137 were excluded after full-text review because of the absence of proper statistics, low performance emphasis, or overlapping circumstances. A total of 39 studies were included in the final dataset.

After applying the inclusion and exclusion criteria, 39 empirical works were subjected to the final analysis. They are diverse in terms of countries represented, factor levels, and measurement methods. Table 1 presents a systematic account of the included works, aggregating details of authors, study context, key entrepreneurial performance parameters, sample sizes, effect sizes (r), and measurement tools.

Table 1. Meta-Analysis of Entrepreneurial Performance Factors (2016–2025)

Author (Year)	Country	Factor Level	Key Factor	Respondents	N	r	Measurement Tool
(Asad et al., 2023)	Pakistan	Business Level	Innovation Capability	SME owners/managers	384	0.40	7-point Likert; validated by α, CR, AVE
(Qi et al., 2023)	China	Environmental Level	Ecosystem Support	University Students	302	0.55	Structured questionnaire; Cronbach's α, CR, HTMT; Pearson correlation
(Indrawati et al., 2025)	Indonesia	Individual Level	Risk Taking	MSMEs	229	0.71	Structured questionnaire; 5-point Likert; SEM-PLS
(Alkahtani et al., 2020)	Pakistan	Business Level	Networking	SMEs (manufacturing)	267	0.24	Structured questionnaire; 5-point Likert; Pearson correlation
(Fu et al., 2024)	Indonesia	Environmental Level	Market Conditions	SME owners/managers	508	0.15	7-point Likert; SEM; Cronbach's α, AVE; GoF = 0.586
(Sadiku-Dushi et al., 2019)	Kosovo	Individual Level	Risk Taking	SME owners/managers	217	0.43	Structured questionnaire; 5-point Likert scale
(Kisubi et al., 2022)	Uganda	Business Level	Innovation Capability	SME owners/managers	314	0.46	5-point Likert scale; Structured questionnaire; Correlation & SEM (SPSS)
(Amraei et al., 2021)	Iran	Individual Level	Creativity	Educational hospital managers	110	0.64	Creativity & Entrepreneurial Skills Questionnaire; 5-point Likert; Pearson's r
(Jang & Lee, 2025)	Republic of Korea	Business Level	Digitalization	SME owners/managers	122	0.30	Online questionnaire; 7-point Likert scale; Smart PLS 4.0
(Shaheen & AL-Haddad, 2018)	Jordan	Individual Level	Self-Efficacy	Entrepreneurs, employees	155	0.73	Questionnaire survey
(Orobia et al., 2020)	Uganda	Business Level	Financial Management	SMEs Manager	314	0.41	Questionnaire; SEM-PLS
(Usoro & Brownson, 2023)	Nigeria	Individual Level	Creativity	SME owners	361	0.71	Likert scale survey; Pearson Product Moment Correlation

continued on following page

Table 1. Continued

Author (Year)	Country	Factor Level	Key Factor	Respondents	N	r	Measurement Tool
(Urban, 2020)	South Africa	Individual Level	Self-Efficacy	Individuals	156	0.65	Questionnaire; 5-point Likert scale
(Pulka et al., 2021)	Nigeria	Environmental Level	Government Support	SME owners/managers	470	0.57	Structured questionnaire; 5-point Likert; SPSS 24; PLS-SEM 3.0
(W. Zhao et al., 2021)	China	Individual Level	Risk Taking	Entrepreneurs/Founders	150	0.12	Questionnaire; 5-point Likert scale
(Somathilake & Pathirawasam, 2020)	Sri Lanka	Business Level	Financial Management	SMEs (manufacturing, service, trade)	245	0.39	Structured questionnaire; Pearson correlation; Multiple regression (SPSS)
(Olaleye et al., 2024)	Nigeria	Environmental Level	Market Conditions	SME managers	402	0.36	Structured questionnaire; 5-point Likert; validated by α, CR, AVE; PLS-SEM
(Obeidat et al., 2016)	Jordan	Business Level	Marketing Strategy	Consultancy firm employees	216	0.88	Likert scale (1–5); Pearson r
(Saleem et al., 2023)	India	Individual Level	Emotional Intelligence	Women entrepreneurs	317	0.41	Survey; 5-point Likert; PLS-SEM
(Li et al., 2020)	Pakistan	Environmental Level	Government Support	Students & SMEs	567	0.38	Survey; 5-point Likert; SEM
(Ebrahimi & Mirbargkar, 2017)	Iran	Business Level	Innovation Capability	SME senior managers	112	0.64	Questionnaire; 5-point Likert; SEM–AMOS
(Anwar et al., 2020)	Pakistan	Environmental Level	Government Support	New ventures	183	0.38	Self-administered questionnaire; SEM (SmartPLS)
(Amofah et al., 2020)	Ghana	Individual Level	Self-Efficacy	MBA students	159	0.42	5-point Likert scale
(Tang et al., 2018)	China	Business Level	Marketing Strategy	Firm managers	188	0.51	Likert scale (1–5); Pearson r
(Karia, 2021)	Malaysia	Individual Level	Emotional Intelligence	SME entrepreneurs	397	0.50	Self-administered questionnaire; Correlation analysis

continued on following page

Table 1. Continued

Author (Year)	Country	Factor Level	Key Factor	Respondents	N	r	Measurement Tool
(Adeyemi & Sajuyigbe, 2017)	Nigeria	Business Level	Financial Management	Women entrepreneurs	114	0.20	Questionnaire (test–retest reliability, expert validity); Pearson correlation; OLS regression
(Mei et al., 2019)	China	Environmental Level	Ecosystem Support	SMEs (electronics, textiles, machinery)	420	0.36	5-point Likert scale; correlations reported
(Parida et al., 2017)	Sweden	Business Level	Networking	Small firms	462	0.49	Likert-scale survey; validated scales
(Machani et al., 2021)	India	Individual Level	Motivation	Micro & small entrepreneurs	134	0.86	Structured questionnaire; 5-point Likert scale
(Abou-Foul et al., 2021)	U.S. & Europe	Business Level	Digitalization	Managers (manufacturing firms)	185	0.66	Survey (validated scales); Descriptive stats & intercorrelations
(Buli, 2017)	Ethiopia	Environmental Level	Market Condition	SME managers	171	0.20	7-point Likert scale; SPSS; Pearson correlation
(Teng et al., 2022)	China	Business Level	Digitalization	SME staff	335	0.40	7-point Likert scale; SPSS & SPSSAU
(Tiwari et al., 2017)	India	Individual Level	Emotional Intelligence	Undergraduate students	230	0.46	7-point Likert scale; Correlation & SEM
(Anwar & Ali Shah, 2020)	Pakistan	Business Level	Networking	Young SME owners/ managers	311	0.52	5-point Likert scale; SEM (AMOS)
(Fazal et al., 2022)	Malaysia	Individual Level	Motivation	Micro-entrepreneurs	403	0.40	Mixed 5- & 7-point Likert; SEM-PLS
(Mai & Nguyen, 2023)	Vietnam	Environmental Level	Ecosystem Support	SME/startup founders/ CEOs	200	0.55	5-point Likert scale; SmartPLS 3.0; PLS-SEM; Pearson's r; Cronbach's α
(Ullah et al., 2022)	Pakistan	Individual Level	Creativity	Managers, engineers, staff	158	0.82	5-point Likert scale; Pearson correlation

continued on following page

Table 1. Continued

Author (Year)	Country	Factor Level	Key Factor	Respondents	N	r	Measurement Tool
(Sari et al., 2023)	Indonesia	Business Level	Marketing Strategy	MSME owners/ managers	290	0.15	Likert scale (1–5); SmartPLS 3.0
(Nakiganda et al., 2025)	Kenya	Individual Level	Motivation	University students	272	0.64	PCA + SEM (PLS); 5-point Likert scale

Source: Author's owns compilation based on empirical studies (2016–2025)

Note: The abbreviation *SME* denotes Small and Medium Enterprises, while *MSME* refers to Micro, Small, and Medium Enterprises. The term *MBA* stands for Master of Business Administration. The symbol *N* represents the sample size, and *r* indicates the correlation coefficient. The Greek letter *α* refers to Cronbach's alpha, a measure of internal consistency(Cronbach, 1951). *CR* corresponds to Composite Reliability (Bagozzi & Yi, 1988). *AVE* indicates the Average Variance Extracted (Fornell & Larcker, 1981). *HTMT* represents the Heterotrait–Monotrait ratio of correlations (Henseler et al., 2015). The term *PLS-SEM* designates Partial Least Squares Structural Equation Modeling(Hair Jr et al., 2017).*AMOS* is an acronym for Analysis of Moment Structures, while *SPSS* signifies the Statistical Package for the Social Sciences. *PCA* stands for Principal Component Analysis. Finally, *GoF* represents the Goodness of Fit index.

Table 1 brings together the 39 empirical studies reviewed by this meta-analysis within the period 2016–2025. They span geographical contexts from South Asia, Far East Asia, and Southeast Asia to Africa, the Middle East, and Europe, and guarantee complete representation of both new and transitioning economies. At the individual level, influential features such as self-efficacy, emotional intelligence, and motivation often appear with fairly strong effect sizes (r = 0.41–0.86). Business-level variables such as innovation capability, networking, digitalization and technology-enabled practices, financial management, and marketing strategy appear to have moderate to strong correlations, although financial management expresses comparatively weak correlations (r = 0.20–0.41). Environmental-level variables, such as government and ecosystem aid, and market conditions, produce mixed findings: government and ecosystem aid exhibit a moderate positive influence (r = 0.36–0.57), while market conditions exhibit a generally weak influence (r = 0.15–0.36). Overall, the table illustrates that entrepreneurial performance is driven by a complex array of individual competences and business and environmental strategies, where individual-level features express the most excellent predictability.

Table 2. Descriptive Statistics of Included Studies by Region (2016–2025)

Region	Countries Covered	No. of Studies	% of Total (N = 39)
South Asia	India, Pakistan, Sri Lanka	10	25.6%
East Asia	China, the Republic of Korea, and Vietnam	7	17.9%
Southeast Asia	Malaysia, Indonesia	5	12.8%
Africa	Nigeria, Uganda, South Africa, Ghana, Ethiopia, Kenya	10	25.6%
Middle East	Iran, Jordan	4	10.3%
Europe/Western	Kosovo, Sweden, U.S. and Europe (combined)	3	7.7%
Total		39	100%

Source: Author's owns compilation

Table 2 presents the regional distribution of the 39 empirical studies included in this meta-analysis, categorised into six geographical regions. South Asia and Africa contributed the largest shares of studies (25.6% each), indicating a rising interest in research and policy regarding entrepreneurship in emerging economies, where SMEs are critical drivers of growth and employment. 17.9% of the studies came from East Asia, reflecting the accelerating digital change and innovation-driven entrepreneurship in China, Korea, and Vietnam. 12.8% of the studies originated from Southeast Asia, with Malaysia and Indonesia providing evidence of entrepreneurial competence in developing economies with growing SME industries. The sample was represented by 10.3% from the Middle East, where most of the work focused on government assistance, creativity, and marketing practices based on transitional cases, such as Iran and Jordan. Finally, Europe/Western countries contributed only 7.7% of the studies, resulting in a reduced focus on developed economy regions compared to limited- or low-income recipient regions. Overall, the regional distribution suggests that most of the evidence has been concentrated within emerging and transitional markets, providing the analysis with rich lessons on entrepreneurship under varying institutional and cultural conditions.

Table 3. Subfactor-Level Frequency, Mean Correlations, and Range (2016–2025)

Dimension	Subfactor	No. of Studies	Unweighted Mean r	Weighted Mean r	Range of r
Individual	Risk Taking	3	0.42	0.49	0.12–0.71
	Creativity	3	0.72	0.73	0.64–0.82
	Self-Efficacy	3	0.60	0.61	0.42–0.73
	Emotional Intelligence	3	0.46	0.46	0.41–0.50
	Motivation	3	0.63	0.65	0.40–0.86
Business	Innovation Capability	3	0.50	0.46	0.40–0.64
	Networking	3	0.42	0.44	0.24–0.52
	Digitalization	3	0.45	0.47	0.30–0.66
	Financial Management	3	0.33	0.37	0.20–0.41
	Marketing Strategy	3	0.51	0.57	0.15–0.88
Environmental	Ecosystem Support	3	0.49	0.47	0.36–0.55
	Market Conditions	3	0.24	0.24	0.15–0.36
	Government Support	3	0.44	0.46	0.38–0.57

Source: Author's owns compilation based on the meta-analytic dataset (2016–2025)

Table 3 consolidates the subfactors into the three principal axes, Individual, Business, and Environmental and the relevant mean correlations between them. On the Individual axis, the strongest predictor of entrepreneurial success was found to be creativity (r = 0.72, weighted r = 0.73), followed by motivation (r = 0.63, weighted r = 0.65) and self-efficacy (r = 0.60, weighted r = 0.61), and therefore cognitive and motivational tendencies featured prominently in the facilitation of success. Risk-taking (r = 0.42–0.49) and emotional intelligence (r = 0.46) also showed moderate but consistent relationships, indicating a supporting yet less central role in facilitating success. At the business-level factors, the top contributor was marketing strategy (r = 0.51, weighted r = 0.57), emphasising the significance of market-driven strategies. Innovation capability (r = 0.50) and digitalisation (r = 0.45–0.47) offered modest contributions. Networking also made a moderate contribution (r = 0.42–0.44), while financial management presented the weakest connection (r = 0.33–0.37); hence, financial conduct in isolation may not be sufficient to improve outcomes. Environmental factors presented moderate contributions with ecosystem support (r = 0.49, weighted r = 0.47) and government support (r = 0.44–0.46), providing a positive contribution to success, but market conditions presented the lowest correlation (r = 0.24), showing limited predictive capacity. Both unweighted and weighted averages are presented, with the weighted estimates taking into account the sample size and thereby providing more robust and reliable conclusions. Both unweighted and weighted means are provided. The unweighted mean is the simple mean of effect sizes per study, while the weighted mean is weighted by sample size and is more influential with larger studies.

7. RESULTS

The results of this meta-analysis, based on 39 empirical studies published from 2016 to 2025 (total N = 10,530), reveal entrepreneurial performance is characterized by the cumulative influence of individual, business, and environmental antecedents. At the individual level, creativity (r = .72; weighted r = .73), motivation (r = .63; weighted r = .65), and self-efficacy (r = .60; weighted r = .61) were the leading predictors and reflected cognitive and motivational abilities to entrepreneurially perform. Risk-taking and emotional intelligence registered moderate and steady contributions (r = .42–.46). Business-level antecedents revealed a more scattered pattern: marketing strategy (r = .51; weighted r = .57) registered the highest association, followed by innovation ability and digitalization (r = .45–.50). Networking registered moderate contributions and financial management the lowest association (r = .33–.37). Environmental-level factors made positive contributions, with government support (r = .49; weighted r = .47) and ecosystem support (r = .44–.46) making a moderate contribution to outcomes, and market conditions showing only a negligible contribution (r = .24). At a geographical level, the evidence base was largely represented by South Asia and Africa (25.6% each), followed by Eastern Asia (17.9%), Southeast Asia (12.8%), the Middle East (10.3%), and Europe/Western contexts (7.7%), which suggests a strong focus on emerging and transitional economies. Providing unweighted and weighted means enhances the robustness of these results by bringing study diversity and sample size considerations within the realm of incorporation. The findings suggest that individual-level competencies have by far the greatest impact on entrepreneurial performance, business strategies are significant enablers at a strategic level, and environmental conditions are significant but supplementary supporters.

8. DISCUSSION

This meta-analysis discloses that entrepreneurial performance is shaped through a multidimensional interplay of person-level, business-level, and environmental variables, with the strongest level being the person-level competencies. The strongest predictors found were creativity, motivation, and self-efficacy that support prior outcomes, demonstrating that they enhance opportunity recognition, persistence, and adaptability (Amraei et al., 2021; Urban, 2020; Usoro & Brownson, 2023). Risk-taking and emotional intelligence showed moderate but persistent relationships, supporting evidence that their contribution is frequently condition-dependent (Indrawati et al., 2025; Saleem et al., 2023). Marketing strategy at the business level became the strongest driver of performance, and market-oriented practices are fundamental in sustaining competitiveness. Innovation capability, digitisation, and networking showed positive relationships that support studies highlighting the contribution of technological adaptation and relational capital in the improvement of firm outcomes (Parida et al., 2017). Financial management demonstrated weaker relationships, indicating that financial practices without strategic and innovative capabilities are insufficient. Environmental variables showed moderate support, with government and ecosystem support both elevating entrepreneurial outcomes. Entrepreneurs cannot rely on external environments for achievement(Kisubi et al., 2022; Saleem et al., 2023), while the sparse representation of Western settings suggests that the majority of existing evidence is informed by resource-scarce and transient economies. The centrality of internal strengths, such as creativity and self-efficacy, and institutional theory, clarifies the facilitative yet supplementary role of government and ecosystem-level assistance in shaping entrepreneurial performance.

9. MANAGERIAL, POLICY, AND DIGITAL TRANSFORMATION IMPLICATIONS FOR ENTREPRENEURIAL PERFORMANCE

The meta-analysis bears important consequences for entrepreneurs, managers and policymakers in the field of AI-augmented hybrid workplaces. Results suggest that elements at the personal level such as self-efficacy, creativity, motivation and emotional intelligence are still the most important drivers of entrepreneurial success. Such competencies facilitate entrepreneurs' adaptation to technological change, handling of uncertainties and sustaining of innovative activities in digitally mediated and hybrid working contexts. Therefore, managers and incubators are advised to acquire digital literacy and emotional intelligence competence through targeted training and coaching programs. Organizational-level results highlight the importance of innovation capability, marketing strategy, networking, and digitalization in translating individual competencies into sustainable performance results. Businesspeople can purposefully employ AI resources and digital channels to achieve a greater market penetration, efficiency of operation and quality of decision making in hybrid settings. Firstly, strong entrepreneurial results in a technology-based setting require institutional settings that include digital facility, funding for innovation and entrepreneurship promotion schemes.

10. LONG-TERM AND CROSS-CULTURAL CONSIDERATIONS IN AI-ENABLED HYBRID WORKPLACES

These findings have some important implications for entrepreneurs, managers, and policymakers operating within AI-enabled hybrid workplaces. The results indicate that individual-level capabilities, self-efficacy, creativity, motivation, and emotional intelligence remain the strongest drivers of entrepreneurial performance. Indeed, these competencies enable entrepreneurs to adapt to technological change, manage uncertainty, and maintain innovative activity in digitally mediated and hybrid work arrangements. In this way, managers and incubators should develop such skills as digital literacy and emotional competence through focused training and mentoring programs.

Results at the business level demonstrate that innovation capacity marketing strategy networking and digitalization serve as mechanisms for converting individual capabilities into sustainable performance results. Since AI tools and digital platforms are now widely used entrepreneurs are in a position to leverage these strategically to profit on market penetration and operational efficiencies and to take decisions in hybrid situations. Facilitating institutional arrangements comprise access to digital infrastructure innovation grants and entrepreneurship development programs that are essential to improve entrepreneurial results in a technology-oriented setting.

11. LIMITATIONS AND FUTURE RESEARCH DIRECTIONS

There are several limitations to this meta-analysis. First, the reliance on published quantitative studies may imply publication bias and limit the representativeness of informal or early-stage entrepreneurial contexts. Second, variations in measurement approaches across studies threaten the comparability of effect sizes. Third, the dominance of studies from emerging and transitional economies suggests that evidence from advanced digital economies remains underrepresented. Future studies should focus on entrepreneurial performance across AI-intensive and platform-based business models with longitudinal designs. Indeed, more importance needs to be given to issues of cross-cultural validation, sector-specific analyses, and the role of advanced AI tools in shaping entrepreneurial decision-making. Other potential avenues for extending the research in this area concern sustainability, ethical considerations, and resilience as shifting determinants of entrepreneurial performance in hybrid and digitally enabled work environments.

12. CONCLUSION

This meta-analysis shows that entrepreneurial performance is the result of interacting influences at the individual, business, and environmental levels, with the strongest predictor being the interaction between creativity, motivation, and self-efficacy. Business-level strengths in marketing strategy, innovation, and digitalisation serve as strong enablers, supplemented by the supportive but weaker role of financial management and networking. Environmental facilitation, particularly through government and ecosystem support, enhances outcomes where market forces have limited impact. The regional focus in South Asia and Africa reveals context-specific issues for emerging economies and offers insight different from Western perspectives Consequently this enhances the resource-based view by emphasizing the primacy of internal resources and capabilities and supports the institutional theory of the mediating role of external factors From a practical standpoint, the results stress the need for the development of entrepreneurial skills digital skills and adaptive strategies for AI- and hybrid work environments Practitioners should also consider the various policies and programs that can enhance entrepreneurial skills and stimulate ecosystems and digital adoption Methodologically this report presents unweighted and weighted means adding to the robustness of the results Future research should move towards longitudinal and cross-cultural comparisons sectorial studies and a more nuanced analysis of digital transformation and sustainability as emerging determinants of entrepreneurial success in AI-enabled settings.

REFERENCES

Abou-Foul, M., Ruiz-Alba, J. L., & Soares, A. (2021). The impact of digitalization and servitization on the financial performance of a firm: An empirical analysis. *Production Planning and Control, 32*(12), 975–989.

Adeyemi, A. Z., & Sajuyigbe, A. S. (2017). Financial Management Practices and Women Entrepreneurs Performance: An Empirical Investigation. *International Journal of Economics and Business Management, 3*(1).

Agrawal, R., Wankhede, V. A., Kumar, A., Upadhyay, A., & Garza-Reyes, J. A. (2022). Nexus of circular economy and sustainable business performance in the cra of digitalization. *International Journal of Productivity and Performance Management, 71*(3), 748–774.

Alkahtani, A., Nordin, N., & Khan, R. U. (2020). Does government support enhance the relation between networking structure and sustainable competitive performance among SMEs? *Journal of Innovation and Entrepreneurship, 9*(1), 14.

Alqahtani, N., & Uslay, C. (2020). Entrepreneurial marketing and firm performance: Synthesis and conceptual development. *Journal of Business Research, 113*, 62–71.

Ameer, F., & Khan, N. R. (2023). Green entrepreneurial orientation and corporate environmental performance: A systematic literature review. *European Management Journal, 41*(5), 755–778.

Amofah, K., Saladrigues, R., & Akwaa-Sekyi, E. K. (2020). Entrepreneurial intentions among MBA students. *Cogent Business & Management, 7*(1), 1832401.

Amraei, M., Rezheh, M., Hamzekhani, M. S., & Faraji-Khiavi, F. (2021). Correlation between Creativity and Entrepreneurial Skills in Managers of Educational Hospitals. *Depiction of Health, 12*(3), 240–250.

Anwar, M., & Ali Shah, S. Z. (2020). Managerial networking and business model innovation: Empirical study of new ventures in an emerging economy. *Journal of Small Business and Entrepreneurship, 32*(3), 265–286.

Anwar, M., Tajeddini, K., & Ullah, R. (2020). Entrepreneurial finance and new venture success-the moderating role of government support. *Business Strategy & Development, 3*(4), 408–421.

Asad, M., Majali, T., Aledeinat, M., Abdelkarim Almajali, D., & Akhorshaideh, A. H. O. (2023). Green entrepreneurial orientation for enhancing SMEs financial and environmental performance: Synergetic moderation of green technology dynamism and knowledge transfer and integration. *Cogent Business & Management, 10*(3), 2278842.

Audretsch, D. B., Belitski, M., & Cherkas, N. (2021). Entrepreneurial ecosystems in cities: The role of institutions. *PLoS One, 16*(3), e0247609.

Bagozzi, R. P., & Yi, Y. (1988). On the evaluation of structural equation models. *Journal of the Academy of Marketing Science, 16*(1), 74–94.

Baron, R. (2006). The Bar-On model of emotional-social intelligence (ESI) 1. *Psicothema*, •••, 13–25.

Baron, R. A. (2006). Opportunity recognition as pattern recognition: How entrepreneurs "connect the dots" to identify new business opportunities. *The Academy of Management Perspectives, 20*(1), 104–119.

Baron, R. A. (2007). Behavioral and cognitive factors in entrepreneurship: Entrepreneurs as the active element in new venture creation. *Strategic Entrepreneurship Journal, 1*(1-2), 167–182.

Beard, D. W., & Dess, G. G. (1981). Corporate-level strategy, business-level strategy, and firm performance. *Academy of Management Journal, 24*(4), 663–688.

Bell-Masterson, J., & Stangler, D. (2015). Measuring an entrepreneurial ecosystem. *Available at SSRN* 2580336.

Buli, B. M. (2017). Entrepreneurial orientation, market orientation and performance of SMEs in the manufacturing industry: Evidence from Ethiopian enterprises. *Management Research Review, 40*(3), 292–309.

Bullough, A., Renko, M., & Myatt, T. (2014). Danger zone entrepreneurs: The importance of resilience and self–efficacy for entrepreneurial intentions. *Entrepreneurship Theory and Practice, 38*(3), 473–499.

Cassar, G. (2009). Financial statement and projection preparation in start-up ventures. *The Accounting Review, 84*(1), 27–51.

Caton, J. L. (2019). Creativity in a theory of entrepreneurship. *Journal of Entrepreneurship and Public Policy, 8*(4), 442–469.

Chedli, M. K. E. (2016). Entrepreneurial motivation and performance of enterprises. *Economics, Management, and Financial Markets, 11*(1), 175–189.

Cronbach, L. J. (1951). Coefficient alpha and the internal structure of tests. *Psychometrika, 16*(3), 297–334.

Crossan, M. M., & Apaydin, M. (2010). A multi-dimensional framework of organizational innovation: A systematic review of the literature. *Journal of Management Studies, 47*(6), 1154–1191.

Danish, R. Q., Asghar, J., Ahmad, Z., & Ali, H. F. (2019). Factors affecting "entrepreneurial culture": The mediating role of creativity. *Journal of Innovation and Entrepreneurship, 8*(1), 1–12.

de Lucas Ancillo, A., & Gavrila, S. G. (2023). The impact of research and development on entrepreneurship, innovation, digitization and digital transformation. *Journal of Business Research, 157*, 113566.

Ebrahimi, P., & Mirbargkar, S. M. (2017). Green entrepreneurship and green innovation for SME development in market turbulence. *Eurasian Business Review, 7*(2), 203–228.

Eggers, F., & Kraus, S. (2011). Growing young SMEs in hard economic times: The impact of entrepreneurial and customer orientations—A qualitative study from Silicon Valley. *Journal of Small Business and Entrepreneurship, 24*(1), 99–111.

Fatoki, O. (2014). The causes of the failure of new small and medium enterprises in South Africa. *Mediterranean Journal of Social Sciences, 5*(20), 922–927.

Fayolle, A., Liñán, F., & Moriano, J. A. (2014). Beyond entrepreneurial intentions: Values and motivations in entrepreneurship. *The International Entrepreneurship and Management Journal, 10*(4), 679–689.

Fazal, S. A., Al Mamun, A., Alshebami, A. S., Muniady, R., Ali, M. H., Al Shami, S. S. A., Al Marri, S. H., Seraj, A. H. A., Thomran, M., & Algobaei, F. (2022). Entrepreneurial motivation, competency and micro-enterprise sustainability performance: Evidence from an emerging economy. *Sustainability, 14*(19), 12615.

Filatotchev, I., Liu, X., Buck, T., & Wright, M. (2009). The export orientation and export performance of high-technology SMEs in emerging markets: The effects of knowledge transfer by returnee entrepreneurs. *Journal of International Business Studies, 40*(6), 1005–1021.

Fornell, C., & Larcker, D. F. (1981). Evaluating structural equation models with unobservable variables and measurement error. *JMR, Journal of Marketing Research, 18*(1), 39–50.

Fu, C.-J., Silalahi, A. D. K., Yang, L.-W., & Eunike, I. J. (2024). Advancing SME performance: A novel application of the technological-organizational-environment framework in social media marketing adoption. *Cogent Business & Management*, *11*(1), 2360509.

Hair, J. F.Jr, Matthews, L. M., Matthews, R. L., & Sarstedt, M. (2017). PLS-SEM or CB-SEM: Updated guidelines on which method to use. *International Journal of Multivariate Data Analysis*, *1*(2), 107–123.

Hameed, I., & Ali, B. (2011). Impact of entrepreneurial orientation, entrepreneurial management and environmental dynamism on firm's financial performance. *Journal of Economics and Behavioral Studies*, *3*(2), 101–114.

Henseler, J., Ringle, C. M., & Sarstedt, M. (2015). A new criterion for assessing discriminant validity in variance-based structural equation modeling. *Journal of the Academy of Marketing Science*, *43*(1), 115–135.

Hmieleski, K. M., & Baron, R. A. (2008). When does entrepreneurial self-efficacy enhance versus reduce firm performance? *Strategic Entrepreneurship Journal*, *2*(1), 57–72.

Hoang, H., & Antoncic, B. (2003). Network-based research in entrepreneurship: A critical review. *Journal of Business Venturing*, *18*(2), 165–187.

Indrawati, N. K., Muljaningsih, S., Juwita, H. A. J., Jazuli, A. M., Nurmasari, N. D., & Fahlevi, M. (2025). The mediator role of risk tolerance and risk perception in the relationship between financial literacy and financing decision. *Cogent Business & Management*, *12*(1), 2468877.

Jack, S. L. (2010). Approaches to studying networks: Implications and outcomes. *Journal of Business Venturing*, *25*(1), 120–137.

Jang, S. H., & Lee, C. W. (2025). Digital Entrepreneurial Orientation, Technology Absorptive Capacity, and Digital Innovation on Business Performance. *Systems*, *13*(4), 300.

Jiang, X., Liu, H., Fey, C., & Jiang, F. (2018). Entrepreneurial orientation, network resource acquisition, and firm performance: A network approach. *Journal of Business Research*, *87*, 46–57.

Karia, N. (2021). A comparative benchmark model for SMEs: Viable entrepreneur emotional intelligence. *Benchmarking*, *28*(3), 813–829.

Keh, H. T., Der Foo, M., & Lim, B. C. (2002). Opportunity evaluation under risky conditions: The cognitive processes of entrepreneurs. *Entrepreneurship Theory and Practice*, *27*(2), 125–148.

Kisubi, M. K., Aruo, F., Wakibi, A., Mukyala, V., & Ssenyange, K. (2022). Entrepreneurial competencies and performance of Ugandan SMEs: The mediating role of firm capabilities. *Cogent Business & Management*, *9*(1), 2115622.

Li, C., Ahmed, N., Qalati, S. A., Khan, A., & Naz, S. (2020). Role of business incubators as a tool for entrepreneurship development: The mediating and moderating role of business start-up and government regulations. *Sustainability*, *12*(5), 1822.

Lumpkin, G. T., & Dess, G. G. (1996). Clarifying the entrepreneurial orientation construct and linking it to performance. *Academy of Management Review*, *21*(1), 135–172.

Machani, M. P., Nagapriya, C., & Kumar, Y. L. (2021). Motives driving the entrepreneurial thought: An empirical study on micro entrepreneurs. *Design Engineering (London)*, *1*, 15271–15281.

Mai, K. N., & Nguyen, V. T. (2023). Entrepreneurial ecosystem affects organisational learning, creativity and success. *Cogent Business & Management*, *10*(3), 2260125.

Mayer, J. D., Salovey, P., & Caruso, D. R. (2008). Emotional intelligence: New ability or eclectic traits? *The American Psychologist*, *63*(6), 503.

Mei, L., Zhang, T., & Chen, J. (2019). Exploring the effects of inter-firm linkages on SMEs' open innovation from an ecosystem perspective: An empirical study of Chinese manufacturing SMEs. *Technological Forecasting and Social Change*, *144*, 118–128.

Miao, C., Qian, S., & Ma, D. (2017). The relationship between entrepreneurial self-efficacy and firm performance: A meta-analysis of main and moderator effects. *Journal of Small Business Management*, *55*(1), 87–107.

Mortan, R. A., Ripoll, P., Carvalho, C., & Bernal, M. C. (2014). Effects of emotional intelligence on entrepreneurial intention and self-efficacy. *Revista de Psicología del Trabajo y de las Organizaciones*, *30*(3), 97–104.

Murphy, G. B., Trailer, J. W., & Hill, R. C. (1996). Measuring performance in entrepreneurship research. *Journal of Business Research*, *36*(1), 15–23.

Nakiganda, R. G., Okello, D. O., & Bett, H. K. (2025). Factors influencing the sustainability of university-incubated agribusinesses: The role of stigma failure, personality and motivation in Kenya. *Cogent Business & Management*, *12*(1), 2447410.

Narkhede, B. E., Nehete, R. S., Raut, R. D., & Mahajan, S. K. (2014). Impact of entrepreneurial skills on the firm's performance: Evidence from manufacturing SMEs in India. *International Journal of Indian Culture and Business Management*, *8*(2), 216–236.

O'Cass, A., & Weerawardena, J. (2009). Examining the role of international entrepreneurship, innovation and international market performance in SME internationalisation. *European Journal of Marketing*, *43*(11/12), 1325–1348.

Obeidat, B. Y., Al-Suradi, M. M., Masa'deh, R., & Tarhini, A. (2016). The impact of knowledge management on innovation: An empirical study on Jordanian consultancy firms. *Management Research Review*, *39*(10), 1214–1238.

Olaleye, B. R., Lekunze, J. N., & Sekhampu, T. J. (2024). Examining structural relationships between innovation capability, knowledge sharing, environmental turbulence, and organisational sustainability. *Cogent Business & Management*, *11*(1), 2393738.

Oriarewo, G. O., Ofobruku, S. A., & Tor, Z. A. (2019). The implications of emotional intelligence on entrepreneurial performance: A discuss. *South Asian Journal of Social Studies and Economics*, *3*(1), 1–13.

Orobia, L. A., Nakibuuka, J., Bananuka, J., & Akisimire, R. (2020). Inventory management, managerial competence and financial performance of small businesses. *Journal of Accounting in Emerging Economies*, *10*(3), 379–398.

Otache, I. (2024). Innovation capability, strategic flexibility and SME performance: The roles of competitive advantage and competitive intensity. *African Journal of Economic and Management Studies*, *15*(2), 248–262.

Page, M. J., McKenzie, J. E., Bossuyt, P. M., Boutron, I., Hoffmann, T. C., Mulrow, C. D., Shamseer, L., Tetzlaff, J. M., Akl, E. A., & Brennan, S. E. (2021). The PRISMA 2020 statement: An updated guideline for reporting systematic reviews. *BMJ (Clinical Research Ed.)*, •••, 372.

Palich, L. E., & Bagby, D. R. (1995). Using cognitive theory to explain entrepreneurial risk-taking: Challenging conventional wisdom. *Journal of Business Venturing*, *10*(6), 425–438.

Parida, V., Pesämaa, O., Wincent, J., & Westerberg, M. (2017). Network capability, innovativeness, and performance: A multidimensional extension for entrepreneurship. *Entrepreneurship and Regional Development*, *29*(1–2), 94–115.

Prashantham, S., & Dhanaraj, C. (2010). The dynamic influence of social capital on the international growth of new ventures. *Journal of Management Studies, 47*(6), 967–994.

Pulka, B. M., Ramli, A., & Mohamad, A. (2021). Entrepreneurial competencies, entrepreneurial orientation, entrepreneurial network, government business support and SMEs performance. The moderating role of the external environment. *Journal of Small Business and Enterprise Development, 28*(4), 586–618.

Qi, R., Wang, D., Yang, Y., & Wu, F. (2023). How does environmental perception affect the willingness of university students to return home to start a business? *Cogent Business & Management, 10*(3), 2288720.

Rauch, A., & Frese, M. (2007). Let's put the person back into entrepreneurship research: A meta-analysis on the relationship between business owners' personality traits, business creation, and success. *European Journal of Work and Organizational Psychology, 16*(4), 353–385.

Rauch, A., Wiklund, J., Lumpkin, G. T., & Frese, M. (2009). Entrepreneurial orientation and business performance: An assessment of past research and suggestions for the future. *Entrepreneurship Theory and Practice, 33*(3), 761–787.

Ribeiro-Navarrete, S., Botella-Carrubi, D., Palacios-Marqués, D., & Orero-Blat, M. (2021). The effect of digitalization on business performance: An applied study of KIBS. *Journal of Business Research, 126*, 319–326.

Rosete, D., & Ciarrochi, J. (2005). Emotional intelligence and its relationship to workplace performance outcomes of leadership effectiveness. *Leadership and Organization Development Journal, 26*(5), 388–399.

Roundy, P. T. (2016). Start-up community narratives: The discursive construction of entrepreneurial ecosystems. *The Journal of Entrepreneurship, 25*(2), 232–248.

Sadiku-Dushi, N., Dana, L.-P., & Ramadani, V. (2019). Entrepreneurial marketing dimensions and SMEs performance. *Journal of Business Research, 100*, 86–99.

Saleem, I., Saleem, A., Hassan, A., Farukh, M. U., & Kamran, H. (2023). Psychological aspects affecting the venture performance of Indian women entrepreneurs. *Cogent* Sari, D., Kusuma, B. A., Sihotang, J., & Febrianti, T. (2023). The role of entrepreneurial marketing & innovation capability in the performance of SMEs during covid-19 pandemic: Evidence of MSMEs in West Java. *Cogent Business & Management, 10*(1), 2194091.

Sarkar, M. B., Echambadi, R. A. J., & Harrison, J. S. (2001). Alliance entrepreneurship and firm market performance. *Strategic Management Journal, 22*(6-7), 701–711.

Saunila, M., & Ukko, J. (2013). Facilitating innovation capability through performance measurement: A study of Finnish SMEs. *Management Research Review*, *36*(10), 991–1010.

Sethna, Z., Jones, R., & Harrigan, P. (2013). *Entrepreneurial marketing: Global perspectives*. Emerald Group Publishing.

Shaheen, N., & AL-Haddad, S. (2018). Entrepreneurial self-efficacy and entrepreneurial behavior. *International Journal of Development and Sustainability*, *7*(10), 2385–2402.

Siahaan, D. T., & Lin Tan, C. S. (2020). Antecedents of Innovation Capability and Firm Performance of Indonesian ICT SMEs. *Asian Journal of Business Research*, *10*(2).

Somathilake, H., & Pathirawasam, C. (2020). The effect of financial management practices on performance of SMEs in Sri Lanka. *International Journal of Scientific Research and Management*, *8*(5), 1789–1803.

Tang, M., Walsh, G., Lerner, D., Fitza, M. A., & Li, Q. (2018). Green innovation, managerial concern and firm performance: An empirical study. *Business Strategy and the Environment*, *27*(1), 39–51.

Teng, X., Wu, Z., & Yang, F. (2022). Research on the relationship between digital transformation and performance of SMEs. *Sustainability*, *14*(10), 6012.

Tiwari, P., Bhat, A. K., & Tikoria, J. (2017). The role of emotional intelligence and self-efficacy on social entrepreneurial attitudes and social entrepreneurial intentions. *Journal of Social Entrepreneurship*, *8*(2), 165–185.

Ullah, Y., Ullah, H., & Jan, S. (2022). The mediating role of employee creativity between knowledge sharing and innovative performance: Empirical evidence from manufacturing firms in emerging markets. *Management Research Review*, *45*(1), 86–100.

Urban, B. (2020). Entrepreneurial alertness, self-efficacy and social entrepreneurship intentions. *Journal of Small Business and Enterprise Development*, *27*(3), 489–507.

Usoro, I. A., & Brownson, C. D. (2023). Creativity and entrepreneurial development. *Open Access Journal of Business and Entrepreneurship*, *1*(2), 64–72.

Waweru, C., & Ngugi, K. (2014). Influence of financial management practices on the performance of micro and small enterprises in Kenya. *European Journal of Business and Management*, *1*(11), 141–161.

Wiklund, J., & Shepherd, D. (2003). Knowledge-based resources, entrepreneurial orientation, and the performance of small and medium-sized businesses. *Strategic Management Journal, 24*(13), 1307–1314.

Zahra, S. A. (2007). Contextualizing theory building in entrepreneurship research. *Journal of Business Venturing, 22*(3), 443–452.

Zhao, H., Seibert, S. E., & Lumpkin, G. T. (2009). The Relationship of Personality to Entrepreneurial Intentions and Performance: A Meta-Analytic Review. *Journal of Management, 36*(2), 324–381. DOI: 10.1177/0149206309335187

Zhao, W., Yang, T., Hughes, K. D., & Li, Y. (2021). Entrepreneurial alertness and business model innovation: The role of entrepreneurial learning and risk perception. *The International Entrepreneurship and Management Journal, 17*(2), 839–864.

Chapter 12
Navigating the Human-AI Blend:
Workforce Challenges in Hybrid Hospitality

Amrik Singh
https://orcid.org/0000-0003-3598-8787
Lovely Professional University, India

ABSTRACT

The rapid proliferation of Artificial Intelligence (AI) is fundamentally reshaping workforce management across industries, and hospitality, with its unique blend of human-centric service and operational complexity, presents a particularly compelling case study. Hospitality establishments such as hotels, resorts, and F&B increasingly adopt AI for tasks ranging from guest services and personalized recommendations to predictive staffing and automated operations, the traditional workforce model is undergoing significant transformation. The chapter explores the complexities of integrating diverse human and AI roles within a hybrid work environment, where both on-site and remote employees interact with AI systems. The key challenges include the need for upskilling and reskilling the existing human workforce to collaborate effectively with AI, addressing potential job displacement concerns, mitigating algorithmic bias in decision-making, and maintaining the quintessential human touch that defines exceptional hospitality.

1. INTRODUCTION

This is changing the hospitality industry significantly as artificial intelligence (AI) has rapidly been integrated into the service industry, which long been known as

DOI: 10.4018/979-8-3373-5871-0.ch012

ht © 2026, IGI Global Scientific Publishing. Copying or distributing in print or electronic forms without written permission of IGI Global Scientific Publishing is prohibited. Use of this chapter to generative artificial intelligence (AI) technologies is expressly prohibited. The publisher reserves all rights to license its use for generative AI training and machine learning model development.

a human-centric industry. It is a new paradigm, so called the Human-AI Blend, that offers an unprecedented opportunity, but a big challenge in workforce appearance (Singh & Kumar, 2021). Although AI will provide increased efficiency, personalized customer experience, and smarter operations, its successful introduction will rely on how well it deals with the intricacies of a hybrid workforce, in which humans and intelligent machines co-exist and collaborate. This introduction elucidates key issues that hospitality companies conceptualize when adopting AI and their capability to uphold their core values of empathy, personalization, or high-touch service. The first one is the risk of job loss, which causes anxiety and opposition in employees (Singh & Ansari, 2024; Ambardar et al., 2023). Some of the roles can be automated, whereas many of them will be enhanced, necessitating new skills and the change of the duties. The most crucial aspect in this regard is training and reskilling efforts to prepare the current workforce to work in this shifting environment so that they can use AI tools, but not be substituted with the latter. Other than the technical abilities, there should also be focus on creating distinctly human qualities such as emotional intelligence, creative problem solving and interpersonal communication, which is also lacking in AI at present. Besides, it is essential to organize the psychological effects of collaboration with AI (Singh & Hassan, 2024; Singh & Kumar, 2024). Job satisfaction and employee morale questions, and the perception of value may occur in case of the human element feeling undervalued or overridden. It is necessary to establish effective communication channels, role definition, and collaborative environment to curb these issues. The aspect of ethical AI implementation, especially in the data privacy and bias in the algorithms, further complicates it. To address these complex issues, it is necessary to take a strategic and sensitive approach to the matter, making sure that the Human-AI Blend in the hospitality industry is more about operational efficiency than about the human touch that the industry is famed to possess (Singh & Kumar, 2024; Singh & Kumar, 2021). There is a paradigm shift in the hospitality sector with the integration of artificial intelligence (AI) radically taking over its activities. AI is transforming the way services are offered, even the automated check-ins or smart concierge services. Nevertheless, this hybrid approach to work where human employees are integrated with AI systems creates a complicated set of workforce issues. It is necessary to balance the human empathy and the efficiency of machines, which can be achieved through a long-term perspective, organizational transformation, and lifelong learning (Supina & Singh, 2024).

1.2 Foundational Theories Underpinning Technology, Work, and Human–AI Interaction

Theoretical strong grounds are needed to comprehend how individuals and organisations are adopting, using and adjusting to the emerging technologies. Technology

Acceptance Model (TAM), Unified Theory of Acceptance and Use of Technology (UTAUT)., Job Demands-Resources (JD-R) model, Socio-technical Systems Theory, and Theories of Human-AI Collaboration and Augmentation. can be used as a comprehensive approach to the study of technology-related changes within modern workplaces. All of these theories are used to explain that of user acceptance, work design, integration with organizations and the changing collaboration between intelligent systems and humans.

Figure 1. Conceptual Framework

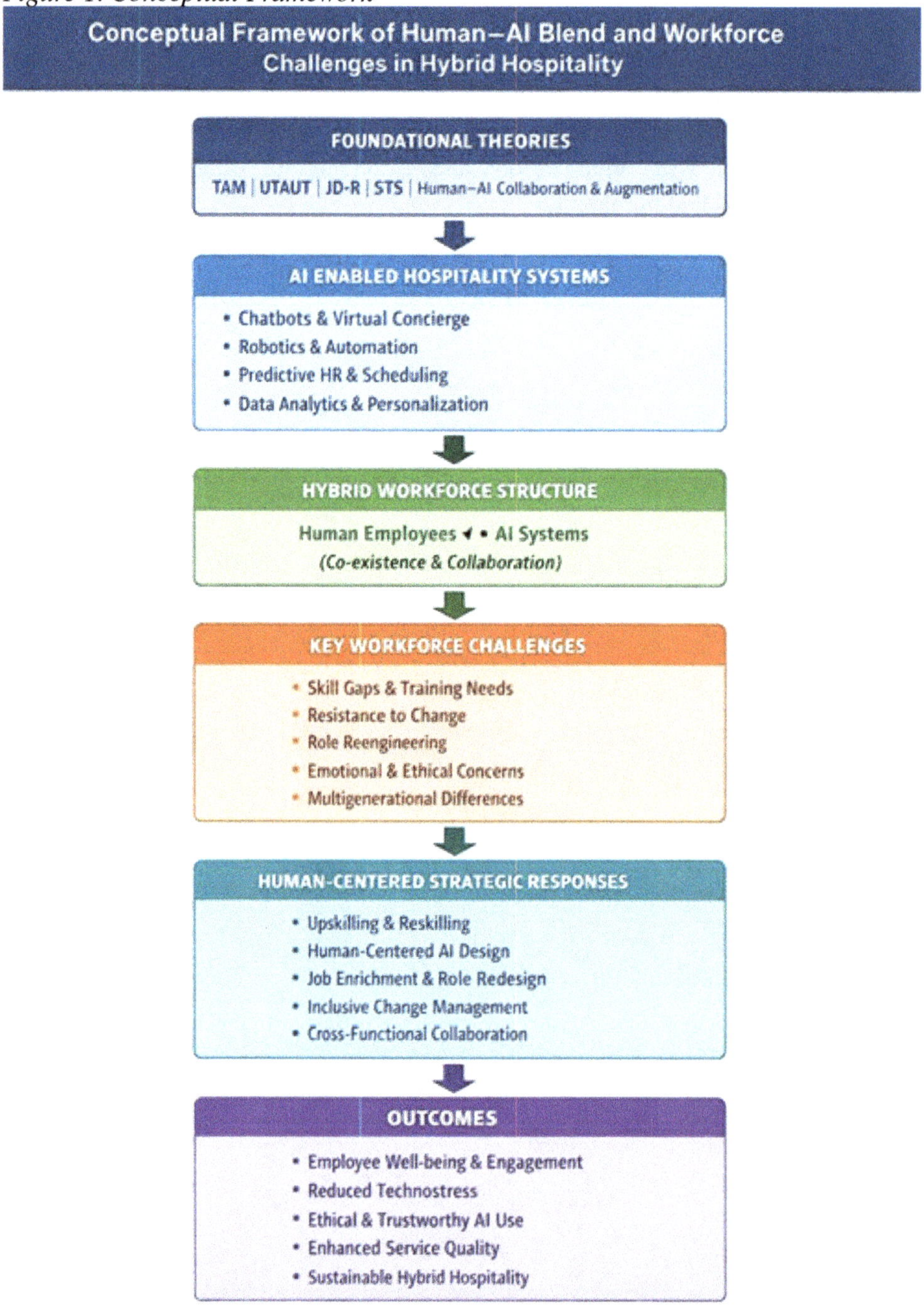

Sources: Author's own elaboration

1.2.1 Technology Acceptance Model (TAM)

One of the most popular models that have been used to explain user acceptance of information systems is the Technology Acceptance Model (TAM) which was proposed by Davis in 1989. TAM assumes that intention to utilize a technology is determined by two major beliefs which are Perceived Usefulness (PU) and Perceived Ease of Use (PEOU). Perceived usefulness is the extent to which an individual believes that the use of a system will improve job performance whereas perceived ease of use is the extent to which the system is thought to be effort free. TAM states that the two beliefs have an impact on attitude towards use, which then has an impact on behavioral intention and eventual behavioral use (El Hajal & Yeoman, 2024). TAM has over the years been expanded to accommodate external variables that include system quality, training, organisational support, and user experience. TAM can be considered a very applicable model in the context of digital transformation and artificial intelligence to predict the acceptance of technologies like self-service kiosk, artificial intelligence chatbots and automation platforms by employees and consumers. Critics have however suggested that TAM simplifies human behavior too much and fails to adequately explain social, organizational and ethical influences resulting in the emergence of more integrative models like UTAUT.

1.2.2 Unified Theory of Acceptance and Use of Technology (UTAUT)

Unified Theory of Acceptance and Use of Technology (UTAUT) is an amalgamation of eight major models of technology acceptance such as TAM, the Theory of Planned Behavior and the Diffusion of Innovations Theory. UTAUT assumes the use of four determinants of technological use, which are: Performance Expectancy, Effort Expectancy, Social Influence, and Facilitating Conditions. Performance expectancy is similar to perceived usefulness and is born out of the extent to which technology is considered to deliver performance benefits. The ease of use is in congruence with effort expectancy. Social influence denotes the effect of peer, supervisor, and organizational culture on adoption choices whereas facilitating conditions are the accessibility of resources and technical support. Another moderating variable brought about by UTAUT is age, gender, experience, and voluntariness of use which provides a more detailed description of technology adoption among various user categories. UTAUT is very useful in contemporary AI-based workplaccs to study the acceptance of intelligent systems of decision support, robotic process automation, and virtual assistants by employees. It emphasizes the role of organizational preparedness and social environment in the formation of adoption, as well as it is especially useful in studies of digital transformation, smart workplaces, and the services industry based on technologies.

1.2.3 Job Demands-Resources (JD-R) Model

Job Demands-Resources (JD-R) is a paradigm associated with the well-being, motivation, and performance of employees that is developed by Demerouti and Bakker. The model categorizes workplace characteristics into two broad groups namely job demands and job resources. Job demands refer to features of work that involve a high degree of physical or mental energy, e.g. workload, emotional work, time pressure, and techno-stress. Job resources, conversely, are defined as physical, psychological, social, and organizational conditions which contribute to meeting work targets, making demands less, and arousing personal growth such as autonomy, social backing, feedback and access to technology (El Hajal & Yeoman, 2024). The JD-R model assumes both parallel processes: the health impairment process, in which the excessive workload causes burnout and strain, and the motivational process, in which work resources help to increase engagement and performance. Digital tools enable digital demands and resources both in technology-intensive settings. As an example, AI systems can decrease routine workload (resource), but can also augment monitoring pressure and cognitive load (demand). JD-R model is increasingly used to analyse the technological stress, remote work, algorithmic management, and resiliency of employees in digital work places. It offers a strong prism to investigate the impact of AI-based redesign of work on burnout, engagement, productivity, and psychological health.

1.2.4 Socio-Technical Systems Theory

The Socio-technical Systems (STS) Theory originated in the mid-20th century at the Tavistock Institute and focuses on the interdependence of social systems (people, structures, culture) and technical systems (tools, machines, processes) in organizations. The STS theory postulates that both systems should be optimized simultaneously and not independently to enable the best performance in organizations (Aziz et al., 2025). The technological change according to STS is unavoidable in transforming work roles, communication patterns, power relations, and organizational culture. Subsequently, participatory planning, involvement of the employees, skill training and alignment with the organizational values are essential in the successful implementation of technology. Technological solutions that are not socialized or adapted tend to resist, lead to inefficiency and have undesirable consequences (Choudhary et al., 2025). The STS theory is particularly important in the epoch of artificial intelligence, automation, and platform-based work. The AI systems do not only change workflows, but also re-establish authority, responsibility, and identity of their jobs. Considering a service industry as an example, algorithmic scheduling modifies technical efficiency and employee discretion, which explains why socio-technical coexistence is needed. STS theory is therefore a critical construct of ethical AI implementation, digital governance, and sustainable organizational innovation.

1.2.5 Human-AI Collaboration and Augmentation Theories

Theories of human-AI collaboration and augmentation address the networks between human beings and intelligent systems, which are becoming more of an augmentation-based concept and less of an automation concept, where the intelligent system complements, instead of replaces, human abilities. The theories are based on cognitive science, human-computer interaction and organizational behavior (Yawson & Goryunova, 2025). The main assumption is that the best results would be achieved when machines are left to process data-intensive, repetitive, and predictive tasks, whereas humans will provide creativity, emotionality, ethical judgment, and contextual knowledge. Centaur models (human-AI collaborating), collaborative intelligence, and hybrid decision-making are some of the key concepts of this domain (Kanwal et al., 2025). AI is considered to be a cognitive co-worker, which will assist employees with real-time suggestions, pattern recognition, and predictive analytics. Nonetheless, efficient cooperation requires trust, transparency, explainability and user control. Human accountability and trust in the AI systems can decrease when the latter are used as black boxes. Continuous learning and skill development are also shown in human-AI augmentation theories. Due to the absorption of routine tasks by AI, human roles become less and less connected with routine and more associated with supervision, interpretation, strategic judgment, and human interactions. The theories play an important role in the reskilling of the workforce, ethical risks, job redesign, and the psychological effects of working alongside intelligent machines.

1.2.6 Overlapping Significance of the Theories

The combination of these five theories gives a multidimensional model of analyzing the technology adoption and its influence on the work and organizations. TAM and UTAUT define how people adapt or who do not adopt technologies. JD-R model explains the impact of technology that transforms the well-being and motivation of employees. The Socio-technical Systems Theory describes the development of technology and social systems in terms of the need to evolve together to achieve a sustainable success, whereas the Human-AI Collaboration theorics describe the future of the work as a collaboration between machine intelligence and human intelligence (Kolbjørnsrud, 2024). In the modern digital workplace, which is marked by AI, automation, remote working, and data-driven management, it is not enough to use a single theoretical lens. A combination of these underlining theories can help researchers and practitioners to discover more about technology-enabled performance, employee experience, organizational resilience, and ethical governance (Fenwick et al., 2024). These theories will be the key ones used to drive responsible innovation and human-centered digital transformation as technological improvement keeps gaining momentum.

2. LITERATURE REVIEW

Hybrid hospitality is the notion of integrating human touchpoints and automation (via AI) into improving service delivery. Hotels, resorts, and restaurants grow more and more dependent on AI to perform such tasks as data on guests' analysis, demand forecasting, chatbots as customer service, and robots. Although these technologies are efficient, lead to cost reductions, and provide personalized experiences, they also transform the role of new jobs and require employees to possess new skills (Singh & Ansari, 2024; Ambardar et al., 2023). The hospitality environment is in the midst of a paradigm shift with the rise of a new paradigm of hospitality in the form of hybrid hospitality which combines the elements of the inimitable human touch with the wonders of AI-powered automation with increased efficiency. This growing idea is quickly transforming the manner in which hotels, resorts as well as restaurants are run, radically changing the historical service delivery paradigm (Wang et al., 2025). The analysis of guest data and accurate forecasting of demand through AI can be taken to the next level, as well as 24/7 chatbots with customers and even robots to do routine jobs, making AI an indispensable part of guest experience optimization (Singh & Supina, 2024; Singh & Kumar, 2024). The fascination of such technologies is complex. To a business, it is an attractive prospect of increased efficiency using automated operations, huge cost reduction due to operational streamlining, and the potential to provide hyper-personalized experiences to each individual guest. When customers are able to book through AI, it is able to process large volumes of data to predict the needs of the guests, provide personalized services, and anticipate possible problems that would cause increased client satisfaction and loyalty (Singh & Kumar, 2021). But this technological integration is not a simple upgrade on operations, it is a complete re-definition of the human role in the industry. With the increased amount of analytical and repetitive tasks mentioned by AI, the nature of job roles in the hospitality sector is changing. An example is front-desk workers, whose role may shift away from the transactional nature of it to more problem-solving or customized concierge (Singh & Supina, 2024; Singh & Kumar, 2024). Robotic cleaning assistance can be added to housekeeping, so that human employees can be concentrated on the complex details and communication with guests. This change requires an active method of developing workforce. Employees are no longer service providers they need to learn how to interact, manage, and utilize AI tools. This requires new skills, such as technological literacy, the ability to interpret data, and a more pronounced attention to uniquely human capabilities of empathy, flexibility, and making complex decisions, which even the most advanced AI is unable to possess at the present.

Table 1. Workforce and AI Adoption Statistics in Hospitality

Variable / Indicator	Statistic / Evidence	Source (Secondary Databases)	Implication for Hybrid Hospitality
AI Adoption in Hospitality	~60–65% large hotel chains use AI-based systems	Scopus, Web of Science (Dwivedi et al., 2023)	AI integration is now mainstream
Workforce Skill Gap	~45% hospitality employees lack AI/digital skills	Industry & Academic Reviews (Bankins et al., 2024)	Strong need for reskilling
Employee Resistance to AI	~40% staff express job insecurity fears	Scopus-indexed surveys (Thomas, 2024)	Change management essential
Reduction in Routine Work	25–30% task automation at front office	Industry reports & WoS studies	Role reengineering required
Increase in Technostress	~35% rise in digital stress indicators	JD-R based studies (El Hajal & Yeoman, 2024)	AI as job demand
Training Effectiveness	20–30% higher engagement post AI training	Scopus empirical studies	Training mitigates resistance
Guest Satisfaction Impact	15–20% improvement with hybrid service	Hospitality analytics reports	Balance AI + human touch
Ethical Concerns Awareness	~50% employees concerned about surveillance	WoS & policy literature	Need for ethical AI governance
Multigenerational Gap	Older staff 2× slower AI adoption	Cross-sector secondary studies	Customized training required
Employee Retention	Hybrid AI models reduce turnover by ~12%	Hospitality workforce studies	Sustainable HR outcomes

Sources: Author's own elaboration

2.1KEY WORKFORCE CHALLENGES

he emergence of hybrid hospitality, in turn, is a promising but also a challenging frontier that requires a careful balance between technological sophistication and development of human capital.

2.1.1 Skill Gaps and Training Needs

The use of AI technologies has introduced a high level of skill shortage. Numerous hospitality experts are not digitally literate and technologically competent enough to collaborate with AI tools. Employee training in the fields of data handling and system troubleshooting along with AI integration is fundamental and should not be under-prioritized (Bankins et al., 2024; Dinker & Rawat, 2025). The rapid adoption of AI technologies in the hospitality sector has put the acute issue of a significant skills gap in the current workforce. The hospitality industry has long been defined by interpersonal service; thus, many people in this industry are now deprived of the required digital literacy and technical skills to communicate and utilize AI effectively (Petrescu & Krishen, 2023; Dwivedi et al., 2023). It is not limited to the basic computer knowledge but includes more specialized knowledge on data handling, interpreting the AI products, and troubleshooting integrated systems (Sağbaş & Aydogan, 2025). Filling this gap with the help of solid upskilling efforts is not only advantageous, but is the key to successful adoption of AI. The staff should be trained on the ways of interpreting guest data that has been analyzed by an AI, the ways of using chatbot interfaces to serve a customer, and even to do basic maintenance or escalate the problem using robotic help. Nevertheless, such comprehensive training is a highly critical element of hospitality that is not given sufficient priority by the organizations (La Sala et al., 2024). The result of this neglect is employee opposition, sub-optimal use of costly AI solutions, and the inability to achieve the promised efficiency and improved guest experiences promised by hybrid hospitality (Thomas, 2024; Babashahi et al., 2024). To close this skill gap, there is a need to make a strategic investment in an approach to lifelong learning and development so that the human workforce can work effectively with their AI counterparts.

2.1.2 Resistance to Change

Employees usually fear AI as something that would take their jobs and tend to resist or lose interest. This emotional obstacle may become an impediment to seamless adoption of hybrid systems, because employees might feel underappreciated or be afraid of being fired. Employee resistance to the introduction of AI in the hospitality industry is usually quite strong, and the root causes of the phenomenon are mostly hidden within the lack of job security. The employees often see AI as a threat to themselves directly, as they think it will replace them and make them useless (Islam et al., 2025; Abaddi, 2025). This resistance could be an insurmountable barrier towards the effective adoption of hybrid systems, which may result in a lack of interest, negative attitude and even outright resistance. An environment of anxiety is formed when employees are undervalued or do not feel that their services are no longer needed. This fear of obsolescence may come in the shape of the unwillingness to acquire new skills and knowledge related to AI, the uncertainty towards the motives of management, and a sense of powerlessness in general (Dinker & Rawat, 2025). In response to this, effective and understanding leadership communication is paramount. It should not be positioned as a substitute to AI but as an extension - the tool that will empower the employees to pay attention to more challenging, creative, and uniquely human features of service and, in the end, improve the work of the employees and guest experience. The trust and willingness to invest in the upskilling of the workforce is also essential to change the resistance into acceptance and even a recommendation to the Human-AI Blend.

2.1.3 Repositioning of Roles and Responsibilities

The scope of most conventional roles is modified by AI. Front-desk employees, such as those, can have a shift to a more supervisory or a guest experience-oriented position. Nevertheless, role redefinitions are not clearly defined, which may lead to confusion, inefficiencies, and decreased morale. The adoption of AI essentially transforms the definition of most of the conventional job positions in the hospitality industry (Abaddi, 2025). Use front-desk employees, as an example: their jobs are becoming less transactional, due to the fact that AI can effectively perform the check-ins and payments, and more customer-centric, based on the experience that guests could have. It may include the transformation into superiors of automated systems, solutions of complicated guest requests, unique problem-solving which artificial intelligence is not capable of, or active communication with guests to add value to their experience (Babashahi et al., 2024). Nevertheless, when these new roles are not well defined, a major challenge is expected. The lack of the clear redefinition of the roles may confuse the staff, making them feel that they are not useful and needed because of the new hybrid environment (Bankins et al., 2024). This ambiguity can be a major source of inefficiency when tasks are duplicated and it can drastically affect the morale of the employees. Employees that lack knowledge on how their efforts are linked to the larger goal will develop feelings of being underappreciated or unnecessary.

2.1.4 Ethical and Emotional Concerns

AI does not possess emotional intelligence and ethical reasoning as human interactions have. The fact that machines cannot sympathize or deal with more complex cases of guest control increases emotional strain on human staff who have to deal with escalations or negative reactions in a service-based industry. Emotional intelligence and ethical reasoning as key elements of AI are absent in the hospitality industry, which is highly service-oriented by nature, posing a major threat. Although AI is an excellent data processing and automating the routine, it has no ability to show a human being a sense of real empathy - one of the keystones of human existence. Robots are not capable of reading between the lines of emotions, interpreting nonverbal messages, and providing an individual with the necessary support and reassurance that a person may feel in a challenging experience (Massaro et al., 2025). This is the basic shortcoming that imparts more emotional stress to human workers. In case an AI chatbot cannot resolve a complicated or emotionally charged guest complaint, or a self-service kiosk breaks, the human staff will have to intervene (Petrescu & Krishen, 2023). They then receive the responsibility of handling issues that have escalated, de-escalating frustration, and regaining guest satisfaction to bear the burden of the poor original experience. This continuous fixation on correcting AI emotional failures may cause more stress and burnout and the perception of being a cleaning team to correct anomalies in technology (Singh & Ansari, 2024). The positive working environment and well-being of the staff makes it necessary to consider the emotional burden and give appropriate support and training in higher order emotional intelligence and conflict management.

2.1.5 Multigenerational Workforce Dynamics

The hospitality employees are of different age groups and vary in terms of e-fluency. Older workers can find it difficult to use AI tools, whereas younger employees can adapt quickly and cause productivity and team cohesion differences. Hospitality employees are diverse in nature and they are made up of different generations with different levels of digital fluency. This is a distinct challenge to the integration of AI in a generation-to-generation dynamic (Li & Duan, 2025; Thomas, 2024). Digital natives, who are usually younger employees, are likely to learn new technologies fast, with their intuition about AI tools and their use. They are familiar with online interfaces and can even accept AI as a source of work simplification and better it. On the other hand, the rapid transition of older workers to AI-related systems may be more overwhelming to them since they may have several decades of experience when it comes to the traditional hospitality skills (Singh & Hassan, 2024; Singh, 2024). They might not have a previous experience with complex digital tools, and it will have a higher learning curve and may feel incompetent or frustrated. Such a digital divide may cause a productivity gap in teams, and, unless it is addressed, may lead to the loss of cohesion in the team. The solution to this generational gap is to have specialized training that addresses the various learning styles, patient mentoring, and emphasis of showing the concrete benefits AI brings to everyone in the organization irrespective of their age. Creating a culture of inclusion, in which experience is appreciated and technological usage is facilitated, is essential to a successful Human-AI Blend.

2.1.6 Research Gap

Although artificial intelligence is quickly being implemented in the operations of hospitality, the process of hybrid human-AI workforce and its scholarly study is still somewhat disjointed and incomplete. Human workforce dimension, especially the psychosocial, ethical, and long-term career aspects, has been given relatively little and unequal attention in existing hospitality research work, as most studies have been based on the technology adoption, service automation, digital customer experience, and operational efficiency. To begin with, the majority of empirical research is still technology-focused, prioritizing acceptance and usage (i.e. self-service technologies, chatbots, and robotics) in terms of models like TAM and UTAUT. Although these models capture the process of early adoption, they do not provide much information on how sustained human-AI interaction transforms job identity, emotional labor, professional autonomy, and service meaning as time progresses. There is a relative lack of longitudinal studies that present the workforce adjustment at various stages of AI adoption. Second, the studies focusing on the well-being of employees, technostress, algorithmic management, and burnout in AI-enabled hospitality settings remain premature. Even though the JD-R model has been implemented in the digital workplace, the available evidence is not sufficient on how AI can be used as a job demand and a job resource to frontline hospitality workers, supervisors, and middle managers alike. Third, the available literature is highly focused on developed economies and major global hotels, and it poses a considerable gap in the context. Empirical studies of growing hospitality markets like India, small and medium-sized hotels, or informal service environments with significantly different digital infrastructure, workforce capabilities and organizational cultures are limited. Fourth, ethical, governance, and trust aspects of human-AI collaboration such as surveillance, data privacy, transparency, and algorithmic bias are a poorly explored area of the hospitality-related literature. Also, the fact that employees feel fair, accountable, and psychologically safe when subjected to algorithmic management regimes has limited information. Lastly, there are no integrative and interdisciplinary models that simultaneously look at the aspects of acceptance, work design, well-being, and socio-technical alignment in hybrid hospitality environments. Majority of the studies follow single-theory orientations, and there is a serious gap in the total and humanistic models. It is necessary to fill these gaps in order to work out evidence-based strategies that would make AI-based transformation of the hospitality industry not only technologically effective but also socially responsible and focused on employees.

3. RESEARCH METHODOLOGY

In this study, we use a systematic secondary-source research approach to explore workforce issues that are arising at the nexus of human labour and artificial intelligence (AI) in hybrid hospitality environment. The method of secondary research is especially proper in this case due to the fact that the sphere is developing rapidly, and the data may be found in academic, industry, and policy levels and the analysis of previous evidence may help to identify tendencies, gaps, and the perspectives of the future primary study. Source selection and search strategy. The search of the literature will be extensive and reproducible. Such databases as multidisciplinary academic databases (e.g., Scopus, Web of Science), specific journals in hospitality and service-management, and repositories of studies on technology and labour are going to be searched. The search of complementary grey literature will include industry reports (consultancies, hotel chains), government and regulatory documents, conference proceedings and reputable trade media. The search terms are comprised of hospitality keywords (e.g., "hotel" or "hospitality workforce" or front desk or housekeeping) + AI and hybrid work keywords (e.g., "artificial intelligence" or "robotics" or "human-AI collaboration" or hybrid service delivery). Thorough search is guaranteed due to the use of the Boolean operators, citation chaining and backward/forward reference checks.

Selection and deselection criteria

Included sources will: (1) deal with workforce/labour topics in the hospitality or any service sector closely related to it; (2) discuss AI, automation, or human-technology interaction in an operational or managerial setting; (3) be written in English; and (4) contain empirical data, theoretical background, or sound industry analysis. Outlined materials will consist of mere promotional marketing contents with no analytical content, opinionated materials that have not been substantiated or materials that do not fall within the specified topic of interest.

Information selection and evaluation

The structured information will be obtained out of each source: research objectives, setting/sample characteristics, the type of AI/technology used, the workforce implications (skills, roles, job structure, health/safety and well being), managerial reactions, regulatory implications, and methodological shortcomings. The adapted tools that will be used in quality appraisal include critical appraisal checklists (empirical studies, assessing their validity, sampling, measurement, and associated problems) and a robustness checklist (assessing transparency, data sources, and possible commercial bias) used in grey literature.

Synthesis approach

Since the types of sources are heterogeneous, convergent qualitative synthesis is an adequate choice. Peering synthesis will find the common themes (skill displacement and augmentation, role redefinition, training and reskilling, labor relations, equity and inclusion, and ethical/regulatory problems). Simple meta-analytic summarisation or narrative aggregation will be cautiously used, where quantitative results are comparably sufficient (e.g. survey measures of job satisfaction or time savings in a task), and heterogeneity is observed. Where the literature is sparse on hospitality-specific issues, cross-sector comparisons (e.g. retail vs. hospitality) will be employed to put the findings into perspective.

Triangulation and reflexivity

The triangulation of academic sources, industry sources and policy sources reduces bias of a source and helps to arrive at balanced conclusions. The study will explicitly describe how positionable the authors are and how there might be biases in publication, specifically, the commercial incentive of vendor reports and the novelty bias of early AI research.

Transparency and restrictions

The secondary research is unable to replicate emergent, location dynamics that primary field research would have identified; temporal delay in published reports can insufficiently publicize the most recent technological rollouts. To optimise the transparency, the search log, inclusion/exclusion list, and data extraction templates will be provided as an appendix to the chapter to allow the readers to evaluate the reproducibility and credibility. Altogether, this approach of secondary sources offers a serious, effective basis of mapping the human-AI workforce environment in hybrid hospitality, identifying empirical evidence, theory building, and practical conclusions to inform managers, policymakers, and future principal research.

4. DISCUSSION AND INTERPRETATION

The multi-pronged, strategic approach to adapting hospitality workforce to the realities of the Human-AI Blend needs. To begin with, it is essential to develop a culture of lifelong learning and leave a training session behind and offer smaller, on-demand courses that are directed at not only learning technical skills, such as AI literacy and data interpretation, but also essential soft ones, such as improved emotional intelligence, ability to find complex solutions, and conflict management (Singh & Kumar, 2024). Second, an AI integration philosophy, that is, human-oriented, allows introducing technology as an enabler and not an attack on people, engaging employees directly in the design and implementation process to create trust and learn how AI will help them in their work (Dwivedi et al., 2023; Singh & Kumar, 2021). Third, it is essential to restructure roles and enrich jobs, redistributing duties to higher-order processes that build the use of human capabilities that cannot be replicated by AI, resulting in job satisfaction and an experience that cannot be offered by AI to the guests. Lastly, change management can be made inclusive by means of open communication, psychological support, and custom-made career paths to reduce resistance and make employees feel more empowered to overcome this change process.

4.1 On-the-Job Learning Process

Companies should establish the culture of life-long education and technological literacy. Training should be modular and on demand and targeted at both technical skills as well as soft skills demanded in a hybrid environment. AI literacy and digital hospitality are also certifications that can be added to the portfolios of employees (Dinker & Rawat, 2025). In order to maneuver in the changing environment of hybrid hospitality organizations need to take the initiative of fostering the culture of continual learning and digital literacy. This is not a single training program, but a continuous promise to train the labor force on the skills that would be required in tomorrow. The training programs are to be modular and on-demand to enable the employees to learn at their own pace and concentrate on the areas that are relevant without interfering with the flow of operations (Singh & Supina, 2024). Importantly, such programs should include not only technical skills, i. e., the knowledge of AI interfaces, data interpretation, and troubleshooting of systems, but also improved soft skills. The more activities are delegated to AI, the more human workers will be expected to utilize their emotional intelligence, critical thinking, problem-solving, and high-level communications skills. In order to offer more incentive to learn and a well-defined career route, organizations may also consider offering AI literacy, digital hospitality, or proficiency with one or more AI tools certifications. Not only do they certify new skills, but they also contribute a lot of value to employee portfolios, increasing morale and retention during technological change (Singh & Hassan, 2024; Singh, 2024). Such a proactive strategy will guarantee the creation of a workforce not only adjusting, but also performing well in the Human-AI Blend.

4.2 Human-Centered AI Implementation

Technology must be implemented as an add-on and not substitution. This will entail enrolling the employees into the implementation process, obtaining feedback and developing systems that complement human roles and not destroy them. To have a real success of AI integration in the hospitality industry, it should be done using a humane philosophy. It implies the perception of technology as a strong enabler of employees rather than an immediate substitute (Singh & Kumar, 2024; Ambardar et al., 2023). More importantly, this includes the active engagement of employees in the implementation process at the very beginning. The knowledge obtained in workshops, surveys, and pilot programs is priceless in terms of determining pain points and making sure that AI solutions truly aid their work. It is highly important to design systems that promote but not destroy human roles. In lieu of merely automating things out, the AI should be set to handle the repetitive or data-heavy parts and leave the human personnel to work on the complex, personal, and creative aspects of service that foster the establishment of authentic guest relationships (Singh & Ansari, 2024). As an example, an AI concierge can give fast responses to frequently asked questions, where a human concierge can use the additional time on personalized recommendations or complex problem-solving. This visionary design will make sure that the AI will build up human capacities, not replace, but make people feel empowered and eventually create a more productive, but yet highly human experience in a hospitality service.

4.3 Role Reengineering and Job Enrichment

To ensure that the content of the first approach is in place, hospitality companies have to invest in role reengineering by adding higher-order roles like engaging guests, resolving conflicts, and being creative, which AI is unable to imitate. This does not only increase the satisfaction of employees but also improves the experience of the guests. The transition to hybrid hospitality requires a radical redesign of the job positions and going beyond the automation of the existing jobs (Singh & Supina, 2024). The hospitality companies have to invest in developing employee roles strategically to incorporate higher-order functions that involve the use of uniquely human capabilities - functions that AI cannot mimic. It involves enabling employees to work on actual interaction with guests, sensitive conflict management, and creative problem-solving. An example is the front-desk staff are not just the processing check-in but can be the active guest experience managers who anticipate guests and design unique memories. On the same note, AI can process basic questions, with human agents working on more difficult conflicts that demand emotional intelligence and negotiation capabilities (Bankins et al., 2024; Singh, 2025). Moreover, they can also assign employees the responsibility of discovering new service opportunities or innovative solutions to improve operations which creates a culture of innovation. This role reengineering does not only result in a higher level of employee satisfaction considering that they end up work on more meaningful and challenging work, but also it goes a long way in improving the guest experience through a personalized, high touch services that make a brand stand out in an ever automated world.

4.4 Inclusive Change Management

Leaders should deal with the transitional process sensitively and provide clear communication and involve everyone in the process. Resistance can be addressed by offering psychological assistance, career advice, and upskilling opportunities to foster confidence in the use of technology. The process of switching to a hybrid human-AI workforce in hospitality requires a strong and sensitive change management strategy (Dinker & Rawat, 2025). The leaders should focus on open communication, stating a clear reason why AI should be adopted, why it will help the business and workers, and how roles will look in the future. This active candor contributes to removing the rumors and concerns related to job security and creating the perception of understanding instead of fear (Supina & Singh, 2024). Most importantly, it is essential to have inclusive planning. This implies the engagement of the employees in the decision making and implementation process at different levels. Their response to new technologies, using their feedback to make changes in workflows, and having them participate in the solution process can change the possible resistance into proactive participation. Employees feel included and appreciated and turn out to be the champions of the change instead of the receiving end. In addition to communication, they should be given overall psychological support. This may be provided with access to counseling services to cope with stress or anxiety caused by job changes, and forums where employees can freely share their issues (Bankins et al., 2024). In combination with this, providing personalized career guidance enables the person to have a better idea of how their skills can be cultivated and what new possibilities may emerge in the hybrid system (Singh & Hassan, 2024). Lastly, the presence of easy and well-organized upskilling opportunities and easy access to the corresponding training and certification are the signs of a true interest in the growth of the employees. Combining these aspects, leaders will be able to eliminate the resistance successfully, establish the base of trust, and develop a workforce willing and eager to pursue the future of human-AI cooperation in the hospitality industry.

4.5 Cross-Functional Collaboration

The hybrid hospitality involves collaboration between the operations managers, IT, as well as the HR departments. The creation of cross-functional task force can be used to make sure that technological and human considerations are made during strategy development. Effective execution of hybrid models of hospitality models is a critical aspect that depends on effective cross-functional cooperation within an organization. IT departments can no longer work in secrecy, and create solutions without a profound understanding of the realities of operations or HR consequences. The same could be said about the HR that cannot simply concentrate on the classic models of staffing without knowing the technological changes that redefine job descriptions and cannot be allowed to operate by the operations managers without consulting on its technical and personnel viability (Dinker & Rawat, 2025). To close these conventional silos, hospitality organizations should be keen to promote the collaboration processes among IT departments, Human Resource departments, and operations managers. The cross-functional task force or steering committees should be an effective strategy (Singh & Sihmar, 2025; Singh & Singh, 2022). These special teams, including the representatives of all the spheres, could be used as the core decision-making, idea-sharing, and control units. By having a combined expertise, they do not seek to make technological developments in isolation but rather, it is tailored to the strategies of human capital and operational efficiencies. As an illustration, IT may discover a new AI-based check-in system, which would subsequently be evaluated by a cross-functional team on its effect to front-desk personnel (HR), on the integration with the current property management systems (Operations), and on the creation of a training program (HR/Operations). This combined solution will make sure that both technological and human factors are taken into account at the same time, avoiding any disconnection that may result in the need to rework, employee dissatisfaction, or even guest dissatisfaction (Singh, 2024; Singh & Supina, 2024). Cross-functional collaboration allows reducing the complex nature of AI integration to a coordinated and strategic benefit that drives seamless transitions and streamlines the Human-AI Blend by breaking departmental boundaries and encouraging maximum understanding of objectives.

5. CASE STUDIES AND EXAMPLES

5.1 Marriott International

Marriott has used AI-oriented chatbots to answer customers, but still has human agents to resolve complicated questions. Their own Digital Learning Hub helps bring the staff closer to AI competency development, so they do not experience anxiety over the risk of technological displacement.

5.2 Japan's Henn-na Hotel

The Henn-na Hotel is known to have suffered because of the lack of satisfaction on the part of the guests and the overdependence on the machine staff. It ultimately brought back human employees to the hotel and this showed the need to balance efficiency and the personal touch.

The introduction of artificial intelligence in the sphere of hospitality functions is transforming the way of providing, organizing and consuming services. Even though AI is seen to be efficient, personalized, and optimized on costs, its integration with human labor has created complicated employment issues. A number of real-life situations in organizations demonstrate how hybrid hospitality models result in the emergence of new tensions concerning skills, job design, ethics, trust, and employee well-being. One of the most striking cases is the implementation of self-service kiosks and check-in bots that are AI-powered in major international hotel chains. The world's leading hotel brand launched the introduction of facial recognition-based check-in at some of the Asian and European hotels to minimize waiting time and staffing expenses. Although the scores of the guest satisfaction were directly enhanced with the faster service, the workers of the front office complained about the feeling of insecurity and guidance ambiguity. Their duties were changed to exception processing and system monitoring, rather than dealing with guests. Employees were anxious about becoming backup robots and not professionals working in the hospitality sector. The case demonstrates that AI has the potential to increase efficiency and at the same time undermine occupational identity and emotional involvement, which are the fundamental aspects of hospitality work (Singh & Hassan, 2024; Singh & Kumar, 2024). The other example vignette is one involving a luxury resort in the Middle East that used AI-based concierge applications to give personalized guest suggestions on where to eat, spa and touring activities. To create custom itineraries, the system took into consideration guest data. Although the convenience was enjoyed by the guests, human concierges complained of displaced skills and lack of autonomy. The powers of decision-making became more algorithm-oriented and did not give employees enough freedom to reach professional judgments. With time, the management noticed that the employee engagement decreased despite the improvement in service consistency. The case is a typical example of the issue of hybrid hospitality: how to balance the precision of algorithms with human instincts and imagination. The third scenario is the use of AI-based workforce management systems through predictive scheduling within big hotel chains. These systems examine occupancy trends, seasonal trends and booking trends in order to optimize staffing. The AI scheduling process saved almost 15 percent in labor costs in one Indian metropolitan hotel group. Nevertheless, employees had unpredictable working schedules, work life imbalance, and digital stress. Employees complained that artificial decision-making was not humanitarian to individual limitations like family or health. This shows that AI could also serve as a productivity-enhancing tool and a psychosocial job demand at the same time. Ethical and psychological issues are also associated with the use of AI-enabled surveillance and performance analytics. As an illustration, computer vision has now been used by some hotels to track the speed of services provided, facial expressions, and interaction with the guests. Though the management can gain advantages through the availability of real-time data on the performance, employees are usually feeling that the systems are meddling in their lives which is unappealing and anxiety provoking. An example of a hotel chain located in the United States showed that the case of constant monitoring caused emotional fatigue and increased employee turnover, especially with frontline service employees. This highlights the health impairment process in the JD-R model, in which the technological surveillance raises the cognitive and emotional load. On the other hand, successful integration of human and AI is also present in positive instances. A hotel chain in Japan installed housekeeping robots that help staff members to move goods and replenish supplies. Instead of taking over workers, robots were set as co-workers. Consequently, there was a reduction in physical workload, increased working tenure of older employees and also employee satisfaction increased. This case shows that AI as a supportive tool and not a control tool can lead to improved well-being and productivity. All these pieces of evidence indicate that hybrid hospitality is not simply a technological change but a fundamental change in the workforce. The main dilemma is to create AI systems that will support human service and not shadow it. In the absence of socio-technical alignment, ethical protection, and constant reskilling, the human-AI combination will pose a threat of technostress and dehumanized service, and human resistance to the workforce. But, with the approach of a human approach, AI can transform the hospitality work towards more sustainable, inclusive and high-performance directions.

6. FUTURE RESEARCH

Hybrid hospitality has no zero-sum game between man and machine. Rather, it will be based on co-creation, with AI working on mechanical tasks, and people concentrating on experiencing something memorable and empathetic. The changing labor force has to be dynamic, emotionally balanced and digitally savvy. Employers need to invest in long-term workforce development strategies, and universities and training institutions need to change the content of their curriculums. The emerging field of hybrid hospitality, despite the abundance of opportunities, is the area where new studies can be conducted (Ambardar et al, 2023). One of the aspects that require more thorough research is the psychological effects of human-AI collaboration in the long term on employees of the hospitality industry. Although the existing discussion also addresses the issue of initial resistance and skills mismatch, more in-depth longitudinal research is required to determine how the continuous engagement with AI influences employee well-being, job satisfaction, identity, and the possibility of new stress or burnout forms (Singh & Ansari, 2024). The studies have the potential to explore such elements of psychological wellbeing as the ideal ratio of AI and human activity, the impact of perceived autonomy on AI-enhanced jobs, and the emergence of coping strategies to address the fears caused by technology.

7. IMPLICATION

The massive adoption of AI in the hospitality industry has a lot of long-term consequences, with it affecting every aspect of the industry, including its operational efficiency and the essence of work. To the Workforce: The first impact that can be realized is job role transformation. The monotonous and data-driven processes, including reservations management, simple customer care questions using chatbots, and regular cleaning, are becoming increasingly automated. This liberates human workers off routine tasks, but requires a major upskilling and reskilling exercise. The employees will be forced to acquire new skills in digital literacy, data analysis, system troubleshooting, and increased attention to the distinctly human competence such as emotional intelligence, empathy communication, and the ability to solve problems creatively. Some may be laid off or rendered job insecure because of the inability to adjust to these new requirements, and others will have their responsibilities and roles expanded and diversified, creating job satisfaction and a more valuable input. The psychological effect, such as the possible anxiety and change resistance, also presupposes the necessity of the empathetic leadership and the strong supportive mechanisms. In the case of Businesses and Operations: AI has the implication of much higher efficiency and cost-saving. The predictive analytics are able to optimize prices, handle inventory as well as forecast demand with greater precision than ever before contributing to the management of revenue. The automation simplifies the check-in/check-out, provision of room services, and cleaning, and cuts through the bottlenecks in the operations. It also means that it is possible to ensure 24/7 availability of services and hyper-personalization of the experiences of guests, which results in higher customer satisfaction and loyalty (Singh & Ansari, 2024). Nonetheless, they are accompanied by the negative aspect of high-upfront costs of the AI technologies and the uncertainty of the data quality control to guarantee the efficacy of AI. To the Guest Experience: The guest implications are usually favorable, which are more individual, smooth, and efficient experiences. AI-based applications will be in a position to predict, make customized suggestions, and give immediate feedback to queries, which makes them more convenient. Yet, the connotation of the possible loss of human touch is also present in case it is not handled properly. The guests might love the efficiency and still want to have a human touch and empathy, especially in complicated or emotional cases. Hospitality businesses need to discover the proper balance, which means that AI will complement instead of harm the personal connection that constitutes the next level of service. Overall, the Human-AI Blend has significant and diverse implications on the hospitality industry, which requires strategically proactive behavior, constant commitment to human assets, and adherence to ethical and humanistic technology application.

CONCLUSION

The human-AI entwining in the hospitality industry is not only a cultural but also an ethical problem as well as a technological issue. Although the potential of AI is enormous and the possibilities of innovation are enormous, human potential must not be criticized but supplemented by it. The businesses in the hospitality industry that understand this and therefore take steps to counter the workforce challenges will be in a better position to be successful in the era of intelligent service. The human-AI fusion of hybrid hospitality is a challenging but interesting frontier to the industry. Although the efficacy, reduced costs, and personalisation supremacy of AI-related technologies cannot be underestimated, the key to successful implementation of the new technologies is taking into consideration the major labour issues. Addressing job displacement fears and skill gaps, as well as redefining jobs and coping with the emotional impact on the employees, the process will consume a fine arrangement between technological progress and people-centric approach. The main idea is simple, AI must be an enabler, not a replacement. The most important is to cultivate a continuous education culture, focus on human-centric AI integration and perform a serious re-engineering of the jobs to take advantage of the unique qualities of humans, such as empathy and creativity. Moreover, it will also be essential that inclusive change management and cross-functional collaboration will contribute to building trust and keeping all stakeholders on track with the changing vision. The future of hospitality is not human versus AI, but it is about the effectiveness of the collaboration between humans and AI to deliver a better experience to the guests and bring more meaningful and valuable positions to the workforce. Through these approaches, the industry will manage to strike the right balance between the strength of artificial intelligence and the inimitable warmth of human touch to make hybrid hospitality a successful and sustainable business in the future.

REFERENCES

Abaddi, S. (2025). AI–human data hybridization: a hybrid approach to unveiling global entrepreneurial motivations, challenges and opportunities. Journal of Ethics in Entrepreneurship and Technology.

Ambardar, A., Singh, A., & Singh, V. (2023). Barriers in Implementing Ergonomic Practices in Hotels- A Study on five star hotels in NCR region. *International Journal of Hospitality and Tourism Systems*, *16*(2), 11–17.

Aziz, M. F., Rajesh, J. I., Jahan, F., McMurrray, A., Ahmed, N., Narendran, R., & Harrison, C. (2025). AI-powered leadership: A systematic literature review. *Journal of Managerial Psychology*, *40*(5), 604–630.

Babashahi, L., Barbosa, C. E., Lima, Y., Lyra, A., Salazar, H., Argôlo, M., & Souza, J. M. D. (2024). AI in the workplace: A systematic review of skill transformation in the industry. *Administrative Sciences*, *14*(6), 127.

Bankins, S., Jooss, S., Restubog, S. L. D., Marrone, M., Ocampo, A. C., & Shoss, M. (2024). Navigating career stages in the age of artificial intelligence: A systematic interdisciplinary review and agenda for future research. *Journal of Vocational Behavior*, •••, 104011.

Choudhary, V., Marchetti, A., Shrestha, Y. R., & Puranam, P. (2025). Human-AI ensembles: When can they work? *Journal of Management*, *51*(2), 536–569.

Dinker, N., & Rawat, N. (2025). Technological Mediation and AI for Agility in Hospitality and Tourism: A Sociological Analysis through the Lens of Structuration and Network Theory. *Nepalese Journal of Management Science and Research*, *8*(1), 126–143.

Dwivedi, Y. K., Kshetri, N., Hughes, L., Slade, E. L., Jeyaraj, A., Kar, A. K., & Wright, R. (2023). Opinion Paper:"So what if ChatGPT wrote it?" Multidisciplinary perspectives on opportunities, challenges and implications of generative conversational AI for research, practice and policy. *International Journal of Information Management*, *71*, 102642.

El Hajal, G., & Yeoman, I. (2024). AI and the future of talent management in tourism and hospitality. *Current Issues in Tourism*, •••, 1–18. DOI: 10.1080/13683500.2024.2439395

Fenwick, A., Molnar, G., & Frangos, P. (2024). The critical role of HRM in AI-driven digital transformation: A paradigm shift to enable firms to move from AI implementation to human-centric adoption. *Discover Artificial Intelligence*, *4*(1), 34.

Islam, M. T., Sepanloo, K., Woo, S., Woo, S. H., & Son, Y. J. (2025). A review of the industry 4.0 to 5.0 transition: Exploring the intersection, challenges, and opportunities of technology and Human–Machine collaboration. *Machines (Basel)*, *13*(4), 267.

Kanwal, P., Malik, P., Purty, J., Rawat, N., Randhawa, S. K., & Kaur, K. (2025). Redefining Work: Global Trends, Hybrid Models, and Strategies for Retaining Gen Z Talent in the Age of AI. In Global Work Arrangements and Outsourcing in the Age of AI (pp. 317-340). IGI Global Scientific Publishing.

Kolbjørnsrud, V. (2024). Designing the Intelligent Organization: Six principles for Human-AI collaboration. *California Management Review*, *66*(2), 44–64.

La Sala, A., Fuller, R., Riolli, L., & Temperini, V. (2024). The rise of hybrids: Plastic knowledge in human–AI interaction. *Journal of Knowledge Management*, *28*(10), 3023–3045.

Massaro, M., Secinaro, S., Bagnoli, C., & Calandra, D. (2025). Guest editorial: Artificial Intelligence (AI) for management decision-making processes. From measurement to strategy. *Management Decision*, *63*(10), 3213–3225.

Petrescu, M., & Krishen, A. S. (2023). Hybrid intelligence: Human–AI collaboration in marketing analytics. *Journal of Marketing Analytics*, *11*(3), 263–274.

Sağbaş, M., & Aydogan, S. (2025). Unveiling the Nuances: How Fuzzy Set Analysis Illuminates Passenger Preferences for AI and Human Agents in Airline Customer Service. *Tourism and Hospitality*, *6*(1), 43.

Singh, A. (2024). Quality of Work-Life Practices in the Indian Hospitality Sector: Future Challenges and Prospects. In Valeri, M., & Sousa, B. (Eds.), *Human Relations Management in Tourism* (pp. 208–224). IGI Global., DOI: 10.4018/979-8-3693-1322-0.ch010

Singh, A. (2025). Analysis of Perceptions on Employment of differently-abled People in the Indian Hotel Industry. *Pasos (El Sauzal)*, *23*(1), 167–183. DOI: 10.25145/j.pasos.2025.23.011

Singh, A., & Ansari, A. I. (2024). Role of Training and Development in Employee Motivation: Tourism and Hospitality Sector. In Mazurowski, T. (Ed.), *Enhancing Employee Motivation Through Training and Development* (pp. 248–261). IGI Global., DOI: 10.4018/979-8-3693-1674-0.ch011

Singh, A., & Hassan, S. C. (2024), "Identifying the Skill Gap in the Workplace and Their Challenges in Hospitality and Tourism Organisations", Thake, A.M., Sood, K., Özen, E. and Grima, S. (Ed.) Contemporary Challenges in Social Science Management: Skills Gaps and Shortages in the Labour Market (Contemporary Studies in Economic and Financial Analysis, Vol. 112B), Emerald Publishing Limited, Leeds, pp. 101-114. DOI: 10.1108/S1569-375920240000112B006

Singh, A., & Kumar, S. (2021). Identifying Innovations in Human Resources: Academia and Industry Perspectives. In Pathak, A., & Rana, S. (Eds.), *Transforming Human Resource Functions With Automation* (pp. 104–120). IGI Global.

Singh, A., & Kumar, S. (2024). Effective Talent Management Practices Implemented in the Hospitality Sector. In Christiansen, B., Aziz, M., & O'Keeffe, E. (Eds.), *Global Practices on Effective Talent Acquisition and Retention* (pp. 126–144). IGI Global., DOI: 10.4018/979-8-3693-1938-3.ch008

Singh, A., & Sihmar, P. (2025). Higher Education Institution Sustainability: Role of Green Human Resource Management. In Adu-Gyamfi, M., Boateng, F., & Atiku, S. (Eds.), *Green HRM Awareness and Training in Higher Education Institutions* (pp. 1–14). IGI Global Scientific Publishing., DOI: 10.4018/979-8-3693-2956-6.ch001

Singh, A., & Singh, V. K. (2022). The impact of ergonomic practices on housekeeping employee retention and efficiency in hotels during COVID-19 in India. Turyzm/Tourism, 32(2), 29–50. DOI: 10.18778/0867-5856.32.2.02

Singh, A., & Supina, S. (2024). Talent Acquisition and Retention in Hospitality Industry: Current Skill Gaps and Challenges. In Christiansen, B., Aziz, M., & O'Keeffe, E. (Eds.), *Global Practices on Effective Talent Acquisition and Retention* (pp. 363–379). IGI Global., DOI: 10.4018/979-8-3693-1938-3.ch020

Supina, S., & Singh, A. (2024). Exploring the Presence and Adoption of Quality of Work-Life Dimensions in the Hotel Industry? *African Journal of Hospitality, Tourism and Leisure*, *13*(2), 421–429. DOI: 10.46222/ajhtl.19770720.524

Thomas, A. (2024). Revolutionizing Events: Exploring the Seamless Integration of Robots in Hybrid and Virtual Experiences. In S. Kulshreshtha & C. Webster (Eds.), New Technologies in Virtual and Hybrid Events (pp. 19-46). IGI Global Scientific Publishing. DOI: 10.4018/979-8-3693-2272-7.ch002

Wang, P. Q., Yan, L., & Santoso, C. (2025). Generational engagement with AI in hospitality: human–AI interaction perspectives across the service process. *Current Issues in Tourism*, •••, 1–14.

Yawson, R. M., & Goryunova, E. (2025). Nested Complexity: A Conceptual Framework for Leveraging AI for Sustainable Organizations and Human Resource Development. *Advances in Developing Human Resources*, •••, 15234223251335908.

KEY TERMS AND DEFINITIONS

Cross-Functional Collaboration: It is a practice whereby people in various departments or functional areas (e.g., IT, HR, Operations) must share common objectives, and this is necessary to align technological implementation with human resource approaches and operational realities in a hybrid environment.

Emotional Intelligence (EI): The skill to recognize, utilize, and control personal feelings in constructive ways to alleviate stress levels, communicate efficiently, empathize with others, conquer obstacles and dissolve conflict - a human important skill that has been mentioned as a contrast to AI. To maintain the inclusiveness of the change management process, the manager ought to consider using an inclusive Change Management: A leadership model of organizational change that centers on open communication, participation of employees in change initiatives, psychological support and customized training whereby all the different groups within the working population feel supported and empowered through such a change management process.

Human-AI Blend: The collaborative paradigm is whereby human employees and artificial intelligence systems co-exist and collaborate to provide services, each bearing responsibility and exploiting the other to fulfill their individual strengths in an integrated operation system.

Human-Centered AI Integration: A strategic concept of integrating AI technology that emphasizes the needs, well-being, and empowerment of the human employee, so that AI systems are created to supplement and not substitute human abilities.

Hybrid Hospitality: An innovative business model in the hospitality sector that effectively incorporates AI-based automation and technology with traditional human-based service and touchpoints to help businesses be more efficient, more personalized, and guest-centric.

Role Reengineering: This is the planned process of redesigning job roles and job accountabilities within an organization, usually as a reaction to technological alterations, with the objective of streamlining performance, taking advantage of new instruments, and diversifying employee input, putting a premium on high-order tasks.

Skill Gaps: This is a difference between the skills that current employees of an organization currently have and the skills that they need to perform their duties in a new or altered environment especially with the emergence of new and sophisticated technologies such as AI.

Upskilling/Reskilling-Upskilling: is the process of imparting new skills to existing employees (upskilling) to better their existing job or of acquiring new skills altogether (reskilling) to be prepared to undertake other jobs in the same organization, frequently due to technological change.

Workforce Challenges: This is a set of complications and challenges that the employees and management of an organization would encounter during a major shift, e.g. the implementation of new technologies, including skills gaps, resistance to change, and new roles.

Chapter 13 Green HRM in the Era of AI-Enabled Hybrid Workplaces: Theoretical Perspectives and Research Trends Toward Sustainable Development

Chandni Rani
https://orcid.org/0009-0009-0806-6147
Galgotias University, Greater Noida, India

Pooja Kansra
https://orcid.org/0000-0003-2229-0662
Lovely Professional University, India

ABSTRACT

Rapid adoption of artificial intelligence and the expansion of hybrid work models are reshaping how HR functions operate and how sustainability initiatives are implemented. This chapter explores the intersection of AI-enabled HR systems, hybrid workplace structures, and GHRM practices, and examines their collective role in supporting sustainable organizational development. Drawing on existing theoretical perspectives and recent research trends, the chapter highlights how green recruitment, training, performance management, employee empowerment, reward systems. It also discusses the organizational, technological, and behavioral challenges associated with implementing GHRM in dynamic work environments. By integrating sustainability, digital transformation, and human-centered management

DOI: 10.4018/979-8-3373-5871-0.ch013

ht © 2026, IGI Global Scientific Publishing. Copying or distributing in print or electronic forms without written permission of IGI Global Scientific Publishing is prohibited. Use of this chapter to generative artificial intelligence (AI) technologies is expressly prohibited. The publisher reserves all rights to license its use for generative AI training and machine learning model development.

perspectives, the chapter offers a comprehensive framework for understanding how organizations can design future-ready HR systems that promote environmental responsibility while maintaining employee well-being and organizational resilience.

1. INTRODUCTION

The increased emphasis on environmental sustainability has basically altered the manner in which organizations design and administer their human resource practices. Green Human Resource Management (GHRM) has also become a strategic practice that has integrated ecological responsibility at the HR management level and activities of the organization in day-to-day human management. In contrast to considering sustainability as a corporate program, GHRM incorporates environmental reasoning into the recruitment and training processes, performance appraisal, rewards program, and employee involvement procedures. GHRM helps organizations to keep business performance and long-term ecological accountability connected by promoting green practices among employees and helping them develop a workplace culture that orientates towards sustainability (Masood, 2018). During the last 20 years, the global business ecosystem has gone through a sharp transformation to the models of operation oriented at achieving sustainability. The idea of a green economy, circular business, environmentally conscious production, and sustainable development have become a rising trend as organizations react to the escalating environmental threats, regulatory demands and growing stakeholder scrutiny and pressure. The agendas of sustainability have been further supported by the urgency factor within the corporate governance and managerial decisions, through the international structures, especially the Sustainable Development Goals (SDGs) by the United Nations (Agenda 2030) (Chamsa and Garcia-Blandon, 2019). With the ever-increasing rate of climate change, biodiversity decline, and water shortage as well as carbon emissions that organizations have continuously implemented, they are increasingly being forced to embrace sustainability-oriented approaches in their management practices instead of mere token compliance to an organization transformation. Previous studies have proven that, multidimensional value is created as a result of environmentally responsible organizational strategies. Companies that are actively involved in sustainability practices tend to enjoy better corporate image, increased investor trust, better stakeholder confidence, operating economies of scale, and increased competitive advantage in the long-run (Christmann, 2000; Shrivastava, 1995). HRM has been identified to play especially a critical role in this wider sustainability agenda. Human resources systems affect the attitudes, skill building and behavior of performance, and cultural norms and place HRM at the center point as a lever to institutionalizing sustainability in the organizational routines (Jackson and Seo, 2010). Opatha and Arulrajah (2014) affirm that GHRM is a systematic arrangement of policies and practices that strive to inspire their employees to be keen on environmental stewardship at the same time addressing their effectiveness in the organization. This strategic role of GHRM has been amplified even further in the emerging economies like India where fast economic growth, demographic surge and digitalization are being accompanied with the alarming environmental issues. The young workforce with a high number of individuals provides scope to combine sustainability goals with the current HR activities like online paperwork, online teamwork, and workflow mechanisms that consume less resources. Researchers opine that HR practices that are sustainability based can help in achieving the objectives of a country to develop environmentally friendly behavior towards the workforce, lessen reliance of an organization in paper-based operations, as well as boost efficiency in operations by green innovation (Pham et al., 2020; Mishra, 2017). Empirical research also suggests that GHRM has been associated with greater engagement of employees, organizational commitment, less turnover intentions, greater job satisfaction, and creation of organizational cultures that are sustainable in nature (Renwick et al., 2013; Mousa and Othman, 2020). These results place GHRM more than as an environmental measure, but rather as a strategic HR capability that enhances the long-term organizational resilience and social legitimacy. Simultaneously organizations are going through radical structural change in the organization and performance of work. The introduction of hybrid work arrangements has radically changed the conventional workplace boundaries. Flexible work arrangements such as hybrid work models that provide employees with flexible on-site and remote work have become a shift in temporary crisis solutions to permanent organizational patterns. This trend is a reflection of what is occurring in the large scale employee expectations related to flexibility, autonomy, and work-life elements. Hybrid work environments change communication habits, collaboration models, leadership behaviors, and performance management systems and they demand an organisation to revamp traditional ways of HR processes. Lauring and Jonasson (2025) theorize hybrid work as a multidimensional scale of attachments, work modality, spatial, and temporal coordination, which have complicated implication of organizational regulation and HR design.

Along with these shifts in the structure of work, there is now the emergence of the transformative technological force of Artificial Intelligence (AI), which changes the HR role. The application of AI-based systems is becoming more widespread in recruitment, talent management, workforce analytics, and learning and development, employee engagement monitoring, and performance evaluation. Recent bibliometric data show that AI-HRM studies and practice are growing quickly in recent years, specifically after 2016, as such themes as automation, predictive analytics, and employee experience personalization have become predominant strategic agenda points (Úbeda-Garcia et al., 2025). These technologies can help organizations to shift towards information-based HR decision-making, ensure the accuracy of workforce planning, lessen the administrative burden, and increase the scalability of HR processes. Notably, the organizational sustainability targets are also quite well aligned with the adoption of AI. Digital Hr tools limit the use of paper-based documents, cut down physical movement in relation to recruitment and training procedures, facilitate remote work, and streamline the use of resources with predictive analytics. In that regard, AI does not only increase the efficiency of operations but also aids the responsibility of the organization environmentally wise. Properly aligned with the GHRM goals, AI can become the catalyst of sustainability performance enhancement, as the green principles are introduced into the daily HR procedures. The intersection of AI-driven HRs and hybrid workplace systems presents a novel organizational ecosystem to the GHRM practices that can be redesigned and intensified. To demonstrate, AI-based green recruitment allows conducting a virtual interview, screening resumes automatically, and providing digital onboarding solutions, which will greatly contribute to the decrease of the use of paper and to the minimization of carbon emission caused by traveling. Equally, AI-based learning systems can achieve ongoing sustainability training of workforces geographically spread, reducing the environmental impact of the physical training infrastructure. Digital performance management systems also enable organizations to incorporate environmental sustainability indicators in the employee appraisal systems which can provide real time feedback to reinforce environmentally responsible conduct (Mishra & Barik, 2024). This integration also has an impact on the organizational culture and identity not only in the manner of improving operations. Employing the sustainability goals into the AI-based HR systems, employees will feel that the organization has an environmentally responsible approach and is willing to embrace the approach that is seen as more of the organizational perception than a separate initiative. Hybrid workplaces intensify this to an even greater extent, as they promote the use of digital collaboration tools facilitating knowledge sharing, innovation and sustainable work across company boundaries. Since employees are gradually becoming more purpose-minded, the kind of organization that is able to incorporate sustainability in the digital HR systems are better placed to attract and maintain environmentally aware talent. But complex ethical, social, and organizational issues are also brought about by the growing use of AI and digital monitoring technologies. The issues connected to the privacy of data, discrimination in the algorithms, the lack of transparency in the automated decision-making, surveillance of the employees, and technostress can now be considered the primary concerns of the modern HR discourse (Úbeda-Garcia et al., 2025). The situations are especially relevant to those working in a hybrid format when workers have to engage closely with digital technology platforms and remote surveillance tools. In the absence of proper governance structures, the implementation of AI can undermine the trust in an employee, diminish the views of fairness and adversely influence the psychological health. Therefore, the development of responsible AI should be characterized by the clarity of system design, ethics, ongoing employee training and development, and effective organizational control systems. Besides that, AI-enabled Green HRM alters the way organizations assess the performance of sustainability. Most of the traditional sustainability measures focus on the operational measures of energy consumption, a reduction in waste, and the reporting of emissions. Nonetheless, the human aspect of sustainability such as involvement of employees in the green programs, development of green skills, behavior modifications, and employee health are areas where more complex methods must be used. New opportunities emerge with AI-powered HR analytics to capture real-time behavioral indicators linked to sustainability since organizations are able to transcend beyond static reporting to dynamic sustainability performance management. New organizational capabilities also have to be established because of the combination of AI, hybrid work, and GHRM. HR professionals are becoming more anticipated as sustainability strategists, agents of digital transformation, and custodians of ethical technology. Such a change necessitates employing active upskilling in data analytics, AI literacy, sustainability models, and responsible technology governance. Leadership commitment is also a key measure that would ascertain sustainability and ethical AI use to become part of organizational culture, especially in hybrid work settings where only a few physical interactions are possible but digital communication prevails. Although the more and more scholars are interested in Green HRM, AI-based HR systems, or hybrid work forms, the research streams are typically analyzed separately. The current GHRM research is mostly oriented at traditional organizational context, whereas AI-HRM research usually prefers efficiency, automation and performance optimization results without redundantly addressing environmental sustainability aspects. Equally, the literature of hybrid work majorly focuses on the flexibility and productivity performance, but this provides limited information about the sustainability-oriented HR practices. This fragmented research situation supports the necessity to develop a comprehensive conceptual approach that addresses the ways the use of AI based hybrid working environment can facilitate the progress of Green HRM and sustainability of organizational development. It is against this backdrop that this present chapter attempts to discuss how Artificial Intelligence intersects with hybrid workplace model, and Green Human Resource Management. Combining the perspectives of sustainability management, digital HRM and future-of-work studies, the chapter should make a significant impact on building a thorough perspective of how organizations can realize future-oriented HR systems that can be both technologically advanced, environmentally responsible, and human-oriented. By doing so, the chapter adds to the scholarly and practical contribution in the field of management by providing strategic information on how a resilient, sustainable, and digitally enabled organization can be constructed.

2. GREEN HUMAN RESOURCE MANAGEMENT (GHRM) OPERATIONS

Behavioral Human Resource Management studies indicate that the attitudes of the employees, motivation and behavior at the work place are of great importance to the outcome of organizational sustainability. The practices of GHRM are at the center of determining such behavioral outcomes through institutionalizing environmental responsibility within HR formal systems. Hameed et al. (2020) empirically show that green employee behavior is greatly contributed by GHRM practices, which align the organizational policies with the sustainability objectives. Another similarity is that the two authors (Ahmad, 2015; Ayeswarya, 2017) emphasize that the efficacy of GHRM may be interpreted in terms of three complementary processes: (1) employee empowerment, (2) green performance outcomes improvement and (3) the way employee is involved in the sustainability initiative. All these mechanisms contribute to making Green Employee Empowerment (GEE) more efficient because they make employees sensitive to topics of environmental responsibility and promote the incorporation of environmentally friendly solutions into the everyday workflow. The conceptualization provided by Ramasamy (2017) explains such a relationship through demonstrating how GHRM practices facilitate the capability, motivation, and opportunity of employees to initiate environmentally responsible behavior. AI-powered HR systems and a hybrid workplace enable such associations to expand their sustainability practices in geographically dispersed teams in digitally transformed organizations (Mishra and Barik, 2024; Úbeda-Garcia et al., 2025).

The discussion on the operational dimensions of GHRM is below.

2.1 Green Recruitment

Green recruitment will be the point at which sustainability values are instilled in the culture of the organisation. It is concerned with minimizing the environmental implication in hiring, and acquires new employees with sustainability oriented skills. According to Sachin and Aradhana (2019), green recruitment is a paperless recruitment approach that focuses on less environmental impact because of the utilization of digital platforms, online application systems, and even virtual interviews. In addition to efficiency on the environment, there is the alignment strategic role of green recruitment. In their argument, Renwick et al. (2013) state that sustainability-related ability to be incorporated into job analysis and role specifications may comprise of familiarity with renewable energy systems, waste management initiatives, environmental compliance regulations, eco-design principles, and sustainable supply chain administration. This will make the process of environment responsibility to be incorporated into the workforce criteria as opposed to an afterthought. Recruitment sites made so by AI also enhance the idea of green hiring, by hiring based on predictive matchmaking of the candidate, automatic screening of resumes and hosting virtual interviews. All these tools can cut the administrative load, decrease travel-related emissions and speed up the process of recruitment (Mishra & Barik, 2024). It is essential to note, however, that researchers indicate that algorithm transparency and ethical governance have a significant part to play to prevent any bias and promote fairness in AI-based recruiting (Úbeda-Garcia et al., 2025).

2.2 Green Orientation and Development

Green orientation and macro-training are fundamental towards developing sustainability politics in organizations. It is observed that companies are gradually moving away the outdated classroom-based training to online learning platforms that minimise use of physical resources and energy usage. The goals of green training programs are to create awareness to employees regarding issues of environmental concern and to acquire technical and behavioral skills of environmental practices through sustainability practices (Manzoor et al., 2019). Such types of programs are usually aimed at managing energy efficiency, reducing mediation, and using clothing water conservation, adopting renewable energy, green manufacturing, circular economy, and eco-innovation. Sustainability-driven training programs also contribute to employee engagement and build organizational brand in terms of an indication of organizational commitment to environmental responsibility according to Al-Abbadi (2021). Another significant element of green orientation is leadership development. Managers and top leaders are also educated to incorporate sustainability issues into the strategic decision-making models, operational planning and performance management models. The AI-based learning management systems also contribute to increasing the effectiveness of training by facilitating learning with a customized path, virtual sustainability courses, and constant knowledge advancement in hybrid-based workplaces (Úbeda-García et al., 2025).

2.3 Green Performance Management and Appraisal

Green performance management is an implementation of environmental goals in the employee assessment mechanisms. The green performance appraisal systems acknowledge the employees acting in commitment towards the sustainability processes like energy conservation, reduction of waste, eco-innovation, and the utilization of resources in a responsible manner. These reward systems can take the form of financial rewards, promotions, career development, or even appreciation of the environmental contribution in front of the general public. Renwick et al. (2013) also stress that integrating sustainability indicators into performance evaluation systems is an indicator of the firm being strongly committed to environmental responsibility. Such performance indicators as carbon emission reduction activities, contribution to eco-innovation, resource efficiency improvement and involvement in sustainability programs are also becoming performance measures. Performance management systems that are based on AI enable an organization to monitor performance indicators related to sustainability in real time. Digital dashboards facilitate processes of evaluating and future feedbacking in the form of data. Ramgolam et al., (2025), however, warn that over digital monitoring can compound workload and technostress even within the hybrid working environment. Consequently, the performance management systems should reflect accountability and the well-being of employees, as well as protection of their privacy.

2.4 Green Employee Empowerment (GEE) and Participation

Green Employee Empowerment (GEE) is the perceived employee independence, opportunities to participate in making decisions affecting sustainability and influence. When employees are empowered, chances of them becoming proactive in environmental programs are higher and so they are more committed to the organization. Simpson and Samson (2010) discover that empowered employees make superior contributions towards the eco-friendly innovation and organizational sustainability programs. Making employees entitled to the information of sustainability, decision-making, as well as collective platforms assist in making people own the environmental responsibility. Mixed working conditions also increase empowerment through the possibility of making decisions on a decentralized basis and through online collaboration. Idea management systems and sustainability portals using AI work to suggest, provide, and engage in cross-functional sustainability projects across geographical boundaries.

2.5 Green Rewards and Remuneration

Green reward and remuneration frameworks help to strengthen the behavior that has a sustainability orientation by associating incentives to the outcome of environmental performance. The use of digital payroll and compensation systems in many organizations has minimized the amount of paper, as well as administration waste. Rewards that can be provided based on the sustainability can relate to performance bonuses based on the green targets, reward programs related to eco-innovation, and the reward can be inspired by non-financial values such as flexible working schedules to reduce commuting emissions. Mousa and Othman (2020) show that green reward systems are very useful in motivating the workers and fostering sustainability-based organizational cultures. Compensation packages that use AI also help in enhancing openness and competence since reward distributions are automated according to set sustainability figures. Nevertheless, the organizations should maintain transparency of the appraisal criterion and ethical management to retain the trust of employees. The second strategy that they can pursue is to collaborate with Green Organizations and Sustainability Networks. The planned partnerships with environmental organizations, NGOs focusing on sustainability, institutions of higher learning, and industry networks reinforce the organizational GHRM efforts. Through these partnerships there is accessibility to sustainability conscious talent bases, growth of sustainability training, and common environmental projects. It is also through collaboration that organizations build on their legitimacy and credibility through showing real commitment with sustainability stakeholders.

2.6 Partnering with Green Organizations and Sustainability Networks

The second strategy that should be implemented is collaborating with Sustainability Networks and Green Organizations. Alliance with environmental organizations, NGOs -sustainability oriented, academic institutions and Industry networks fortify organizational GHRM efforts. These joint ventures access clean-conscience pools of talent, co-created sustainability training programs and shared sustainability projects. Collaborations also improve the legitimacy and credibility of organizations in that they show active involvement of the organizations with the sustainability stakeholders.

2.7 Integration with Conceptual Framework

The paper will be correlated with the conceptual framework and will make sure that its consistency to its major principles is maintained. In line with the suggestive conceptual framework, GHRM practices will serve as the mediating variable that AI-based hybrid workplaces impact sustainability. The HR infrastructure based on AI and the hybrid workplace environments contribute to the effectiveness of green recruitment and training, performance management, empowerment, rewards, and external collaboration practices in collaboration. The strength of the relations between AI adoption, the implementation of GHRM, and the outcomes of sustainability is conditioned by the moderating effect of responsible AI governance and leadership commitment (Ubeda-Garcia et al., 2025). In cases where ethical protection, transparency tools, and leadership possessiveness are high, AI-enabled GHRM activities are more likely to produce favorable environmental, social, and organizational performances. Finally, according to the framework it is the combination of the technological capabilities, flexible work structures, and green HR practices that allow the sustainable performance of organizations when they are not applied separately but with each other.organizational performance outcomes. Ultimately, the framework suggests that sustainable organizational performance is achieved when technological capabilities, flexible work structures, and green HR practices are strategically aligned rather than implemented independently.

Table 1. Integration of GHRM Practices, AI Enablers, and Sustainability Outcomes

GHRM Practice	AI Enablers in Hybrid Workplaces	Sustainability Outcomes
Green Recruitment	AI resume screening, virtual interviews, applicant tracking systems	Reduced paper usage, lower carbon emissions, sustainability-aligned talent acquisition
Green Orientation & Development	AI learning platforms, personalized training modules, virtual workshops	Improved sustainability skills, reduced training-related energy consumption
Green Performance Management	AI dashboards, real-time sustainability metrics, predictive analytics	Improved environmental performance, accountability, continuous improvement
Green Employee Empowerment	Digital collaboration tools, AI idea management systems	Higher employee engagement, innovation in sustainability practices
Green Rewards & Remuneration	Automated compensation systems, sustainability-linked incentive analytics	Stronger motivation for green behavior, transparent reward systems
Green Partnerships	Digital collaboration platforms, data-sharing networks	Expanded sustainability impact, cross-sector environmental collaboration

3. GREEN HRM AND SUSTAINABLE DEVELOPMENT

Given the significance of paperless work systems and pro-environment offices, this specific section will be essential in this study. One of the most obvious sustainability efforts on the current offices is the incorporation of pro-environment practices. Paperless office systems are digital based whereby documents are stored using cloud storage, electronic approvals, virtual communication platforms among others with a significant reduction in the usage of papers. Studies indicate that not only do paperless work processes save forest resources, but it also enhances operational efficiency and availability of data (Sachin and Aradhana, 2019). Regarding the GHRM concept, the paperless offices foster the environmental friendliness of the employees by promoting the digital working habits, CPs would use less physical documentation. A further enhancement of sustainable working practices is online recruitment, electronic payroll systems, online training, and virtual performance appraisals (Mishra and Barik, 2024).

3.1 Conserving Energy

Conservation of energy is one of the best sustainability strategies that organizations have implemented. To minimize carbon footprints in its operations, many companies have GoPro to use energy-saving lighting systems, smart energy-efficient technologies, low-energy consuming electrical appliances. The International Energy Agency (2022) claims that building management can not only decrease energy use in commercial buildings by up to 30-60 percent with energy efficiency technology. Indian firms including Tata Motors have ventured on electric vehicle production and compressed natural gas (CNG) to minimize the use of fossil fuels and promote the system of transportation with low emission. Through these projects, it is possible to see how corporate sustainability measures can be realised to open up to wider consumption patterns in society, as opposed to particular internal functions.

3.2 Green Printing and Digital Documentation

Green printing programs are aimed at reducing physical printing when switching to an online system of documents, e-contracts, e-statements, and electronic certificate systems. Electronic records minimize the level of paper wastes, storage needs, and efficient ways of retrieving information (Renwick et al., 2013). Under the HR perspective, digital documentation facilitates the operations under sustainable HR, as it allows online employee records, electronic performance management systems, and online training materials. The practices also ease the burden on the administration and enhance eco-friendly organization habits.

3.3 Green Building and Sustainable Infrastructure

Green buildings have come to be a significant element of corporate sustainability policies. This type of building has included energy efficient lighting systems, rain water harvesting systems and natural ventilation systems and sustainable building construction material. The studies show that besides conserving resources, green buildings can also enhance employee well-being and productivity due to the ability to create healthier interiors (World Green Building Council, 2021). Such frameworks as Global Reporting Initiative (GRI) have been implemented by organizations like ONGC to improve their transparency and stakeholder engagement and reinforce their environmental accountability. Sustainability in the investment of infrastructure is also an indication of long-term organizational compliance towards environmental responsibility.

3.4 Resource Optimization and Water conservation

The water shortage has become a major sustainability threat to industrial organizations. Some examples of effective water management practices are the presence of leakage sensors in water management, recycling of wastewater, optimization in processes and the infrastructures of rainwater harvesting. Tata motors has embraced Water footprint Network approaches in keeping track and managing the water usage within manufacturing plants and ONGC has also been awarded nationally due to its big water conservation initiatives. These initiatives do not only minimise the amount of water used during operations, but also influence the employees to behave responsibly in the usage of water, which enhances the GHRM role in instilling sustainability awareness among the employees at work.

3.5 Recycling and Waste Management Practices

Waste management and recycling programs are also very important to facilitate the central economic ideas of relying on the raw materials that can be recycled, avoiding the reliance on a virgin one, and they also contribute to the environmental pollution reduction. ITC has also introduced joint waste recycling schemes on carbon, water, and solid waste management and ITC Hotels are all too well known to run responsible environments as far as hospitality businesses are concerned. Other companies like Mamaearth campaign about plastic recycling that increases awareness to the consumer and helps them use plastic to package products in a sustainable manner. In the same regard, Maruti Suzuki has also introduced recycling initiatives to allow reprocessing of the manufacturing waste as well as the reuse of recycled water in the manufacturing plants. These efforts provide insights into the ways sustainability activities may be incorporated as part of business and they do not constitute isolated environmental initiatives.

3.6 Energy Integration of Electricity Preservation and Renewable Energy

Due to these increases, organizations are more willing to conserve electricity through encouraging energy saving habits in the employees, and through investment in renewable energy facilities. Use of smart and energy monitoring systems, rooftop solar panels, natural-light optimization and natural building design can minimize the use of electricity and carbon emissions. Conservation energies are based on the idea of responsible usage of the existing resources, not stealing it to its full extent (IEA, 2022). Within GHRM viewpoint, electricity conservations can still be enhanced through employee awareness programs and sustainability trainings that promote responsible workplace actions by employees. In Australia, rainwater harvesting initiatives are encouraged in rural regions to maintain water supplies during periods of drought.

3.7 Rainwater Harvesting

Rainwater harvesting is a new sustainability activity that has been a popular trend among Indian corporate campuses. Tata Motors has installed massive rainwater harvesting systems and ground water recharge reservoirs at manufacturing plants. Infosys has put up recharging wells and rooftop harvesting to aid groundwater and irrigation. ITC limited, Mahindra and Hindustan Unilever Limited (HUL) are companies that have also invested in rain water harvesting infrastructure due to the need to limit reliance on municipal water supply. The initiatives help in ensuring long term water security besides enhancing corporate environmental stewardship.

3.8 Tree Plantation and conservation of biodiversity

Tree plantation programs are high impact and visible programs of sustainability that companies take. The farm forestry projects of ITC have helped to green close to 142,000 hectares of land besides helping the rural people sustain their livelihoods. In a comparable initiative, Mamaearth campaign titled Plant Goodness tries to incorporate one million trees with the help of NGOs. Tata Motors has set up plantation programs, which associate soil sapling planting with vehicle sales. These programs help in conserving biodiversity, capturing carbon and involving communities, as well as motivating employees to participate in environmental initiatives.

4. CHALLENGES OF GREEN HUMAN RESOURCE MANAGEMENT

Despite the fact that GHRM has gained considerable popularity as a significant avenue, which organizations are likely to sustain their operations, implementing the concept of green HR in a daily routine is not that easy. Most organizations have difficulties in transitioning the intentions to sustainability into actual behavioural change in the workplace. This loophole is present due to the fact that GHRM does not merely presuppose new policies and technologies but profound changes in the mentality of employees and the behavior of leaders as well as in the organizational culture (Renwick et al., 2013).

Organization changes in employee habits have been labeled as one of the most immediate challenges facing organizations. The habits in the work place concerning the use of print, energy, commuting, and the resources are usually deeply entrenched. It is not realistic to expect employees to start behaving in an environmentally friendly manner at once. It is also demonstrated that employees can be reluctant to embrace green initiatives at the start of the business since they believe that this will be an extra burden or a change that will cause them to alter their working habits (Hameed et al., 2020). This opposition is more prominent when sustainability programs are unveiled without proper communication and participation of employees. This forces the need to have long-term behavioral change through sustained leadership support and regular awareness programs. Another primary obstacle is the test of cultural change. Creating a sustainability-based organizational culture is a slow process that involves balancing such aspects as values, leadership behavior, HR systems, and the daily management process. Ahmad (2015) points out that when sustainability is confined to the policy documents or corporate reports, the sustainability values are not internalized by the employees. Green initiatives cannot be sustained by a token commitment by the leadership and not reinforced on a regular basis by HR practices, they will become symbolic instead of being meaningful. Organizations must therefore take the time and effort to establish cultures that embrace environmental responsibility as one of the aspects of how work is done and not an activity. There are also practical challenges of recruitment.

Although green recruitment seeks to hire individuals who are environmental conscious, it is not always feasible to find an individual who has technical skills and environmental awareness. There is a shortage of enough professionals in most labor markets that specialize in environmental management, renewable energy, and sustainability analytics, and regulatory compliance areas (Renwick et al., 2013). Moreover, there is an intensification of competition in the skill of sustainability talent with more organizations employing green strategies. This tends to cause lengthening recruitment processes and increase in recruitment expenses. Another complicated problem is the measurement of sustainability performance at the employee level. Environmental performance may be hard to measure unlike the traditional performance measures like sales targets or productivity measures. It is necessary to devise measurement systems to assess the role of a particular employee in conserving energy, decreasing waste, or original innovations that are environmentally friendly (Mousa and Othman, 2020). Most organizations find it difficult to deploy equitable and open sustainability measures that are able to measure individual contribution as well as group contribution without placing undue administrative strain. The matter of measuring behavioral change is closely connected with performance measurement. Although organizations may implement green training programs and create awareness policies, it is not always evident that it causes permanent green behavior in the organization.

The interactions between employees are susceptible to various factors, among which there are personal values, peer norms, leadership signals, and workplace culture (Hameed et al., 2020). This complicates the separation of the direct effect of GHRM practices, and necessitates feedback and constant monitoring. Another factor that makes GHRM implementation difficult is the financial constraints. Numerous green projects require considerable initial expenses, e.g. infrastructure upgrades, the implementation of renewable energy technologies, and acquisition of environmentally friendly equipment. Even though such investments can result into long term cost-saving in terms of increased efficiency and reduction in the resource-consumption, organizations fear to take the risks as it may result in uncertainty concerning short term financial returns (Shrivastava, 1995). The smaller organizations and startups have even more difficulty as they have fewer financial resources. This financial challenge is noted by the use of renewable energy solutions, especially the use of solar power systems. The cost of installing solar panels, altering infrastructure and sustainability of renewable energy systems is costly in the initial investment. Although such costs can be offset with government incentives and long-term energy savings, the viability of such undertakings and beneficial return on investments requires careful consideration before any organization gamble on them (IEA, 2022). The contextual problems are particularly apparent in the emerging economies. In other countries like India, a good percentage of the workforce resides in either the rural or semi-urban areas where the traditional working practice is still dominant. The GHRM practices are not readily applied to a large group of people because of limited digital infrastructure, reduced environmental awareness, and unequal access to sustainability education (Mishra, 2017). These facts underscore the need to come up with contextualized green HR strategies as opposed to merely copying the sustainability models being practiced in the developed economies.

There is an additional layer of complexity because of the growing application of digital HR systems, artificial intelligence, and hybrid work arrangements. Although these technologies facilitate a paperless experience and remote sustainability training, issues of employee surveillance, data confidentiality, and algorithm discrimination as well as digital exhaustion are also brought up (Ubeda-Garcia et al., 2025). The need to engage employees and sustainability culture in hybrid working environments becomes a more complicated task since teams do not spend as much time together physically. Organizations should therefore come up with new digital leadership and communication approaches to make sustainability initiatives conspicuous and significant. Lastly, long term commitment to GHRM is something that is always difficult to maintain. When companies are facing a recession or reorganizing their structures to compete with the business environment, sustainability efforts tend to be in conflict with short-term business objectives. The absence of ongoing leadership engagement, observable accountability procedures, and alignment of the goals on sustainability and business strategy can mean that green HR activities slowly fade away (Jackson & Seo, 2010). On the whole, these issues indicate that the adoption of Green HRM is not a single initiative but a continuous change in the organisation. To be successful, a company must have patience, steadfastly supporting leadership, engagement of employees, investment in the development of capabilities, and introduction of sustainability as a part of every decision-making. Those organizations that view GHRM as a long-term cultural process and not solely as a compliance process stand a better chance to enjoy material and long term responsiveness.

5. CONCLUSION

GHRM is a long term change in the organization and not a short term managerial programme. Although it is not always possible to see the direct effect of GHRM practices, its overall impact on employee behavior, organizational culture, and performance in the environment becomes more pronounced with time. Incorporation of green practices in the recruitment, training, performance management, and reward systems are already underway in a lot of organizations, and this shows an increasing trend towards sustainability. Nevertheless, to produce significant and sustained results, GHRM should go beyond individual projects and go holistic in a manner that environmental responsibility is integrated throughout the entire HR processes.

Cultural fit and top management dedication are key to the success of the GHRM. To change the organizational culture towards sustainability, green values need to be reinforced on a regular basis by policies, leadership behavior and practice of day-to-day management. When sustainability is incorporated in the organizational identity and not as a point of compliance, the employees reduce the chances of internalizing green values and significantly contribute to the environmental agenda. This cultural migration is not immediate and should be a matter of lifelong learning, participation of employees and strategic commitment over long period. The effects of GHRM are further reinforced by its operational sustainability programs like implementation of renewable energy, use of rainwater harvesting, recycling programs, and production processes that are environmentally friendly. As these initiatives are combined with HR practices, employees receive the opportunities to directly engage in the process of sustainability, so the environmental responsibility becomes a common organizational mission. This kind of integration is also prone to the realization of global sustainability goals such as the United Nations Sustainable Development

Goals (UN SDGs) in the 2030 Agenda which focuses on responsible consumption, climate action, decent work, and sustainable industrial growth.

Change in HR management practices and workplace model is accelerated by the COVID-19 pandemic. Remote and hybrid work arrangements have become common, which has led to new possibilities to minimize commuting-based emissions, office energy usage, and flexible working organizations.

Simultaneously, the pandemic has also created some bonus problems associated with employee health, digital burnout, solitude, and work-life balance. Companies should thus weigh between HR practices based on technology and on humans. Sustainable HR systems require green employee engagement, psychological wellness, and work-life balance. In future, the incorporation of automated intelligence and hybrid work organization will keep on changing the design and implementation of GHRM. The AI-based HR may facilitate sustainability through better utilization of resources, the ability to track performance data-driven, and conducting sustainability training programs at scale. Nevertheless, effective governance, accountable technologies, and open decision making will become mandatory to make sure that the digital transformation will help to foster sustainability and profitability of the environment and society but not identities or the stress-related issues. Lastly, to have significant sustainability results, there must be concerted action. GHRM implementation in organizations cannot be done in isolation. The development of the sustainable ecosystems depends on the cooperation of the business leaders, employees, policymakers, and educational institutions with community stakeholders. As the stakeholders collaborate on common objectives on environmental matters, the GHRM is transformed into not a company practice but a societal phenomenon that leads to the overall planetary well-being.

6. IMPLICATIONS AND FUTURE SCOPE

The emerging trend of Green Human Resource Management has significant impacts not only to the organization but also to the employee, communities and the entire society. Its core is that GHRM warns organizations that being sustainable is not only a matter of saving energy or decreasing the amount of waste -it is building healthier, meaningful and more balanced work environments. High attention to the well-being of employees and the work-life balance is one of the most evident advantages of GHRM. Hybrid work, work-from-home, and compressed workweeks are a few examples of flexible work arrangements that enable employees to dedicate less time to work and other productive and personal activities. Such changes decrease the negative influence on the environment, as well as increase the quality of life and job satisfaction. On the managerial side, GHRM proposes that managers bring to mind the fact that they should not rely on the conventional models of command-and control but they ought to employ more responsible or people-oriented leadership styles. There is a growing demand on managers to strike a balance between the business achievement and sustainability objectives as well as the welfare of the employees. The transition necessitates such new skills as understanding sustainability, digital skills, making ethical decisions and being emotionally intelligent. Organizations that invest in leadership growth and sustainability educational programs have higher probabilities of building confidence, intensifying staff dedication and establishing long organizational endurance.

The implication of GHRM to a second significant point is that its effect is not limited within the boundaries of organizations. Sustainability activities can reach out to the supply chains and business relations. By persuading suppliers and vendors to use sustainable practices, the organizations produce a wave effect that spreads their sustainability to a greater extent. Even basic measures like choosing suppliers who are environmentally certified, lessening the amount of waste used in packaging, and encouraging responsible sourcing policies can have enormous effects on environmental performance on a value chain scale. GHRM also enhances corporate social responsibility agenda by integrating the concept of sustainability to daily HR activities. In terms of aligning recruitment, training, performance evaluation systems and rewards with sustainability objectives, CSR will be incorporated in organizational everyday life, instead of a special PR activity. This uniformity assists the organizations to develop the sense of credibility and authenticity to the customer, investors, staffing, and regulators. In terms of talent management, the commitment to sustainability by the organizations is also usually reflected in a better employer branding. A variety of employees today, particularly youthful professionals, are adorning themselves on employers whose moral tendencies are corresponding to their own. There are higher chances that companies with a focus in environmental responsibility and ethical conduct will attract motivated and purpose-oriented talent and maintain employees who wish to add to a meaningful work. This builds the reputation of the organization as time goes by and forms a cycle of engagement and performance. In the future perspective, it is expected that the future of GHRM will be affected by the technology. The digital HR platform, artificial intelligence, and data analytics provide the potent means to facilitate sustainability by enhancing efficiency, decreasing paperwork, promoting virtual collaboration, and assists in real-time tracking of sustainability performance.

Simultaneously, companies should be careful and accountable when utilizing technology. To ensure a high level of trust and well-being, it will be necessary to protect the privacy of employees, not overmonitor them, and make sure that AI will be used ethically. Constant learning and skill improvement is also going to become the future of GHRM. The emerging knowledge associated with climate change, green innovation, and circular economy practices and environmental risk management will be required by employees as sustainability issues are turning complex. The organizations that invest into the sustainability education and green skills development will be in a better position to adjust to the changes in regulations and market expectations. Support of policies will be very important in the new stage of adoption of GHRM. Organizations can be motivated to invest in green HR practices through government incentives, sustainability reporting guidelines and ESG regulations. As one of the solutions, collaboration between policymakers, educational organizations, and industry executives can aid in the development of training systems and certification programs that contribute to the creation of a sustainable workforce.

REFERENCES

Ahmad, S. (2015). Green human resource management: Policies and practices. *Cogent Business & Management*, *2*(1), 1030817.

Al-Abbadi, L. H. (2021). The effect of employee sustainable training on sustainable performance. *Journal of Management Information and Decision Sciences*, *24*(6), 1–12.

Ayeswarya, R. B. (2017). *A Study on Green Human Resource Management practices and its impact on organizations. International Journal of Advanced Research in Management, Architecture, Technology and Engineering*. IJARMATE.

Chamsa, J., & García-Blandón, J. (2019). On the importance of sustainable human resource management for the adoption of sustainable development goals. *Resources, Conservation and Recycling*, *141*, 109–122. DOI: 10.1016/j.resconrec.2018.10.006

Chamsa, N., & García-Blandón, J. (2019). On the importance of sustainable human resource management for the adoption of sustainable development goals. *Resources, Conservation and Recycling*, *141*, 109–122.

Christmann, P. (2000). Effects of "best practices" of environmental management on cost advantage: The role of complementary assets. *Academy of Management Journal*, *43*(4), 663–680. DOI: 10.2307/1556360

Hameed, Z., Khan, I. U., Islam, T., Sheikh, Z., & Naeem, R. M. (2020). Green HRM practices and employee environmental performance. *Journal of Cleaner Production*, *256*, 120123.

International Energy Agency. (2022). *World energy outlook*. IEA.

Jackson, S. E., & Seo, J. (2010). The greening of strategic HRM scholarship. *Organizational Management Journal*, *7*(4), 278–290.

Lauring, J., & Jonasson, C. (2025). What is hybrid work? Towards greater conceptual clarity of a common term and understanding its consequences. *Human Resource Management Review*, *35*(1), 101044. Advance online publication. DOI: 10.1016/j.hrmr.2024.101044

Manzoor, F., Wei, L., Bányai, T., Nurunnabi, M., & Subhan, Q. A. (2019). An examination of sustainable HRM practices on job performance: An application of training as a moderator. *Sustainability*, *11*(8), 2263.

Masood, A. (2018). Green human resource management: Policies and practices. *International Journal of Management Studies*, *5*(3), 12–20.

Mishra, A., & Barik, R. (2024). The role of artificial intelligence in augmenting green HRM for sustainable development: A bibliometric perspective. *Srusti Management Review, 17*(1), 117–126.

Mishra, P. (2017). Sustainable development in India: Challenges and opportunities. *The International Journal of Environmental Studies, 74*(2), 207–220. DOI: 10.1080/00207233.2016.1245678

Mishra, P. (2017, September). Green Human Resource Management: A framework for sustainable organizational development in an emerging economy. *The International Journal of Organizational Analysis.*

Mousa, S. K., & Othman, M. (2020). The impact of green human resource management practices on sustainable performance in organizations. *Journal of Cleaner Production, 243*, 118595. DOI: 10.1016/j.jclepro.2019.118595

Opatha, H. H. D. N. P., & Arulrajah, A. A. (2014). Green human resource management: Simplified general reflections. *International Business Research, 7*(8), 101–112. DOI: 10.5539/ibr.v7n8p101

Pham, N. T., Tučková, Z., & Jabbour, C. J. C. (2020). Greening the hospitality industry: How do green human resource management practices influence organizational citizenship behavior? *Tourism Management, 72*, 386–399. DOI: 10.1016/j.tourman.2018.12.005

Ramasamy, A. (2017). A Study on Implications of Implementing Green HRM in the Corporate Bodies with Special Reference to Developing Nations. *International Journal of Business and Management, 12*(9), 117.

Renwick, D. W. S., Redman, T., & Maguire, S. (2013). Green human resource management: A review and research agenda. *International Journal of Management Reviews, 15*(1), 1–14. DOI: 10.1111/j.1468-2370.2011.00328.x

Sachin, B. S., & Aradhana, N. M. (2019). Green Human Resource Management: Best practice of Attaining Sustainable Development Goals. *Journal of Emerging Technologies and Innovative Research, 6*(4), 15–23.

Shrivastava, P. (1995). Environmental technologies and competitive advantage. *Strategic Management Journal, 16*(S1), 183–200.

Simpson, D., & Samson, D. (2010). Environmental strategy and low waste operations: Exploring complementarities. *Business Strategy and the Environment, 19*(2), 104–118.

Úbeda-García, M., Marco-Lajara, B., Zaragoza-Sáez, P. C., & Poveda-Pareja, E. (2025). Artificial intelligence, knowledge and human resource management: A systematic literature review of theoretical tensions and strategic implications. *Journal of Innovation & Knowledge*, *10*, 100809. Advance online publication. DOI: 10.1016/j.jik.2025.100809

United Nations. (2015). *Transforming our world: The 2030 agenda for sustainable development.* United Nations General Assembly. https://sdgs.un.org/2030agenda

WCED. (1987). *Our common future*. Oxford University Press. World Green Building Council. (2021). *The business case for green buildings.*

Chapter 14

The Future of Gender Equality in Hybrid Workplace:
Ethical Implications and AI Governance in Workforce Management

Ashu
https://orcid.org/0009-0003-3322-8706
Lovely Professional University, India

Pooja Kansra
https://orcid.org/0000-0003-2229-0662
Lovely Professional University, India

Shyam Sunder Agrawal
Lovely Professional University, India

ABSTRACT

The integration of artificial intelligence (AI) and the hybrid work model changed the old style of work model by providing more job opportunities of remote work. This hybrid model is more flexible, increases employee's productivity, autonomy, and job satisfaction. This working model also raises opportunities for women and decreases the gender equality problem in organizations. The present study tries to understand the paradoxical role of AI and the hybrid work model system, shows how this integration increases gender equality, opportunities, and poses challenges for the hybrid model with the help of a gendered lens. It also helps to understand the importance of governance and AI in workforce development and management. It is

DOI: 10.4018/979-8-3373-5871-0.ch014

…nt © 2026, IGI Global Scientific Publishing. Copying or distributing in print or electronic forms without written permission of IGI Global Scientific Publishing is prohibited. Use of this chapter to …generative artificial intelligence (AI) technologies is expressly prohibited. The publisher reserves all rights to license its use for generative AI training and machine learning model development.

found out that gender equality did not depend only on policy flexibility but is also depends on responsibility, ethical use of AI, and a good framework in workforce governance.

1. INTRODUCTION

The hybrid work model transforms the traditional work culture into a new working procedure. Before the COVID-19 pandemic, hybrid mode of work was limited to only a few sectors and companies. During lockdown, many companies adopted this method of work, but after the pandemic, this working model became a common, popular, and standard way of work. The hybrid working model is a model of work in which workers can choose where they feel they work best. It's a flexible working method that balances remote and office work. Hybrid work permits employees to split their time between working in a physical office and working from another location. According to a report by Archie (2025) it was observed that 64 percent of leaders report that their organization use a hybrid model of work model that offers greater flexibility and independence for employees. Using these organizations is reducing expenses such as office space, electricity, the hybrid model, and furniture while boosting profits. Hybrid work provides transformative potential to further gender equality by breaking down structural barriers that have long hindered women's entry into the labour force. Hybrid work structure reduces the major barriers of place of employment, journey time, and routine office hours, which simplifies women in managing professional and personal life (Deloitte, 2024).

For women who have the caregiving responsibilities, hybrid work setups enable them to remain engaged in their careers without stepping away from the workforce. Additionally, this has historically contributed to wider gender gaps in career progression and earnings. Moreover, hybrid work models create new opportunities for women in rural and semi-urban areas, providing access to corporate jobs that were previously available mainly in urban regions. This supports greater inclusion and economic empowerment (IWWAGE, 2023).

Even after all these advantages, hybrid work raises the concern about, how equity in employees is managed (Choudhury et al., 2021). During the time of automation, AI is not only technology about it is an effective tool which help people to modify their group dynamics, way of doing work, and help them to develop their skills (Dheer & Pareek, 2025). The combination of hybrid work model with AI has a great potential to increase gender equality in workforce by providing flexibility in work and help them to increase their skills as required for the jobs. However, these advancements also bring new challenges in systems where biases, discrimination, and surveillance can occur, which will affect women and gender minorities. (International Labour Organization, 2021; World Economic Forum, 2023)

These technological advancements change the way firms handle their collaboration, planning, and task distribution, particularly for teams that are distributed across multiple locations (Davenport & Ronanki, 2018). A significant transition that promotes sustainability, accountability, and more control over technology in contemporary enterprises is the move toward hybrid work arrangements (World Economic Forum, 2023). In this regard, the discussion of gender equality is altered when artificial intelligence is included into mixed work environments. The advantage of drawback of AI is totally dependent on how they are used; AI-driven workforce data and performance reviews have the potential to either strengthen current disparities or advance justice (Cappelli et al., 2020).

2. IMPORTANCE OF GENDER EQUALITY IN THE EVOLVING WORKPLACE

Depending on the way they are introduced, flexible and hybrid work forms could be utilized to empower women or make them marginalized, thus throwing the spotlight again on the issue of gender equity. Hybrid work is normally conceptualized or promoted as a way of improving the balance between work and life, especially for women, who tend to perform excessive unpaid caring and household work (ILO, 2022). Flexible work forms, when used together with the promotion of the best possible workplace culture, could help women across all life or career circles gain increased labour force participation, career continuity, or overall happiness. Yet, hybrid work, unaccompanied by gender perspectives, could help accentuate gender, legitimize the absence of women's presence within the labour force, and restrict them from social capital and leadership positions. (Williams et al. 2023)

Gender equality is essential to change the workplace environment, as it is morally right also. In today's modern workplace promoting gender equality is a wise and ethically required approach. It is not only a matter of doing what is right, but also a wise business choice to ensure fair working conditions in different situations. Ensuring that everyone, regardless of their gender, has equal chances, support, and the ability to take part in making decisions can help eliminate long-standing problems that have negatively impacted women. Policies that effectively support gender equality led to greater teamwork and creativity. According to Betts (1990) and McKinsey & Company (2022), including a variety of people in a group leads to better problem-solving.

Bringing in people who have been sidelined, such as women, into the workplace can create a positive work environment that reflects the value of fairness. In this context, it can be said that the issue of gender differences, which are not addressed in policies related to learning opportunities in mathematics, may unintentionally be reinforced through the teaching of math-related ideas in many countries. These work environments often combine different elements, where employees may have different levels of access to support systems, whether through guidance from mentors or the availability of physical or online resources. For starters, women are among the group of individuals who are likely to find it harder to multitask while working from a distance and taking care of family and/or home responsibilities, compared to men, which could contribute disproportionally to their being held back in their profession, (Chung et al.,2021). Gender equality takes prominence since it formulates a strategic or ethical imperative for organizations. First, it mirrors the values of inclusiveness and fairness in the society in which it operates. The work environments increase employee retention rates, as well as happiness levels, thus creating an effective feedback loop of loyalty and productivity (Sharma & Sinha, 2022).

3. FROM FLEXIBILITY TO FAIRNESS: HYBRID WORK AND GENDER INCLUSION

The introduction of the mixed work system has improved gender equality. According to a study conducted by the International Workplace Group (IWG), 66% of women believe that working in hybrid relationships opens new career options, but 53% of women are more optimistic about getting promoted. Shell's opportunities for job growth are due to its increased flexibility. Additionally, the hybrid model has made women more inclusive in the workforce, according to over 70% of women with disabilities, suggesting that women feel included in organizational activities (IWG, 2022). Better work-life balance, which includes less travel expense and more time for personal interests, is also valued by 38% of respondents (ILO, 2023). Even though such flexibilities afford some advantages many benefits, but it does not substitute for Equal opportunity. When operating in a hybrid environment, there are several hurdles to overcome. In comparison to their office-going counterparts, whose members are usually men, women who opt for telecommuting opportunities more often may face issues of such as impaired visibility, fewer opportunities for advancement, and limited access to leadership networks (Mumford, 2024) Therefore, in addition to the apparent advantages of flexibility, firms must implement inclusive policies that guarantee fairness in promotion, pay, and recognition.

However, when AI systems are put together with equity, they provide hope for balancing the playing field by reducing biases in personal evaluations and providing data driven inclusion. Hybrid technology's transition from flexibility to fairness, the last phase in the process is to implement intentional governance structures that acknowledge the moral importance of gender inclusion (Yeke et al., 2024; Bearman et al., 2025). In keeping with that, it will include developing hybrid systems that facilitate women's multi-role balancing and provide them with the same opportunities as men to achieve, lead, and influence the future of work. Gender inclusivity is considered an essential element of the workforce strategy, which outlines how a company should operate, rather than being a result of flexible working arrangements. This approach integrates fairness into the core of the company's operations (Yeke et al., 2024). Despite the many benefits it offers, there are ethical concerns about using AI in workforce management. If the government does not develop proper policies for AI, it could lead to increased inequality for marginalized groups and women (Davenport & Miller, 2022). Laws related to transparency and regular audits are important in ensuring fairness and equality when using AI, helping to create equal opportunities and prevent unfair use of AI advantages, which is vital for maintaining gender inclusivity in a modern workplace that combines AI with a hybrid model (OECD, 2023).

4. GENDER EQUALITY CHALLENGES IN HYBRID WORK ENVIRONMENTS

Hybrid models at work offer promising aspects and challenges in the pursuit for achieving gender equality at work. The concept of flexible work arrangement enables women, and specifically those who are caregivers, by eliminating barriers that hindered them, thus enabling more women to join the workforce movement (Chung & van der Lippe, 2020). Conversely, hybrid models at work also contribute to gender inequality at workplaces as women are mostly involved in remote work that makes them underrepresented at the workforce. Moreover, these models ignore the fact that women are mostly barred from critical decision-making and indirectly eliminate the opportunities for women to network and climb up the promotional ladder (Adisa et al.,2022). Apart from these challenges, societal constructed gender roles also tend to underscore the disparities in undertaking home and caregiving responsibilities in remote working environments (Craig & Churchill,2021).

Although hybrid working has shown promise in promoting gender equality, inclusivity still depends on how organizations handle this cultural challenge. Women often take on caregiving responsibilities, which makes them more likely to choose remote work. However, as remote employees often get neglected in favour of office-based employees, this option might inadvertently encourage less committed employees. Although the presence in the organization has been shown to be related to work productivity and commitment, research proves that the views of the management on the matter are still largely conditioned by “face time” (Chung & van der Lippe,

2020; Fazackerley, 2021). The imbalanced distribution of resources in the hybrid work model is another hurdle. Remote employees may encounter limited chances for professional growth, mentorship, and career advancement (Craig & Churchill, 2021).

5. HARNESSING ARTIFICIAL INTELLIGENCE TO PROMOTE GENDER EQUITY IN HYBRID WORK ENVIRONMENTS

Artificial intelligence (AI) presents significant opportunities to enhance gender equality in contemporary hybrid work environments. A primary advantage is its ability to minimize human bias anonymizing in recruitment and advancement procedures by anonymizing applications using uniform assessment criteria, which restricts the impact of gender stereotypes (Raghavan et al., 2020). AI evaluation, similarly, compensation, and Career can identify the difference in progress and provide data-manual insights to organizations So that this dissatisfaction can be dealt with properly (Capley et al., 2020). In hybrid workplaces, AI technologies training, Development, and the help of remote employees, often women and professional caregivers, provide fair access to duties. AI evaluation, similarly, compensation, and Career can identify the difference in progress and provide data-manual insights to organizations so that this dissatisfaction can be dealt with properly (Capley et al., 2020). In mixed workplaces, AI methods training, development, and support of remote workers, often women and professional care provide proper access to duties in keeps the chances of career progress (World Economic Forum, 2023). Artificially scheduling and assignment work may rise equal opportunity by minimizing the over-the-top quantity of unpaid homework burdened by women (ILO, 2021). Further, AI makes inclusive business conduct in the workplace and supports accountability and transparency within decision-making (Bogen & Rieke, 2018). All these advantages come with a price: strict regulation, fair administration, and ethical design. But properly applied, it can eliminate structural barriers at work and create more equal opportunities for men and women in mixed workplaces.

6. ETHICAL GOVERNANCE OF AI FOR GENDER-INCLUSIVE HYBRID WORKPLACES

To create an inclusive workplace in the hybrid model of employment, we must pay particular attention to the control of artificial intelligence systems. According to a 2020 study by Raghavan et al., AI is making several in addition to the fact that refugees entering the local or remote team would suffer, the user will unintentionally impose segregation bias based on training data or by personnel in the hybrid environment, whether it is or is not (Bogen and Rieke, 2018). Full openness of AI decisions, placing the responsibility on executives, audits for any negative outputs, and frequent modifications to reduce or eliminate biases are all necessary for the creation of strong governance regimes (Cappelli et al., 2020). To ensure that the AI marriage with organizational goals was harmonious, it is paramount that key stake holders from HR, data scientists, and employee advocates have a say in the initial framework (World Economic Forum, 2023). To stop backdoor stigma like compromise of work distribution or disparity in promotions (ILO, 2021), continuous monitoring is essential technology can further be used to support women and minorities career opportunities, through equal representation efforts and helping out with impediments in hybrid workplace practices by enforcing oversight with ethical principles that therefore Allowing genderized friendly AI for robotics in ensuring a nontoxic and fair resulting in the development of more corporate and organizational based end to end equities.

Conclusively, the practice of responsible AI governance thus becomes a central part of organization's workforce management system in conclusion Organizational advancement in gender equality within AI- driven hybrid jobs work system demands a coordinated strategy that incorporate ethical technology, policy inclusions and work based organization should be willing to honest to end audits, the introduction of anonymized candidate portfolios, and implementing fairness-constrained techniques to avoid discriminatory outcome (Raghavan et al., 2020; Bogen & Rieke, 2018). Creating equal access to mentoring, growth opportunities, and the chance to advance in leadership for remote and in-office employees is a strategy that can assist in reducing propinquity bias for the AI-driven fixing of fringes moved by force and pay and appropriations between the workers in the settlement (World Economic Forum, 2023), To make headway with the organizations goals with the use of technology AI governance needs to be part of conversations held by all stakeholders which include HR teams, the data scientist, employees (ILO, 2021). Frequent audits and employee feedback techniques guarantee that companies are fulfilling all policy modification criteria. By implementing strategic, ethical AI allowed decisions making and promoting target-driven methods of defining employee's interaction phases, hybrid workplaces can pull technology to increase productivity and promote equitable career improvement, inclusivity, and a gender-friendly, supportive work environment (Ashok et al., 2025).

For the aspect of governing the issue of using AI for achieving gender equity within the context of the hybrid work environment, there is a need for robust institutional frameworks that integrate ethical principles of the use of AI with policy frameworks on gender equity and labor law. Companies should carry out gender impact assessments before using AI systems, create committees with diverse expertise to oversee AI initiatives, and put in place ways to hold people accountable for any unfair results (WEF, 2023). It is important to involve women and people of diverse gender identities in the creation, use, and review of AI technologies to prevent solutions that are focused only on male experiences and ignore a wide range of perspectives. Strong leadership is also key, as AI alone cannot change a company's culture if it does not value inclusion, openness, and justice.

7. IMPACTS ON PRIVACY, AUTONOMY, AND FAIR TREATMENT OF EMPLOYEES

The operation of cold-blooded work and its heavy reliance on online communication and digital platforms have raised issues about autonomy for staff members, confidentiality, and equal treatment. Although these technologies can help companies in making opinions, assessing productivity, and relating plant inefficiencies, they also carry the eventuality of protrusive data collection and the coupling of scores, both particular and professional (Ball, 2021). Since women and marginalized groups are frequently scanned more in technologically advanced workplaces, similar practices may limit freedom and, in some cases, worsen being Injuries (Ajunwa, 2020). The use of statistical analysis in performance evaluations, elevations, and hiring is growing. This generally ignores pivotal contextual factors and simplifies complex mortal features to numerical data (Boddy & Taplin, 2017; Crawford, 2021). We can lessen negative goods and ameliorate a terrain where workers are motivated, treated fairly, and feel valued by promoting the generalities of data and organizational justice and enforcing lower strict and high trust monitoring procedures (Ball, 2021; Datta et al., 2024; Nawaz, 2024).

Excessive surveillance is connected to increased anxiety, reduced satisfaction with work, and decreased organizational commitment, particularly when individuals believe that their independence may be in danger (Glavin, 2024; Siegel, 2022). Open and broadly inclusive use of technology for justice, coupled with time and space independence, is not only necessary for ethical regulatory goals but also for maintaining a healthy and productive society. Stricter privacy laws are also needed for the hybrid employment model. Due to this, enabling fair treatment requires open governance structures. Ethical supervision practices and ensuring that organizational effectiveness is aligned with maintaining employees' rights and dignity.

8. GOVERNANCE FRAMEWORKS FOR ETHICAL WORKFORCE MANAGEMENT

Ethical hybrid work and AI workforce management is an area requiring frameworks to constantly improve responsibility and transparency with decisions being made by automated systems. The governance framework must improve emphasis on transparency with respect to the collection, administration, and use of employees' data, and allocating responsibility and measures opportunities in inappropriate use situations (Taylor and Broders, 2022). European Union emphasize the important law like General Data Protection Regulation (GDPR) of data minimization, are appropriate for employees and agreed to protect the rights (Voigt and von Dame Busha, 2017). Routine evaluations, equity assessments through systematic methodologies for measuring equity and opportunity and the processes for addressing data confidentiality, as well as those that sought to counteract unintended bias, promoting procedural justice for employees, are integral to modern organizations. In correlation with compliance with regulatory requirements, there are other practices that businesses must incorporate if they are to embrace fairness analyses and are continually evaluating their impacts to avoid the dangers of discrimination and bias. Discriminatory practices, especially against women and minority groups (Raghavan et al., 2020). Adherence to the principles of autonomy and respect within the framework of incorporating the principles into the business management offers inclusivity and supports building trust in technology-driven business organizations.

9. CONCLUSION

The hybrid work model will reshape gender parity in today's workplace by promoting equal opportunities for flexible working conditions and encouraging meaningful interactions between all co-workers. This shift contributes to better work-life balance, increased involvement of women in the labour force, and other positive outcomes. Examples of these significant changes include the removal of traditional barriers alongside adaptable laws and more progressive societies that consider the moral implications of technological decisions. However, it is crucial to understand that the freedom to work from anywhere does not automatically mean equality. Issues such as bias, lack of qualified promotion opportunities, digital monitoring innovation, and AI-based decision-making are still a reality and need active monitoring and ethical regulation. To reach gender equality, companies should work on mentorship and sponsorship activities with marginalized groups of employees; promote flexible and fair policies of work; and design a criterion assessment to determine what effect a diverse schedule of work may have on gender inclusion. It is expected that future frameworks should emphasize intersectionality and the value of achieving gender equity on the job by understanding the correlation between racial inequity, child care tasks, and economic inequities. In order to ensure a smooth change through the implementation of hybrid work as a facilitator of gender equality and the empowerment of women to lead and innovate through work, there will be a need to develop a culturally responsible AI system. As such, it is recommended that there be a development of a transparent AI-based performance system to ensure fair assessment and a less biased workplace. There are also training programs for companies to promote inclusivity with team development and a conducive environment for a hybrid setup. It is necessary for a safe and healthy hybrid workplace with limited times and a balanced monitoring system for companies to sustain employee loyalty.

REFERENCES

Adisa, T. A., Gbadamosi, G., & Adekoya, O. D. (2022). The implications of the COVID-19 pandemic on the gender pay gap in the United Kingdom: Advocating a sustainable policy response. *Employee Relations: The International Journal*, *44*(2), 408–426. DOI: 10.1108/ER-05-2020-0234

Ajunwa, I. (2020). The paradox of automation as anti-bias intervention. *Cardozo Law Review*, *41*(5), 1671–1714.

Ashok, S., Saranya, T. S., & Gupta, S. K. (2025). Gender Inclusion in the Workplace Using AI for Sustainable Management. *Atlantis Press*, 19-27. DOI: 10.2991/978-94-6463-898-1_3

Ball, K. (2021). Workplace surveillance: An overview. *Routledge*, 4(3), 1-12.

Bearman, M., Howard, S., & Caouette, S. (2025). Artificial intelligence in day-to-day professional practice: implications for higher education. In *Handbook of Artificial Intelligence in Higher Education* (pp. 475–487). Edward Elgar Publishing.

Boddy, C., & Taplin, R. (2017). A note on workplace psychopathic bullying–Measuring its frequency and severity. *Aggression and Violent Behavior*, *34*, 117–119.

Bogen, M., & Rieke, A. (2018). Help wanted: An examination of hiring algorithms, equity, and bias. *Upturn*. Retrieved from https://www.upturn.org

Cappelli, P., Tambe, P., & Yakubovich, V. (2020). Artificial intelligence in human resources management: Challenges and a path forward. *California Management Review*, *62*(4), 15–42. DOI: 10.1177/0008125620949070

Choudhury, P., Foroughi, C., & Larson, B. Z. (2021). Work-from-anywhere: The productivity effects of geographic flexibility. *Strategic Management Journal*, *42*(4), 655–683. DOI: 10.1002/smj.3251

Chung, H., & van der Lippe, T. (2020). Flexible working, work–life balance, and gender equality: Introduction. *Social Indicators Research*, *151*(2), 365–381. DOI: 10.1007/s11205-018-2025-x PMID: 33029036

Craig, L., & Churchill, B. (2021). Dual-earner parent couples' work and care during COVID-19. *Gender, Work and Organization*, *28*(S1), 66–79. DOI: 10.1111/gwao.12497 PMID: 32837023

Crawford, K. (2021). Atlas of AI: Power, politics, and the planetary costs of artificial intelligence. *Yale University Press*, 7(3), 1-14.

Datta, S.. (2024). Measuring autonomy in hybrid work: Scale development. *Psychology Research and Behavior Management*, *38*(8), 1–11. https://www.scielo.br/j/prc/a/yY3fwfVCFdr3c6ZwdqJNdTh/?format=pdf&lang=en PMID: 40153183

Davenport, T. H., & Miller, S. M. (2022). *Working with AI: real stories of human-machine collaboration*. MIT Press.

Davenport, T. H., & Ronanki, R. (2018). Artificial intelligence for the real world. *Harvard Business Review*, *96*(1), 108–116.

Deloitte. (2024). Women @ Work 2024: A global outlook. *Deloitte*. https://www.deloitte.com/global/en/issues/work/content/women-at-work-global-outlook.html

Glavin, P., ... (2024). Private Eyes, They See Your Every Move:Workplace surveillance and worker well-being. *PMC*, 11(4), 327-345. https://journals.sagepub.com/doi/epub/10.1177/23294965241228874

Indian Institute for Human Settlements (IWWAGE). (2023). *Hybrid work and its effect on women's labour force participation* (Policy review). https://iwwage.org/wp-content/uploads/2023/06/Hybrid-Work-and-its-Effect.pdf

International Labour Organization (ILO). (2021). *World employment and social outlook: The role of digital labor platforms in transforming the world of work*. Geneva: ILO. Retrieved from https://www.ilo.org/publications/flagship-reports/role-digital-labour-platforms-transforming-world-work

International Labour Organization (ILO). (2023). *The future of work and gender equality*. Geneva: ILO. Retrieved from https://www.ilo.org/publications/flagship-reports/role-digital-labour-platforms-transforming-world-work

International Workplace Group (IWG). (2022). *The Hybrid Work Report*. IWG. Retrieved from https://www.iwgplc.com/en-gb/think-hybrid/people

McKinsey & Company. (2022). Women in the workplace 2022. *McKinsey & Company and LeanIn.Org*. Retrieved from https://www.mckinsey.com

Nawaz, N. (2024). The adoption of artificial intelligence in human resources management. *Journal of Business Research*, *4*, 1–11. https://www.sciencedirect.com/science/article/pii/S266709682300054X

Organisation for Economic Co-operation and Development (OECD). (2021). *The gender gap in employment: Challenges and policy responses*. OECD Publishing. Retrieved from https://www.oecd.org/employment/the-gender-gap-in-employment.html

Organisation for Economic Co-operation and Development (OECD). (2023). *AI, gender and work: Building inclusive workplaces*. OECD Publishing. Retrieved from https://www.oecd.org/en/topics/sub-issues/ai-and-work.html

Pareek, A., & Dheer, P. (2025). CSR and Sustainability in the Cement Industry of Rajasthan: A Comparative Study of Company Performance and Stakeholders' Engagement (Based on Secondary Survey Reports). *International Journal of Scientific Research in Science and Technology*, *12*(2), 450–458.

Raghavan, M., Barocas, S., Kleinberg, J., & Levy, K. (2020). Mitigating bias in algorithmic hiring: Evaluating claims and practices. *Proceedings of the 2020 Conference on Fairness, Accountability, and Transparency*, 469–481. https://doi.org/ DOI: 10.1145/3351095.3372828

Sharma, R., & Sinha, V. (2022). Gender equality and hybrid work: A pathway to inclusive organizational development. *Journal of Business Ethics*, *176*(3), 543–556.

Siegel, R.. (2022). The impact of electronic monitoring on employees' job satisfaction, stress, performance, and counterproductive work behavior: A meta-analysis. *Computers in Human Behavior Reports*, *8*, 1–13. DOI: 10.1016/j.chbr.2022.100227

Taylor, L., & Broeders, D. (2022). In the name of AI? Limits of data-driven governance. *Information Communication and Society*, *25*(1), 1–18.

World Economic Forum. (2023). *Global gender gap report 2023*. Geneva: World Economic Forum. Retrieved from https://www.weforum.org/reports

Yeke, D., Ibrahim, M., Tuncay, G. S., Farrukh, H., Imran, A., Bianchi, A., & Celik, Z. B. (2024, May). Wear's my data? understanding the cross-device runtime permission model in wearables. In *2024 IEEE Symposium on Security and Privacy (SP)* (pp. 2404-2421). IEEE.

Compilation of References

Abaddi, S. (2025). AI–human data hybridization: a hybrid approach to unveiling global entrepreneurial motivations, challenges and opportunities. Journal of Ethics in Entrepreneurship and Technology.

Abbasi, M. M. H., & Rasheed, M. R. (2024). Media for sustainable tourism growth in Pakistan: An analysis of traditional and new media channels. *Social Science Review Archives*, *2*(2), 25–29.

Abhishek, K. L., Niranjanamurthy, M., Aric, S., Ansarullah, S. I., Sinha, A., Tejani, G., & Shah, M. A. (2025). Developing an Intelligent Resume Screening Tool With AI-Driven Analysis and Recommendation Features. *Applied AI Letters*, *6*(2), e116.

Abou-Foul, M., Ruiz-Alba, J. L., & Soares, A. (2021). The impact of digitalization and servitization on the financial performance of a firm: An empirical analysis. *Production Planning and Control*, *32*(12), 975–989.

Accenture. (2023, June 13). *Accenture to invest $3 billion in AI to accelerate clients' reinvention*. Accenture Newsroom. https://newsroom.accenture.com/news/2023/accenture-to-invest-3-billion-in-ai-to-accelerate-clients-reinvention

Accenture. (2024, March 5). *Accenture launches Accenture LearnVantage to help clients and their people gain essential skills and achieve greater business value in the AI economy*. Accenture Newsroom. https://newsroom.accenture.com/news/2024/accenture-launches-accenture-learnvantage-to-help-clients-and-their-people-gain-essential-skills-and-achieve-greater-business-value-in-the-ai-economy

Acemoglu, D., Manera, A., & Restrepo, P. (2020). Does the US tax code favor automation? (No. w27052). National Bureau of Economic Research.

ACM. (2025). Emotion AI will not fix the workplace. *Interactions*. Retrieved from https://interactions.acm.org/archive/view/march-april-2025/emotion-ai-will-not-fix-the-workplace

Adeyemi, A. Z., & Sajuyigbe, A. S. (2017). Financial Management Practices and Women Entrepreneurs Performance: An Empirical Investigation. *International Journal of Economics and Business Management, 3*(1).

Adisa, T. A., Gbadamosi, G., & Adekoya, O. D. (2022). The implications of the COVID-19 pandemic on the gender pay gap in the United Kingdom: Advocating a sustainable policy response. *Employee Relations: The International Journal, 44*(2), 408–426. DOI: 10.1108/ER-05-2020-0234

Agrawal, R., Wankhede, V. A., Kumar, A., Upadhyay, A., & Garza-Reyes, J. A. (2022). Nexus of circular economy and sustainable business performance in the era of digitalization. *International Journal of Productivity and Performance Management, 71*(3), 748–774.

Ahmad, S. (2015). Green human resource management: Policies and practices. *Cogent Business & Management, 2*(1), 1030817.

Ahmed, N., & Wahed, M. (2020). The de-democratization of AI: Deep learning and the compute divide in artificial intelligence research. arXiv. Available at: https://arxiv.org/abs/2010.15581

Ajunwa, I. (2020). An auditing imperative for automated hiring systems. *Harv. JL & Tech., 34*, 621.

Ajunwa, I. (2020). The paradox of automation as anti-bias intervention. *Cardozo Law Review, 41*(5), 1671–1714.

Ajunwa, I., Crawford, K., & Schultz, J. (2017). Limitless worker surveillance. *California Law Review, 105*(3), 735–776. DOI: 10.15779/Z38BR8MF94

Al Naqbi, H., Bahroun, Z., & Ahmed, V. (2024). Enhancing work productivity through generative artificial intelligence: A comprehensive literature review. *Journal unspecified.*

Al-Abbadi, L. H. (2021). The effect of employee sustainable training on sustainable performance. *Journal of Management Information and Decision Sciences, 24*(6), 1–12.

Al-Abdullatif, A. M. (2025, June). Auditing AI Literacy Competency in K–12 Education: The Role of Awareness, Ethics, Evaluation, and Use in Human–Machine Cooperation. *Systems, 13*(06). Advance online publication. DOI: 10.3390/systems13060490

Alam, M. Z., Hu, W., & Barua, Z. (2018). Using the UTAUT model to determine factors affecting acceptance and use of mobile health (mHealth) services in Bangladesh. *Journal of Studies in Social Sciences, 17*(2).

Aldoseri, A., Al-Khalifa, K. N., & Hamouda, A. M. S. (2024). Methodological approach to assessing the current state of organizations for ai-based digital transformation. *Applied System Innovation*, *7*(1), 14. DOI: 10.3390/asi7010014

Alghizzawi, M., Ahmed, E., Ezmigna, I., Ezmigna, A. A. R., & Omeish, F. (2024). The relationship between artificial intelligence and digital marketing in business companies. In Awwad, B. (Ed.), *The AI Revolution: Driving Business Innovation and Research* (Vol. 525, pp. 885–895). Springer Nature Switzerland., DOI: 10.1007/978-3-031-54383-8_67

Al-Issawi, A. M. A. A. (2024). The impact of artificial intelligence in supporting risk management and performance evaluation. *World Economics & Finance Bulletin*, 36.

Alkahtani, A., Nordin, N., & Khan, R. U. (2020). Does government support enhance the relation between networking structure and sustainable competitive performance among SMEs? *Journal of Innovation and Entrepreneurship*, *9*(1), 14.

Allal-Chérif, O., Aránega, A. Y., & Sánchez, R. C. (2021). Intelligent recruitment: How to identify, select, and retain talents from around the world using artificial intelligence. *Technological Forecasting and Social Change*, *169*, 120822.

Allen, D. W., Berg, A., Berg, C., Markey-Towler, B., & Potts, J. (2019). Some economic consequences of the GDPR. *Allen DWE, Berg A, Berg C, Markey-Towler B and Potts J (2019) 'Some Economic Consequences of the GDPR'. Economic Bulletin*, *39*(2), 785–797. DOI: 10.2139/ssrn.3160404

Almaiah, M. A., Alfaisal, R., Salloum, S. A., Hajjej, F., Shishakly, R., Lutfi, A., & Al-Maroof, R. S. (2022). Measuring institutions' adoption of artificial intelligence applications in online learning environments: Integrating the innovation diffusion theory with technology adoption rate. *Electronics (Basel)*, *11*(20), 3291.

Almeida, F., Junça Silva, A., Lopes, S. L., & Braz, I. (2025). Understanding recruiters' acceptance of artificial intelligence: Insights from the Technology Acceptance Model. *Applied Sciences (Basel, Switzerland)*, *15*(2), 746.

Alnsour, A. S., Kanaan, O. A., Salah, M., Alfayyad, L., Hijazi, Y., & Alsharif, D. (2024). The impact of implementing AI in recruitment on human resource management efficiency and organizational development effectiveness. Journal of Infrastructure. *Policy and Development*, *8*(8), 6186.

Alqahtani, N., & Uslay, C. (2020). Entrepreneurial marketing and firm performance: Synthesis and conceptual development. *Journal of Business Research*, *113*, 62–71.

Ambardar, A., Singh, A., & Singh, V. (2023). Barriers in Implementing Ergonomic Practices in Hotels- A Study on five star hotels in NCR region. *International Journal of Hospitality and Tourism Systems*, *16*(2), 11–17.

Ambarwati, R., Harja, Y. D., & Thamrin, S. (2020). The role of facilitating conditions and user habits: A case of Indonesian online learning platform. *The Journal of Asian Finance, Economics and Business*, *7*(10), 481–489.

Ameer, F., & Khan, N. R. (2023). Green entrepreneurial orientation and corporate environmental performance: A systematic literature review. *European Management Journal*, *41*(5), 755–778.

Ami-Narh, J. T., & Williams, P. A. (2012). A revised UTAUT model to investigate E-health acceptance of health professionals in Africa. *Journal of Emerging Trends in Computing and Information Sciences*, *3*(10), 1383–1391.

Amoadu, M., Agyare, D. F., Doe, P. F., & Abraham, S. A. (2025). Examining the impact of psychosocial safety climate on working conditions, well-being and safety of healthcare providers: A scoping review. *BMC Health Services Research*, *25*(1), 90.

Amofah, K., Saladrigues, R., & Akwaa-Sekyi, E. K. (2020). Entrepreneurial intentions among MBA students. *Cogent Business & Management*, *7*(1), 1832401.

Amraei, M., Rezheh, M., Hamzekhani, M. S., & Faraji-Khiavi, F. (2021). Correlation between Creativity and Entrepreneurial Skills in Managers of Educational Hospitals. *Depiction of Health*, *12*(3), 240–250.

Amy, A. (2025, May 06). *IBM Accelerates Enterprise Gen AI Revolution with Hybrid Capabilities*. Retrieved Aug 15, 2025, from https://newsroom.ibm.com/2025-05-06-ibm-accelerates-enterprise-gen-ai-revolution-with-hybrid-capabilities: https://newsroom.ibm.com/2025-05-06-ibm-accelerates-enterprise-gen-ai-revolution-with-hybrid-capabilities

Anagnoste, S., Biclesanu, I., D'Ascenzo, F., & Savastano, M. (2021). The role of chatbots in end-to-end intelligent automation and future employment dynamics. In Business Revolution in a Digital Era: 14th International Conference on Business Excellence, ICBE 2020, Bucharest, Romania (pp. 287-302). Springer International Publishing.

Andrews, J. E., Ward, H., & Yoon, J. (2021). UTAUT as a model for understanding intention to adopt AI and related technologies among librarians. *Journal of Academic Librarianship*, *47*(6), 102437.

Angelopoulos, A., Michailidis, E. T., Nomikos, N., Trakadas, P., Hatziefremidis, A., Voliotis, S., & Zahariadis, T. (2019). Tackling faults in the industry 4.0 era—A survey of machine-learning solutions and key aspects. *Sensors (Basel)*, *20*(1), 109. PMID: 31878065

Anika, S. (2025, Mar 28). *Standard Chartered unveils AI platform SC GPT*. Retrieved Aug 15, 2025, from https://www.privatebankerinternational.com: https://www.privatebankerinternational.com/news/standard-chartered-unveils-ai-platform-sc-gpt/

Anwar, M., & Ali Shah, S. Z. (2020). Managerial networking and business model innovation: Empirical study of new ventures in an emerging economy. *Journal of Small Business and Entrepreneurship*, *32*(3), 265–286.

Anwar, M., Tajeddini, K., & Ullah, R. (2020). Entrepreneurial finance and new venture success-the moderating role of government support. *Business Strategy & Development*, *3*(4), 408–421.

Aragão, A. (2024). Towards a Typology of Imaginary Skyscrapers. In *Vision and Verticality: A Multidisciplinary Approach* (pp. 145–154). Springer International Publishing., DOI: 10.1007/978-3-031-39884-1_12

Arias, J. A., Beltran, J. A., & Bedoya, S. (2020). RPA Implementation for automation of managenment process of personal in Compañía Nacional de Empaques S.A. *15th Iberian Conference on Information Systems and Technologies, CISTI 2020*. Seville: IEEE Computer Society. DOI: 10.23919/CISTI49556.2020.9140994

Armstrong, L., & Metaxa, D. (2025). Navigating Automated Hiring: Perceptions, Strategy Use, and Outcomes Among Young Job Seekers. *Proceedings of the ACM on Human-Computer Interaction*, *9*(2), 1–26.

Arpita, A., & Saurabh, B. (2024, Jan 09). Artificial Intelligence for Hiring and Induction: The Unilever Experience. *Business Cases*. 10.4135/9781071921470

Arslan, A., Cooper, C., Khan, Z., Golgeci, I., & Ali, I. (2022). Artificial intelligence and human workers interaction at team level: A conceptual assessment of the challenges and potential HRM strategies. *International Journal of Manpower*, *43*(1), 75–88.

Aryan, F., Valença, L., & de Souza Santos, R. (2025). Exploring Fairness Debt Through Evidence from Studies on Algorithmic Discrimination. *8th IEEE/ACM International Conference on Technical Debt, TechDebt 2025* (pp. 34-39). Ottawa: Institute of Electrical and Electronics Engineers Inc. DOI: 10.1109/TechDebt66644.2025.00011

Asad, M., Majali, T., Aledeinat, M., Abdelkarim Almajali, D., & Akhorshaideh, A. H. O. (2023). Green entrepreneurial orientation for enhancing SMEs financial and environmental performance: Synergetic moderation of green technology dynamism and knowledge transfer and integration. *Cogent Business & Management, 10*(3), 2278842.

Ashby, A., Leat, M., & Hudson-Smith, M. (2012). Making connections: A review of supply chain management and sustainability literature. *Supply Chain Management, 17*(5), 497–516. DOI: 10.1108/13598541211258573

Ashkanasy, N. M., & Daus, C. S. (2005). Rumors of the death of emotional intelligence in organizational behavior are vastly exaggerated. *Journal of Organizational Behavior, 26*(4), 441-452. Ashkanasy, N. M., & Daus, C. S. (2005). Rumors of the death of emotional intelligence in organizational behavior are vastly exaggerated. *Journal of Organizational Behavior, 26*(4), 441–452.

Ashok, S., Saranya, T. S., & Gupta, S. K. (2025). Gender Inclusion in the Workplace Using AI for Sustainable Management. *Atlantis Press*, 19-27. DOI: 10.2991/978-94-6463-898-1_3

Ashok, M., Madan, R., Joha, A., & Sivarajah, U. (2022). Ethical framework for Artificial Intelligence and Digital technologies. *International Journal of Information Management, 62*, 102433.

Ashri, R. (2019). *The AI-Powered workplace: How Artificial Intelligence, Data, and Messaging Platforms Are Defining the Future of Work.* Apress.

Audretsch, D. B., Belitski, M., & Cherkas, N. (2021). Entrepreneurial ecosystems in cities: The role of institutions. *PLoS One, 16*(3), e0247609.

Awasthi, L. S., Awasthi, K. S., & Rai, A. K. (2024). Integrating human expertise and decision-making with artificial intelligence systems. In *Sustainability Principles and Applications in Engineering Practice* (pp. 217–236). Nova Science Publishers, Inc., 2-s2.0-85202112091

Ayanponle, L. O., Elufioye, O. A., Asuzu, O. F., Ndubuisi, N. L., Awonuga, K. F., & Daraojimba, R. E. (2024). The future of work and human resources: A review of emerging trends and HR's evolving role. *International Journal of Science and Research Archive, 11*(2), 113–124. DOI: 10.30574/ijsra.2024.11.2.0151

Ayeswarya, R. B. (2017). *A Study on Green Human Resource Management practices and its impact on organizations. International Journal of Advanced Research in Management, Architecture, Technology and Engineering*. IJARMATE.

Azeroual, O. (2024). Smart Data Stewardship: Innovating Governance and Quality with AI. *16th International Conference on Knowledge Management and Information Systems, KMIS 2024 as part of 16th International Joint Conference on Knowledge Discovery, Knowledge Engineering and Knowledge Management, IC3K 2024. 03*, pp. 187 - 196. Porto: Science and Technology Publications, Lda. DOI: 10.5220/0012918200003838

Aziz, M. F., Rajesh, J. I., Jahan, F., McMurrray, A., Ahmed, N., Narendran, R., & Harrison, C. (2025). AI-powered leadership: A systematic literature review. *Journal of Managerial Psychology*, *40*(5), 604–630.

Babashahi, L., Barbosa, C. E., Lima, Y., Lyra, A., Salazar, H., Argôlo, M., & Souza, J. M. D. (2024). AI in the workplace: A systematic review of skill transformation in the industry. *Administrative Sciences*, *14*(6), 127.

Babina, T., Fedyk, A., He, A., & Hodson, J. (2024). Artificial intelligence, firm growth, and product innovation. *Journal of Financial Economics*, *151*, 103745.

Bagozzi, R. P., & Yi, Y. (1988). On the evaluation of structural equation models. *Journal of the Academy of Marketing Science*, *16*(1), 74–94.

Baharm, S. F., Sharma, P., & Gupta, P. (2024). AI work tracker: Monitoring time and productivity. *International Journal of Advanced Research in Science. Tongxin Jishu*, *4*(2).

Balasundaram, S., & Venkatagiri, S. (2020). A structured approach to implementing Robotic Process Automation in HR. *3rd National Conference on Computational Intelligence, NCCI 2019. 1427*. Bangalore, Karnataka: Journal of Physics: Conference Series. DOI: 10.1088/1742-6596/1427/1/012008

Balasundaram, S., Venkatagiri, S., & Sathiyaseelan, A. (2022). Using AI to enhance candidate experience in high volume hiring: A conceptual review and case study. Proceedings of the Replenish, Restructure & Reinvent: Technology Fueled Transformation for Sustainable Future, 21-22.

Baldwin, T. T., & Ford, J. K. (1988). Transfer of training: A review and directions for future research. *Personnel Psychology*, *41*(1), 63–105. DOI: 10.1111/j.1744-6570.1988.tb00632.x

Ball, K. (2021). Workplace surveillance: An overview. *Routledge*, 4(3), 1-12.

Ball, K. (2021). Workplace surveillance: An overview. *Labor History*, *62*(4), 440–456. DOI: 10.1080/0023656X.2021.1915038

Bankins, S., Jooss, S., Restubog, S. L. D., Marrone, M., Ocampo, A. C., & Shoss, M. (2024). Navigating career stages in the age of artificial intelligence: A systematic interdisciplinary review and agenda for future research. *Journal of Vocational Behavior*, •••, 104011.

Baradaran, M., Zohari, P., Mahyar, A., Motamednia, H., Rahmati, D., & Gorgin, S. (2024, March). Cultural-Aware AI Model for Emotion Recognition. In *2024 13th Iranian/3rd International Machine Vision and Image Processing Conference (MVIP)* (pp. 1-6). IEEE.

Barath, G. V., Sanjev, R., & Saranya, S. (2025, May). AI-Driven Recruitment: Resume Screening and Skill Matching with NLP. In *2025 IEEE International Conference on Computer, Electronics, Electrical Engineering & their Applications (IC2E3)* (pp. 1-6). IEEE.

Barocas, S., Hardt, M., & Narayanan, A. (2019). Fairness and machine learning. fairmlbook.org

Barocas, S., & Selbst, A. D. (2016). Big data's disparate impact. *California Law Review*, *104*(3), 671–732. DOI: 10.2139/ssrn.2477899

Baron, R. (2006). The Bar-On model of emotional-social intelligence (ESI) 1. *Psicothema*, •••, 13–25.

Bar-On, R. (2006). The Bar-On model of emotional-social intelligence (ESI) 1. *Psicothema*, 13-25. Bar-On, R. (2006). The Bar-On model of emotional-social intelligence (ESI) 1. *Psicothema*, •••, 13–25.

Baron, R. A. (2006). Opportunity recognition as pattern recognition: How entrepreneurs "connect the dots" to identify new business opportunities. *The Academy of Management Perspectives*, *20*(1), 104–119.

Baron, R. A. (2007). Behavioral and cognitive factors in entrepreneurship: Entrepreneurs as the active element in new venture creation. *Strategic Entrepreneurship Journal*, *1*(1-2), 167–182.

Barrier, T. (Ed.). (2001). *Human computer interaction development & management*. IGI Global.

Barry, M., Haque, A. A., & Jan, M. T. (2024). From Expectancy to Acceptance: The Impact of Performance and Effort Expectations on Mobile Commerce Intentions. *SRIWIJAYA INTERNATIONAL JOURNAL OF DYNAMIC ECONOMICS AND BUSINESS*, 65-86.

Baruah, A., Shaikh, M., Kumar, R. M., Shaikh, I. A. K., & Thomas, S. N. (2024, April). Artificial Intelligence Influence on Leadership Styles in Human Resource Management for Employee Engagement. In *2024 Ninth International Conference on Science Technology Engineering and Mathematics (ICONSTEM)* (pp. 1-5). IEEE. https://doi.org/DOI: 10.1109/ICONSTEM60960.2024.10568819

Basnet, S. (2024). AI-ML algorithm for enhanced performance management: A comprehensive framework using backpropagation (BP) algorithm. *International Journal of Science and Research Archive, 11*(1), 1111–1127.

Batool, A., Zowghi, D., & Bano, M. (2023). *Responsible AI governance: A systematic literature review*. arXiv. /arXiv.2401.10896DOI: 10.48550

Bauer, T., Erdogan, B., Caughlin, D., & Truxillo, D. (2023). *Human resource management: People, data, and analytics*. Sage Publications.

Bayan, F., & Ali, A. N. (2025). EXPLORING THE FUTURE OF WORK: HOW AI IS RESHAPING INDUSTRIES. *International Journal of Professional Business Review, 10*(10), e05106. DOI: 10.26668/businessreview/2025.v10i10.5106

Beard, D. W., & Dess, G. G. (1981). Corporate-level strategy, business-level strategy, and firm performance. *Academy of Management Journal, 24*(4), 663–688.

Bearman, M., Howard, S., & Caouette, S. (2025). Artificial intelligence in day-to-day professional practice: implications for higher education. In *Handbook of Artificial Intelligence in Higher Education* (pp. 475–487). Edward Elgar Publishing.

Behare, N. (2025). Embracing AI: Fostering employee engagement and satisfaction in the digital era. In *Innovative Approaches for International Competitiveness Through Human Resource Management* (pp. 155-168). IGI Global. DOI: 10.4018/979-8-3373-1005-3.ch006

Bell-Masterson, J., & Stangler, D. (2015). Measuring an entrepreneurial ecosystem. *Available at SSRN* 2580336.

Bellucci, M., Delestre, N., Malandain, N., & Zanni-Merk, C. (2022). Combining an explainable model based on ontologies with an explanation interface to classify images. *Procedia Computer Science, 207*, 2395–2403. DOI: 10.1016/j.procs.2022.09.298

Belz, F. M., & Peattie, K. (2012). *Sustainability Marketing: A Global Perspective* (2nd ed.). Wiley United Kingdom.

Benbya, H., Davenport, T. H., & Pachidi, S. (2020). Artificial intelligence in Organizations: current state and future opportunities. SSRN Electronic Journal. DOI: 10.2139/ssrn.3741983

Benjamin, D. J. (2019). Errors in probabilistic reasoning and judgment biases. Handbook of Behavioral Economics: Applications and Foundations 1, 2, 69-186.

Bennett, T. M. (2009). *Development and performance of distributed teams: Examining differences between asynchronous and synchronous communication in planning task execution* (Doctoral dissertation, Capella University).

Bergefurt, L., van den Boogert, P. F., Appel-Meulenbroek, R., & Kemperman, A. (2024). The interplay of workplace satisfaction, activity support, and productivity support in the hybrid work context. *Building and Environment*, *261*, 111729. DOI: 10.1016/j.buildenv.2024.111729

Bersin, J. (2019a). *A new model of talent management: The internal talent marketplace* (HR People + Strategy White Paper). Society for Human Resource Management. https://www.shrm.org/content/dam/en/shrm/executive-network/A%20New%20Model%20of%20Talent%20Management-%20The%20Internal%20Talent%20Marketplace.pdf

Bersin, J. (2019b, July 17). *The company as a talent network: Unilever and Schneider Electric show the way*. Josh Bersin. https://joshbersin.com/2019/07/the-company-as-a-talent-network-unilever-and-schneider-electric-show-the-way/

Berta, M. (2024). *Towards a Gender Inclusive Neural Network for Automatic Gender Recognition* (Doctoral dissertation, Politecnico di Torino).

Bhanot, A. (2022). A novel review on the adaptation of artificial intelligence in human resources management by organizations in gulf countries. In *Handbook of Research on Innovative Management Using AI in Industry 5.0* (pp. 19–38). IGI Global.

Bharathi, K. V., & Krithika, M. (2024). Investigating the Impact of Evolving Work Culture on Employee Productivity in the Post-Pandemic Period. *10th International Conference on Smart Computing and Communication, ICSCC 2024*. Bali: Institute of Electrical and Electronics Engineers Inc. DOI: 10.1109/ICSCC62041.2024.10690698

Bhardwaj, G., Singh, S. V., & Kumar, V. (2020). An empirical study of artificial intelligence and its impact on human resource functions. *2020 International Conference on Computation, Automation and Knowledge Management (ICCAKM).*

Bhatt, M., & Shah, P. (2023). Acceptance of Artificial intelligence in human resource practices by employees. In The Adoption and Effect of Artificial Intelligence on Human Resources Management, Part B (pp. 13-30). Emerald Publishing Limited.

Bhattacharya, T. (2024). *A critical study on the work from home facility and its impact on employees' satisfaction and performance in the service sector* (Doctoral dissertation, ICFAI University Jharkhand). ICFAI University.

Bhukya, R., & Paul, J. (2023). Social influence research in consumer behavior: What we learned and what we need to learn?–A hybrid systematic literature review. *Journal of Business Research, 162*, 113870.

Billett, S. (2002). Toward a Workplace Pedagogy: Guidance, Participation, and Engagement. *Adult Education Quarterly, 53*(1), 27–43. DOI: 10.1177/074171302237202

Binns, R. (2018). Fairness in machine learning: Lessons from political philosophy. In *Proceedings of the 2018 Conference on Fairness, Accountability, and Transparency* (pp. 149–159). DOI: <ALIGNMENT.qj></ALIGNMENT>10.1145/3287560.3287592

Binns, R. (2018). Fairness in Machine Learning: Lessons from Political Philosophy. *Proceedings of the 2018 Conference on Fairness, Accountability, and Transparency*, 149-159.

Biswal, S. S., Ganesh, A., & Madhavan, P. (2020, April). Robotic automation of employee onboarding using neural computing. *International Journal of Scientific and Technology Research, 09*(04), 353–357. Retrieved August 01, 2025, from https://www.scopus.com/pages/publications/85083461419

Black, J. S., & van Esch, P. (2020). AI-enabled recruiting: What is it and how should a manager use it? *Business Horizons, 63*(2), 215–226.

Boddy, C., & Taplin, R. (2017). A note on workplace psychopathic bullying–Measuring its frequency and severity. *Aggression and Violent Behavior, 34*, 117–119.

Bodie, M. T., Cherry, M. A., McCormick, M. L., & Tang, A. (2021). The law and policy of people analytics. *University of Colorado Law Review, 92*(1), 1–56.

Bogen, M., & Rieke, A. (2018). Help wanted: An examination of hiring algorithms, equity, and bias. Upturn. https://www.upturn.org/reports/2018/hiring-algorithms/

Bogen, M., & Rieke, A. (2018). Help wanted: An examination of hiring algorithms, equity, and bias. *Upturn*. Retrieved from https://www.upturn.org

Bosse, S., & Pournaras, E. (2017, August). A ubiquitous multi-agent mobile platform for distributed crowd sensing and social mining. In *2017 IEEE 5th International Conference on Future Internet of Things and Cloud (FiCloud)* (pp. 280-287). IEEE. DOI: DOI: 10.1109/FiCloud.2017.44

Boughanem, H., Ghazouani, H., & Barhoumi, W. (2023). Facial emotion recognition in-the-wild using deep neural networks: A comprehensive review. *SN Computer Science, 5*(1), 96.

Bouncken, R. B., & Reuschl, A. J. (2018). Coworking-spaces: How a phenomenon of the sharing economy builds a novel trend for the workplace and for entrepreneurship. *Review of Managerial Science, 12*, 317–334. DOI: 10.1007/s11846-016-0215-y

Boyd, K. L., & Andalibi, N. (2023). Automated emotion recognition in the workplace: How proposed technologies reveal potential futures of work. *Proceedings of the ACM on human-computer interaction, 7*(CSCW1), 1-37.

Bozkurt, A., Xiao, J., Farrow, R., Bai, J. Y. H., Nerantzi, C., Moore, S., Dron, J., Stracke, C. M., Singh, L., Crompton, H., Koutropoulos, A., Terentev, E., Pazurek, A., Nichols, M., Sidorkin, A. M., Costello, E., Watson, S., Mulligan, D., Honeychurch, S., & Asino, T. I. (2024). The manifesto for teaching and learning in a time of generative ai: A critical collective stance to better navigate the future. *Open Praxis, 16*(4), 487–513. DOI: 10.55982/openpraxis.16.4.777

Bristol-Alagbariya, B., Ayanponle, O. L., & Ogedengbe, D. E. (2022). Integrative HR approaches in mergers and acquisitions ensuring seamless organizational synergies. *Magna Scientia Advanced Research and Reviews, 6*(1), 78–85.

Brock, D. (2019). The impact of artificial intelligence on strategic decision-making. *Strategic Direction, 35*(5), 16–20.

Brynjolfsson, E., Li, D., & Raymond, L. R. (2023). *Generative AI at work* (NBER Working Paper No. 31161). National Bureau of Economic Research. DOI: 10.3386/w31161

Brynjolfsson, E., & McAfee, A. (2017). *Machine, platform, crowd: Harnessing our digital future*. W. W. Norton & Company.

Budhwar, P., Chowdhury, S., Wood, G., Aguinis, H., Bamber, G. J., Beltran, J. R., & DeNisi, A. (2023). Human resource management in the age of generative artificial intelligence: Perspectives and research directions on ChatGPT. *Human Resource Management Journal, 33*(3), 606–659.

Budhwar, P., Malik, A., De Silva, M. T., & Thevisuthan, P. (2022). Artificial intelligence–challenges and opportunities for international HRM: A review and research agenda. *International Journal of Human Resource Management, 33*(6), 1065–1097.

Buli, B. M. (2017). Entrepreneurial orientation, market orientation and performance of SMEs in the manufacturing industry: Evidence from Ethiopian enterprises. *Management Research Review, 40*(3), 292–309.

Bullough, A., Renko, M., & Myatt, T. (2014). Danger zone entrepreneurs: The importance of resilience and self–efficacy for entrepreneurial intentions. *Entrepreneurship Theory and Practice, 38*(3), 473–499.

Buolamwini, J., & Gebru, T. (2018, January). Gender shades: Intersectional accuracy disparities in commercial gender classification. In Conference on fairness, accountability and transparency (pp. 77-91). PMLR.

Burnett, J. R., & Lisk, T. C. (2019, January 02). The Future of Employee Engagement: Real-Time Monitoring and Digital Tools for Engaging a Workforce. *International Studies of Management & Organization*, *49*(01), 108–119. DOI: 10.1080/00208825.2019.1565097

Burnett, J. R., & Lisk, T. C. (2021). The future of employee engagement: Real-time monitoring and digital tools for engaging a workforce. In *International Perspectives on Employee Engagement* (pp. 117–128). Routledge.

Burns, J., Chang, L., Hardware, A., Scaling, A., Martineau, K., & Generative, A. (2022). Meet the ibm artificial intelligence unit. *IBM Research.[Online]. Available: https://research. ibm. com/blog/ibm-artificial-intelligence-unit-aiu*

Burrell, J. (2016). How the machine "thinks": Understanding opacity in machine learning algorithms. *Big Data & Society*, *3*(1), 1–12. DOI: 10.1177/2053951715622512

Bygrave, L. A. (2021). The 'Strasbourg Effect' on data protection in light of the 'Brussels Effect': Logic, mechanics and prospects. *Computer Law & Security Review*, *40*, 105460. DOI: 10.1016/j.clsr.2020.105460

Cabinet Office. (2025, June 2). *Microsoft 365 Copilot experiment: Cross-government findings report*. GOV.UK. https://assets.publishing.service.gov.uk/media/683db42bd23a62e5d32680d0/M365_Copilot_Experiment_Findings_Report.pdf

Calders, T., & Verwer, S. (2010). Three naive bayes approaches for discrimination-free classification. *Data Mining and Knowledge Discovery*, *21*, 277–292. DOI: 10.1007/s10618-010-0190-x

Caldwell, S., Sweetser, P., O'donnell, N., Knight, M. J., & Aitchison, M. (2022, July 26). An Agile New Research Framework for Hybrid Human-AI Teaming: Trust, Transparency, and Transferability. *ACM Transactions on Interactive Intelligent Systems*, *12*(03). Advance online publication. DOI: 10.1145/3514257

Cao, X., Yu, L., Liu, Z., Gong, M., & Adeel, L. (2018). Understanding mobile payment users' continuance intention: A trust transfer perspective. *Internet Research*, *28*(2), 456–476.

Cappelli, P., Tambe, P., & Yakubovich, V. (2019). *Artificial intelligence in human resources management: Challenges and a path forward. SSRN*. DOI: 10.2139/ssrn.3263878

Cappelli, P., Tambe, P., & Yakubovich, V. (2020). Artificial intelligence in human resources management: Challenges and a path forward. *California Management Review*, *62*(4), 15–42. DOI: 10.1177/0008125620949070

Cassar, G. (2009). Financial statement and projection preparation in start-up ventures. *The Accounting Review*, *84*(1), 27–51.

Caton, J. L. (2019). Creativity in a theory of entrepreneurship. *Journal of Entrepreneurship and Public Policy*, *8*(4), 442–469.

Celestin, M., & Sujatha, S. (2024). Analyzing the long-term impact of remote work on organizational efficiency and employee performance: Exploring key technologies and management practices. *International Journal of Applied and Advanced Scientific Research*, *9*(2), 102–112.

Cetindamar, D., Kitto, K., Wu, M., Zhang, Y., Abedin, B., & Knight, S. (2022). Explicating AI literacy of employees at digital workplaces. *IEEE Transactions on Engineering Management*, *71*, 810–823. DOI: 10.1109/TEM.2021.3138503

Chamsa, J., & García-Blandón, J. (2019). On the importance of sustainable human resource management for the adoption of sustainable development goals. *Resources, Conservation and Recycling*, *141*, 109–122. DOI: 10.1016/j.resconrec.2018.10.006

Chamsa, N., & García-Blandón, J. (2019). On the importance of sustainable human resource management for the adoption of sustainable development goals. *Resources, Conservation and Recycling*, *141*, 109–122.

Chandratreya, A. (2025). Digital transformation and the future workforce. In *Transforming the Service Sector With New Technology* (pp. 19–40). IGI Global., DOI: 10.4018/979-8-3693-7447-4.ch002

Chattu, V. K. (2021). A review of artificial intelligence, big data, and blockchain technology applications in medicine and global health. *Big Data and Cognitive Computing*, *5*(3), 41. DOI: 10.3390/bdcc5030041

Chawla, U., Mohnot, R., Singh, H. V., & Banerjee, A. (2023). The mediating effect of perceived trust in the adoption of cutting-edge financial technology among digital natives in the post-COVID-19 era. *Economies*, *11*(12), 286.

Chedli, M. K. E. (2016). Entrepreneurial motivation and performance of enterprises. *Economics, Management, and Financial Markets*, *11*(1), 175–189.

Chen, J.-H., Ha, N. T. T., Tai, H.-W., & Chang, C.-A. (2020). The willingness to adopt the internet of Things (IoT) conception in Taiwan's construction industry. *Journal of Civil Engineering and Management*, *26*(6), 534–550. DOI: 10.3846/jcem.2020.12639

Chen, Z. (2024). Responsible AI in Organizational Training: Applications, Implications, and Recommendations for Future Development. *Human Resource Development Review, 23*(4), 498–521. DOI: 10.1177/15344843241273316

Cherniss, C. (2010). Emotional intelligence: Toward clarification of a concept. *Industrial and Organizational Psychology: Perspectives on Science and Practice, 3*(2), 110–126.

Chiriatti, M., Bergamaschi Ganapini, M., Panai, E., Wiederhold, B. K., & Riva, G. (2025, July 01). System 0: Transforming Artificial Intelligence into a Cognitive Extension. *Cyberpsychology, Behavior, and Social Networking, 28*(07), 534–542. DOI: 10.1089/cyber.2025.0201 PMID: 40504761

Chiu, Y. T., Zhu, Y. Q., & Corbett, J. (2021). In the hearts and minds of employees: A model of pre-adoptive appraisal toward artificial intelligence in organizations. *International Journal of Information Management, 60*, 102379. DOI: 10.1016/j.ijinfomgt.2021.102379

Choosetheperk. (2024). Boost leadership with trust and emotional intelligence. Retrieved from https://www.choosetheperk.com/blog/boost-leadership-with-trust-and-emotional-intelligence

Choudhary, V., Marchetti, A., Shrestha, Y. R., & Puranam, P. (2025). Human-AI ensembles: When can they work? *Journal of Management, 51*(2), 536–569.

Choudhury, P., Foroughi, C., & Larson, B. Z. (2021). Work-from-anywhere: The productivity effects of geographic flexibility. *Strategic Management Journal, 42*(4), 655–683. DOI: 10.1002/smj.3251

Chowdhury, S., Dey, P., Joel-Edgar, S., Bhattacharya, S., Rodriguez-Espindola, O., Abadie, A., & Truong, L. (2023). Unlocking the value of artificial intelligence in human resource management through AI capability framework. *Human Resource Management Review, 33*(1), 100899.

Christmann, P. (2000). Effects of "best practices" of environmental management on cost advantage: The role of complementary assets. *Academy of Management Journal, 43*(4), 663–680. DOI: 10.2307/1556360

Chrusciak, C. B., Szejka, A. L., & Canciglieri, O., Junior. (2023). A Preliminary Digital Transformation Framework to Support Business Management Processes and Human Factors Impacts: Systematic Review and Gap Analysis. In *Lecture Notes in Computer Science (including subseries Lecture Notes in Artificial Intelligence and Lecture Notes in Bioinformatics)* (Vol. 14316 LNCS, pp. 308-329). Springer Science and Business Media Deutschland GmbH. DOI: 10.1007/978-3-031-50040-4_23

Chung, H., & van der Lippe, T. (2020). Flexible working, work–life balance, and gender equality: Introduction. *Social Indicators Research*, *151*(2), 365–381. DOI: 10.1007/s11205-018-2025-x PMID: 33029036

Cohen, B., Cowie, A., Babiker, M., Leip, A., & Smith, P. (2021). Co-benefits and trade-offs of climate change mitigation actions and the Sustainable Development Goals. *Sustainable Production and Consumption*, *26*, 805–813. DOI: 10.1016/j.spc.2020.12.034

Colette, S. (2023, Apr). *From AI in Teams Premium to updates for Viva—here's what's new in Microsoft 365*. Retrieved Aug 19, 2025, from https://www.microsoft.com: https://www.microsoft.com/en-us/microsoft-365/blog/2023/02/28/from-ai-in-teams-premium-to-updates-for-viva-heres-whats-new-in-microsoft-365/?msockid=3a60cb3d05b66d9b3435dd2a042d6c09

Cornelia, D., & Nasution, N. (2024). The influence of remote work on the performance of remote workers: The mediating role of work-family conflict and work-life balance. *Ekombis Review: Jurnal Ilmiah Ekonomi dan Bisnis*, 12(1).

Coupe, T. (2019). Automation, job characteristics and job insecurity. *International Journal of Manpower*, *40*, 1288–1304. DOI: 10.1108/ijm-12-2018-0418

Cowgill, B., & Tucker, C. E. (2019). Economics, fairness and algorithmic bias. *preparation for. The Journal of Economic Perspectives*.

Craig, L., & Churchill, B. (2021). Dual-earner parent couples' work and care during COVID-19. *Gender, Work and Organization*, *28*(S1), 66–79. DOI: 10.1111/gwao.12497 PMID: 32837023

Crawford, K. (2021). Atlas of AI: Power, politics, and the planetary costs of artificial intelligence. *Yale University Press*, 7(3), 1-14.

Cronbach, L. J. (1951). Coefficient alpha and the internal structure of tests. *Psychometrika*, *16*(3), 297–334.

Crossan, M. M., & Apaydin, M. (2010). A multi-dimensional framework of organizational innovation: A systematic review of the literature. *Journal of Management Studies*, *47*(6), 1154–1191.

Csaba, M., Miklós, I., & Ákos, H. (2025). Hybrid work in the public and competitive sectors: Implications and challenges (Lessons from a pilot research). *Statisztikai Szemle*, *103*(06), 545–567. DOI: 10.20311/stat2025.06.hu0545

Cunningham-Sereque, M., Gordon, N., & Vaezi, R. (2023). Flying Blind: Recruiter Trust in Automated Employment Decision Tools. *29th Annual Americas Conference on Information Systems: Diving into Uncharted Waters, AMCIS 2023.* Panama City: Association for Information Systems. Retrieved Aug 02, 2025, from https://www.scopus.com/pages/publications/85192865952

Dajani, L., Ferraro, A., Maruyama, F., & Cheng, Y. (2024). Human Rights and Ethics Guiding Human-Machine Teaming. *14th IEEE Global Humanitarian Technology Conference, GHTC 2024.* Radnor: Institute of Electrical and Electronics Engineers Inc. DOI: 10.1109/GHTC62424.2024.10771558

Danish, R. Q., Asghar, J., Ahmad, Z., & Ali, H. F. (2019). Factors affecting "entrepreneurial culture": The mediating role of creativity. *Journal of Innovation and Entrepreneurship*, *8*(1), 1–12.

Darwish, H., Yalabik, Z. Y., & Gustafsson, S. (2025). BEING A GOOD CITIZEN IN A HYBRID WORK SETTING: WHAT DOES IT MEAN FOR PROFESSIONALS? *85th Annual Meeting of the Academy of Management, AOM 2025.* 2025. Copenhagen: Academy of Management. DOI: 10.5465/AMPROC.2025.332bp

Dash, G., & Paul, J. (2021). CB-SEM vs PLS-SEM methods for research in social sciences and technology forecasting. *Technological Forecasting and Social Change*, *173*(121092), 121092. DOI: 10.1016/j.techfore.2021.121092

Dastin, J. (2018, October 10). Amazon scraps secret AI recruiting tool that showed bias against women. Reuters. https://www.reuters.com/article/amazon-ai-idUSKCN1MK08G

Datta, S.. (2024). Measuring autonomy in hybrid work: Scale development. *Psychology Research and Behavior Management*, *38*(8), 1–11. https://www.scielo.br/j/prc/a/yY3fwfVCFdr3c6ZwdqJNdTh/?format=pdf&lang=en PMID: 40153183

Davenport, T. H., & Miller, S. M. (2022). *Working with AI: real stories of human-machine collaboration.* MIT Press.

Davenport, T. H., & Ronanki, R. (2018). Artificial intelligence for the real world. *Harvard Business Review*, *96*(1), 108–116.

de Lucas Ancillo, A., & Gavrila, S. G. (2023). The impact of research and development on entrepreneurship, innovation, digitization and digital transformation. *Journal of Business Research*, *157*, 113566.

Deepthi, P., Shaikh, M., Nargunde, A. S., Faldu, R., & Goli, G. (2024, April). Deep learning-enabled human resource analytics in predicting employee performance. In *2024 Ninth International Conference on Science Technology Engineering and Mathematics (ICONSTEM)* (pp. 1-5). IEEE.https://doi.org/DOI: 10.1109/ICONSTEM60960.2024.10568716

Delina, G., Badada, B., Krishnaraj, R., Thiruthuvanathan, M. M., & Kumar, R. M. (2024). A Narrative Synthesis on the Role of Affective Computing in Fostering Workplace Well-Being Using a Deep Learning Model. In *International Conference on Innovations in Computational Intelligence and Computer Vision* (pp. 431-445). Springer, Singapore.

Deloitte. (2024). Women @ Work 2024: A global outlook. *Deloitte.* https://www.deloitte.com/global/en/issues/work/content/women-at-work-global-outlook.html

Dhamija, P. (2012). E-recruitment: A roadmap towards e-human resource management. *Research World*, *3*(3), 33.

Dhand, S., Pandey, A., Mishra, S., Sharma, K., & Kadanga, A. (2025). Role of artificial intelligence in enhancing employee well-being at the workplace. In *Global Work Arrangements and Outsourcing in the Age of AI* (pp. 25–46). IGI Global., DOI: 10.4018/979-8-3373-1270-5.ch002

Dinker, N., & Rawat, N. (2025). Technological Mediation and AI for Agility in Hospitality and Tourism: A Sociological Analysis through the Lens of Structuration and Network Theory. *Nepalese Journal of Management Science and Research*, *8*(1), 126–143.

Disco. (2025, August 11). How to assess the ROI of AI-driven upskilling initiatives. Blog post. https://www.disco.co/blog/how-to-assess-the-roi-of-ai-driven-upskilling-initiatives

disprz, Deloitte, & MindID (n.d). Disprz x Deloitte x MindID: Workforce transformation and learning culture case study. FeaturedCustomers. https://cdn.featuredcustomers.com/CustomerCaseStudy.document/Case_Study__disprz_x_Deloitte_x_MindID_.pdf

Dixit, S., Sharma, N., Maurya, M., & Dharwal, M. (2022). AI power: making recruitment smarter. In *Evolution of Digitized Societies Through Advanced Technologies* (pp. 165–180). Springer Nature Singapore.

Duarte, A., & Dias, P. (2025). How artificial intelligence is changing organizations: Portuguese CEOs' perspective. *Journal of Communication Management*, 01-18. DOI: 10.1108/JCOM-10-2024-0204

Duchek, S. (2020). Organizational resilience: A capability-based conceptualization. *Business Research, 13*, 215–246. DOI: 10.1007/s40685-019-0085-7

Dutta, D., Mishra, S. K., & Tyagi, D. (2023). Augmented employee voice and employee engagement using artificial intelligence-enabled chatbots: A field study. *International Journal of Human Resource Management, 34*(12), 2451–2480.

Dwivedi, D., & Agarwal, S. (2024). Evaluating the Effectiveness of Leadership Decision Making by Data Analytics and Reporting Technologies. In *Advancing the Marketing Technology (MarTech) Revolution* (pp. 207-232). IGI Global. DOI: 10.4018/979-8-3693-4361-6.ch008

Dwivedi, Y. K., Kshetri, N., Hughes, L., Slade, E. L., Jeyaraj, A., Kar, A. K., & Wright, R. (2023). Opinion Paper:"So what if ChatGPT wrote it?" Multidisciplinary perspectives on opportunities, challenges and implications of generative conversational AI for research, practice and policy. *International Journal of Information Management, 71*, 102642.

Dwork, C. (2008, April). Differential privacy: A survey of results. In *International conference on theory and applications of models of computation* (pp. 1-19). Berlin, Heidelberg: Springer Berlin Heidelberg. https://doi.org/DOI: 10.1007/978-3-540-79228-4_1

Dwork, C., & Roth, A. (2014). The algorithmic foundations of differential privacy. *Foundations and Trends in Theoretical Computer Science, 9*(3–4), 211–407. DOI: 10.1561/0400000042

Ebrahimi, P., & Mirbargkar, S. M. (2017). Green entrepreneurship and green innovation for SME development in market turbulence. *Eurasian Business Review, 7*(2), 203–228.

Edmondson, A. (1999). Psychological safety and learning behavior in work teams. *Administrative Science Quarterly, 44*(2), 350–383.

Edmondson, A. C. (2018). *The fearless organization: Creating psychological safety in the workplace for learning, innovation, and growth.* John Wiley & Sons.

Eggers, F., & Kraus, S. (2011). Growing young SMEs in hard economic times: The impact of entrepreneurial and customer orientations—A qualitative study from Silicon Valley. *Journal of Small Business and Entrepreneurship, 24*(1), 99–111.

Eisenberger, R., Stinglhamber, F., Vandenberghe, C., Sucharski, I. L., & Rhoades, L. (2002). Perceived Supervisor Support. *The Journal of Applied Psychology, 87*(3), 565–573. https://psycnet.apa.org/doi/10.1037/0021-9010.87.3.565

Eke, C. I., & Shuib, L. (2024). The role of explainability and transparency in fostering trust in AI healthcare systems: A systematic literature review, open issues and potential solutions. *Neural Computing & Applications*, •••, 1–36.

Ekuma, K. (2024). Artificial intelligence and automation in human resource development: A systematic review. *Human Resource Development Review*, *23*(2), 199–229.

El Hajal, G., & Yeoman, I. (2024). AI and the future of talent management in tourism and hospitality. *Current Issues in Tourism*, •••, 1–18. DOI: 10.1080/13683500.2024.2439395

Elumilade, O. O., Ogundeji, I. A., Achumie, G. O., Omokhoa, H. E., & Omowole, B. M. (2022). Optimizing corporate tax strategies and transfer pricing policies to improve financial efficiency and compliance. *Journal of Advance Multidisciplinary Research*, *1*(2), 28–38. https://www.synstojournals.com/multi/article/view/147

Emanuel, N., & Harrington, E. (2024). Working remotely? Selection, treatment, and the market for remote work. *American Economic Journal. Applied Economics*, *16*(4), 528–559.

Erickson, A. (2018). Comparative analysis of the EU's GDPR and Brazil's LGPD: Enforcement challenges with the LGPD. *Brooklyn Journal of International Law*, *44*(2), 859–888. https://brooklynworks.brooklaw.edu/bjil/vol44/iss2/9

Ermel, A. P. C., Lacerda, D. P., Morandi, M. I. W., & Gauss, L. (2021). *Literature reviews: modern methods for investigating scientific and technological knowledge*. Springer Nature.

Ernst, A. T., Jiang, H., Krishnamoorthy, M., & Sier, D. (2004b). Staff scheduling and rostering: A review of applications, methods and models. *European Journal of Operational Research*, *153*(1), 3–27. DOI: 10.1016/S0377-2217(03)00095-X

European Commission. (2021). *Proposal for a regulation laying down harmonised rules on artificial intelligence (Artificial Intelligence Act)*. https://eur-lex.europa.eu/legal-content/EN/TXT/?uri=CELEX%3A52021PC0206

Fakhabi, M. M., Hamidian, S. M., & Aliehyaei, M. (2024). Exploring the role of the Internet of Things in green buildings. *Energy Science & Engineering*, *12*(9), 3779–3822. DOI: 10.1002/ese3.1840

Fan, C. (2022). Evaluating employee performance with an improved clustering algorithm. *Informatica (Vilnius)*, *46*(5), 123–128.

Farah, T., & Trajković, L. (2013, June). Anonym: A tool for anonymization of the Internet traffic. In *2013 IEEE International Conference on Cybernetics (CYBCO)* (pp. 261-266). IEEE. https://doi.org/DOI: 10.1109/CYBConf.2013.6617434

Fatima, H., Javaid, Z. K., Arshad, Z., Ashraf, M., & Batool, H. (2024). A systematic review on the impact of remote work on employee engagement. *Bulletin of Business and Economics*, *13*(2), 117–126.

Fatoki, O. (2014). The causes of the failure of new small and medium enterprises in South Africa. *Mediterranean Journal of Social Sciences*, *5*(20), 922–927.

Fayolle, A., Liñán, F., & Moriano, J. A. (2014). Beyond entrepreneurial intentions: Values and motivations in entrepreneurship. *The International Entrepreneurship and Management Journal*, *10*(4), 679–689.

Fazal, S. A., Al Mamun, A., Alshebami, A. S., Muniady, R., Ali, M. H., Al Shami, S. S. A., Al Marri, S. H., Seraj, A. H. A., Thomran, M., & Algobaei, F. (2022). Entrepreneurial motivation, competency and micro-enterprise sustainability performance: Evidence from an emerging economy. *Sustainability*, *14*(19), 12615.

Feng, C. M., Botha, E., & Pitt, L. (2024). From HAL to GenAI: Optimizing chatbot impacts with CARE. *Business Horizons*, *67*(5), 537–548. DOI: 10.1016/j.bushor.2024.04.012

Fenwick, A., Molnar, G., & Frangos, P. (2024). The critical role of HRM in AI-driven digital transformation: A paradigm shift to enable firms to move from AI implementation to human-centric adoption. *Discover Artificial Intelligence*, *4*(1), 34.

Ferneborg, S., Napolitano, F., Vaarst, M., Mejdell, C. M., Waiblinger, S., & De Oliveira, D. (2020). Methodology for studying human attitudes and behaviour to cow– calf contact systems. *The Journal of Dairy Research*, *87*(S1), 122–127.

Filatotchev, I., Liu, X., Buck, T., & Wright, M. (2009). The export orientation and export performance of high-technology SMEs in emerging markets: The effects of knowledge transfer by returnee entrepreneurs. *Journal of International Business Studies*, *40*(6), 1005–1021.

Filippucci, F., Gal, P., Jona-Lasinio, C., Leandro, A., & Nicoletti, G. (2024). *The impact of artificial intelligence on productivity, distribution and growth: Key mechanisms, initial evidence and policy challenges*. OECD Artificial Intelligence Papers.

Financial News London. (2025, April 8). *Deloitte triples number of auditors using AI chatbot*. https://www.fnlondon.com/articles/deloitte-triples-number-of-auditors-using-ai-chatbot-42086859

Financial Times. (2025, June 2). *UK civil servants who used AI saved two weeks a year, government study finds.* https://www.ft.com/content/7c2aa19d-4c92-490d-bb35-f329a246fe5b

Fishbein, M., & Ajzen, I. (1975). Beliefs, attitude, intention, and behavior: An introduction to theory and research.

Fisher, D. A., Seetoh, T., May-Lin, H. O., Viswanathan, S., Toh, Y., Yin, W. C., & Dempsey, M. (2013). Automated measures of hand hygiene compliance among healthcare workers using ultrasound: Validation and a randomized controlled trial. *Infection Control and Hospital Epidemiology*, *34*(9), 919–928. DOI: 10.1086/671738

Floridi, L., & Cowls, J. (2019). A unified framework of five principles for AI in society. *Harvard Data Science Review*, *1*(1). Advance online publication. DOI: 10.1162/99608f92.8cd550d1

Floridi, L., Cowls, J., Beltrametti, M., Chatila, R., Chazerand, P., Dignum, V., & Vayena, E. (2018). AI4People—An ethical framework for a good AI society: Opportunities, risks, principles, and recommendations. *Minds and Machines*, *28*(4), 689–707.

Floridi, L., Cowls, J., Beltrametti, M., Chatila, R., Chazerand, P., Dignum, V., & Vayena, E. (2018). AI4People—an ethical framework for a good AI society: Opportunities, risks, principles, and recommendations. *Minds and Machines*, *28*, 689–707. DOI: 10.1007/s11023-018-9482-5

Ford, D. K., & Bauer, T. N. (2024). Onboarding During Transformational Times. Systems of Psychotherapy: A Transtheoretical Analysis, 162.

Fornell, C., & Larcker, D. F. (1981). Evaluating structural equation models with unobservable variables and measurement error. *JMR, Journal of Marketing Research*, *18*(1), 39–50.

Frey, C. B., & Osborne, M. A. (2016). The future of employment: How susceptible are jobs to computerisation? *Technological Forecasting and Social Change*, *114*, 254–280. DOI: 10.1016/j.techfore.2016.08.019

Friedman, B., & Nissenbaum, H. (1996). Bias in computer systems. ACM Transactions on information systems (TOIS), 14(3), 330-347.

Fu, C.-J., Silalahi, A. D. K., Yang, L.-W., & Eunike, I. J. (2024). Advancing SME performance: A novel application of the technological-organizational-environment framework in social media marketing adoption. *Cogent Business & Management*, *11*(1), 2360509.

Fu, Y., & Weng, Z. (2024). Navigating the ethical terrain of AI in education: A systematic review on framing responsible human-centered AI practices. *Computers and Education: Artificial Intelligence*, *7*, 100306. DOI: 10.1016/j.caeai.2024.100306

Gallup. (2024).*State of the global workplace: 2024 report*. Retrieved from https://gallup.com/workplace/349484/state-of-the-global-workplace.aspx

Ganapathy, A. (2021). ROBOTIC PROCESS AUTOMATION: END FROM ENTREPRENEURIAL CONTENT EDITING TO GO LIVE. *Academy of Entrepreneurship Journal*, *27*(03), 1–11. Retrieved August 12, 2025, from https://www.scopus.com/pages/publications/85109437774

García-Madurga, M.-Á., Gil-Lacruz, A.-I., Saz-Gil, I., & Gil-Lacruz, M. (2024). The Role of Artificial Intelligence in Improving Workplace Well-Being: A Systematic Review. *Businesses*, *4*(3), 389–410. DOI: 10.3390/businesses4030024

García-Pérez, L., García-Garnica, M., & Olmedo-Moreno, E. M. (2021). Skills for a working future: How to bring about professional success from the educational setting. *Education Sciences*, *11*(1), 27.

Gärtner, C., & Kern, D. (2021). Smart HRM in 2030: Conversational HR, Connected Robotics, and Controlled Analytics. Managing Work in the Digital Economy: Challenges, Strategies and Practices for the Next Decade, 203-221.

George, A. S. (2024). Artificial Intelligence and the Future of Work. *Job Shifting Not Job Loss.*, *02*, 17–37. DOI: 10.5281/zenodo.10936490

Ghazzawi, K., & Accoumeh, A. (2014). Critical success factors of the e-recruitment system. *Journal of Human Resources Management and Labor Studies*, *2*(2), 159–170.

Gibbs, M. B. (2022). How is new technology changing job design? *IZA World of Labor: Evidence-Based Policy Making*.

Glavin, P., ... (2024). Private Eyes, They See Your Every Move:Workplace surveillance and worker well-being. *PMC*, 11(4), 327-345. https://journals.sagepub.com/doi/epub/10.1177/23294965241228874

Goleman, D. (2005). *Emotional intelligence: Why it can matter more than IQ*. Bantam.

Govindarajan, S., & Ananthanpillai, B. (2023) IMPACT OF AI DRIVEN PREDICTIVE SCHEDULING ON EMPLOYEES ENGAGEMENT AND PRODUCTIVITY. https://doi.org/DOI: 10.17605/OSF.IO/RM6DS

Grassini, S., Aasen, M. L., & Møgelvang, A. (2024). Understanding university students' acceptance of ChatGPT: Insights from the UTAUT2 model. *Applied Artificial Intelligence*, *38*(1), 2371168.

Greenleaf, G., & Cottier, B. (2022). International and regional commitments in African data privacy laws: A comparative analysis. *Computer Law & Security Review*, *44*, 105638. DOI: 10.1016/j.clsr.2021.105638

Gryncewicz, W., Zygała, R., & Pilch, A. (2023). AI in HRM: Case study analysis. Preliminary research. *Procedia Computer Science*, *225*, 2351–2360.

Guenole, N., & Feinzig, S. (2018). *The business case for AI in HR. With Insights and Tips on Getting Started*. IBM Smarter Workforce Institute, IBM Corporation.

Guide, T. (2014). *The convention on the rights of persons with disabilities*. United Nations of Human Rights.

Gundage, V., Deshmukh, M. T., Kolape, R., Kate, A., & Narve, N. G. (2025, April). Enhancing Manufacturing Efficiency and Safety through Human-Robot Collaboration: A Comprehensive Review. *Journal of Mines. Metals and Fuels*, *43*(04), 943–950. DOI: 10.18311/jmmf/2025/48270

Guodong, Z., Huanhuan, Y., & Yuanzhong, X. (2021). *Metaverse. BEIJING BOOK CO*. INC.

Gupta, A., & Mishra, M. (2023). Artificial Intelligence for Recruitment and Selection. In The Adoption and Effect of Artificial Intelligence on Human Resources Management, Part B (pp. 1-11). Emerald Publishing Limited.

Gupta, R. (2024). Impact of artificial intelligence (AI) on human resource management (HRM). *International Journal For Multidisciplinary Research, doi, 10.*

Gupta, K. P. (2019, July). Artificial intelligence for governance in india: Prioritizing the challenges using analytic hierarchy process (AHP). *International Journal of Recent Technology and Engineering*, *09*(02), 3756–3762. DOI: 10.35940/ijrte.B3392.078219

Gursoy, D., Chi, O. H., Lu, L., & Nunkoo, R. (2019). Consumers acceptance of artificially intelligent (AI) device use in service delivery. *International Journal of Information Management*, *49*, 157–169.

Guyot, G., Sherman, M. H., & Walker, I. S. (2018). Smart ventilation energy and indoor air quality performance in residential buildings: A review. *Energy and Building*, *165*, 416–430. DOI: 10.1016/j.enbuild.2017.12.051

Hair, J. F., Hult, G. T. M., Ringle, C. M., & Sarstedt, M. (2022). A Primer on Partial Least Squares Structural Equation Modeling (PLS-SEM). *Sage (Atlanta, Ga.)*.

Hair, J. F.Jr, Matthews, L. M., Matthews, R. L., & Sarstedt, M. (2017). PLS-SEM or CB-SEM: Updated guidelines on which method to use. *International Journal of Multivariate Data Analysis*, *1*(2), 107–123.

Halid, H., Ravesangar, K., Mahadzir, S. L., & Halim, S. N. A. (2024). Artificial Intelligence (AI) in Human Resource Management (HRM). In *Building the Future with Human Resource Management* (pp. 37–70). Springer International Publishing.

Hamadneh, S., Alshurideh, M. T., Alquqa, E. K., Al Kassem, A., Agha, K., & Alzoubi, H. M. (2024, February). AI-driven talent acquisition systems: transforming recruitment strategies in the digital age. In *2024 2nd International Conference on Cyber Resilience (ICCR)* (pp. 1-6). IEEE.

Hameed, I., & Ali, B. (2011). Impact of entrepreneurial orientation, entrepreneurial management and environmental dynamism on firm's financial performance. *Journal of Economics and Behavioral Studies*, *3*(2), 101–114.

Hameed, Z., Khan, I. U., Islam, T., Sheikh, Z., & Naeem, R. M. (2020). Green HRM practices and employee environmental performance. *Journal of Cleaner Production*, *256*, 120123.

Hammad, A., & Abu-Zaid, R. (2024). Applications of AI in decentralized computing systems: Harnessing artificial intelligence for enhanced scalability, efficiency, and autonomous decision-making in distributed architectures. *Applied Research in Artificial Intelligence and Cloud Computing*, *7*(6), 161–187.

Hamon, R., Junklewitz, H., & Sanchez, I. (2020). Robustness and explainability of artificial intelligence. *Publications Office of the European Union*, *207*(40), 2020. DOI: 10.2760/57493

Hamouche, S., Rofa, N., & Parent-Lamarche, A. (2025). Systematic bibliometric review of artificial intelligence in human resource development: Insights for HRD researchers, practitioners and policymakers. *European Journal of Training and Development*, *49*(1-2), 43–62.

Hasan, M. R., Chowdhury, F. R., & Ray, R. K. (2024). Employee performance prediction: An integrated approach of business analytics and machine learning. *Journal of Business and Management Studies*, *6*(1).

Hasbullah, H., Tullah, R. H., & Farhan, R. (2023). Factors Affecting The Quality of Financial Reports: A Systematic Literature Review. *INTERNATIONAL JOURNAL OF TRENDS IN ACCOUNTING RESEARCH*, *4*(1), 59–58.

Hasija, S., Shen, Z. J. M., & Teo, C. P. (2020). Smart city operations: Modeling challenges and opportunities. *Manufacturing & Service Operations Management, 22*(1), 203–213. DOI: 10.1287/msom.2019.0823

Henseler, J., Ringle, C. M., & Sarstedt, M. (2015). A new criterion for assessing discriminant validity in variance-based structural equation modeling. *Journal of the Academy of Marketing Science, 43*(1), 115–135.

Herrera, F. (2025, September). Reflections and attentiveness on eXplainable Artificial Intelligence (XAI). The journey ahead from criticisms to human–AI collaboration. *Information Fusion, 121*. Advance online publication. DOI: 10.1016/j.inffus.2025.103133

Hickey, G., McGilloway, S., O'Brien, M., Leckey, Y., Devlin, M., & Donnelly, M. (2018). Strengthening stakeholder buy-in and engagement for successful exploration and installation: A case study of the development of an area-wide, evidence-based prevention and early intervention strategy. *Children and Youth Services Review, 91*, 185–195. DOI: 10.1016/j.childyouth.2018.06.008

Hmieleski, K. M., & Baron, R. A. (2008). When does entrepreneurial self-efficacy enhance versus reduce firm performance? *Strategic Entrepreneurship Journal, 2*(1), 57–72.

Hoang, H., & Antoncic, B. (2003). Network-based research in entrepreneurship: A critical review. *Journal of Business Venturing, 18*(2), 165–187.

Hofeditz, L., Clausen, S., Rieß, A., Mirbabaie, M., & Stieglitz, S. (2022, December). Applying XAI to an AI-based system for candidate management to mitigate bias and discrimination in hiring. *Electronic Markets, 32*(04), 2207–2233. DOI: 10.1007/s12525-022-00600-9 PMID: 36568961

Hölzle, K., Rose, R., & Kaschub, V. L. (2024, December 01). The Interplay of Humans, Technology, and Organizations in Realizing AI's Productivity Promise. *The Economists' Voice, 21*(02), 357–362. DOI: 10.1515/ev-2024-0053

Hosseini, M., Bodaghi, M., Bhupatiraju, R. T., Maida, A., & Gottumukkala, R. (2023). Multimodal stress detection using facial landmarks and biometric signals. *Frontiers in Physiology*.

Huang, L., Zhao, X., & Huang, K. (2020, April). Global track: A simple and strong baseline for long-term tracking. In *Proceedings of the AAAI conference on artificial intelligence* (Vol. 34, No. 07, pp. 11037-11044). https://doi.org/ . v34i07.6758DOI: 10.1609/aaai

Huang, X., Yang, F., Zheng, J., Feng, C., & Zhang, L. (2023). Personalized human resource management via HR analytics and artificial intelligence: Theory and implications. *Asia Pacific Management Review, 28*(4), 598–610.

Hunkenschroer, A. L., & Luetge, C. (2022). Ethics of AI-enabled recruiting and selection: A review and research agenda. *Journal of Business Ethics, 178*(4), 977–1007.

Hussain, M. A. (2024). The impact of artificial intelligence on workforce automation and skill development. *J. Artif. Intel. Mach. Learn. Neural Netw., 44*, 11–21. DOI: 10.55529/ jaimlnn.44.11.21

Hu, Z., Song, C., Xu, C., Jin, G., Chen, Y., Xu, X., & Shen, H. (2020). Clinical characteristics of 24 asymptomatic infections with COVID-19 screened among close contacts in Nanjing, China. *Science China. Life Sciences, 63*, 706–711. DOI: 10.1007/s11427-020-1661-4

Ilgin, E., & Aslantamer, Ö. N. (2024). Comparative analysis of space efficiency in contemporary tall buildings: Residential, office, hotel and mixed-use functions. *International Journal of Architectural Engineering Technology, 11*, 60–79. DOI: 10.15377/2409-9821.2024.11.4

Ilieva, I., Matthews, R., Tobin, P., Valor, C., Moreno, V. K., & Ruiz, L. (2025). Adaptable customer engagement strategy for utilising energy flexibility. *International Journal of Sustainable Energy Planning and Management, 44*, 30–46. DOI: 10.54337/ijsepm.8521

Indian Institute for Human Settlements (IWWAGE). (2023). *Hybrid work and its effect on women's labour force participation* (Policy review). https://iwwage.org/wp-content/uploads/2023/06/Hybrid-Work-and-its-Effect.pdf

Indrawati, N. K., Muljaningsih, S., Juwita, H. A. J., Jazuli, A. M., Nurmasari, N. D., & Fahlevi, M. (2025). The mediator role of risk tolerance and risk perception in the relationship between financial literacy and financing decision. *Cogent Business & Management, 12*(1), 2468877.

International Energy Agency. (2022). *World energy outlook*. IEA.

International Labour Organization (ILO). (2021). *World employment and social outlook: The role of digital labor platforms in transforming the world of work*. Geneva: ILO. Retrieved from https://www.ilo.org/publications/flagship-reports/role-digital-labour-platforms-transforming-world-work

International Labour Organization (ILO). (2023). *The future of work and gender equality*. Geneva: ILO. Retrieved from https://www.ilo.org/publications/flagship-reports/role-digital-labour-platforms-transforming-world-work

International Workplace Group (IWG). (2022). *The Hybrid Work Report*. IWG. Retrieved from https://www.iwgplc.com/en-gb/think-hybrid/people

Ipsen, C., Kirchner, K., Andersone, N., & Karanika-Murray, M. (2022). Becoming a Distance Manager: Managerial Experiences, Perceived Organizational Support, and Job Satisfaction During the COVID-19 Pandemic. *Frontiers in Psychology*, *13*(916234), 1–11. DOI: 10.3389/fpsyg.2022.916234

Islam, M. T., Sepanloo, K., Woo, S., Woo, S. H., & Son, Y. J. (2025). A review of the industry 4.0 to 5.0 transition: Exploring the intersection, challenges, and opportunities of technology and Human–Machine collaboration. *Machines (Basel)*, *13*(4), 267.

Islam, M., Mamun, A. A., Afrin, S., Ali Quaosar, G. A., & Uddin, M. A. (2022). Technology adoption and human resource management practices: The use of artificial intelligence for recruitment in Bangladesh. *SA Journal of Human Resource Management*, *9*(2), 324–349.

Islam, M., Rahman, M. M., Taher, M. A., Quaosar, G. A. A., & Uddin, M. A. (2024). Using artificial intelligence for hiring talents in a moderated mechanism. *Future Business Journal*, *10*(1), 13.

Jaakkola, H., Henno, J., Mäkelä, J., & Thalheim, B. (2019, May). Artificial intelligence yesterday, today and tomorrow. In 2019 42nd International Convention on Information and Communication Technology, Electronics and Microelectronics (MIPRO) (pp. 860-867). IEEE.

Jack, S. L. (2010). Approaches to studying networks: Implications and outcomes. *Journal of Business Venturing*, *25*(1), 120–137.

Jackson, S. E., & Seo, J. (2010). The greening of strategic HRM scholarship. *Organizational Management Journal*, *7*(4), 278–290.

Jahun, I., Said, I., El-Imam, I., Ehoche, A., Dalhatu, I., Yakubu, A., Greby, S., Bronson, M., Brown, K., Bamidele, M., & Boyd, A. T. (2021). Optimizing community linkage to care and antiretroviral therapy Initiation: Lessons from the Nigeria HIV/AIDS Indicator and Impact Survey (NAIIS) and their adaptation in Nigeria ART Surge. *PLoS One*, *16*(9), e0257476. DOI: 10.1371/journal.pone.0257476

Jai, G. M. (2025, Mar 27). *Standard Chartered rolls out SC GPT, advancing AI-driven innovation in banking*. Retrieved Aug 12, 2025, from https://www.sc.com: https://www.sc.com/en/press-release/standard-chartered-rolls-out-sc-gpt-advancing-ai-driven-innovation-in-banking/

Jain, R., Garg, N., & Khera, S. N. (2023). Effective human–AI work design for collaborative decision-making. *Kybernetes*, *52*(11), 5017–5040.

Jain, V., & Mitra, A. (2025). Digital transformation and organizational culture: A sociological examination of employee interactions in modern workplaces. In *Organizational Sociology in the Digital Age* (pp. 203–218). IGI Global., DOI: 10.4018/979-8-3693-7398-9.ch012

James, A., Plank, M. J., Hendy, S., Binny, R., Lustig, A., Steyn, N., & Verrall, A. (2021). Successful contact tracing systems for COVID-19 rely on effective quarantine and isolation. *PLoS One*, *16*(6), e0252499. DOI: 10.1371/journal.pone.0252499

Jang, S. H., & Lee, C. W. (2025). Digital Entrepreneurial Orientation, Technology Absorptive Capacity, and Digital Innovation on Business Performance. *Systems*, *13*(4), 300.

Jaspin, K., Kiruba, G. M., Nivedha, V., Priyadharshini, S., & Sivaraman, D. (2024, October). AI Assisted Career Guidance and Resume Screening System. In *2024 5th IEEE Global Conference for Advancement in Technology (GCAT)* (pp. 1-7). IEEE.

Javaid, M., Haleem, A., Singh, R. P., & Suman, R. (2022). Artificial intelligence applications for industry 4.0: A literature-based study. *Journal of Industrial Integration and Management*, *7*(01), 83–111.

Jiang, X., Liu, H., Fey, C., & Jiang, F. (2018). Entrepreneurial orientation, network resource acquisition, and firm performance: A network approach. *Journal of Business Research*, *87*, 46–57.

Jin, G., Jiang, J., & Liao, H. (2024). The work affective well-being under the impact of AI. *Scientific Reports*, *14*(1), 25483.

Jobin, A., Ienca, M., & Vayena, E. (2019). The global landscape of AI ethics guidelines. *Nature Machine Intelligence*, *1*(9), 389–399. DOI: 10.1038/s42256-019-0088-2

Johansson, J., & Herranen, S. (2019). The application of artificial intelligence (AI) in human resource management: Current state of AI and its impact on the traditional recruitment process.

John, B., Alsamarra'i, Z., & Panteli, N. (2025, March). Reconfiguring digital embeddedness in hybrid work: The case of employee experience management platforms. *Information Systems Journal*, *35*(02), 450–479. DOI: 10.1111/isj.12545

Jonathan, H., Magd, H., & Khan, S. A. (2024). Artificial intelligence and augmented reality: a business fortune to sustainability in the digital age. In *Navigating the digital landscape: Understanding customer behaviour in the online world* (pp. 85–105). Emerald Publishing Limited.

Joshi, S. (2025). The Role of AI in Enhancing Teamwork, Resilience and Decision-Making: Review of Recent Developments. *International Journal of Computer Applications*, •••, 9.

Juglan, K. C., Sharma, B., Gehlot, A., Singh, S. P., & Hussein, A. (2023). Exploring the Effectiveness of Natural Language Processing in Customer Service. *3rd International Conference on Advance Computing and Innovative Technologies in Engineering, ICACITE 2023* (pp. 814-818). Greater Noida: Institute of Electrical and Electronics Engineers Inc. DOI: 10.1109/ICACITE57410.2023.10183107

Kadioglu, M. A., & Takci, H. (2022). A data science project management methodology: From development to production (p.2). *Proceedings Book 2*

Kadioglu, M. A., & Alatas, B. (2023). Enhancing Call Center Efficiency: Data Driven Workload Prediction and Workforce Optimization. *The Eurasia Proceedings of Science Technology Engineering and Mathematics*, *24*, 96–100. DOI: 10.55549/epstem.1406245

Kadirov, A., Shakirova, Y., Ismoilova, G., & Makhmudova, N. (2024, April). AI in human resource management: reimagining talent acquisition, development, and retention. In *2024 International Conference on Knowledge Engineering and Communication Systems (ICKECS)* (Vol. 1, pp. 1-8). IEEE.

Kairouz, P., McMahan, H. B., Avent, B., Bellet, A., Bennis, M., Bhagoji, A. N., ... & Zhao, S. (2021). Advances and open problems in federated learning. Foundations and Trends® in Machine Learning, 14(1–2), 1–210. https://doi.org/DOI: 10.1561/2200000083

Kamau, J. N. (2025). Generative Artificial Intelligence and Mental Well-Being of University Students. A Structural Equation Modeling (SEM) Based-Analysis. African. *Journal of Business and Development Studies*, *1*(2), 344–358. DOI: 10.70641/ajbds.v1i2.135

Kambur, E., & Akar, C. (2022). Human resource developments with the touch of artificial intelligence: A scale development study. *International Journal of Manpower*, *43*(1), 168–205.

Kanwal, P., Malik, P., Purty, J., Rawat, N., Randhawa, S. K., & Kaur, K. (2025). Redefining Work: Global Trends, Hybrid Models, and Strategies for Retaining Gen Z Talent in the Age of AI. In Global Work Arrangements and Outsourcing in the Age of AI (pp. 317-340). IGI Global Scientific Publishing.

Kapoor, R., & Agarwal, S. (2020). How artificial intelligence is changing the face of operational efficiency. *Business Horizons*, *63*(1), 53–64.

Karia, N. (2021). A comparative benchmark model for SMEs: Viable entrepreneur emotional intelligence. *Benchmarking*, *28*(3), 813–829.

Karyamsetty, H. J., Khan, S. A., & Nayyar, A. (2024). *Envisioning toward modernization of society 5.0—A prospective glimpse on status, opportunities, and challenges with XAI. XAI Based Intelligent Systems for Society 5.0*. Elsevier.

Kassa, B. Y., & Worku, E. K. (2025). The impact of artificial intelligence on organizational performance: The mediating role of employee productivity. *Journal of Open Innovation*, *11*(1), 100474.

Kassim, N. M., Ramayah, T., & Kurnia, S. (2012). Antecedents and outcomes of human resource information system (HRIS) use. *International Journal of Productivity and Performance Management*, *61*(6), 603–623.

Kaur, J., Devgon, R., & Chaudhary, D. (2022). Work of Fiction: Using Speculative Design to Deliberate on the Future of Hiring. *25th ACM Conference on Computer-Supported Cooperative Work and Social Computing, CSCW 2022* (pp. 23-26). Online: Association for Computing Machinery. DOI: 10.1145/3500868.3559442

Kaur, M. P., Smith, S., Pazour, J. A., & Schumacher, A. D. (2022). Optimization of volunteer task assignments to improve volunteer retention and nonprofit organizational performance. *Socio-Economic Planning Sciences*, *84*, 101392. DOI: 10.1016/j.seps.2022.101392

Keh, H. T., Der Foo, M., & Lim, B. C. (2002). Opportunity evaluation under risky conditions: The cognitive processes of entrepreneurs. *Entrepreneurship Theory and Practice*, *27*(2), 125–148.

Kelan, E. K. (2024, July). Algorithmic inclusion: Shaping the predictive algorithms of artificial intelligence in hiring. *Human Resource Management Journal*, *34*(03), 694–707. DOI: 10.1111/1748-8583.12511

Kennedy, D. (2003). The methods and the politics. In Legrand, P., & Munday, R. (Eds.), *Comparative legal studies: Traditions and transitions* (1st ed., pp. 345–434). Cambridge University Press., DOI: 10.1017/CBO9780511522260.011

Khalilzadeh, J., Ozturk, A. B., & Bilgihan, A. (2017). Security-related factors in extended UTAUT model for NFC based mobile payment in the restaurant industry. *Computers in Human Behavior*, *70*, 460–474.

Khan, M. R. (2024). Application of artificial intelligence for talent management: Challenges and opportunities. Intelligent Human Systems Integration (IHSI 2024): Integrating People and Intelligent Systems, 119(119).

Khan, S. A., & Naim, A. (2024). XAI in Society 5.0 through the lens of marketing and HRM. In *XAI based intelligent Systems for Society 5.0* (pp. 327-363). Elsevier.

Khanam, L., & Mahfuz, M. A. (2017). Employee acceptance of knowledge management systems in Bangladesh: Integrating Utaut and Kms diffusion model. *Independent Business Review*, *10*(1/2), 85–109.

Khanna, D., Edison, H., Nguyen-Duc, A., & Kemell, K.-K. (2024). Software Companies' Responses to Hybrid Working. *50th Euromicro Conference on Software Engineering and Advanced Applications, SEAA 2024* (pp. 244 - 251). Paris: Institute of Electrical and Electronics Engineers Inc. DOI: 10.1109/SEAA64295.2024.00045

Khan, R., Hussain, A., & Ahmad, S. (2023). Revolutionizing Human Resource Management: The Transformative Impact of Artificial Intelligence (AI) Applications. *International Journal of Social Science & Entrepreneurship*, *3*(4), 306–326.

Khan, S. A., Epoc, F., Gangwar, V., Ligori, T. A. A., & Ansari, Z. A. (2021). Will online banking sustain in Bhutan post COVID-19? A quantitative analysis of the customer e-satisfaction and e-loyalty in the Kingdom of Bhutan. *Transnational Marketing Journal*, *9*(3), 607–624.

Khan, S. A., Khatri, B., Jonathan, H., Naim, A., & Arora, S. (2025). Revolutionizing Agriculture: Harnessing High-Performance Computing and Artificial Intelligence for Innovative Farming Practices. In *Circular Economy and Technological Innovation: The Regional Implications* (pp. 237–252). Springer Nature Singapore.

Khatri, B., Shrimali, H., Khan, S. A., & Naim, A. (2023). Role of HR analytics in ensuring psychological wellbeing and job security: Learnings from COVID-19. In *HR analytics in an era of rapid automation* (pp. 36-53). IGI Global.

Kim, Y., & Ployhart, R. E. (2018). The strategic value of selection practices: Antecedents and consequences of firm-level selection practice usage. *Academy of Management Journal*, *61*(1), 46–66.

Kisubi, M. K., Aruo, F., Wakibi, A., Mukyala, V., & Ssenyange, K. (2022). Entrepreneurial competencies and performance of Ugandan SMEs: The mediating role of firm capabilities. *Cogent Business & Management*, *9*(1), 2115622.

Kniffin, K. M., Narayanan, J., Anseel, F., Antonakis, J., & Ashford, S. P. (2021, January). COVID-19 and the workplace: Implications, issues, and insights for future research and action. *The American Psychologist*, *76*(01), 63–77. DOI: 10.1037/amp0000716 PMID: 32772537

Kochhar, R. (2023). Which U.S. workers are more exposed to AI on their jobs? Pew Research Center. https://www.pewresearch.org/wp-content/uploads/sites/20/2023/07/st_2023.07.26_ai-and-jobs-1.pdf.Raghavan, M., Barocas, S., Kleinberg, J., & Levy, K. (2020). Mitigating bias in algorithmic hiring: Evaluating claims and practices. Proceedings of the 2020 Conference on Fairness, Accountability, and Transparency.

Koedinger, K. R., Corbett, A. T., & Perfetti, C. (2012). The knowledge–learning–instruction framework: Bridging the science–practice chasm to enhance robust student learning. *Cognitive Science*, *36*(5), 757–798. DOI: 10.1111/j.1551-6709.2012.01245.x PMID: 22486653

Koeszegi, S. T. (2023). AI @ work: Human empowerment or disempowerment? In *Introduction to Digital Humanism: A Textbook* (pp. 175–196). Springer Nature., DOI: 10.1007/978-3-031-45304-5_12

Kolbjørnsrud, V. (2024). Designing the Intelligent Organization: Six principles for Human-AI collaboration. *California Management Review*, *66*(2), 44–64.

Korzynski, P., Kim, S., & Egan, T. (2024). *Bridging human resource development processes through generative Artificial Intelligence* (Vol. 35). Wiley Online Library.

Kovach, K. A., & Cathcart, C. E.Jr. (1999). Human resource information systems (HRIS): Providing business with rapid data access, information exchange and strategic advantage. *Public Personnel Management*, *28*(2), 275–282.

Krishnan, S., Haas, D., Franklin, M. J., & Wu, E. (2016, June). Towards reliable interactive data cleaning: A user survey and recommendations. In *Proceedings of the Workshop on Human-In-the-Loop Data Analytics* (pp. 1-5). https://doi.org/DOI: 10.1145/2939502.2939511

Kuberkar, S., & Singhal, T. K. (2020). Factors Influencing Adoption Intention of AI Powered Chatbot for Public Transport Services within a Smart City. *International Journal of Emerging Technologies in Learning*, *2020*, 948–958.

Kumar, A. (2025). Research methodology and artificial intelligence: An integrated approach. *Inspira–Journal of Commerce, Economics &. Computer Science*, *11*(2), 111–122.

Kuner, C. (2020). The GDPR and international organizations.

Kusý, Š. (2021). Artificial intelligence as a tool in human research management—potential and current use. *Journal of HRM*, *24*(2).

Kytainyk, V. V., Yushchenko, A. G., & Lyalin, D. Y. (2025). AI - human cooperation in "Second Brain" Technology, as a modern implementation of general evolution in human-machine interaction. *7th International Congress on Human-Computer Interaction, Optimization and Robotic Applications, ICHORA 2025*. Ankara: Institute of Electrical and Electronics Engineers Inc. DOI: 10.1109/ICHORA65333.2025.11017255

La Sala, A., Fuller, R., Riolli, L., & Temperini, V. (2024). The rise of hybrids: Plastic knowledge in human–AI interaction. *Journal of Knowledge Management*, *28*(10), 3023–3045.

Lai, P. C. (2017). The literature review of technology adoption models and theories for the novelty technology. *JISTEM-Journal of Information Systems and Technology Management*, *14*(1), 21–38.

Langer, M., König, C. J., & Papathanasiou, M. (2019). Highly automated job interviews: Acceptance under the influence of stakes. *International Journal of Selection and Assessment*, *27*(3), 217–234.

Latané, B. (1981). The psychology of social impact. *The American Psychologist*, *36*(4), 343.

Lauring, J., & Jonasson, C. (2025). What is hybrid work? Towards greater conceptual clarity of a common term and understanding its consequences. *Human Resource Management Review*, *35*(1), 101044. Advance online publication. DOI: 10.1016/j.hrmr.2024.101044

Lee, C. C., Li, Y. S., Yeh, W. C., & Yu, Z. (2022). The effects of leader emotional intelligence, leadership styles, organizational commitment, and trust on job performance in the real estate brokerage industry. *Frontiers in Psychology*, *13*, 881725.

Lee, D., & Lee, S. T. (2023). Artificial intelligence enabled energy-efficient heating, ventilation and air conditioning system: Design, analysis and necessary hardware upgrades. *Applied Thermal Engineering*, *235*, 121253. DOI: 10.1016/j.applthermaleng.2023.121253

Lee, J. D., & See, K. A. (2004). Trust in automation: Designing for appropriate reliance. *Human Factors*, *46*(1), 50–80. DOI: 10.1518/hfes.46.1.50_30392 PMID: 15151155

Lee, M. K. (2018). Understanding perception of algorithmic decisions: Fairness, trust, and emotion in response to algorithmic management. *Big Data & Society*, *5*(1), 2053951718756684.

Lee, M., Yun, J. J., Pyka, A., Won, D., Kodama, F., Schiuma, G., & Zhao, X. (2018). How to respond to the fourth industrial revolution, or the second information technology revolution? Dynamic new combinations between technology, market, and society through open innovation. *Journal of Open Innovation*, *4*(3), 21.

Lee, S. H., Peña-Mora, F., & Park, M. (2006). Dynamic planning and control methodology for strategic and operational construction project management. *Automation in Construction*, *15*(1), 84–97. DOI: 10.1016/j.autcon.2005.02.008

Lenka, R., & Chanda, R. (2025). Generative AI for Predicting Employee Engagement in HR Analytics: A Bibliometric Analysis. *9th International Conference on ICT for Sustainable Development, ICT4SD 2024. 1162 LNNS*, pp. 201-209. Goa: Springer Science and Business Media Deutschland GmbH. DOI: 10.1007/978-981-97-8605-3_19

Leonardi, P. M., Parker, S. H., & Shen, R. (2024). How Remote Work Changes the World of Work. *Annual Review of Organizational Psychology and Organizational Behavior*, *11*, 193–219. DOI: 10.1146/annurev-orgpsych-091922-015852

Liang, S. Z., Xu, J. L., & Huang, E. (2024). Comprehensive analysis of the effect of social influence and brand image on purchase intention. *SAGE Open*, *14*(1), 21582440231218771.

Li, C., Ahmed, N., Qalati, S. A., Khan, A., & Naz, S. (2020). Role of business incubators as a tool for entrepreneurship development: The mediating and moderating role of business start-up and government regulations. *Sustainability*, *12*(5), 1822.

Lihua, D. (2022). An extended model of the theory of planned behavior: An empirical study of entrepreneurial intention and entrepreneurial behavior in college students. *Frontiers in Psychology*, *12*, 627818.

Li, L. (2022). Reskilling and upskilling the future-ready workforce for industry 4.0 and beyond. *Information Systems Frontiers*, •••, 1–16.

Lilly, A., Rajkumar, R., & Amudha, R. (2022). Aggrandizing the human resource development with underpinning artificial intelligence. *Journal of Statistics and Management Systems*, *25*(5), 1083–1094.

Linde, S., Walker, R. J., Campbell, J. A., & Egede, L. E. (2025). Structural inequalities and chronic disease health outcomes: Impact of AI on health equity. In *Structural Inequalities and Health Outcomes for Chronic Disease* (pp. 587–616). Elsevier., DOI: 10.1016/B978-0-443-23750-8.00029-1

Li, Y., Tolosa, L., Rivas-Echeverria, F., & Marquez, R. (2025). *Integrating AI in education: Navigating UNESCO global guidelines, emerging trends, and its intersection with sustainable development goals. ChemRxiv*. DOI: 10.26434/chemrxiv-2025-wz4n9

Lo, L. S. (2023). The art and science of prompt engineering: A new literacy in the information age. *Internet Reference Services Quarterly*, *27*(4), 203–210. DOI: 10.1080/10875301.2023.2227621

Loy, R. W., Christiansen, N. D., Tett, R. P., Klein, K., & Toich, M. (2025). Personality Test Validity Differs Between Low-Stakes and High-Stakes Employment Settings. *International Journal of Selection and Assessment*, *33*(3), e70018.

Lumpkin, G. T., & Dess, G. G. (1996). Clarifying the entrepreneurial orientation construct and linking it to performance. *Academy of Management Review*, *21*(1), 135–172.

Machani, M. P., Nagapriya, C., & Kumar, Y. L. (2021). Motives driving the entrepreneurial thought: An empirical study on micro entrepreneurs. *Design Engineering (London)*, *1*, 15271–15281.

Madanchian, M. (2024, December). From Recruitment to Retention: AI Tools for Human Resource Decision-Making. *Applied Sciences (Switzerland)*, *14*(24). Advance online publication. DOI: 10.3390/app142411750

Madanchian, M., Taherdoost, H., & Mohamed, N. (2023). AI-based human resource management tools and techniques; a systematic literature review. *Procedia Computer Science*, *229*, 367–377.

Madhumithaa, N., Sharma, A., Adabala, S. K., Siddiqui, S., & Kothinti, R. R. (2025). Leveraging AI for personalized employee development: A new era in human resource management. *Advances in Consumer Research. Association for Consumer Research (U. S.)*, *2*(1).

Maertz, C. P.Jr, Griffeth, R. W., Campbell, N. S., & Allen, D. G. (2007). The effects of perceived organizational support and perceived supervisor support on employee turnover. *Journal of Organizational Behavior: The International Journal of Industrial. Occupational and Organizational Psychology and Behavior*, *28*(8), 1059–1075. DOI: 10.1002/job.472

Magd, H., Jonathan, H., Khan, S. A., & El Geddawy, M. (2022). Artificial intelligence—the driving force of industry 4.0. *A roadmap for enabling industry 4.0 by artificial intelligence*, 1-15.

Magd, H., Ansari, M. S. A., & Khan, S. A. (2024). Need for explainable artificial intelligence ethnic decision-making in society 5.0. In *XAI Based Intelligent Systems for Society 5.0* (pp. 103–127). Elsevier.

Magd, H., Khan, S. A., Khatri, B., Sharma, N., & Arora, S. (2023). Understanding the relationship between IoT and digital marketing: a bibliometric analysis. In *Global applications of the internet of things in digital marketing* (pp. 123–140). IGI Global.

Magesh, N., Thangaraj, P., Sivagobika, S., Praba, S., & Mohana Priya, R. (2013). Evaluating the performance of an employee using decision tree algorithm. *International Journal of Engineering Research & Technology (Ahmedabad), 2*(4).

Maier, D., Maier, A., A chilean, I., Anastasiu, L., & Gavri , O. (2020). The relationship between innovation and sustainability: A bibliometric review of the literature. *Sustainability, 12*(10), 4083.

Mai, K. N., & Nguyen, V. T. (2023). Entrepreneurial ecosystem affects organisational learning, creativity and success. *Cogent Business & Management, 10*(3), 2260125.

Maisha, K., & Shetu, S. N. (2023). Influencing factors of e-learning adoption amongst students in a developing country: The post-pandemic scenario in Bangladesh. *Future Business Journal, 9*(1), 37.

Makarius, E. E., Mukherjee, D., Fox, J. D., & Fox, A. K. (2020). Rising with the machines: A sociotechnical framework for bringing artificial intelligence into the organisation. *Journal of Business Research, 120*, 262–273.

Malik, A., Budhwar, P., & Mohan, H., & NR, S. (2023). Employee experience–the missing link for engaging employees: Insights from an MNE's AI-based HR ecosystem. *Human Resource Management, 62*(1), 97–115.

Malik, P., & Malik, P. (2024). Mitigating destructive deviance in organisations: Assessing the role of perceived HRM practices and perceived organisational support. *The International Journal of Organizational Analysis, 32*(7), 1242–1263.

Manzoor, F., Wei, L., Bányai, T., Nurunnabi, M., & Subhan, Q. A. (2019). An examination of sustainable HRM practices on job performance: An application of training as a moderator. *Sustainability, 11*(8), 2263.

Ma, Q., & Liu, L. (2004). The technology acceptance model: A meta-analysis of empirical findings. [JOEUC]. *Journal of Organizational and End User Computing, 16*(1), 59–72.

Margherita, A. (2021). Human resources analytics: A systematization of research topics and directions for future research. *Human Resource Management Review, 31*(2), 100795. DOI: 10.1016/j.hrmr.2020.100795

Marler, J. (2016). An evidence-based review of HR Analytics. *International Journal of Human Resource Management*. Advance online publication. DOI: 10.1080/09585192.2016.1244699

Marozva, R. R., & Pelser, A. M. (2025). Social employee well-being challenges of academics in the hybrid work environment. *Frontiers in Psychology, 16*, 1524804. PMID: 39989635

Masayuki, M. 2017. Who are afraid of losing their jobs to artificial intelligence and robots? Evidence from a survey. RIETI Discussion Paper Series 17-E-069.

Masood, A. (2018). Green human resource management: Policies and practices. *International Journal of Management Studies, 5*(3), 12–20.

Massaro, M., Secinaro, S., Bagnoli, C., & Calandra, D. (2025). Guest editorial: Artificial Intelligence (AI) for management decision-making processes. From measurement to strategy. *Management Decision, 63*(10), 3213–3225.

Mayer, J. D., Salovey, P., & Caruso, D. R. (2008). Emotional intelligence: New ability or eclectic traits? *The American Psychologist, 63*(6), 503.

McCausland, T. (2023). Creating psychological safety in the workplace. *Research Technology Management, 66*(2), 56–58.

McCoy, B. R. (2016). Digital distractions in the classroom phase II: Student classroom use of digital devices for non-class related purposes.

McKinsey & Company. (2022). Women in the workplace 2022. *McKinsey & Company and LeanIn.Org*. Retrieved from https://www.mckinsey.com

McKinsey & Company. (2025). The state of AI in 2025: Agents, innovation, and transformation. https://www.mckinsey.com/capabilities/quantumblack/our-insights/the-state-of-ai

McStay, A. (2018). Emotional AI: The rise of empathic media.

Mehrabi, N., Morstatter, F., Saxena, N., Lerman, K., & Galstyan, A. (2021). A survey on bias and fairness in machine learning. *ACM Computing Surveys, 54*(6), 1–35. DOI: 10.1145/3457607

Mei, L., Zhang, T., & Chen, J. (2019). Exploring the effects of inter-firm linkages on SMEs' open innovation from an ecosystem perspective: An empirical study of Chinese manufacturing SMEs. *Technological Forecasting and Social Change, 144*, 118–128.

Meltzer, J., Tielemans, A., & Brookings Institution. (2022). THE EU AI ACT: NEXT STEPS AND ISSUES FOR BUILDING INTERNATIONAL COOPERATION. In *Brookings Institution* [Policy brief]. https://www.brookings.edu/wp-content/uploads/2022/05/FCAI-Policy-Brief_Final_060122.pdf

Mennella, C., Maniscalco, U., De Pietro, G., & Esposito, M. (2024). Ethical and regulatory challenges of AI technologies in healthcare: A narrative review. *Heliyon*. PMID: 38384518

Miao, C., Humphrey, R. H., & Qian, S. (2017). A meta-analysis of emotional intelligence and work attitudes. *Journal of Occupational and Organizational Psychology, 90*(2), 177–202.

Miao, C., Qian, S., & Ma, D. (2017). The relationship between entrepreneurial self-efficacy and firm performance: A meta-analysis of main and moderator effects. *Journal of Small Business Management, 55*(1), 87–107.

Michael, M. T. (2020). Unconscious emotion and free-energy: A philosophical and neuroscientific exploration. *Frontiers in Psychology, 11*, 984.

Michelle, S. (2024, Mar 05). *AI-native learning platform uses recommendation engine to deliver personalized learning experiences for technical teams, business users, C-suite and board members*. Retrieved Aug 19, 2025, from https://newsroom.accenture.com: https://newsroom.accenture.com/news/2024/accenture-launches-accenture-learnvantage-to-help-clients-and-their-people-gain-essential-skills-and-achieve-greater-business-value-in-the-ai-economy

Microsoft. (2025). *Advanced analysis privacy: Viva Insights documentation*. https://learn.microsoft.com/en-us/viva/insights/advanced/privacy/privacy

Microsoft. (n.d.). *Microsoft Viva privacy*. Microsoft. https://www.microsoft.com/en-in/microsoft-viva/privacy

Milhem, M., Ayyash, M. M., Ateeq, A., Alzaghal, Q., & Alzoraiki, M. (2024). Emotional intelligence in leadership: Its role in fostering employee engagement in Palestine's ICT sector. *Problems and Perspectives in Management, 22*(1), 338.

Mishra, S., Choubey, S., Choubey, A., Yogeesh, N., & Rao, J. D. (2022). Data Extraction Approach using Natural Language Processing for Sentiment Analysis. *1st IEEE International Conference on Automation, Computing and Renewable Systems, ICACRS 2022* (pp. 970-972). Pudukkottai: Institute of Electrical and Electronics Engineers Inc. DOI: 10.1109/ICACRS55517.2022.10029216

Mishra, A., & Barik, R. (2024). The role of artificial intelligence in augmenting green HRM for sustainable development: A bibliometric perspective. *Srusti Management Review*, *17*(1), 117–126.

Mishra, P. (2017). Sustainable development in India: Challenges and opportunities. *The International Journal of Environmental Studies*, *74*(2), 207–220. DOI: 10.1080/00207233.2016.1245678

Mishra, P. (2017, September). Green Human Resource Management: A framework for sustainable organizational development in an emerging economy. *The International Journal of Organizational Analysis*.

Mitchell, M., Wu, S., Zaldivar, A., Barnes, P., Vasserman, L., Hutchinson, B., & Gebru, T. (2021). Model cards for model reporting. In *Proceedings of the Conference on Fairness, Accountability, and Transparency (FAT'19)* (pp. 220–229). https://doi .org/DOI: 10.1145/3287560.3287596

Mittal, P., Jora, R. B., Sodhi, K. K., & Saxena, P. (2023). A Review of The Role of Artificial Intelligence in Employee Engagement. *9th International Conference on Advanced Computing and Communication Systems, ICACCS 2023* (pp. 2502-2506). Coimbatore: Institute of Electrical and Electronics Engineers Inc. DOI: 10.1109/ ICACCS57279.2023.10112957

Mittelstadt, B. D., Allo, P., Taddeo, M., Wachter, S., & Floridi, L. (2016). The ethics of algorithms: Mapping the debate. *Big Data & Society*, *3*(2). Advance online publication. DOI: 10.1177/2053951716679679

Mohammad, S. M. (2020). Artificial intelligence in information technology. Available at *SSRN* 3625444.

Mohammad, S. M. (2022). Ethics sheet for automatic emotion recognition and sentiment analysis. *Computational Linguistics*, *48*(2), 239–278.

Mohammed, D. A. Q. (2019). HR analytics: A modern tool in HR for predictive decision making. *Journal of Management*, *6*(3).

Moore, P. V., Upchurch, M., & Whittaker, X. (2018). *Humans and machines at work: Monitoring, surveillance and automation in contemporary capitalism*. Palgrave Macmillan.

Morariu, C., Morariu, O., Răileanu, S., & Borangiu, T. (2020). Machine learning for predictive scheduling and resource allocation in large scale manufacturing systems. *Computers in Industry, 120*, 103244. DOI: 10.1016/j.compind.2020.103244

Mortan, R. A., Ripoll, P., Carvalho, C., & Bernal, M. C. (2014). Effects of emotional intelligence on entrepreneurial intention and self-efficacy. *Revista de Psicología del Trabajo y de las Organizaciones, 30*(3), 97–104.

Mourad, Z., Noura, A., Mohamed, C., & Abdelhamid, B. (2024). Enhancing employee performance management: A data-driven decision support model using machine learning algorithms. *International Journal of Advanced Computer Science and Applications, 15*(3).

Mousa, S. K., & Othman, M. (2020). The impact of green human resource management practices on sustainable performance in organizations. *Journal of Cleaner Production, 243*, 118595. DOI: 10.1016/j.jclepro.2019.118595

Moussy, C., Burfield, I. J., Stephenson, P. J., Newton, A. F., Butchart, S. H., Sutherland, W. J., & Donald, P. F. (2022). A quantitative global review of species population monitoring. *Conservation Biology, 36*(1), e13721. DOI: 10.1111/cobi.13721

Mudunuri, L. N. R., & Bhattacharya, P. (2025). Ethical Considerations Balancing Emotion and Autonomy in AI Systems. In *Humanizing Technology With Emotional Intelligence* (pp. 443–456). IGI Global Scientific Publishing.

Muller, M., & Weisz, J. (2022). Extending a Human-AI Collaboration Framework with Dynamism and Sociality. *1st Annual Meeting of the Symposium on Human-Computer Interaction for Work, CHIWORK 2022*. Virtual, Online: Association for Computing Machinery. DOI: 10.1145/3533406.3533407

Muris, J. E. M., Herder, E., Hoppenbrouwers, S. J. B. A., & Strieker, M. (2021). The Consequences of Artificial Intelligence in Human Capital Management in the Next Five to Ten Years (Doctoral dissertation, Thesis. Faculty of Science. Nijmegen: Radboud University).

Murphy, G. B., Trailer, J. W., & Hill, R. C. (1996). Measuring performance in entrepreneurship research. *Journal of Business Research, 36*(1), 15–23.

Murugesan, U., Subramanian, P., Srivastava, S., & Dwivedi, A. (2023). A study of artificial intelligence impacts on human resource digitalization in industry 4.0. *Decision Analytics Journal, 7*, 100249.

Muthusubramanian, M., Jangoan, S., Sharma, K. K., & Krishnamoorthy, G. (2024). Demystifying explainable AI: Understanding, transparency and trust. *International Journal for Multidisciplinary Research*, *6*(2), 1–13. DOI: 10.36948/ijfmr.2024.v06i02.14597

Mwita, K. M., & Kitole, F. A. (2025, December). Potential benefits and challenges of artificial intelligence in human resource management in public institutions. *Discover Global Society*, *03*(01). Advance online publication. DOI: 10.1007/s44282-025-00175-8

Naim, A., Khan, S. A., Mohammed, A. B., & Malik, P. K. (2024b). Applications of high performance computing and AI in green digital marketing. In *AI Applications for Business, Medical, and Agricultural Sustainability* (pp. 47-67). IGI Global Scientific Publishing.

Naim, A., Mohammed, A. B., Fatima, N., Khan, S. A., Alnfiai, M. M., & Malik, P. K. (2024a). Applications of artificial intelligence in environmental resource business management and sustainability. In *AI Applications for Business, Medical, and Agricultural Sustainability* (pp. 1-22). IGI Global Scientific Publishing.

Nakiganda, R. G., Okello, D. O., & Bett, H. K. (2025). Factors influencing the sustainability of university-incubated agribusinesses: The role of stigma failure, personality and motivation in Kenya. *Cogent Business & Management*, *12*(1), 2447410.

Narayanan, A., & Shmatikov, V. (2008, May). Robust de-anonymization of large sparse datasets. In 2008 IEEE Symposium on Security and Privacy (sp 2008) (pp. 111-125). IEEE.

Narkhede, B. E., Nehete, R. S., Raut, R. D., & Mahajan, S. K. (2014). Impact of entrepreneurial skills on the firm's performance: Evidence from manufacturing SMEs in India. *International Journal of Indian Culture and Business Management*, *8*(2), 216–236.

Nawaz, N. (2024). The adoption of artificial intelligence in human resources management. *Journal of Business Research*, *4*, 1–11. https://www.sciencedirect.com/science/article/pii/S266709682300054X

Nedumaran, C., Shyam, S. S., Sham Kumar, S., Nithish, K. R., & Rajan, R. G. (2023). An Intelligent Agent to Automate HR Process. *2023 IEEE World Conference on Communication and Computing, WCONF 2023.* Raipur: IEEE. DOI: 10.1109/WCONF58270.2023.10235110

Newman, A., Donohue, R., & Eva, N. (2017). Psychological safety: A systematic review of the literature. *Human Resource Management Review*, *27*(3), 521–535.

Nguyen, T. D., Le, H. S., Lam, H. T., Tran, T. A., & Tran, Q. T. (2023). A survey of AI-based robotic process automation for businesses and organizations. *Science and Technology Development Journal*, *26*(3), 2959–2966.

Nguyen, T.-H. D., Chen, Z., & El-Nasr, M. S. (2015). Analytics-based AI techniques for a better gaming experience. *Game AI Pro*, *2*, 481–500.

Nielsen, K., & Shepherd, R. (2022). Understanding the outcomes of training to improve employee mental health: A novel framework for training transfer and effectiveness evaluation. *Work and Stress*, *36*(4), 377–391. DOI: 10.1080/02678373.2022.2028318

Nieves, J. C., Osorio, M., Rojas-Velazquez, D., Magallanes, Y., & Brännström, A. (2024). Digital companions for well-being: challenges and opportunities. *Journal of Intelligent & Fuzzy Systems*, JIFS-219336.

Nocker, M., & Sena, V. (2019). Big data and human resources management: The rise of talent analytics. *Social Sciences*, *8*(10), 273.

Noy, S., & Zhang, W. (2023). Experimental Evidence on the Productivity Effects of Generative Artificial Intelligence. *Science*, *381*(6654), 187–192.

Noy, S., & Zhang, W. (2023). Experimental evidence on the productivity effects of generative artificial intelligence. *Science*, *381*(6654), 187–192. DOI: 10.1126/science.adh2586 PMID: 37440646

Nuswantoro, B., Richter, A., & Riemer, K. (2023). Conceptualizing Visibility in Hybrid Work. *44th International Conference on Information Systems: Rising like a Phoenix: Emerging from the Pandemic and Reshaping Human Endeavors with Digital Technologies, ICIS 2023*. Hyderibad: Association for Information Systems. Retrieved Aug 08, 2025, from https://www.scopus.com/pages/publications/85192500405

Nuswantoro, B., Richter, A., & Riemer, K. (2023). Conceptualizing visibility in hybrid work. https://doi.org/DOI: 10.25455/wgtn.27092125

O'Cass, A., & Weerawardena, J. (2009). Examining the role of international entrepreneurship, innovation and international market performance in SME internationalisation. *European Journal of Marketing*, *43*(11/12), 1325–1348.

O'Neil, C. (2016). *Weapons of math destruction: How big data increases inequality and threatens democracy*. Crown.

O'Sullivan, D. T. J., Keane, M. M., Kelliher, D., & Hitchcock, R. J. (2004). Improving building operation by tracking performance metrics throughout the building lifecycle (BLC). *Energy and Building*, *36*(11), 1075–1090. DOI: 10.1016/j.enbuild.2004.03.003

Obeidat, B. Y., Al-Suradi, M. M., Masa'deh, R., & Tarhini, A. (2016). The impact of knowledge management on innovation: An empirical study on Jordanian consultancy firms. *Management Research Review*, *39*(10), 1214–1238.

Oben, U. F., Gozukara, E., & Tezcan, L. (2022). The Moderating Roles of Remote, Hybrid, and Onsite Working on the Relationship between Work Engagement and Organizational Identification during the COVID-19 Pandemic. *Sustainability*, *14*(24), 16828. DOI: 10.3390/su142416828

Obiuto, N. C., Adebayo, R. A., Olajiga, O. K., & Festus-Ikhuoria, I. C. (2024). Integrating artificial intelligence in construction management: Improving project efficiency and cost-effectiveness. *Int. J. Adv. Multidisc. Res. Stud*, *4*(2), 639–647.

Ochmann, J., & Laumer, S. (2020, March). AI Recruitment: Explaining job seekers' acceptance of automation in human resource management. In *Wirtschaftsinformatik (Zentrale Tracks)* (pp. 1633-1648).

OECD. (2023). *OECD Employment Outlook 2023: Artificial Intelligence and the Labour Market*. OECD Publishing., DOI: 10.1787/08785bba-

Oguamanam, C. (2020). Indigenous peoples, data sovereignty, and self-determination: Current realities and imperatives. *The African Journal of Information and Communication*, *26*, 1–20.

Olaleye, B. R., Lekunze, J. N., & Sekhampu, T. J. (2024). Examining structural relationships between innovation capability, knowledge sharing, environmental turbulence, and organisational sustainability. *Cogent Business & Management*, *11*(1), 2393738.

Oliveira, T., Thomas, M., Baptista, G., & Campos, F. (2016). Mobile payment: Understanding the determinants of customer adoption and intention to recommend the technology. *Computers in Human Behavior*, *61*, 404–414.

Opatha, H. H. D. N. P., & Arulrajah, A. A. (2014). Green human resource management: Simplified general reflections. *International Business Research*, *7*(8), 101–112. DOI: 10.5539/ibr.v7n8p101

Open, A. I. (2023). GPT-4 Technical Report. https://cdn.openai.com/papers/gpt-4.pdf

Organisation for Economic Co-operation and Development (OECD). (2021). *The gender gap in employment: Challenges and policy responses.* OECD Publishing. Retrieved from https://www.oecd.org/employment/the-gender-gap-in-employment .html

Organisation for Economic Co-operation and Development (OECD). (2023). *AI, gender and work: Building inclusive workplaces*. OECD Publishing. Retrieved from https://www.oecd.org/en/topics/sub-issues/ai-and-work.html

Organisation for Economic Co-operation and Development. (2024). *Using AI in the workplace: Opportunities, risks and policy responses.*

Oriarewo, G. O., Ofobruku, S. A., & Tor, Z. A. (2019). The implications of emotional intelligence on entrepreneurial performance: A discuss. *South Asian Journal of Social Studies and Economics*, *3*(1), 1–13.

Orobia, L. A., Nakibuuka, J., Bananuka, J., & Akisimire, R. (2020). Inventory management, managerial competence and financial performance of small businesses. *Journal of Accounting in Emerging Economies*, *10*(3), 379–398.

Orr, A. E., & Savage, T. (2021). Expanding access to and ensuring equity in the benefits of remote work following the COVID-19 pandemic. *Journal of Science Policy & Governance*, *18*(4), 1–8. DOI: 10.38126/JSPG180413

Otache, I. (2024). Innovation capability, strategic flexibility and SME performance: The roles of competitive advantage and competitive intensity. *African Journal of Economic and Management Studies*, *15*(2), 248–262.

Owen, R., Stilgoe, J., Macnaghten, P., Gorman, M., Fisher, E., & Guston, D. (2013). A framework for responsible innovation. Responsible innovation: managing the responsible emergence of science and innovation in society, 27-50.

Özkiziltan, D., & Hassel, A. (2021). Artificial Intelligence at Work: An Overview of the literature. SSRN Electronic Journal. DOI: 10.2139/ssrn.3796746

Pagán-Castaño, E., Maseda-Moreno, A., & Santos-Rojo, C. (2020). Wellbeing in work environments. *Journal of Business Research*, *115*, 469–474.

Page, M. J., McKenzie, J. E., Bossuyt, P. M., Boutron, I., Hoffmann, T. C., Mulrow, C. D., Shamseer, L., Tetzlaff, J. M., Akl, E. A., & Brennan, S. E. (2021). The PRISMA 2020 statement: An updated guideline for reporting systematic reviews. *BMJ (Clinical Research Ed.)*, ●●●, 372.

Palich, L. E., & Bagby, D. R. (1995). Using cognitive theory to explain entrepreneurial risk-taking: Challenging conventional wisdom. *Journal of Business Venturing*, *10*(6), 425–438.

Pandey, S. (2020). Exploring the role of Artificial Intelligence (AI) in transforming HR functions: An Empirical Study in the Indian Context. *International Journal of Scientific Research and Engineering Development*, *3*(5).

Pan, Y., & Froese, F. J. (2023). An interdisciplinary review of AI and HRM: Challenges and future directions. *Human Resource Management Review*, *33*(1), 100924.

Papamitsiou, Z., & Economides, A. A. (2014). Learning Analytics and Educational Data Mining in Practice: A Systematic Literature Review of Empirical Evidence. *Journal of Educational Technology & Society*, *17*(4), 49–64. https://www.jstor.org/stable/jeductechsoci.17.4.49

Pareek, A., & Dheer, P. (2025). CSR and Sustainability in the Cement Industry of Rajasthan: A Comparative Study of Company Performance and Stakeholders' Engagement (Based on Secondary Survey Reports). *International Journal of Scientific Research in Science and Technology*, *12*(2), 450–458.

Parida, V., Pesämaa, O., Wincent, J., & Westerberg, M. (2017). Network capability, innovativeness, and performance: A multidimensional extension for entrepreneurship. *Entrepreneurship and Regional Development*, *29*(1–2), 94–115.

Park, J. S., Shin, J., & Lee, T. (2024). To believe or not to believe: Leader's belief about emotion usefulness and its impact on team dynamics. *BMC Psychology*, *12*(1), 737.

Park, W. (2018). *Artificial intelligence and human resource management: new perspectives and challenges*. Japan Institute for Labour Policy and Training.

Patel, V., Chesmore, A., Legner, C. M., & Pandey, S. (2022). Trends in workplace wearable technologies and connected-worker solutions for next-generation occupational safety, health, and productivity. *Advanced Intelligent Systems*, *4*(1), 2100099. DOI: 10.1002/aisy.202100099

Pathak, S., & Solanki, V. K. (2021). Impact of internet of things and artificial intelligence on human resource development. In *Further advances in internet of things in biomedical and cyber physical systems* (pp. 239–267). Springer.

Patil, D. (2024). Impact of artificial intelligence on employment and workforce development: Risks, opportunities, and socioeconomic implications. DOI: 10.2139/ssrn.5010441

Patil, P., Tamilmani, K., Rana, N. P., & Raghavan, V. (2020). Understanding consumer adoption of mobile payment in India: Extending Meta-UTAUT model with personal innovativeness, anxiety, trust, and grievance redressal. *International Journal of Information Management*, *54*, 102144.

Patil, S., Upadhye, P., Khandekar, S. R., Darekar, P., & Ghewari, A. (2024). Artificial Intelligence and Data Science Approaches to Analyzing Human Resource Management in Hybrid and Remote Work Models. *Proceedings of the 2024 International Conference on Innovative Computing, Intelligent Communication and Smart Electrical Systems, ICSES 2024.* Chennai: Institute of Electrical and Electronics Engineers Inc. DOI: 10.1109/ICSES63760.2024.10910810

Pereira, V., Hadjielias, E., Christofi, M., & Vrontis, D. (2024). A systematic literature review on the impact of artificial intelligence on workplace outcomes: A multi-process perspective. *Human Resource Management Review.*

Petrescu, M., & Krishen, A. S. (2023). Hybrid intelligence: Human–AI collaboration in marketing analytics. *Journal of Marketing Analytics, 11*(3), 263–274.

Pham, N. T., Tučková, Z., & Jabbour, C. J. C. (2020). Greening the hospitality industry: How do green human resource management practices influence organizational citizenship behavior? *Tourism Management, 72*, 386–399. DOI: 10.1016/j.tourman.2018.12.005

Picard, R. W. (2000). *Affective computing*. MIT press.

Pitchforth, J., & Mengersen, K. (2013). A proposed validation framework for expert elicited Bayesian Networks. *Expert Systems with Applications, 40*(1), 162–167. DOI: 10.1016/j.eswa.2012.07.026

Pittet, D. (2008). Hand hygiene: It's all about when and how. *Infection Control and Hospital Epidemiology, 29*(10), 957–959. DOI: 10.1086/592218

Ponce-Bobadilla, A. V., Mensing, S., Schmitt, V., & Stodtmann, S. (2024). Practical guide to SHAP analysis: Explaining supervised machine learning model predictions in drug development. *Clinical and Translational Science.*

Poser, M., & Bittner, E. A. (2021). (Re)Designing IT Support: How Embedded and Conversational AI Can Augment Technical Support Work. *42nd International Conference on Information Systems: Building Sustainability and Resilience with IS: A Call for Action, ICIS 2021 TREOs.* Austin: Association for Information Systems. Retrieved Aug 15, 2025, from https://www.scopus.com/pages/publications/85152125922

Prasanth, A., Densy, J. V., Surendran, P., & Bindhya, T. (2023). Role of artificial intelligence and business decision making. *International Journal of Advanced Computer Science and Applications, 14*(6). Advance online publication. DOI: 10.14569/ijacsa.2023.01406103

Prashantham, S., & Dhanaraj, C. (2010). The dynamic influence of social capital on the international growth of new ventures. *Journal of Management Studies, 47*(6), 967–994.

Pratama, I. (2025). THE FUTURE OF WORK: EXPLORING THE IMPACT OF AUTOMATION AND AI ON THE LABOR MARKET AND ETHICAL BUSINESS PRACTICES. International Conference "Actual Economy: Local Solutions for Global Challenges", 280-282.

Prem, P. S. (2024). Machine learning in employee performance evaluation: A HRM perspective. *International Journal of Science and Research Archive, 11*(1), 1573–1585.

Pulka, B. M., Ramli, A., & Mohamad, A. (2021). Entrepreneurial competencies, entrepreneurial orientation, entrepreneurial network, government business support and SMEs performance. The moderating role of the external environment. *Journal of Small Business and Enterprise Development, 28*(4), 586–618.

Qamar, F., Afshan, G., & Rana, S. A. (2023). Sustainable HRM and well-being: systematic review and future research agenda. Management review quarterly, 1-51.

Qamar, Y., Agrawal, R. K., Samad, T. A., & Chiappetta Jabbour, C. J. (2021). When technology meets people: The interplay of artificial intelligence and human resource management. *Journal of Enterprise Information Management, 34*(5), 1339–1370.

Qin, F., & Kochan, T. A. (2020). *The learning system at IBM: A case study* (MIT Sloan School of Management Working Paper). MIT Sloan School of Management. https://mitsloan.mit.edu/sites/default/files/2022-06/Qin%20and%20Kochan%20The%20Learning%20System%20at%20IBM%2012%202020.pdf

Qin, S., Jia, N., Luo, X., Liao, C., & Huang, Z. (2023). Perceived fairness of human managers compared with artificial intelligence in employee performance evaluation. *Journal of Management Information Systems, 40*(4), 1039–1070.

Qi, R., Wang, D., Yang, Y., & Wu, F. (2023). How does environmental perception affect the willingness of university students to return home to start a business? *Cogent Business & Management, 10*(3), 2288720.

Raghavan, M., Barocas, S., Kleinberg, J., & Levy, K. (2020). Mitigating bias in algorithmic hiring: Evaluating claims and practices. In *Proceedings of the 2020 Conference on Fairness, Accountability, and Transparency* (pp. 469–481). https://doi.org/DOI: 10.1145/3351095.3372828

Raikov, A. N., & Pirani, M. (2022). Contradiction of modern and social-humanitarian artificial intelligence. *Kybernetes, 51*(13), 186–198. DOI: 10.1108/K-01-2022-0057

Rajan, A., & Nagajothi, V. (2024). AI-Powered Talent Management Strategies in HR: An Analytical Study. *International Journal of Scientific Research in Modern Science and Technology, 3*(12).

Rajeswari, A., & Gomathi, S. (2022, December 20). Wearable Technology: A Stimulant for Employee Engagement in a Hybrid Work model. *International Journal of Intelligent Systems and Applications in Engineering, 10*(04), 689–694. Retrieved August 09, 2025, from https://www.scopus.com/pages/publications/85164813799

Rajni, D. R. J., Rajvanshi, A., Shaikh, M., Tiwari, V., & Alaskar, K. (2023). Impact of Artificial Intelligence (AI) on Selected Human Resource Management (HRM) Functions in Pharmaceutical Industry in India. *Migration Letters : An International Journal of Migration Studies, 20*(S13), 629–646.

Ramasamy, A. (2017). A Study on Implications of Implementing Green HRM in the Corporate Bodies with Special Reference to Developing Nations. *International Journal of Business and Management, 12*(9), 117.

Ramkumar, G., Sujatha, V., & Raja, B., TamilSelvi, M., Balaji, A., & Kumar, A. K. (2023, November). An Experiment to Develop an Enhanced Medical Image Security by using Deep Learning Assisted Crypto Policy. In 2023 *International Conference on Research Methodologies in Knowledge Management, Artificial Intelligence and Telecommunication Engineering (RMKMATE)* (pp. 1-8). IEEE.https://doi.org/ DOI: 10.1109/RMKMATE57356.2023.10123456

Ramos, I. F., Gianini, G., Leva, M. C., & Damiani, E. (2024, November). Collaborative Intelligence for Safety-Critical Industries: A Literature Review. *Information (Switzerland), 15*(11). Advance online publication. DOI: 10.3390/info15110728

Rana, E. K. (2020). Bringing emotional intelligence to technology with Rana el-Kaliouby

Rane, N. L., Paramesha, M., Choudhary, S. P., & Rane, J. (2024). Artificial intelligence, machine learning, and deep learning for advanced business strategies: A review. *Partners Universal International Innovation Journal*, 2(3).

Rao, T. V. N., Patel, G. S., Bhavana, S., & Swetha, C. (2025). AI-Driven Decision Support System for Workplace Wellbeing. In *Insights on Wellbeing and Happiness in the Workplace* (pp. 1–18). IGI Global Scientific Publishing.

Rathinaswamy, J., Sengottaiyan, K., & Duraisamy, B. (2020). A qualitative approach towards adoption of information and communication technology by medical doctors applying utaut model. Xi'an Jianzhu Keji Daxue Xuebao/J. Xi'an. *Univ. Archit. Technol, 2020*, 4689–4703.

Rauch, A., & Frese, M. (2007). Let's put the person back into entrepreneurship research: A meta-analysis on the relationship between business owners' personality traits, business creation, and success. *European Journal of Work and Organizational Psychology, 16*(4), 353–385.

Rauch, A., Wiklund, J., Lumpkin, G. T., & Frese, M. (2009). Entrepreneurial orientation and business performance: An assessment of past research and suggestions for the future. *Entrepreneurship Theory and Practice, 33*(3), 761–787.

Rawls, J. (1971). A Theory of Justice. 2. The Law of Peoples, 67.

Reddy, M. S., Deepthi, S., Bhattaru, S., Srilakshmi, V., & Singh, H. (2024). Harmony in HR: Exploring the Synergy of Artificial Intelligence and Green Practices for Sustainable Workplaces". In *MATEC Web of Conferences* (Vol. 392, p. 01039). EDP Sciences. https://doi.org/DOI: 10.1051/matecconf/202439201039

Renwick, D. W. S., Redman, T., & Maguire, S. (2013). Green human resource management: A review and research agenda. *International Journal of Management Reviews, 15*(1), 1–14. DOI: 10.1111/j.1468-2370.2011.00328.x

Rhue, L. (2019). Beauty is in the AI of thc beholder: How artificial intelligence anchors human decisions on subjective vs. Objective measures. *40th International Conference on Information Systems, ICIS 2019*. Munich: Association for Information Systems. Retrieved Aug 20, 2025, from https://www.scopus.com/pages/publications/85136806761

Ribeiro-Navarrete, S., Botella-Carrubi, D., Palacios-Marqués, D., & Orero-Blat, M. (2021). The effect of digitalization on business performance: An applied study of KIBS. *Journal of Business Research, 126*, 319–326.

Ringle, C. M., Sarstedt, M., Sinkovics, N., & Sinkovics, R. R. (2023). A perspective on using partial least squares structural equation modelling in data articles. *Data in Brief, 48*(109074), 109074. DOI: 10.1016/j.dib.2023.109074

Roemmich, K., Schaub, F., & Andalibi, N. (2023, April). Emotion AI at work: Implications for workplace surveillance, emotional labor, and emotional privacy. In *Proceedings of the 2023 CHI Conference on Human Factors in Computing Systems* (pp. 1-20).

Rönkkö, M., & Cho, E. (2022). An updated guideline for assessing discriminant validity. *Organizational Research Methods, 25*(1), 6–14. DOI: 10.1177/1094428120968614

Rosete, D., & Ciarrochi, J. (2005). Emotional intelligence and its relationship to workplace performance outcomes of leadership effectiveness. *Leadership and Organization Development Journal, 26*(5), 388–399.

Rostamzadeh, R., Alizadeh, F. K., Keivani, S., & Isavi, H. (2025). The Role of Artificial Intelligence in Improving Organizational Behavior: A Systematic Study. *Human Behavior and Emerging Technologies, 2025*(01). DOI: 10.1155/hbe2/8094428

Roundy, P. T. (2016). Start-up community narratives: The discursive construction of entrepreneurial ecosystems. *The Journal of Entrepreneurship, 25*(2), 232–248.

Russo, F., & Comi, A. (2012). City characteristics and urban goods movements: A way to environmental transportation system in a sustainable city. *Procedia: Social and Behavioral Sciences, 39*, 61–73. DOI: 10.1016/j.sbspro.2012.03.091

Rustan, A. F., Rahayu, M. K. P., & Surwanti, A. (2024). A review of work-life balance trends in remote work. *International Research Journal of Multidisciplinary Scope, 5*(4), 316–330.

Sachin, B. S., & Aradhana, N. M. (2019). Green Human Resource Management: Best practice of Attaining Sustainable Development Goals. *Journal of Emerging Technologies and Innovative Research, 6*(4), 15–23.

Sadeghi, S. (2024). Employee Well-being in the Age of AI: Perceptions, Concerns, Behaviors, and Outcomes. *arXiv preprint arXiv:2412.04796.*

Sadeghi, S. (2024). Employee well-being in the age of AI: Perceptions, concerns, behaviors, and outcomes. *World Economics & Finance Bulletin*, 36.

Sadiku-Dushi, N., Dana, L.-P., & Ramadani, V. (2019). Entrepreneurial marketing dimensions and SMEs performance. *Journal of Business Research, 100*, 86–99.

Sætra, H. S. (2021). A Framework for Evaluating and Disclosing the ESG Related Impacts of AI with the SDGs. *Sustainability, 13*(15), 8503. DOI: 10.3390/su13158503

Sağbaş, M., & Aydogan, S. (2025). Unveiling the Nuances: How Fuzzy Set Analysis Illuminates Passenger Preferences for AI and Human Agents in Airline Customer Service. *Tourism and Hospitality, 6*(1), 43.

Şahin, Y., & Dogru, İ. (2023). An enterprise data privacy governance model: Security-centric multi-model data anonymization. *International Journal of Engineering Research and Development, 15*(2), 574–583. DOI: 10.29137/umagd.1272085

Sahyaja, C., Shankar, C., Zeeshan, K., & Nagaraj, N. (2024). Artificial Intelligence and Remote Work: Transforming Human Resource Management in a Post-Pandemic World. *3rd International Conference on Automation, Computing and Renewable Systems, ICACRS 2024* (pp. 1555 - 1560). Pudukkottai: Institute of Electrical and Electronics Engineers Inc. DOI: 10.1109/ICACRS62842.2024.10841784

Sakka, F., El Maknouzi, M. E. H., & Sadok, H. (2022). Human resource management in the era of artificial intelligence: Future HR work practices, anticipated skill set, financial and legal implications. *Academy of Strategic Management Journal, 21*, 1–14.

Saleem, I., Saleem, A., Hassan, A., Farukh, M. U., & Kamran, H. (2023). Psychological aspects affecting the venture performance of Indian women entrepreneurs. *Cogent* Sari, D., Kusuma, B. A., Sihotang, J., & Febrianti, T. (2023). The role of entrepreneurial marketing & innovation capability in the performance of SMEs during covid-19 pandemic: Evidence of MSMEs in West Java. *Cogent Business & Management, 10*(1), 2194091.

Salovey, P. E., & Sluyter, D. J. (1997). *Emotional development and emotional intelligence: Educational implications*. Basic Books.

Salovey, P., & Mayer, J. D. (1990). Emotional intelligence. *Imagination, Cognition and Personality*, *9*(3), 185–211.

Samson, B. D., Mama, B. R.-Z., Luriaga, R. L., & Ebardo, R. A. (2024). Barriers to Hybrid Work Among IT Professionals: A TOE Perspective From a Developing Economy. *4th International Conference on Advances in Computational Science and Engineering, ICACSE 2023* (pp. 505 - 520). Manila: Springer Science and Business Media Deutschland GmbH. DOI: 10.1007/978-981-97-2977-7_32

Sana'a, Y. (2016). A critical review of models and theories in field of individual acceptance of technology. *International journal of hybrid information technology, 9*(6), 143-158.

Sanni, B. (2023). An Integrated Framework for Mitigating IT Industry Burnout: Leveraging AI-Driven Work Pattern Monitoring to Enhance Workforce Wellbeing.

Santoso, A., & Surya, Y. (2024). Maximizing decision efficiency with edge-based AI systems: Advanced strategies for real-time processing, scalability, and autonomous intelligence in distributed environments. *Quarterly Journal of Emerging Technologies and Innovations*, *9*(2), 104–132.

Sanyaolu, E., & Atsaboghena, R. (2022). Role of Artificial Intelligence in Human Resource Management: Overview of its benefits and challenges. *ResearchGate*, (December), 1–8.

Saragih, H. (2025). The role of digital transformation in enhancing performance and security of technology infrastructure in public institutions. *Edelweiss Applied Science and Technology*, *09*(06), 679–686. DOI: 10.55214/25768484.v9i6.7865

Saravi, B., Hassel, F., Ülkümen, S., Zink, A., Shavlokhova, V., Couillard-Despres, S., & Lang, G. M. (2022). Artificial intelligence-driven prediction modeling and decision making in spine surgery using hybrid machine learning models. *Journal of Personalized Medicine, 12*(4), 509. DOI: 10.3390/jpm12040509

Saritha, T., & Akthar, P. (2024). The Impact of Hybrid Work Models on Employee Well-being and Engagement. *Communications on Applied Nonlinear Analysis, 31*(55), 97–104. DOI: 10.52783/cana.v31.1003

Sarkar, M. B., Echambadi, R. A. J., & Harrison, J. S. (2001). Alliance entrepreneurship and firm market performance. *Strategic Management Journal, 22*(6-7), 701–711.

Sarrionandia, A., Ramos-Díaz, E., & Fernández-Lasarte, O. (2018). Resilience as a mediator of emotional intelligence and perceived stress: A cross-country study. *Frontiers in Psychology, 9*, 2653.

Sarstedt, M., Ringle, C. M., & Hair, J. F. (2025). Partial least squares structural equation modeling. In *Handbook of Market Research* (pp. 1–56). Springer Nature Switzerland.

Saunila, M., & Ukko, J. (2013). Facilitating innovation capability through performance measurement: A study of Finnish SMEs. *Management Research Review, 36*(10), 991–1010.

Schein, E. H. (2010). *Organizational culture and leadership* (Vol. 2). John Wiley & Sons.

Schlippe, T., & Bothmer, K. (2023). Skill scanner: An AI-based recommendation system for employers, job seekers and educational institutions. *International Journal of Advanced Corporate Learning, 16*(1), 55.

Schwartz, P. M., & Solove, D. J. (2011). The PII problem: Privacy and a new concept of personally identifiable information. NYUL rev., 86, 1814.

Sekaran, K., & Shanmugam, S. (2022, March). Interpreting the factors of employee attrition using explainable AI. In 2022 *International Conference on Decision Aid Sciences and Applications (DASA)* (pp. 932-936). IEEE. https://doi.org/DOI: 10.1109/DASA54658.2022.9765067

Seletedi, C., Mwalemba, G., & Mashingaidze, K. (2024). A Bunch of Sheep Running Towards Somewhere" - Implications of Digital Transformation on the Workforce. *18th IFIP WG 9.4 International Conference on the Implications of Information and Digital Technologies for Development, ICT4D 2024. 709*, pp. 03-15. Cape Town: Springer Science and Business Media Deutschland GmbH. DOI: 10.1007/978-3-031-66986-6_1

Sethna, Z., Jones, R., & Harrigan, P. (2013). *Entrepreneurial marketing: Global perspectives*. Emerald Group Publishing.

Shaheen, N., & AL-Haddad, S. (2018). Entrepreneurial self-efficacy and entrepreneurial behavior. *International Journal of Development and Sustainability, 7*(10), 2385–2402.

Shaikh, Z. P. (2025). Artificial Intelligence-Based Emotional Intelligence and Effective Leadership: Applications, Implications, and Ethical Bias. In *Emotionally Intelligent Methods for Meaningful Leadership* (pp. 223-254). IGI Global Scientific Publishing.

Sharma, A., Lin, I. W., Miner, A. S., Atkins, D. C., & Althoff, T. (2023). Human–AI collaboration enables more empathic conversations in text-based peer-to-peer mental health support. *Nature Machine Intelligence, 5*(1), 46–57.

Sharma, N., Khatri, B., Khan, S. A., & Shamsi, M. S. (2023). Extending the UTAUT model to examine the influence of social media on tourists' destination selection. *Indian Journal of Marketing, 53*(4), 47–64.

Sharma, R. K. (2025). Ethics in AI: Balancing innovation and responsibility. *International Journal of Science and Research Archive, 14*(1), 544–551. DOI: 10.30574/ijsra.2025.14.1.0122

Sharma, R., & Sinha, V. (2022). Gender equality and hybrid work: A pathway to inclusive organizational development. *Journal of Business Ethics, 176*(3), 543–556.

Sheikh, H., Prins, C., & Schrijvers, E. (2023). Artificial intelligence: definition and background. In Mission, A. I. (Ed.), *The new system technology* (pp. 15–41). Springer International Publishing.

Shet, S. V., Poddar, T., Samuel, F. W., & Dwivedi, Y. K. (2021). Examining the determinants of successful adoption of data analytics in human resource management–A framework for implications. *Journal of Business Research, 131*, 311–326.

Shrivastava, P. (1995). Environmental technologies and competitive advantage. *Strategic Management Journal, 16*(S1), 183–200.

Siahaan, D. T., & Lin Tan, C. S. (2020). Antecedents of Innovation Capability and Firm Performance of Indonesian ICT SMEs. *Asian Journal of Business Research, 10*(2).

Siegel, R.. (2022). The impact of electronic monitoring on employees' job satisfaction, stress, performance, and counterproductive work behavior: A meta-analysis. *Computers in Human Behavior Reports, 8*, 1–13. DOI: 10.1016/j.chbr.2022.100227

Silva, P., & Costa, E. (2025). Assessing large language models for automated feedback generation in learning programming problem solving. *arXiv preprint*.

Sima, V., Gheorghe, I. G., Subić, J., & Nancu, D. (2020). Influences of the Industry 4.0 Revolution on the human capital Development and Consumer Behavior: A Systematic review. *Sustainability*, *12*(10), 4035. DOI: 10.3390/su12104035

Simpson, D., & Samson, D. (2010). Environmental strategy and low waste operations: Exploring complementarities. *Business Strategy and the Environment*, *19*(2), 104–118.

Singh, A., & Hassan, S. C. (2024), "Identifying the Skill Gap in the Workplace and Their Challenges in Hospitality and Tourism Organisations", Thake, A.M., Sood, K., Özen, E. and Grima, S. (Ed.) Contemporary Challenges in Social Science Management: Skills Gaps and Shortages in the Labour Market (Contemporary Studies in Economic and Financial Analysis, Vol. 112B), Emerald Publishing Limited, Leeds, pp. 101-114. DOI: 10.1108/S1569-37592024000112B006

Singh, A., & Singh, V. K. (2022). The impact of ergonomic practices on housekeeping employee retention and efficiency in hotels during COVID-19 in India. Turyzm/Tourism, 32(2), 29–50. DOI: 10.18778/0867-5856.32.2.02

Singh, A. (2024). Quality of Work-Life Practices in the Indian Hospitality Sector: Future Challenges and Prospects. In Valeri, M., & Sousa, B. (Eds.), *Human Relations Management in Tourism* (pp. 208–224). IGI Global., DOI: 10.4018/979-8-3693-1322-0.ch010

Singh, A. (2025). Analysis of Perceptions on Employment of differently-abled People in the Indian Hotel Industry. *Pasos (El Sauzal)*, *23*(1), 167–183. DOI: 10.25145/j.pasos.2025.23.011

Singh, A., & Ansari, A. I. (2024). Role of Training and Development in Employee Motivation: Tourism and Hospitality Sector. In Mazurowski, T. (Ed.), *Enhancing Employee Motivation Through Training and Development* (pp. 248–261). IGI Global., DOI: 10.4018/979-8-3693-1674-0.ch011

Singh, A., & Kumar, S. (2021). Identifying Innovations in Human Resources: Academia and Industry Perspectives. In Pathak, A., & Rana, S. (Eds.), *Transforming Human Resource Functions With Automation* (pp. 104–120). IGI Global.

Singh, A., & Kumar, S. (2024). Effective Talent Management Practices Implemented in the Hospitality Sector. In Christiansen, B., Aziz, M., & O'Keeffe, E. (Eds.), *Global Practices on Effective Talent Acquisition and Retention* (pp. 126–144). IGI Global., DOI: 10.4018/979-8-3693-1938-3.ch008

Singh, A., & Sihmar, P. (2025). Higher Education Institution Sustainability: Role of Green Human Resource Management. In Adu-Gyamfi, M., Boateng, F., & Atiku, S. (Eds.), *Green HRM Awareness and Training in Higher Education Institutions* (pp. 1–14). IGI Global Scientific Publishing., DOI: 10.4018/979-8-3693-2956-6.ch001

Singh, A., & Singh, G. (2025). Leveraging AI-powered predictive analytics for proactive risk management and business resilience in SMEs: Harnessing predictive insights to strengthen decision-making in SMEs. In *Incentives and Benefits for Adopting Green Entrepreneurship Practices* (pp. 265–294). IGI Global., DOI: 10.4018/979-8-3693-9306-2.ch011

Singh, G., Bhardwaj, G., Singh, S. V., & Kumar, V. (2020). Technology Acceptance Model to Assess Employee's Perception and Intention of Integration of Artificial Intelligence and Human Resource Management in IT Industry. *Int. J. Adv. Sci. Technol, 2020*, 11485–11490.

Soleimani, M., Intezari, A., & Pauleen, D. J. (2022, January 01). Mitigating cognitive biases in developing ai-assisted recruitment systems: A knowledge-sharing approach. *International Journal of Knowledge Management, 18*(01). Advance online publication. DOI: 10.4018/IJKM.290022

Somathilake, H., & Pathirawasam, C. (2020). The effect of financial management practices on performance of SMEs in Sri Lanka. *International Journal of Scientific Research and Management, 8*(5), 1789–1803.

Soni, V. (2023). Impact of generative AI on small and medium enterprises' revenue growth: The moderating role of human, technological, and market factors. *Reviews of Contemporary Business Analytics, 6*(1), 133–153.

Soni, V. (2024, April). AI in Job Matching and Recruitment: Analyzing the Efficiency and Equity of Automated Hiring Processes. In *2024 International Conference on Knowledge Engineering and Communication Systems (ICKECS)* (Vol. 1, pp. 1-5). IEEE.

Soomro, K., Bhutta, M. N. M., Khan, Z., & Tahir, M. A. (2019). Smart city big data analytics: An advanced review. *Wiley Interdisciplinary Reviews. Data Mining and Knowledge Discovery, 9*(5), e1319. DOI: 10.1002/widm.1319

Squire, D., Gonzalez, L., & Shayan, C. (2024). Enhancing sense of belonging in nursing student clinical placements to advance learning and identity development. *Journal of Professional Nursing, 51*, 109–114.

Stanbery, K., Lindley, K., & Huffman, C. (2023, January 01). The Feasibility of Using Net Promoter Score to Measure Real-Time Employee Engagement. *The Journal of Nursing Administration*, *53*(01), 34–39. DOI: 10.1097/NNA.0000000000001239 PMID: 36542442

Stanford Workplace Dynamics Lab. (2025). *AI research reveals hidden costs of workplace emotional labor*. https://sanj.dev/post/ai-research-emotional-labor-workplace-impact

Strohmeier, S. (2020). HR Digitalisation Technologies. T. Bondarouk & S. Fisher (Ed.), Encyclopedia of Electronic HRM, 14-19.

Sucharita, K. (2024). Navigating The Ai Frontier: A Study Of Ai Integration In It Employee Training And Development. *Educational Administration: Theory and Practice*, *30*(5), 1079–1085.

Supina, S., & Singh, A. (2024). Exploring the Presence and Adoption of Quality of Work-Life Dimensions in the Hotel Industry? *African Journal of Hospitality, Tourism and Leisure*, *13*(2), 421–429. DOI: 10.46222/ajhtl.19770720.524

Surve, A. A. (2020). Impact Of Artifical Intelligence In Human Resource Management (Doctoral dissertation, Doctoral Dissertation]. University of Mumbai).

Suryawanshia, S., Bhosale, D., Vishwakarma, S., Patila, K., Harwania, V., & Bhosalec, A. (2024). A Comprehensive Survey on Smart Wearables: Real-time Health and Workplace Monitoring, Alerting, and Analysis in the Industrial Context. *Transactions C: Aspects, 37(12)*, 2473.

Suvedhaa, A., Imranmohamed, M., & Sudhipth, V., & M., T. (2025). AI-Powered Workforce Management for Automated Appraisals and Task Allocation. *6th International Conference on Innovative Trends in Information Technology, ICITIIT 2025*. Kottayam: Institute of Electrical and Electronics Engineers Inc. DOI: 10.1109/ICITIIT64777.2025.11041265

Sýkorová, Z., Hague, D., Dvouletý, O., & Procházka, D. A. (2024). Incorporating artificial intelligence (AI) into recruitment processes: ethical considerations. *Vilakshan-XIMB Journal of Management*, (ahead-of-print).

T.S. S., Babhuti, K., Jyoti, D., Kaur, H., & Kapoor, T. (2025). The evolving role of Artificial Intelligence (AI) in Human Resource Management (HRM). In *Sustainable Management Practices for Employee Retention and Recruitment* (pp. 301-309). IGI GLobal. DOI: 10.4018/979-8-3693-8679-8.ch015

Tadajewski, M., & Jones, B. (2021). The ethics of digital workplace surveillance. *Journal of Business Ethics*, *174*(4), 731–747. DOI: 10.1007/s10551-020-04620-3

Taherdoost, H. (2021). Importance of technology acceptance assessment for successful implementation and development of new technologies. *Global Journal of Engineering Sciences.*

Talmage-Rostron, M. (2024). How will artificial intelligence affect jobs 2024-2030. Nexford University. Retrieved from https://www.nexford.edu/insights/how-will-ai-affect-jobs

Tanantong, T., & Wongras, P. (2024). A UTAUT-based framework for analyzing users' intention to adopt artificial intelligence in human resource recruitment: A case study of Thailand. *Systems*, *12*(1), 28.

Tang, M., Walsh, G., Lerner, D., Fitza, M. A., & Li, Q. (2018). Green innovation, managerial concern and firm performance: An empirical study. *Business Strategy and the Environment*, *27*(1), 39–51.

Tatiparti, S., Goli, G., & Reddy, T. B. P. (2025). Exploring the ethical implications of AI in talent management: Perspectives from medium and large enterprises. *Business Process Management Journal.*

Taylor, L., & Broeders, D. (2022). In the name of AI? Limits of data-driven governance. *Information Communication and Society*, *25*(1), 1–18.

Teece, D. J. (2007). Explicating dynamic capabilities: The nature and microfoundations of (sustainable) enterprise performance. *Strategic Management Journal*, *28*(13), 1319–1350. DOI: 10.1002/smj.640

Teng, X., Wu, Z., & Yang, F. (2022). Research on the relationship between digital transformation and performance of SMEs. *Sustainability*, *14*(10), 6012.

TERENTIEVA, N., PAVLOV, D., & TVERDOKHLIB, M. (2024). INTEGRATION OF DIGITAL TOOLS AND ARTIFICIAL INTELLIGENCEINTO HR MANAGEMENT PROCESSES. *Herald of Khmelnytskyi National University. Economic sciences, 334*(5), 624-629.

Thakur, A., & Konde, A. (2021). Fundamentals of neural networks. *International Journal for Research in Applied Science and Engineering Technology*, *9*(VIII), 407–426.

The Guardian. (2024, June 23). Are you 80% angry and 2% sad? Why 'emotional AI' is fraught with problems. *The Guardian*. Retrieved from https://www.theguardian.com/technology/article/2024/jun/23/emotional-artificial-intelligence-chatgpt-4o-hume-algorithmic-bias

Thomas, A. (2024). Revolutionizing Events: Exploring the Seamless Integration of Robots in Hybrid and Virtual Experiences. In S. Kulshreshtha & C. Webster (Eds.), New Technologies in Virtual and Hybrid Events (pp. 19-46). IGI Global Scientific Publishing. DOI: 10.4018/979-8-3693-2272-7.ch002

Thompson, R. L., Higgins, C. A., & Howell, J. M. (1991). Personal computing: Toward a conceptual model of Utilization1. *Management Information Systems Quarterly*, *15*(1), 125–143. DOI: 10.2307/249443

Tian, X., Pavur, R., Han, H., & Zhang, L. (2023). A machine learning-based human resources recruitment system for business process management: Using LSA, BERT and SVM. *Business Process Management Journal*, *29*(1), 202–222.

Tiwari, P., Bhat, A. K., & Tikoria, J. (2017). The role of emotional intelligence and self-efficacy on social entrepreneurial attitudes and social entrepreneurial intentions. *Journal of Social Entrepreneurship*, *8*(2), 165–185.

Tomašev, N., Cornebise, J., Hutter, F., Mohamed, S., Picciariello, A., Connelly, B., & Clopath, C. (2020). AI for social good: Unlocking the opportunity for positive impact. *Nature Communications*, *11*(1), 2468. DOI: 10.1038/s41467-020-15871-z

Triansyah, F. A., Hejin, W., & Stefania, S. (2023). Factors affecting employee performance: A systematic review. *Journal Markcount Finance*, *1*(3), 150–159. DOI: 10.55849/jmf.v1i2.102

Tuffaha, M. (2022). Adoption factors of artificial intelligence in human resource management (Doctoral dissertation, Universitat Politècnica de València).

Tuffaha, M. (2023). The Impact of Artificial Intelligence Bias on Human Resource Management Functions: Systematic Literature Review and Future Research Directions. *European Journal of Business and Innovation Research*, *11*(4), 35–58.

Úbeda-García, M., Marco-Lajara, B., Zaragoza-Sáez, P. C., & Poveda-Pareja, E. (2025). Artificial intelligence, knowledge and human resource management: A systematic literature review of theoretical tensions and strategic implications. *Journal of Innovation & Knowledge*, *10*, 100809. Advance online publication. DOI: 10.1016/j.jik.2025.100809

Uddin, M. A., Alam, M. S., Mamun, A. A., Khan, T.-U.-Z., & Akter, A. (2020). A study of the adoption and implementation of enterprise resource planning (ERP): Identification of moderators and mediator. *Journal of Open Innovation*, *6*(1), 2. DOI: 10.3390/joitmc6010002

Ullah, Y., Ullah, H., & Jan, S. (2022). The mediating role of employee creativity between knowledge sharing and innovative performance: Empirical evidence from manufacturing firms in emerging markets. *Management Research Review, 45*(1), 86–100.

Uma, V. R., Velchamy, I., & Upadhyay, D. (2023). Recruitment analytics: Hiring in the era of artificial intelligence. In *The adoption and effect of artificial intelligence on human resources management, part A* (pp. 155–174). Emerald Publishing Limited.

Unilever & WIRED Consulting. (2022). *The Future of Work Is Flexible*. Unilever. https://www.unilever.com/files/4bbfab9a-54aa-4493-a9b0-146c1c4aa738/glo-wired-x-unilever-workplace.pdf

Unilever. (2020, June 23). *An exciting new normal for flexible working.* https://www.unilever.com/news/news-search/2020/an-exciting-new-normal-for-flexible-working/

United Nations. (2015). *Transforming our world: The 2030 agenda for sustainable development*. United Nations General Assembly. https://sdgs.un.org/2030agenda

Urban, B. (2020). Entrepreneurial alertness, self-efficacy and social entrepreneurship intentions. *Journal of Small Business and Enterprise Development, 27*(3), 489–507.

Usman, M., Srivastava, P., Fatma, A., & Devi, M. K. (2025). AI-Based Forecasting of Staffing Requirements Using Market and Business Trend Data. *International Journal (Toronto, Ont.), 9*(5).

Usoro, I. A., & Brownson, C. D. (2023). Creativity and entrepreneurial development. *Open Access Journal of Business and Entrepreneurship, 1*(2), 64–72.

van de Fliert, E., Christiana, B., Hendayana, R., & Murray-Prior, R. (2010). Pilot Roll-out: Adaptive Research in Farmers' Worlds. *Extension Farming Systems Journal, 6*(1), 63–71. DOI: 10.3316/479036039691084

Vanlehn, K. (2011). The Relative Effectiveness of Human Tutoring, Intelligent Tutoring Systems, and Other Tutoring Systems. *Educational Psychologist*. Advance online publication. DOI: 10.1080/00461520.2011.611369

Varsha, P. S., Chakraborty, A., & Kar, A. K. (2024). How to undertake an impactful literature review: Understanding review approaches and guidelines for high-impact systematic literature reviews. *South Asian Journal of Business and Management Cases, 13*(1), 18–35.

Vartak, M., Ortiz, P., Siegel, K., Subramanyam, H., Madden, S., & Zaharia, M. (2015). Supporting fast iteration in model building. In *NIPS Workshop Learnings* (pp. 1-6).

Vashishth, T. K., Sharma, V., Tomer, T., Kumar, A., & Kaushik, S. (2025). AI in HRM: Transforming employee engagement and satisfaction amidst challenges and opportunities. In *Human Resource Management in the Age of Generative AI* (pp. 157-187). IGI Global. DOI: 10.4018/979-8-3693-7693-5.ch006

Vaswani, A., Shazeer, N., Parmar, N., Uszkoreit, J., Jones, L., Gomez, A. N., Kaiser, Ł., & Polosukhin, I. (2017). Attention is All you Need. https://papers.nips.cc/paper_files/paper/2017/hash/3f5ee243547dee91fbd053c1c4a845aa-Abstract.html

Venkatachalam, S. (2024, September). Artificial Intelligence and Big Data Applications in Recruitment Process Management. In 2024 4th International Conference on Soft Computing for Security Applications (ICSCSA) (pp. 68-72). IEEE.

Venkatesh, V., Morris, M. G., Davis, G. B., & Davis, F. D. (2003). User acceptance of information technology: Toward a unified view. *Management Information Systems Quarterly*, *27*(3), 425–478. DOI: 10.2307/30036540

Venkatesh, V., Thong, J. Y. L., & Xu, X. (2012). Consumer acceptance and use of information technology: Extending the unified theory of acceptance and use of Technology1. *Management Information Systems Quarterly*, *36*(1), 157–178. DOI: 10.2307/41410412

Vermeulen, B., Kesselhut, J., Pyka, A., & Saviotti, P. P. (2018). The impact of automation on employment: Just the usual structural change? *Sustainability*, *10*(5), 1661.

Vichare, S., Gawade, A., & Mangrulkar, R. (2024). Qgen: A Unique Question Generation and Answer Evaluation Technique Using Natural Language Processing. *Journal of Engineering Education Transformations*, *38*(1).

Vishwanath, B., & Vaddepalli, S. (2023). The Future of Work: Implications of Artificial Intelligence on Hr Practices. Tuijin Jishu/Journal of Propulsion Technology, 44(3), 1711-1724.

Voigt, P., & Von dem Bussche, A. (2017). *The EU General Data Protection Regulation (GDPR): A practical guide*. Springer., DOI: 10.1007/978-3-319-57959-7

Votto, A. M., Valecha, R., Najafirad, P., & Rao, H. R. (2021). Artificial intelligence in tactical human resource management: A systematic literature review. *International Journal of Information Management Data Insights*, *1*(2), 100047.

Vrontis, D., Christofi, M., Pereira, V., Tarba, S., Makrides, A., & Trichina, E. (2023). Artificial intelligence, robotics, advanced technologies and human resource management: a systematic review. *Artificial intelligence and international HRM*, 172-201.

Wachter, S., & Mittelstadt, B. (2019). A right to reasonable inferences: re-thinking data protection law in the age of big data and AI. Colum. Bus. L. Rev., 494.

Wahab, F., Shah, A., Ullah, I., Adhikari, D., & Khan, I. (2024). Applications of artificial intelligence in smart distributed processing and big data mining. In *Artificial Intelligence for Intelligent Systems* (pp. 69–85). CRC Press.

Walambe, R., Nayak, P., Bhardwaj, A., & Kotecha, K. (2021). [Retracted] Employing Multimodal Machine Learning for Stress Detection. *Journal of Healthcare Engineering*, *2021*(1), 9356452.

Walter, S. (2023). AI impacts on supply chain performance: A manufacturing use case study. *Discover Artificial Intelligence*, *3*(1), 18. DOI: 10.1007/s44163-023-00061-9

Wang, B. Y., Boell, S. K., Riemer, K., & Peter, S. (2023). Human Agency in AI Configurations Supporting Organizational Decision-making. *34th Australasian Conference on Information Systems, ACIS 2023.* Wellington: Association for Information Systems. Retrieved Aug 10, 2025, from https://www.scopus.com/pages/publications/85198754646

Wang, C., Jiang, W., Yang, K., Yu, D., Newn, J., Sarsenbayeva, Z., & Kostakos, V. (2021). Electronic monitoring systems for hand hygiene: Systematic review of technology. *Journal of Medical Internet Research*, *23*(11), e27880. DOI: 10.2196/27880

Wang, P. Q., Yan, L., & Santoso, C. (2025). Generational engagement with AI in hospitality: human–AI interaction perspectives across the service process. *Current Issues in Tourism*, •••, 1–14.

Waweru, C., & Ngugi, K. (2014). Influence of financial management practices on the performance of micro and small enterprises in Kenya. *European Journal of Business and Management*, *1*(11), 141–161.

WCED. (1987). *Our common future*. Oxford University Press. World Green Building Council. (2021). *The business case for green buildings.*

Weiner, B. J. (2009). A theory of organizational readiness for change. *Implementation Science : IS*, *4*, 67. DOI: 10.1186/1748-5908-4-67 PMID: 19840381

Weiss, H. M., & Cropanzano, R. (1996). Affective events theory. *Research in Organizational Behavior*, *18*(1), 1–74.

Wiklund, J., & Shepherd, D. (2003). Knowledge-based resources, entrepreneurial orientation, and the performance of small and medium-sized businesses. *Strategic Management Journal*, *24*(13), 1307–1314.

Wood, A. J., Graham, M., Lehdonvirta, V., & Hjorth, I. (2019). Good gig, bad gig: Autonomy and algorithmic control in the global gig economy. *Work, Employment and Society*, *33*(1), 56–75.

Workhuman. (2025, April). AI praise-giving tool promises 'authentic' insights. Retrieved from https://www.ft.com/content/abee0887-f723-464e-9cd8-c429b171abc8

World Economic Forum. (2020a). Recession and automation changes our future of work, but there are jobs coming, report says.

World Economic Forum. (2020b). The Future of Jobs Report 2020. https://www3.weforum.org/docs/WEF_Future_of_Jobs_2020.pdf

World Economic Forum. (2023). Future of Jobs Report 2023. In Future of Jobs Report. https://www3.weforum.org/docs/WEF_Future_of_Jobs_2023.pdf

World Economic Forum. (2023). *Global gender gap report 2023.* Geneva: World Economic Forum. Retrieved from https://www.weforum.org/reports

Wu, Y. J., Antone, B., DeChurch, L., & Contractor, N. (2023, July 01). Information sharing in a hybrid workplace: Understanding the role of ease-of-use perceptions of communication technologies in advice-seeking relationship maintenance. *Journal of Computer-Mediated Communication*, *28*(04). Advance online publication. DOI: 10.1093/jcmc/zmad025

Xu, J., Wan, S., Li, Y., Luo, S., Chen, Z., Shao, Y., Huang, S., & Song, L. (2025). Cooperative multi-model training for personalized federated learning over heterogeneous devices. *IEEE Journal of Selected Topics in Signal Processing*, *19*, 195–207. DOI: 10.1109/JSTSP.2024.3497660

Yam, K. C., Tang, P. M., Jackson, J. C., Su, R., & Gray, K. (2023). The rise of robots increases job insecurity and maladaptive workplace behaviors: Multimethod evidence. *The Journal of Applied Psychology*, *108*, 850–870. DOI: 10.1037/apl0001045

Yang, C. H., Lee, K. C., & Chen, H. C. (2016). Incorporating carbon footprint with activity-based costing constraints into sustainable public transport infrastructure project decisions. *Journal of Cleaner Production*, *133*, 1154–1166. DOI: 10.1016/j.jclepro.2016.06.014

Yang, T., & Jiang, J. (2025). Dcsigning job characteristics for effective hybrid intelligence: Insights from job design and human–AI collaboration. *Personnel Review*. Advance online publication. DOI: 10.1108/PR-03-2024-0229

Yawson, R. M., & Goryunova, E. (2025). Nested Complexity: A Conceptual Framework for Leveraging AI for Sustainable Organizations and Human Resource Development. *Advances in Developing Human Resources*, •••, 15234223251335908.

Yeke, D., Ibrahim, M., Tuncay, G. S., Farrukh, H., Imran, A., Bianchi, A., & Celik, Z. B. (2024, May). Wear's my data? understanding the cross-device runtime permission model in wearables. In *2024 IEEE Symposium on Security and Privacy (SP)* (pp. 2404-2421). IEEE.

Yesufu, L., & Alajlani, S. (2025). Enhancing Strategic Decision-Making With AI: Unveiling the Untapped Potential. In *Economic and Political Consequences of AI: Managing Creative Destruction* (pp. 415 - 436). IGI Global. DOI: 10.4018/979-8-3693-7036-0.ch018

Yue, L., Song, L., Zhu, S., Fu, X., Li, X., He, C., & Li, J. (2024). Machine learning assisted rational design of antimicrobial peptides based on human endogenous proteins and their applications for cosmetic preservative system optimization. *Scientific Reports*, *14*(1), 947. DOI: 10.1038/s41598-023-50832-8

Zahra, S. A. (2007). Contextualizing theory building in entrepreneurship research. *Journal of Business Venturing*, *22*(3), 443–452.

Zaman, K. (2022). Transformation of marketing decisions through artificial intelligence and digital marketing. *Journal of Marketing Strategies*, *4*(2), 353–364. DOI: 10.52633/jms.v4i2.210

Zareen, S., & Khan, S. A. (2023). Exploring dependence of human resource management (HRM) on internet of things (IoT) and digital marketing in the digital era. In *Global applications of the internet of things in digital marketing* (pp. 51-66). IGI Global.

Zeidner, M., Matthews, G., & Roberts, R. D. (2004). Emotional intelligence in the workplace: A critical review. *Applied Psychology*, *53*(3), 371–399.

Zhang, J., & Tao, D. (2020). Empowering things with intelligence: A survey of the progress, challenges, and opportunities in artificial intelligence of things. *IEEE Internet of Things Journal*, *8*(10), 7789–7817.

Zhang, R., Flathmann, C., Musick, G., Schelble, B., & McNeese, N. J. (2024, February 05). I Know This Looks Bad, But I Can Explain: Understanding When AI Should Explain Actions In Human-AI Teams. *ACM Transactions on Interactive Intelligent Systems*, *14*(01). Advance online publication. DOI: 10.1145/3635474

Zhang, Y., Liu, G., Zhang, L., Xu, S., & Cheung, M. W. L. (2021). Psychological ownership: A meta-analysis and comparison of multiple forms of attachment in the workplace. *Journal of Management, 47*(3), 745–770.

Zhang, Y., Liu, X., Yan, Q., & Na, M. (2025). Empowering workforces in AI-driven environments: Co-skilling, organizational support, and mitigating job insecurity. *Frontiers in Psychology, 16*, 1700129. DOI: 10.3389/fpsyg.2025.1700129

Zhao, H., Seibert, S. E., & Lumpkin, G. T. (2009). The Relationship of Personality to Entrepreneurial Intentions and Performance: A Meta-Analytic Review. *Journal of Management, 36*(2), 324–381. DOI: 10.1177/0149206309335187

Zhao, W., Yang, T., Hughes, K. D., & Li, Y. (2021). Entrepreneurial alertness and business model innovation: The role of entrepreneurial learning and risk perception. *The International Entrepreneurship and Management Journal, 17*(2), 839–864.

Ziakis, C., & Vlachopoulou, M. (2023). Artificial intelligence in digital marketing: Insights from a comprehensive review. *Information (Basel), 14*(12), 664. DOI: 10.3390/info14120664

Zirar, A., Ali, S. I., & Islam, N. (2023). Worker and workplace Artificial Intelligence (AI) coexistence: Emerging themes and research agenda. *Technovation, 124*, 102747. 10.1016/j.technovation.2023.102747

Ződi, Z. (2022). Algorithmic explainability and legal reasoning. *The Theory and Practice of Legislation, 10*(1), 67–92. DOI: 10.1080/20508840.2022.2033945

Zuboff, S. (2019). *The Age of Surveillance Capitalism: The Fight for a Human Future at the New Frontier of Power*. Public Affairs.

Zuboff, S. (2019). *The age of surveillance capitalism: The fight for a human future at the new frontier of power*. PublicAffairs.

About the Contributors

Preeti Mehra, a Business Instructor at Campbell College and a Sessional Instructor at Keyano College (May–Sept 2024), holds a PhD from Guru Nanak Dev University, Amritsar, on "Consumers Perception and Purchase Decision Making for Micro Packs – A Study of FMCGs in Punjab" (2017). She has guided multiple PhD scholars in marketing and digital consumer behavior and has extensively published in Scopus and ABDC-indexed journals on topics such as social media marketing, AI in business, electric vehicles, blockchain, and consumer engagement. Dr. Mehra has edited books, including Integrating Sustainability and Autonomous Transportation for Enhanced Urban Mobility, Incentives and Benefits for Adopting Green Entrepreneurship Practices, Unlocking Growth and Sustainability for SMEs with AI, and Reimagining Inclusion: Transforming Policies and Practices for Sustainable and Equitable Futures. She has also authored several book chapters on branding, e-commerce, digital marketing, and pandemic-driven consumer behavior, establishing herself as a leading researcher in business and marketing strategies.

Ergunova Olga Titovna, PhD, is an esteemed Associate Professor at the Higher School of Production Management, Peter the Great St. Petersburg Polytechnic University, and an expert at the Russian Academy of Sciences. She also holds an associate professorship at Lovely Professional University (India) and serves as President of the Ural Union of Tourism Industry. With over 21 years of experience in marketing, strategic communications, and project management, her expertise spans digital transformation, sustainable development, smart cities, tourism, and HoReCa. She has held leadership roles in academia and industry, contributing to major branding, tourism, and economic development projects. An accomplished researcher, she has authored numerous publications indexed in RSCI, Web of Science, and Scopus. She has played a pivotal role in initiatives such as the Russian Union of Young Scientists and the Federation of Hospitality Auditors, as well as various national and regional tourism and strategic development projects. A recognized thought leader, she is a jury member and speaker at international forums and contributes to leading Russian media outlets. Her work has been honored with prestigious awards, including the Russian Event Awards and national recognitions in education, tourism, and science.

Shyam Sunder Agrawal, Assistant Professor, Mittal school of Business, Lovely Professional University, Phagwara, Punjab. He has been associated with the education industry since 2015. He has presented papers in various reputed IIM conferences and published several research papers in UGC CARE, SCOPUS and ABDC Journals. His field of interest are Behavioral finance, Sustainable finance, Capital Market, Banking and Insurance, Fintech. He has published and granted 2 patents from Govt of India. He got International Case Study award in 2022. He is reviewer of Emerald, Springer and UGC care Journals.

Pooja Kansra is a distinguished academician and researcher with extensive contributions to health economics, trade specialization, consumer behavior, and digital marketing. She has presented her research at esteemed international and national conferences, including the Maharaja Agrasen Institute of Management Studies, NIT Srinagar, and ICFAI Business School, covering topics such as health insurance perceptions, India's trade specialization in the healthcare sector, and online shopping behavior. A prolific author, she has written and co-authored several books on blockchain applications, socio-economic issues, and health insurance, published by renowned international publishers such as Emerald, IGI Global, and Weser Books. Her research has been featured in Scopus-indexed and high-impact journals like the International Journal of Quality & Reliability Management, Economic and Political Weekly (EPW), and Global Business Review. With a distinguished career, she has served as a Lecturer at Government College, Ajnala, and later held academic positions at Lovely Professional University, where she currently serves as a professor. She has taught a diverse range of courses across undergraduate and postgraduate programs, specializing in economics, statistical methods, and business analytics. Dr. Kansra's dedication to academia and research continues to shape the fields of economics, public policy, and business studies.

Stefanovic Miladin is a distinguished academic, researcher, and consultant with extensive contributions to quality management, ICT, e-learning, university-enterprise cooperation, and innovation management. As the author or co-author of over 200 papers, six technical solutions, six books, and seven book chapters—including 40 manuscripts published in SCI Thompson-listed journals—he has played a pivotal role in advancing his field. He has actively participated in numerous projects, including seven TEMPUS, two ERASMUS+, five national scientific projects, and three Innovation Fund-funded initiatives, alongside over 50 industry collaborations. A key figure in business and technology transfer, he contributed to the establishment of the Business Start-Up Center (BIC) in Kragujevac and serves as a leading consultant for management systems, having implemented ISO standards in over 30 companies. As Manager of the Center for Quality and the Center for Knowledge Transfer at the University of Kragujevac, he has mentored six PhD candidates and overseen 75 MSc and over 120 BSc theses. A member of prestigious organizations such as IFIP, the Engineering Academy of Serbia, and AQSS, he also serves on the editorial boards of eight international journals, further solidifying his impact in academia and industry.

***

Rahmath Nisha A, Driven by her passion for teaching, Rahmath Nisha transitioned into academia, drawing on her background as an Engineer specializing in Electronics and Communication. Her academic achievements include ranking as a Gold Medalist in her MBA (HR and Hospital Management) from Saveetha University, where she was also recognized as the Best Outgoing Student. Rahmath Nisha's aspiration is to equip students with industry-ready skills through real-time teaching methods, thereby bridging the gap between academic knowledge and practical application in the workplace.

A.K. Subramani is a distinguished academic with a PhD in Business Administration from Manonmaniam Sundaranar University, Tirunelveli, India. With 18 years of teaching experience, he has made significant contributions to the field of human resource management and organisational behaviour. He has an impressive publication record with 80 articles in international journals, including two papers in the ABDC-A category, eight in the ABDC-B category, three in the ABDC-C category, 30 in Scopus-indexed journals, and eight in Web of Science journals. He has served as a resource person for various training workshops on SPSS and AMOS software packages

Nitesh Behare is an accomplished academician, author, and researcher with over 16 years of experience in higher education. He currently serves as an Associate Professor at the Balaji Institute of International Business (BIIB), Sri Balaji University, Pune (SBUP), India. Dr. Behare has made significant contributions to academia through the publication of numerous research papers and book chapters in reputed SCOPUS, Web of Science (WoS), and UGC CARE–listed journals and edited books, establishing himself as a recognized scholar in his field. His work reflects a strong commitment to academic excellence, innovation, and impactful knowledge creation. He is also the holder of multiple national and international patents, highlighting his engagement in applied research, innovation, and industry-oriented problem solving.Dr. Behare continues to contribute actively to the academic and professional community through teaching, research, and collaborative initiatives that effectively bridge theory and practice.

Ujjal Bhuyan, Currently working as an assistant professor in the department of Commerce, Jagannath Barooah University, Jorhat. Specialized in the field of finance and entrepreneurship.

Dolly Gaur is currently associated with GLA University as an Assistant Professor. She has been awarded Ph.D. in Finance in 2021 from Amity College of Commerce and Finance, Amity University, Uttar Pradesh, NOIDA. Her research work has been published in journals indexed and ranked with Web of Science, Scopus and ABDC. Dr. Gaur is a Post-Graduate from Department of Commerce, University of Delhi and has completed her graduation from Kamla Nehru College, University of Delhi. She can be reached at dolly.gaur2608@gmail.com.

Kanishka Gupta is an academician and researcher with over 5 years of teaching experience in Accounting and Finance. She is currently serving as an Assistant Professor at the Vivekananda School of Business Studies, Vivekananda Institute of Professional Studies - Technical Campus, Delhi. Dr. Kanishka holds a Ph.D. in Commerce from Amity University, where she researched the relationship between intellectual capital and firm performance. Her academic portfolio includes over 20 research publications in reputed journals indexed in Scopus, Web of Science, and ABDC. Her work spans areas such as intellectual capital, FinTech adoption, ESG performance, and financial risk. A recognised contributor to the academic community, she has presented research at 19 national and international conferences, winning 9 Best Paper Awards. Kanishka is also actively involved in mentoring, journal editing, and organising academic and cultural events. She is proficient in statistical tools including SPSS, AMOS, STATA, and MS Excel, and continues to explore the intersection of finance, technology, and sustainable development in her research.

Shainima Islam is an academic and researcher in Business and Management with a specialization in Human Resource Management, Organizational Psychology, and Social Identity. She holds a Ph.D. in Business Management from Universitas Jenderal Soedirman (Indonesia), where her doctoral research introduced the concept of Professional Psychology to explain professional commitment under job stress in developing-country contexts. She is currently a Lecturer in Business Communication at the American University of Phnom Penh (AUPP), Cambodia, and also serves as an Honorary Adjunct Faculty Member at Maryam Abacha American International University of Nigeria (MAAUN), Kano. Her research interests include leadership and social identity, entrepreneurial psychology, Green HRM, diversity and inclusion, virtual work, and crisis-driven organizations. She has extensive experience in international research collaboration across Asia and Africa and is actively engaged in academic publishing, curriculum design, and postgraduate supervision.

Shad Ahmad Khan is a distinguished academic leader, and researcher, whose work spans the Middle East and Asia. Recognized globally for his scholarly influence, he has been listed among the Top 2% of Scientists worldwide for both 2024 and 2025. With close to fifteen years of experience in higher education, Dr. Khan has contributed significantly to institutional development, research advancement, and program leadership. He is serving as Associate Professor, Faculty of Business & Management, American University of Phnom Penh, and International Professor, University of Arizoan, USA. During his term at the University of Buraimi, Oman he has been central to strengthening the research culture, leading initiatives that resulted in a 100% increase in Scopus-indexed publications across the College of Business. He also played an essential role in the university's successful OAAAQA institutional accreditation, reflecting his strength in academic governance and strategic planning. His research profile is equally strong. Dr. Khan has published 84 Scopus-indexed articles, authored/edited 14 books, and contributed 78 book chapters, with more than 1,100 citations across major scholarly platforms. His work focuses on sustainable business practices, digital marketing, consumer loyalty, and higher education systems, fields in which he continues to be widely cited and consulted. Dr. Khan's academic reach extends internationally. He serves as International Professor for University of Arizona, USA; Doctoral Supervisor in Rushford Business School, Switzerland, a Research Fellow at INTI International University, Malaysia, and a Visiting Professor in the Lyceum of the Philippines University. He is also Associate Editor-in-Chief of the International Journal of Pluralism and Economics Education (Scopus indexed) and a member of the Editorial Board of Humanities and Social Sciences Communications (Scopus & Web of Science indexed). He is also the Research Brand Ambassador & International Advisory Board member for International Association of Technology and Management-USA. Alongside his academic roles, he has secured multiple funded research projects, including a major grant from The Research Council of Oman (Ministry of Higher Education, Research and Innovation), and completed consultancy assignments for organizations in Bhutan and Oman. His teaching performance has been consistently strong, reflected in an average appraisal score above 93. Dr. Khan holds a PhD in Business Administration (E-Marketing) from Aligarh Muslim University, India. He is well-versed in advanced research tools such as SmartPLS, SPSS, AMOS, NVivo, and VOSviewer, and is frequently invited as a keynote speaker at international conferences, including the QS Higher Ed Summit.

M. Monisha Devi completed her undergraduate degree in Biomedical Engineering (B.Tech) and is currently pursuing a postgraduate degree in Management Studies. With a multidisciplinary academic background, she offers a unique perspective connecting technology, healthcare, and management. Actively engaged in research, she demonstrates a strong commitment to innovation and collaboration across disciplines. Her core competencies include data science and data analysis She applies these skills to generate data-driven insights and develop intelligent solutions, particularly in biomedical and management domains.

A. Ancy Micheal is currently working as an Assistant Professor in the Institute of Computer Science and Digital Innovation (ICSDI) at UCSI University, Malaysia. She earned her Ph.D. from the College of Engineering, Anna University, Chennai. She holds a Master's degree in Computer Science and Engineering from Anna University, Chennai. Her research interests include Artificial Intelligence, Image Processing, Computer Vision, UAVs, Pattern Recognition, and Machine Learning.

Habib Mohammed earned a Bachelor of Arts in English Language and Literature from Jigjiga University in 2014 and a Master of Arts in Public Relations and Corporate Communications from Jimma University in 2018. Since August 2014, he as served as a lecturer at Samara University, teaching courses such Sociolinguistics, Public Relations, Afar Morphology and Syntax, Afar Oral Communication, Research Methods, and Discourse Analysis, Advanced Translation and Interpreting for both undergraduate and graduate students respectively. He has held several leadership roles, including Head of the Department of Afar Language and Literature (2018-2020), Coordinator of Postgraduate Programs for the College of Social Sciences and Humanities (2020-2022), and Dean of the same college (2022-2025). He is prominent member and Vice President of the Afar Intellectual Association (AFIA), His research focuses on Afar oral traditions, society, and communication, with a growing emphasis on African studies, particularly concerning the Afar people and diaspora. He has contributed to projects aimed at preserving Afar oral literature and investigating community atrocities, and currently lead multidisciplinary research addressing Afar cultural studies, pastoralism, and social capital. His professional mission is to preserve and advocate for indigenous knowledge, culture, language, and history through scholarship, promoting an Afrocentric perspective in Afar studies.

Keerthana N V is an Assistant Professor with 8 Years of experience in teaching and 1-year experience in research (IUCAA LIGO Data Centre, Pune). Her area of interest is Network Security, Blockchain Security, and Machine Learning

Algorithms. She is pursuing PhD at Anna University in Security in Blockchain. She has a working experience in High-Performance Computing (HTCondor) in LIGO INDIA Project. She has written many research articles in Network Security and assisted Scientists in analyzing Datasets in HTCondor.

Nidhi Oswal, Currently working as Head of the Human Resource Management department, Faculty of Business at Liwa College AbuDhabi, UAE. Program Leader and Assistant Professor for the Business Administration department at Khawarizmi International College, UAE. I worked as a lecturer at Punjab Institute of Management and Technology, India. In addition, she has been a recruitment consultant for companies in UAE and India. She has earned the SHRM Certified Professional® (SHRM-CP) credential. Nidhi has attended various conferences within and outside the UAE. She holds an ABA level 1 certification through KHDA. She specializes in recruitment, selection, and training & development. The main research areas are recruitment, technology implications in HR, human behaviour, and Sustainable HR development. Furthermore, she serves as a reviewer for a range of reputable journals.

Purigilla Pradyumna Sri Ram is studying M.Tech. (Integrated) Computer Science and Engineering with Specialization in Business in Vellore Institute of technology, Chennai . His research interests includes, Data analytics, Business Analytics, Machine learning and Deep learning.

Suresh P is currently working as Senior Associate Professor in the School of Computer Science and Engineering at Vellore Institute of Technology, Vellore, Tamil Nadu, India. He has 19 years of teaching and academic experience. He has completed Ph.D in Anna University, Chennai. He has published around 60 research papers in reputed international journals indexed by Scopus/SCI/WoS and presented around 35 papers in National and International Conferences. He has authored 6 books and 20 book chapters. His areas of interest include Networks, Cloud Computing, Data Analytics, Machine Learning and Deep Learning. He has received grants from various funding agencies like DRDO, ICMR, and CSIR towards the conduct of seminars and workshops. He has received Best Faculty Award and Best Performer in Academics, Research and consultancy from Kongu Engineering College, Erode, Tamil Nadu. He has received Faculty Research Award for the year 2022 from Vellore Institute of Technology, Vellore. He is serving as Reviewer and Editorial Board member in reputed journals.

Baiju P S currently working as an Assistant Professor in the Department of Electronics & Communication at LBS College of Engineering Kasaragod which is affiliated to APJ Abdul Kalam Technological University. He received Ph.D. in Electronics & Communication Engineering from National Institute of Technology

Calicut. He holds Master's degree in Signal processing and Bachelor's degree in Electronics & Communication Engineering from University of Kerala. He has over 17 years of teaching experience and has published several papers in reputed international journals. His research interests include Image and Video Processing, Computer Vision, Machine Learning, Deep Learning, Compressed Sensing, Data Science and Artificial Intelligence.

Abhinav Pal, Senior Assistant Professor of Economics at Symbiosis Centre for Management Studies, NOIDA, Symbiosis International (Deemed University) Pune, India has over a decade of experience in Teaching, Research, Corporate Development, and Consultancy. His teaching areas include Global Economic Analysis, Financial Literacy, Personal Finance and Financial Planning.

Lakshmi Harika Palivela completed her B.Tech in Computer Science and Engineering from Jawaharlal Nehru Technological University Kakinada in 2009, M.Tech in Computer Science and Engineering from Jawaharlal Nehru Technological University Kakinada in 2011, and Ph.D. in the faculty of Information and Communication Engineering MIT Campus, Anna University, Chennai in 2020. She is currently working as an Assistant Professor (Sr.) at Vellore Institute of Technology, Chennai. Her research interests include Machine Learning, Distributed systems, Image processing, Data Analytics and Video Analytics

Majdi Quttainah is Associate Professor in Kuwait University College of Business Administration. He is having 10 plus years of experience.

R. Durai Pandian is a Professor of Finance & Accounting at Saveetha School of Management, Saveetha University, Chennai. He previously served as Professor & Head (Research) at Garden City University (2019–2022) and held a similar role at PES University, Bangalore (2007–2019). Beginning his academic career in 2000, he held positions at Karunya University after initial industry experience in the hotel sector. With 26 years in teaching and research, he holds degrees in Commerce, an MBA from Manipal University, and a Ph.D. from Alagappa Institute of Management. A UGC Junior Research Fellow, he also completed an FDPM at IIM-A. Dr. Pandian has published over 55 research papers, led academic initiatives, and mentored Ph.D. scholars. His interests include history and sustainable agriculture, especially organic farming.

Purushothaman R, is a dedicated researcher and academician, currently serving as a Research Assistant at the Srinivasa Ramanujan Center, SASTRA University, Kumbakonam. His research interests span across multiple disciplines, including circular economy, supply chain management, operations management, general management, and human resource management. With a passion for advancing knowledge in these fields, he actively contributes to academia through research and scholarly pursuits.

R. Alamelu is working as a Senior Assistant Professor in the Department of Commerce and Management Studies, Srinivasa Ramanujan Centre, SASTRA Deemed University, Kumbakonam, Thanjavur, Tamil Nadu, India. She is a passionate management enabler with a blend of research and academic experience and competency in developing and delivering learner-centric pedagogy with a teaching experience of 25 years. She contributed articles and research papers at different conferences at national and international levels, and written case studies, and published 83 papers in SCOPUS--indexed international journals. She pursued her doctoral degree in Quality Management and coordinated several seminars, conferences and conducted Quality improvement programmes for over a decade. She has authored a book titled 'Management Information System' and is actively involved as a consultant for selected tiny industries in Tamil Nadu. Currently, she supervises two part-time research scholars, and her research areas are Supply Chain Management, Human Resource Analytics, and Circular economy.

Chandni Rani is an Assistant Professor at the School of Business, Galgotias university, Greater Noida,India. With over three years of teaching experience, her research interests span Human Resources, HR analytics, Organizational behavior, green HRM, and the application of artificial intelligence and virtual reality in HR and the healthcare sector. She is a lifetime member of the International Teachers Association. She is an avid researcher and has presented papers at national and international conferences. Dr. Rani has also played a pivotal role in curriculum development and pedagogy design, enhancing the learning experience at Galgotias university.

Poonam Abhijit Rawat is an academic professional with a strong foundation in Human Resource Management and Organizational Behavior. Currently serving as an Assistant Professor at Maharashtra Education Society's Senior College, Pune she has over 15 years of experience in teaching, research, and academic administration. She holds a Ph.D. in HRM from Savitribai Phule Pune University, and is UGC-NET qualified in HRM. Her research interests include employee engagement, organizational culture, and HR practices, with several papers published in reputed national and international journals. She has also contributed significantly to academic conferences, presenting papers on diverse topics such as the role of HR in innovation, entrepreneurship, and education. With a strong commitment to continuous learning, she has completed various faculty development programs and certifications, further enhancing her skills in management education. She has played a pivotal role in organizing national and international conferences, seminars, and workshops, fostering academic discourse and collaboration within the management field

Amrik Singh is working as Professor in the School of Hotel Management and Tourism at Lovely Professional University, Punjab, India. He obtained his Ph.D. degree in Hotel Management from Kurukshetra University, Kurukshetra. He started his academic career at Lovely Professional University, Punjab, India in the year 2007. He has published more than 40 research papers in UGC and peer-reviewed and Scopus/Web of Science) journals. He has published 12 patents and 01 patent has been granted in the inter-disciplinary domain. Dr. Amrik Singh participated and acted as a resource person in various national and international conferences, seminars, research workshops, and industry talks. His area of research interest is accommodation management, ergonomics, green practices, human resource management in hospitality, waste management, AR VR in hospitality, etc. He is currently guiding 8Ph.D. scholars and 2 Ph.D. scholars have been awarded Ph.D.

Abdul Wajid is a faculty member at MIE-SPPU Institute of Higher Education, Doha, Qatar, with several years of teaching experience. He holds a Ph.D. in Commerce from Amity University and has multiple research publications in reputed journals indexed in Web of Science, Scopus, ABDC, and other databases. His research expertise spans various areas of finance, with a strong focus on research, analysis, and academic writing. He actively contributes to the academic community through impactful research and scholarly engagements. He can be contacted at abdulwajid000@gmail.com.

Index

A

D

E

F

G

H

I

J

L

M

O

P

R

S

T

U

W

www.ingramcontent.com/pod-product-compliance
Lightning Source LLC
LaVergne TN
LVHW062333300926
849161LV00007B/1680